Advances in GPU
Research and Practice

Advances in GPU Research and Practice

Edited by

Hamid Sarbazi-Azad

AMSTERDAM • BOSTON • HEIDELBERG • LONDON
NEW YORK • OXFORD • PARIS • SAN DIEGO
SAN FRANCISCO • SINGAPORE • SYDNEY • TOKYO

Morgan Kaufmann is an imprint of Elsevier

Morgan Kaufmann is an imprint of Elsevier
50 Hampshire Street, 5th Floor, Cambridge, MA 02139, United States

Library of Congress Cataloging-in-Publication Data
A catalog record for this book is available from the Library of Congress

British Library Cataloguing-in-Publication Data
A catalogue record for this book is available from the British Library

ISBN: 978-0-12-803738-6

For information on all Morgan Kaufmann publications
visit our website at https://www.elsevier.com/

Working together
to grow libraries in
developing countries

www.elsevier.com • www.bookaid.org

Publisher: Todd Green
Acquisition Editor: Brian Romer
Editorial Project Manager: Amy Invernizzi
Production Project Manager: Punithavathy Govindaradjane
Cover Designer: Maria Inês Cruz

Typeset by SPi Global, India

To my wife and son for their endless love and support.

Contents

PART 3   ARCHITECTURE AND PERFORMANCE

List of Contributors

S.L. Alarcon
Rochester Institute of Technology, Rochester, NY, United States

R. Andonov
University of Rennes 1, Rennes, France

M. Arjomand
Sharif University of Technology, Tehran, Iran

R. Ausavarungnirun
Carnegie Mellon University, Pittsburgh, PA, United States

R. Bashizade
Sharif University of Technology, Tehran, Iran

A. Bhowmick
Carnegie Mellon University, Pittsburgh, PA, United States

N. Bombieri
University of Verona, Verona, Italy

V. Boyer
Graduate Program in Systems Engineering, Universidad Autónoma de Nuevo León, Mexico

M. Burtscher
Texas State University, San Marcos, TX, United States

F. Busato
University of Verona, Verona, Italy

G. Chapuis
LANL, Los Alamos, NM, United States

Y.-C. Chen
National Tsing Hua University, Hsinchu City, Taiwan

N. Chong
Imperial College London, London, United Kingdom

J. Coplin
Texas State University, San Marcos, TX, United States

C. Das
Pennsylvania State University, State College, PA, United States

A.C.M.A. de Melo
University of Brasilia, Brasilia, Brazil

H. Djidjev
LANL, Los Alamos, NM, United States

A.F. Donaldson
Imperial College London, London, United Kingdom

D. El Baz
LAAS-CNRS, Université de Toulouse, CNRS, Toulouse, France

H. Esmaeilzadeh
Georgia Institute of Technology, Atlanta, GA, United States

X. Fu
University of Houston, Houston, TX, United States

A. Ganguly
Rochester Institute of Technology, Rochester, NY, United States

S. Ghose
Carnegie Mellon University, Pittsburgh, PA, United States

G. Gopalakrishnan
University of Utah, Salt Lake City, UT, United States

M. Gopi
University of California, Irvine, CA, United States

F. Hesaaraki
Texas State University, San Marcos, TX, United States

B. Jang
University of Mississippi, Oxford, MS, United States

G. Jo
Seoul National University, Seoul, Korea

A. Jog
Pennsylvania State University, State College, PA, United States

W. Jung
Seoul National University, Seoul, Korea

M. Kandemir
Pennsylvania State University, State College, PA, United States

J. Ketema
Imperial College London, London, United Kingdom

F. Khunjush
Shiraz University, Shiraz; Institute for Research in Fundamental Sciences (IPM), Tehran, Iran

H. Kim
Seoul National University, Seoul, Korea

J. Kim
Seoul National University, Seoul, Korea

D. Lavenier
University of Rennes 1, Rennes, France

J. Lee
Seoul National University, Seoul, Korea

Y.-J. Lee
Seoul National University, Seoul, Korea

C.-R. Lee
National Tsing Hua University, Hsinchu City, Taiwan

G. Li
University of Utah, Salt Lake City, UT, United States

J. Li
University of Florida, Gainesville, FL, United States

P. Li
University of Utah, Salt Lake City, UT, United States

A. Lokhmotov
dividiti, Cambridge, United Kingdom

P. Lotfi-Kamran
Institute for Research in Fundamental Sciences (IPM), Tehran, Iran

N. Mansoor
Rochester Institute of Technology, Rochester, NY, United States

T. Mitra
National University of Singapore, Singapore, Singapore

N. Moreano
Federal University of Mato Grosso do Sul, Campo Grande, Brazil

T.C. Mowry
Carnegie Mellon University, Pittsburgh, PA, United States

H. Mukka
Texas State University, San Marcos, TX, United States

O. Mutlu
Carnegie Mellon University, Pittsburgh, PA, United States

R. Nath
University of California, San Diego, La Jolla, CA, United States

J. Park
Georgia Institute of Technology, Atlanta, GA, United States

J. Park
Seoul National University, Seoul, Korea

A. Pathania
National University of Singapore, Singapore, Singapore

G. Pekhimenko
Carnegie Mellon University, Pittsburgh, PA, United States

A. Prakash
National University of Singapore, Singapore, Singapore

S. Qadeer
Microsoft Research, Redmond, WA, United States

S. Ranka
University of Florida, Gainesville, FL, United States

S. Sahni
University of Florida, Gainesville, FL, United States

M.A. Salazar-Aguilar
Graduate Program in Systems Engineering, Universidad Autónoma de Nuevo León, Mexico

M.H. Samavatian
Sharif University of Technology, Tehran, Iran

H. Sarbazi-Azad
Institute for Research in Fundamental Sciences (IPM); Sharif University of Technology, Tehran, Iran

H. Sharma
Georgia Institute of Technology, Atlanta, GA, United States

X. Shen
North Carolina State University, Raleigh, NC, United States

K. Skadron
University of Virginia, Charlottesville, VA, United States

T. Ta
University of Mississippi, Oxford, MS, United States

J. Tan
University of Houston, Houston, TX, United States

D. Troendle
University of Mississippi, Oxford, MS, United States

D. Tullsen
University of California, San Diego, La Jolla, CA, United States

N. Vijaykumar
Carnegie Mellon University, Pittsburgh, PA, United States

J. Wadden
University of Virginia, Charlottesville, VA, United States

B. Wu
Colorado School of Mines, Golden, CO, United States

A. Yang
Texas State University, San Marcos, TX, United States

A. Yazdanbakhsh
Georgia Institute of Technology, Atlanta, GA, United States

P. Zardoshti
Shiraz University, Shiraz; Institute for Research in Fundamental Sciences (IPM), Tehran, Iran

Preface

It is known that increasing the number of cores in a multicore central processing unit (CPU) to thousands is not possible due to architectural and power limitations, while a graphics processing unit (GPU) can easily exploit thousands of simple and efficient cores each executing a single thread of instructions.

The enormous appetite for both computation and bandwidth of graphic applications has led to the emergence of GPUs as the dominant massively parallel architecture. Today, general-purpose GPUs (GPGPU) with floating-point computation capability are widely used for general purpose computations in most of the top machines with hybrid CPU-GPU architectures. A recent product of such GPGPUs, NVIDIA Pascal, has 3840 cores.

The main problem with such powerful computing chips is the management of such a huge number of cores. New architectural techniques to further increase the number of cores, while considering the technological limitations affecting their reliability, performance, and energy characteristics, for future needs are of great importance. And the lack of efficient programming models and system software to exploit the full capabilities of such a huge number of cores in real applications is the most challenging problem.

This book focuses on the research and practices in GPU-based systems and tries to address their important issues. The topics cover a range of issues from hardware and architectural issues to high-level issues immediately concerning the application or system users, including parallel programming tools and middleware support for such computing systems. The book is divided into four parts, with each including chapters authored by known researchers, who have shared their recent research findings under the topic of that part.

Part 1 deals with different programming issues and tools. This part is comprised of five chapters: 1–5. Chapter 1 discusses how to program a GPU in a reliable manner. Although GPU programs provide high-computational throughput in distinct areas, it is somehow difficult to correctly optimize the codes. This is due to the subtleties of GPU concurrency. For this reason, the focus of this chapter is to discuss and address several things to make the GPU programming easier. The chapter also provides some insights into the recent progress on rigorous methods for the formal analysis of GPU software. The latter is an important issue, with the advances in GPU programming. Therefore verification methods should be taught to new GPU programmers.

Chapter 2 introduces a unified Open Computing Language (OpenCL) framework for heterogeneous clusters (SnuCL). It is a freely available, open-source OpenCL framework for heterogeneous clusters. Basically, OpenCL is a programming model for heterogeneous parallel computing systems, and it defines an abstraction layer between traditional processors and accelerators. The pros of using OpenCL is that programmers write an OpenCL application once and run it on any system that is OpenCL compatible. However, it lacks the ability to target a heterogeneous cluster.

SnuCL provides the programmer with the illusion of a single, unified OpenCL platform image for the cluster. With the help of SnuCL, OpenCL applications are able to utilize compute devices in a compute node as if they were in the host node. Moreover, with SnuCL, it is possible to integrate multiple OpenCL platforms from different vendors into a single platform. Therefore OpenCL objects are shared among compute devices from different vendors and are able to achieve high performance and ease of programming for heterogeneous systems.

Chapter 3 discusses on-thread communication and synchronization on massively parallel GPUs. On GPUs, where thousands of threads run simultaneously, the performance of the processor largely depends on the efficiency of communication and synchronization among threads. Understanding which mechanisms are supported on modern GPUs and their implication on algorithm design is a key issue in writing efficient GPU codes. Due to the fact that conventional GPGPU workloads are massively parallel, with little cooperation among threads, early GPUs supported only coarse-grained thread communication and synchronization. Nowadays, the current trend is to accelerate more diverse workloads and that means coarse-grained mechanisms are a major limiting factor in exploiting the parallelism. The latest industry standard programming framework, OpenCL 2.0, introduces fine-grained thread communication and synchronization support to address this issue. In this chapter, both coarse-grained and fine-grained thread synchronization and communication mechanisms available on modern GPUs are discussed.

Chapter 4 focuses on software-level task scheduling on GPUs. To exploit the full potential of the many-core processor, task scheduling is a critical issue. Contrary to CPUs, GPUs lack the necessary APIs for the programmers or compilers to control scheduling. As a result, it is difficult to use the hardware scheduler on modern GPUs in a flexible manner. This chapter presents a compiler and runtime framework to automatically transform and optimize GPU programs to enable controllable task scheduling to the streaming multiprocessors (SMs). In the center of the framework is SM-centric transformation, which addresses the complexities of the hardware scheduler and provides the scheduling capability. The framework opens many opportunities for new optimizations, of which this chapter presents three of them for optimizing parallelism, locality, and processor partitioning. Extensive experiments reveal that the optimizations can substantially improve the performance of a set of GPU programs in multiple scenarios.

Chapter 5 investigates the complexity of data placement on GPUs and introduces PORPLE, a software framework, to show how to automatically resolve the complexity of a given GPU application. The concept of data placement is an important issue because modern GPU memory systems consist of a number of components with different properties and the question is how to place data on various memory components.

Part 2 presents some useful algorithms and applications for GPUs. It includes nine chapters: 6–14. Chapter 6 focuses on biological sequences' analyses. High-throughput techniques for DNA sequencing have led to an exponential growth of biological databases. These biological sequences have to be analyzed and interpreted in order to determine their function and structure. The problem is that the growth of biological databases is faster than the performance of a single-core processor. With the emergence of many-core processors, it is possible to take advantage of biological sequence analysis tools. This chapter discusses the recent advances in GPUs for two main sequence comparison problems: pairwise sequence comparison and sequence-profile comparison.

Chapter 7 discusses graph algorithms on GPUs. It is started by presenting and comparing the main data structures and techniques applied for representing and analyzing graphs on GPUs. The chapter is followed by theory and updated reviews on efficient graph algorithms for GPUs. The algorithms focused on in the chapter are mainly traversal algorithms (breadth-first search), single-source shortest path (Djikstra, Bellman-Ford, delta stepping, hybrids), and all-pair shortest path (Floyd-Warshall). Later, the chapter discusses load balancing and memory access techniques, with an overview of their main issues and management techniques.

Chapter 8 considers the alignment of sequences where authors consider the optimal alignment of two and three sequences using GPUs. The problem of aligning two sequences is commonly referred to as pairwise alignment. Experimental results on the NVIDIA Tesla C2050 are then presented.

Chapter 9 introduces the Augmented Block Cimmino Distributed (ABCD) algorithm for solving tri-diagonal systems on GPU. Tri-diagonal systems with their special structures mostly appear in scientific and engineering problems, such as Alternating Direction Implicit methods, fluid simulation, and Poisson's equation. This chapter presents the parallelization of the ABCD method for solving tri-diagonal systems on GPU. Among various aspects, this chapter investigate the boundary padding technique to eliminate the execution branches on GPU. Various performance optimization techniques, such as memory coalescing, are also incorporated to further enhance the performance. Performance evaluation shows over 24 times speedups of the GPU implementation over the traditional CPU version.

Chapter 10 discusses linear and mixed-integer programming methods. It shows that the complex problems in the operations research (OR) community can take great benefit of GPUs. Authors also present a survey on the main contributions to the field of GPU computing applied to linear and mixed-integer programming by highlighting how different authors overcome the difficulties of implementation.

Chapter 11 considers the accelerated implementation of the shortest path computation for planar graphs. Three algorithms and their associated GPU implementations are described for two types of shortest path problems. The first algorithm solves the All-Pairs Shortest Path problem while the second algorithm trades this ability for better parallel scaling properties and memory access. The third algorithm solves the Single-Pair Shortest Path query problem. The implementation results show that the computational power of 256 GPUs are exploited simultaneously. Therefore the improvement gap is an order of magnitude more than existing parallel approaches.

Chapter 12 discusses the sort algorithms on GPUs. There is a brief introduction on CUDA programming, memory, and computation models, and on generic GPU programming strategies. Then current GPU implementations of common and popular parallel sorting algorithms including Bitonic, Radix, And Merge Sorts are studied in details while other algorithms including Quicksort and Warp sort are briefly discussed.

In Chapter 13, Massively Parallel Compression (MPC), an effective floating-point compression algorithm for GPUs is introduced. Lossless compression algorithms for single- and double-precision floating-point values are considered in this chapter. Authors also compare the algorithms to choose the best one, explain why it compresses efficiently, and derive the MPC algorithm from them. This algorithm requires little internal state, and roughly matches the best CPU-based algorithms in compression ratio. The result shows that MPC outperforms others by one to two orders of magnitude in throughput and energy efficiency.

Chapter 14 discusses sparse matrix-vector multiplication (SpMV), which is a fundamental computational kernel used in scientific and engineering applications. The nonzero elements of sparse matrices are represented in various formats, and a single sparse matrix representation is not suitable for all sparse matrices with different sparsity patterns. This chapter first introduces an adaptive representation approach for SpMV. The proposed adaptive GPU-based SpMV scheme is based on the configuration and characteristics of GPU cores and chooses the best representation for the given input matrix. The effect of various parameters and different settings on the performance of SpMV applications when employing different sparse formats are studied. Compared to the state-of-the-art sparse library and the latest GPU SpMV method, the proposed adaptive scheme improves the performance of SpVM by $2.1\times$ for single-precision and $1.6\times$ for double-precision formats, on average.

Part 3 focuses on the architecture and performance issues and it includes four chapters: 15–18. In Chapter 15, a framework is introduced to accelerate the bottlenecks in GPU application. The hard part is that there are different bottlenecks during the execution since heterogeneous application requirements are different and hence they create imbalances in the utilization of resources in a GPU. In this chapter, the Core-Assisted Bottleneck Acceleration (CABA) framework is introduced which employs idle on-chip resources to eliminate different bottlenecks in GPU execution. CABA provides flexible mechanisms for generating "assist warps" automatically that execute on GPU cores to perform specific tasks. In other words, it enables the use of idle computational units and pipelines to alleviate the memory bandwidth bottleneck. Therefore it improves the GPU performance and efficiency. CABA architecture is then discussed and evaluated thoroughly to perform effective and flexible data compression in the GPU memory subsystem hierarchy. Results show that using CABA for data compression, provides an average performance improvement of 41.7% (maximum $2.6\times$) across a wide range of memory-bandwidth-sensitive GPGPU applications.

Chapter 16 considers the acceleration of GPUs through neural algorithmic transformation. Basically, the high-performance gain of GPUs is achieved by exploiting large degrees of data-level parallelism and employing the single instruction multiple thread (SIMT) execution model. Many application domains benefit from GPU, including recognition, gaming, data analytics, weather prediction, and multimedia. Most of the above-mentioned applications are good candidates for approximate computing. Therefore, GPU performance and energy efficiency are improved with such a feature. Among approximation techniques, neural accelerators yield significant performance and efficiency gains. This chapter describes a neurally accelerated GPU (NGPU) architecture that embeds neural acceleration within GPU accelerators without hurting their SIMT execution.

The authors, in Chapter 17, introduce a heterogeneous photonic network-on-chip with dynamic bandwidth allocation for GPUs. It is predicted that future multicore chips will have hundreds of heterogeneous components, including processing nodes, distributed memory, custom logic, GPU units, and programmable fabrics. Knowing the fact that future chips are expected to run varied, multiple parallel workloads simultaneously, different communicating cores will require different bandwidths. Therefore the existence of a heterogeneous Network-on-Chip (NoC) architecture is a must. Recent research has shown that photonic interconnects are capable of achieving high-bandwidth and energy-efficient on-chip data transfer. This chapter discusses a dynamic heterogeneous photonic NoC (d-HetPNOC) architecture with dynamic bandwidth allocation for better performance and energy-efficiency compared to a homogeneous photonic NoC architecture.

Chapter 18 presents some models for GPGPU frequency scaling, including CRISP, the first runtime analytical model of performance in the presence of variable frequency in a GPGPU. Prior models failed to account for important characteristics of GPGPU execution since they did not target the GPGPU. The shortcomings include the high degree of overlap between memory access and computation and the frequency of store-related stalls. The accuracy of CRISP is much higher than prior runtime performance models, being within 4%, on average, when scaling the frequency by up to $7\times$. The result reveals a 10.7% improvement in energy-delay product versus a 6.2% difference via the best of prior methods.

Part 4 considers power consumption and reliability issues and includes five chapters: 19–23. Chapter 19 addresses the energy and power issues of GPUs. The discussion includes different algorithm implementations, program inputs, core and memory clock frequencies, and the effect of source-code optimizations on energy and power consumption, and the performance of a modern compute GPU. Important things to note is that authors distinguish between compute intensive and memory intensive codes as well as regular and irregular codes. Therefore the focus is on the behavioral differences between these classes of programs. Some examples of software approaches used to modify the energy, power, and runtime of GPU kernels are examined and it is explained how they can be used to improve energy efficiency.

Chapter 20 introduces STT-RAM based L2 cache architecture for GPUs. The key to achieve a high level of performance is the large number of threads that helps

GPUs to hide memory access latency with maximum thread-level parallelism (TLP). The downside, however, is that by increasing the TLP and the number of cores, the performance does not necessarily increase due to contentions among threads to access shared resources, such as the last-level cache. For such a reason, future GPUs should have larger last-level cache (L2 in GPU). However, based on the current trends in VLSI technology and GPU architectures, the trend is to increase the number of processing cores. This chapter presents an efficient L2 cache architecture for GPUs based on STT-RAM technology. The positive side of such technology is "high density and low power consumption," making the STT-RAM technology a good candidate to fulfill the limited area for on-chip memory banks. The downsides, though, are high energy and latency of write operations. Low-retention (LR) time STT-RAMs can reduce the energy and delay of write operations. Investigations show that it is possible to design a two-parted STT-RAM based L2 cache with LR and high-retention (HR) parts. The cache architecture proposed in this chapter is able to improve IPC by up to 171% (20% on average), and reduce the average consumed power by 28.9% in comparison with a conventional L2 cache architecture with equal on-chip area.

Chapter 21 highlights power management in mobile GPUs. Such processors in mobile devices have come a long way in the recent years in terms of their capabilities to accelerate various applications from graphic-specific applications, such as games, to traditional general purpose applications. The downside is the significant power consumption when executing such a wide range of applications. This necessitates sophisticated power management techniques for the GPUs in order to save power and energy in mobile devices that typically have a limited power budget and battery capacity. This chapter first discusses the pros and cons of the state-of-the-art power management techniques for both graphic-specific and general-purpose applications running on GPUs. Particularly, it shows that existing approaches suffer from the lack of coordination in power management between the CPU and the GPU that reside on the same silicon die in the mobile application processors. The authors present a recently proposed power management solution to address these shortcomings through synergistic CPU-GPU execution and power management.

Chapter 22 addresses some recent advances in GPU-reliability research. While the popularity of using GPUs as massively parallel coprocessors has increased dramatically over the last 10 years, improvements in GPU reliability has lagged behind adoption. GPUs are the first candidate for gaming applications where they need attention regarding high reliability. GPUs are now being used to accelerate applications in medical imaging, nuclear science, materials science, social science, finance, etc., and all of them require a high level of reliability. GPUs are also considered a good candidate for high-node-count data centers and many of the fastest supercomputers in the world, exacerbating system failure rates.

Chapter 23 discusses the hardware reliability challenges in GPGPUs. On one hand, graphic applications effectively mask errors and have relaxed requests on computation correctness and that means there has been little attention given to error detection and the fault tolerance of GPUs. On the other hand, HPC applications have some hard limits on execution correctness, and for that reason, reliability is a growing concern in GPGPU architecture design. To address this issue, there is a need to characterize and address the reliability concept in GPGPU design. It is known that there exists two important hardware reliability challenges in GPGPUs. The first is particle strikes that induce soft errors and the second is manufacturing process variations. This chapter explores a set of mechanisms to effectively improve the GPGPUs reliability.

Acknowledgments

I should first thank the authors and acknowledge their contributions to the book, as well as their support and patience. I would also like to thank the reviewers for their useful comments and suggestions that helped in improving the earlier outline of the book and presentation of the material. I should extend my deepest thanks to Professor Hamid R. Arabnia (the series editor of Emerging Trends in Computer Science and Applied Computing) for his encouragement and support to start this project, and Amy Invernizzi (the editorial project manager) for her collaboration, guidance, and patience in finalizing this volume. Last but not the least, I am very grateful to the lovely team from Elsevier's production department for their extensive efforts during the many phases of this project and the timely fashion in which the book was produced.

Programming and tools

Formal analysis techniques for reliable GPU programming: current solutions and call to action

1

A.F. Donaldson[1], G. Gopalakrishnan[2], N. Chong[1], J. Ketema[1], G. Li[2], P. Li[2], A. Lokhmotov[3], S. Qadeer[4]

Imperial College London, London, United Kingdom[1] University of Utah, Salt Lake City, UT, United States[2] dividiti, Cambridge, United Kingdom[3] Microsoft Research, Redmond, WA, United States[4]

1 GPUs IN SUPPORT OF PARALLEL COMPUTING

When the stakes are high, money is no object in a nation's quest for computing power. For instance, the SAGE air-defense network [1] was built using a computing system with 60,000 vacuum tubes, weighing 250 tons, consuming 3 MW of power, and at a cost of over $8 billion, in 1964. Now (five decades later), a door-lock computer often exceeds SAGE in computing power, and more than ever, we are critically dependent on computers becoming faster as well as more energy efficient. This is true not only for defense but also for every walk of science and engineering and the social sector.

Graphics processing units (GPUs) are a natural outgrowth of the computational demands placed by today's applications on such stringently power-capped and bounded wire-delay hardware [2]. GPUs achieve higher computational efficiency than CPUs by employing simpler cores and hiding memory latency by switching away from stalled threads. Overall, the GPU throughput-oriented execution model is a good match for many data-parallel applications.

The rate of evolution of GPUs is spectacular: from the 3M transistor Nvidia NV3 in 1997, their trajectory is marked by the 7B transistor Nvidia GK110 (Kepler) in 2012 [3]. Nvidia's CUDA programming model, introduced in 2007, provided a dramatic step up from the baroque notation associated with writing pixel and vertex shaders, and the recent CUDA 7.5 [4] offers versatile concurrency primitives.

Advances in GPU Research and Practice. http://dx.doi.org/10.1016/B978-0-12-803738-6.00001-X

OpenCL, an industry standard programming model [5] supported by all major device vendors, including Nvidia, AMD, ARM, and Imagination Technologies, provides straightforward, portable mapping of computational intent to tens of thousands of cores.

GPUs now go far beyond graphics applications, forming an essential component in our quest for parallelism, in diverse areas such as gaming, web search, genome sequencing, and high-performance supercomputing.

Bugs in parallel and GPU code

Correctness of programs has been a fundamental challenge of computer science even from the time of Turing [6]. Parallel programs written using CPU threads or message passing (e.g., MPI) are more error prone than sequential programs, as the programmer has to encode the logic of synchronization and communication among the threads and arrange for resources (primarily the memory) to be shared. This situation leads to bugs that are very difficult to locate and rectify.

In contrast to general concurrent programs, GPU programs are "embarrassingly parallel," with threads being subject to structured rules for control and synchronization. Nevertheless, GPU programs pose certain unique debugging challenges that have not received sufficient attention, as will be clear in Sections 2 and 3 where we discuss GPU bugs in detail. Left unchecked, GPU bugs can become showstoppers, rendering simulation results produced by multimillion-dollar scientific projects utterly useless. Sudden inexplicable crashes, irreproducible executions, as well as irreproducible scientific results are all the dirty laundry that often goes unnoticed amid the din of exascale computing.

Yet these bugs do occur, and they seriously worry experts who often struggle to bring up newly commissioned machines or are pulled away from doing useful science. The purpose of this chapter is to describe some of these challenges, provide an understanding of the solutions being developed, and characterize what remains to be accomplished.

After introducing GPUs at a high level (Section 2), we survey some key GPU correctness issues in a manner that the program analysis and verification community can benefit from (Section 3). The key question addressed is: *What are the correctness challenges, and how can we benefit from joint efforts to address scalability and reliability?* We then address the question: *How can we build rigorous correctness checking tools that handle today's as well as upcoming forms of heterogeneous concurrency?* To this end we discuss existing tools that help establish correctness, providing a high-level description of how they operate and summarizing their limitations (Section 4). We conclude with our perspective on the imperatives for further work in this field through a call to action for (a) research-driven advances in correctness checking methods for GPU-accelerated software, motivated by open problems and (b) dissemination and technology transfer activities to increase uptake of analysis tools by industry (Section 5).

2 A QUICK INTRODUCTION TO GPUs

GPUs are commonly used as parallel co-processors under the control of a host CPU in a heterogeneous system. In this setting, a task with abundant parallelism can be offloaded to the GPU as a kernel: a template specifying the behavior of an arbitrary thread. Fig. 1 presents a CUDA kernel for performing a parallel dot product of two vectors, adapted from the CUDA 5.0 SDK [7], which we use as a running example.

We provide a brief overview of the GPU programming model. As we introduce each concept and component, we give the CUDA term for the concept or component, followed by the OpenCL term in parentheses if it is different, and use of the CUDA term thereafter.

Organization of threads

Kernels are executed on a GPU by many lightweight *threads* (*work-items*) organized hierarchically as a *grid* (*NDRange*) of *thread-blocks* (*work-groups*), as illustrated in

```
1    #define ACCUM_N 1024
2    __global__ void dotProduct(float *d_A, float *d_B,
3                               float *d_c, int n) {
4      __shared__ float accumResult[ACCUM_N];
5      int tid = threadIdx.x;
6      int bdim = blockDim.x;
7
8      // (a) Compute partial sums
9      for (int i = tid; i < ACCUM_N; i += bdim) {
10       float sum = 0;
11       for (int j = i; j < n; j += ACCUM_N) {
12         sum += d_A[j] * d_B[j];
13       }
14       accumResult[i] = sum;
15     }
16
17     // (b) Reduce
18     for (int stride = ACCUM_N / 2; stride > 0;
19          stride >>= 1) {
20       __syncthreads();
21       for (int i = tid; i < stride; i += bdim) {
22         accumResult[i] += accumResult[stride + i];
23       }
24     }
25
26     if (tid == 0) *d_c = accumResult[0];
27   }
```

FIG. 1

Dot product kernel adapted from the CUDA 5.0 SDK.

Fig. 2. For example, a grid of 4 thread-blocks with each of 256 threads results in 1024 threads, each running a copy of a kernel. The `__global__` annotation in Fig. 1 indicates that dotProduct is a kernel function.

Within the kernel, a thread can query its position within the grid hierarchy (as well as the grid and thread-block dimensions) using built-ins such as `threadIdx` (`get_local_id`) and `blockDim`(`get_local_size`). Grids and blocks can be multidimensional, and for example, `blockDim.x` (`get_local_size(0)`) and `threadIdx.x` (`get_local_id(0)`) provide, respectively, the size of a thread-block and the id of a thread within its block in the first dimension. This allows threads to operate on distinct data and to follow distinct execution paths through the kernel.

Memory spaces

Threads on a GPU can access data from multiple memory spaces arranged in a hierarchy that reflects thread organization, as shown in Fig. 2. In descending order of size, scope-visibility and latency, they are

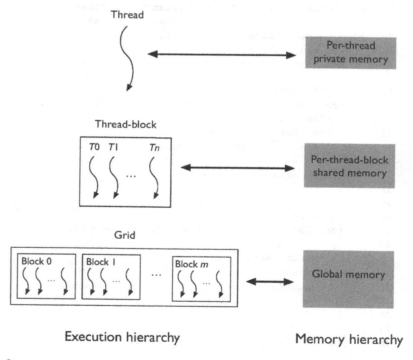

FIG. 2

GPU thread and memory hierarchy.

Adapted from Ref. [4].

- A large global memory visible to all threads in a grid. In CUDA pointer
  parameters to a kernel refer to global memory arrays, thus d_a, d_b, and d_c in
  Fig. 1 are global arrays. The kernel computes the dot product of the arrays d_A
  and d_B and stores the result in d_c (a one-element array).
- A per-thread-block *shared* (*local*) memory visible to all threads within the same
  thread-block. The __**shared**__ annotation in Fig. 1 specifies that the
  accumResult array resides in shared memory. Each thread-block has a distinct
  copy of this array, which is used for accumulating partial dot product values.
- A small per-thread *private* memory. Loop variables i, j, and stride in Fig. 1
  reside in private memory. Each thread has a separate copy of these variables.

It is the programmer's responsibility to orchestrate data movement between the
global and shared memory spaces. Memory *coalescing* is an important property for
performance reasons. When adjacent threads access contiguous memory locations,
the hardware can coalesce these accesses into fewer memory transactions and
therefore increase bandwidth.

While threads share certain memory spaces, memory writes do not become
instantaneously visible to all threads (as this would severely impede performance). In
computer architecture, the concept of memory consistency models is used to clearly
explain when threads may observe the writes of other threads. GPU programming
models specify a *weak memory consistency model* [4,5]. That is, the updates and
order of accesses of a given thread are not guaranteed to be observable by other
threads.

Barrier synchronization
Barriers facilitate safe communication between threads of the same thread-block.
A barrier operation causes a thread to stall until all threads in the thread-block have
reached the same barrier. In fact, the barrier must be reached under the same control-
flow by all threads in order to avoid the problem of *barrier divergence*, which results
in undefined behavior. The dot product kernel uses barrier synchronization, indicated
by __**syncthreads**(), to ensure proper ordering of updates to the shared array
accumResult.

Barriers cannot be used for synchronization between threads in distinct thread-
blocks. Instead, this requires the programmer to split the workload into multiple
kernels that are invoked in sequence. Threads in different thread-blocks can use
atomic operations to communicate via global memory.

Warps and lock-step execution
On Nvidia GPUs the hardware executes a thread-block by dynamically partitioning
it into sets of *warps*; AMD GPUs have a similar notion of a *wavefront*. Currently,
Nvidia specifies that a warp is a set of 32 adjacent threads of the thread-block.
Threads within the same warp execute in *lockstep* and so are implicitly synchronized;
we comment on the opportunities and dangers presented by this phenomenon in
Section 3.

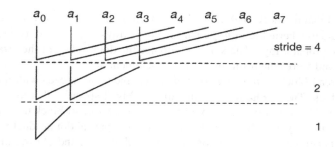

FIG. 3

A tree reduction as used in the kernel of Fig. 1.

Dot product example

We are now suitably equipped to discuss the kernel in Fig. 1. Consider the kernel when it is invoked with a single thread-block of 128 threads (i.e., `blockDim.x = 128`) where the length n of the input arrays equals 4096.

The kernel has two parallel phases. In the first phase, partial products are accumulated into the shared array `accumResult`. The outer loop assigns a distinct thread to each element of the `accumResult` array. Because there are more elements (ACCUM_N) than threads, the outer loop assigns `ACCUM_N/blockDim.x = 8` elements per thread. For example, thread 0 is assigned elements 0, 128, 256, ..., 896. The result for each element i of the output is accumulated in the thread-private variable `sum` and accumulated by the inner loop. The inner loop performs n /ACCUM_N = 4 partial products at ACCUM_N intervals. For example, the inner loop for thread 0 when $i = 0$ will compute $\Sigma a_j b_j$ for j in {0, 1024, 2048, 3072}. The stride of accesses ensures coalesced memory accesses to global memory.

In the second phase, the partial products are reduced into the final expected result. Instead of summing ACCUM_N elements serially, the kernel uses a parallel tree reduction. The reduction is performed using a logical tree. A simplified reduction tree for eight elements is given in Fig. 3. Each iteration of the loop—using descending power-of-two `stride` values—corresponds to a different level of the tree. The barrier ensures that the updates of a given level are ordered before any access at the next level and is thus a form of inter-thread communication.

3 CORRECTNESS ISSUES IN GPU PROGRAMMING

We now outline four key classes of correctness issues that can make the transition from CPUs to GPUs difficult.

Data races

Insufficient or misplaced barriers can lead to *data races*. A data race occurs if two threads access the same memory location (in global or shared memory) where at least one access is nonatomic, at least one access modifies the location, and there is no intervening barrier synchronization that involves both threads. (In OpenCL 2.0, synchronization between certain atomic operations can also be used to avoid races; we do not delve into the details of this here.) For example, consider the in-place tree reduction of the dot product kernel in Fig. 1. The barrier at line 20 ensures that all accesses at a given iteration (when stride = k, say) are ordered before any accesses at the next iteration (when stride = $k/2$). If the barrier is omitted then data races are possible. For example, thread 0 with stride 2 and thread 2 with stride 4 will race on accumResult [8].

In most concurrent programs, races are tell-tale indicators that something is seriously wrong with the code, including the potential for nondeterministic results or semantically incoherent updates because of insufficient atomicity. GPU programming models (e.g., OpenCL) require the programmer to write data race-free code. Programs containing data races have undefined semantics. Consequently, many compiler optimizations assume race-freedom; in the presence of races they may produce unexpected results.

One can guard against data races through conservative barrier placement, but excessive use of barriers can be problematic for two reasons. First, barriers are expensive to execute, so that superfluous synchronization introduces an unnecessary performance overhead. Second, placing barriers in conditional code can be dangerous because of the problem of barrier divergence discussed in Section 2.

On Nvidia GPUs, many CUDA programmers choose to elide barriers in the case where synchronization is required only between threads in the same warp. For instance, the last six iterations of the tree reduction loop in phase two of the dot product kernel (see Fig. 1) might be replaced with the following sequence of statements, to avoid explicit synchronization when the stride is less than or equal to 32:

```
if(tid < 32)   accumResult[tid] += accumResult[tid + 32];
if(tid < 16)   accumResult[tid] += accumResult[tid + 16];
if(tid <  8)   accumResult[tid] += accumResult[tid +  8];
if(tid <  4)   accumResult[tid] += accumResult[tid +  4];
if(tid <  2)   accumResult[tid] += accumResult[tid +  2];
if(tid <  1)   accumResult[tid] += accumResult[tid +  1];
```

This practice relies on the compiler preserving implicit intra-warp synchronization during optimization. It is not clear whether this is the case. Advice related to intra-warp synchronization was removed in version 5.0 of the CUDA Programming Guide, and there is disagreement among practitioners about the guarantees provided by current platforms in this regard (see, e.g., a Nvidia forum discussion on the topic [9]).

Nevertheless, some samples that ship with the CUDA 5.0 SDK rely on implicit intra-warp synchronization. More surprisingly, OpenCL kernels in open-source benchmark suites such as Parboil [10] and SHOC [11] elide barriers in the preceding manner. This is clearly erroneous since the notion of lock-step warps is not part of the OpenCL specification.

Recent work has shown that Nvidia and AMD GPUs exhibit weak memory behaviors (as discussed in Section 2), whereby nonsequentially consistent executions can be observed, and that this is a source of subtle software defects [12]. Bugs arising because of weak memory effects will become increasingly relevant as GPU applications move toward exploiting fine-grained concurrency in place of barrier synchronization.

Lack of forward progress guarantees

The lack of fair scheduling of threads on GPU architectures is another source of defects.

Fig. 4 shows an attempt to implement an inter-block barrier in CUDA. The idea behind this well-known strategy is as follows. Each thread synchronizes within its block (line 3) after which the *leader* of each thread-block (the thread with threadIdx.x = 0) atomically decrements a counter (line 5). Assuming the counter was initialized to the total number of thread-blocks (comment on line 1), it might appear that spinning until the counter reaches zero (line 6) would suffice to ensure that every leader has passed the decrement (line 5). (Note that the counter value is retrieved by atomically adding zero to the counter; atomicAdd returns the old value of the location operated upon. Using an atomic operation, rather than a plain load operation, avoids data races between accesses to the counter.) If spinning until the counter reaches zero would indeed ensure that every leader has passed the decrement, then a global synchronization would have been achieved, and the leader could resynchronize with the rest of its block (line 8), allowing execution to recommence. The purpose of the fences (lines 2 and 9) is to ensure that memory access operations before the global synchronization point take effect before memory access operations after the global synchronization point. For a community discussion of the strategy and its problems, see, for example, Ref. [13].

The problem with this barrier implementation is that it assumes forward progress between thread-blocks. However, if a sufficient number of CUDA blocks are requested, then they will be scheduled in *waves*: a number of blocks will be scheduled

```
1    // Pre: 'count' initialized to #thread-blocks
2    __threadfence();
3    __syncthreads();
4    if(threadIdx.x == 0) {
5      atomicDec(count);
6      while(atomicAdd(count, 0) > 0) { }
7    }
8    __syncthreads();
9    __threadfence();
```

FIG. 4

An attempt to implement an inter-block barrier in CUDA is foiled by lack of progress guarantees between thread-blocks.

and must run to completion before compute units are freed for further blocks to be scheduled. This scenario leads to deadlock: leaders of the blocks scheduled in the first wave get stuck spinning at line 6, waiting for the counter to be decremented by leaders of additional blocks; these blocks in turn cannot be scheduled until the initial blocks complete execution. An analogous attempt to implement global synchronization in OpenCL does not work either, for the same reason.

This example illustrates unfair scheduling across thread-blocks. Similar lack of progress issues arise between threads *within* a CUDA thread-block because, as discussed in Section 2, a thread-block is subdivided into warps such that threads in the same warp execute in lockstep, executing identical instruction sequences. This leads to deadlock if a programmer attempts to force a thread to busy-wait for another thread in the same warp; progress would require the threads to genuinely execute distinct instructions at runtime. This defeats the naïve implementation of an intra-block critical section based on busy waiting. For an example of this issue, with a community discussion, see Ref. [14].

Floating-point accuracy

Achieving equivalence to a reference implementation can be especially challenging for kernels that compute on floating-point data, which are commonplace in high-performance computing.

It can be convenient to assume that floating-point operators have the algebraic properties of real numbers when designing parallel algorithms. For instance, the sum reduction operation, in which all elements of an array are added, can be parallelized through a computation tree illustrated by the diagrams of Fig. 5. A tree-based approach allows reduction in a logarithmic number of steps if the number of parallel processing elements exceeds the size of the array. The figure shows two possible computation trees for an eight-element array. If addition were *associative*, that is, if the law $(x + y) + z = x + (y + z)$ held for all floating-point values x, y, and z, with $+$ denoting floating-point addition, the computation trees would yield identical results,

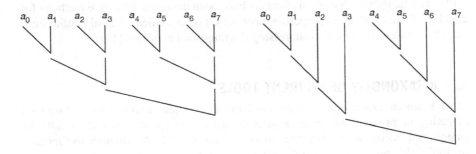

FIG. 5

Both reduction trees compute a sum over a_i but can yield different results because floating-point addition is not associative.

and the result would be the same as that of the left-associative sum obtained from a straightforward sequential implementation. However, it is well known that floating-point addition is not associative so that results are expected to differ depending on how the parallel algorithm is structured.

While these issues are shared by CPUs, perhaps what makes these concerns particularly important for GPUs is the fact that GPUs are throughput oriented, and have much smaller caches. Thus the added penalty of using double-precision arithmetic everywhere (instead of single-precision almost everywhere) tends to be higher with GPUs, especially since the number of double-precision units on a GPU is typically small. There are also language-specific issues related to floating-point accuracy in the context of GPUs. For example, the question of whether *denormal* numbers are accurately represented in OpenCL is implementation-defined, and OpenCL provides a *half precision* data type, specifying only *minimal* (not exact) accuracy requirements for associated operators. Implementation differences make it hard to write high-performance floating-point code that behaves with an acceptable degree of precision on multiple GPU platforms.

4 THE NEED FOR EFFECTIVE TOOLS

The issues discussed in Section 3 show that practitioners working at the level of OpenCL and CUDA cannot avoid being exposed to the "sharp edges" of concurrency. In some application areas, it may be possible for nonexpert programmers to bypass these issues through the use of domain-specific languages with associated compilers that generate low-level code automatically (e.g., [15]), at the price of flexibility and generality. For programmers who require the flexibility afforded by writing lower-level code directly, help is needed in easing the GPU programming task in various forms. These include clearer formal documentation and "best practices" guides, as well as *tool support* for correctness checking.

We now detail state-of-the-art research in methods for data race analysis of GPU kernels, for which custom checkers have been designed. Effective methods for checking forward progress properties have not yet been studied, and only initial steps have been taken in relation to addressing floating-point concerns [16].

4.1 A TAXONOMY OF CURRENT TOOLS

Most research and tooling efforts on GPU correctness issues have focused on detecting or proving the absence of data races. The techniques can broadly be categorized according to dynamic analysis methods [17–20] (though the method of Ref. [19] combines dynamic and static analysis), symbolic execution-based approaches [16,21,22], and methods that use static, logic-based verification [23–27].

Table 1 presents a top-level summary of the capabilities of a selection of publicly available tools for analyzing CUDA and OpenCL kernels. The table focuses on tools

Table 1 A Summary of the Features of Several Dynamic and Symbolic Bug-Finders and Verifiers for CUDA and OpenCL

| | Dynamic Bug-Finders | | Symbolic Bug-Finders | | Verifiers |
	CMC	Oclgrind	GKLEE	GKLEE$_p$	GPUVerify
OpenCL/CUDA support	CUDA	OpenCL	CUDA	CUDA	CUDA + OpenCL
Analysis coverage	Low	Low	Medium	Medium	High
Precise bug reports	✓	✓	✓	✗	✗
Correctness guarantees	✗	✗	✗	✗	✓
Scalability to large thread counts	High	Medium	Low	Medium	High
Degree of automation	High	High	Medium	Medium	Low

that are actively maintained and is not meant to be exhaustive; indeed, we discuss some further tools in the following text.

Dynamic bug-finding tools, including Oclgrind [28,29] and CUDA-MEMCHECK (CMC) [30], detect defects during dynamic analysis, either while running a kernel on hardware (CMC) or in emulation mode (Oclgrind). These tools are easy to apply automatically and are precise in the bugs they report because defects are directly observed. They provide low analysis coverage (and no correctness guarantees) because they check a kernel with respect to a single input. Scalability to large thread counts is limited: Oclgrind serializes execution; the overhead of dynamic race instrumentation with CMC is modest, at the price that only races on shared memory, not global memory, can be detected.

Symbolic bug-finding tools, including GKLEE [21] and KLEE-CL [16], retain bug-finding precision but improve on analysis coverage compared with purely dynamic techniques. This is achieved through *symbolic execution*, whereby a constraint solver is used to check for defects along a path for input values, providing correctness guarantees on a per-path basis. State-of-the-art tools build on the KLEE symbolic execution engine [31]. These tools tend to scale poorly to large thread counts: the bottleneck for symbolic execution is a constraint-solving overhead, and analysis of a large number of threads requires very large sets of constraints to be solved. (In Section 4.3 we discuss GKLEE$_p$, an extension of GKLEE that uses *parametric flows* to scale to larger thread counts.) Automation is basically as high as with dynamic approaches; a little more work may be required to decide which inputs to a kernel should be treated as symbolic, though dependence analysis can partially automate this process [32].

Verification tools, including GPUVerify [24,25] and PUG [23], provide the highest degree of analysis coverage and are able to guarantee absence of certain types of defects under well-defined conditions. (The words "verification" and "guarantee" are arguably contentious since both tools have known limitations and sources of unsoundness. We use these terms because a key aim of these tools is to guarantee full behavioral coverage, in contrast to bug-finding methods that do not aim to verify correctness and instead prioritize defect detection.) The price for high coverage is a lack of precision in bug reporting: both tools suffer from a high false to positive rate, and it may be necessary for developers to manually analyze bug reports and write annotations, in the form of preconditions, loop invariants, and barrier invariants [33] to eliminate false alarms.

We now explain how state-of-the-art tools exploit the traditional GPU programming model to achieve scalable analyses (Section 4.2), and describe two such tools, GKLEE and GPUVerify, in more detail (Sections 4.3 and 4.4, respectively).

4.2 CANONICAL SCHEDULES AND THE TWO-THREAD REDUCTION

Most existing program analysis tools for GPU kernels are restricted to "traditional" GPU programs, where barrier synchronization is the only means for communication between threads. The tools leverage the simplicity of this setting to achieve scalable analyses, as we now explain. For ease of presentation, we assume in the following that all threads are in a single thread-block so that all threads synchronize at a barrier.

Race freedom implies determinism
Suppose that a traditional kernel is free from data races. From the initial state of the kernel, a thread executes until it reaches its first barrier without interacting with other threads: any such interaction would constitute a data race. The threads either reach different barriers, in which case the kernel suffers from barrier divergence, or all threads reach the *same* barrier. Thus the initial state of the kernel uniquely determines the state of the kernel when all threads reach their first barrier. If the threads all reach the same barrier, then, by a similar argument, the threads execute deterministically until they reach another barrier (or the end of the kernel), and so on. The series of barriers at which the threads will synchronize, and the state of the kernel at each of these barriers, and at kernel exit, are independent of the order in which threads are scheduled. The argument is presented more formally in Ref. [34] and requires that the internal actions of threads are deterministic (e.g., threads should not employ randomization).

Detecting races: "all for one and one for all"
Suppose a kernel exhibits a data race with respect to some input and thread schedule. Then *every thread schedule exhibits a data race with respect to this input*. A formal argument for this result is presented in Ref. [21]. Informally, if a kernel can exhibit a race for a given input, then a nonempty set of *earliest* races for the input exists: races that are guaranteed to occur, independent of whether any race has already occurred. Every schedule is guaranteed to expose an earliest race.

Restricting to a canonical schedule

The "race freedom implies determinism" and "all for one and one for all" properties combine to yield a powerful schedule reduction method: when analyzing a traditional GPU kernel, it suffices to consider a *single* schedule, as long as data races are detected for this schedule and reported as errors. As a result, the astronomical schedule space of a GPU kernel executed by thousands of threads can be collapsed so that just one *canonical schedule* is considered. Reduction to a canonical schedule is an example of *partial order reduction* [35], a key state space reduction technique used by many model checking tools.

Reduction to a pair of threads

Because a data race always involves a pair of threads, further scalability can be achieved by restricting race analysis to consider the execution of a single, arbitrary thread pair, using abstraction to overapproximate the behavior of other threads. If pairwise race-freedom can be demonstrated then, because the thread pair under consideration was arbitrary, the kernel is race-free for all threads. If on the other hand a race is detected, the race may be genuine or may be a false alarm induced by the abstraction process. As part of the case studies in Sections 4.3 and 4.4, we discuss next how this *two-thread reduction* is employed by the GKLEE$_p$ and GPUVerify tools.

4.3 SYMBOLIC BUG-FINDING CASE STUDY: GKLEE

GKLEE is based on *symbolic execution* [36] and builds on the execution mechanisms provided by the KLEE tool [31].

Consider a program fragment for which control flow depends on the evaluation of a predicate f applied to a program input:

```
if (f(input)) {
  /* branch 1 */
} else {
  /* branch 2 */
}
```

Traditional testing requires explicitly supplied concrete inputs that cover both branches. The power of *symbolic* execution is that the variable input can be marked as symbolic, and thus treated initially as unconstrained. On reaching the conditional, a constraint solver determines whether concrete values exist for input such that f evaluates to *true*, and such that f evaluates to *false*. If inputs exist such that both branches are feasible, then "branch 1" is explored under the constraint f(input) and "branch 2" is explored under the constraint ¬f(input), ensuring that both branches are covered. The KLEE tool implements symbolic execution of LLVM bit code and has shown to be very effective in detecting subtle bugs in systems code that evaded manual testing for several years [31].

We use the following example to illustrate how GKLEE [21] evolves the sequential analysis capabilities of KLEE to achieve race checking for CUDA (following a first step in which a CUDA kernel is compiled into LLVM bit code). In the following, we use `tid` and `bdim` as shorthand for `threadIdx.x` and `blockDim.x`, respectively, and we do not specify the behavior of function `f`.

```
__global__ void race(int *v, int x) {
  v[tid] = v[(tid + x) % bdim];
  __syncthreads();
  if (tid % 2 == 0) {
    ... = v[tid];
  } else {
    v[f(tid)] = ...;
  }
}
```

GKLEE adapts KLEE's memory organization to realize the hierarchical organization shown in Fig. 2. Based on the idea of canonical scheduling (Section 4.2), GKLEE symbolically executes the given GPU threads *sequentially* between two barriers, recording potentially racing accesses. A constraint solver is then queried to detect scenarios in which races actually manifest. In the preceding example, the following instruction precedes the first barrier:

```
v[tid] = v[(tid + x) % bdim];
```

If this instruction is sequentially executed from the point of view of two threads with ids 0 and 1 (for example), we have

```
v[0] = v[(0 + x) % bdim]; v[1] = v[(1 + x) % bdim];
```

In this execution, a potential racing pair of accesses consists of a read from `v[(0 + x) % bdim]` by thread 0 and a write to `v[1]` by thread 1. A constraint solver easily determines that this pair indeed races for $x = 1$.

By default, GKLEE explicitly models all threads that execute a kernel; this approach does not scale to large thread counts. An extension to GKLEE, named GKLEE$_p$ [22], employs the two-thread reduction (Section 4.2) to perform *parameterized* race analysis between an arbitrary pair of threads. Regardless of the number of threads that actually execute a kernel, data race detection between barriers can be performed with respect to two threads with symbolic ids, representative of the full thread population.

In the preceding example, the code after the barrier exhibits *thread divergence*: the even-numbered threads read from `v[tid]`, while the odd-numbered threads write to `v[f(tid)]`. GKLEE$_p$ handles thread divergence as follows: (1) it creates a separate *flow group* for each branch target, in this case, one for all even-numbered threads and one for all odd-numbered threads; (2) within each flow group, GKLEE$_p$ conducts pairwise symbolic execution; and (3) the tool checks whether a race is possible *within* each flow group, as well as *across* flow groups. In our example, if `f` is injective (one-to-one), then there are no races within flow groups, whereas if `f` yields the same value for two odd-numbered threads, then there is a write-write race on v in the second flow group. There is a potential race *across* flow groups if it is possible for f(tid) under condition tid % 2 ≠ 0 to be equal to tid under condition tid % 2 = 0. The power of a symbolic solver lies in the fact that it can, very often, find solutions for such equalities by analyzing the function body of functions such as f and generating the necessary set of constraints.

A drawback of parameterized checking is that using the two-thread reduction necessitates abstraction of additional threads. This means that, unlike GKLEE, $GKLEE_p$ can yield false alarms. Another potential drawback is that the number of flow groups can grow exponentially. Recent work has shown that static analysis can be used to overcome this problem in several practical examples [32].

4.4 VERIFICATION CASE STUDY: GPUVerify

The GPUVerify tool [24,25,37] aims for full verification of race-freedom for OpenCL and CUDA kernels. As with GKLEE, a kernel is first translated to LLVM bit code. The canonical scheduling idea (Section 4.2) is exploited to transform the kernel into a *sequential* program in the Boogie intermediate verification language [38]. During this transformation, memory access instructions are instrumented so that the conditions for checking race-freedom are encoded as assertions to be checked in the Boogie program. Thus proving race-freedom of a kernel amounts to verifying the sequential Boogie program generated by this process. This allows for reuse of the Boogie verification framework (widely used by other verification tools, including VCC [39] and Spec# [40]), where a program is checked by generating a verification condition that can be discharged to an SMT solver. Verification of programs with loops requires loop invariants, and GPUVerify uses the Houdini candidate-based invariant generation algorithm [41] for this purpose.

To achieve scalability to large numbers of threads, GPUVerify employs a two-thread reduction (see Section 4.2). Unlike $GKLEE_p$, which handles thread-divergent control flow by considering multiple pairs of threads, GPUVerify symbolically encodes all control flow scenarios with respect to a single thread pair via *predicated execution* [24,25,42]. Because additional threads are modeled abstractly when the two-thread reduction is employed, analysis using GPUVerify can yield false alarms. Another source of false alarms stems from a lack of preconditions describing constraints on kernel execution; to some extent this can be overcome through interception of kernels at runtime to capture details of their execution environment [43]. A large experimental evaluation with respect to publicly available benchmark suites has demonstrated that GPUVerify is able to handle many practical GPU kernels [37], and the tool has been used to find numerous defects in these benchmark suites (see, e.g., a confirmed and fixed SHOC bug report [44] and acknowledgments to Jeroen Ketema in the Rodinia 3.1 release notes [45]). For kernels whose correctness depends on richer shared state properties, GPUVerify supports *barrier invariant* annotations [33]. These allow the precision of the shared state abstraction to be increased, at the expense of manual effort.

5 CALL TO ACTION

We have discussed a number of issues that affect GPU program correctness and the capabilities of current solutions. We now consider the future role GPUs will play in software systems and the extent to which the current analysis techniques can be effective in improving the quality of this software.

GPUs will become more pervasive

The high development cost associated with application-specific processors makes the idea of removing such processors from an embedded chip, and implementing its functionality as software running on a GPU, an appealing one. The idea that GPUs may gain traction in, for example, the automotive domain further underscores the need to consider safe GPU programming. We may be comfortable with GPU-powered infotainment systems of cars being developed without rigorous correctness analysis, but we are likely less comfortable with this situation if next-generation GPUs play a more fundamental role.

As James Larus points out in a recent CACM letter to the editor [46], for reasons of liability manufacturers will be increasingly required to demonstrate that software has been rigorously developed, and will thus turn their attention to the best available tools and practices. As GPUs become more pervasive, there will be an even greater need for the sorts of tools surveyed in this article.

Current tools show promise

Existing tools for GPU program analysis have demonstrated that they can help improve the quality of GPU software. For example, GKLEE and GPUVerify have found numerous bugs in kernels shipped with the Lonestar, Parboil, Rodinia, and SHOC suites.

However, many challenges lie ahead. We conclude with a call to action on what we believe to be some of the most pressing issues for researchers and industry.

Solving basic correctness issues

While today's tools show that analysis for GPU correctness issues related to mis-synchronization is tractable, Table 1 shows that no single method provides high analysis coverage and precise bug reporting while scaling to large thread counts. We issue a call to researchers for innovation in this regard, through clever combinations of methods or via new approaches to the analysis problem. A particular challenge is reasoning about fine-grained concurrency; support for reasoning about atomic operations in mature tools is limited [47,48], though recent methods for reasoning about atomics via concurrent separation logic show promise [8]. Fully supporting fine-grained concurrency will require accounting for the relaxed memory behavior of GPU architectures [12].

Equivalence checking

A GPU program is often the evolution of a CPU program, via several optimizing transformations. For floating-point code, these transformations may be "fuzzy," preserving functionality within an acceptable margin of error and not providing bit-level equivalent results. A fascinating open research challenge is to provide assistance in this transformation process via formal equivalence-checking methods that tolerate an acceptable degree of fuzziness; this will require coping with the combined challenges of reasoning about floating-point and concurrency.

Clarity from vendors and standards bodies

Recent research into GPU memory consistency [12] indicates that vendor documentation and open standards are not clear on subtle details related to the concurrency semantics of GPU kernels. These subtleties are of essential importance to compiler writers, expert programmers, and developers of formal analysis techniques. We issue a call to vendors and standards bodies to engage further with the programming languages research community to achieve better clarity.

User validation of tools

Despite their promise, the current analysis tools for GPU programming have only a modest following of professional developers. Higher user engagement is needed to better understand the most pressing problems that developers face. One preliminary success story here is a recent integration of GPUVerify into the Graphics Debugger 2.0 for the ARM Mali GPU series [49]. We call on other platform vendors to similarly promote uptake and continued development of promising research tools.

Concerted community action coupled with dialog with industry is a sure-footed way to attain these objectives. After all, future exascale machines and intelligent navigation systems must trust GPUs to safely accelerate computing, and this safety requires tools to aid in systematic software development, about which this chapter only scratches the surface.

ACKNOWLEDGMENTS

We are grateful to Geof Sawaya, Tyler Sorensen, and John Wickerson for feedback on a draft of this chapter, and to Daniel Poetzl for guidance regarding the placement of memory fences in Fig. 4.

We thank Geof Sawaya, Tyler Sorensen, Ian Briggs, and Mark Baranowski for testing and improving the robustness of GKLEE.

REFERENCES

[1] SAGE: The First National Air Defense Network 2016, http://www-03.ibm.com/ibm/history/ibm100/us/en/icons/sage/ (retrieved Jan. 19).

[2] S. Borkar, A.A. Chien, The future of microprocessors, Commun. ACM 54 (5) (2011) 67–77.

[3] J. Sanders, E. Kandrot, CUDA by Example: An Introduction to General-Purpose GPU Programming, Addison-Wesley, Boston, MA, 2010.

[4] NVIDIA, CUDA C Programming Guide, version 7.5, 2015.

[5] Khronos, The OpenCL C specification, 2013.

[6] F.L. Morris, C.B. Jones, An early program proof by Alan Turing, Ann. Hist. Comput. 6 (2) (1984) 139–143.

[7] NVIDIA, CUDA code samples 2016, https://developer.nvidia.com/gpu-computing-sdk (retrieved Jan. 19).

[8] A. Amighi, S. Darabi, S. Blom, M. Huisman, Specification and verification of atomic operations in GPGPU programs, in: SEFM, 2015, pp. 69–83.

[9] Nvidia CUDA ZONE forum, 2016, https://devtalk.nvidia.com/default/topic/632471/is-syncthreads-required-within-a-warp- (retrieved Jan. 19).

[10] J. Stratton, et al., Parboil: a revised benchmark suite for scientific and commercial throughput computing, Tech. Rep. IMPACT-12-01, UIUC, 2012.

[11] A. Danalis, et al., The scalable heterogeneous computing (SHOC) benchmark suite, in: GPGPU 2010, 2010, pp. 63–74.

[12] J. Alglave, M. Batty, A.F. Donaldson, G. Gopalakrishnan, J. Ketema, D. Poetzl, T. Sorensen, J. Wickerson, GPU concurrency: weak behaviours and programming assumptions, in: ASPLOS, 2015, pp. 557–591.

[13] Stack Overflow: Inter-Block Barrier in CUDA, 2016, http://stackoverflow.com/questions/7703443/inter-block-barrier-on-cuda (retrieved Jan. 19).

[14] Stack Overflow: How to implement a critical section in CUDA?, 2016, http://stackoverflow.com/questions/2021019/how-to-implement-a-critical-section-in-cuda (retrieved Jan. 19).

[15] S. Verdoolaege, J.C. Juega, A. Cohen, J.I. Gómez, C. Tenllado, F. Catthoor, Polyhedral parallel code generation for CUDA, TACO 9 (4) (2013) 54.

[16] P. Collingbourne, C. Cadar, P.H.J. Kelly, Symbolic crosschecking of data-parallel floating-point code, IEEE Trans. Software Eng. 40 (7) (2014) 710–737.

[17] M. Boyer, K. Skadron, W. Weimer, Automated dynamic analysis of CUDA programs, in: Proceedings of the Third Workshop on Software Tools for MultiCore Systems (STMCS), 2008.

[18] M. Zheng, V.T. Ravi, F. Qin, G. Agrawal, GMRace: detecting data races in GPU programs via a low-overhead scheme, IEEE Trans. Parallel Distrib. Syst. 25 (1) (2014) 104–115.

[19] A. Leung, M. Gupta, Y. Agarwal, et al., Verifying GPU kernels by test amplification, in: PLDI, 2012, pp. 383–394.

[20] P. Li, C. Ding, X. Hu, T. Soyata, LDetector: a low overhead race detector for GPU programs, in: Proceedings of the 5th Workshop on Determinism and Correctness in Parallel Programming (WODET), 2014.

[21] G. Li, P. Li, G. Sawaya, G. Gopalakrishnan, I. Ghosh, S.P. Rajan, GKLEE: Concolic verification and test generation for GPUs, in: PPoPP, 2012, pp. 215–224.

[22] P. Li, G. Li, G. Gopalakrishnan, Parametric flows: automated behavior equivalencing for symbolic analysis of races in CUDA programs, in: SC, 2012, pp. 29:1–29:10.

[23] G. Li, G. Gopalakrishnan, Scalable SMT-based verification of GPU kernel functions, in: FSE, 2010, pp. 187–196.

[24] A. Betts, N. Chong, A.F. Donaldson, J. Ketema, S. Qadeer, P. Thomson, J. Wickerson, The design and implementation of a verification technique for GPU kernels, ACM Trans. Program. Lang. Syst. 37 (3) (2015) 10.

[25] A. Betts, N. Chong, A.F. Donaldson, S. Qadeer, P. Thomson, GPUVerify: a verifier for GPU kernels, in: OOPSLA, 2012, pp. 113–132.

[26] S. Blom, M. Huisman, M. Mihelcic, Specification and verification of GPGPU programs, Sci. Comput. Program. 95 (2014) 376–388.

[27] R. Sharma, M. Bauer, A. Aiken, Verification of producer-consumer synchronization in GPU programs, in: PLDI, 2015, pp. 88–98.

[28] J. Price, S. McIntosh-Smith, Oclgrind: an extensible OpenCL device simulator, in: IWOCL, 2015.

[29] Oclgrind, 2016, https://github.com/jrprice/Oclgrind (retrieved Jan. 19).

[30] Nvidia, CUDA-MEMCHECK, 2016, https://developer.nvidia.com/CUDA-MEMCHECK (retrieved Jan. 19).

[31] C. Cadar, D. Dunbar, D.R. Engler, KLEE: unassisted and automatic generation of high-coverage tests for complex systems programs, in: OSDI, 2008, pp. 209–224.

[32] P. Li, G. Li, G. Gopalakrishnan, Practical symbolic race checking of GPU programs, in: SC, 2014, pp. 179–190.

[33] N. Chong, A.F. Donaldson, P. Kelly, J. Ketema, S. Qadeer, Barrier invariants: a shared state abstraction for the analysis of data-dependent GPU kernels, in: OOPSLA, 2013.

[34] N. Chong, A.F. Donaldson, J. Ketema, A sound and complete abstraction for reasoning about parallel prefix sums, in: POPL, 2014, pp. 397–410.

[35] P. Godefroid, Partial-Order Methods for the Verification of Concurrent Systems, Lecture Notes in Computer Science, vol. 1032, Springer Verlag Berlin Heidelberg.

[36] C. Cadar, K. Sen, Symbolic execution for software testing: three decades later, Commun. ACM 56 (2) (2013) 82–90.

[37] E. Bardsley, A. Betts, N. Chong, P. Collingbourne, P. Deligiannis, A.F. Donaldson, J. Ketema, D. Liew, S. Qadeer, Engineering a static verification tool for GPU kernels, in: CAV, 2014, pp. 226–242.

[38] M. Barnett, Boogie: a modular reusable verifier for object-oriented programs, in: FMCO, 2005, pp. 364–387.

[39] E. Cohen, M. Dahlweid, M.A. Hillebrand, D. Leinenbach, M. Moskal, T. Santen, W. Schulte, S. Tobies, VCC: a practical system for verifying concurrent C, in: TPHOLs, 2009, pp. 23–42.

[40] M. Barnett, M. Fähndrich, K.R.M. Leino, P. Müller, W. Schulte, H. Venter, Specification and verification: the Spec# experience, Commun. ACM 54 (6) (2011) 81–91.

[41] C. Flanagan, K.R.M. Leino, Houdini, an annotation assistant for ESC/Java, in: FME, 2001, pp. 500–517.

[42] P. Collingbourne, A.F. Donaldson, J. Ketema, S. Qadeer, Interleaving and lock-step semantics for analysis and verification of GPU kernels, in: ESOP, 2013, pp. 270–289.

[43] E. Bardsley, A.F. Donaldson, J. Wickerson, KernelInterceptor: automating GPU kernel verification by intercepting kernels and their parameters, in: IWOCL, 2014, pp. 7:1–7:5.

[44] SHOC project bug report, 2016, https://github.com/vetter/shoc/issues/30 (retrieved Jan. 19).

[45] Rodinia version history, 2016, https://www.cs.virginia.edu/~skadron/wiki/rodinia/index.php/TechnicalDoc (retrieved Jan. 19).

[46] J. Larus, Responsible programming not a technical issue, in: Commun. ACM, 2014, p. 8, Letter to the Editor.

[47] W.F. Chiang, G. Gopalakrishnan, G. Li, Z. Rakamaric, Formal analysis of GPU programs with atomics via conflict-directed delay-bounding, in: NFM, 2013, pp. 213–228.

[48] E. Bardsley, A.F. Donaldson, Warps and atomics: beyond barrier synchronization in the verification of GPU kernels, in: NFM, 2014, pp. 230–245.

[49] ARM, Debugging OpenCL Applications with Mali Graphics Debugger V2.1 and GPU-Verify, 2016, https://community.arm.com/groups/arm-mali-graphics/blog/2015/04/14/debugging-opencl-applications-with-mali-graphics-debugger-v21-and-gpuverify (retrieved Jan. 19).

SnuCL: A unified OpenCL framework for heterogeneous clusters

2

J. Lee, G. Jo, W. Jung, H. Kim, J. Kim, Y.-J. Lee, J. Park
Seoul National University, Seoul, Korea

1 INTRODUCTION

A general-purpose computing on graphics processing units (GPGPU) system typically consists of a general-purpose CPU and one or more GPUs. The GPGPU system has been a great success so far and is continuously widening its user base. It is a typical example of heterogeneous computing systems. A heterogeneous computing system refers to a system that contains different types of computational units, such as multicore CPUs, GPUs, DSPs, FPGAs, and ASICs. The computational units in a heterogeneous system typically include a general-purpose processor that runs an operating system. Processors other than the general-purpose processor are called accelerators because they accelerate a specific type of computation by assisting the general-purpose processor. Each accelerator in the system is best suited to a different type of task. The program execution and data are distributed among these computational units. Introducing such additional, specialized computational resources in a single system enables users to gain extra performance and power efficiency. In addition, exploiting different capabilities of the wide range of accelerators enables users to solve difficult and complex problems efficiently and easily.

As of Nov. 2015, 21% of the supercomputers in TOP500 are heterogeneous systems [1], and it is expected that the number will increase continuously. To exploit heterogeneity in the system, new programming models, such as Compute Unified Device Architecture (CUDA) [2,3] and Open Computing Language (OpenCL) [4] have been proposed and widely used. Although CUDA works only for NVIDIA GPUs, OpenCL is supported by many vendors, including Altera, AMD, Apple, ARM, IBM, Imagination, Intel, MediaTek, NVIDIA, Qualcomm, Samsung, TI, Xilinx, and so on. OpenCL works for any device that provides an OpenCL framework. OpenCL has code portability for different processors from different vendors. The processors include multicore CPUs, GPUs, and other accelerators, such as Intel Xeon Phi coprocessors and FPGAs.

Advances in GPU Research and Practice. http://dx.doi.org/10.1016/B978-0-12-803738-6.00002-1

OpenCL is a unified programming model for different types of processors. OpenCL provides a common hardware abstraction layer across them. Programmers can write OpenCL applications once and run them on any OpenCL-compliant hardware. This portability is one of the major advantages of OpenCL. It allows programmers to focus their efforts on the functionality of their application rather than the lower-level details of the underlying architecture. This makes OpenCL a standard for general-purpose and heterogeneous parallel programming models.

However, one of the limitations of OpenCL is that it is a programming model for a single operating system instance. That is, it is restricted to a single node in a cluster system. An OpenCL application does not work for a cluster of multiple nodes unless the application developer explicitly inserts communication libraries, such as MPI, into the application. The same thing is true for CUDA [2,3].

For example, a GPU cluster contains multiple GPUs across its nodes to solve bigger problems within an acceptable timeframe. Application developers for the clusters are forced to turn to a mix of two programming models, OpenCL + MPI or CUDA + MPI. Thus the application becomes a mixture of a communication API and OpenCL/CUDA. This makes the application more complex, less portable, and harder to maintain.

The mixed programming model requires the hierarchical distribution of the workload and data across nodes and across accelerators in a node. MPI functions are used to communicate between the nodes in the cluster. Therefore the resulting application may not be executed in a single node.

Another limitation comes from OpenCL's installable client driver (ICD). It enables different OpenCL platforms from different vendors to coexist under a single operating system instance. However, to use different processors from different vendors in the same application, programmers need to explicitly choose a vendor-specific OpenCL platform for each processor in the application. Moreover, OpenCL objects (buffers, events, and so on) cannot be shared across different vendor platforms without explicit data copying through the host main memory.

In this chapter, we present an OpenCL framework called SnuCL. SnuCL overcomes aforementioned limitations of OpenCL and is a unified programming model for heterogeneous clusters. The target cluster architecture is shown in Fig. 1. Each node in the cluster contains one or more multicore CPUs and accelerators, such as GPUs. The nodes are connected by an interconnection network, such as Gigabit Ethernet and InfiniBand. One of the nodes is designated as the host node by the SnuCL runtime. The host node executes the host program in an OpenCL application. Other nodes are designated as compute nodes. In a compute node, a set of CPU cores or an accelerator becomes an OpenCL compute device. If the accelerator is a discrete GPU, data are transferred between the compute device memory and the main memory through a PCI-E bus.

SnuCL naturally extends the original OpenCL semantics to the heterogeneous cluster environment. As shown in Fig. 1, SnuCL gives the programmer an illusion of a single OpenCL platform image for the whole heterogeneous cluster. It allows the application to utilize compute devices in a compute node as though they were

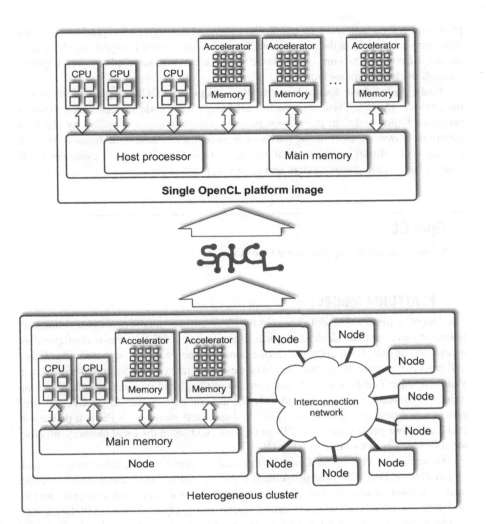

FIG. 1

SnuCL's target cluster architecture. It gives the user an illusion of a single OpenCL platform image.

in the host node. The user can launch a kernel to a compute device or manipulate a memory object in a remote node using only OpenCL API functions. This enables OpenCL applications written for a single operating system instance (a single node) to run on the cluster without any modification. That is, with SnuCL, an OpenCL application becomes portable not only between heterogeneous computing devices in a single node but also between those in the entire cluster environment. Moreover, programmers do not need to explicitly choose different vendor platforms to use different accelerators in the same OpenCL application. OpenCL objects can be shared across different platforms in the same application without explicit data copying through the host main memory.

Many studies have focused on enabling OpenCL or CUDA applications to run on a cluster [5–18]. These approaches all have a host node that executes the host program. Other nodes in the cluster perform computations controlled by the host program. However, most of the previous approaches evaluate their framework with a small-scale cluster with less than 16 nodes. Only SnuCL [12,13] evaluates itself using a large-scale cluster system and shows its practicality.

2 OpenCL

In this section, we briefly introduce OpenCL.

2.1 PLATFORM MODEL

The OpenCL platform model shown in Fig. 2 consists of a host processor connected to one or more *compute devices*. An accelerator or a set of CPU cores is configured as a compute device. Each compute device contains one or more compute units (CUs) and has the compute device memory. The device memory of a compute device is not visible to other compute devices and consists of the global memory and the constant memory. Constant memory is read-only for the compute device. Each CU contains one or more *processing elements* (PEs) and the local memory. A PE is a processor and has its own private memory. PEs in the same CU share the local memory, and the local memory is not visible to other CUs.

As shown in Fig. 3, an OpenCL application consists of a *host program* and *OpenCL programs*. The host program is typically written in C and executes on the host processor. It creates one or more *command-queues* for each compute device and submits *commands* to a command-queue using OpenCL host API functions. Command-queues are attached to a compute device and maintained by the OpenCL runtime. Note that different compute devices may not share the same command-queue. If the command-queue is an in-order queue, enqueued commands are issued by the OpenCL runtime in the order they were enqueued and complete in that order. Otherwise, if the command-queue is an out-of-order queue, a command may begin execution before all its previous commands in the command-queue are complete.

The OpenCL program is a set of *kernels*. A kernel is a function and is written in OpenCL C. It performs computation on the PEs within a compute device. It is submitted to a command-queue in the form of a kernel execution command by the host program. The OpenCL runtime dequeues the kernel command and issues it to the target compute device. OpenCL C is a subset of C99 with some extensions that include support for vector types, images, and memory hierarchy qualifiers. It also

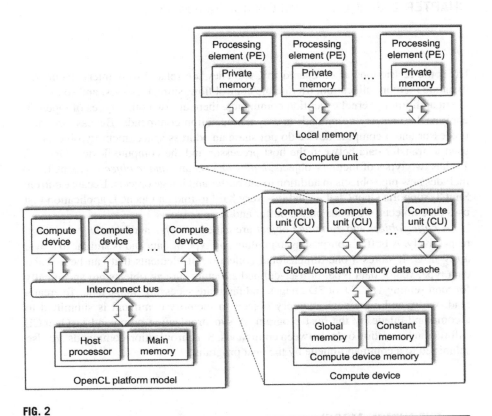

FIG. 2

The OpenCL platform model.

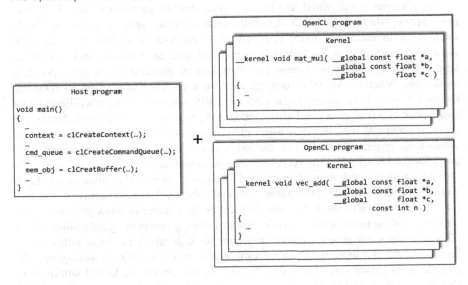

FIG. 3

An OpenCL application.

has some restrictions as compared to C99. They are related to pointers, recursion, dynamic memory allocation, irreducible control flow, storage classes, and so on.

In addition to kernel execution commands, there are two other types of OpenCL commands: memory commands and synchronization commands. Because the host processor and a compute device do not share an address space, memory objects are used to transfer data between the host processor and the compute device. OpenCL 1.2 has two types of memory objects: *buffer objects* and *image objects*. OpenCL 2.0 includes new pipe objects in addition to the buffer and image objects. Because current SnuCL supports OpenCL 1.x, and it is very hard to find an OpenCL application that uses pipe objects, we focus on the buffer and image objects.

A *buffer object* and an *image object* are called a *buffer* and an *image* for short, respectively. A buffer's purpose is to contain any type of data and is similar to a byte array in C. It stores a one-dimensional collection of elements that can be a scalar data type, vector data type, or user-defined structure. Image objects are specifically for representing 1D, 2D, or 3D images and facilitate accessing image data. To create, read, write, and copy such memory objects, a memory command is submitted to a command-queue by the host program. A synchronization command in OpenCL enforces an execution order between commands. Synchronization commands are also submitted to a command-queue by the host program.

2.2 EXECUTION MODEL

Before a kernel is submitted, the host program defines an N-dimensional abstract index space, where $1 \leq N \leq 3$. A two-dimensional index space is shown in Fig. 4. Each point in the index space is specified by an N-tuple of integers with each dimension starting at 0. Each point is associated with an execution instance of the kernel, which is called a *work-item*. The N-tuple is the global ID of the corresponding work-item. When the kernel is running, each work-item is able to query its ID using OpenCL C built-in functions. It can perform a different task and access different data based on its ID (i.e., data parallelism and single program, multiple data). An integer array of length N (i.e., the dimension of the index space) specifies the number of work-items in each dimension of the index space. The host program prepares the array for the kernel when the kernel command is enqueued.

One or more work-items are grouped in *work-groups* in the index space. Each work-group also has a unique ID that is also an N-tuple. An integer array of length N (i.e., the dimension of the index space) specifies the number of work-groups in each dimension of the index space. A work-item in a work-group is assigned a unique local ID within the work-group, treating the entire work-group as the local index space. The global ID of a work-item can be computed with its local ID, its work-group ID, and the work-group size. The OpenCL runtime distributes the kernel workload to CUs in the target device. The granularity of the distribution is a work-group. Work-items in a work-group execute *concurrently* on the PEs of the CU.

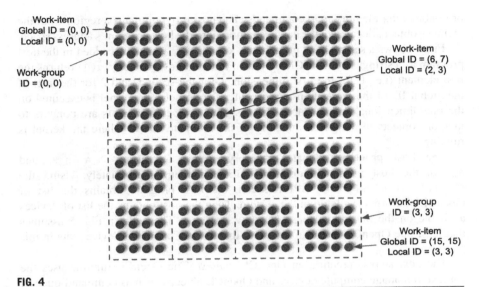

FIG. 4

A two-dimensional kernel index space.

2.3 MEMORY MODEL

OpenCL C defines four distinct memory regions in a compute device according to the platform model (Fig. 2): global, constant, local, and private. These regions are accessible to work-items, and OpenCL C has four address space qualifiers to distinguish these memory regions: __global, __constant, __local, and __private. They are used in variable declarations in the kernel code. Accesses to the global memory or the constant memory may be cached in the global/constant memory data cache if such a cache exists in the device.

The host program enqueues memory commands to manipulate memory objects. Only the host program can dynamically create memory objects (i.e., buffers and images) in the global or constant memory using OpenCL API functions. A kernel may statically allocate constant memory space. Pointers to the memory objects are passed as arguments to a kernel that accesses the memory objects. Local memory spaces are shared by all work-items in the same work-group. The host program can dynamically allocate a local memory space using a clSetKernelArg() host API function. A kernel may statically allocate a local memory space. The private memory is local to each work-item. A kernel statically allocates a private memory space. The host program may not access the private memory space.

Using OpenCL API functions or pointers, only the host program can transfer data between the main memory and the memory objects allocated in the compute device memory. The host program enqueues blocking (synchronous) or nonblocking (asynchronous) memory transfer commands. Another way is enqueueing blocking or nonblocking memory map commands. The host program maps a region from the memory object allocated in the device memory into the host program's address space.

Fig. 5 shows a sample host program. A kernel, vec_add, is embedded in the host program as a string. The OpenCL C built-in function get_global_id(0) returns the first element (i.e., 0 for the first dimension, 1 for the second, and 2 for the last) of the global ID of the work-item that executes the kernel. The kernel is executed on the one-dimensional index space. The first three kernel arguments are pointers to memory objects in the global memory of the compute device where the kernel is running.

The host program allocates memory spaces for arrays h_A, h_B, and h_C in the host main memory and initializes them appropriately. Using the clGetPlatformIDs() host API function, the host program obtains the list of OpenCL platforms available in the system. Then the host obtains the list of devices available on the platform using clGetDeviceIDs(). The code in Fig. 5 assumes that least one OpenCL platform exits and that at least one GPU device exits in this platform.

The next step is creating an OpenCL *context*. The OpenCL runtime uses the context to manage compute devices and OpenCL objects, such as command-queues, memory, program, and kernel objects. A context to which a kernel object belongs is an execution environment for the kernel. Using clCreateContext(), the host creates a context. In the context, the host creates a command-queue on the GPU device using clCreateCommandQueue() and an OpenCL program object using clCreateProgramWithSource(). An OpenCL program executable is compiled and linked by clBuildProgram(). Then the host API function clCreateKernel() creates a kernel object from the program executable.

To execute the kernel, the host prepares memory objects for the kernel. Using the clCreateBuffer() API function, the host creates three buffers, buff_A, buff_B, and buff_C. Because of CL_MEM_COPY_HOST_PTR flag, the contents of h_A and h_B are copied to buff_A and buff_B, respectively, when buff_A and buff_B are created.

Kernel arguments are set by clSetKernelArg(). After defining work-group size, lws[0], and the kernel index space, gws[0], the host enqueues a kernel command using the nonblocking API function clEnqueueNDRangeKernel() to execute the kernel on the GPU device. The OpenCL runtime issues the kernel to the target GPU device. Then the kernel executes on the GPU. The synchronization API function clFinish() blocks until the kernel command in the command-queue is issued to the GPU and has completed. The blocking memory command clEnqueueReadBuffer() reads the contents of buff_C to h_C. It is blocking because of the flag CL_TRUE. After reading the contents, the host prints the contents of h_C. Finally, the host releases OpenCL objects and frees dynamically allocated host memory spaces.

2.4 SYNCHRONIZATION

A *work-group barrier* used in the kernel synchronizes work-items in the same work-group. Every work-item in the work-group must execute the barrier and cannot

```c
#include <stdio.h>
#include <stdlib.h>
#include <math.h>
#include <CL/opencl.h>

#define N 10000

const char *kernel_str =              // The OpenCL kernel source is embedded in the host program
   "__kernel void vec_add( __global float *a, __global float *b, __global float *c, \n"
   "                       const unsigned int n)                                    \n"
   "{                                                                               \n"
   "    int id = get_global_id(0);  // Get global ID                                \n"
   "                                                                                \n"
   "    if (id < n)                      // Bound checking                          \n"
   "        c[id] = a[id] + b[id];                                                  \n"
   "}                                                                               \n";

int main( int argc, char* argv[] )
{
    size_t bytes = N * sizeof(float);

    // Allocate host memory for the host-side vectors and initialize them
    float *h_A = (float*)malloc(bytes);
    float *h_B = (float*)malloc(bytes);
    float *h_C = (float*)malloc(bytes);

    ...

    cl_platform_id platform;
    cl_int err = clGetPlatformIDs(1, &platform, NULL);                    // Obtain the platform

    cl_device_id device_id;
    err = clGetDeviceIDs(platform, CL_DEVICE_TYPE_GPU, 1, &device_id, NULL);    // Get the GPU device ID

    cl_context context = clCreateContext(0, 1, &device_id, NULL, NULL, &err);   // Create a context

    cl_command_queue queue = clCreateCommandQueue(context, device_id, 0, &err); // Create a command-queue

    // Create a program object from the kernel source
    cl_program program = clCreateProgramWithSource(context, 1, (const char **) & kernel_str, NULL, &err);

    err = clBuildProgram(program, 1, &device_id, NULL, NULL, NULL);  // Compile and link the program

    cl_kernel kernel = clCreateKernel(program, "vec_add", &err); // Create a kernel object form the program

    // Create buffers and copy the vectors in the host side to the buffers
    cl_mem buff_A = clCreateBuffer(context, CL_MEM_READ_ONLY | CL_MEM_COPY_HOST_PTR, bytes, h_A, NULL);
    cl_mem buff_B = clCreateBuffer(context, CL_MEM_READ_ONLY | CL_MEM_COPY_HOST_PTR, bytes, h_B, NULL);
    cl_mem buff_C = clCreateBuffer(context, CL_MEM_WRITE_ONLY, bytes, NULL, NULL);

    unsigned int n = N;

    // Set the arguments to the kernel
    err = clSetKernelArg(kernel, 0, sizeof(cl_mem), &buff_A);
    err = clSetKernelArg(kernel, 1, sizeof(cl_mem), &buff_B);
    err = clSetKernelArg(kernel, 2, sizeof(cl_mem), &buff_C);
    err = clSetKernelArg(kernel, 3, sizeof(unsigned int), &n);

    size_t lws[1] = {64};                          // Number of work-items in each work group
    size_t gws[1] = {ceil(n/(float)lws[0])*lws[0]}; // Number of total work-items

    // Execute the kernel
    err = clEnqueueNDRangeKernel(queue, kernel, 1, NULL, gws, lws, 0, NULL, NULL);

    clFinish(queue); // Wait for all the commands in queue to be finished

    // Read the result from the device
    err = clEnqueueReadBuffer(queue, buff_C, CL_TRUE, 0, bytes, h_C, 0, NULL, NULL );

    // Print the result
    ...

    clReleaseMemObject(buff_A);   // Release OpenCL resources and host memory
    free(h_A);
    ...

    return 0;
}
```

FIG. 5

An OpenCL host program.

proceed beyond the barrier until all other work-items in the work-group reach the barrier. No synchronization mechanism is available between work-groups in OpenCL.

Synchronization between commands in a single command-queue can be specified by a *command-queue barrier* using clEnqueueBarrierWithWaitList(). To synchronize commands in different command-queues, *event objects* are used. Each OpenCL API function that enqueues a command returns an event object that encapsulates one of the four distinct states of the command: CL_QUEUED, CL_SUBMITTED, CL_RUNNING, and CL_COMPLETE. It also takes an *event wait list* as an argument. This command cannot be issued for execution until the states of all the commands in the event wait list go to CL_COMPLETE. A user-defined event can be used to trigger some action when the host program detects that a certain condition is met.

2.5 MEMORY CONSISTENCY

OpenCL [4] defines a relaxed memory consistency model [19,20] for the consistent memory view. An update to a device memory location by a work-item may not be visible to all the other work-items at the same time. Instead, the local view of memory from each work-item in the same work-group is guaranteed to be consistent at work-group barriers. The work-group barrier enforces a global memory fence for the consistent view of the global memory or a local memory fence for the consistent view of the local memory.

Updates to a shared memory object across different command-queues (e.g., different compute devices) are visible at synchronization points. The synchronization points defined in OpenCL include the following:

- The end of a blocking API function that enqueues a command
- A command-queue barrier
- The end of clFinish()
- The point when a kernel is launched onto a device after all events on which the kernel is waiting have been set to CL_COMPLETE
- The point when a kernel completes after all of its work-groups have completed

2.6 OpenCL ICD

OpenCL implementations are provided as ICD. This mechanism enables multiple OpenCL implementations to coexist under the same operating system instance. Users should choose the specific OpenCL platform for use in their applications, as shown in Fig. 6. At each OpenCL API function call, the ICD loader in the OpenCL runtime infers the vendor ICD function to call using the arguments to the function. Then it dispatches the OpenCL API call to the particular vendor implementation using a function pointer dispatch table.

Even though OpenCL ICD provides users with a convenient way of using multiple platforms in a single OpenCL application, there are some limitations in the current OpenCL ICD implementation. Fig. 7 shows an example of using ICD.

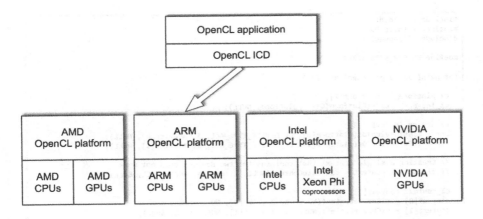

FIG. 6

Using OpenCL ICD.

We assume there are two OpenCL implementations available in the system, and each platform has only one compute device. Because each compute device belongs to a different OpenCL platform, the current OpenCL implementation does not allow creating a single context for the two devices. We need to create a context for each of them. In addition, to copy the contents of one buffer (`buffer[0]`) to another buffer (`buffer[1]`) that belongs to a different context (`context[1]`), we may not use `clEnqueueCopyBuffer()`. Instead, a temporary host-side memory space, `tmp`, is allocated. The buffers are copied through `tmp` with `clEnqueueReadBuffer()` and `clEnqueueWriteBuffer()`.

3 OVERVIEW OF SnuCL FRAMEWORK

In this section, we address limitations of OpenCL and present the methods to overcome them.

3.1 LIMITATIONS OF OpenCL

As mentioned before, one of the limitations of OpenCL comes from its ICD. Even though ICD enables different OpenCL platforms from different vendors to coexist under a single operating system instance, programmers need to explicitly choose a specific OpenCL platform for each compute device in the application to use different compute devices from different vendors in the same application. As a result, an OpenCL context needs to be created for each vendor-specific platform. Thus a compute device may not access memory objects that belong to a different context without explicit data copying through a temporary space in the host main memory

```
#include <stdio.h>
#include <stdlib.h>
#include <CL/opencl.h>

#define BUFFER_SIZE 16384

int main( int argc, char* argv[] )
{
  cl_platform_id platform[2];
  cl_int err = clGetPlatformIDs(2, platform, NULL);

  cl_device_id device[2];
  err = clGetDeviceIDs(platform[0], CL_DEVICE_TYPE_ALL, 1, &device[0], NULL);
  err = clGetDeviceIDs(platform[1], CL_DEVICE_TYPE_ALL, 1, &device[1], NULL);

  // Creating a single context that contains the two devices does not work
  // cl_context context = clCreateContext(NULL, 2, device, NULL, NULL, &err);

  cl_context context[2];
  context[0] = clCreateContext(NULL, 1, &device[0], NULL, NULL, &err);
  context[1] = clCreateContext(NULL, 1, &device[1], NULL, NULL, &err);

  cl_command_queue queue[2];
  queue[0] = clCreateCommandQueue(context[0], device[0], 0, &err);
  queue[1] = clCreateCommandQueue(context[1], device[1], 0, &err);

  size_t bytes = BUFFER_SIZE * sizeof(int);
  ...

  cl_mem buffer[2];
  buffer[0] = clCreateBuffer(context[0], CL_MEM_READ_WRITE, bytes, NULL, &err);
  buffer[1] = clCreateBuffer(context[1], CL_MEM_READ_WRITE, bytes, NULL, &err);
  ...

  // Directly copying the contents of buffer[0] to buffer[1] does not work
  // err = clEnqueueCopyBuffer(queue[1], buffer[0], buffer[1], 0, 0, bytes, 0, NULL, NULL);

  // To copy buffer[0] to buffer[1], a temporary host-side memory space is needed
  int *tmp = (int *)malloc(bytes);
  err = clEnqueueReadBuffer(queue[0], buffer[0], CL_TRUE, 0, bytes, tmp, 0, NULL, NULL);
  err = clEnqueueWriteBuffer(queue[1], buffer[1], CL_TRUE, 0, bytes, tmp, 0, NULL, NULL);
  ...

  clReleaseMemObject(buffer[0]); // Release OpenCL resources and host memory
  ...

  free(tmp);
  ...

  return 0;
}
```

FIG. 7

Using OpenCL ICD.

(Fig. 7). In addition, commands for different compute devices from different vendors cannot be synchronized using event objects. It is also impossible to share other OpenCL objects (programs, kernels, and so on) across different contexts.

To overcome this limitation, SnuCL integrates multiple OpenCL platforms from different vendors into a single platform. Using OpenCL ICD, SnuCL enables an

OpenCL application to share objects (buffers, events, and so on) between different compute devices from different vendors.

For example, the code shown in Fig. 7 can be rewritten to the code shown in Fig. 8 using SnuCL. The SnuCL framework provides a unified platform called SnuCL Single under a single operating system instance. Because the two devices from two different vendor-specific OpenCL platforms belong to SnuCL Single, we create only one context for the two devices. As a result, to copy the contents of one buffer (buffer[0]) to another buffer (buffer[1]), we just use clEnqueueCopyBuffer(). An extra host-side memory space in the host program is not needed to transfer data from one buffer to another.

Another limitation of current OpenCL is that it is a programming model under a single operating system instance. An OpenCL application does not work for a cluster of multiple nodes each of which runs an operating system instance. Programmers are required to use communication libraries, such as MPI, in addition to OpenCL. This mixed programming model complicates workload and data distribution. The resulting application may not be executed under a single operating system instance.

SnuCL provides the programmer with an illusion of a single OpenCL platform image as shown in Fig. 1. SnuCL designates a node in the cluster as the host node where the OpenCL host program runs. SnuCL allows the OpenCL application to utilize compute devices in a remote node as they were in the host node. Using SnuCL, OpenCL applications written for multiple compute devices under a single operating system instance can run on the cluster without any modifications.

As shown in Fig. 9, SnuCL provides three different OpenCL platforms: SnuCL CPU, SnuCL Single, and SnuCL Cluster.

- SnuCL CPU platform is for general-purpose multicore CPUs under a single operating system instance. A set of CPU core in the system can be configured as an OpenCL compute device. The platform provides an ICD dispatch table. Thus SnuCL Single or SnuCL Cluster chooses this platform for CPU devices.
- SnuCL Single is a unified OpenCL platform that integrates all ICD-compatible OpenCL implementations installed under a single operating system instance.
- SnuCL Cluster is another unified OpenCL platform for heterogeneous clusters. It integrates all ICD-compatible OpenCL implementations in the cluster nodes and provides the programmer with an illusion of a single OpenCL platform image.

Assume that the developer uses a mix of OpenCL and MPI as a programming model for a heterogeneous cluster. The developer wants to launch a kernel to an OpenCL-compliant compute device in an OpenCL application. Assume that the kernel accesses a buffer, buff_A, that has been written by another compute device in a different compute node. Then the developer needs to explicitly insert communication and data transfer operations using MPI in the OpenCL application. To do so, as shown in Fig. 10A, the developer makes the source device to copy buff_A into a main memory space tmp using clEnqueueReadBuffer(). The source node sends the data to the target node using MPI_Send(). The target node receives the data in its own tmp from the source node using MPI_Recv(). The contents

```c
#include <stdio.h>
#include <stdlib.h>
#include <CL/opencl.h>

#define BUFFER_SIZE 16384

int main( int argc, char* argv[] )
{
  cl_uint num_platforms;

  // Check the number of platforms available in the system
  cl_int err = clGetPlatformIDs(0, NULL, &num_platforms);
  cl_platform_id *platforms = (cl_platform_id *)malloc(sizeof(cl_platform_id) * num_platforms);

  // Obtaining all the platforms available in the system
  err = clGetPlatformIDs(num_platforms, platforms, NULL);

  char buf[1024];

  // Obtaining the platform provided by SnuCL. "SnuCL Single" or "SnuCL Cluster"
  cl_platform_id snucl_platform;
  for (i = 0; i < num_platforms; i++) {
    err = clGetPlatformInfo(platforms[i], CL_PLATFORM_NAME, 1024, buf, NULL);
    if (strcmp(buf, "SnuCL Single") == 0) {
      snucl_platform = platforms[i];
      break;
    }
  }

  cl_device_id device[2];
  err = clGetDeviceIDs(snucl_platform, CL_DEVICE_TYPE_ALL, 2, device, NULL);

  // Creating a single context for the two devices
  cl_context context = clCreateContext(NULL, 2, device, NULL, NULL, &err);

  cl_command_queue queue[2];
  queue[0] = clCreateCommandQueue(context, device[0], 0, &err);
  queue[1] = clCreateCommandQueue(context, device[1], 0, &err);

  size_t bytes = BUFFER_SIZE * sizeof(int);

  …

  cl_mem buffer[2];
  buffer[0] = clCreateBuffer(context, CL_MEM_READ_WRITE, bytes, NULL, &err);
  buffer[1] = clCreateBuffer(context, CL_MEM_READ_WRITE, bytes, NULL, &err);

  …

  // Directly copying the contents of buffer[0] to buffer[1]
  err = clEnqueueCopyBuffer(queue[1], buffer[0], buffer[1], 0, 0, bytes, 0, NULL, NULL);
  …

  clReleaseMemObject(buffer[0]); // Release OpenCL resources and host memory
  …

  return 0;
}
```

FIG. 8

Using SnuCL for the code in Fig. 7.

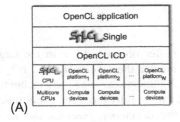

(A)

OpenCL application				
SnuCL Single				
OpenCL ICD				
SnuCL CPU	OpenCL platform₁	OpenCL platform₂	...	OpenCL platform_N
Multicore CPUs	Compute devices	Compute devices	...	Compute devices

(B)

OpenCL application														
SnuCL Cluster														
OpenCL ICD					OpenCL ICD					OpenCL ICD				
SnuCL CPU	OpenCL platform₁	OpenCL platform₂	...	OpenCL platform_N	SnuCL CPU	OpenCL platform₁	OpenCL platform₂	...	OpenCL platform_N	SnuCL CPU	OpenCL platform₁	OpenCL platform₂	...	OpenCL platform_N
Multicore CPUs	Compute devices	Compute devices	...	Compute devices	Multicore CPUs	Compute devices	Compute devices	...	Compute devices	Multicore CPUs	Compute devices	Compute devices	...	Compute devices

FIG. 9

SnuCL framework. (A) SnuCL CPU and SnuCL Single. (B) SnuCL Cluster.

```
...
void *tmp = malloc(…);
cl_mem buff_B = clCreateBuffer(…);
if (rank == SRC_DEV) {
    clEnqueueReadBuffer(queue[0], buff_A, …, tmp, …);
    MPI_Send(tmp, …, DST_DEV, …);
} else if (rank == DST_DEV) {
    MPI_Recv(tmp, …, SRC_DEV, …);
    clEnqueueWriteBuffer(queue[1], buff_B, …, tmp, …);
}
...
clSetKernelArg(kernel, …, sizeof(cl_mem), &buff_B);
...
clEnqueueNDRangeKernel(queue[1],…, …);

...
```

(A)

```
...

clSetKernelArg(kernel, …, sizeof(cl_mem), &buff_A);
...
clEnqueueNDRangeKernel(queue[1], …, …);

...
```

(B)

FIG. 10

Ease of programming with SnuCL. (A) OpenCL+MPI. (B) SnuCL Cluster.

of `tmp` is copied to a new buffer object `buff_B` in the target device memory by `clEnqueueWriteBuffer()`. Finally, the developer sets `buff_B` as an argument of the kernel and invokes `clEnqueueNDRangeKernel()` to execute the kernel.

On the other hand, SnuCL Cluster fully hides the communication and data transfer from the developer. Thus the developer executes the kernel by invoking only `clEnqueueNDRangeKernel()` without any additional data movement operations (`clEnqueueReadBuffer()`, `MPI_Send()`, `MPI_Recv()`, and `clEnqueueWriteBuffer()`). This improves software developers' productivity and increases portability. As a result, SnuCL achieves both high performance and ease of programming for a system running a single operating system instance and a cluster running multiple operating system instances.

3.2 SnuCL CPU

SnuCL CPU's target architecture is a system that consists of multicore CPUs and that runs a single operating system instance. The user may use a vendor-specific OpenCL implementation for the multicore CPU instead of using SnuCL CPU. While vendor-specific OpenCL implementations typically use some kind of lightweight context switching to run OpenCL kernels on multicore CPUs [21], SnuCL CPU uses a source-to-source loop transformation technique called work-item coalescing [22].

The runtime for SnuCL CPU defines a mapping between the components of the OpenCL platform model and those of the target architecture. The mapping is summarized in Table 1. A set of CPU cores is configured as a compute device. Each CPU core in the set becomes a CU. Because there is no component in a CPU core that is similar to a PE in the OpenCL platform model, the core emulates the PEs using a kernel transformation technique. This technique is called work-item coalescing [22] and is provided by the SnuCL OpenCL-C-to-C translator. The runtime maps all of the memory components in the compute device to disjoint regions in the main memory.

Table 1 Mapping Between the OpenCL Platform Model and the Multicore CPU System

OpenCL Platform Model	Multicore CPU System
Compute device	A set of CPU cores
Compute unit	A CPU core
Processing element	Emulated by a CPU core
Global memory	Main memory
Constant memory	Main memory
Local memory	Main memory
Private memory	Main memory and registers
Global/constant memory data cache	Data caches and coherence mechanism between cores

```
__kernel void vec_add(__global const float *a,
                      __global const float *b,
                      __global float *c)
{
    int id = get_global_id(0);
    c[id] = a[id] + b[id];
}
```

(A)

```
#define get_global_id(N) \
  (__global_id[N] + (N == 0 ? __i : (N == 1 ? __j : __k)))

void vec_add(const float *a, const float *b, float *c)
{
    for (int __k = 0; __k < __local_size[2]; __k++) {
        for (int __j = 0; __j < __local_size[1]; __j++) {
            for (int __i = 0; __i < __local_size[0]; __i++) {
                int id = get_global_id(0);
                c[id] = a[id] + b[id];
            }
        }
    }
}
```

(B)

FIG. 11

Emulating PEs using the work-item coalescing technique. (A) The kernel code. (B) After applying the work-item coalescing to the kernel code.

The work-item coalescing technique makes the CPU core execute each work-item in a work-group sequentially, one by one. It uses a loop that iterates over the local work-item index space (i.e., inside a work-group). The triple-nested loop in Fig. 11B is such a loop. The code in Fig. 11B is obtained after the work-item coalescing technique has been applied to the kernel code in Fig. 11A. The size of the local work-item index space is determined by the array __local_size provided by the SnuCL runtime. It is the array passed to the runtime through clEnqueueNDRangeKernel(). The runtime also provides the array __global_id that contains the global ID of the first work-item in the work-group.

When work-group barriers are in the kernel, the work-item coalescing technique divides the kernel code into work-item coalescing regions (WCRs) [22]. A WCR is a code region that does not contain any work-group barrier. Because a work-item private variable whose value is defined in one WCR and used in another needs a separate location for each work-item to transfer the value across different WCRs, a code transformation technique called variable expansion [22] is applied to WCRs. Then the work-item coalescing technique executes each WCR using a loop that iterates over the local work-item index space.

In SnuCL CPU, the kernel workload is dynamically distributed across different CPU cores (i.e., CUs) in a compute device. The unit of workload distribution is a work-group. Work-group scheduling across different CPU cores is similar to parallel loop scheduling for traditional multiprocessor systems because each work-group is essentially a loop because of the work-item coalescing technique.

SnuCL CPU uses the conventional parallel loop scheduling algorithm, called *factoring*, proposed by Ref. [23]. The runtime of SnuCL CPU groups one or more work-groups together and dynamically assigns them to a currently idle CPU cores in order to balance the load. The set of work-groups assigned to a CPU core is called a *work-group assignment*. To minimize the scheduling overhead, the size of each work-group assignment is large at the beginning, and the size decreases progressively. When there are N remaining work-groups, the size S of the next work-group assignment to an idle CPU core is computed by $S = \lceil N/(2P) \rceil$, where P is the number of all CPU cores in the CPU device [23]. The runtime repeatedly schedules the remaining work-groups until N is equal to zero. Factoring [23] is similar to *guided self-scheduling* (GSS) proposed by Ref. [24], where S is given by $\lceil N/P \rceil$. Factoring is better than GSS when the variation of the workload in each iteration is large.

3.3 SnuCL SINGLE

Every ICD-compatible OpenCL implementation has an ICD dispatch table that contains all OpenCL API function pointers. The runtime for SnuCL Single keeps the ICD dispatch tables of all available OpenCL platforms under a single operating system instance. It uses the tables to direct calls to a particular vendor implementation. The unified OpenCL platform, SnuCL Single, can be obtained with `clGetPlatformIDs()` in the host program. SnuCL Single implements `clEnqueueCopyBuffer()` using a temporary host main memory space if the source buffer and the destination buffer are allocated to two different compute devices that belong to different OpenCL platforms.

3.4 SnuCL CLUSTER

Fig. 12 shows the organization of the runtime for SnuCL Cluster. The runtime designates a node in the cluster as the host node where the host program runs. It consists of two different parts: the runtime for the host node and the runtime for other compute nodes. The runtime for the host node consists of two threads: *host thread* and *command scheduler thread*. When an OpenCL application executes on the host node, the host thread in the host node executes the host program in the application. The host thread and the command scheduler share command-queues. A compute device may have one or more command-queues as shown in Fig. 12. The host thread enqueues a command to a command-queue (❶ in Fig. 12). The command scheduler schedules enqueued commands across compute devices in the cluster one by one (❷).

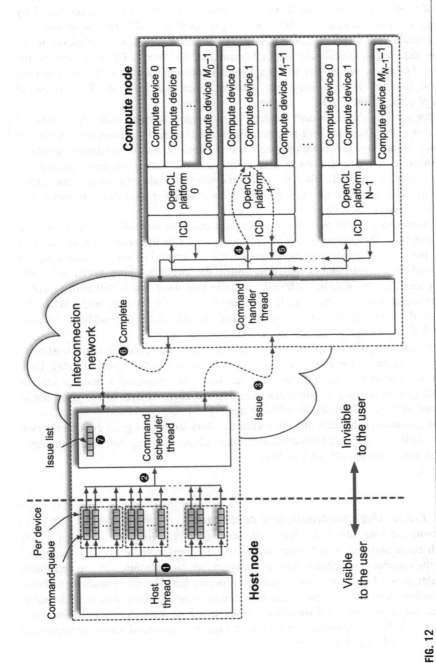

FIG. 12

The organization of the runtime for SnuCL Cluster.

The command scheduler visits all the command-queues in a round-robin manner. After dequeueing a command from a command-queue, it *issues* the command by sending a *command message* (❸) to the target compute node. The target compute node contains the target compute device. A command message contains the information required to execute the original command. To identify OpenCL objects, the runtime assigns a unique ID to each OpenCL object, such as contexts, compute devices, memory objects, programs, kernels, events, and so on. The command message contains these IDs.

After sending the command message to the target compute node, the command scheduler calls a nonblocking receive communication API function to wait for the completion message sent from the target node. The command scheduler encapsulates this information in an event object. To communicate the status of commands, an event object is used in OpenCL. Then the command scheduler adds the event object in the *issue list*. The issue list contains event objects associated with the commands that have been issued but have not been completed.

A *command handler thread* resides in each compute node. It receives command messages from the command scheduler and executes them across compute devices in the node. After extracting the target device information from the message, the command handler dispatches the command to the target compute device using the vendor-specific OpenCL ICD (❹). We assume that there are N different OpenCL platforms and that platform i has M_i compute devices in a compute node. When the compute device completes executing the command (❺), the command handler sends a completion message to the host node (❻).

After receiving the completion message, the command scheduler in the host node updates the status of the associated event in the issue list to CL_COMPLETE (❼). Then it removes the event object from the issue list. The command scheduler repeats scheduling commands and continues checking the event objects in the issue list in turn until the OpenCL application terminates.

The command scheduler and command handlers are in charge of communication between different nodes. This communication mechanism is implemented with a low-level communication API, such as MPI.

3.4.1 Processing synchronization commands

The command scheduler in the host node honors the type (in-order or out-of-order) of each command-queue and event synchronization enforced by the host program. When the command scheduler dequeues a synchronization command, the command scheduler uses it for determining execution ordering between commands in different command-queues. It maintains a data structure to store the events that are associated with queued commands and maintains bookkeeping of the ordering between those commands. When there is no event for which a queued command waits, the command is dequeued and issued to its target.

4 MEMORY MANAGEMENT IN SnuCL CLUSTER

In this section, we describe how SnuCL Cluster manages memory objects and executes memory commands.

4.1 SPACE ALLOCATION TO MEMORY OBJECTS

In OpenCL, the host program creates a memory object by invoking an API function, `clCreateBuffer()`. Even though the space for a buffer is allocated in the global memory of a specific device, the buffer is not bound to the compute device in OpenCL [4]. Binding a buffer and a compute device is implementation-dependent. As a result, `clCreateBuffer()` has no parameter that specifies a compute device. This implies that when a buffer is created, the runtime has no information about which compute device accesses the buffer.

The SnuCL runtime does not allocate any memory space to a buffer when the host program invokes `clCreateBuffer()`. Instead, when the host program issues to a compute device a memory command that manipulates the buffer or a kernel-execution command that accesses the buffer, the runtime checks whether a space is allocated to the buffer in the target device's global memory. If not, the runtime allocates a global memory space to the buffer.

However, there is an exception to this rule. When `clCreateBuffer()` is invoked with the `CL_MEM_COPY_HOST_PTR` flag, the application wants to allocate a space to the buffer and copy data from the host main memory to the buffer. If the runtime delays the space allocation until the buffer binds to a specific compute device, the runtime may lose the original data because the data may have been updated. To avoid this situation, the runtime allocates a temporary space in the host main memory and copies the data to the temporary space. After the buffer binds to a compute device, the runtime allocates a space in the device's global memory and copies the data from the temporary space to the allocated space. Then the temporary space is discarded.

4.2 MINIMIZING COPYING OVERHEAD

To efficiently handle buffer sharing between multiple compute devices, the SnuCL runtime maintains a *device list* for each buffer. The device list contains compute devices that have the same latest copy of the buffer in their global memory. It is empty when the buffer is created. When a command that accesses the buffer completes, the command scheduler updates the device list of the buffer. If the buffer contents are modified by the command, it empties the list and adds the device that has the modified copy of the buffer in the list. Otherwise, it just adds in the list the device that has recently obtained a copy of the buffer because of the command.

When the command scheduler dequeues a memory command or kernel-execution command, it checks the device list of each buffer that is accessed by the command. If the target compute device is in the device list of a buffer, the compute device has a copy of the buffer. Otherwise, the runtime checks whether a space is allocated to the buffer in the target device's global memory. If not, the runtime allocates a space for the buffer in the global memory of the target device. Then it copies the buffer contents from a device in the device list of the buffer to the allocated space.

To minimize the memory copy overhead, the runtime selects a source device in the device list that incurs the minimum copying overhead. For example, memory copy overhead in a node increases in the following order: a GPU to the same GPU, a CPU to the same CPU, a CPU to a GPU, a GPU to a CPU, and a GPU to another GPU. The copying overhead between two different nodes is usually much higher than that between two devices in the same node. The overhead also increases as the amount of copy increases. The runtime prefers a source device that has a latest copy of the buffer and resides in the same node as that of the target device. If there are multiple such devices, a CPU device is preferred. When all of the potential source devices reside in other nodes, a CPU device is also preferred to other compute devices. This is because the lower-level communication API does not typically support reading directly from the device memory of an accelerator, such as GPUs. It requires one more copying step from the compute device memory to a temporary space in the node's main memory.

To avoid such an unnecessary memory copy overhead, we define a distance metric between compute devices as shown in Table 2. We assume that there are two types of compute devices in the cluster: CPUs and GPUs. Based on this metric, the runtime selects the nearest compute device in the device list of the buffer and copies the buffer contents to the target device from the selected device.

4.3 PROCESSING MEMORY COMMANDS

There are three representative memory commands in OpenCL: write (`clEnqueueWriteBuffer()`), read (`clEnqueueReadBuffer()`), and copy (`clEnqueueCopyBuffer()`). When the runtime executes a write command, it copies the buffer contents from the host main memory to the global memory of the target device. When the runtime executes a read command, it copies the buffer contents from the global memory of a compute device in the device list of the buffer to the host main

Table 2 Distance Between Compute Devices

Distance	Compute Devices
0	Within the same device
1	A CPU and another CPU in the same node
2	A CPU and a GPU in the same node
3	A GPU and another GPU in the same node
4	A CPU and another CPU in a different node
5	A CPU and a GPU in a different node
6	A GPU and another GPU in a different node

memory. A CPU device is preferred to avoid the unnecessary memory copy overhead. When the runtime executes a copy command, based on the distance metric (Table 2), it selects the nearest device to the target device in the device list of the source buffer. Then it copies the buffer contents from the global memory of the source device to that of the target device.

4.4 CONSISTENCY MANAGEMENT

In OpenCL, multiple kernel-execution and memory commands can be executed simultaneously, and each of them may access a copy of the same memory object (e.g., a buffer). If they update the same set of locations in the memory object, we may choose any copy as the last update for the memory object according to the OpenCL memory consistency model. However, when they update different locations in the same memory object, the case is similar to the false sharing problem that occurs in a traditional, page-level software shared virtual memory system [25].

One solution to this problem is introducing a multiple writer protocol [25] that maintains a twin for each writer and updates the original copy of the memory object by comparing the modified copy with its twin. Each node that contains a writer device performs the comparison and sends the result (e.g., diffs) to the host that maintains the original memory object. The host updates the original memory object with the diffs. However, this introduces significant communication and computation overhead in the cluster environment if the degree of sharing is high.

Instead, the SnuCL runtime solves this problem by executing kernel-execution and memory commands atomically in addition to keeping the most up-to-date copies using the device list. When the command scheduler issues a memory command or kernel-execution command, say C, it records the memory objects that are written by the command C in a list called *written-memory-object list*. When the command scheduler dequeues another command D, and D writes to any memory object in the written-memory-object list, it delays issuing D until the memory objects accessed by D are removed from the written-memory-object list. This mechanism is implemented by adding those commands that write to the memory objects and have not completed yet into the event wait list of the dequeued command D. Whenever a kernel-execution or memory command completes its execution, the command scheduler removes memory objects written by the command from the written-memory-object list.

4.5 DETECTING MEMORY OBJECTS WRITTEN BY A KERNEL

The consistency management described before requires detecting memory objects that are written by an OpenCL kernel. In OpenCL, each memory object has a flag that represents its read/write permission: CL_MEM_READ_ONLY, CL_MEM_WRITE_ONLY, and CL_MEM_READ_WRITE. Thus the runtime may use the read/write permission of each memory object to obtain the necessary information. However, this may be too

```
int vec_add_memory_flags[3] =
{
    CL_MEM_READ_ONLY, // a
    CL_MEM_READ_ONLY, // b
    CL_MEM_WRITE_ONLY // c
}
```

FIG. 13

The buffer access information of the kernel vec_add in Fig. 11A.

conservative. When a memory object has CL_MEM_READ_WRITE and the kernel does not write to it at all, relying on read/write permission cannot detect this case.

Instead, SnuCL performs a conservative pointer analysis on the kernel source when the kernel is built. A simple and conservative pointer analysis [26] is enough to obtain the necessary information because OpenCL 1.2 imposes a restriction on the usage of global memory pointers used in a kernel. Specifically, a pointer to address space A can be assigned only to a pointer to the same address space A. Casting a pointer to address space A to a pointer to another address space B ($\neq$ A) is illegal.

When the host builds a kernel by invoking clBuildProgram(), the SnuCL OpenCL-C-to-C translator at the host node generates the memory object access information from the OpenCL kernel code. Fig. 13 shows the information generated from the OpenCL kernel in Fig. 11A. It is an array of integer for each kernel. The ith element of the array represents the access information of the ith buffer argument of the kernel. Fig. 13 indicates that the first and second buffer arguments (a and b) are read and that the third buffer argument (c) is written by kernel vec_add. The runtime uses this information to manage memory object consistency. When the source code of the kernel is not available (e.g., the kernel is built from binary), the runtime conservatively uses each buffer's read/write permission flag.

5 SnuCL EXTENSIONS TO OpenCL

In this section, we describe SnuCL's collective communication extensions to OpenCL. Although a buffer copy command (clEnqueueCopyBuffer()) is available in OpenCL and can be used for point-to-point communication in a cluster environment, OpenCL does not provide any collective communication mechanisms that facilitate exchanging data between many devices. SnuCL provides collective communication operations between buffers. These are similar to MPI collective

Table 3 Collective Communication Extensions

sniCL	MPI Equivalents
clEnqueueAlltoAllBuffer	MPI_Alltoall
clEnqueueBroadcastBuffer	MPI_Bcast
clEnqueueScatterBuffer	MPI_Scatter
clEnqueueGatherBuffer	MPI_Gather
clEnqueueAllGatherBuffer	MPI_Allgather
clEnqueueReduceBuffer	MPI_Reduce
clEnqueueAllReduceBuffer	MPI_Allreduce
clEnqueueReduceScatterBuffer	MPI_Reduce_scatter
clEnqueueScanBuffer	MPI_Scan

```
cl_int
clEnqueueAlltoAllBuffer( cl_command_queue *cmd_queue_list,
                         cl_uint           num_buffers,
                         cl_mem           *src_buffer_list,
                         cl_mem           *dst_buffer_list,
                         size_t           *src_offset_list,
                         size_t           *dst_offset_list,
                         size_t            cb,
                         cl_uint           num_events_in_wait_list,
                         const cl_event   *event_wait_list,
                         cl_event         *event );
```

FIG. 14

The format of `clEnqueueAlltoAllBuffer()`.

communication operations. They can be efficiently implemented with the lower-level communication API or multiple `clEnqueueCopyBuffer()` commands. Table 3 lists each collective communication operation and its MPI equivalent.

For example, the format of `clEnqueueAlltoAllBuffer()` operation is shown in Fig. 14.

It is similar to the MPI collective operation `MPI_Alltoall()`. The first argument, `cmd_queue_list`, is the list of command-queues that are associated with the compute devices where the destination buffers (`dst_buffer_list`) are located. The command is enqueued to the first command-queue in the list. The meaning of this API function is the same as enqueueing N-independent `clEnqueueCopyBuffer()`s to each command-queue in `cmd_queue_list`, where N is the number of buffers. An example of this operation is shown in Fig. 15.

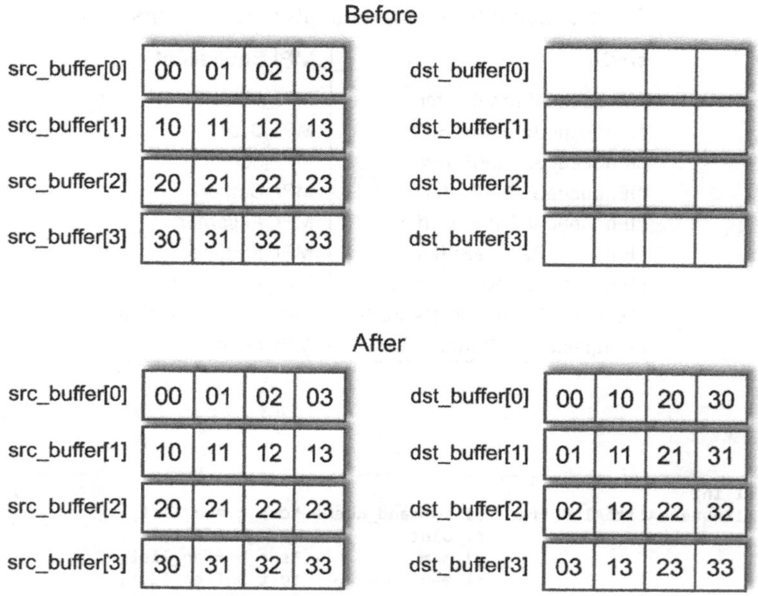

Before

| src_buffer[0] | 00 | 01 | 02 | 03 |

dst_buffer[0]
dst_buffer[1]
dst_buffer[2]
dst_buffer[3]

src_buffer[0] 00 01 02 03
src_buffer[1] 10 11 12 13
src_buffer[2] 20 21 22 23
src_buffer[3] 30 31 32 33

After

src_buffer[0] 00 01 02 03
src_buffer[1] 10 11 12 13
src_buffer[2] 20 21 22 23
src_buffer[3] 30 31 32 33

dst_buffer[0] 00 10 20 30
dst_buffer[1] 01 11 21 31
dst_buffer[2] 02 12 22 32
dst_buffer[3] 03 13 23 33

FIG. 15

A `clEnqueueAlltoAllBuffer()` operation for four source buffers and four destination buffers.

6 PERFORMANCE EVALUATION

This section describes the performance evaluation result of SnuCL. SnuCL implementation is open to the public at http://snucl.snu.ac.kr.

6.1 EVALUATION METHODOLOGY

We evaluate SnuCL using a medium-scale GPU cluster and a large-scale CPU cluster. Configurations of the clusters are summarized in Tables 4 and 5. Applications used in the evaluation are from the SNU NAS Parallel Benchmarks (NPB) suite [27], PARSEC [28], NVIDIA SDK [29], AMD [30], and Parboil [31]. Table 6 summarizes the applications used. The SNU NPB suite is an OpenCL implementation of the NPB suite [32]. It provides OpenCL NPB applications for multiple compute devices. Blackscholes, BinomialOption, CP, N-body, and MatrixMul are manually translated to OpenCL applications for multiple compute devices.

Table 4 System Configuration of the Medium-Scale GPU Cluster

Medium-Scale GPU Cluster	
Number of nodes	36
CPU	2 × Intel 2.0 GHz octa-core Xeon E5-2650 for each node
GPU	4 × AMD Radeon HD 7970 (2 GB RAM each) for each node
Memory	128 GB for each node
OS	Red Hat Enterprise Linux 6.3
Interconnect	Mellanox Infiniband QDR
OpenCL	AMD APP SDK v2.8
MPI	Open MPI 1.6.4
C compiler	GCC 4.4.6

Table 5 System Configuration of the Large-Scale CPU Cluster

Large-Scale CPU Cluster	
Number of nodes	512
CPU	2 × Intel 2.93 GHz quad-core Xeon X5570 for each node
Memory	24 GB for each node
OS	Red Hat Enterprise Linux 5.3
Interconnect	Mellanox Infiniband QDR
OpenCL	AMD APP SDK v2.9
MPI	Open MPI 1.6.3
C compiler	GCC 4.4.6
Fortran compiler	GNU Fortran 3.4.6

Table 6 Applications Used

Application	Source	Input	
		CPU Cluster	GPU Cluster
Blackscholes	PARSEC	64M options	128M options
BinomialOption	AMD SDK	1M samples	1M samples
CP	Parboil	16K × 16K	16K × 16K
N-body	NVIDIA	2.5M bodies	10M bodies
MatrixMul	NVIDIA	16K × 16K	10,752 × 10,752
EP	NPB	Class E	Class E
FT	NPB	Class D	Class C
CG	NPB	Class E	Class C
MG	NPB	Class E	Class C
SP	NPB	Class E	Class D
BT	NPB	Class E	Class D

6.2 PERFORMANCE

For all applications but FT, CG, MG, SP, and BT, SnuCL on a GPU cluster is an order to three orders of magnitude faster than a CPU core depending on the number of GPUs used [12,13]. For FT, CG, MG, SP, and BT, it is a few times faster than a CPU core. On a CPU cluster, SnuCL is a few times or an order of magnitude faster than a CPU core depending on the number of nodes used. They report that the performance of SnuCL for NPB is comparable to MPI-Fortran on a CPU cluster that consists of up to 64 nodes.

6.2.1 Scalability on the medium-scale GPU cluster

To show the scalability of SnuCL, we evaluate it on a 36-node GPU cluster. Fig. 16 shows the evaluation result. The x-axis shows the number of nodes. The number of GPUs used is recorded in parentheses. The y-axis shows the speedup over two nodes (eight GPUs) in logarithmic scale. It is better to show the speedup over a single GPU device, but a single GPU device cannot satisfy the memory requirement of the applications. Note that SP and BT require the number of devices to be a perfect square number. The speedups of SP and BT are obtained over 4 nodes (16 GPU devices) and 9 nodes (36 GPU devices), respectively. Because BT's memory footprint

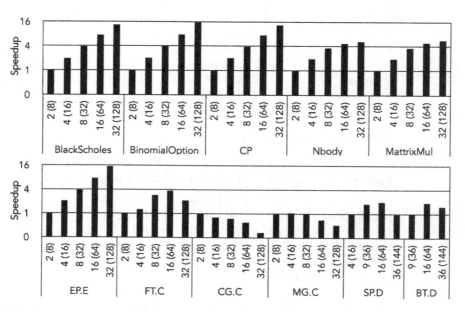

FIG. 16

Performance of SnuCL on the medium-scale GPU cluster (speedup over 256 MPI processes on 32 nodes with 256 CPU cores). The *number in the parentheses* represents the total number of GPUs.

exceeds the available memory in 4 nodes (16 GPUs), we do not execute BT on 4 nodes (16 GPUs).

Because Blackscholes, BinomialOptions, and CP are applications that scale well, SnuCL shows good scalability. The total amount of transferred data in N-body and MatrixMul increases as the number of devices increases. Thus the speedup increases slowly when the number of devices becomes large. Because EP is an embarrassingly parallel application, it also scales well with SnuCL.

The OpenCL kernels in FT, CG, MG, SP, and BT contain a relatively small amount of work. The amount of work in each kernel is too small to amortize the node-local, vendor-specific OpenCL runtime overhead. When the number of GPU devices increases, the amount of work in each kernel decreases because the total amount of work remains constant. In turn, the node-local, vendor-specific OpenCL runtime overhead becomes relatively large compared to the kernel workload. Because the total amount of memory in a GPU is limited (e.g., 2 GB), we cannot increase the input size further. Moreover, CG, MG, SP, and BT execute a large number of commands. Thus the command-scheduling and delivery overhead to remote devices dominates their performance. These are the reasons why SnuCL does not scale well with FT, CG, MG, SP, and BT on the GPU cluster.

6.2.2 Scalability on the large-scale CPU cluster

We compare the performance of SnuCL with that of MPI. The original NPB applications are written in Fortran using MPI. Fig. 17 shows the result. The x-axis shows the number of nodes, and the y-axis shows speedup over 256 MPI processes running on 32 nodes (i.e., 256 CPU cores) in logarithmic scale. Because E-class NPB applications do not run with less than 32 nodes because of the memory size, we run the applications on 32, 128, and 512 nodes. An exception is FT. Because E-class FT requires the memory size that is bigger than the total amount of memory of 32 nodes, we use the D-class input for FT (Table 6). The bars labeled MPI-Fortran and SnuCL show the performance of MPI and SnuCL, respectively. Because Blackscholes, BinomialOption, CP, N-body, and MatrixMul do not have an MPI version, we just obtain their speedup over SnuCL on 32 nodes (i.e., 256 CPU cores).

Blackscholes, BinomialOption, CP, N-body, MatrixMul, and EP execute a relatively small number of commands. Thus they scale well, except for MatrixMul at 512 nodes. MatrixMul initializes large 16,384 × 16,384 float-type matrices and multiplies them. The host should transfer at least 1 GB to each compute node without regard to the number of nodes to perform the matrix multiplication. As a result, MatrixMul does not scale well at 512 nodes.

SnuCL does not scale at all for FT. MPI-Fortran is much faster than SnuCL when the number of node is large. The performance of SnuCL decreases as the number of nodes increases. Because clEnqueueAlltoAllBuffer() commands used in FT make the host to deliver a point-to-point communication message to each compute node one by one, the amount of communication overhead between the centralized host and compute nodes becomes much more severe as the number of nodes becomes large.

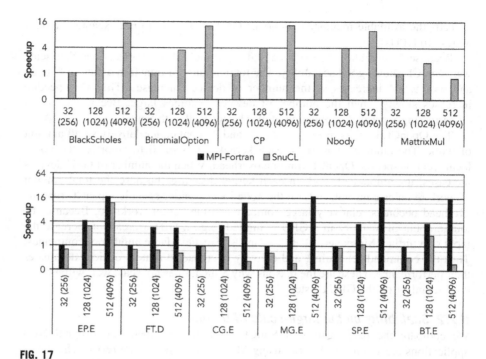

FIG. 17

Comparison between MPI-Fortran and SnuCL on the large-scale CPU cluster (speedup over 256 MPI processes on 32 nodes with 256 CPU cores). The *number in the parentheses* represents the total number of CPU cores.

As mentioned before, CG, MG, SP, and BT execute a large number of commands. Thus command-scheduling and delivery overhead dominate their performance in SnuCL. In addition, because the amount of work in the OpenCL kernel for 512 nodes is much smaller than that in the kernel for 32 or 128 nodes, the execution time of a kernel is not big enough to amortize the inherent overhead of the local, vendor-specific OpenCL runtime. On the contrary, MPI just executes the code immediately. Because the largest input class allowed for the NPB applications is class E, we cannot increase the input size further. In addition, the buffer-copy overhead of SnuCL is much bigger for a large number of nodes, and CG, MG, SP, and BT execute many buffer-copy commands. This is another reason why they do not scale well with SnuCL.

Overall, we see that SnuCL does not scale well for applications that have the following characteristics:

- The amount of work contained in kernels is too small, and a large number of such kernels are executed. As a result, the local, vendor-specific OpenCL runtime overhead and the command-scheduling overhead to remote devices dominate performance.

- A large number of memory commands are executed. The data movement overhead to remote devices dominates performance.

Actually, applications having these characteristics do not fit well with any heterogeneous programming model, such as CUDA and OpenCL.

7 CONCLUSIONS

In this chapter, we introduced the design and implementation of SnuCL. SnuCL unifies multiple OpenCL platforms from different vendors into a single OpenCL platform. It provides the single OpenCL platform image of a heterogeneous cluster to the programmer. Unlike OpenCL, SnuCL's unified OpenCL platform enables an OpenCL application to share OpenCL objects between compute devices of different OpenCL platforms from different vendors. It allows the OpenCL application to utilize compute devices in a remote compute node as though they were in the host node. The user launches a kernel to any compute device in the cluster and manipulates memory objects using standard OpenCL API functions. SnuCL shows that OpenCL can be a unified programming model for heterogeneous clusters with different types of accelerators. Moreover, SnuCL's collective communication extensions to OpenCL facilitate achieving high performance and provide ease of programming. SnuCL achieves high performance, ease of programming, and comparable scalability to MPI-Fortran for medium-scale clusters. However, applications that contain many small kernels and execute many memory commands do not scale well with SnuCL. These applications do not seem to fit well with any heterogeneous programming model, such as CUDA and OpenCL. For large-scale clusters, SnuCL may lead to performance degradation because of its centralized command-scheduling model. SnuCL source files are freely downloadable from the website http://snucl.snu.ac.kr.

ACKNOWLEDGMENTS

This work was supported by Grant No. 2013R1A3A2003664 (Creative Research Initiatives: Center for Manycore Programming) from the National Research Foundation of Korea funded by the Korean Government (Ministry of Science, ICT, and Future Planning). ICT at Seoul National University provided research facilities for this study.

REFERENCES

[1] TOP500, TOP500 The List, 2015, http://top500.org/lists/.
[2] NVIDIA, CUDA C Programming Guide, NVIDIA, 2013.
[3] NVIDIA, CUDA Runtime API, NVIDIA, 2013.
[4] Khronos Group, OpenCL 2.0 Specification, Khronos Group, 2013, http://www.khronos.org/registry/cl/specs/opencl-2.0.pdf.

[5] A. Alves, J. Rufino, A. Pina, L.P. Santos, clOpenCL: supporting distributed heterogeneous computing in HPC clusters, in: Proceedings of the 18th International Conference on Parallel Processing Workshops, Euro-Par'12, Springer-Verlag, Berlin, Heidelberg, ISBN 978-3-642-36948-3, 2013, pp. 112–122, http://dx.doi.org/10.1007/978-3-642-36949-0_14.

[6] R. Aoki, S. Oikawa, R. Tsuchiyama, T. Nakamura, Hybrid OpenCL: connecting different OpenCL implementations over network, in: Proceedings of the 2010 10th IEEE International Conference on Computer and Information Technology, CIT '10, IEEE Computer Society, Washington, DC, USA, ISBN 978-0-7695-4108-2, 2010, pp. 2729–2735, http://dx.doi.org/10.1109/CIT.2010.457.

[7] A. Barak, T. Ben-Nun, E. Levy, A. Shiloh, A package for OpenCL based heterogeneous computing on clusters with many GPU devices, in: 2010 IEEE International Conference on Cluster Computing Workshops and Posters (CLUSTER WORKSHOPS), 2010, pp. 1–7, http://dx.doi.org/10.1109/CLUSTERWKSP.2010.5613086.

[8] Casten, SocketCL, 2013, http://sourceforge.net/projects/socketcl.

[9] J. Duato, A.J. Pena, F. Silla, R. Mayo, E.S. Quintana-Orti, rCUDA: Reducing the number of GPU-based accelerators in high performance clusters, in: 2010 International Conference on High Performance Computing and Simulation (HPCS), 2010, pp. 224–231, http://dx.doi.org/10.1109/HPCS.2010.5547126.

[10] I. Grasso, S. Pellegrini, B. Cosenza, T. Fahringer, LibWater: heterogeneous distributed computing made easy, in: Proceedings of the 27th International ACM Conference on International Conference on Supercomputing, ICS '13, ACM, New York, NY, USA, ISBN 978-1-4503-2130-3, 2013, pp. 161–172, http://dx.doi.org/10.1145/2464996.2465008.

[11] P. Kegel, M. Steuwer, S. Gorlatch, dOpenCL: towards a uniform programming approach for distributed heterogeneous multi-/many-core systems, in: Proceedings of the 26th IEEE International Parallel and Distributed Processing Symposium Workshops & PhD Forum (IPDPSW), 2012, pp. 174–186, http://dx.doi.org/10.1145/2464996.2465008.

[12] J. Kim, S. Seo, J. Lee, J. Nah, G. Jo, J. Lee, OpenCL as a programming model for GPU clusters, in: Proceedings of the 24th International Workshop on Languages and Compilers for Parallel Computing, LCPC '11, 2011.

[13] J. Kim, S. Seo, J. Lee, J. Nah, G. Jo, J. Lee, SnuCL: an OpenCL framework for heterogeneous CPU/GPU clusters, in: Proceedings of the 26th ACM International Conference on Supercomputing, ICS '12, ACM, New York, NY, USA, ISBN 978-1-4503-1316-2, 2012, pp. 341–352, http://dx.doi.org/10.1145/2464996.2465008.

[14] B. König, CLara—OpenCL across the net, 2013, http://sourceforge.net/projects/clara.

[15] J. Lee, J. Kim, S. Seo, J. Lee, An OpenCL framework for homogeneous manycores with no hardware cache coherence, in: Proceedings of the 20th International Conference on Parallel Architectures and Compilation Techniques, PACT '11, 2011, pp. 56–67.

[16] C. Reano, A.J. Pea, F. Silla, J. Duato, R. Mayo, E.S. Quintana-Orti, CU2rCU: towards the complete rCUDA remote GPU virtualization and sharing solution, in: 2012 19th International Conference on High Performance Computing (HiPC), 2012, pp. 1–10, http://dx.doi.org/10.1109/HiPC.2012.6507485.

[17] A. Tupinamba, DistributedCL, 2013, https://github.com/andrelrt/distributedcl.

[18] A. Woodland, CLuMPI (OpenCL under MPI), 2013, http://sourceforge.net/projects/clumpi.

[19] S.V. Adve, M.D. Hill, Weak ordering: a new definition, in: Proceedings of the 17th Annual International Symposium on Computer Architecture, 1990, pp. 2–14.

[20] K. Gharachorloo, D. Lenoski, J. Laudon, P. Gibbons, A. Gupta, J. Hennessy, Memory consistency and event ordering in scalable shared-memory multiprocessors, in: Proceedings of the 17th Annual International Symposium on Computer Architecture, ISCA '90, ISBN 0-89791-366-3, 1990, pp. 15–26.

[21] J. Gummaraju, L. Morichetti, M. Houston, B. Sander, B.R. Gaster, B. Zheng, Twin peaks: a software platform for heterogeneous computing on general-purpose and graphics processors, in: Proceedings of the 19th International Conference on Parallel Architectures and Compilation Techniques, PACT '10, ACM, New York, NY, USA, ISBN 978-1-4503-0178-7, 2010, pp. 205–216, http://dx.doi.org/10.1145/1854273.1854302.

[22] J. Lee, J. Kim, S. Seo, S. Kim, J. Park, H. Kim, T.T. Dao, Y. Cho, S.J. Seo, S.H. Lee, S.M. Cho, H.J. Song, S.-B. Suh, J.-D. Choi, An OpenCL framework for heterogeneous multicores with local memory, in: Proceedings of the 19th International Conference on Parallel Architectures and Compilation Techniques, PACT '10, 2010, pp. 193–204.

[23] S.F. Hummel, E. Schonberg, L.E. Flynn, Factoring: a method for scheduling parallel loops, Commun. ACM 35 (8) (1992) 90–101, ISSN 0001-0782, http://dx.doi.org/10.1145/135226.135232.

[24] C.D. Polychronopoulos, D.J. Kuck, Guided self-scheduling: a practical scheduling scheme for parallel supercomputers, IEEE Trans. Comput. 36 (12) (1987) 1425–1439, ISSN 0018-9340, http://dx.doi.org/10.1109/TC.1987.5009495.

[25] C. Amza, A.L. Cox, S. Dwarkadas, P. Keleher, H. Lu, R. Rajamony, W. Yu, W. Zwaenepoel, TreadMarks: shared memory computing on networks of workstations, Computer 29 (1996) 18–28.

[26] B. Steensgaard, Points-to analysis in almost linear time, in: Proceedings of the 23rd ACM SIGPLAN-SIGACT Symposium on Principles of Programming Languages, POPL '96, 1996, pp. 32–41.

[27] S. Seo, G. Jo, J. Lee, Performance characterization of the NAS Parallel Benchmarks in OpenCL, in: 2011 IEEE International Symposium on Workload Characterization (IISWC), 2011, pp. 137–148, http://dx.doi.org/10.1109/IISWC.2011.6114174.

[28] C. Bienia, S. Kumar, J.P. Singh, K. Li, The PARSEC benchmark suite: characterization and architectural implications, in: PACT '08: Proceedings of the 17th International Conference on Parallel Architectures and Compilation Techniques, ACM, New York, NY, USA, 2008, pp. 72–81, doi:http://doi.acm.org/10.1145/1454115.1454128.

[29] NVIDIA, NVIDIA CUDA Toolkit 7.0, 2015, http://developer.nvidia.com/cuda-toolkit.

[30] AMD, AMD Accelerated Parallel Processing (APP) SDK, 2014, http://developer.amd.com/tools-and-sdks/opencl-zone/amd-accelerated-parallel-processing-app-sdk/.

[31] J.A. Stratton, C. Rodrigues, I.-J. Sung, N. Obeid, V.W. Chang, N. Anssari, G.D. Liu, W.M.W. Hwu, Parboil: a revised benchmark suite for scientific and commercial throughput computing, Tech. Rep., University of Illinois at Urbana-Champaign, 2012.

[32] NASA, NAS Parallel Benchmarks version 3.3, 2015, http://www.nas.nasa.gov/Resources/Software/npb.html.

Thread communication and synchronization on massively parallel GPUs

3

T. Ta, D. Troendle, B. Jang

University of Mississippi, Oxford, MS, United States

1 INTRODUCTION

Thread communication and synchronization play an important role in parallel computing. Thread communication refers to information exchange among concurrent threads either via shared memory or a message passing mechanism. In shared memory systems, a thread can update variables and make them visible to other threads. In contrast, a message passing mechanism allows threads in separate memory spaces to communicate with each other. Graphics processing unit (GPUs) adopt a shared memory model; thus threads communicate through memories such as local and global memory. As with other shared memory parallel systems, GPUs encounter the following main issues associated with shared memory access:

[Mutual exclusion:] Concurrently running threads may attempt to update the same memory location simultaneously. Without a mechanism to guarantee mutual exclusion, shared variables may become corrupted, causing an indeterministic result. Such a scenario is called a *race condition* or *data race*. One way to avoid it is to protect shared memory using *atomic* operations. An atomic operation grants serialized exclusive access to shared data. Another way is to divide a program into phases so that threads in a phase can update shared data safely without any interference from the execution of other phases. A *barrier* divides a program into phases, ensuring that all threads must reach the barrier before any of them can proceed past the barrier. Therefore phases before and after the barrier cannot be concurrent with each other [1].

[Ordering:] Shared memory may appear inconsistent among threads without an ordering policy. This type of problem usually arises when the compiler or hardware reorders load and store operations within a thread or among threads. A memory consistency model is used to resolve this issue. GPUs adopt

Advances in GPU Research and Practice. http://dx.doi.org/10.1016/B978-0-12-803738-6.00003-3

57

a relaxed consistency model where ordering is guaranteed only when the programmer explicitly uses a mechanism called a *fence*.

Thread synchronization is a mechanism to resolve the problems arising from concurrent access to shared memory. It prevents data corruption caused by unconstrained shared memory accesses. In this chapter, we present thread communication and synchronization mechanisms found in modern GPUs. We also discuss the performance implications of some techniques and include examples. Understanding thread communication and synchronization is essential not only to writing correct code but also to fully exploiting GPU's parallel computation power.

Throughout the chapter, we use OpenCL terminology, except when Compute Unified Device Architecture (CUDA)-specific techniques are presented. The rest of the chapter is structured as follows: Section 2 discusses coarse-grained synchronization operations using explicit barriers and implicit hardware thread batch. Section 3 presents native atomic functions available for shared variables with regular data types. Section 4 presents fine-grained synchronization operations supported in OpenCL 2.0.

2 COARSE-GRAINED COMMUNICATION AND SYNCHRONIZATION

In parallel programming, it is quite common that work within a group of threads must be done in separate and distinct phases. For example, on GPUs each thread in a work-group may load some data from global to local memory before doing computation on the data in local memory. In this scenario, we have two separate execution phases: loading global data to local memory and computation. All threads in a work-group need to complete the first phase before any thread in the second phase attempts to access local memory. A synchronization mechanism called a *barrier* implements such separation within a group of threads.

Separating execution phases within a group of threads implies two requirements. First, all threads must reach or execute a barrier before any thread is allowed past that barrier. This requirement constrains the execution order among the group of threads. Since data can be cached and memory instructions can be reordered around a synchronization point, there may not be a consistent view of memory shared among threads once they clear the barrier. This fact leads to the second requirement that all threads after a barrier must have the same view of shared memory. The second constraint can be implemented through a special memory operation called a *fence*. Since a barrier is applied to a group of threads (typically at least 32 threads on current GPUs), it is considered as a coarse-grained synchronization. In following sections, we discuss barrier operations at the kernel and work-group and wavefront levels in the context of GPU programming.

2.1 GLOBAL BARRIER AT THE KERNEL LEVEL

A global barrier synchronizes all threads across all work-groups in an NDRange, and it must satisfy the aforementioned two requirements: execution order constraints and memory consistency. A global barrier requires that all threads across all work-groups reach the barrier before any thread proceeds past the global barrier. This requires the suspension of work-groups that have already reached the barrier so that other work-groups can be scheduled and execute to the global barrier. Work-group suspension carries significant overhead as it involves the context switching of many threads. For that reason, there is no built-in global barrier function supported on GPUs. The effects of global barrier, however, can be achieved by splitting a kernel into multiple kernels and launching them in order. When a kernel terminates, all threads reach the end of the kernel, and data in caches are flushed to memory, which gives a consistent view of global memory among all threads in the successor kernel. However, a global synchronization at the kernel level comes with significant overhead. First, launching a new kernel instance incurs initialization cost. It takes significant time to send a kernel launch request to the host command queue via a device driver call and to warm up the hardware. On AMD GPUs, it usually takes hundreds of microseconds up to 1 ms to launch a kernel instance. Second, since all data are flushed to global memory between kernel launches, threads need to load data back to shared memory, L1/L2 caches, and registers. Third, this technique synchronizes all threads, even when only a smaller number of threads require synchronization.

A possible workaround that partially hides kernel launch overhead is to use out of order command queue execution. Fig. 1 shows the strategy. The idea is that instead of launching a new kernel instance after the previous one completes (Fig. 1A), all instances of a kernel are launched at the beginning and then the order of their execution is ensured using OpenCL events. OpenCL event objects can be used to define the sequence of the actual execution of the commands in the host queue. Fig. 1B illustrates how it works. Kernel 1 executes exactly as before, but the launch overhead of Kernel 2 is hidden by Kernel 1's execution as it is queued in advance. Kernel 2 does not start its execution until Kernel 1 completes. This reduces the overall execution time.

Listing 1 shows an example skeletal host code that uses events and two kernels to achieve the effect of a global barrier. Lines 5–6 declare an out-of-order command

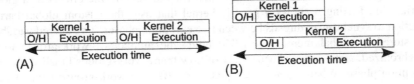

FIG. 1

Out of order execution using OpenCL event to hide kernel launch overhead (O/H). (A) In-order kernel execution. (B) Out-of-order kernel execution.

queue. Lines 9–11 launch *kernel1*, and OpenCL runtime posts its completion to *event1*. Lines 13–15 launch *kernel2*, but it is not executed until *event1* is posted. The overhead associated with *kernel2*'s launch is hidden while *kernel1* is executing. Line 18 waits for *kernel2* to post *event2*. Lines 20–21 release the events created by the launches.

There are some other attempts to "mimic" the effects of global barrier on GPUs at the software level. Xiao and Feng [2] proposed three implementations that synchronize threads across work-groups: (1) a GPU simple synchronization, (2) a GPU tree-based synchronization, and (3) a GPU lock-free synchronization.[1] In order to illustrate the main idea of their proposed techniques, we discuss the first one here. The other two implementations provide some improvements in performance, but they are left to readers for further reading.

```
1    ...
2    cl_int retCode;
3    cl_event event1, event2;
4    // create an out-of-order command queue.
5    cl_command_queue cmdQueue = clCreateCommandQueue(<context>, <device>,
6      CL_QUEUE_OUT_OF_ORDER_EXEC_MODE_ENABLE, &retCode);
7    ...
8    // launch the first kernel.
9    retCode = clEnqueueNDRangeKernel (cmdQueue, kernel1, <work_dim>,
10     <global_work_offset>, <global_work_size>, <local_work_size>,
11     0, NULL, event1);
12   // immediately launch second kernel, but wait for first kernel's event.
13   retCode = clEnqueueNDRangeKernel (cmdQueue, kernel2, <work_dim>,
14     <global_work_offset>, <global_work_size>, <local_work_size>,
15     1, {event1}, event2);
16   ...
17   // wait for the second kernel to finish.
18   retCode = clWaitForEvents(1, {event2});
19   // at this point, both kernels are complete.
20   ...
21   retCode = clReleaseEvent(event1);
22   retCode = clReleaseEvent(event2);
```

LISTING 1

An example of global synchronization at the kernel level using OpenCL events.

Listing 2 shows a custom function[2] that tries to achieve the effects of a global barrier, and Listing 3 shows a generic kernel that uses the custom global barrier function to synchronize threads between two execution phases. Two shared variables are stored in global memory: *goalVal* holds the number of work-groups to be synchronized, and *g_mutex* keeps track of how many work-groups finished the first execution phase. When *g_mutex* is equal to *goalVal*, all work-groups have already

---

[1] We use equivalent OpenCL terms instead of CUDA ones that the authors used in their paper.
[2] We have rewritten the original CUDA function in OpenCL.

reached the global synchronization point, and then they can start their second execution phase. In the *gpu_sync* function, the first thread of each work-group communicates with other work-groups by atomically incrementing the *g_mutex* variable to notify that this work-group has just finished the first phase. After that, it must wait at the synchronization point until all other work-groups finish their first execution phase. The first thread continuously checks the *g_mutex* variable in a tight while loop until *g_mutex* is equal to *goalVal*. It is likely that at the beginning of kernel execution, some work-groups are not scheduled to any compute units (CUs) right away, so the function will fail if threads in some active work-groups must wait for unscheduled work-groups without releasing computing resources on GPUs. To solve this problem, Xiao and Feng place a constraint that requires that the number of work-groups be less than or equal to the number of available CUs on GPU and that one work-group be mapped to one CU by allocating all local memory space in a unit to a work-group [2].

```
1   void gpu_sync(int* g_mutex, int goalVal)
2   {
3        // thread ID in a work-group
4        int tid_in_wg = get_local_id(0);
5        // only thread 0 is used for synchronization
6        if (tid_in_wg == 0){
7             atomic_add(g_mutex, 1);
8             // only when all blocks add 1 to g_mutex will
9             // g_mutex equal to goalVal
10            while (g_mutex != goalVal) {
11                 // a simple spin lock
12            }
13       }
14       barrier(CLK_LOCAL_MEM_FENCE|CLK_GLOBAL_MEM_FENCE);
15  }
```

LISTING 2

Another global synchronization proposed in Ref. [2].

```
1   __kernel void SampleKernel(..., // input and output parameters
2                        const int goalVal,
3                        __global int* g_mutex) // initialized to 0 by host program
4   {
5        ... // first execution phase
6        gpu_sync(g_mutex, goalVal); // global barrier
7        ... // second execution phase
8   }
```

LISTING 3

Using GPU simple synchronization barrier in a generic kernel.

However, there are some critical limitations in this technique. First, a deadlock is still possible since it is up to the hardware work-group scheduler to determine how to schedule work-groups to available CUs. Experiments on both AMD and

NVIDIA GPUs verify this. On NVIDIA GPUs, these requirements are enough to avoid the deadlock since the work-group scheduler distributes all work-groups evenly to all available CUs. However, on AMD GPUs, the work-group scheduler may not schedule work-groups to all available CUs, which leads to some unscheduled work-groups at the beginning of kernel execution. Second, this technique only guarantees the order of execution among threads but not the consistency of global memory. In the *gpu_sync* function, there is a local barrier (we discuss this in Section 2.2) that synchronizes all threads in a work-group. As explained in Section 2.2, the memory fence option used inside the local barrier ensures that local and global memory are consistent only with threads in the same work-group. That fence fails to guarantee the consistency among threads across work-groups, so the *gpu_sync* function does not behave exactly as a true global barrier does.

2.2 LOCAL BARRIER AT THE WORK-GROUP LEVEL

OpenCL provides a scope-limited, built-in barrier function for threads within a work-group. It guarantees the synchronization among threads in the same work-group but not threads across work-groups. (See the discussion on overhead in Section 2.1.) Since its scope is restricted to threads within a work-group, it is also called a *local barrier*. A local barrier delineates two execution phases—before and after the barrier function. It does this by enforcing all threads in a work-group to execute the barrier function before any thread can proceed past the barrier. Listing 4 shows a simple kernel that uses a local barrier function to separate two phases across the threads of a work-group. Since a local barrier is placed between the input[gid]++ and output[gid] = input[gid] statements, no thread is allowed to update the output buffer until all threads in a work-group execute the barrier function. Hence the order of execution among threads in the same work-group is guaranteed.

```
1  __kernel void localBarrier (__global float* input,
2                              __global float* output)
3  {
4      int gid = get_global_id(0);
5      input[gid]++;
6      barrier(CLK_GLOBAL_MEM_FENCE);
7      output[gid] = input[gid];
8      return;
9  }
```

LISTING 4

An example of how to use local barrier in OpenCL.

In addition, the consistency of shared memory regions is guaranteed by an explicit memory fence implemented inside the local barrier function. Section 4 discusses in more detail how a fence can ensure the memory consistency among threads. Recall that threads in a work-group share two memory regions: local and global memory. Because their latency is significantly different, ensuring consistency in global memory is generally more expensive than having threads in a work-group see a consistent view of local memory. Therefore OpenCL allows programmers to choose in which memory region they want to implement consistency. The *CLK_LOCAL_MEM_FENCE* flag ensures that all threads in a work-group have a consistent view of local memory after a local barrier, while the *CLK_GLOBAL_MEM_FENCE* flag ensures consistency in global memory. Both flags may be used together if consistency is required in both local and global memory.

A deadlock may occur when the local barrier is incorrectly placed inside branching statements. Listing 5 shows an example of such a scenario in which the local barrier is placed inside the if statement that allows only threads with even thread IDs to execute the barrier function. Threads with odd IDs will never be able to reach the barrier because of the branching statement.

```
1   __kernel void deadLock (__global float* input,
2                           __global float* output)
3   {
4       int gid = get_global_id(0);
5       if (gid % 2 == 0){
6               input[gid]++;
7               barrier(CLK_GLOBAL_MEM_FENCE);
8       }
9       output[gid] = input[gid];
10      return;
11  }
```

LISTING 5

A deadlock caused by an inappropriate use of local barrier.

Local barriers at the work-group level are widely used in GPU programs. Listing 6 shows an example of using a barrier to implement a simple work donation algorithm among threads in the same work-group. On GPUs load imbalance could become a critical performance issue when workload per thread cannot be determined at compile time. When the workload is not evenly distributed, only a few threads may do most of work, while others may finish early because they have little work to do. Nasre et al. [3] presents a general work donation scheme to balance workloads among threads in the same work-group. The main idea of work donation is that the amount of work assigned to a thread should be roughly equal to the average workload for all threads.

In this algorithm, a donation box is shared by all work-items in a work-group so that threads assigned too much work can "donate" or transfer their extra tasks to others. Three phases are separated by local barriers in this algorithm. First, each thread determines the number of tasks assigned to it, and then the per-thread workload is atomically added to the total number of tasks assigned to all threads in the work-group. In the second phase, the average workload per thread is calculated by dividing the total work for all tasks by the number of threads in a work-group. Since each thread must finish calculating its workload and update the total number of tasks before any thread proceeds to the next phase, a local barrier is used to separate the two phases. Without this barrier, some threads could compute the average workload before all threads have contributed their workload to the task total. If any thread gets too many tasks (i.e., greater than the average plus a certain threshold), the excess work will be donated to the shared box. Another barrier is placed at the end of this phase to ensure the donation box is updated and visible to all threads in the work-group. Lastly, all work-items do their assigned jobs and then get some extra tasks from the donation box if the box is not empty. Since work-items exchange tasks within the scope of work-group, shared variables are placed in local memory instead of global memory to minimize access latency. CL_LOCAL_MEM_FENCE is chosen to avoid the unnecessary overhead of making global memory consistent.

```
1   donate_kernel():
2         shared donationbox[...], totalwork = 0;
3         // determine whether I should donate
4         for all tasks assigned to me
5               mywork += estimated work per task
6         atomicAdd(totalwork, mywork)
7         barrier();
8         // donate
9         averagework = totalwork / threads_per_work-group
10        if mywork > averagework + threshold
11              push excess work into donationbox
12        barrier();
13        // normal processing
14        for all tasks assigned to me
15              process task
16        // empty donation box
17        while donationbox is not empty
18              task = pop work from donationbox in a critical section
19              process task
```

LISTING 6

A work donation algorithm on GPUs [3].

In this example, the work-group barriers impact the algorithm's correctness in two ways. First, they order the three phases so that no instruction in later phases is executed until all threads finish all instructions in their current phase. Second, after the synchronization point, the local barriers guarantee that all threads in a work-group have a consistent view of shared variables including the donation box and total work. If the consistency was not ensured at the barriers, threads would see different values in the donation box and total workload.

2.3 IMPLICIT BARRIER AT THE WAVEFRONT LEVEL

In addition to the built-in local barrier discussed in Section 2.2, GPU hardware intrinsically implements another smaller-scoped barrier. We call it an *implicit barrier*. To understand how an implicit barrier works, we need to go back to how threads are organized and executed on a GPU. A GPU is composed of multiple computing cores called *CUs* in OpenCL terminology (or equivalently *streaming multiprocessors* in CUDA terminology). Since hardware vendors use different terminologies to describe their architectures, for the purpose of this discussion, we explain the AMD GPU architecture and use its corresponding terminology. Fig. 2 shows the hierarchical structure of AMD Southern Islands GPUs. Each CU is further divided into smaller hardware blocks called processing elements (PEs). The way PEs are structured within a CU is an architecture design choice. For example, in AMD Southern Islands architecture, each CU consists of 4 vector units, each of which contains a group of 16 PEs [4]. These 16 PEs are able to handle 16 work-items in parallel, which is called the single instruction multiple data (SIMD) unit. All elements in an SIMD unit share a single instruction but operate on 16 possibly different operands.

To hide latency, SIMD units are further grouped to form a hardware thread batch called *wavefront* (equivalently *warp* in NVIDIA's terminology). On AMD GPUs, the wavefront size is 4 SIMD units (i.e., 64 threads), and all 64 work-items in a wavefront execute the same instruction in a lock-step fashion, completing one before moving on to the next instruction. They are always implicitly synchronized with each other, and no explicit barrier is required to synchronize them.

When branching causes divergent thread paths within a wavefront, the hardware maintains lock-step execution by either disabling some threads that are not in the current branch or forcing all threads to execute all branches and masking invalid results. Fig. 3 visualizes a simple case where an if statement splits the control flow inside a wavefront and some threads not on the current branch are disabled. No matter how hardware deals with thread divergence, all threads in a wavefront always stay synchronized.

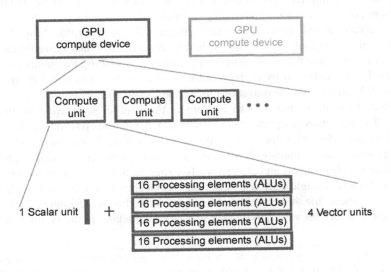

FIG. 2

Hardware architecture of AMD Southern Islands GPUs [4].

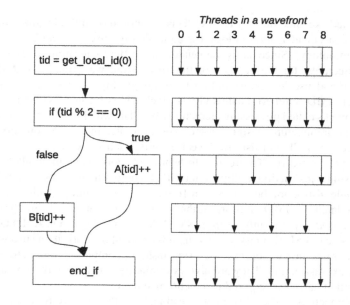

FIG. 3

Thread divergence in a wavefront.

Since threads in a wavefront automatically and implicitly stay synchronized, there is no synchronization overhead as is the case with explicit barriers. Several algorithms have already exploited this characteristic for efficiency. We discuss two scenarios where implicit synchronization is used efficiently: (1) a fast parallel scan algorithm and (2) a software prefetching scheme.

Sengupta et al. [5] proposed a better GPU parallel scan algorithm.[3] Fig. 4 shows the original scan algorithm that uses explicit local barrier to synchronize threads in a block. Assuming that the work-group size is 256 (i.e., $n = 256$), the number of local barriers that are executed by each thread is 16 (i.e., 8 iterations and 2 barriers per iteration). Such local synchronizations incur runtime overhead.

Let us look at another way to implement the parallel scan using an implicit barrier. The algorithm is separated into two phases: (1) intrawarp scan (Fig. 5) and (2) intrablock scan (Fig. 6). First, each warp does the scanning on its own threads. After the intrawarp scan is complete in all warps of a block, a single thread in each warp (e.g., *lane == 31*) collects and consecutively writes partial results from each warp to an array. Finally, a single warp does scanning on that array to get the final result. With this improvement, the number of local barriers required is only 5 compared to 16 in the original algorithm with 256 threads in a block. In addition, the number of local

---

[3]We use CUDA terminology to explain this algorithm. A warp is equivalent to wavefront and consists of 32 threads. A block is equivalent to a work-group. In CUDA __syncthreads is a local barrier function.

```
template<class OP, class T>
__device__ T scan(T *values)
{
    unsigned int i = threadIdx.x;   // ID of this thread
    unsigned int n = blockDim.x;    // number of threads in block

    for(unsigned int offset=1; offset<n; offset *= 2)
    {
        T t;

        if(i>=offset)  t = values[i-offset];
        __syncthreads();

        if(i>=offset)  values[i] = OP::apply(t , values[i]);
        __syncthreads();
    }
}
```

FIG. 4

The original parallel scan algorithm on GPU [5].

```
template<class OP, ScanKind Kind, class T>
__device__ T scan_warp(volatile T *ptr, const unsigned int idx=threadIdx.x)
{
    const unsigned int lane = idx & 31; // index of thread in warp (0..31)

    if (lane >=  1)  ptr[idx] = OP::apply(ptr[idx -  1] , ptr[idx]);
    if (lane >=  2)  ptr[idx] = OP::apply(ptr[idx -  2] , ptr[idx]);
    if (lane >=  4)  ptr[idx] = OP::apply(ptr[idx -  4] , ptr[idx]);
    if (lane >=  8)  ptr[idx] = OP::apply(ptr[idx -  8] , ptr[idx]);
    if (lane >= 16)  ptr[idx] = OP::apply(ptr[idx - 16] , ptr[idx]);

    if( Kind==inclusive ) return ptr[idx];
    else                  return (lane>0) ? ptr[idx-1] : OP::identity();
}
```

FIG. 5

Intrawarp scan [5].

barriers in the improved parallel scan does not increase with the block size. Therefore the second way improves the performance by reducing the number of local barriers needed.

The preceding example shows how to avoid expensive explicit local barriers by using implicit barriers. In another work, Bauer et al. [6] discussed a way to prefetch data into local memory in parallel with computation. The idea is to preload data into local memory before the data is actually used. To do that, they separated wavefronts in a work-group into two different groups.[4] The first group called *DMA-wavefronts* (*DMA-warps* as in the original paper) was dedicated to loading data from global

---

[4]The authors used CUDA terminology to explain this algorithm.

```
template<class OP, ScanKind Kind, class T>
__device__ T scan_block(volatile T *ptr, const unsigned int idx=threadIdx.x)
{
    const unsigned int lane   = idx & 31;
    const unsigned int warpid = idx >> 5;

    // Step 1: Intra-warp scan in each warp
    T val = scan_warp<OP,Kind>(ptr, idx);
    __syncthreads();

    // Step 2: Collect per-warp partial results
    if( lane==31 )  ptr[warpid] = ptr[idx];
    __syncthreads();

    // Step 3: Use 1st warp to scan per-warp results
    if( warpid==0 ) scan_warp<OP,inclusive>(ptr, idx);
    __syncthreads();

    // Step 4: Accumulate results from Steps 1 and 3
    if (warpid > 0) val = OP::apply(ptr[warpid-1], val);
    __syncthreads();

    // Step 5: Write and return the final result
    ptr[idx] = val;
    __syncthreads();

    return val;
}
```

FIG. 6

Intrablock scan [5].

into local memory for the next computation iteration, while wavefronts in the second group called *compute-wavefronts* (*compute-warps* as in the original paper) did actual computation on the data preloaded in local memory. The numbers of compute and DMA wavefronts were not necessarily equal. The authors discussed three ways to implement the prefetching: (1) single-buffering, (2) double-buffering, and (3) manual double-buffering. Here we discuss only the third, manual double-buffering.

Two buffers named *A* and *B* are kept in local memory. The DMA wavefronts load data from global memory into one buffer while the compute wavefronts do computation on the other buffer. Fig. 7 shows how two groups of wavefronts interchange buffers in each iteration. At the end of each iteration, an explicit local barrier ensures compute and DMA wavefronts are in sync and data in the two buffers are not corrupted.

3 BUILT-IN ATOMIC FUNCTIONS ON REGULAR VARIABLES

Sharing memory across concurrent threads becomes problematic when one thread attempts an unsynchronized update. This is called a *data race*. A data race happens when (1) at least two threads are concurrently accessing the same memory location; (2) at least one thread is trying to update the value stored in that location; and (3) there

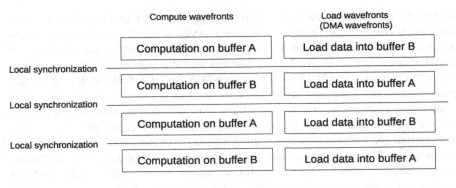

FIG. 7

Software prefetching with manual double-buffering [6].

is no synchronization mechanism to ensure that these accesses are mutually exclusive [7]. Listing 7 shows a very simple kernel in which a data race problem results in an unpredictable final value of the variable *counter*. Suppose two threads *A* and *B* try to increment *counter*. Both threads must read *counter* first, add one to it, and then write the new value back to *counter*. The final new value will be incorrect if a thread reads *counter* after the other one reads it but has not yet written the new value back. Such an indeterministic data race can occur unless operations are guaranteed to be mutually exclusive.

```
1   __kernel void dataRace (__global int* counter)
2   {
3         (*counter)++;
4   }
```

LISTING 7

An OpenCL kernel with a data race problem.

Since a data race can lead to corrupted shared memory and indeterministic program behavior, most parallel and distributed computing systems, including GPUs, provide built-in atomic functions. These functions ensure that memory operations are indivisible and not interrupted by any other concurrent threads. The list of atomic functions supported in OpenCL and CUDA can be found in their specifications [7,8]. These atomic functions can work on shared variables declared with a regular data type in both local and global memory, and guarantee mutually exclusive access to the variable across all threads without constraining in which order concurrent memory operations occur. We call them regular atomic functions to differentiate them from the atomic operations discussed later in Section 4.

Atomic operations come at a price. An atomic operation serializes memory accesses from different threads. While a thread is accessing a shared location, a lock is issued on that location until the occupying thread completes its atomic update. Other threads must wait on the lock, and the order in which they occur is undefined. The overhead of atomic functions can vary across different access patterns and hardware implementations. Consider the microbenchmark kernels in Listings 8 and 9 adopted from Ref. [9]. Listing 8 shows four different atomic access patterns on global memory. The first kernel, *CoalescedAtomicOnGlobalMem*, has all threads access consecutive memory addresses (aka, coalesced memory accesses) without contentions among threads. The second and third kernels, *AddressRestrictedAtomicOnGlobalMem* and *ThreadRestrictedAtomicOnGlobalMem*, have all threads within a wavefront (or warp) access consecutive memory addresses and the same address, respectively. The last kernel, *SameAddressAtomicOnGlobalMem*, has all threads access the same address, causing high contentions among threads. Table 1 shows their performance measured on modern AMD and NVIDIA GPUs.

```
1   #define NUM 7
2   #define WF_SIZE 64      // if AMD GPU is used
3   // #define WF_SIZE 32 // if NVIDIA GPU is used
4   __kernel void CoalescedAtomicOnGlobalMem(__global int* data, int nElem)
5   {
6       unsigned int tid = get_global_id(0);
7       for (unsigned int i = tid; i < nElem; i += get_global_size(0)){
8           atomic_add(data + i, NUM);
9       }
10  }
11  __kernel void AddressRestrictedAtomicOnGlobalMem(__global int* data, int nElem)
12  {
13      unsigned int tid = get_global_id(0);
14      for (unsigned int i = tid; i < nElem; i += get_global_size(0)){
15          // WF_SIZE is an arbitrary restriction size
16          atomic_add(data + (i & (WF_SIZE - 1)), NUM);
17      }
18  }
19  __kernel void ThreadRestrictedAtomicOnGlobalMem(__global int* data, int nElem)
20  {
21      unsigned int tid = get_global_id(0);
22      for (unsigned int i = tid; i < nElem; i += get_global_size(0)){
23          atomic_add(data + (i / WF_SIZE), NUM);
24      }
25  }
26  __kernel void SameAddressAtomicOnGlobalMem(__global int* data, int nElem)
27  {
28      unsigned int tid = get_global_id(0);
29      for (unsigned int i = tid; i < nElem; i += get_global_size(0)){
30          atomic_add(data, NUM);
31      }
32  }
```

LISTING 8

Global memory atomic operations with different access patterns.

Listing 9 shows microbenchmark kernels that perform atomic operations on local memory with the same patterns as in Listing 8, and Table 2 shows their corresponding performance.

Table 1 Performance of Global Atomic Operations With Different Access Patterns (Numbers in Milliseconds)

Kernels	AMD Radeon R9 290[a]	NVIDIA GTX 980[b]
CoalescedAtomicOnGlobalMem	1.485	1.820
AddressRestrictedAtomicOnGlobalMem	2.155	9.712
ThreadRestrictedAtomicOnGlobalMem	6.393	2.722
SameAddressAtomicOnGlobalMem	33.614	25.908

[a]*WF_SIZE is set to 64.*
[b]*WF_SIZE is set to 32 (warp size in NVIDIA GPU).*

Table 2 Performance of Local Atomic Operations With Different Access Patterns (Numbers in Milliseconds)

Kernels	AMD Radeon R9 290[a]	NVIDIA GTX 980[b]
CoalescedAtomicOnLocalMem	0.181	0.114
AddressRestrictedAtomicOnLocalMem	0.192	0.085
ThreadRestrictedAtomicOnLocalMem	2.037	1.474
SameAddressAtomicOnLocalMem	2.089	1.474

[a]*WF_SIZE is set to 64.*
[b]*WF_SIZE is set to 32 (warp size in NVIDIA GPU).*

```
1   #define NUM 7
2   #define WF_SIZE 64      // if AMD GPU is used
3   // #define WF_SIZE 32 // if NVIDIA GPU is used
4   __kernel void CoalescedAtomicOnLocalMem(__global int* data, int nElem)
5   {
6       __local int lmem_data[256];
7       unsigned int gtid = get_global_id(0);
8       unsigned int ltid = get_local_id(0);
9       for (unsigned int i = gtid; i < nElem; i += get_global_size(0)){
10          atomic_add(lmem_data + get_local_id(0), NUM);
11      }
12      data[gtid] = lmem_data[ltid];
13  }
14  __kernel void AddressRestrictedAtomicOnLocalMem(__global int* data, int nElem)
15  {
16      __local int lmem_data[256];
17      unsigned int gtid = get_global_id(0);
18      unsigned int ltid = get_local_id(0);
19      for (unsigned int i = gtid; i < nElem; i += get_global_size(0)){
20          // WF_SIZE is an arbitrary restriction size
21          atomic_add(lmem_data + (ltid & (WF_SIZE - 1)), NUM);
22      }
23      data[gtid] = lmem_data[ltid];
24  }
25  __kernel void ThreadRestrictedAtomicOnLocalMem(__global int* data, int nElem)
26  {
```

```
27        __local int lmem_data[256];
28        unsigned int tid = get_global_id(0);
29        unsigned int ltid = get_local_id(0);
30        for (unsigned int i = gtid; i < nElem; i += get_global_size(0)){
31            atomic_add(lmem_data + (ltid / WF_SIZE), NUM);
32        }
33        data[gtid] = lmem_data[ltid];
34    }
35    __kernel void SameAddressAtomicOnLocalMem(__global int* data, int nElem)
36    {
37        __local int lmem_data[256];
38        unsigned int gtid = get_global_id(0);
39        unsigned int ltid = get_local_id(0);
40        for (unsigned int i = gtid; i < nElem; i += get_global_size(0)){
41            atomic_add(lmem_data, NUM);
42        }
43        data[gtid] = lmem_data[ltid];
44    }
```

LISTING 9

Local memory atomic operations with different access patterns.

4 FINE-GRAINED COMMUNICATION AND SYNCHRONIZATION

The coarse-grained synchronization operations discussed in Section 2 are applied to a group of threads in an NDRange, a work-group, or a wavefront. They are efficient if communication needs involve all threads in the group. In regular workloads, whose computation patterns and execution dependencies are known at compile time, programmers can pack threads that need synchronization into as small a group as possible to minimize the cost of triggering barriers. The fast parallel scan algorithm discussed in Section 2.3 is a good example of such regular programs. However, redesigning an algorithm to reduce the cost of barrier is a difficult and sometimes even impossible task. There are many algorithms whose computation pattern and control flow cannot be determined at compile time. So where a barrier should be placed and how large its scope should be are hard to know. In such situations, programmers must use a wide-scoped barrier that synchronizes only a few threads in order to make their programs run correctly. This incurs very high overhead. Therefore more fine-grained communication among threads is desirable in general-purpose workloads on GPUs. Fortunately, the OpenCL 2.0 memory model (aka, memory consistency) includes new synchronization operations that allow fine-grained thread communication on GPUs. In Section 4.1, we first revisit briefly the concept of memory consistency and explain two general memory models: sequential and relaxed consistency. Section 4.2 discusses the details of the OpenCL 2.0 memory model and how to synchronize threads using a stand-alone fence and new atomic operations.

4.1 MEMORY CONSISTENCY MODEL

A memory model helps programmers ensure the correctness of their programs in multicore (or multiprocessor) systems by ordering the visibility of the effects of load and store instructions from different cores. To understand why a memory model is important, consider the typical producer-consumer code shown in Table 3. Assume that only two cores are sharing a single memory space.

Programmers expect that variable $R2$ will eventually store the *NEW*'s value because they assume $S1$ is always executed before $S2$, as shown in the program order. In fact, without an additional mechanism to strictly order $S1$ and $S2$, these instructions can be reordered by either the compiler (e.g., through instruction scheduling) or hardware (e.g., through out-of-order execution). If $S1$ and $S2$ are reordered, *flag* is set before *data* gets *NEW*'s value. Thus it is possible that $R2$ will get the old value stored in *data* on Core 2. Notice that $L1$ and $L2$ could also be reordered on Core 2 for similar reasons. This example shows the importance of a consistency model in a multicore system because it ensures the correctness of multithreaded programs. Based on how strictly a memory model enforces the order of load and store instructions, memory models are categorized into two groups: (1) sequential consistency that strictly preserves memory instructions' order and (2) relaxed consistency that allows memory instructions to be reordered to some extent for better performance. OpenCL 2.0 implements a relaxed memory consistency model.

4.1.1 Sequential consistency

Lamport [11] first introduced the sequential consistency model. On multicore systems with shared memory, it ensures the runtime order of memory instructions in the order specified in the program. Sequential consistency is the most intuitive model—the hardware follows the order of instructions specified in the program. Lamport specified two requirements for the sequential consistency model: (1) all memory requests issued by a single core (processor) execute in the order specified by programmer and (2) the memory system must service memory requests from different cores in an FIFO order [11]. Going back to the example shown in Table 3, a programmer expects the system to execute instruction $S1$ before $S2$ on Core 1. That order is specified by the programmer and is called the *program order* [10]. If

Table 3 An Indeterministic Program on Dual-Core System Without Consistency Model [10]

Core 1	Core 2
S1: data ← NEW	
S2: flag ← SET	L1: R1 ← flag
	B1: if (R1 != SET) goto L1
	L2: R2 ← data

sequential consistency is applied, Core 1 must issue $S1$ before $S2$, and also $S1$ must be executed before $S2$ since $S1$ arrives at the memory system before $S2$ does.

4.1.2 Relaxed consistency

Sequential consistency is a conservative memory model that does not allow any instruction reordering on each core. This prevents many optimizations and degrades performance. However, not all memory instructions on a single core need to preserve their program order. Some memory instructions can be reordered, achieving better performance without losing correctness. This is the motivation for more relaxed or weaker memory models. In order to do that, programmers are responsible for specifying program order through fence instructions. A memory fence is basically a special instruction that orders memory operations around it. In relaxed models, without an explicit fence, load and store instructions are assumed to be order-independent and thus eligible for reordering [10]. All memory instructions before a fence must be issued and executed before any one after the fence. Table 4 shows an example of how to place fence instructions to guarantee that $R2$ will eventually get *NEW* value.

4.2 THE OPENCL 2.0 MEMORY MODEL

Inherited from previous OpenCL versions, the coarse-grained barriers and regular built-in atomic functions are still available in OpenCL 2.0. In addition to these synchronization mechanisms, OpenCL 2.0 provides stand-alone fence and special atomic functions that can order memory instructions around them. This support allows programmers to do fine-grained thread communication. In this section, we first define relationships that may exist between any two memory operations (i.e., load or store instructions). These relationships help us precisely discuss (1) special atomic operations and stand-alone memory fences (Section 4.2.2), (2) acquire/release semantics (Section 4.2.3), and (3) memory ordering options (Section 4.2.4). Lastly, we present memory scope options that help reduce synchronization overhead.

Table 4 Two Fence Instructions, F1 and F2, Are Placed to Ensure *NEW* Value Is Assigned to R2 [10]

Core 1	Core 2
S1: data ← NEW F1: fence S2: flag ← SET	
	L1: R1 ← flag B1: if (R1 != SET) goto L1 F2: fence L2: R2 ← data

4.2.1 Relationships between two memory operations

OpenCL 2.0 defines the following relationships between two memory operations in a single thread or multiple threads. They can be applied to operations on either global or local memory.

- *Sequenced-before relationship.* In a single thread (or unit of execution), a memory operation A is sequenced before a memory operation B if A is executed before B. All effects made by the execution of A in memory are visible to operation B. If the sequenced-before relationship between A and B is not defined, A and B are neither sequenced nor ordered [7]. This defines a relationship between any two memory operations in a single thread and how the effects made by one operation are visible to the other (Fig. 8).
- *Synchronizes-with relationship.* When two memory operations are from different threads, they need to be executed in a particular order by the memory system. Given two memory operations A and B in two different threads, A synchronizes with B if A is executed before B. Hence all effects made by A in shared memory are also visible to B [7] (Fig. 9).
- *Happens-before relationship.* Given two memory operations A and B, A happens before B if
  - A is sequenced before B, or
  - A synchronizes with B, or
  - For some operation C, A happens before C, and C happens before B [7] (Fig. 10).

4.2.2 Special atomic operations and stand-alone memory fence

The regular atomic functions discussed in Section 3 ensure only that concurrent accesses to a shared memory location are mutually exclusive. They can be applied to a shared variable declared with a regular data type so that it can be protected from race condition. Special atomic operations in OpenCL 2.0 are able to do more than just ensuring mutually exclusive access to a shared location. They place ordering

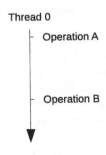

FIG. 8

Sequenced-before relationship.

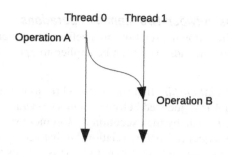

FIG. 9

Synchronizes-with relationship.

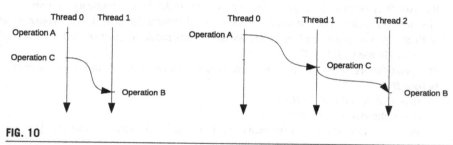

FIG. 10

Happens-before relationship.

constraints on memory instructions before and after them in program order. The ordering constraints are discussed in detail in later sections. These special atomic operations must work on a predefined subset of shared variables called *atomic objects*. These objects are declared with special atomic data types (e.g., atomic_int, atomic_float, etc.). Programmers have to declare, initialize, and use these objects through special built-in functions. For example, *atomic_init* initializes an atomic object to a constant, and *atomic_load* returns the value stored in an atomic object [7]. The full list of available special atomic functions can be found in the OpenCL 2.0 C specification.

Section 2.2 described the memory fence implemented inside a local barrier to order memory instructions before and after the barrier. The OpenCL 2.0 memory model supports a stand-alone fence function, *atomic_work_item_fence*, with more ordering constraint and scope options. There is a difference between a special atomic operation and a memory fence. No specific atomic object is associated with a fence. In contrast, any special atomic operation requires a corresponding atomic object [7]. A special atomic operation, in addition to its capability of ordering memory instructions, provides globally exclusive access to its corresponding atomic object. Programmers can do a read-modify-write operation on an atomic object atomically through a special atomic operation (e.g., *atomic_fetch_add* function).

Table 5 An Example of Acquire and Release Semantics

Producer Thread	Consumer Thread
LS1: Some loads and stores in shared memory F1: Release fence Atomic S1: flag ← SET	
	Atomic L1: R1 ← flag B1: if (R1 != SET) goto L1 F2: Acquire fence LS2: Some loads and stores in shared memory

4.2.3 Release and acquire semantics

In OpenCL 2.0, release and acquire semantics specify the aforementioned relationships between two memory operations through either a stand-alone fence or a special atomic operation. They are mostly used to broadcast a change(s) made by a thread in shared memory to one or more other threads. Let us go back to the producer-consumer pattern in which a producer thread wants to broadcast to consumer thread(s) all values it has written to shared memory through fence and atomic instructions (we use fence and atomic function as stand-alone operations in this example for the purpose of clarification). We give an example of OpenCL 2.0 code in which they are fused into a single atomic function in a later section (Table 5).

The release fence F1 guarantees that *LS*1 is **sequenced before** *Atomic S*1 instructions. Therefore, all changes made by *LS*1 are visible in shared memory when *Atomic S*1 is executed. Without the release fence, the problem discussed in Section 4.1 would happen. Similarly, the acquire fence F2 ensures that *Atomic L*1 is **sequenced before** *LS*2 instructions. In this case, the release fence F1 **synchronizes with** the acquire fence F2. In short, the execution chain will be LS1 → F1 → Atomic S1 → Atomic L1 → F2 → LS2 (operation at the left of the arrow **happens before** the one at the right of the arrow).

4.2.4 Memory order parameters

In either a memory fence or a special atomic operation, programmers can pass one of the following enumeration constants to specify how they want to order memory instructions around a synchronization operation.

- *memory_order_relaxed*. This constant implies that there is no order constraint specified among memory instructions [7]. Only the atomicity of operations is guaranteed. This option can be used to implement a global counter as shown next.

```
1  __kernel void threadCounter(__global atomic_uint* globalCounter)
2  {
3        uint old_val = atomic_fetch_add_explicit(globalCounter,
4                                                          1,
```

```
5                                              memory_order_relaxed ,
6                                              memory_scope_device );
7          return;
8  }
```

A global atomic variable named *globalCounter* that is initialized by the host program is incremented by each thread. Since addition is commutative, the order threads increment *globalCounter* does not matter. So we only need *memory_order_relaxed* to enforce the atomicity of that operation. Since no ordering constraint is specified, this option would yield the best performance.

- *memory_order_acquire and memory_order_release.* These two constants specify the release and acquire semantics as discussed in Section 4.2.3. They can be used in parallel code that have a producer-consumer pattern, like the following example.

```
1   __kernel void kernel( __global atomic_uint* lock ,
2                          __global int* sharedBuffer )
3   {
4      atomic_init(lock , 0);
5      int local_thread_id = get_local_id (0);
6      int work_group_id = get_group_id (0);
7      // producer
8      if (work_group_id == get_num_groups(0)−1 && local_thread_id == 0) {
9             sharedBuffer [0] = 123;
10            atomic_store_explicit(lock ,
11                                    1,
12                                    memory_order_release ,
13                                    memory_scope_device );
14     }
15     // consumer
16     else if (work_group_id == 0 && local_thread_id == 0) {
17         while (atomic_load_explicit(lock ,
18                                       memory_order_acquire ,
19                                       memory_scope_device) == 0){};
20         sharedBuffer [1] = sharedBuffer [0];
21     }
22     return;
23  }
```

In this example, a single global atomic lock variable is used to notify consumer thread(s) that a producer thread has updated shared memory with its results. The first thread in work-group 0 is a consumer who waits for the output returned by the first thread in the last work-group (i.e., the producer). The producer writes a value to a global variable, and then the consumer loads the value and stores it in a different variable. A tight while loop is used to guarantee that the release operation (i.e., atomic_store_explicit) synchronizes with the acquire operation (i.e., atomic_load_explicit). Without that loop, the load acquire may happen earlier than the store release, and thus no synchronization is achieved. Note that this kind of producer-consumer paradigm could fail and lead to a deadlock situation. For example, consider the situation where there are many consumer threads in multiple work-groups waiting on the lock that is supposed to be updated by a single producer thread. Because of some resource constraints, the work-group that has the producer thread could never be scheduled and executed. In that case, all consumer threads are executing a tight loop waiting for the producer to give them work. Since no consumer thread completes and frees resources, the producer cannot be scheduled. Therefore, when using fine-grained thread communication, programmers need to carefully design their algorithms to avoid such a deadlock.

- *memory_order_acq_rel*. This option implies both *acquire* and *release* orderings on load and store instructions around a synchronization point. It can be used in a read-modify-write atomic operation. For example, in OpenCL 2.0, the function *atomic_fetch_key* can first load a value in a shared variable, do an operation on it, and then update that variable with the modified value [7].
- *memory_order_seq_cst*. This constant specifies that sequential consistency is desired for all load and store instructions from different units of execution. No reordering is allowed for these instructions in a single thread. The program order from multiple threads appears to be interleaved [7]. Choosing this option will lead to additional overhead because no instruction ordering is allowed.

4.2.5 Memory scope parameters

Another parameter passed to OpenCL 2.0 synchronization operations is *memory scope*. The OpenCL execution model groups threads into different scopes (wavefront, work-group, NDRange, etc.). As reasoned in Section 2, communication among threads under a larger scope is generally more expensive than one under a smaller scope. Therefore programmers can improve performance by specifying as small a scope as possible under which threads communicate with each other. Any two threads involved in a synchronization must be under the same scope. Otherwise, the runtime would result in undefined behaviors. The memory scope constants used in synchronization operation are

- *memory_scope_work_item*. Ordering constraints are applied within a single work-item.
- *memory_scope_work_group*. Ordering constraints are applied to work-items within a work-group. Any synchronization across work-groups leads to undefined behaviors.
- *memory_scope_device*. Ordering constraints are applied to work-items across work-groups and running within a device.
- *memory_scope_all_svm_devices*. Ordering constraints are applied to work-items across devices provided that those devices share the same memory address space.

5 CONCLUSION AND FUTURE RESEARCH DIRECTION

Throughout the chapter, we discussed various thread communication and synchronization mechanisms available in current GPUs. We presented several ways to achieve coarse-grained synchronization among threads under different scopes, and the performance implications of each technique in particular situations. We discussed built-in atomic operations on regular, shared variables to avoid data race problems and also the impact of such atomic functions on performance for different GPUs. We presented the current trend toward more fine-grained thread communication and synchronization that have been recently introduced as core functionalities in OpenCL 2.0 and HSA standards. We described the release-consistency-based memory model in OpenCL 2.0 by discussing concepts underlying that model and explaining how to correctly use newly introduced OpenCL 2.0 functions to achieve fine-grained communication at the thread level.

There is interesting ongoing research on fine-grained thread communication and synchronization that is essential in order for current GPUs to handle irregular workloads efficiently at both the software and the architecture levels. Various lock-free concurrent data structures (doubly ended queue, linked list, skip list, etc.) that have been implemented using traditional coarse-grained synchronization and atomic operations on GPUs [12,13] can be more easily and efficiently implemented using fine-grained synchronization. The new HSA memory model opens more optimization opportunities for a class of irregular graph-based and mesh-based workloads whose performance is limited by coarse-grained synchronization. At the architecture level, implementation of such fine-grained thread communication mechanisms and the choice of a memory model for GPUs are interesting research directions [14–16]. As GPUs become more tightly coupled with CPUs, supporting a single memory model for these different processors becomes an increasingly important and challenging research topic.

REFERENCES

[1] J. DeNero, Composing Programs, 2015, http://www.composingprograms.com/.
[2] S. Xiao, W.C. Feng, Inter-block GPU communication via fast barrier synchronization, in: 2010 IEEE International Symposium on Parallel & Distributed Processing (IPDPS), IEEE, 2010, pp. 1–12.
[3] R. Nasre, M. Burtscher, K. Pingali, Data-driven versus topology-driven irregular computations on GPUs, in: 2013 IEEE 27th International Symposium on Parallel & Distributed Processing (IPDPS), IEEE, 2013, pp. 463–474.
[4] AMD, AMD Accelerated Parallel Processing: OpenCL Programming Guide, 2013, http://developer.amd.com/wordpress/media/2013/07/AMD_Accelerated_Parallel_Processing_OpenCL_Programming_Guide-rev-2.7.pdf.
[5] S. Sengupta, M. Harris, M. Garland, Efficient parallel scan algorithms for GPUs, Tech. Rep. NVR-2008-003 (1), NVIDIA, Santa Clara, CA, 2008.

[6] M. Bauer, H. Cook, B. Khailany, CudaDMA: optimizing GPU memory bandwidth via warp specialization, in: Proceedings of 2011 International Conference for High Performance Computing, Networking, Storage and Analysis, SC'11, ACM, New York, NY, USA.

[7] Khronos OpenCL Working Group, The OpenCL Specification, Version: 2.0, Revision: 26, 2014, https://www.khronos.org/registry/cl/specs/opencl-2.0-openclc.pdf.

[8] NVIDIA, CUDA C Programming Guide, 2015, http://docs.nvidia.com/cuda/cuda-c-programming-guide/index.html.

[9] Stack Overflow Forum, CUDA atomic operation performance in different scenarios, 2014, http://stackoverflow.com/questions/22367238/cuda-atomic-operation-performance-in-different-scenarios.

[10] D.J. Sorin, M.D. Hill, D.A. Wood, A primer on memory consistency and cache coherence, Synth. Lect. Comput. Architect. 6 (3) (2011) 1–212.

[11] L. Lamport, How to make a multiprocessor computer that correctly executes multiprocess programs, IEEE Trans. Comput. 100 (9) (1979) 690–691.

[12] D. Cederman, B. Chatterjee, P. Tsigas, Understanding the performance of concurrent data structures on graphics processors, in: Euro-Par 2012 Parallel Processing, Springer, 2012, pp. 883–894.

[13] P. Misra, M. Chaudhuri, Performance evaluation of concurrent lock-free data structures on GPUs, in: 2012 IEEE 18th International Conference on Parallel and Distributed Systems (ICPADS), Dec., 2012, pp. 53–60.

[14] B. Hechtman, S. Che, D.R. Hower, Y. Tian, B.M. Beckmann, M.D. Hill, S.K. Reinhardt, D. Wood, et al., Quickrelease: a throughput-oriented approach to release consistency on GPUs, in: 2014 IEEE 20th International Symposium on High Performance Computer Architecture (HPCA), IEEE, 2014, pp. 189–200.

[15] D.R. Hower, B.A. Hechtman, B.M. Beckmann, B.R. Gaster, M.D. Hill, S.K. Reinhardt, D.A. Wood, Heterogeneous-race-free memory models, ACM SIGPLAN Not. 49 (4) (2014) 427–440.

[16] M.S. Orr, S. Che, A. Yilmazer, B.M. Beckmann, M.D. Hill, D.A. Wood, Synchronization using remote-scope promotion, in: Proceedings of the Twentieth International Conference on Architectural Support for Programming Languages and Operating Systems, ACM, 2015, pp. 73–86.

Software-level task scheduling on GPUs

4

B. Wu[1], X. Shen[2]

Colorado School of Mines, Golden, CO, United States[1] North Carolina State University, Raleigh, NC, United States[2]

1 INTRODUCTION, PROBLEM STATEMENT, AND CONTEXT

Graphics processing units (GPUs) integrate thousands of cores onto a single chip and support the simultaneous execution of tens of thousands of threads. This massive parallelism greatly improves peak throughput compared to central processing units (CPUs). However, the sustainable performance for many GPU applications, especially data-intensive applications, is below 30% of the peak throughput [1–5]. One source of such inefficiency comes from the difficulty of scheduling the huge number of threads.

Thread scheduling comprises two dimensions: temporal scheduling and spatial scheduling. Temporal scheduling decides when the threads should run; spatial scheduling decides where the threads should run. On CPUs, many studies explored both dimensions and showed scheduling's central role for tapping into the full power of processors [6–10] and for enforcing fairness for co-running applications [11–13]. The operating system provides flexible APIs to bind CPU threads to specific cores, which serve as the building blocks to apply various software-level scheduling strategies. However, scheduling on the GPU is complicated by the thread hierarchy: Some threads compose a warp, some warps compose a thread block (i.e., a CTA)[1] and some thread blocks compose a grid. The threads in a grid execute the same kernel function. The hardware scheduler, despite being able to quickly schedule thread blocks to processors, cannot be controlled by compilers or programmers. Furthermore, the mechanism of the scheduler is not disclosed, which manifests obscure and nondeterministic behaviors.

The hardware scheduler on modern GPUs makes suboptimal decisions in both the temporal and spatial dimensions, seriously slowing down various applications,

---

[1] We use Compute Unified Device Architecture (CUDA) terminology from NVIDIA. The OpenCL equivalents of warp and thread block are wavefront and work-group, respectively.

Advances in GPU Research and Practice. http://dx.doi.org/10.1016/B978-0-12-803738-6.00004-5

as shown in previous research [2,14,15]. In the temporal dimension, the hardware scheduler always schedules thread blocks, each of which contains the same number of threads and represents a unit for scheduling, to GPU processors, whenever there are enough hardware resources—such as registers and shared memory—to support their execution. The rationale behind such a *greedy* scheduling strategy is that a higher level of utilization should lead to better performance. Unfortunately, as previous work showed [14], the greedy scheduling approach results in up to 4.9× increase in performance degradations on a set of applications, because all the threads compete for memory bus accesses or data caches, slowing down each other's performance. In the spatial dimension, the hardware scheduler randomly distributes thread blocks to processors, ignoring the different amounts of data sharing among them. Such arbitrary schedules forfeit some locality optimizations. For example, an NVIDIA Tesla M2075 GPU contains 14 streaming multiprocessors (SMs), each having a private data cache. If some thread blocks share a common data set, scheduling them to the same SM may improve data reuse significantly, because some blocks may act as data prefetchers for others.

In this chapter, we describe a framework consisting of a code transformation component (SM-centric transformation) and three optimizations enabled by it. The SM-centric transformation comprises two techniques. The first technique, *SM-based task selection*, breaks the mapping between thread blocks and tasks, but directly associates tasks to GPU processors. In a traditional GPU kernel execution, with or without persistent threads, what task a thread block executes is usually based on the block's ID; whereas with SM-based task selection, what task a thread block executes is based on the ID of the SM that the block runs on. By replacing the binding between tasks and threads with the binding between tasks and SMs, the scheme enables a direct, precise control of task placement on the SM.

The second technique is a *filling-retreating scheme*, which offers flexible control of the number of concurrent thread blocks on an SM. Importantly, the control is resilient to the randomness and obscuration in GPU hardware thread scheduling. It helps SM-centric transformation in two aspects. First, it ensures an even distribution of active threads across SMs for load balancing. Second, it facilitates online determination of the parallelism level suitable for a kernel, which not only helps kernels with complicated memory reference patterns but also benefits multiple kernel co-runs.

The optimizations, namely *parallelism control*, *affinity-based scheduling*, and *SM partitioning*, are enabled by the flexible scheduling support and are made applicable to off-the-shelf GPUs. The central challenges are to find the optimal task scheduling parameters in both spatial and temporal dimensions to optimize parallelism, data locality, and hardware resource allocation. We present both static and dynamic analysis to efficiently search for the appropriate parameters for each optimization or their combinations.

In the remainder of this chapter, we first show the complexities from the hardware scheduler and then describe the detailed idea and implementation of SM-centric transformation, which circumvents the complexities. We then show two use cases that benefit from the three optimizations, together with some evaluation results. Finally, we draw a conclusion.

2 NONDETERMINISTIC BEHAVIORS CAUSED BY THE HARDWARE

Although a software-level control may enable interesting optimizations, modern hardware scheduler design, however, presents a set of complexities. What makes the scheduling-based optimizations harder is that the scheduling mechanism is never disclosed. Nevertheless, our investigations [16–18] showed that the GigaThread engine in NVIDIA Fermi GPUs [19] has the following properties.

2.1 P1: GREEDY

The scheduler always distributes thread blocks to an SM if that SM has enough hardware resources to support the blocks' execution. This design choice is not surprising, as the design philosophy of GPUs is to hide memory access latency through multithreading among a large number of threads. It has been shown that achieving high occupancy (i.e., the number of active threads on a device) is one of the key factors to obtaining high performance for streaming applications [20,21]. However, as GPU computing went mainstream, its scope expanded quickly, covering many more domains, such as data mining [22,23], machine learning [24,25], database [26,27], and graph analytics [28–32]. A common characteristic of those applications is their strong reliance on efficient data cache performance. Unfortunately, the greedy scheduling always tries to achieve the highest level of utilization, which may degrade cache performance significantly due to cache contention.

2.2 P2: NOT ROUND-ROBIN

Various studies [3,5,33,34] assumed that the mapping between thread blocks and SMs is round-robin style. That is, the ith thread block should be scheduled with the $(i \bmod M)$th SM, where M represents the number of SMs. However, our investigation shows that this common perception does not hold. For example, in an execution of MD (a benchmark for molecular dynamics simulation from the SHOC [35] benchmark suite) on a 14-SM NVIDIA M2075 GPU, we generated 14 thread blocks but found that one SM obtained 2 thread blocks, while another SM got no thread blocks. This property leads to serious load balancing problems for persistent threads, as the generated small number of threads do not utilize the SMs evenly.

2.3 P3: NONDETERMINISTIC ACROSS RUNS

Even with the same input, the mapping between thread blocks and SMs may change across executions of the same program. As such, it is not feasible to rely on traditional techniques, such as offline profiling and intelligent data-to-thread block mapping, to explore the benefits.

2.4 P4: OBLIVIOUS TO NONUNIFORM DATA SHARING

In many applications, the data sharing among threads is nonuniform. For instance, in MD the simulated atoms form neighborhood relations with one another according to their positions. The processing of one atom needs to access its neighbors. Therefore, if two groups of atoms have many of the same neighbors, the thread blocks, which process those atoms, share a lot of data. Scheduling these blocks to the same SM would enhance the private data cache performance because of efficient data reuses. Unfortunately, the scheduler is oblivious to the nonuniform data sharing among thread blocks, as shown in Wu et al. [17].

2.5 P5: SERIALIZING MULTIKERNEL CO-RUNS

Fermi and newer generation GPUs support concurrent kernel executions. However, if the number of thread blocks exceeds the maximum number of supported concurrent thread blocks, the executions of different kernels are serialized [15]. As shown in multiple studies [14,15,36], this property forfeits optimizations on enforcing fairness, exploiting nonuniform frequencies of SMs and handling different scaling properties of the co-run kernels.

In the next section, we present compiler and runtime techniques to circumvent these complexities for a flexible software-level task scheduler.

3 SM-CENTRIC TRANSFORMATION

3.1 CORE IDEAS

3.1.1 SM-centric task selection

We present a code transformation technique to enable spatial scheduling. It is based on the observation that what matters is the mapping between tasks and processors rather than that the mapping between thread blocks to processors. The transformation binds tasks to SMs instead of thread blocks as in traditional GPU programming. We illustrate the basic idea by using an abstract model of GPU kernel executions.

The GPU threads are organized in a hierarchy. Many threads compose a thread block; many thread blocks compose a grid. We view a thread block as a worker, which needs to finish a task. As Fig. 1A shows, in the original kernel, a worker uses its ID to select a task to process. Persistent threads, as illustrated in Fig. 1B, breaks the mapping between workers and tasks. It creates one shared task queue, containing all tasks that should be processed. When a worker is scheduled for execution, it fetches a task in the queue. Because the thread block scheduling is not round-robin and nondeterministic (P2 and P3), persistent threads cannot enable spatial scheduling, as they cannot control the mapping between workers and SMs.

The central idea of *SM-centric task selection* is to directly map tasks to SMs. As shown in Fig. 1C, it creates a task queue for each SM (the tasks in the queues depend on optimizations and will be discussed in Section 4). A worker first retrieves

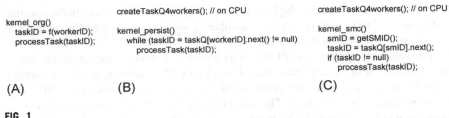

```
                    createTaskQ4workers(); // on CPU          createTaskQ4workers(); // on CPU
kernel_org()                                                 kernel_smc()
   taskID = f(workerID);     kernel_persist()                   smID = getSMID();
   processTask(taskID);         while (taskID = taskQ[workerID].next() != null)   taskID = taskQ[smID].next();
                                   processTask(taskID);         if (taskID != null)
                                                                   processTask(taskID);
(A)                       (B)                                (C)
```

FIG. 1

Conceptual relations among tasks, workers, and SMs. (A) Original kernel. (B) With persistent thread. (C) With SM-centric task selection.

the ID of its host SM[2] and then uses it to fetch a task in the corresponding queue. The association of a task to a specific SM is simple: just place the ID of that task to the preferred task queue. Note that the transformation introduces extra overhead (around 1–2% of the original kernel execution time), which, as will be shown in Section 4, is usually outweighed by the performance benefits.

Correctness issues

The idea is straightforward. One worker processes exactly one task from a queue of the SM it runs on. However, since block scheduling is nondeterministic, it causes a correctness issue: The task queue is created before the kernel's invocation, but an SM may not obtain enough workers to process all tasks in its queue. For example, on a NVIDIA Tesla M2075 card of 14 SMs, a kernel's execution creates 1400 tasks (i.e., thread blocks) evenly distributed in 14 queues. However, the number of workers scheduled to each SM varies from 92 to 110. The SMs, which obtained less than 100 workers, could not finish all tasks, leading to incorrect results.

To address these issues, as well as provide temporal scheduling support, we propose a second technique to complement *SM-centric task selection*.

3.1.2 Filling-retreating scheme

The correctness issue comes from the mismatch between the number of assigned tasks and the number of distributed thread blocks to an SM. The one-to-one mapping between tasks and thread blocks requires that the number of thread blocks should be no less than the assigned tasks. The basic idea of filling-retreating is to run a small number of workers on each SM, which keep fetching and processing tasks in the task queues until all tasks are finished.

There are two challenges to realizing the idea. First, how can each SM run the same number of workers on each SM? This is important for load balancing but is hard to enforce because of P2 (the randomness of the hardware-controlled scheduling). Second, how can the exact number of workers on each SM be specified?

---

[2]Currently, only NVIDIA GPUs support SMID retrieval, which limits the scope of the use of the transformation.

As discussed in Section 2, the highest level of parallelism may not lead to the optimal performance. The flexibility to set the number of workers on each SM is critical for several optimizations, as shown in Section 4.

The solution leverages the P1 (Greedy) nature of the hardware scheduler. Since the scheduler always distributes thread blocks to SMs as long as the remaining hardware resource permits, we generate only the number of workers the GPU can accommodate at the same time. This can be easily done by analyzing the generated parallel thread execution (PTX) code (i.e., assembly code for CDUA devices) to obtain the hardware resources that one thread block's execution requires. We hence guarantee that each SM runs the maximum number of concurrent workers. This process is called *Filling*.

To precisely control the number of concurrent workers on each SM, we stop some workers by using atomic operations, as illustrated in Fig. 2. We maintain a global variable for each SM to record how many workers have been distributed to it. Whenever a worker begins execution, it first figures out its host SM and updates the corresponding variable through an atomic increase. If the number of workers already exceeds a predefined threshold, that worker immediately exits its execution. Otherwise, the worker belongs to the set of active workers, which should process the tasks.

The simple design of the filling-retreating scheme not only solves the correctness issue raised by *SM-centric task selection* but also provides the flexibility to control the exact number of concurrent workers on each SM.

3.2 IMPLEMENTATION

Thanks to its simplicity, we can easily apply SM-centric transformation either manually or through a compiler. We extend the Cetus [37] compiler to include SM-centric transformation as a pass to transform CUDA code. Before showing its full details, we next highlight two important considerations in the design.

First, although the while loop in Fig. 2 illustrates the basic idea of SM-centric transformation, it has serious performance problems: Its dequeue operation involves an atomic operation in each iteration. All these atomic operations are serialized as

```
createTaskQ4sms(); // on CPU

kernel_smc()
  smID = getSMID();
  workers = workerCounters[smID]++; // atomic
  if (workers > wantedNumPerSM)
    return;
  while (taskID = taskQ[smID].next() != null)
    processTask(taskID);
```

FIG. 2

Psuedo code of a GPU kernel in a *filling-retreating* scheme.

they access the same global variable. We circumvent this problem by parallelizing the atomic operations over the SMs. According to the design of the filling-retreating scheme, each SM processes exactly W jobs. If an SM is supposed to concurrently run L workers, a worker should then process W/L jobs. We put the index range of the jobs assigned to an SM into a global index array in which each worker running on that SM can obtain the beginning and ending indices of its section of jobs. When a worker is distributed to an SM, it first checks whether the SM already obtains enough workers via an atomic operation. Hence, different SMs modify different global variables, providing better performance than the original design. Based on this idea, we transform the code to be something like lines 9–16 in Listing 1. Each worker, if needed by the SM, attains the starting and ending indices in the index array and processes corresponding jobs.

Second, we leverage the property of C-like features of CUDA to efficiently obtain the IDs of SMs. We insert PTX code, which is similar to assembly code, into the CUDA program. As shown in line 27 in Listing 1, one "mov" instruction copies the value in a register %smid, which stores the SM ID, to an integer variable.

```
1   #define __SMC_init \
2   unsigned int * __SMC_workersNeeded = __SMC_numNeeded(); \
3   unsigned int * __SMC_newChunkSeq = __SMC_buildChunkSeq(); \
4   unsigned int * __SMC_workerCount= __SMC_initiateArray();
5
6   #define __SMC_Begin \
7   __shared int __SMC_workingCTAs; \
8   __SMC_getSMid; \
9   if(offsetInCTA == 0) \
10      __SMC_workingCTAs = \
11        atomicInc (&__SMC_workerCount[__SMC_smid], INT_MAX); \
12  synchthreads(); \
13  if(__SMCS_workingCTAs >= __SMC_workersNeeded) return; \
14  int __SMC_chunksPerCTA = \
15      __SMC_chunksPerSM / __SMC_workersNeeded; \
16  int __SMC_startChunkIDidx = __SMC_smid * __SMC_chunksPerSM + \
17      __SMC_workingCTAs * __SMC_chunksPerCTA;\
18  for (int __SMC_chunkIDidx = __SMC_startChunkIDidx; \
19      __SMC_chunkIDidx < __SMC_startChunkIDidx+\
20              __SMC_chunksPerCTA ; \
21      __SMC_chunkIDidx++) { \
22      __SMC_chunkID = __SMC_newChunkSeq[__SMC_chunkIDidx];
23
24  #define __SMC_End  }
25
26  // get the ID of the current SM
27  #define __SMC_getSMid \
28  uint __SMC_smid;\
29  asm("mov.u32 %0, %smid;" : "=r"(__SMC_smid) )
```

LISTING 1

Macros that materialize SM-centric transformation (N jobs; M SMs).

```
1    /**** CPU–side code ****/
2    main (){
3        ...
4        __SMC_init;
5        invoke original kernel with three extra arguments:
6            __SMC_chunkCount, __SMC_newChunkSeq, K/M .
7        ...
8    }
9
10   /**** GPU–side code ****/
11   __global__ kernel (...,
12   unsigned int *__SMC_chunkCount,
13   unsigned int *__SMC_newChunkSeq,
14   unsigned int __SMC_chunksPerSM)
15   {
16   __SMC_Begin
17       // the original kernel with the ID of CTA
18       // replaced with __SMC_chunkID
19       ... ...
20   __SMC_End
21   }
```

LISTING 2

GPU program after SM-centric transformation (N vector elements; K job chunks; M SMs).

3.2.1 Details

On GPUs, a CTA is the unit for spatial scheduling. Since a CTA processes a job chunk in the original program, the thread ID is used to distinguish jobs. Our design concerns the distribution of jobs to SMs, thereby assigning job chunks as units to SMs.

We encapsulate SM-centric transformation into four macros to minimize changes on the original GPU program. Listing 2 shows the application of the macros on the CPU-side code. The macro __SMC_init is inserted before the invocation of the GPU kernel to initialize the transformation, such as filling up the index array. Note that we append three arguments to the kernel call in order to pass in necessary information for the job assignment. The change to the kernel code is also minimal. Two macros, __SMC_Begin and __SMC_End, are inserted at the beginning and end of the kernel code, respectively. We also replace the appearance of the ID of the CTA with __SMC_chunkID. Our compiler can easily transform the code in one pass.

The preceding four macros are defined in Listing 1. The first macro, __SMC_init, initiates the three variables with the number of needed workers on each SM, the index array to indicate job chunks, and an all-zero counter array to count active workers. The functions used to initiate the first two variables depend on specific optimizations, which can be provided by the programmer or the optimizing compiler/runtime. __SMC_Begin obtains the SM ID of the host SM by calling the fourth macro and checks whether the SM already has enough active CTAs; then it obtains the section of job chunks the CTA should work on if it is active. The third macro, __SMC_End, just appends the ending bracket of the for loop in the second macro for syntax correctness.

4 SCHEDULING-ENABLED OPTIMIZATIONS

Flexible scheduling removes restrictions from hardware and opens opportunities for many optimizations. We investigate three novel optimizations not previously applicable on modern GPUs. We describe their basic ideas and main challenges to bring them to realization, as well as some experiment results.

4.1 PARALLELISM CONTROL

The many cores on GPUs can accommodate a large number of threads, which on one hand hides memory latency through multithreading, but on the other hand competes for limited hardware resources—such as private or shared data cache. Several studies have shown that cache performance is critical for many GPU applications [5,38,39]. However, a GPU's scheduler always tries to achieve the maximum parallelism, while, as Kayiran et al. [14] show in simulations, choosing the appropriate level of parallelism results in a speedup of around five times that of the default speed.

By limiting the number of concurrent thread blocks on the GPU, our scheduling framework enables flexible control of parallelism. The main challenge is to find the optimal number of concurrent thread blocks to maximize performance. Since most benchmarks invoke the same kernel many times, we leverage a typical hill-climbing process in the first several invocations. For example, given M as the maximum allowed concurrent thread blocks on an SM, we first run M thread blocks on each SM for the first invocation and decrease the number by one for each following invocation. We stop once we observe decreased performance.

Because of limited space, we show the evaluation results of parallelism control with the other two optimizations in the following sections.

4.2 AFFINITY-BASED SCHEDULING

Many scientific applications (e.g., molecular dynamic simulation and computational fluid dynamic) and graph algorithms have complicated memory reference patterns. As such, the threads often manifest nonuniform data sharing among threads: some tasks share a lot of data, while some other tasks share no data. With flexible scheduling support, to better utilize the private data cache, we can schedule the tasks that share more data to the same SM and set them as data prefetchers for each other.

We present a graph-based approach to model the nonuniform data sharing and an efficient partitioning algorithm for the task assignment. In the graph construction stage, we establish an affinity graph, in which a vertex represents a task and the weight of an edges represents the affinity score between two tasks. Affinity score is defined as follows. Let $S1$ and $S2$ be the set of cache lines accessed by two tasks $T1$ and $T2$, respectively. Their affinity score is defined as $\frac{|S1 \cap S2|}{|S1 \cup S2|}$. For instance, three tasks (A, B, and C) of a kernel each access 10 cache lines during their execution. The number of overlapped cache lines for A and B is 2, while this number is 4 and 6 for the task pairs B and C, and A and C, respectively. We have affinity_score(A,B) = 2/18, affinity_score(B,C) = 4/16, and affinity_score(A,C) = 6/14. There is no edge between two vertices when their affinity score is less than a threshold (0.05 in the experiments). It is hence possible to have multiple disconnected subgraphs, which makes the next stage more efficient.

With the established affinity graph, the goal is to partition the tasks to SMs. Graph partitioning is an NP-complete problem in general. Most existing graph partitioning algorithms are quite costly, as they prefer high-quality partitioning. However, for online use, the overhead can easily outweigh the benefit. Therefore we design an algorithm to carefully balance the partitioning overhead and quality. The algorithm has three steps. The first step is *seed selection*. Let C denote the number of disconnected subgraphs in the affinity graph and M the number of SMs. If $C \geq M$, we random select M vertices as seeds, each in a different subgraph. If $C < M$, we randomly select a vertex in each subgraph and iterate the remaining vertices for the remaining $M - C$ seeds. In each iteration, we include the vertex if its affinity score for any seed is less than or equal to a threshold. We stop the iteration once we have M seeds. Initially, we set the threshold as 0 and increase it by 0.1 if we find less than M seeds. At most, we increase the threshold by 10 times to successfully select M seeds, but usually no more than two rounds is needed. The second step is *sorted list creation*, which, for each seed, creates a sorted list of all remaining vertices according to their affinity score to that seed. The third step, *cluster enlargement*, repetitively iterates all the sorted lists. In each iteration, it draws the vertex, whose affinity score with the corresponding seed is the largest, to join the same cluster. The process stops once all vertices are partitioned.

4.2.1 Evaluation

We experiment with a NVIDIA M2075 GPU hosted by an Intel 8-core Xeon X5672 machine with 48 GB of main memory. We run a 64-bit Redhat Enterprise 6.2 Linux operating system with a 4.2 CUDA runtime. We repeat each experiment 10 times and report the average.

We adopt four commonly used irregular benchmarks to evaluate both parallelism control and affinity-based scheduling. We give a very brief description of the benchmarks. IRREG is extracted from a partial differential solver. NBF is the key component of molecular dynamics simulation. These two benchmarks were rewritten from C to CUDA. SPMV calculates sparse matrix vector multiplication, which comes from the SHOC benchmark suite. CFD, from the RODINIA benchmark suite, simulates fluid dynamics.

We compare SM-centric transformation to persistent threads. Persistent threads run a fixed number of concurrent thread blocks through the whole execution. The difference is that persistent threads, because of the complexity from the hardware scheduler described in Section 2, cannot bind threads and hence tasks to specific SMs. To enable affinity-based scheduling with persistent threads, we generate M (the number of SMs) persistent thread blocks and make sure the thread block size is the maximum size supported by the hardware resources. The tasks partitioned to the same SM are consumed by the same thread block.

Fig. 3A shows the performance results. The baseline is the original benchmark. Persistent threads without affinity-based scheduling suffers a 22% performance degradation caused by insufficient parallelism and poor data sharing among tasks running on the same SM. Affinity-based scheduling helps persistent threads by reducing its slowdown to 11%. The results show that persistent threads cannot balance locality and parallelism well. Though running only one thread block on one SM improves locality, the benefit is not enough to compensate for the degradation caused by insufficient parallelism. SM-centric transformation, together with affinity-based scheduling, runs multiple thread blocks on an SM, which execute tasks with a great affinity for data. On average, it brings a 21% speedup over the baseline. It is worth noticing that CFD is an anomaly, for which persistent threads with affinity-based scheduling produce the best result. A plausible reason is that warp scheduling affects the performance significantly, but neither approach has any control over it.

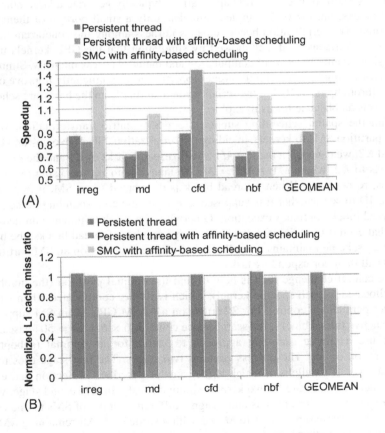

FIG. 3

Performance results on irregular benchmarks. (A) Speedups of single-kernel runs. (B) Normalized L1 miss ratios.

Fig. 3B shows normalized L1 cache miss ratios collected through the CUDA hardware performance monitor. The trend aligns well with the performance results, which confirms that the improved performance of L1 cache is the main contributor to the gain in performance.

4.3 SM PARTITIONING FOR MULTI-KERNEL CO-RUNS

Modern GPUs are embracing more features from CPUs to target general purpose computing, in which an important one is multiprogram co-runs. Although GPUs do not support the concurrent execution of different programs yet, they can support multikernel co-runs in the same execution context (i.e., within the same program). Unfortunately, as Sreepathi et al. [15] showed, the executions of different kernels are often serialized, because GPU applications typically generate a large number of thread blocks, but the GPU can accommodate only a small portion of them at the same time. The serialization hence impedes fairness among the concurrent kernels. Moreover, Adriaens et al. [2] showed by simulation that the GPU kernels usually differ significantly in terms of computation and memory access intensity. Simultaneously co-running kernels with different properties may significantly improve overall system throughput (STP), but the serialization resulting from the hardware scheduler design sets an obstacle for us to explore.

With the spatial scheduling support from SM-centric transformation, we can easily partition SMs to kernels, avoiding the serialization. Given two co-run kernels, $K1$ and $K2$, we can assign the first $M1$ SMs to execute tasks of $K1$ and the remaining $M2$ SMs to $K2$, where $M1 + M2 = M$. We launch both kernels using two CUDA streams, respectively. When a thread block is distributed to an SM, it first obtains the SM ID to see whether it is supposed to execute the corresponding kernel. If so, the thread block continues execution. Otherwise, the block terminates immediately. Note that even if the original kernel has a large number of thread blocks, the filling-retreating scheme maintains a small number of thread blocks on an SM partition to process all their corresponding tasks.

The central challenge then is how to find the optimal partition (the number of SMs allocated to each specific kernel), which is further complicated when we also consider parallelism control. For 2 kernels on a 14-SM GPU, if an SM supports at most 6 active thread blocks, the search space contains $6 \times 6 \times 14 = 504$ cases.

We use a simple sampling approach to search for an optimal (suboptimal) configuration online. The process contains two stages. The first stage tries to find the best level of parallelism, which is the same as described in Section 4.1, except that we need to take care of two kernels simultaneously. In the second stage, we fix the number of concurrent CTAs and assign a different number of SMs to one co-run kernel, which increases from 1 to $M - 1$ with a stride of 3. All remaining SMs are partitioned to the other kernel.

4.3.1 Evaluation

Since current GPUs do not support more than one execution context, we combine the kernels of two different programs into one, which are executed by two different streams. To cover various co-run scenarios, we experiment with every pair out of the selected nine benchmarks, as shown in Table 1. We use two metrics, STP and average normalized turnaround time (ANTT), to consider both overall throughput and responsiveness. These two metrics are defined in the equations [40]

$$STP = \sum_{i=1}^{n} \frac{C_i^{SP}}{C_i^{MP}}$$

$$ANTT = \frac{1}{n} \sum_{i=1}^{n} \frac{C_i^{MP}}{C_i^{SP}}$$

where n is the number of co-running kernels and C_i^{SP} and C_i^{MP} are the execution times of single-run and co-run of program i, respectively.

Since we are only interested in the overlapped execution, we launch the two co-run kernels together and restart a kernel once it is finished. The process stops when both kernels are executed at least seven times. Note that we discard the last instance of the kernel, which is finished after the seven invocations of the other kernel, as its execution is not fully overlapped.

We still compare SM-centric transformation with persistent threads because the latter can indirectly partition SMs to the two kernels. We launch M thread blocks of the largest possible size and assign P CTAs to execute the tasks of one kernel and the remaining $M - P$ ones for the other kernel. Because of the randomness of hardware scheduling, it is not guaranteed that each SM obtains exactly one CTA. We run the experiments multiple times until each SM happens to obtain one CTA. We

Table 1 Benchmarks

Benchmark	Source	Description	Irregular
irreg	Maryland [41]	Partial diff. solver	Y
nbf	Maryland [41]	Force field	Y
md	SHOC [42]	Molecular dynamics	Y
spmv	SHOC [42]	Sparse matrix vector multi	Y
cfd	Rodinia [43]	Finite volume solver	Y
nn	Rodinia [43]	Nearest neighbor	N
pf	Rodinia [43]	Dynamic programming	N
mm	CUDA SDK	Dense matrix multiplication	N
reduce	CUDASDK	Reduction	N

enumerate all possible choices for P and report the best performance to compare with SM-centric transformation.

Fig. 4 shows the speedups defined as the ratio between the original ANTT and the optimized ANTT. To obtain the original ANTT, we run the co-running kernels in the default way: each original kernel is executed by a separate CUDA stream. "SMC Predicted" and "SMC Optimal" represent the speedups brought by SM-centric transformation using predicted configurations and optimal configurations, respectively. We obtain the optimal configuration by exhaustively searching the entire space. We observe that the potential performance gain from SM-centric transformation is around 38%. Our prediction successfully exploits most of the benefit by producing $1.36\times$ speedup on average. The performance, however, varies greatly across benchmarks from $2.35\times$ speedup to a 2% slowdown. The benchmarks cannot benefit much from SM partitioning and parallelism control for two reasons. First, the original scalability is already good with few wasted computational resources. Second, the benchmarks are not sensitive to cache-level locality improvement because of the small amount of data reuses. Persistent threads, on the other hand, slow down the benchmarks by around 18% on average. To enable SM partitioning, persistent threads can support only concurrent execution of M thread blocks, which is not sufficient to fully leverage the many GPU cores.

Fig. 5 shows the improved performance in terms of STP. SM-centric transformation consistently outperforms persistent threads by producing an extra 17% throughput gain. One interesting observation is that, different from the ANTT result, persistent threads provide an 11% improvement on average over the baseline. Because STP and ANTT measure different aspects of the system, an optimization may improve one but degrade the other, which was also observed by Eyerman and Eeckhout [40]. The results show that SM-centric transformation consistently outperforms persistent threads, and hence is a better choice for SM partitioning.

5 OTHER SCHEDULING WORK ON GPUs

5.1 SOFTWARE APPROACHES

Kato et al. [44] considered GPU command scheduling in multitasking environments, in which many applications shared the same GPU. Their scheduler, TimeGraph, implemented two scheduling polices: predictable response time (PRT) and high throughput (HT), to optimize response time and throughput, respectively. Their model allows flexible implementation of other scheduling policies to optimize for different objectives. However, TimeGraph does not allow two applications to simultaneously run on the same GPU. Once off-the-shelf GPUs support co-running of multiple applications, SM-centric transformation can work together with TimeGraph to exploit a much larger scheduling space.

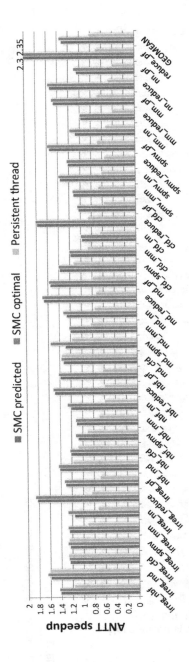

FIG. 4

Speedup of average normalized turnaround time.

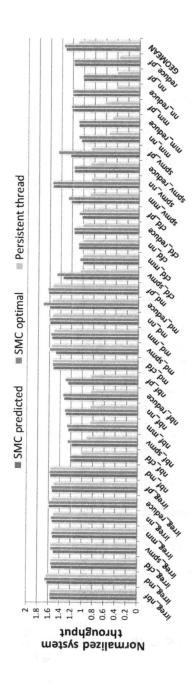

FIG. 5

Improvement on system throughput.

Prior work on software-level scheduling for single application runs mainly focused on persistent threads with static or dynamic partitioning of tasks [45–49]. The approach runs maximum possible concurrent threads on the GPU and enforces a mapping of tasks to those persistent threads. Gupta et al. [50] showed that by leveraging persistent threads, they significantly improved the performance of producer-consumer applications and irregular applications. SM-centric transformation is inspired by the work on persistent threads, but shows one salient distinction. Persistent threads assign tasks to threads, while SM-centric transformation assigns tasks to SMs. Hence SM-centric transformation enables two optimizations that persistent threads cannot: interthread block locality enhancement and SM partitioning between concurrent kernels.

Two independent studies, Kernelet [29] and Elastic Kernels [15] investigated software scheduling for optimal kernel co-runs. Kernelet sliced multiple kernels from the same application into small pieces. Pieces of different characteristics (compute-intensive and memory-intensive ones) were scheduled for concurrent execution on the GPU. Sreepathi et al. [15] developed the framework to transform GPU kernels into an elastic form, enabling flexible online tuning of resource allocation for each co-run kernel to fully utilize the hardware. Spatial scheduling (i.e., scheduling tasks to SMs) enabled by SM-centric transformation is complementary to these approaches.

5.2 HARDWARE APPROACHES

Thread block scheduling recently gained some attention from the computer architecture community. Nath et al. [51] exploited the thermal heterogeneity across kernels and mixed them in the scheduling to reduce thermal hotspots. Adriaens et al. [2] proposed a hardware-based SM partitioning framework to enable spatial multitasking. Similar to Kernelet's work [29], kernels of different characteristics simultaneously shared one GPU. Kayiran et al. [14] designed a hardware thread block scheduler to dynamically adapt to the monitored memory access intensity and to throttle concurrent thread blocks. To the contrary, SM-centric transformation enabled spatial multitasking and thread block scheduling without hardware support.

There is abundant work on warp scheduling targeting improvements in memory performance. Narasiman et al. [52] proposed to use large warps and dynamically form small warps for single instruction multiple data execution to minimize memory divergence. Rogers et al. [39] observed the subtle interaction between warp scheduling and data reuses in the L1 data cache. Round-robin warp scheduling led to early eviction of L1 cache lines which will be used by some warps in the near future. They proposed cache-conscious warp scheduling to improve intrawarp locality through monitoring thread-level data reuse inside each warp, and they prefer to schedule warps whose data are already present in the L1 data cache. Jog et al. [5] used a similar idea to prioritize warps to improve L1 cache hit ratios. Furthermore, they scheduled consecutive thread blocks on the same SM to enhance memory bank-level parallelism.

6 CONCLUSION AND FUTURE WORK

We have shown that the SM-centric transformation successfully circumvents the complexities of the GPU hardware scheduler and enables flexible task scheduling. We designed three optimizations to leverage the transformation to optimize for parallelism, locality, and SM resource partitioning. The experiments on a Fermi GPU demonstrate that the optimizations can be easily applied to widely used GPU benchmarks and can improve their performance significantly.

Possible future work can go in two directions. The first direction is to further develop our compiler to cover more complicated GPU programs, especially the ones with multiple kernels. The second direction is to design more optimizations to utilize the framework. For example, we could apply SM partitioning with individual SM voltage scaling. The SMs partitioned to memory-intensive kernels can scale down their voltage to save power.

ACKNOWLEDGMENTS

This material is based upon work supported by the National Science Foundation under Grant No. 1464216. Any opinions, findings, conclusions, or recommendations expressed in this material are those of the author(s) and do not necessarily reflect the views of the National Science Foundation.

REFERENCES

[1] E.Z. Zhang, Y. Jiang, Z. Guo, K. Tian, X. Shen, On-the-fly elimination of dynamic irregularities for GPU computing, in: The International Conference on Architectural Support for Programming Languages and Operating Systems, 2011.

[2] J.T. Adriaens, K. Compton, N.S. Kim, M.J. Schulte, The case for GPGPU spatial multi-tasking, in: The International Symposium on High-Performance Computer Architecture, 2012.

[3] A. Jog, O. Kayiran, A.K. Mishra, M.T. Kandemir, O. Mutlu, R. Iyer, C.R. Das, Orchestrated scheduling and prefetching for GPGPUs, in: The International Symposium on Computer Architecture, 2013.

[4] T.G. Rogers, M. O'Connor, T.M. Aamodt, Divergence-aware warp scheduling, in: The International Symposium on Microarchitecture, 2013.

[5] A. Jog, O. Kayiran, N.C. Nachiappan, A.K. Mishra, M.T. Kandemir, O. Mutlu, R. Iyer, C.R. Das, OWL: cooperative thread array aware scheduling techniques for improving GPGPU performance, in: The International Conference on Architectural Support for Programming Languages and Operating Systems, 2013.

[6] M. Dashti, A. Fedorova, J. Funston, F. Gaud, R. Lachaize, B. Lepers, V. Quema, M. Roth, Traffic management: a holistic approach to memory placement on NUMA systems, in: The International Conference on Architectural Support for Programming Languages and Operating Systems, 2013.

[7] J. Chen, L.K. John, Efficient program scheduling for heterogeneous multi-core processors, in: The Design Automation Conference, 2009.

[8] S. Peter, A. Schupbach, P. Barham, R. Baumann, A. Isaacs, T. Harris, T. Roscoe, Design principles for end-to-end multicore schedulers, in: The USENIX Workshop on Hot Topics in Parallelism, 2010.

[9] Y. Jiang, X. Shen, J. Chen, R. Tripathi, Analysis and approximation of optimal co-scheduling on chip multiprocessors, in: The International Conference on Parallel Architecture and Compilation Techniques, 2008.

[10] K.K. Pusukuri, R. Gupta, L.N. Bhuyan, ADAPT: a framework for coscheduling multi-threaded programs, ACM Trans. Archit. Code Optim. 9 (4) (2013) 45.

[11] J. Aas, Understanding the Linux 2.6.8.1 CPU scheduler, SGI 22 (2005) 1–38.

[12] T. Li, D. Baumberger, S. Hahn, Efficient and scalable multiprocessor fair scheduling using distributed weighted round-robin, in: The ACM SIGPLAN Symposium on Principles and Practice of Parallel Programming, 2009.

[13] C.S. Wong, I. Tan, R.D. Kumari, F. Wey, Towards achieving fairness in the Linux scheduler, ACM SIGOPS Oper. Syst. Rev. 42 (5) (2008) 34–43.

[14] O. Kayiran, A. Jog, M.T. Kandemir, C.R. Das, Neither more nor less: optimizing thread-level parallelism for GPGPUs, in: The International Conference on Parallel Architecture and Compilation Techniques, 2013.

[15] P. Sreepathi, M.J. Thazhuthaveetil, R. Govindarajan, Improving GPGPU concurrency with elastic kernels, in: The International Conference on Architectural Support for Programming Languages and Operating Systems, 2013.

[16] B. Wu, G. Chen, D. Li, X. Shen, J. Vetter, Enabling and exploiting flexible task assignment on GPU through SM-centric program transformations, in: The International Conference on Supercomputing, 2015.

[17] B. Wu, W. Wang, X. Shen, Software-level scheduling to exploit non-uniformly shared data cache, in: ACM SIGPLAN Workshop on Memory Systems Performance and Correctness, 2013.

[18] B. Wu, G. Chen, D. Li, X. Shen, J. Vetter, SM-centric transformation: circumventing hardware restrictions for flexible GPU scheduling, in: The International Conference on Parallel Architecture and Compilation Techniques, 2014.

[19] NVIDIA, NVIDIA's Next Generation CUDA Computer Architecture: Fermi.

[20] Y. Liu, E.Z. Zhang, X. Shen, A cross-input adaptive framework for GPU program optimizations, in: The IEEE International Parallel & Distributed Processing Symposium, 2009.

[21] A.R. Brodtkorb, T.R. Hagen, M.L. Sætra, Graphics processing unit (GPU) programming strategies and trends in GPU computing, J. Parallel Distrib. Comput. 73 (1) (2013) 4–13.

[22] W. Fang, K.K. Lau, M. Lu, X. Xiao, C.K. Lam, P.Y. Yang, B. He, Q. Luo, V.S. Pedro, K. Yang, Parallel data mining on graphics processors, Tech. Rep., Hong Kong University of Science and Technology, 2008.

[23] V. Kysenko, K. Rupp, O. Marchenko, S. Selberherr, A. Anisimov, GPU-accelerated non-negative matrix factorization for text mining, in: NLDB, Lecture Notes in Computer Science, vol. 7337, 2012, pp. 158–163.

[24] A. Coates, B. Huval, T. Wang, D.J. Wu, B.C. Catanzaro, A.Y. Ng, Deep learning with COTS HPC systems, in: The International Conference on Machine Learning, 2013.

[25] N. Lopes, B. Ribeiro, GPUMLib: an efficient open-source GPU machine learning library, Int. J. Comput. Inf. Syst. Ind. Manag. Appl. 3 (2011) 355–362.

[26] P. Bakkum, K. Skadron, Accelerating SQL database operations on a GPU with CUDA, in: Proceedings of the 3rd Workshop on General-Purpose Computation on Graphics Processing Units, 2010, 94–103.

[27] H. Wu, G. Diamos, S. Cadambi, S. Yalamanchili, Kernel weaver: automatically fusing database primitives for efficient GPU computation, in: The International Symposium on Microarchitecture, 2012.

[28] A. Gharaibeh, L.B. Costa, E. Santos-Neto, M. Ripeanu, A yoke of oxen and a thousand chickens for heavy lifting graph processing, in: The International Conference on Parallel Architecture and Compilation Techniques, 2012.

[29] J. Zhong, B. He, Medusa: simplified graph processing on GPUs, IEEE Trans. Parallel Distrib. Syst. 25 (6) (2013) 1543–1552.

[30] D. Merrill, M. Garland, A. Grimshaw, Scalable GPU graph traversal, in: The ACM SIGPLAN Symposium on Principles and Practice of Parallel Programming, 2012.

[31] S. Che, B.M. Beckmann, S.K. Reinhardt, K. Skadron, Pannotia: understanding irregular GPGPU graph applications, in: The IEEE International Symposium on Workload Characterization, 2013.

[32] F. Khorasani, K. Vora, R. Gupta, L.N. Bhuyan, CuSha: vertex-centric graph processing on GPUs, in: The International ACM Symposium on High-Performance Parallel and Distributed Computing, 2014.

[33] J. Zhong, B. He, Kernelet: High-Throughput GPU Kernel Executions with Dynamic Slicing and Scheduling, IEEE Trans. Parallel Distrib. Syst., 25 (6) (2014) 1522–1532.

[34] S. Kato, M. McThrow, C. Maltzahn, S. Brandt, Gdev: first-class GPU resource management in the operating system, in: Proceedings of the 2012 USENIX Conference on Annual Technical Conference, 2012.

[35] A. Danalis, G. Marin, C. McCurdy, J.S. Meredith, P.C. Roth, K. Spafford, V. Tipparaju, J.S. Vetter, The scalable heterogeneous computing (SHOC) benchmark suite, in: The International Workshop on General Purpose Processing Using GPUs, 2010.

[36] P. Aguilera, J. Lee, A. Farmahini-Farahani, K. Morrow, M. Schulte, N.S. Kim, Process variation-aware workload partitioning algorithms for GPUs supporting spatial-multitasking, in: Proceedings of the Conference on Design, Automation & Test in Europe, 2014.

[37] S. Lee, T. Johnson, R. Eigenmann, Cetus—an extensible compiler infrastructure for source-to-source transformation, in: The International Workshop on Languages and Compilers for Parallel Computing, 2003, pp. 539–553.

[38] W. Jia, K.A. Shaw, M. Martonosi, Characterizing and improving the use of demand-fetched caches in GPUs, in: The International Conference on Supercomputing, 2012.

[39] T.G. Rogers, M. O'Connor, T.M. Aamodt, Cache-conscious wavefront scheduling, in: The International Symposium on Microarchitecture, 2012.

[40] S. Eyerman, L. Eeckhout, System-level performance metrics for multiprogram workloads, IEEE Micro 28 (3) (2008).

[41] H. Han, C.-W. Tseng, Exploiting locality for irregular scientific codes, IEEE Trans. Parallel Distrib. Syst. 17 (7) (2006) 606–618.

[42] A. Danalis, G. Marin, C. McCurdy, J.S. Meredith, P.C. Roth, K. Spafford, V. Tipparaju, J.S. Vetter, The scalable heterogeneous computing (SHOC) benchmark suite, in: The International Workshop on General Purpose Processing Using GPUs, 2010.

[43] S. Che, M. Boyer, J. Meng, D. Tarjan, J.W. Sheaffer, S.-H. Lee, K. Skadron, Rodinia: a benchmark suite for heterogeneous computing, in: The IEEE International Symposium on Workload Characterization, 2009.

[44] S. Kato, K. Lakshmanan, R. Rajkumar, Y. Ishikawa, TimeGraph: GPU scheduling for real-time multi-tasking environments, in: Proceedings of the 2011 USENIX Conference on USENIX Annual Technical Conference, USENIXATC'11, 2011.

[45] K. Gupta, J.A. Stuart, J.D. Owens, A study of persistent threads style GPU programming for GPGPU workloads, in: Innovative Parallel Computing, 2012.

[46] L. Chen, O. Villa, S. Krishnamoorthy, G.R. Gao, Dynamic load balancing on single- and multi-GPU systems, in: The IEEE International Parallel & Distributed Processing Symposium, 2010.

[47] S. Xiao, W.C. Feng, Inter-block GPU communication via fast barrier synchronization, in: The IEEE International Parallel & Distributed Processing Symposium, 2010.

[48] T. Aila, S. Laine, Understanding the efficiency of ray traversal on GPUs, in: Proceedings of the Conference on High Performance Graphics 2009, HPG '09, 2009.

[49] M. Steinberger, M. Kenzel, P. Boechat, B. Kerbl, M. Dokter, D. Schmalstieg, Whipple-tree: task-based scheduling of dynamic workloads on the GPU, ACM Trans. Comput. Syst. 33 (6) (2014) 1–11.

[50] K. Gupta, J.A. Stuart, J.D. Owens, A study of persistent threads style GPU programming for GPGPU workloads, in: The Innovative Parallel Computing: Foundations & Applications of GPU, Manycore, and Heterogeneous Systems, 2012.

[51] R. Nath, R. Ayoub, T.S. Rosing, Temperature aware thread block scheduling in GPGPUs, in: Proceedings of the 50th Annual Design Automation Conference, DAC '13, ISBN 978-1-4503-2071-9, 2013.

[52] V. Narasiman, M. Shebanow, C.J. Lee, R. Miftakhutdinov, O. Mutlu, Y.N. Patt, Improving GPU performance via large warps and two-level warp scheduling, in: The International Symposium on Microarchitecture, 2011.

Data placement on GPUs

5

X. Shen[1], B. Wu[2]

North Carolina State University, Raleigh, NC, United States[1] Colorado School of Mines, Golden, CO, United States[2]

1 INTRODUCTION

To meet the relentless demands for data by the large number of cores, graphics processing unit (GPU) memory systems are by necessity complex and sophisticated. They are typically heterogeneous memory systems (HMS). One HMS often consists of a number of components, with each having some different properties (e.g., access bandwidth, access latency, endurance, memory organization, preferable access patterns, and programming paradigms). For example, on a NVIDIA Kepler GPU, there are more than eight types of memories (global, texture, shared, constant, and various caches), with some on-chip, some off-chip, some directly manageable by software, and some not. The trend of memory heterogeneity is stressed by the emergence of new memory technologies (e.g., 3D stacked memory) that are getting into GPUs.

The sophistication of an HMS is a double-edged sword. It has the potential for narrowing the gap between a GPU and data by meeting the demands from different types of applications. At the same time, its complexity and fast evolvement make that potential extremely difficult to tap into. For instance, recent studies show that many memory-intensive GPU applications carefully written by developers sometimes cannot yet reach half of the performance that they could achieve with a better memory system [1]. The studies all indicate that relying on programmers to match an application with HMS such that it taps into its full potential is impractical, yet that is what existing programming systems (e.g., CUDA, OpenCL, OpenACC, OpenMP) all require. Lack of systematic support needed for applications to best benefit HMS is a key reason for the poor memory performance of today's applications. As future memory systems get more complicated and multicore process become get more thirsty for solving data, the solve in order to maintain a sustained improvement of computing efficiency will become more pressing.

Advances in GPU Research and Practice. http://dx.doi.org/10.1016/B978-0-12-803738-6.00005-7

One solution explored by researchers [2] was to use autotuning to search for the best way to use HMS for a program. It is time-consuming and more importantly cannot easily adapt the memory usage to changes in program inputs or memory systems. Some prior work tried to come up with high-level rules to guide the usage of an HMS [3]. These rules are easy to follow, but they often fail to produce suitable placements, and their effectiveness degrades further when memory systems evolve across generations (as shown later in Section 6).

In this chapter, we describe a systematic solution for automatically tapping into the full potential of an HMS. The new solution is a software framework with a set of novel compiler and runtime techniques included. We name the solution PORPLE, which stands for a *por*table data *pl*acement *e*ngine. With PORPLE, programmers will be freed from concerns about tailoring their programs to different memory systems, and at the same time, the sophisticated designs of memory systems can become fully translated into computing efficiency of modern applications. PORPLE transforms the programs such that they are customized—in terms of where data are placed in memory—to the underlying HMS at runtime and attain near-optimal memory usage. Evolvement of memory systems is not problem but an opportunity; applications can automatically tap into the full power of the new system without the need of refactoring or retuning (given the specifications of the new system). By closing the gap between memory design and memory usage, PORPLE is promising to raise the capability of existing programming systems to a new level, opening up many new opportunities for addressing memory performance issues, which is a serious bottleneck in modern computing.

2 OVERVIEW

PORPLE leverages a synergy between a source-to-source compiler and a runtime library. To use PORPLE, an application just needs to go through its compiler before being compiled into the native code. Then, during the execution of the application, the runtime library will be activated and will automatically enhance the data placement of the program (including migration of data if necessary) on the fly such that the execution can match up with the current program inputs and underlying memory systems, translating the sophisticated design of HMS into the best performance or energy efficiency of the application.

Fig. 1 provides a conceptual overview of the major components of PORPLE and their relations. At a high level, PORPLE contains three key components: the specification language MSL that provides specifications of a memory system, the source-to-source compiler PORPLE-C that reveals the data access patterns of the program and that stages the code for runtime adaptation, and the online data placement engine *Placer* that consumes the specifications and access

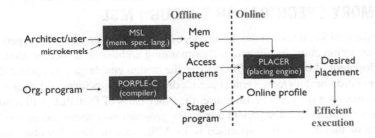

FIG. 1

High-level structure of PORPLE.

patterns to find the best data placements at runtime. Working together, these systems equip PORPLE with several appealing properties:

- *User-transparency*: PORPLE enhances data placement and memory usage without the involvement of programmers. All analysis and transformations are enabled by the compiler and runtime support.
- *Portability*: With PORPLE an application that executes on different memory systems will automatically run with the data placements appropriate to the respective memory system, which happens because PORPLE is able to determine and materialize the best data placements at runtime on the fly.
- *Adaptivity*: The on-the-fly enhancement of data placement also makes PORPLE optimizations able to adapt to program input changes.
- *Extensibility*: It is easy to add support to a new memory system. Architects just need to put in a specification of the memory system written in MSL, a language that will be designed in this project. When applications run on the new system, PORPLE will automatically adjust the data placement to fit its properties.[1] No code refactoring or retuning of applications is necessary.
- *Generality*: PORPLE can support both regular and irregular applications. It uses compiler analysis for finding out data access patterns in regular programs and uses lightweight online profiling for irregular programs. It leverages a novel semantic-aware hardware profiling mechanism to further enrich the profiled information to effectively guide data placement decisions.

We next elaborate on each component of PORPLE and how all of them work as a synergy to enhance memory usage with these appealing properties.

---

[1] If the new memory system requires new kinds of statements to use, the PORPLE compiler will need to be extended.

3 MEMORY SPECIFICATION THROUGH MSL

We introduce MSL, a specification language in which the architect or expert users develop an architecture specification. By separating architectural specifications from the development of other parts of PORPLE, the design enables a good portability of the optimization of data management across different architectures: When the target program runs on a different architecture, the other parts of PORPLE will automatically optimize the data management during the program executions, according to the properties of that architecture specified in its MSL specification. No changes need to be made to either the program or the other components of PORPLE (except some minor extensions to the compiler when new kinds of statements are introduced with the new memory system).

An important part of MSL is the specification of the memory system, which provides a simple, uniform way to specify a type of memory and its relationships with other pieces of memory in a system. Fig. 2 shows the design, including the keywords,

---

Keywords:
address1, address2, index1, index 2, banks, blockSize, warp, block, grid, sm, core, tpc, die, clk, ns, ms, sec, na, om, ?;
                         // na: not applicable; om: omitted; ?: unknown;
                         // om and ? can be used in all fields

Operators:
C-like arithmetic and relational operators, and a scope operator { };

Syntax:
- specList ::= processorSpec memSpec*
- processorSpec ::= die=Integer tpc; tpc=Integer sm; sm=Integer core; end-of-line
- memSpec ::= name id swmng rw dim size blockSize banks latency upperLevels
          lowerLevels shareScope concurrencyFactor serialCondition ; end-of-line
- name ::= String
- id ::= Integer
- swmng ::= Y | N *// software manageable or not*
- rw ::= R|W|RW *// allow read or write accesses*
- dim ::= na | Integer *// special for arrays of a particular dimensionality*
- sz ::= Integer[K|M|G|T|ε][E|B] *// E for data elements*
- size ::= sz | <sz sz> | <sz sz sz>
- blockSize ::= sz | <sz sz> | <sz sz sz>
- lat ::= Integer[clk|ns|ms|sec] *// clk for clocks*
- latency ::= lat | <lat lat>
- upperLevels ::= <[id | name]*>
- lowerLevels ::= <id*>
- shareScope ::= core | sm | tpc | die
- concurrencyFactor ::= < Number Number>
- serialCondition ::= scope{RelationalExpr}
- scope ::= warp | block | grid

FIG. 2

Syntax of MSL, some token rules omitted.

operators, and syntax written in BackusNaur Form. The memory part of an MSL specification contains an entry for the processor and a list of entries for memory. The processor entry shows the composition of a die, an streaming multiprocessor (SM), and other scopes. Each memory spec corresponds to one type of memory, indicating the name of the memory (started with letters) and a unique ID (in numbers), and other attributes.

The name and ID could be used interchangeably; having both is just a convenience. The field "swmng" indicates whether the memory is software manageable. The data placement engine can put an explicit data array onto a software-manageable memory (vs hardware-managed cache for instance). The field "rw" indicates whether a GPU kernel can read or write the memory. The field "dim," if it is not "?," indicates that the spec entry is applicable only when the array dimensionality equals the value of "dim." The field after "dim" indicates memory size. Because a GPU memory typically consists of a number of equal-sized blocks or banks, "blockSize" (which could be multidimensional) and the number of banks are the next two fields in a spec. Then the next field describes memory access latency. To accommodate the access latency difference between read and write operations, the spec allows the use of a tuple to indicate both. We use "upperLevels" and "lowerLevels" to indicate memory hierarchy; they contain the names or IDs of the memories that sit above (i.e., closer to computing units) or blow the memory of interest. The "shareScope" field indicates in what scope the memory is shared. For instance, "sm" means that a piece of the memory is shared by all cores on an SM. The "concurrencyFactor" is a field that indicates parallel transactions a memory (e.g., global memory and texture memory) may support for a GPU kernel. Its inverse is the average number of memory transactions that are serviced concurrently for a GPU kernel. As shown in previous studies [4], such a factor depends on not only memory organization and architecture but also kernel characterization. MSL broadly characterizes GPU kernels as compute-intensive and memory-intensive and allows the "concurrencyFactor" field to be a tuple containing two elements, respectively, corresponding to the values for memory-intensive and compute-intensive kernels (e.g., $\langle 0.1, 0.5 \rangle$). The field "serialCondition" allows the use of simple logical expressions to express the special conditions, under which multiple accesses to a memory are serialized. MSL has three special tokens: the question mark "?" indicating that the information is unavailable, "om" indicating that the information is omitted because it appears in some other entries, and "na" indicating that the field is not applicable to the entry. A default value predefined for each field allows the use of "?" for unknowns (e.g., 1 for the concurrencyFactor field).

A distinctive feature of MSL design is the concept of "serialization condition." The introduction of this feature is based on our following observation: many HMS have special characteristics. How to allow simple but yet well-structured descriptions of these various properties such that they can be easily exploited by the other parts of data management frameworks is a big challenge. For example, accesses to *global memory* could be coalesced, accesses to *texture memory* could come with a 2D locality (i.e., caching benefits accesses in a 2D neighborhood), accesses to

```
Mem spec of Tesla M2075:

 die =1 tpc; tpc = 16 sm; sm = 32 core;
 globalMem 8 Y rw na 5375M 128B ? 600clk <L2 L1> <> die <0.1 0.5> warp{⌊address1/blockSize⌋ != ⌊address2/blockSize⌋};
 L1 9 N rw na 16K 128B ? 80clk <> <L2 globalMem> sm ? warp{⌊address1/blockSize⌋ != ⌊address2/blockSize⌋};
 L2 7 N rw na  768K 32B ? 390clk om om die ? warp{⌊address1/blockSize⌋ != ⌊address2/blockSize⌋};

 constantMem 1 Y r na 64K ? ? 360clk <cL2 cL1> <> die ? warp{address1 != address2};
 cL1 3 N r na 4K 64B ? 48clk <> <cL2 constantMem> sm ? warp{⌊address1/blockSize⌋ != ⌊address2/blockSize⌋};
 cL2 2 N r na 32K 256B ? 140clk <cL1> <cL2 constantMem> die ? warp{⌊address1/blockSize⌋ != ⌊address2/blockSize⌋};

 sharedMem 4 Y rw na 48K ? 32 48clk <> <> sm ? block{word1!=word2 && word1%banks ==word2%banks};

 ...  ...
```

FIG. 3

Part of the memory specification of Tesla M2075 in MSL.

shared memory could suffer from bank conflicts, accesses to *constant memory* could get broadcast, and so on. A challenge is how to allow simple but well-structured descriptions of these various properties such that they can be easily exploited by the other parts of data management frameworks. The MSL design addresses the problem based on an important insight: All of those special properties are essentially about the conditions through which concurrent access requests are serialized. A "serialization condition" field is introduced in the design of MSL, which allows the specification of all those special properties in logical expressions of a simple format.

Fig. 3 demonstrates how MSL can be used for specifying the memory systems of Tesla M2075 GPU. The bottom line in the example, for instance, indicates that the specification is about the "shared memory" in the system: Its ID is 4; it is software manageable (e.g., directly allocated at user level), readable and writeable; its size is 48 KB; it has 32 banks; access latency is 48 clock cycles; it is shared by all cores on one SM; its serialization condition indicates that two accesses to shared memory from the same thread block will get serialized if they access different memory locations on the same bank.

4 COMPILER SUPPORT

The compiler has two main functionalities: getting the data access patterns of GPU kernels that the runtime can use to figure out the best data placement and preparing the code such that it can work well regardless how data are placed in memory at runtime.

4.1 DERIVING DATA ACCESS PATTERNS: A HYBRID APPROACH

The first functionality is to derive the data access patterns of the given program. Data access patterns include how frequently a data object is accessed, in regular strides or not, the number of reads versus the number of writes, and so on. Knowing these patterns is essential for deciding the appropriate ways to organize, place, and migrate data in memory.

PORPLE employs a hybrid approach to attaining data access patterns. In particular, this approach includes the compiler framework PORPLE-C that analyzes the source code of a GPU program to figure out the patterns for accessing data. For an irregular kernel whose patterns are hard to know at compile time, this approach derives a *shadow kernel*, which is a CPU function that involves much less work than the original kernel, but at the same time captures the data access patterns of the original kernel. During an execution of the target program, the runtime support will collect the size of data objects, and invoke the shadow kernels to find the missing info about the data access patterns of the program.

4.1.1 Reuse distance model

One important part of the data access patterns is the data reuse distance histogram of each array in a GPU kernel. Such a histogram is important for PORPLE to determine how many accesses of the array could be hits in a higher level memory hierarchy (e.g., cache), which in turn, is essential for the PORPLE runtime to estimate the quality of a particular data placement.

Reuse distance is a classical way to characterize data locality [5]. The reuse distance of an access A is defined as the number of distinct data items accessed between A and a prior access to the same data item as accessed by A. For example, the reuse distance of the second access to "b" in a trace "b a c c b" is two because two distinct data elements "a" and "c" are accessed between the two accesses to "b." If the reuse distance is no smaller than the cache size, enough data have been brought into cache such that A is a cache miss. Although this relation assumes a fully associative cache, prior studies have shown that it is also effective for approximating the cache miss rates for set-associative cache [6,7].

What PORPLE builds, from the data access patterns of an array, is a reuse distance histogram, which records the percentage of data accesses whose reuse distances fall into each of a series of distance ranges. For example, the second bar in Fig. 4 shows that 17% of the references to the array have reuse distances in the range [2K, 4K). With the histogram, it is easy to estimate the cache miss rate for an arbitrary cache size: it is simply the sum of the heights of all the bars appearing on the right side of the cache size, as shown in Fig. 4.

The histogram-based cache miss rate estimation comes in handy especially for the runtime search for the best data placement by PORPLE. During the search, PORPLE needs to assess the quality of many placement plans, some of which have multiple arrays sharing a single cache. Following a common practice [8], upon the cache contention, the effects can be modeled as each array (say array i) gets a portion of the cache, the size of which is proportional to the array size. That is, the cache it gets equals $size_i / \sum_j size_j$, where $size_j$ is the size of the jth array that shares the cache. PORPLE then can immediately estimate the cache miss rates of the array by comparing that size to the bars in the reuse distance histogram. In one run of a GPU program, PORPLE needs to construct the histogram for a GPU kernel only once,

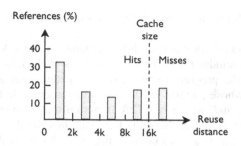

FIG. 4

Illustration of a reuse distance histogram and its relationship with cache miss rate estimation.

which can be used many times in that run for estimating the cache performance of all possible data placements during the search by PORPLE. With the cache miss rates estimated, PORPLE knows the portions of accesses to an array that get a hit at each level of a memory hierarchy.

Many methods have been developed for constructing reuse distance histograms that leverage affine reference patterns [9] or reference traces [10]. Construction from a trace has a near-linear time complexity [10]; construction from a pattern is even faster. Overall, the time overhead is only a small portion of the online profiling process. The collection of the trace could take some time, which will be discussed in the later section on online profiling.

In the data access patterns derived by the compiler, some parameters (e.g., the data size, thread numbers) are often symbolic, because their values remain unknown until the execution time. The compiler inserts some simple recording instructions into the GPU program to obtain such values at the program's execution time such that the data access patterns can get substantialized at runtime.

4.1.2 Staging code to be agnostic to placement

The second functionality is to transform the original program such that it can work with an arbitrary data placement decided by the data placement engine at runtime. A program written on a system with multiple types of memory typically does not meet the requirement because of its hardcoded data access statements that are valid only under a particular data placement (e.g., declaration "_shared_" for an array on GPU shared memory). The source-to-source compiler PORPLE-C that we will develop will transform a program into a *placement-agnostic form*. The form is equipped with some guarding statements which ensure that executions of the program can automatically select the appropriate version of code to access data according to the current data placement. A problem with this solution is the tension between the size of the generated code and the overhead of the guarding statements, which is addressed in our solution by a combination of coarse-grained and fine-grained versioning.

Fig. 5 shows this idea. The coarse-grained versioning creates multiple versions of the GPU kernel, with each corresponding to one possible placement of the arrays (e.g., in Fig. 5B; *kernel_1* is for the case when A0 is in texture and A1 is in shared memory). The appropriate version is invoked through a runtime selection based on the result from the runtime decisions on appropriate data placement, as Fig. 5A shows. When there are too many possible placements, the coarse-grained versions are created for only some of the placements (e.g., five most likely ones); for all other placements, a special copy of the kernel is invoked. This copy has fine-grained versioning on data accesses, as shown in Fig. 5C. The combination of the two levels of versioning helps strike a balance between code size and runtime overhead.

The compiler follows these steps to generate the placement-agnostic form of the code:

Step 1: Find all arrays that are on global memory in the kernel functions, assign ID numbers, and generate access expressions for the arrays.

Step 2: Identify the feasible placement options for each array to avoid generating useless code in the follow-up steps.

Step 3: Create global declarations for the constant buffer and texture references (as shown in Fig. 5A).

Step 4: Customize PROPLE_place function accordingly (as shown in Fig. 5B).

```
host code
...
// coarse-grained version selection
// TXR: texture; SHR: shared mem
if (memSpace[A0_id]==TXR &&
memSpace[A1_id]==SHR)
    kernel_1(...); // Version 1
else
    kernel_others(...); // Version 2
```

(A)

```
// Version 1 code (kernel_1)
{...
    // code for statement:  A1[j] = A0[i]
    sA1[...] = tex1Dfetch(A0tex, i);
...}
```

(B)

```
// Version 2 code (kernel_others)
{...
    // code for statement:  A1[j] = A0[i]
    switch (memSpace[A0_id]){
        case GLB: _tempA0 = A0[i]; break;
        case GLR: _tempA0 = __ldg(&A0[i]); break;
        case SHR: _tempA0 = sA0[...]; break; // use local index
        case CST: _tempA0 = cBuffer[i]; break;
    } // GLB: global; GLR: read-only global; TXR: texture;
    // SHR: shared; CST: constant

    if (memSpace[A1_id]==SHR)
        sA1[...] = _tempA0; // use local index
    else
        A1[j] = _tempA0;
....}
```

(C)

FIG. 5

Illustration of placement-agnostic code. The combination of coarse-grained kernel-level versioning and fine-grained statement-level versioning strikes a balance between code size and runtime overhead. (A) Host code. (B) Implementation of $A1[j] = A0[i]$ in Version 1. (C) Implementation of $A1[j] = A0[i]$ in Version 2.

Step 5: Insert code at the start and end of each kernel function and change data access statements (as shown in Fig. 5C).

In addition, the compiler inserts invocations of the PORPLE runtime library calls (e.g., the invocation of the online profiling function, the call to trigger the search for the best data placement) at the appropriate places in the program of interest such that the runtime support is invoked in an execution of the program.

5 RUNTIME SUPPORT

This section describes *Placer*, PORPLE's runtime engine for finding the appropriate placement for the data of a kernel at runtime.

5.1 LIGHTWEIGHT PERFORMANCE MODEL

An important component of the *Placer* is a performance model through which, for a given data placement plan and data access patterns (or traces), the Placer can easily approximate the memory throughput, and hence assess the quality of the plan.

PORPLE features a lightweight memory performance model for fast assessment of different data placement plans. The model takes as input the program data access patterns and architecture specifications (written in MSL), and outputs the estimated memory performance of the given program if it uses a certain data placement. Unlike prior GPU performance models that focus on accuracy [4], the lightweight model is easy to build and can quickly meet the requirements of online usage. The model is path-based. It estimates the amount of time taken by data transfers over each of the data transfer paths in the system. On NVIDIA Kapler GPUs, for instance, there are three data transfer paths: one between a core and the global memory, one between a core and the texture memory, and one between a core and the constant memory. Note that the first one also covers accesses between a core and the shared memory since those transfers take a part of that first path. Similarly, the second one also covers accesses to and from the read-only cache. Because the three paths transfer data concurrently, the performance model uses the maximum times estimated on those paths to assess the quality of a data placement.

Specifically, letting P be the set of paths, $A(p)$ be the set of arrays whose accesses take path p, N_{ij} be the number of memory transactions of array i that happen on memory whose ID equals j, PORPLE assesses the quality of a data placement plan through the following performance model:

$$\max_{p \in P} \left\{ \sum_{i \in A(p)} \sum_{j \in memHier(i)} N_{ij} * T_j * \alpha_j \right\}$$

The inner summation estimates the total time that accesses to array i occur, and the outer summation sums across all arrays going through path p. In the formula, *memHier*(i) is the memory hierarchy that accesses to array i go through (which can be estimated through the reuse distance histogram mentioned earlier in the compiler section), and T_j is the latency of a memory transaction on memory j. The parameter α_j is the concurrency factor of the memory, which takes into account that multiple memory transactions may be served concurrently. For instance, multiple memory transactions can be served concurrently on the global and texture memories (hence for them, $0 < \alpha_j < 1$), while only one memory transaction occurs on the constant memory ($\alpha_j = 1$). The values of the concurrency factor are given in the MSL specification; in our experiments, we use 0.2 for the global and texture memories and 1 for others.

5.2 FINDING THE BEST PLACEMENTS

With the lightweight model, Placer can quickly determine the quality of an arbitrary data placement plan. For a given GPU kernel, to find the best data placements for the kernel, Placer could just enumerate all possible plans and apply the model to each of them. It could employ some sampling or fast search algorithms for better efficiency.

PORPLE could use many search algorithms, such as A^*-search, simulated annealing, genetic algorithm, branch-and-bound algorithm, and so on. PORPLE has an open design by offering a simple interface; any search algorithm that is compatible with the interface can be easily plugged into PORPLE. The interface includes a list of IDs of software-managed memory, a list of array IDs, and a data structure for a data placement plan. PORPLE offers a built-in function (i.e., the memory performance model) that a search algorithm can directly invoke to assess the quality of a data placement plan. Users of PORPLE can configure it to use any search algorithm. All the aforementioned algorithms can find the placement plan that has the lowest total latency; they could differ in empirical computational complexity.

5.2.1 Dealing with phases

Some complexities arise when a GPU program contains the invocations of multiple kernels. These kernels may need different data placements; if Placer gives different data placements for them, there could be some overhead in moving data from one placement to another. To determine the best data placements for the entire GPU program, *Placer* must take these complexities into account.

A solution could center on a representation named *Data Placement and Migration Graph (DPMG)*. Some representations have been used for data reorganizations, such as Data Layout Graph [11]. But these representations are for homogeneous systems and mostly about cache performance, failing to accommodate the new constraints from hybrid memory systems (e.g., differences in memory sizes, latency, migration cost) DPMG is an acyclic directed graph and is shown in Fig. 6. For a program with K phases (e.g., K kernels for a GPU program), the nodes in the program's DPMG, except for two special ones (e.g., n_0 and n_9 in Fig. 6), fall into K

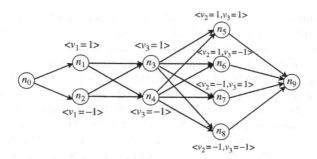

FIG. 6

A DPMG of a program with three phases on a memory system consisting of two kinds of memory. (Edge weights are omitted for readability.)

groups. Every group corresponds to the set of legitimate (i.e., meeting the size and other constraints of various types of memory) data placements for one phase of the program. Here a *data placement* is an A-dimensional vector, $\langle v_1, v_2, \ldots, v_A \rangle$, where the value of v_i indicates the type of memory that the ith container object (e.g., an array) resides on, and A is for the total number of container objects in the program.

Every node in group i represents one legitimate placement—represented by an integer vector shown in the angle parentheses in Fig. 6—of all the program data on memory in the ith phase of the program. Each integer value corresponds to one type of memory (e.g., global memory, texture memory, constant memory). The nodes in adjacent phases are fully connected; the edges represent all possible data migrations across phases. Every edge in the graph carries a weight. The weight on the edge from node$_i$ in group l to node$_j$ in group $(l + 1)$ (denoted as $w_{i \leftarrow j}$) equals the cost of the $(l + 1)$th kernel when it uses node$_j$'s data placement, plus the cost of the data migrations needed for changing node$_i$'s data placement to node$_j$'s. The definition of cost shall combine energy and performance (e.g., production of energy and delay to evaluate energy efficiency).

By capturing various constraints in a graph form, DPMG simplifies the problem of data placement to a shortest path problem. A path here refers to a route from the starting node to the ending node in the graph. The length of a path is the sum of the weights of all edges on the path, which equals the total cost when the data placements represented by the nodes on the path are used for the program phases. A shortest path in a DPMG hence gives a data placement that minimizes the accumulated cost.

A complexity is to effectively minimize the size of DPMG, which is essential for the solution to be applicable at runtime. The size of DPMG grows with the number of phases, number of arrays, and number of types of memory. However, for most programs, many possible data placements can be filtered out as unlikely choices through the use of heuristics.

6 RESULTS

This section reports some experimental results of PORPLE on three generations of GPUs; their memory latencies are listed in Table 1.

We evaluate PORPLE on a diverse set of benchmarks, as shown in Table 2. The experiments focus on only one kernel per program; the benefits on multiple kernels (including data migrations) are not covered in the experimental results. These benchmarks include all of the level-1 benchmarks from the SHOC benchmark suite [12] that come from various application domains. To further evaluate PORPLE with complicated memory access patterns, we add three benchmarks from the RODINIA benchmark suite [13] and three from CUDA SDK. The bottom five benchmarks in Table 2 have irregular memory accesses. Their memory access patterns depend highly on inputs and can be known only during runtime. Hence

Table 1 Memory Latency Description

Machine Name	Constant	cL2	cL1	Global	gL2	gL1	Read-Only	Texture	tL2	tL1	Shared
Tesla K20c	250	120	48	345	222	N/A	141	351	222	103	48
Tesla M2075	360	140	48	600	390	80	N/A	617	390	208	48
Tesla C1060	545	130	56	548	N/A	N/A	N/A	546	366	251	38

Notes: cL1 and cL2 are L1 and L2 caches for constant memory, respectively. gL1 and gL2 are L1 and L2 caches for global memory, respectively. tL1 and tL2 are L1 and L2 caches for texture memory, respectively.

Table 2 Benchmark Description

Benchmark	Source	Description	Irregular
mm	SDK	Dense matrix multiplication	N
convolution	SDK	Signal filter	N
trans	SDK	Matrix transpose	N
reduction	SHOC	Reduction	N
fft	SHOC	Fast Fourier transform	N
scan	SHOC	Scan	N
sort	SHOC	Radix sort	N
traid	SHOC	Stream triad	N
kmeans	Rodinia	kmeans clustering	N
particlefilter	Rodinia	Particle filter	Y
cfd	Rodinia	Computational fluid	Y
md	SHOC	Molecular dynamics	Y
spmv	SHOC	Sparse matrix vector multi	Y
bfs	SHOC	Breadth-first search	Y

static analysis cannot work for them, and online profiling must be employed. They all have a loop surrounding the GPU kernel call. The loop in *bfs* has a fixed number of iterations (100), while the number of iterations of the loops in the other four benchmarks are decided by the input argument of the benchmark. In our experiments, we use 100 for all of them. We focus on the optimization of the most important kernel in each of the benchmarks. To optimize data placement for multiple kernels, PORPLE would need to consider the data movements that might possibly be required across the kernels.

The results were compared with the state-of-the-art memory selection algorithm on GPU by Jang et al. [3]. In their algorithm, the data placement decisions were made according to several high-level rules derived from some empirical studies. For data arrays whose access patterns cannot be inferred through static analysis, the algorithm simply leaves them in the global memory space. We call this algorithm, the *rule-based approach*. Another comparison counterpart is the optimal data placement obtained through an offline exhaustive search, which produces the best speedup a data placement method can achieve.

6.1 RESULTS WITH IRREGULAR BENCHMARKS

The results on the irregular benchmarks are shown in Fig. 7. The rule-based approach and the optimal data placement are labeled as "Rule-Based" and "POTENTIAL" in the figure, respectively.

Simply relying on limited static analysis and without cooperative detection of memory access patterns and prediction of data placement results, the rule-based approach favors one type of memory (i.e., global memory) and cannot determine optimal data placement for HMS. This fact is especially pronounced in the benchmarks *bfs* and *particlefilter*. In contrast, PORPLE appropriately spread data between diverse memory systems. In general, PORPLE provides 59% performance improvement on average over the original, only 9% less than the optimal, but 26% more than the rule-based approach. This salient performance improvement comes from accurate characterization of memory access patterns and lightweight runtime management. Furthermore, we notice that PORPLE works consistently well across different GPU architectures and across different input problem sizes. This demonstrates the good portability of PORPLE.

6.2 RESULTS WITH REGULAR BENCHMARKS

Fig. 8 shows the performance results for regular benchmarks on Tesla K20c. POR-PLE provides on average 13% speedup, successfully exploiting almost all potential (i.e., 14%) from data array placement. The rule-based approach, however, provides only a 5% improvement in performance. We observe that for all benchmarks, except mm, trans, and triad, the data placement strategies in the original programs are optimal or close to optimal, as the benchmark developers manually optimized the

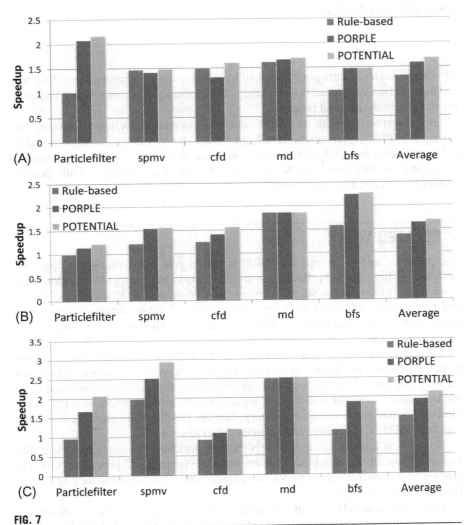

FIG. 7

Benefits of GPU for improving performance of GPU. (A) Speedup of some irregular benchmarks on Tesla K20c. (B) Speedup on Tesla M2075. (C) Speedup on Tesla C1060.

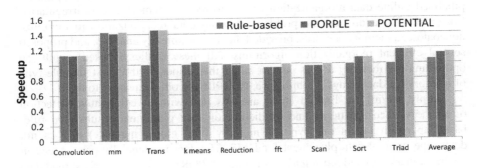

FIG. 8

Speedup of regular benchmarks on Tesla K20c.

GPU kernels. Hence little potential (<10%) exits for further improvement. PORPLE and the rule-based approach both find the optimal placement strategy, which is almost the same as in the original programs.

The experiments are all on CUDA benchmarks on NVIDIA devices because the current PORPLE implementation is CUDA-based. However, the method is applicable to OpenCL and other GPUs. For instance, after manually applying the transformation to the program in OpenCL SDK, we saw 1.76× speedups on K20c. Fully porting PORPLE to OpenCL is future work.

7 RELATED WORK

The previous sections compared PORPLE with a rule-based placement approach designed by Jang et al. [3]. Besides that related work, Ma et al. [14] considered the optimal data placement on shared memory only. Wang et al. [15] studied the energy and performance tradeoff for placing data on DRAM versus nonvolatile memory. Other work has focused on easing GPU programming when the data working set is too large to fit into GPU memory [16,17].

Data placement is also a significant problem for CPUs with heterogeneous memory architectures. Jevdjic et al. [18] designed a server CPU that has 3D stacked memory. Because of the various technical constraints, especially heat dissipation, the stacked memory has a limited size and is managed by hardware like traditional cache. Similarly, some heterogeneous memory designs [19,20] involving phase change memory (PCM) also use hardware-managed data placement.

To our best knowledge, PORPLE is the first portable, extensible optimizer that systematically allows data placement on various types of GPU programs, which is enabled by its novel design of the memory specification language and the placement-agnostic code generator.

GPU programs rely heavily on memory performance; therefore memory optimizations have received lots of attention [21–24]. Yang et al. [25] designed a source-to-source offline compiler to enhance memory coalescing or shared memory use. Zhang et al. [26] focused on irregular memory references and proposed a pipelined online data reorganization engine to reduce memory access irregularity. Wu et al. [27] addressed the problem of using data reorganization to minimize noncoalesced memory accesses, provided the first complexity analysis, and proposed several efficient reorganization algorithms. All these studies focused mainly on optimizing the memory access pattern rather than choosing the most suitable type of memory for data arrays. In this sense, PORPLE is complementary to them.

Simply relying on limited static analysis and without cooperative detection of memory access patterns and prediction of data placement results, the rule-based approach favors one type of memory (i.e., global memory) and cannot determine optimal data placement for HMS. This fact is especially pronounced in the benchmarks *bfs* and *particlefilter*. In contrast, PORPLE appropriately spread data between diverse memory systems. In general, PORPLE provides a 59% performance improvement over the original, only 9% less than the optimal, but 26% more than the rule-based approach. This salient improvement in performance comes from accurate characterization of memory access patterns and lightweight runtime management. Furthermore, we notice that PORPLE works consistently well across different GPU architectures and across different input problem sizes, which demonstrates the good portability of PORPLE.

8 SUMMARY

Good system software support is essential for translating carefully designed memory systems into actual program performance. The PORPLE system described in this chapter demonstrates a promising solution. Its use of MSL helps separate hardware complexities from other concerns, enabling cross-device portability of the optimization. Its carefully designed compiler-and-runtime synergy helps address input sensitivity of data placements. Future memory systems are expected to become even more sophisticated and complex, evidenced by the various emerging memory technologies (e.g., PCM, stacked memory). Because of its distinctive advantages on portability, the PORPLE approach may open up many other opportunities for tapping into the full power of future memory systems.

REFERENCES

[1] G. Chen, B. Wu, D. Li, X. Shen, PORPLE: an extensible optimizer for portable data placement on GPU, in: Proceedings of the Annual IEEE/ACM International Symposium on Microarchitecture, 2014.

[2] Y. Zhang, F. Mueller, Auto-generation and auto-tuning of 3D stencil codes on GPU clusters, in: Proceedings of the Tenth International Symposium on Code Generation and Optimization, CGO '12, ISBN 978-1-4503-1206-6, 2012, pp. 155–164.

[3] B. Jang, D. Schaa, P. Mistry, D. Kaeli, Exploiting memory access patterns to improve memory performance in data-parallel architectures, IEEE Trans. Parallel Distrib. Syst. 22 (1) (2011) 105–118, ISSN 1045-9219.

[4] S. Hong, H. Kim, An analytical model for a GPU architecture with memory-level and thread-level parallelism awareness, in: International Symposium on Computer Architecture, 2009.

[5] A.P. Batson, A.W. Madison, Measurements of major locality phases in symbolic reference strings, in: Proceedings of the ACM SIGMETRICS Conference on Measurement & Modeling Computer Systems, Cambridge, MA, 1976.

[6] A.J. Smith, On the effectiveness of set associative page mapping and its applications in main memory management, in: Proceedings of the 2nd International Conference on Software Engineering, 1976, pp. 286–292.

[7] Y. Zhong, S.G. Dropsho, C. Ding, Miss rate prediction across all program inputs, in: Proceedings of the 12th International Conference on Parallel Architectures and Compilation Techniques, New Orleans, LA, 2003.

[8] S. Manegold, P. Boncz, M.L. Kersten, Generic database cost models for hierarchical memory systems, in: Proceedings of VLDB, 2002, pp. 191–202.

[9] G.C. Cascaval, Compile-time performance prediction of scientific programs, Ph.D. thesis, University of Illinois at Urbana-Champaign, 2000.

[10] C. Ding, Y. Zhong, Predicting whole-program locality with reuse distance analysis, in: Proceedings of ACM SIGPLAN Conference on Programming Language Design and Implementation, San Diego, CA, 2003, pp. 245–257.

[11] R. Bixby, K. Kennedy, U. Kremer, Automatic data layout using 0–1 integer programming, in: Proceedings of International Conference on Parallel Architectures and Compilation Techniques, 1994.

[12] A. Danalis, G. Marin, C. McCurdy, J.S. Meredith, P.C. Roth, K. Spafford, V. Tipparaju, J.S. Vetter, The Scalable Heterogeneous Computing (SHOC) benchmark suite, in: GPGPU, 2010.

[13] S. Che, M. Boyer, J. Meng, D. Tarjan, J.W. Sheaffer, S.-H. Lee, K. Skadron, Rodinia: a benchmark suite for heterogeneous computing, in: IISWC, 2009.

[14] W. Ma, G. Agrawal, An integer programming framework for optimizing shared memory use on GPUs, in: PACT, 2010, pp. 553–554.

[15] B. Wang, B. Wu, D. Li, X. Shen, W. Yu, Y. Jiao, J.S. Vetter, Exploring hybrid memory for GPU energy efficiency through software-hardware co-design, in: Proceedings of the 22nd International Conference on Parallel Architectures and Compilation Techniques, PACT '13, IEEE Press, Piscataway, NJ, USA, ISBN 978-1-4799-1021-2, 2013, pp. 93–102.

[16] J. Lee, M. Samadi, S. Mahlke, VAST: the illusion of a large memory space for GPUs, in: Proceedings of the International Conference on Parallel Architectures and Compilation Techniques, PACT'14, 2014, pp. 443–454.

[17] R. Mokhtari, M. Stumm, BigKernel—high performance CPU-GPU communication pipelining for big data-style applications, in: Proceedings of International Parallel and Distribute Processing Symposium (IPDPS), 2014.

[18] D. Jevdjic, S. Volos, B. Falsafi, Die-stacked DRAM caches for servers: hit ratio, latency, or bandwidth? Have it all with footprint cache, in: ISCA, 2013, pp. 404–415.

[19] L.E. Ramos, E. Gorbatov, R. Bianchini, Page placement in hybrid memory systems, in: Proceedings of the International Conference on Supercomputing, ICS '11, ISBN 978-1-4503-0102-2, 2011, pp. 85–95.

[20] M.K. Qureshi, V. Srinivasan, J.A. Rivers, Scalable high performance main memory system using phase-change memory technology, in: Proceedings of the 36th Annual International Symposium on Computer Architecture, ISCA '09, ISBN 978-1-60558-526-0, 2009, pp. 24–33.

[21] S. Che, J.W. Sheaffer, K. Skadron, Dymaxion: optimizing memory access patterns for heterogeneous systems, in: Proceedings of the ACM/IEEE conference on Supercomputing, 2011.

[22] M.M. Baskaran, U. Bondhugula, S. Krishnamoorthy, J. Ramanujam, A. Rountev, P. Sadayappan, A compiler framework for optimization of affine loop nests for GPGPUs, in: ICS'08: Proceedings of the 22nd Annual International Conference on Supercomputing, 2008, pp. 225–234.

[23] I.-J. Sung, J.A. Stratton, W.-M.W. Hwu, Data layout transformation exploiting memory-level parallelism in structured grid many-core applications, in: Proceedings of the 19th International Conference on Parallel Architectures and Compilation Techniques, PACT '10, ISBN 978-1-4503-0178-7, 2010, pp. 513–522.

[24] W. Jia, K.A. Shaw, M. Martonosi, Characterizing and improving the use of demand-fetched caches in GPUs, in: Proceedings of the 26th ACM international conference on Supercomputing, ICS '12, 2012.

[25] Y. Yang, P. Xiang, J. Kong, H. Zhou, A GPGPU compiler for memory optimization and parallelism management, in: PLDI, 2010.

[26] E. Zhang, Y. Jiang, Z. Guo, K. Tian, X. Shen, On-the-fly elimination of dynamic irregularities for GPU computing, in: Proceedings of the International Conference on Architectural Support for Programming Languages and Operating Systems, 2011.

[27] B. Wu, Z. Zhao, E. Zhang, Y. Jiang, X. Shen, Complexity analysis and algorithm design for reorganizing data to minimize non-coalesced memory accesses on GPU, in: Proceedings of the ACM SIGPLAN symposium on Principles and practice of parallel programming, 2013.

Algorithms and applications

Biological sequence analysis on GPU

N. Moreano[1], A.C.M.A. de Melo[2]

Federal University of Mato Grosso do Sul, Campo Grande, Brazil[1] University of Brasilia, Brasilia, Brazil[2]

1 INTRODUCTION

Bioinformatics represents an interdisciplinary and rapidly evolving area of science that applies mathematics, statistics, computer science, and biology to the understanding of living systems. Bioinformatics is driven by the advent of fast and reliable technology for sequencing nucleic acids and proteins that results in an ever-increasing volume of experimental data to be analyzed. Many of the recent developments in the field use algorithmic techniques in order to reach answers to key challenges in molecular biology research, including understanding the mechanisms of genome evolution, elucidating the structure of protein interaction networks, and determining the genetic basis for susceptibility to disease [1].

A major application of Bioinformatics is the analysis of the DNA and protein sequences of organisms that have been sequenced. Sequence comparison is one of the basic operations in Bioinformatics, serving as a basis for many other more complex manipulations. It provides important information for solving many key problems, such as determining the function of a newly discovered sequence, determining the evolutionary relationships among genes and proteins, and predicting the structure and function of proteins [2].

When a new biological sequence is discovered, its function and structure must be determined. A common approach is to compare the new sequence to known sequences belonging to biological databases, in search for similarities. We can compare a sequence to another sequence, performing a pairwise sequence comparison, which consists of deciding whether a pair of sequences are evolutionary related, that is, whether they share a common evolutionary history. We can also compare a sequence to a profile that models a family of sequences, performing a sequence-profile comparison, which consists of deciding whether a sequence is evolutionarily related to a known evolutionary family sequence.

Advances in GPU Research and Practice. http://dx.doi.org/10.1016/B978-0-12-803738-6.00006-9

When we recognize a significant similarity between a new sequence and a known sequence or sequence family, we can transfer information about structure and/or function to the new sequence. We say that the sequences are homologous and that we are transferring information by homology [3].

Comprehensive databases of DNA and protein sequences are now established as major tools in current molecular biology research. Given the advances in sequencing technologies, the significant amount of biological sequence data produced, and the effectiveness of sequence comparison, it is logical to systematically organize and store the biological sequences to be compared. As a consequence, sequence databases have grown exponentially in the last decade.

The most accurate algorithms for solving the problems of pairwise sequence comparison and sequence-profile comparison are usually based on the dynamic programming technique. Because of the quadratic time and memory complexity of these algorithms and usually the long length of biological sequences, the task of searching large databases can lead to very lengthy execution times with huge memory requirements.

High-performance computing resources and techniques can be used to accelerate these operations. Several solutions for parallel sequence comparison have been proposed, targeting different high-performance platforms, such as multicore architectures, clusters, and field-programmable gate arrays (FPGAs).

Graphics processing units (GPUs) have evolved into highly parallel platforms due to their vast number of simple, data-parallel, deeply multithreaded cores. Their impressive computational power, high memory bandwidth, and comparatively low cost make them an attractive platform to solve problems based on computationally intensive algorithms. Moreover, GPUs are becoming increasingly programmable, offering the potential of significant speedups for a wide range of applications compared to general-purpose processors (CPUs).

The goal of this chapter is to discuss in detail and compare the recent advances in GPU solutions for some biological sequence analysis applications. The problems discussed are two classes of biological sequence comparison: pairwise sequence comparison and sequence-profile comparison. The first one is widely used as a first step in the solution of complex problems such as the determination of the evolutionary history of the species. The second one is extremely important because it is used to decide whether a recently sequenced protein belongs to a particular protein family. For both problems, several GPU solutions have been proposed that obtained substantial speedups over the sequential implementation and over solutions in other parallel platforms.

The remainder of the chapter is organized as follows. In Section 2, we introduce the pairwise sequence comparison and sequence-profile comparison problems and present the most widely used algorithms to solve them. Section 3 presents the main design aspects that are considered in the development of GPU solutions for sequence comparison. In Section 4, several state-of-the-art GPU solutions to the pairwise sequence comparison problem are discussed and compared. In Section 5, we discuss and compare several state-of-the-art GPU solutions for the sequence-profile comparison problem. Finally, Section 6 concludes the chapter, presenting the future tendencies in this research area.

2 PAIRWISE SEQUENCE COMPARISON AND SEQUENCE-PROFILE COMPARISON

A biological sequence comprises a single and continuous molecule of either nucleic acid or protein. A DNA sequence is a chain of simpler molecules called nucleotide bases. Only four different bases are used in DNA sequences, and they are represented by the residues A, C, T, and G. A protein is also a chain of smaller molecules called amino acids, and there are 20 different amino acids, represented by 20 different residues. Therefore we can model a biological sequence (DNA or protein sequence) as a linear list of residues.

One goal of sequence comparison is to enable the researcher to determine whether two sequences or a sequence and a sequence family display sufficient similarity such that an inference of homology can be made. Homology refers to a conclusion drawn from these data that the sequences are evolutionarily related. The changes that occur during the course of the evolutionary process can be categorized as residue substitutions, insertions, and deletions [4].

2.1 PAIRWISE SEQUENCE COMPARISON

Pairwise biological sequence comparison is a very important operation in Bioinformatics projects, often being used to define the similarity between two sequences. In a broad sense, the sequences compared are (a) a protein sequence versus a protein sequence that belongs to a genomic database, (b) a small DNA sequence versus a reference genome, or (c) two long DNA sequences. Pairwise sequence comparison is also used as a building block to solve Bioinformatics problems such as DNA assembly and phylogenetic tree construction, among others. Nowadays, such comparisons are executed daily, thousands of times, all over the world.

The algorithm used to perform pairwise sequence comparisons can be exact, either providing the optimal result as output, or heuristic, or providing as output a result that is not guaranteed to be optimal but that is a good solution for the problem.

The pairwise sequence comparison produces a score as output, which is a measure of the similarity between the sequences and an alignment that highlights the parts of the sequences that are similar/distinct. An alignment can be (A) global, composed of all the characters of the sequences; (B) local, composed of a subset of the characters of the sequences; or (C) semiglobal, where the prefix or suffix of one of the sequences is discarded. Fig. 1 illustrates these types of alignments between sequences $S_1 =$ GCATTCGATC and $S_2 =$ ACGAT.

In order to calculate the score of an alignment, punctuations are given to matches (identical characters), mismatches (different characters), and gaps. If DNA or RNA sequences are compared, matches and mismatches usually have a unique punctuation,

G	C	A	T	T	C	G	A	T	C
–	–	A	–	–	C	G	A	T	–
−2	−2	+1	−2	−2	+1	+1	+1	+1	−2

score = −5

(A)

C	G	A	T
C	G	A	T
+1	+1	+1	+1

score = 4

(B)

A	T	T	C	G	A	T	C
A	–	–	C	G	A	T	–
+1	−2	−2	+1	−1	+1	+1	−2

score = −3

(C)

FIG. 1

Global, local, and semiglobal alignments. The punctuations for matches, mismatches, and gaps are +1, −1, and −2, respectively. (A) Global alignment. (B) Local alignment. (C) Semiglobal alignment.

regardless of the characters compared (i.e., the match A, A is equal to the match C, C). On the other hand, the punctuation of matches and mismatches for the amino acids that compose protein sequences is usually retrieved from substitution matrices that contain punctuations for individual cases. The most popular substitution matrices are PAM and BLOSUM [5].

In all pairwise sequence comparison algorithms, the addition of gaps in the alignment results in a penalty, which is calculated using two distinct gap models: linear and affine gap. In the linear model, each gap has the same penalty, which is a negative value. In the affine gap model, the penalties for gaps are also negative, but the penalty for the first gap is higher than the penalty for the subsequent gaps. The affine gap model produces alignments that are more biologically significant than the linear model since gaps tend to occur together in nature [6].

The most widely used exact algorithms that compare two sequences are (a) Needleman-Wunsch (NW) [7], which is used to obtain optimal global alignments with linear gap penalties; (b) Smith-Waterman (SW) [8], which obtains optimal local alignments with linear gap penalties; (c) Gotoh [9], which computes the affine gap model to obtain optimal global alignments, and (d) Myers-Miller (MM) [10], which computes optimal global alignments in linear memory space.

These four algorithms use the dynamic programming technique to calculate similarity matrices and have quadratic time complexity $O(m \times n)$, where m and n are the lengths of the sequences. Also, they have the same data dependency, where the value of each cell (i, j) in the matrix depends on the values of three previously calculated cells: $(i-1, j-1)$, $(i-1, j)$, and $(i, j-1)$. Algorithms [7–9] execute in two phases, where Phase 1 computes the dynamic programming matrices and obtains the optimal score and Phase 2 obtains the optimal alignment. Algorithm [10] executes in one phase, in a divide-and-conquer recursive manner.

The most widely used heuristic algorithms to compare two sequences are Basic Local Alignment Tool (BLAST) [11] and FASTA [12]. Both algorithms combine exact pattern matching with statistical analysis in order to obtain good alignments quickly.

In order to compare the performance of pairwise sequence comparison applications, the metric GCUPS (billion cells update per second) is often used. This metric is calculated by $(m \times n)/(t \times 10^9)$, where m and n are the lengths of the sequences and t is the total time to execute the comparison.

In the next sections, we detail the SW algorithm and BLAST.

2.1.1 Smith-Waterman algorithm

The SW algorithm [8] is an exact method based on dynamic programming to obtain the best local alignment between two sequences in quadratic time and space. It is divided into two phases: create the similarity matrix and obtain the best local alignment.

Phase 1: Create the similarity matrix

The first phase receives as input sequences s and t, with $|s| = m$ and $|t| = n$, where $|s|$ represents the length of sequence s. The notation used to represent the nth character of a sequence seq is $seq[n]$, and to represent a prefix with n characters, from the beginning of the sequence, we use $seq[1 \ldots n]$. The similarity matrix is denoted $A_{m+1,n+1}$, where $A_{i,j}$ contains the similarity score between prefixes $s[1 \ldots i]$ and $t[1 \ldots j]$.

At the beginning, the first row and column are filled with zeros. The remaining elements of A are obtained from Eq. (1), where ma is the punctuation for matches, mi is the punctuation for mismatches, and g is the gap penalty. The SW score between sequences s and t is the highest value contained in matrix A.

$$A_{i,j} = \max \begin{cases} A_{i-1,j-1} + (\text{if } s[i] = t[j] \text{ then } ma \text{ else } mi) \\ A_{i,j-1} - g \\ A_{i-1,j} - g \\ 0 \end{cases} \tag{1}$$

Phase 2: Obtain the best local alignment

The second phase is executed to obtain the best local alignment. The algorithm starts from the cell that contains the highest value and follows the arrows until a zero-valued cell is reached (Fig. 2). A left arrow in $A_{i,j}$ indicates the alignment of $s[i]$ with a gap in t. An up arrow represents the alignment of $t[j]$ with a gap in s. Finally, an arrow on the diagonal indicates that $s[i]$ is aligned with $t[j]$.

```
       *  G  A  G  C  T  A  T  G  A  G  G
   *   0  0  0  0  0  0  0  0  0  0  0  0
   T   0  0  0  0  0  1  0  1  0  0  0  0
   A   0  0  1  0  0  0  2  0  0  1  0  0
   T   0  0  0  0  0  1  0  3  1  0  0  0
   A   0  0  1  0  0  0  2  1  2  2  0  0
   G   0  1  0  2  0  0  0  1  2  1  3  1
   G   0  1  0  1  1  0  0  0  2  1  2  4
   T   0  0  0  0  0  2  0  1  0  1  0  2
   A   0  0  0  1  0  0  0  3  1  0  1  0  0
   G   0  1  0  0  2  0  0  1  2  2  0  2  1
   C   0  0  0  0  0  3  1  0  0  1  1  0  1
   T   0  0  0  0  0  1  4  2  1  0  0  0  0
   A   0  0  1  0  0  2  5  3  1  1  0  0
```

FIG. 2

Smith-Waterman similarity matrix for pairwise comparison. In this example, the alignment has *score* = 5.

Smith-Waterman variations

Here we describe two variations of SW that are widely used: (a) affine-gap comparison and (b) linear space alignment retrieval.

The original SW algorithm assigns a single penalty for gaps, using the linear gap model. However, in nature gaps tend to occur together. Therefore, in order to better represent the biological phenomena, the penalty for the first gap (*gap open*) must be higher than the penalty for the remaining gaps (*gap extend*) in a sequence of consecutive gaps. This is called the affine gap model. Gotoh [9] proposed an algorithm that implements the affine gap model by using three dynamic programming matrices instead of one. Even so, time and space complexity remain quadratic.

The SW algorithm runs on quadratic space, which prevents it from being executed to compare long sequences. Hirschberg [13] proposed an algorithm that computes the long common subsequence in linear space, using a divide and conquer technique. MM [10] adapted Hirshberg's algorithm to execute the Gotoh algorithm in linear space.

2.1.2 Basic Local Alignment Tool

BLAST was proposed by Ref. [11], and it is based on a heuristic algorithm designed to run fast while still maintaining high sensibility. The BLAST algorithm assumes that significant alignments have words of length w in common, and it is divided into three well-defined phases: seeding, extension, and evaluation.

Phase 1: Seeding

In the first phase, BLAST compares a query sequence s against all sequences t that compose a genomic database, using exact pattern matching for a given length w of substrings. For instance, if w is 3, the locations of all shared w-letter words between sequences s and t are determined. These locations are known as identical words and are used as seed candidates. The list of locations is evaluated using a substitution matrix and the concept of neighborhood. The neighbor of a word includes the word itself and every other word whose score is at least equal to T (cut-off score), when compared with a substitution matrix. A list of seeds is produced as output.

Phase 2: Extension
The goal of this phase is to extend the seeds generated in Phase 1, including some mismatches. This is done by inspecting the characters near each seed in both directions and concatenating them to the seed until a drop-off score X is reached. The drop-off score defines how much the score can be reduced. At the end of this phase, a list of local alignments is produced.

Phase 3: Evaluation
The alignments generated in Phase 2 are evaluated in order to remove those that are not significant. The significant alignments, called high-score segment pairs (HSPs), are the ones whose scores are higher than or equal to a threshold S. Also, consistent HSP groups are generated that include nonoverlapped HSPs. The consistent HSP groups are compared to a final threshold, known as the E-value, and only the alignments that are above this threshold are the output.

BLAST
Basically, BLAST has two versions, which compare proteins (BLASTP) and nucleotides (BLASTN), respectively. The original BLAST algorithm searched for local alignments without considering gaps. In 1994 and 1997, improved gapped versions of the original BLAST, WU-BLAST2 [14] and NCBI-BLAST2 [15] were proposed.

Because of the success in obtaining significant alignments fast, many BLAST variations and wrappers were proposed. Mega-BLAST [16], BLASTZ [17], and MPBLAST [18] form a nonexhaustive list of these variations. The goal of Mega-BLAST is to align very similar DNA sequences faster than BLAST. In order to achieve this goal, Mega-BLAST uses a greedy algorithm to reduce the execution time of the extension phase. BLASTZ is a variation of BLAST which requires that matching regions must occur in the same order in both sequences. Multiplexing BLAST (MPBLAST) concatenates small query sequences into one single query, thus reducing the BLAST search time.

2.2 SEQUENCE-PROFILE COMPARISON
A sequence family is a set of sequences with a similar biological function, or a similar two- or three-dimensional structure, or a known common evolutionary history [5].

Many sequence analysis methods are based on determining the relationship of a newly discovered sequence to a known sequence family. If we recognize a significant similarity between the new sequence and the sequence family, we can infer that the new sequence belongs to the family and transfer information about the family structure and/or function to the new sequence.

In this analysis, we want to compare the sequence to the family using statistical features of the whole set of sequences in the family (and not features of each sequence in the family individually). Similarly, when the family membership is established, a more accurate alignment between the sequence and the family can be obtained by concentrating on features that are conserved on the whole family [3]. Therefore a representation that captures the features of the set of sequences in a family is necessary.

A simple representation of a family of related sequences is given by their multiple alignment and the corresponding profile. Hidden Markov models (HMMs) extend the profile representation of a multiple alignment of a family of sequences and provide a statistical representation of a family of sequences [19]. A profile HMM to model a given sequence family can be built from the multiple alignment of the sequences in the family.

In a typical application, we have a sequence family represented by a profile HMM and we want to identify new family members from a sequence database. Then we perform a database search, performing a sequence-profile comparison between each sequence from the database and the profile HMM.

The sequence-profile comparison produces as output a score and an alignment. The score is a measure of the similarity between the sequence and the family, while the alignment emphasizes the parts of the sequence that are similar/distinct to the family represented by the profile HMM. Most of the solutions to the sequence-profile comparison are based on an important algorithm called Viterbi algorithm [20] and its variations.

The Pfam database [21] is a large collection of protein families, represented by multiple sequence alignments and profile HMMs. It enables the comparison of protein sequences of interest to protein families, in search of additional homologous sequences.

HMMER [22] is a set of tools for the analysis of biological sequences using profile HMMs. One of its main tools is *hmmsearch* [23], which compares the sequences in a protein sequence database to a profile HMM representing a protein sequence family, in order to identify new homologous sequences. HMMER is widely used and many optimizations have been proposed to improve its performance.

The *hmmsearch* tool uses the following strategy: Each sequence passes through a chain of filters, where each filter computes a score for the sequence using a different algorithm for sequence-profile comparison. Depending on the score, the sequence is discarded (because we conclude the sequence is not homologous to the family) or forwarded to the next filter in the chain (because a more thorough analysis of the sequence is necessary). Therefore the initial filters are able to discard a certain amount of the sequences being compared, forwarding to the next filters only a fraction of them. The initial filters, which receive more sequences, use less precise and faster algorithms; while the final filters, which receive fewer sequences, use more precise and slower algorithms.

In HMMER2 (HMMER version 2), the *hmmsearch* tool uses the Viterbi algorithm as its main step. In HMMER3, the Multiple Segment Viterbi (MSV) algorithm is the first filter in the chain of filters of the *hmmsearch* tool. The Viterbi algorithm is a posterior filter in the chain. The MSV algorithm is a simplified version of the Viterbi algorithm, in which the profile HMM structure is reduced.

2.2.1 Hidden Markov models

HMMs are a probabilistic model based on Markov processes and have been applied to other research areas, such as speech recognition [24]. They have been widely used in many Bioinformatics problems.

The profile HMM representing a sequence family and used for sequence-profile comparison represents statistically the similarities and differences among the sequences in the family, extending the multiple alignment of these sequences into a position-specific scoring system. It consists of a set of states, the states' transition probabilities, and the residue emission probabilities at each state. These states correspond to evolutionary possibilities, such as residue insertions and deletions, or to matches between the sequences in the multiple alignment of the sequences in the family.

Krogh et al. [25] proposed a profile HMM with a regular topology for modeling protein families, consisting of Match (M), Insert (I), and Delete (D) states. It has one state M for every conserved column of the multiple alignment of the family. The states I and D model gapped alignments, that is, alignments including residue insertions and deletions in the multiple alignment, respectively. Each state I allows one or more residues to be inserted between two consecutive states M. Each state D allows a residue deletion by skipping over a state M.

The transition probabilities associated with the state transitions also represent specific information about each column in the multiple alignment of the family. The profile HMM can model position-specific gap penalties, with different probabilities for entering different states I and D, representing that certain regions of the multiple alignment allow more insertions and deletions than others. Affine gap penalties can also be modeled with different transition probabilities for entering a state I for the first time and for staying in it.

Residue emission probabilities are associated with states M and I. Each state M emits a single residue, with an emission probability determined by the frequency that the residues are observed in the corresponding column of the multiple alignment. Each state I also emits a residue. This way each state M and I can have different emission probabilities for each different residue (the 4 nucleotide bases in DNA sequences or the 20 amino acids in protein sequences). D states do not emit any residues.

Eddy [26] introduced the Plan7 profile HMM architecture extending this basic profile HMM topology with the addition of special states B (Begin), E (End), N, C, and J (Joining) in order to allow different alignment algorithms to be applied, such as global alignment, local alignment with respect to the profile HMM, local alignment with respect to the sequence being compared, and multiple hit alignment.

The group of states M, I, and D corresponding to the same column in the multiple alignment is called a node of the profile HMM, and the length of the profile HMM is

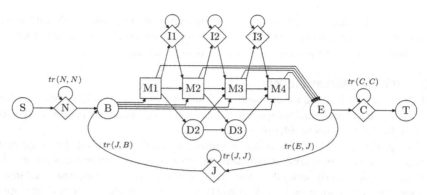

FIG. 3

Plan7 profile HMM with four nodes.

measured as the number of nodes in it. Fig. 3 illustrates a Plan7 profile HMM with four nodes. The labels in the state transitions represent some transition probabilities.

A local alignment with respect to the profile HMM is possible through transitions from state B to internal state M and from these states to state E. A local alignment with respect to the sequence is possible using the loop transitions on the special states N and C, which can emit residues. Multiple hits of the sequence to the profile HMM are allowed by transitions through the special state J [26].

2.2.2 The Viterbi algorithm

The Viterbi algorithm [20] is an optimal algorithm for finding the most likely sequence of states that result in a sequence of observed events, in the context of HMM. It has been applied in a variety of areas, such as digital communications and speech recognition. The Viterbi algorithm is used for the comparison between a sequence S and a profile HMM H, aligning the residues of S to the states of H, beginning at the state Start (S) and finishing at the state Termination (T). It applies the dynamic programming technique in order to find the best path of states in H that emits the sequence S, that is, the one with the maximum probability.

The logarithm of the probabilities is used in order to obtain an additive scoring system (instead of a multiplicative one), producing log-odds scores [3]. The algorithm computes score matrices and vectors corresponding to the states of the profile HMM, as shown here:

- Matrices M, I, and D, for Match, Insert, and Delete states, respectively, where the element $[i,j]$ of each matrix contains the score of the best alignment that emits the first i residues of S and reaches the corresponding state in node j.
- Vectors N, B, E, C, and J for the special states, where the ith element of each vector contains the score of the best alignment that emits the first i residues of S and reaches the state associated with the vector.

Recurrence Eq. (2) describe the Viterbi algorithm for the comparison of a sequence $S = s_1 \ldots s_L$ of length L to a Plan7 profile HMM of length Q, where $tr(q_1, q_2)$ is the transition probability from state q_1 to q_2 and $em(q, s)$ is the emission probability of residue s at state q. The score of the best alignment between S and H is given by $C[L] + tr(C, T)$. The algorithm has time complexity $O(L \times Q)$.

$$M[i,j] = em(M_j, s_i) + \max \begin{cases} M[i-1, j-1] + tr(M_{j-1}, M_j) \\ I[i-1, j-1] + tr(I_{j-1}, M_j) \\ D[i-1, j-1] + tr(D_{j-1}, M_j) \\ B[i-1] + tr(B, M_j) \end{cases}$$

$$I[i,j] = em(I_j, s_i) + \max \begin{cases} M[i-1, j] + tr(M_j, I_j) \\ I[i-1, j] + tr(I_j, I_j) \end{cases}$$

$$D[i,j] = \max \begin{cases} M[i, j-1] + tr(M_{j-1}, D_j) \\ D[i, j-1] + tr(D_{j-1}, D_j) \end{cases}$$

$$N[i] = N[i-1] + tr(N, N) \qquad (2)$$

$$E[i] = \max_{1 \leq j \leq Q} (M[i,j] + tr(M_j, E))$$

$$J[i] = \max \begin{cases} J[i-1] + tr(J, J) \\ E[i] + tr(E, J) \end{cases}$$

$$B[i] = \max \begin{cases} N[i] + tr(N, B) \\ J[i] + tr(J, B) \end{cases}$$

$$C[i] = \max \begin{cases} C[i-1] + tr(C, C) \\ E[i] + tr(E, C) \end{cases}$$

After computing the similarity between the sequence and the profile HMM and concluding that the sequence belongs to the family modeled by the HMM, we can obtain the best alignment of the sequence to the profile HMM in order to add the sequence into the multiple alignment of the family (and into the profile HMM representation of the family). The alignment is obtained by tracing back on the Viterbi data structures.

Analyzing the Viterbi algorithm recurrence equations, we identify many data dependencies for computing the scores. For instance, the cells $M[i-1, j-1]$, $I[i-1, j]$, and $D[i, j-1]$ are needed for computing the cells $M[i,j]$, $I[i,j]$, and $D[i,j]$, respectively. These dependencies prevent the parallel computation of cells in the same row, column, or diagonal as the matrices.

The state J of the profile HMM links the end of the profile HMM core to its beginning, forming a feedback loop. This link creates the dependency chain $M[i-1, 1 \ldots Q] \rightarrow E[i-1] \rightarrow J[i-1] \rightarrow B[i-1] \rightarrow M[i,j]$, which prevents the parallel computation of cells in a same antidiagonal of the matrices.

2.2.3 The MSV algorithm
The MSV algorithm is a simplification of the Viterbi algorithm, obtained by removing from the Plan7 profile HMM the states I and D and considering transition

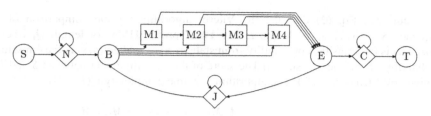

FIG. 4

Profile HMM used by MSV algorithm.

probability of 1.0 for all transitions $M_{j-1} \to M_j$ [23]. The resulting profile HMM is shown in Fig. 4.

Recurrence Eq. (3) describe the MSV algorithm for the comparison of a sequence S of length L to a profile HMM (with the structure shown in Fig. 4) of length Q. The score of the best alignment between S and H is given by $C[L] + tr(C, T)$. The algorithm has time complexity $O(L \times Q)$.

$$M[i,j] = em(M_j, s_i) + \max \begin{cases} M[i-1, j-1] \\ B[i-1] + tr(B, M_j) \end{cases}$$

$$N[i] = N[i-1] + tr(N, N)$$

$$E[i] = \max_{1 \le j \le Q} (M[i,j])$$

$$J[i] = \max \begin{cases} J[i-1] + tr(J, J) \\ E[i] + tr(E, J) \end{cases} \quad (3)$$

$$B[i] = \max \begin{cases} N[i] + tr(N, B) \\ J[i] + tr(J, B) \end{cases}$$

$$C[i] = \max \begin{cases} C[i-1] + tr(C, C) \\ E[i] + tr(E, C) \end{cases}$$

Although it has the same time complexity as the Viterbi algorithm, the MSV algorithm performs fewer computations and has fewer data dependencies because of the removal of states I and D. As a consequence, all cells in the same row of matrix M can be computed in parallel, while successive rows must still be computed sequentially.

3 DESIGN ASPECTS OF GPU SOLUTIONS FOR BIOLOGICAL SEQUENCE ANALYSIS

While each proposal brings different contributions for the solution of the pairwise sequence comparison or sequence-profile comparison using GPUs, some optimization techniques and approaches are used in several solutions. We enumerate these techniques here.

3.1 TASK-PARALLELISM VS DATA-PARALLELISM

The solutions for pairwise and sequence-profile comparisons adopt one or a combination of the two approaches to exploit parallelism: task-parallelism or data-parallelism. In general, if task-parallelism is used, a thread is associated with each sequence from the sequence database and is responsible for performing the comparison between that database sequence and the query sequence (pairwise sequence comparison) or query profile HMM (sequence-profile comparison). Since the comparison of distinct database sequences to the same query (i.e., the execution of the appropriate SW, BLAST, Viterbi, or MSV algorithm) involves independent tasks, the corresponding threads can execute in parallel (coarse-grained parallelism). In this case, we say that the solution exploits sequence parallelism. This strategy has the advantage of removing the need of interthread communication and is adopted by the solutions in Refs. [27–31] for pairwise sequence comparison and in Refs. [32–37] for sequence-profile comparison.

When data-parallelism is adopted, the comparison of a sequence from the sequence database with the query sequence or with the query profile HMM is assigned to multiple threads, each thread being responsible for computing one or more cells of the dynamic programming matrices (fine-grained parallelism). Since the cells computed by one thread are needed for computing cells assigned to different threads, there is intense need of interthread communication in this strategy. For pairwise comparison, the solutions in Refs. [38–43] exclusively exploit data-parallelism. Among the sequence-profile solutions, only Ref. [44] exclusively exploit data-parallelism.

Finally, both forms of parallelism can be combined. In general, we have a set of threads associated with each sequence from the sequence database, each thread being responsible for computing one or more cells of the dynamic programming matrices. And different sequences of the database are compared in parallel, by different sets of threads, to the query sequence or query profile HMM. The solutions in Refs. [45–48] adopt this strategy to perform pairwise comparisons, while the solutions in Refs. [49,50] also use both forms of parallelism to compute sequence-profile comparisons.

3.2 SORTING SEQUENCE DATABASE TO ACHIEVE LOAD BALANCE

The Viterbi, MSV, SW, and BLAST algorithms are sensitive to the length of the target sequence, which in conjunction with the profile HMM or the subject sequence length, determines the execution time of the algorithms. A typical sequence database usually contains sequences with very different lengths and does not have the sequences ordered by their length, that is, short sequences may be close to long sequences.

Therefore solutions that exploit task-parallelism (combined or not with data-parallelism) can have unbalanced workloads among threads, since threads processing shorter sequences finish first and stay idle, waiting while the longest sequence is processed.

In order to minimize this problem, the works in Refs. [29,31–33,35–37,45–48, 50] sort the sequences from the sequence database by sequence length, usually in decreasing order. This is accomplished in a preprocessing step executed on the CPU, previous to the sequence-profile or pairwise comparison. As a result, sequences with similar lengths are assigned to threads in a same warp or in a same block, thereby achieving a better workload balance among them.

3.3 USE OF GPU MEMORY HIERARCHY

GPU memory hierarchy includes several memories with very different features, such as latency, bandwidth, read-only or read-write access, and so on. For instance, in the CUDA architecture, there are registers, shared, global, constant, and texture memories [51].

Memory accesses usually have a great impact on GPU programs performance; therefore most proposals try to optimize the memory layout and usage patterns of the data structures used by the implemented algorithm. SW, BLAST, Viterbi, and MSV algorithms include several large data structures, such as the dynamic programming score matrices and the sequences. The last two algorithms also include the transition and emission probabilities of the profile HMM.

The memory where each data structure is allocated is chosen based on the size of that structure and the types of access performed on it (few or many accesses, only reads or reads and writes, several threads reading from the same position, etc.). A particular data structure may be reorganized in order to provide a better usage pattern regarding the memory it is allocated.

Several solutions for pairwise or sequence-profile comparison [33–37,43–45,49, 50] allocate their data structures in GPU global memory and some of them rearrange the memory accesses of threads into favorable patterns in order to achieve memory coalescing. The idea is that when the threads in a warp access consecutive global memory locations, the hardware is able to combine all accesses into a single memory request. Such coalesced accesses allow GPU global memory to deliver data at a rate close to its peak bandwidth [51].

Registers, shared, constant, and texture memories can be highly effective in reducing the number of accesses to global memory. However, these memories have limited capacity, which may also restrict the number of threads executing simultaneously on a GPU streaming multiprocessor.

Accessing GPU shared memory is very fast and highly parallel; therefore several proposals [29,31,33,34,36,38,39,43,45,48,50,52] use this memory to hold the portion of GPU global memory data that is heavily used in an execution phase of the algorithm. In a further step, the algorithm used may be reorganized in order to create execution phases that focus heavily on small portions of global memory data.

With appropriate access patterns, accessing constant memory is very fast and parallel. This memory provides short-latency, high-bandwidth, and read-only access by the device when all threads simultaneously access the same location, and broadcasts the data accessed to all threads in a warp [51]. Constant memory is used by the works in Refs. [28,29,31,33,36,45].

Texture memory can also be used to avoid global memory bandwidth limitations and handle memory accesses with certain access patterns. Although texture memory was originally designed for traditional graphics applications, it can also be used quite effectively in some general-purpose GPU computing applications. The solutions in Refs. [27,29,32–35,37,39,50] allocate data structures in this memory.

3.4 GPU SOLUTION USED AS A FILTER

The recurrence equations executed in the SW, BLAST, Viterbi, and MSV algorithms present a dependency pattern in such a way that, in order to compute only the best alignment score, it is not necessary to store the whole dynamic programming matrices and vectors. Actually, only two rows of these data structures are needed, the current row (which is being computed) and the previous one. However, in order to execute the traceback operation and produce the best alignment, the whole structures must be stored, requiring a space of $O(m \times n)$, where m and n are the lengths of the sequences in a pairwise comparison, or $O(L \times Q)$ for a profile HMM with Q nodes and a sequence of length L, in a sequence-profile comparison, for each sequence from the database. Given the long length of the biological sequences and the large number of sequences in sequence databases, the amount of memory space required is usually substantial and can exhaust the memory of the GPU.

The traceback is needed only when the comparison results in a hit, that is, the best alignment score is superior to a significance threshold and a homology is detected. Experiments reported indicate that less than 2% of the database sequences result in hits [53] for sequence-profile comparison, and similar results are obtained for pairwise comparisons with genomic databases.

Considering the high demand for memory space and low homology hit ratio, the solutions in Refs. [27,28,30,31,38,39,42,43,45–47] for pairwise comparison and in Refs. [32–37,44,49,50] for sequence-profile comparison work as a first phase filter that computes only the best alignment score (through the SW, BLAST, Viterbi, or MSV algorithm). This filter, implemented in the GPU and taking advantage of its parallel computing capabilities, processes all the database sequences in order to discard the low-scoring sequences. For the small fraction of sequences that produce significant best-alignment scores, the entire comparison (pairwise or sequence-profile) is reprocessed in the CPU in order to generate the corresponding alignment. This time the SW, BLAST, or Viterbi algorithm is executed keeping the entire necessary data structures to produce the best alignment.

4 GPU SOLUTIONS FOR PAIRWISE SEQUENCE COMPARISON

Recently, the use of GPUs to implement pairwise biological sequence comparison algorithms has become very popular. This happens mainly because GPUs are able to attain very good performance at low cost. In this section, we present several GPU solutions for the pairwise sequence comparison problem.

4.1 GPU SOLUTIONS USING EXACT ALGORITHMS

The SW algorithm and its variations have quadratic time complexity, and for this reason, they are excellent candidates for parallelization. In this section, we will present first the approaches that compare one protein sequence to all sequences in a sequence database (Sections 4.1.1–4.1.6). In this case, a protein query sequence q will be compared to a set of y protein sequences $(d_1, d_2, \ldots, d_y)$ that belongs to a genomic database. This comparison is known as coarse-grained since each thread calculates a different dynamic programming matrix, thus there is usually no communication among the threads. In Section 4.1.7, we present a solution that compares two long DNA sequences, computing huge dynamic programming matrices, to multiple threads.

Most of the GPU approaches use two techniques that were initially proposed to run in CPUs, taking advantage of single instruction multiple data (SIMD) instruction sets such as AltiVec (PowerPC) and SSE (Intel). In this case, vector instructions are executed that calculate a set of elements in parallel. The first technique is called *query profile* [54], and it targets the case where a single protein sequence is compared to a genomic database. Since the same protein sequence (query) will be compared to different sequences that belong to a genomic database, the algorithm computes a small specific vector Q based on the query sequence and a given substitution matrix. Therefore the access of punctuations for matches/mismatches is sequential, instead of random. The second technique is called *striped processing* [55], and instead of calculating consecutive cells of the matrix with the same vector instruction, it calculates at the same time cells that are separated by a stripe factor. With this technique, the dependencies of the innermost loop are broken, accelerating the computation.

The comparison of exact pairwise sequence comparison approaches is usually made by using the metrics GCUPS. This metric is calculated by dividing the size of the dynamic programming matrices $(m \times n)$ by the execution time in seconds multiplied by 10^9. In this section, we use GCUPS to express the performance of the solutions.

4.1.1 Manavski and Valle [27]

A multi-GPU-accelerated version of SW in CUDA was proposed in Ref. [27]. In order to optimize the access to the substitution matrix, the authors used query profile. Scores were restricted to 16-bit values. The database was sorted by size and blocks of 256 sequences were created.

The memory hierarchy of the NVIDIA GPU was carefully studied in order to decide where to place the most critical data. Since the query profile is highly accessed, the authors decided to place it in the GPU texture memory. Because of its size, the genomic database was placed into the global memory, and the dynamic programming cell values (matrices H and E) were also stored in global memory.

Each GPU thread computes the whole alignment between the query sequence and one target sequence (task-parallelism). Query sequences of up to 2050 amino acids were compared to the *SwissProt* genomic database, containing 250,296 protein sequences. Results of 1.889 GCUPS and 3.612 GCUPS were obtained for one and two GPUs NVIDIA GeForce 8800 GTX, respectively. When compared to the serial SW implementation called SSEARCH, this approach achieved a speedup of 15.81.

4.1.2 Ligowski and Rudnicki [38]

The approach proposed by Ref. [38] compares a query sequence against a database with SW, returning the best score obtained by each alignment. For a single comparison, the dynamic programming matrix is divided in groups of 12 rows, which are computed by a set of threads (data-parallelism). Each step processes 12 cells that are placed in shared memory and registers with only two global memory transactions, giving additional speedup. This is an improvement over Manavski and Valle (see Section 4.1.1), which placed all cells in the slow global memory.

Results of 7.5 GCUPS and 14.5 GCUPS were obtained for one and two GPUs (NVIDIA 9800 GX2, dual-GPU), respectively, when comparing sequences of up to 1000 amino acids to the SwissProt genomic database containing 388,517 proteins.

4.1.3 Blazwicz et al. [29]

Blazwicz et al. [29] proposed a strategy to run SW (first and second phases) in multiple GPUs. Since the SW algorithm executes in quadratic space, only short sequences ($\leq$2000 amino acids) were compared. In this proposal, coarse-grained parallelization is used in the top level. The algorithm executes as follows. Each idle GPU retrieves one window (set of tasks that can be executed in one kernel invocation) from the top of the queue until the queue is empty, on a self-scheduling (SS) basis. A task is defined to be a single comparison between q and d_i.

The data structures are placed in the NVIDIA GPU memories as follows. Four additional boolean matrices, which are used in the second phase of the SW algorithm, are packed into 32-bit words and placed in global memory. The cells of matrices H and E are also placed in global memory. The cells of matrix F that are being calculated at a given moment are placed in shared memory. The substitution matrix is placed in constant memory, whereas the sequences are placed into texture memory.

In the tests, sets of randomly selected sequences from the Ensembl database were used. The maximum number of database sequences was 1600 and the maximum size of the query sequence was 1103 amino acids. With four homogeneous GPUs (NVIDIA Tesla S1070), a maximum of 11.5 GCUPS was attained. Note that this metric does not include the execution of the second phase of the SW algorithm. When compared to the Farrar SIMD CPU solution [55], this approach achieved speedups of 3.06 (one GPU) and 12.20 (four GPUs).

4.1.4 Li et al. [52]

Li et al. [52] proposed optimized strategies to compute SW scores or/and alignments of long sequences with the affine gap function. The first two strategies, called *StripedScore* and *BlockedAntidiagonal*, divide the DP matrix in strips of equal size and process the matrix by antidiagonals. The differences between these two strategies are mainly related to synchronization and block assignment.

The authors also proposed three strategies to retrieve the alignment. *StripedAlignment* retrieves the alignment in three phases. In the first phase, all DP matrices are calculated by antidiagonals, information is stored about the boundary columns of each strip in global memory, and the optimal score and its position are found. The values of the DP matrices that are being computed are stored in shared memory. The second phase executes serially, finding the cells that are the start and the end of the optimal alignment in each strip. Having these cells, each strip can recalculate its part of the DP matrices, producing the optimal alignment.

In the strategy *ChunkedAlignment1*, the DP matrices are divided into columns and rows, reducing the area reprocessed, as compared to *StripedAlignment*. This reduction in the reprocessed area is due to an additional data structure (horizontal buffer), which is stored in global memory. *ChunkedAlignment2* stores more information in Phase 1, allowing Phase 3 to be executed in parallel.

The authors did an extensive evaluation of their strategies using the NVIDIA Tesla C2050, with query sequences of up to 51,030 amino acids. The proposed strategies were compared with three state-of-the-art tools, including CUDASW++ 2.0 (Section 4.1.6). The authors showed that their approach outperformed the state-of-the-art tools for long sequences. Also, the authors concluded that *ChunkedAlignment1* provides the best performance for most cases. The results showed a maximum performance of 7.1 GCUPS.

4.1.5 Ino et al. [28,30]

Ino et al. [28] proposed the use of an undedicated grid composed of multiple heterogeneous GPUs to execute SW. When the screen saver was activated, coarse-grained SW tasks were executed. The authors proposed a master/slave architecture with three components: grid resources, resource manager server, and clients, where the resource manager server is the master and the grid resources are the slaves.

Given x query sequences to be compared to a genomic database composed of y sequences, each task was responsible for the comparison of one query sequence to the whole database. Tasks were distributed using an SS policy. In the slaves, the GPU SW comparison was done by an OpenGL program. In the tests, 64 query sequences of size 367 were compared to the Swiss-Prot database release 51.0 (241,242 sequences). The platform was composed of eight heterogeneous GPUs (NVIDIA 8800 and 7900 series). In this platform, a maximum of 3.09 GCUPS was obtained.

The work of Ref. [28] was extended by Ref. [30] in order to take advantage of shorter idle periods, so in this case, the screensaver was not used. As in Ref. [28], a master/slave architecture was used, and idle resources executed coarse-grained SW tasks. Tasks were then divided into small subtasks of size 32K, and these subtasks were executed by the GPU. SW subtasks were distributed to the workers in a modified SS fashion, where resources with longer idle periods received tasks first. SW subtasks can be canceled if the resource changes its state to busy. In this case, the subtask was reassigned to another idle resource. Because the subtasks were very small, the sequences being compared were placed in constant memory.

The tests compared iteratively a set of query sequences ranging from 63 to 511 amino acids to a genomic database. The results obtained in a platform composed of eight heterogeneous NVIDIA GPUs (five GTX 285, one GTX 295, one FX 5800, and one 8800 GTX), each one connected to a host machine, show that 64 GCUPS can be achieved.

4.1.6 Liu et al. [45–47]

CUDASW++ 1.0 was proposed in Ref. [45], and it executed SW with affine gap in single and multiple GPUs, obtaining the optimal score. Two levels of parallelism (intertask and intratask) were proposed. Intertask parallelization is coarse-grained and assigns each query × database sequence comparison to a different thread. On the other hand, intratask parallelization uses multiple threads in a single query × database comparison (data-parallelism). Small query sequences were compared with intertask parallelization, whereas long query sequences used the intratask mode. In order to achieve load balancing, query sequences were ordered by their lengths. Also, great care was taken with the manipulation of the GPU memory hierarchy. Database sequences were placed in global memory and then accessed through a coalesced access pattern. Global memory was also used to store the DP matrices, which were organized in a way that allowed coalesced accesses. The DP cells that were being calculated in a given moment were stored in registers. Shared memory was used to store the substitution matrix, and the query sequence was placed in constant memory. Results of 16.08 GCUPS were obtained for the NVIDIA GeForce GTX 295 (dual-GPU), for a maximum query size of 5478 amino acids. Twenty-five query sequences were compared to the genomic database *SwissProt*, release 56.6, with 405,506 protein sequences. A speedup of 1.46 was obtained when comparing CUDASW++ 1.0 with the vectorized tool SWPS3 running on two Intel Xeon dual-core (four cores).

CUDASW++ 2.0 [46] integrated SIMD optimizations such as query profile and striped pattern into its design. Query profile was used in the intertask parallelization mode, and the striped pattern was used in both modes. Two implementations of SW were proposed. The first implementation was an optimized Single Instruction Multiple Thread (SIMT) version for the intertask parallelization, which used a sequential query profile and a packed data format. The second implementation was a variant of the striped SW described in Ref. [55] that divided the query sequences into small partitions that are aligned, one by one, with the subject sequence. Twenty query sequences were compared to *SwissProt*, release 56.6. Results with query sequences of up to 5478 amino acids were shown, achieving 16.9 GCUPS on NVIDIA GTX 280 and 28.8 GCUPS on GTX 295 (dual-GPU). With high gap penalties, CUDASW++ 2.0 achieved 17.8 GCUPS on GTX 280 and 29.7 GCUPS on GTX 295.

CUDASW++ 3.0 [47] proposed a hybrid approach that used both CPUs and GPUs to compare sequences. Load was distributed statically, considering the clock frequencies and number of cores (CPUs) and the number of symmetric multiprocessors and the number of cores (GPUs). The CPU code used query profile and the striped pattern and the GPU code used CUDA PTX SIMD instructions (low-level programming) combined with the idea of a striped pattern to accelerate the computation.

Results were collected on an Intel i7 (quad-core) combined with three GPUs (one NVIDIA GTX 680 and a NVIDIA GTX 690, dual-GPU). Query sequences of up to 5478 amino acids were compared to the SwissProt genomic database (538,585 protein sequences), achieving a maximum GCUPS of 185.6 (4 cores + GTX 690).

4.1.7 Sandes and de Melo [39–41] and Sandes et al. [42]

CUDAlign 1.0 [39] compares two huge DNA sequences (fine-grained) to SW, assigning blocks to threads in a parallelogram shape, and provides the optimal score as the output. In order to increase performance, it divides the code that runs on GPU into two kernels, optimized for specific situations. The input sequences are placed in texture memory, and global memory is used to store border elements of the DP matrices. The DP cells that are being calculated are stored in shared memory and registers. In the study by Sandes et al., results were collected in the NVIDIA GTX 280 GPU, and sequences with lengths up to 32 millions of base pairs (MBP), achieving a maximum GCUPS of 20.37.

CUDAlign 2.0 [40] retrieves the alignment between two huge DNA sequences with an adapted version of the MM algorithm, executing in linear space. It executes in six stages, where stage 1 obtains the optimal score with CUDAlign 1.0, saving some rows to disk. Stages 2–5 execute a modified version of MM (see Section 2.1.1), retrieving the coordinates of the points that belong to the optimal alignment in a divide-and-conquer way. Stage 6 is used optionally to visualize the alignment. In the Sandes et al. studies, the results collected in the NVIDIA GTX 285 comparing sequences with sizes up to 33 MBP showed a maximum GCUPS of 23.63. When compared to the z-aligned nonvectorized cluster tool running on a cluster of 64 cores, CUDAlign achieved a speedup of 19.52.

CUDAlign 2.1 [41] calculates the alignment as in CUDAlign 2.0, with the block pruning optimization, which is able to eliminate the computation of matrix cells that surely will not contribute to the optimal alignment. The results collected in the NVIDIA GTX 560 Ti comparing sequences with sizes up to 33 MBP showed a maximum GCUPS of 58.21.

CUDAlign 3.0 [42] executes SW with affine gap in multiple GPUs with fine-grained parallelism and outputs the optimal score. It uses circular buffers to overlap computation and communication, connecting the GPU nodes with TCP sockets. In the Sandes et al. studies, the results collected with up to 64 GPUs NVIDIA Tesla M2090 presented a maximum GCUPS of 1726 when comparing DNA sequences of 228 MBP × 249 MBP.

4.1.8 Comparative overview

Table 1 presents a comparative view of the solutions discussed in this section. Five solutions [27,29,30,38,42] use more than one GPU (2–64), four use one GPU [39–41,52], three use one dual-GPU [38,45,46], and one solution [47] combines one GPU with one CPU to compare biological sequences.

Table 1 Summary of GPU Solutions for SW Execution

Solution	GPU	Variation	Filter	Parallelism Task	Data	Maximum GCUPS
Manavski et al. [27]	2 × 8800 GTX	Affine-gap	Yes	•		3.61
Ino et al. [28]	8 × (8800, 9800)	Affine-gap	Yes	•		3.09
Ligowski et al. [38]	9800 GX2 (dual)	Affine-gap	Yes		•	14.50
Liu et al. [45]	GTX 295 (dual)	Affine-gap	Yes	•	•	16.08
Sandes and de Melo [39]	GTX 280	Affine-gap	Yes		•	20.37
Liu et al. [46]	GTX 295 (dual)	Affine-gap	Yes	•	•	29.70
Blazwicz et al. [29]	4 × Tesla S1070	Affine-gap	No	•		11.50
Sandes and de Melo [40]	GTX 285	Affine-gap MM	No		•	23.63
Li et al. [52]	Tesla C2050	Affine-gap	No		•	7.10
Ino et al. [30]	10 × GTX 285–295, FX 5800, 8800 GTX	Affine-gap	Yes	•		64.00
Sandes and de Melo [41]	GT 560Ti	Affine-gap MM	No		•	58.21
Liu et al. [47]	GTX 295 (dual) CPU (4 cores)	Affine-gap	Yes	•	•	185.60
Sandes et al. [42]	64 × Tesla M2090	Affine-gap	Yes		•	1726.00

All solutions implement the affine-gap model, and most of them act as a filter, retrieving only the best score. Two solutions [40,41] retrieve the best alignment in linear space in GPU with the MM algorithm (see Section 2.1.1), and one solution [29] retrieves the optimal alignment of two small sequences in GPU in quadratic space.

Most solutions either use data-parallelism, computing one comparison in a multithreaded way, or task-parallelism, assigning a different comparison to each thread. CUDASW++ 1.0 [45], 2.0 [46], and 3.0 [47] use both data- and task-parallelism to accelerate the computation.

Performance comparison of SW solutions is a critical issue because the results of each solution are collected in different hardware/software platforms. In order to address this problem, the metrics of GCUPS were proposed, and this is the metric currently used to compare GPU solutions for SW. In the last column of Table 1, we included the GCUPS achieved by each solution. We can observe an astonishing improvement on the performance of GPU solutions for SW, ranging from 3.09 (2009) to 1726.00 GCUPS (2014). In our opinion, this was possible due to a combination of two factors: (a) the great technological advancement in GPU technology and (b) the advancements in GPU-based parallelization techniques for the SW algorithm, which were able to generate highly optimized parallel versions.

4.2 GPU SOLUTIONS USING BLAST

As discussed in Section 2.1.2, BLAST is a heuristic algorithm that retrieves local alignments much faster than SW. Therefore the execution times of BLAST are usually low. However, in the last decade the genomic databases have experienced exponential growth, and many of these databases now have more than 20,000,000 sequences. In such scenarios, GPUs are a good alternative because they can be used to produce BLAST results faster. In the literature, we can find some solutions that use GPUs to compute BLAST alignments. These solutions are discussed in the next sections.

4.2.1 Vouzis and Sahinidis [31]

GPU-BLAST [31] targets BLASTP, and it is one of the most popular BLAST tools based on GPU. The authors determined that the first and second steps, seeding and extension (see Section 2.1.2), are more computationally intensive and thus decided to parallelize these steps.

Both the GPU and CPU compared a protein query sequence to protein sequences that belonged to a database (subject). Each thread received a different query × subject pair (task-parallelism), and sequences were sorted according to their lengths. The placement of data structures in the GPU memory were carefully designed so that small bit vectors were stored in shared memory to accelerate the computation. Large data tables and the database sequences were placed in global memory, whereas constant memory was used to store the query sequence.

The experimental results were collected in a machine with a NVIDIA Tesla C2050 GPU and a 6-core Intel Xeon. The sequences were distributed between the CPU and GPU proportional to their computing power. The genomic database env_nr (more than 6 million sequences) was compared to 51 query sequences whose lengths ranged from 2 to 4998 amino acids. GPU-BLAST (6-core and GPU) achieved a speedup of 1.6 when compared to the 6-core BLAST version and 4.0 when compared to the serial BLAST implementation.

4.2.2 Liu et al. [48]

In Ref. [48], the authors proposed mpiCUDA-BLASTP, which uses a distributed master-slave architecture that explores data-parallelism in a GPU cluster. Sequences are sorted by their lengths, and the genomic database is split into batches of approximately the same size. Stages 1 and 2 (see Section 2.1.2) are processed independently by each thread (task-parallelism), whereas stage 3 is processed using data-parallelism, where each GPU thread computes a set of diagonals for each HSP. In order to improve performance, this set of diagonals was stored in shared memory.

In the tests, 14 sequences with sizes ranging from 505 to 2512 amino acids were compared to the *nr* database (more than 21 million sequences) in a GPU cluster composed of six nodes, each containing an AMD Opteron quad-core and one NVIDIA Tesla S1060. The tool mpiCUDA-BLASTP (six GPUs) was compared to GPU-BLAST (see Section 4.2.1) with one GPU, achieving a speedup of 6.6.

When compared to the serial BLAST implementation, mpiCUDA-BLASTP achieved approximately a speedup of 26.

4.2.3 Zhang et al. [43]

A data-parallel approach called cuBlastP was proposed in Ref. [43] to execute BLAST on GPU. In stage 1, each thread detected hit positions for a different word of size w in the current query $\times$ subject comparison, respecting the coalesced memory access pattern and using a data structure organized as bins over the columns. Since the bins index columns, there is an additional phase called hit reorganization that maps bins on diagonals. The second phase is also executed in a fine-grained way, and the authors use a hierarchical buffer to place data structures in shared and global memory. Accesses to the global memory are coalesced.

Experimental results were collected separately in two machines. The first machine had an Intel i5 connected to the NVIDIA K20c GPU, and the second machine had the same CPU processor connected to a NVIDIA Fermi board. Two genomic databases were used in the tests: *nr*, with 6 million sequences, and *SwissProt*, with 300,000 sequences. Three query sequences with 127, 517, and 1054 amino acids were compared to these databases. When compared to GPU-BLAST, cuBlastP achieved a maximum speedup of 2.8. A speedup of 7.8 was obtained when compared to the serial FSA-BLAST.

4.2.4 Comparative overview

Table 2 presents a comparative overview of BLAST solutions for GPUs. As can be seen, all solutions implement BLASTP, comparing protein query sequences to genomic databases.

Two solutions [31,43] act as filters, retrieving only the BLAST score. The BLAST algorithm is executed entirely in GPU by Ref. [48], giving as output the alignments that have score greater than a given threshold. One solution [31] takes advantage of data-parallelism, one solution [43] targets task-parallelism, and one solution [48] exploits both forms of parallelism. When compared to the serial BLAST algorithm, the best speedup achieved was 26.0 [31], using six GPUs.

Table 2 Summary of GPU Solutions for BLAST Execution

Solution	GPU	Algorithm	Filter	Parallelism Task	Parallelism Data	Maximum Speedup
Vouzis et al. [31]	Tesla C2050 6-core CPU	BLASTP	Yes	•		4.0
Liu et al. [48]	6 × Tesla S1060	BLASTP	No	•	•	26.0
Zhang et al. [43]	K20c	BLASTP	Yes		•	7.8

5 GPU SOLUTIONS FOR SEQUENCE-PROFILE COMPARISON

Given the high acceptance of pairwise sequence comparison solutions on GPUs, several implementations of sequence-profile comparison algorithms, targeting GPUs as a parallel computing platform, have also been proposed. In this section, we describe several GPU solutions for the sequence-profile comparison problem.

5.1 GPU SOLUTIONS USING THE VITERBI ALGORITHM

We present first the GPU solutions proposed for sequence-profile comparison targeting the Viterbi algorithm. These solutions are based on HMMER2, where the *hmmsearch* tool uses the Viterbi algorithm as its main step. Because the Viterbi algorithm has quadratic time complexity, it is an excellent candidate to parallelization.

5.1.1 Horn et al. [32]

ClawHMMer [32] is an implementation of HMMER2 *hmmsearch* tool on GPU, exploiting sequence parallelism. It is based on the Brook stream programming language for GPUs, not on the CUDA programming model, which was not yet available at the time of the implementation. It implements the Viterbi algorithm based on profile HMMs, which do not have the complete Plan7 structure. There are no states N and C; therefore local alignments (with respect to the sequence) between the sequence and the profile HMM are not allowed.

In a preprocessing step performed on the CPU, the sequence database was sorted by sequence length in order to provide load balance. The sequence database was also divided into smaller parts (usually denominated batches) that fitted in the GPU memory. This way, sequences in the same batch would have similar lengths, and different batches were executed sequentially on the GPU. The GPU solution worked as a filter, storing only two rows of the score matrices. Therefore if an homology hit was detected, the Viterbi algorithm would be reexecuted on the CPU, followed by the traceback operation. The transition probabilities were allocated into registers, while the emission probabilities were stored in the GPU texture memory.

The performance evaluation executed the GPU solution on different GPUs (ATI 9800XT, ATI X800XT PE, NVIDIA 6800 Ultra, NVIDIA 7800 GTX, ATI R520) and compared it to the HMMER 2.3.2 *hmmsearch* tool running on an Intel Pentium 4 Xeon and on a PowerPC G5 (with AltiVec vector instructions enabled or not). The experiments compared 2.4 million proteins from the NCBI protein database [56] to profile HMMs (with 139–3271 states—not nodes) from the Pfam database [21]. The best results for ClawHMMer were obtained on the GPU ATI R520, which outperformed HMMER2 on the three platforms. It reached average speedups of 26.5 and 2.7, compared to HMMER2 executing on Intel Pentium 4 and on PowerPC G5 (with AltiVec vector instructions enabled), respectively.

The authors also performed experiments on a 16-node cluster with a GPU Radeon 9800 Pro in each node. A scheme to distribute the sequence database among the nodes was applied in order to provide load balance and achieve scalability of the solution. According to the authors, for 16 nodes, the achieved speedup was 95% of the ideal speedup.

5.1.2 Du et al. [44]

Du et al. [44] implemented the Viterbi algorithm on GPU, based on a profile HMM structure with only the states M, I, and D. They used the CUDA programming model and exploited a data-parallelism approach. Since the profile HMM structure does not have the state J, the data dependency chain $M[i - 1, 1 \ldots Q] \rightarrow \cdots \rightarrow J[i - 1] \rightarrow \cdots \rightarrow M[i,j]$, described in Section 2.2.2, is broken. Therefore the cells in the same antidiagonal of the dynamic programming score matrices M, I, and D become independent of each other. As a result, all cells in the same antidiagonal are computed in parallel, while successive antidiagonals are computed sequentially, respecting the dependencies. In this case, we say that the solution exploits antidiagonal parallelism. This approach enables exploiting fine-grained parallelism at the expense of accuracy loss, because multihit alignments between the sequence and the profile HMM are not possible without the state J.

The authors implement three different approaches, wavefront, streaming, and tile-based. In the wavefront approach, the score matrices are stored completely in the GPU memory and computed exploiting antidiagonal parallelism. These matrices are organized in a skewed form, so that an antidiagonal can be treated as a row, and the cells in the same antidiagonal occupy contiguous positions in the memory. As a consequence, when the parallel threads access the cells in a same antidiagonal, contiguous positions in memory are accessed, producing a more efficient memory transfer. Global memory is used, respecting the coalesced memory access pattern. The traceback operation is performed in the GPU. Because the entire score matrices are allocated in the GPU memory, this first solution is not able to handle sequences with length longer than 1000.

In the streaming solution, only three antidiagonals of the score matrices are allocated in the GPU memory, the current one being calculated and the two previous ones. The complete matrices are stored in the CPU memory. When the GPU finishes computing an antidiagonal, it is transferred to the CPU, while the next antidiagonal is computed, overlapping GPU computation and GPU-CPU transfers. Because the GPU memory does not store the whole score matrices, the traceback operation is executed on the CPU. The streaming approach provides a solution that is able to handle longer sequences; however, the GPU-CPU transfers can have a negative impact on performance.

The tile-based solution applies a preprocessing step on the CPU to find homologous segments between the sequences. The homologous segments are locally aligned and used to divide the score matrices into smaller and independent tiles that correspond to submatrices of the score matrices. As long as a tile fits entirely in the GPU memory, the tiles are compared on the GPU, sequentially or in parallel, depending on the tile sizes. The tile-based approach presents a solution that is able to handle longer sequences and that is faster than the streaming approach, because it needs to calculate only a portion of the score matrices. The authors describe this approach based on pairwise comparison, and the extension of this method for sequence-profile comparison is not provided.

The performance evaluation executed the GPU solutions on a GPU NVIDIA GeForce 9800 GTX and compared them to a serial implementation of the Viterbi algorithm running on an Intel dual-core processor. The experiments compared artificially generated sequences (lengths between 100 and 1000) and profile HMMs. The wavefront, streaming, and tile-based approaches achieved speedups of 22.3, 20.8, and 24.5, on average, respectively.

5.1.3 Walters et al. [33]

Walters et al. [33] proposed an implementation of HMMER2 *hmmsearch* tool on GPU, using the CUDA programming model. They implemented the Viterbi algorithm based on Plan7 profile HMMs and exploited sequence parallelism, with each thread operating on a different sequence from the sequence database. The number of parallel threads (and, as a consequence, the number of sequences that can be compared in parallel) was limited by the number of registers used by each thread. In a preprocessing step performed on the CPU, the sequence database was sorted by sequence length, in order to provide load balance.

Only two rows of the score matrices were stored in GPU global memory, and the GPU solution worked as a filter. Therefore if an homology hit was detected, the Viterbi algorithm was reexecuted on the CPU, followed by the traceback operation. Loop unrolling of the inner loop (which iterates over the profile HMM nodes) was applied; however, it had the impact of increasing the register pressure.

The allocation of the data structures in the GPU memory hierarchy was carefully designed. Score matrices were organized in a way to provide coalesced access to global memory. Transition and emission probabilities were kept in GPU constant and texture memories, while the sequences were allocated in texture memory. Shared memory was used to store temporarily the current symbol of the sequence of each thread, which was used to index the emission probabilities.

The performance evaluation executed the GPU solution on a GPU NVIDIA GeForce 8800 GTX Ultra and compared it to a serial implementation of the Viterbi algorithm running on an AMD Athlon 275. The experiments compared over 5.5 million from the NCBI nonredundant database [56] (with sequence lengths from 6 to 37,000) to five profile HMMs (with 779–1431 nodes) from the HMMER suite and the Pfam database [21]. The final optimized solution achieved a speedup of 27.7, on average.

5.1.4 Yao et al. [34]

CuHMMer [34] also presents an implementation of the HMMER2 *hmmsearch* tool on GPU, using the CUDA programming model. It implements the Viterbi algorithm based on Plan7 profile HMMs and exploits sequence parallelism. In a preprocessing step performed on the CPU, the sequences from the sequence database were organized, based on their length, in groups corresponding to length ranges.

In the same way as in the sequence database sorting technique, the goal was to provide load balance.

The GPU solution worked as a filter, consequently, if a homology hit was detected, the Viterbi algorithm was reexecuted on the CPU, followed by the traceback operation. The sequences were allocated on GPU global memory, while the score matrices were stored in shared and texture memories. The authors developed a multithreaded solution for the CPU, which could also process sequences while the GPU was executing. This way, the workload was partitioned between the CPU and the GPU, and the CPU did not stay idle while the GPU was executing.

The performance evaluation executed CuHMMer on a GPU NVIDIA GeForce 8800 GTX attached to an Intel Core2 E7200, and compared it to the HMMER2 *hmmsearch* tool running on an AMD Athlon64 X2 Dual Core 3800+. The experiments compared four different sequence databases to four profile HMMs (with 37–461 nodes) from the Pfam database [21]. The best results were achieved with the UniProtKB/Swiss-Prot sequence database [57], producing a speedup of 35.5, on average.

5.1.5 Ganesan et al. [49]

Ganesan et al. [49] proposed an implementation of the HMMER2 *hmmsearch* tool on GPU, using the CUDA programming model. They implemented the Viterbi algorithm based on Plan7 profile HMMs and exploited task- and data-parallelism. The comparison of a sequence from the sequence database to the profile HMM was assigned to multiple threads, and different sequences from the database were compared in parallel by different sets of threads.

The authors implemented a method to parallelize the evaluations of the Viterbi algorithm recurrence equations by partitioning the chain of dependencies in a regular manner. Using this method, they calculated cells of the same row of score matrices in parallel, while successive rows were computed sequentially. The method started by dividing each row into partitions, where a partition is a set of contiguous cells, and by computing the anchors, where an anchor is the initial cell of each partition. The anchors were computed sequentially, with each anchor depending only on the previous one in the row. Then all cells in the row were computed in parallel, each one depending only on the anchor of its partition. Coalesced accesses to global memory were achieved by storing lookup data of the profile HMM contiguously.

The performance evaluation executed the GPU solution on four GPUs with NVIDIA Tesla C1060s and compared it to the Walters et al. [33] proposal running on the same platform, as well as to a serial implementation of the Viterbi algorithm running on an AMD Opteron. The experiments compared the NCBI nonredundant database [56] (with 10.54 million sequences) to three profile HMMs (with 128–507 nodes) from the Pfam database [21]. The proposed approach achieved speedups of 5–8, with respect to [33], and 100, compared to the serial implementation.

5.1.6 Ferraz and Moreano [36]

Ferraz and Moreano [36] presented an implementation of the HMMER2 *hmmsearch* tool on GPU, using the OpenCL [58] programming model, and evaluated several optimizations. They implemented the Viterbi algorithm based on Plan7 profile HMMs and exploited sequence parallelism. In a preprocessing step performed on the CPU, the sequences from the sequence database were sorted, based on their length. Only two rows of the score matrices were stored in GPU memory, and the GPU solution worked as a filter. Therefore if a homology hit was detected, the Viterbi algorithm was reexecuted on the CPU, followed by the traceback operation.

The memory hierarchy of the GPU was carefully studied in order to decide where to allocate the data structures. The score matrices were allocated in GPU local memory, which provided coalesced access in a more effective way and simplified index computations, in comparison to global memory. The sequences were stored in GPU global memory and organized in a way to provide coalesced access. Regular transition probabilities (for states M, I, and D) were stored in constant memory, while special transition probabilities (for special states) were kept in shared memory and replicated for each warp, so that no barrier synchronization was needed. Emission probabilities were stored in global memory.

The authors applied instruction scheduling and register renaming in the GPU implementation of the Viterbi algorithm in order to increase the distance between dependent instructions and to eliminate false dependencies between instructions. They also applied loop unrolling to the Viterbi algorithm inner loop (which iterates over the profile HMM nodes) with unroll factor 8, combined with instruction scheduling, in order to reduce the loop overhead and facilitate instruction scheduling.

The performance evaluation executed the GPU solution on a GPU NVIDIA GeForce GTX 460 and compared it to the Walters et al. [33] proposal running on the same GPU, and to the HMMER2 *hmmsearch* tool running on an AMD Athlon II X3. The experiments compared the entire UniProtKB/Swiss-Prot sequence database [57] (with more than 500,000 sequences) to the *Top-20* profile HMMs (with 23–488 nodes) from the Pfam database [21]. The optimized solution achieved speedups of 15.3 and 49.3, on average, compared to [33] and to HMMER2, respectively. The authors also reported a maximum of 0.21, 0.67, and 10.05 GCUPS for HMMER2, [33], and the proposed GPU solution, respectively.

5.2 GPU SOLUTIONS USING THE MSV ALGORITHM

We present here the GPU solutions for sequence-profile comparison targeting the MSV algorithm. These solutions are based on HMMER3, where the *hmmsearch* tool uses the MSV algorithm as its first filter in the chain of filters. The MSV algorithm is a simplified version of the Viterbi algorithm and also has quadratic time complexity; therefore it is an excellent candidate for parallelization, too.

5.2.1 Li et al. [35]

Li et al. [35] implemented the HMMER3 *hmmsearch* tool on GPU, using the CUDA programming model and exploiting sequence parallelism. In a preprocessing step performed on the CPU, the sequences from the sequence database were sorted, in decreasing order, based on their length. The authors developed a multithreaded solution for the CPU, which can also process sequences while the GPU is executing, overlapping GPU computation and GPU-CPU transfers. The GPU executed only the MSV algorithm, which is the first filter in the chain of filters of HMMER3, and the CPU executed the MSV algorithm and the other filters in the chain.

The score matrices of the MSV algorithm were stored in GPU global memory and organized in a way to provide coalesced access. Emission probabilities were allocated in texture memory. The outer loop of the MSV algorithm (which iterated over the sequence residues) was unrolled by a factor of 2. The score $B[i]$ of the second unrolled iteration was computed speculatively without considering the transition $J \rightarrow B$. This way, several memory accesses were eliminated, because intermediate values are kept in registers. The correct value of $B[i]$ was also computed and compared to the speculative value. If the speculation were to fail, the sequence would be tagged for recalculation, and the MSV algorithm would be executed again for this sequence on the CPU. According to the authors, at most, 1% of the sequences in their test cases failed the speculation.

The performance evaluation executed the GPU solution on a GPU NVIDIA Tesla C2050 attached to an Intel Xeon E5506 Quad Core and compared it to the HMMER3 *hmmsearch* tool running on a single core with SSE instructions enabled. The experiments compared the NCBI nonredundant database [56] (with 15.2 million sequences with lengths from 5 to 41,943) to six profile HMMs (with 63–1774 nodes) from the Pfam database [21]. The best speedup achieved was 6.5, obtained with a profile HMM of length 423.

5.2.2 Cheng and Butler [37]

Cheng and Butler [37] implemented the HMMER3 MSV algorithm on GPU, using the CUDA programming model and exploiting sequence parallelism. In a preprocessing step performed on the CPU, the sequences from the sequence database were sorted, in decreasing order, based on their length. The CPU also processed sequences while the GPU was executing, instead of staying idle while the GPU was processing. The workload was partitioned between the CPU and GPU in such a way that the longest sequences from the database were assigned to the CPU, in order to save GPU memory allocated to sequences and reduce the CPU-GPU transfer overhead. The score matrices were stored in GPU global memory and organized so that coalesced access was provided. Emission probabilities were allocated in texture memory. SIMD video instructions of the GPU were used, providing a limited form of data-parallelism.

The performance evaluation executed the GPU solution on a GPU NVIDIA Quadro K4000 attached to an Intel Core i7-3960X and compared it to the HMMER3 *hmmsearch* tool running on a single core with SSE instructions enabled. The experiments compared the entire UniProtKB/Swiss-Prot sequence database [57] (with 540,958 sequences with lengths from 2 to 35,213) to the Pfam family database [21] (with 14,831 profile HMMs with 7–2207 nodes). The solution achieved a speedup of 1.8, on average, compared to HMMER3. The authors also reported the results of 8.05 and 14.25 GCUPS for HMMER3 and the proposed GPU solution, respectively.

5.2.3 Araújo Neto and Moreano [50]

Araújo Neto and Moreano [50] implemented the HMMER3 *hmmsearch* tool on GPU, using the CUDA programming model, and evaluated several optimizations. In a preprocessing step performed on the CPU, the sequences from the sequence database were sorted, based on their length. The GPU executed the MSV algorithm, which was the first filter in the chain of filters of HMMER3, and the CPU executed the other filters in the chain. They exploited task-parallelism assigning distinct sequences from the sequence database to distinct CUDA blocks; therefore several sequences were compared simultaneously by executing several blocks concurrently on the GPU. The cells in the same row of the score matrix M were computed in parallel by the threads of a block, exploiting data-parallelism, while successive rows were calculated sequentially.

After computing each row of matrix M, a reduction operation was performed to obtain score $E[i]$ as the maximum among the cells in this row (as described in Section 2.2.3). Usually, a reduction operation on Q values was performed in parallel, in $\log_2 Q$ sequential steps separated by barrier synchronizations. The authors optimized this reduction operation, applying the loop unrolling technique on the $\log_2 Q$ steps, in order to simplify index computations, reduce loop overhead, and for the last six steps, remove the barrier synchronizations between them, because the threads in a warp (group of 32 threads) execute synchronously.

The data structures were allocated in the GPU memory hierarchy comparing the results of several experiments. Accesses to global memory were coalesced, the score matrix was stored in shared memory, while emission probabilities are allocated in texture memory.

They applied the tiling technique to the GPU solution, with each thread being associated with several cells, instead of only one. This way, the solution could handle input cases with profile HMM model and sequence lengths longer than the maximum number of threads the GPU used, and the GPU occupancy was improved, because the workload assigned to each thread was increased.

Other optimizations applied were: loop unrolling (factor 8) of the outer loop (which iterated over the residues of the sequence) of the MSV algorithm overlapping GPU computation and CPU-GPU transfers; using pinned memory in CPU-GPU transfers; representing scores with natural numbers; vectorized access to emission probabilities; keeping frequently used data in registers; and reducing thread divergences.

The performance evaluation executed the GPU solution on a GPU NVIDIA GeForce GTX 570 attached to an Intel Core i7-3770S and compared it to the HMMER3 *hmmsearch* tool running on this CPU with SSE instructions enabled. The experiments compared the entire UniProtKB/Swiss-Prot sequence database [57] (with 540,732 sequences with lengths from 2 to 35,213) to 10 profile HMMs (with 256–1774 nodes) from the Pfam family database [21]. The solution achieved speedups of 5.3 and 16.0, on average, compared to HMMER3 1-core/SSE and 4-cores/SSE configurations, respectively. The authors also reported a maximum of 26.27, 82.30, and 372.06 GCUPS for HMMER3 1-core/SSE, HMMER3 4-cores/SSE, and the proposed GPU solution, respectively.

5.3 COMPARATIVE OVERVIEW

Table 3 summarizes the GPU-based sequence-profile comparison proposals discussed in this section, presenting a comparative overview of them. Only two solutions [32,49] use more than one GPU, and three solutions [34,35,37] also execute the sequence-profile comparison algorithm (Viterbi or MSV) on the CPU in parallel to the GPU execution.

All solutions based on the Viterbi algorithm act as a filter, retrieving only the best alignment score. Because the MSV algorithm is the first filter on the chain of filters of HMMER3, the solutions based on it produce only a similarity score, based on which the sequence is discarded or forwarded to the next filter in the chain. One of the approaches proposed in Ref. [44] perform the traceback operation in the GPU, and therefore obtained the optimal alignment. However, it was not able to handle long sequences.

The reported speedup was measured by each individual research group through different experiments. Different input data sets (profile HMMs and sequence database) were used. The GPU solutions were compared to different baseline solutions, executed on different computers (exclusively serial solution, multicore

Table 3 Summary of GPU Solutions for Sequence-Profile Comparison

Solution	GPU	Algorithm and HMM Structure	Filter	Task	Data	Maximum Speedup
				Parallelism		
Horn et al. [32]	ATI R520	Viterbi incomplete Plan7	Yes	•		26.5
Du et al. [44]	9800 GTX	Viterbi only M, I, D	Yes		•	24.5
Walters et al. [33]	8800 GTX Ultra	Viterbi Plan7	Yes	•		27.7
Yao et al. [34]	8800 GTX Intel Core 2	Viterbi Plan7	Yes	•		35.5
Ganesan et al. [49]	4 × Tesla C1060s	Viterbi Plan7	Yes	•	•	100.0
Ferraz and Moreano [36]	GTX 460	Viterbi Plan7	Yes	•		49.3
Li et al. [35]	Tesla C2050 Intel Xeon Quad-core	MSV	Yes	•		6.5
Cheng and Butler [37]	Quadro K4000 Intel Core i7	MSV	Yes	•		1.8
Araújo Neto and Moreano [50]	GTX 570	MSV	Yes	•	•	16.0

solution, solution using SIMD instructions, etc.). Unfortunately, most works do not present the throughput GCUPS results, which would enable a more adequate comparison between them. Only three solutions [36,37,50] present GCUPS results.

Even though the achieved speedups cannot be directly compared due to the variations in the experimental setups, some observations can be drawn from this table. Among the solutions targeting the Viterbi algorithm, the best result is produced by the only proposal [49] that exploits both task- and data-parallelism. Also, this result is based on the use of four GPUs, while all other results are based on the use of only one GPU. Among the solutions targeting the MSV algorithm, the best result is also produced by the only proposal [50] that exploits both task- and data-parallelism.

Finally, there is a significant difference between the performance results achieved by the GPU solutions based on the Viterbi algorithm, compared to those targeting the MSV algorithm. The main reason is that the results of the solutions based on the MSV algorithm are compared to HMMER3 implementation of this algorithm using SIMD SSE instructions, while the results of the solutions targeting the Viterbi algorithm are compared to a serial implementation of the algorithm or to HMMER2 implementation, without SIMD instructions.

6 CONCLUSION AND PERSPECTIVES

In Bioinformatics, we find several problems which are affected by huge processing times and memory consumption because of the sizable biological data sets and the inherent complexity of the corresponding algorithms. Therefore exploiting parallelism approaches becomes necessary in problems such as sequence comparison. Current GPUs are highly parallel platforms, offering performance and power efficiency at comparatively low cost. In this chapter we showed how GPUs can be used efficiently to accelerate pairwise sequence comparison and sequence-profile comparison problems.

Even though the first GPU-based solutions for sequence comparison appeared in 2005 and significant speedups have been obtained since then, this is still a very active research area, with many challenging problems yet to be investigated. An important issue that must be addressed is the long development time to produce correct and high-performance GPU programs. Although the software tools and programming models (such as CUDA and OpenCL) have made programming on GPUs much easier than before, the design of an efficient GPU solution still requires both a long development time and good skills in parallel programming, algorithm and compiler optimization techniques, and computer architectures. Higher-level programming models (such as OpenACC) offer an alternative; however, they also bring a trade-off between productivity and high performance.

Today's developers face a major current problem with performance portability on high-performance platforms. Because architectural features, such as memory resources, vary among different GPU generations, performance portability has become a serious problem for developers.

Usually, the performance and scalability of the GPU solutions are limited by GPU memory capacity and by the bandwidth of the CPU-GPU connecting bus. If the bandwidth to feed the GPU with sequences and profile HMMs is insufficient, it will likely become a severe bottleneck, with the GPU remaining bandwidth-constrained and unable to process data at its maximum potential capacity.

A current trend in high-performance computing is the adoption of heterogeneous computing systems, that is, large-scale computing clusters of heterogeneous nodes equipped with multicore CPUs, GPUs, and FPGAs. However, such systems require a combination of multiple and different programming paradigms, making application development very challenging. Therefore there is a need for a complete programming framework that comprehends the difficulties of parallel systems with heterogeneous computing units and that combines a simplified programming model, support for different devices, and support for high-performance internode communication.

REFERENCES

[1] I.I. Mandoiu, A. Zelikovsky (Eds.), Bioinformatics Algorithmics—Techniques and Applications, John Wiley & Sons, Inc., New Jersey, 2008.

[2] D.E. Krane, M.L. Raymer, Fundamental Concepts of Bioinformatics, Benjamin Cummings, San Francisco, 2003.

[3] R. Durbin, S. Eddy, A. Krogh, G. Mitchison, Biological Sequence Analysis, Cambridge University Press, Cambridge, 1998.

[4] A.D. Baxevanis, B.F.F. Ouellette (Eds.), Bioinformatics—A Practical Guide to the Analysis of Genes and Proteins, John Wiley & Sons, Inc., New York, 2005.

[5] D. Gusfield, Algorithms on Strings, Trees, and Sequences: Computer Science and Computational Biology, Cambridge University Press, Cambridge, 1997.

[6] D.W. Mount, Bioinformatics: sequence and genome analysis, Cold Spring Harbor Laboratory Press, Cold Spring Harbor, NY, 2004.

[7] S.B. Needleman, C.D. Wunsch, A general method applicable to the search for similarities in the amino acid sequence of two proteins, J. Mol. Biol. 48 (3) (1970) 443–453.

[8] T.F. Smith, M.S. Waterman, Identification of common molecular subsequences, J. Mol. Biol. 147 (1) (1981) 195–197.

[9] O. Gotoh, An improved algorithm for matching biological sequences, J. Mol. Biol. 162 (3) (1982) 705–708.

[10] E.W. Myers, W. Miller, Optimal alignments in linear space, Comput. Appl. Biosci. 4 (1) (1988) 11–17.

[11] S.F. Altschul, W. Gish, W. Miller, E.W. Myers, D.J. Lipman, Basic Local Alignment Search Tool, J. Mol. Biol. 215 (3) (1990) 403–410.

[12] D.J. Lipman, W.R. Pearson, Rapid and sensitive protein similarity search, Science 227 (1985) 1435–1441.

[13] D.S. Hirschberg, A linear space algorithm for computing maximal common subsequences, Commun. ACM 18 (6) (1975) 341–343.

[14] D.J. States, W. Gish, Combined use of sequence similarity and codon bias for coding region identification, J. Comput. Biol. 1 (1) (1994) 39–50.

[15] S.F. Altchul, et al., Gapped BLAST and PSI-BLAST: a new generation of protein database search programs, Nucl. Acids Res. 25 (17) (1997) 3389–3402.

[16] Z. Zhang, S. Schwartz, L. Wagner, W. Miller, A greedy algorithm for aligning DNA sequences, J. Comput. Biol. 7 (1) (2000) 203–214.

[17] S. Schwartz, et al., Human-mouse alignments using BLASTZ, Genome Res. 13 (1) (2003) 103–107.

[18] I. Korf, W. Gish, MPBLAST: improved BLAST performance with multiplexed queries, Bioinformatics 16 (11) (2000) 1052–1053.

[19] N.C. Jones, P.A. Pevzner, An Introduction to Bioinformatics Algorithms, The MIT Press, Cambridge, 2004.

[20] G.D. Forney Jr., The Viterbi Algorithm, Proc. IEEE 61 (1973) 268–278.

[21] R.D. Finn, A. Bateman, J. Clements, P. Coggill, R.Y. Eberhardt, S.R. Eddy, A. Heger, K. Hetherington, L. Holm, J. Mistry, E.L.L. Sonnhammer, J. Tate, M. Punta, Pfam: the protein families database, Nucl. Acids Res. 42 (D1) (2014) 222–230.

[22] Howard Hughes Medical Institute, HMMER: biosequence analysis using profile hidden Markov models, http://hmmer.janelia.org/ (accessed July 14, 2015).

[23] S.R. Eddy, Accelerated profile HMM searches, PLoS Comput. Biol. 7 (10) (2011) 1–16.

[24] L.R. Rabiner, A tutorial on hidden Markov models and selected applications in speech recognition, Proc. IEEE 77 (2) (1989) 257–286.

[25] A. Krogh, M. Brown, I.S. Mian, K. Sjölander, D. Haussler, Hidden Markov models in computational biology—applications to protein modeling, J. Mol. Biol. 235 (5) (1994) 1501–1531.

[26] S.R. Eddy, Profile hidden Markov models, Bioinformatics Rev. 14 (9) (1998) 755–763.

[27] S. Manavski, G. Valle, CUDA compatible GPU cards as efficient hardware accelerators for Smith-Waterman sequence alignment, BMC Bioinformatics 9 (Suppl 2) (2008) 9.

[28] F. Ino, Y. Kotani, Y. Munekawa, K. Hagihara, Harnessing the power of idle GPUs for acceleration of biological sequence alignment, Parallel Process. Lett. 19 (4) (2009) 513.

[29] J. Blazewicz, W. Frohmberg, M. Kierzynka, E. Pesch, P. Wojciechowski, Protein alignment algorithms with an efficient backtracking routine on multiple GPUs, BMC Bioinformatics 12 (1) (2011) 181.

[30] F. Ino, Y. Munekawa, K. Hagihara, Sequence homology search using fine grained cycle sharing of idle GPUs, IEEE Trans. Parallel Distrib. Syst. 23 (4) (2012) 751–759.

[31] P.D. Vouzis, N. Sahinidis, GPU-BLAST: using graphics processors to accelerate sequence alignment, Bioinformatics 2 (27) (2011) 182–188.

[32] D.R. Horn, M. Houston, P. Hanrahan, ClawHMMER: a streaming HMMer-search implementation, in: Proceedings of the ACM/IEEE Supercomputing Conference (SC), 2005, pp. 11.

[33] J.P. Walters, V. Balu, S. Kompalli, V. Chaudhary, Evaluating the use of GPUs in liver image segmentation and HMMER database searches, in: Proceedings of the IEEE International Parallel & Distributed Processing Symposium (IPDPS), 2009, pp. 1–12.

[34] P. Yao, H. An, M. Xu, G. Liu, X. Li, Y. Wang, W. Han, CuHMMer: a load-balanced CPU-GPU cooperative bioinformatics application, in: Proceedings of the International Conference on High Performance Computing and Simulation (HPCS), 2010, pp. 24–30.

[35] X. Li, W. Han, G. Liu, H. An, M. Xu, W. Zhou, Q. Li, A speculative HMMER search implementation on GPU, in: Proceedings of the IEEE International Parallel & Distributed Processing Symposium Workshops & PhD Forum (IPDPSW), 2012, pp. 735–741.

[36] S. Ferraz, N. Moreano, Evaluating optimization strategies for HMMer acceleration on GPU, in: Proceedings of the International Conference on Parallel and Distributed Systems (ICPADS), 2013, pp. 59–68.

[37] L. Cheng, G. Butler, Accelerating search of protein sequence databases using CUDA-enabled GPU, in: Database Systems for Advanced Applications, Lecture Notes in Computer Science, vol. 9049, Springer International Publishing, 2015 pp. 279–298.

[38] L. Ligowski, W. Rudnicki, An efficient implementation of Smith-Waterman algorithm on GPU using CUDA, for massively parallel scanning of sequence databases, in: Proceedings of the IEEE International Symposium on Parallel & Distributed Processing (IPDPS-HiCOMB), 2009, pp. 1–8.

[39] E.F.O. Sandes, A.C.M.A. de Melo, CUDAlign: using GPU to accelerate the comparison of megabase genomic sequences, in: Proceedings of the 15th ACM SIGPLAN Symposium on Principles and Practice of Parallel Programming (PPOPP), 2010, pp. 137–146.

[40] E.F.O. Sandes, A.C.M.A. de Melo, Smith-Waterman alignment of huge sequences with GPU in linear space, in: Proceedings of the IEEE International Symposium on Parallel and Distributed Processing (IPDPS), 2011, pp. 1199–1211.

[41] E.F.O. Sandes, A.C.M.A. de Melo, Retrieving Smith-Waterman alignments with optimizations for megabase biological sequences using GPU, IEEE Trans. Parallel Distrib. Syst. 24 (5) (2013) 1009–1021.

[42] E.F.O. Sandes, G. Miranda, A.C.M.A. de Melo, X. Martorell, E. Ayguade, CUDAlign 3.0: parallel biological sequence comparison in large GPU clusters, in: Proceedings of the IEEE/ACM Symposium on Cluster, Cloud and Grid Computing (CCGrid), 2014, pp. 160–169.

[43] J. Zhang, H. Wang, H. Lin, W. Feng, cuBLASTP: fine-grained parallelization of protein sequence search on a GPU, in: Proceedings of the IEEE International Parallel & Distributed Processing Symposium (IPDPS), 2014, pp. 251–260.

[44] Z. Du, Z. Yin, D.A. Bader, A tile-based parallel Viterbi algorithm for biological sequence alignment on GPU with CUDA, in: Proceedings of the IEEE International Parallel & Distributed Processing Symposium (IPDPS), 2010, pp. 1–8.

[45] Y. Liu, D. Maskell, B. Schmidt, CUDASW++: optimizing Smith-Waterman sequence database searches for CUDA-enabled graphics processing units, BMC Res. Notes 2 (1) (2009) 73.

[46] Y. Liu, B. Schmidt, D. Maskell, CUDASW++2.0: enhanced Smith-Waterman protein database search on CUDA-enabled GPUs based on SIMT and virtualized SIMD abstractions, BMC Res. Notes 3 (1) (2010) 93.

[47] Y. Liu, A. Wirawan, B. Schmidt, CUDASW++ 3.0: accelerating Smith-Waterman protein database search by coupling CPU and GPU SIMD instructions, BMC Bioinformatics 14 (2013) 117.

[48] W. Liu, B. Schmidt, Y. Liu, G. Voss, W. Muller-Wittig, Mapping of BLASTP algorithm onto GPU clusters, in: Proceedings of the International Conference on Parallel and Distributed Systems (ICPADS), 2011, pp. 236–246.

[49] N. Ganesan, R.D. Chamberlain, J. Buhler, M. Taufer, Accelerating HMMER on GPUs by implementing hybrid data and task parallelism, in: Proceedings of the ACM International Conference on Bioinformatics and Computational Biology (BCB), 2010, pp. 418–421.

[50] A. Araújo Neto, N. Moreano, Acceleration of single- and multiple-segment Viterbi algorithms for biological sequence-profile comparison on GPU, in: Proceedings of the 21st International Conference on Parallel and Distributed Processing Techniques and Applications (PDPTA), 2015.

[51] D. Kirk, W. Hwu, Programming Massively Parallel Processors: A Hands-On Approach, Morgan Kaufmann, Burlington, MA, USA, 2010.

[52] J. Li, S. Ranka, S. Sahni, Pairwise sequence alignment for very long sequences on GPUs, in: Proceedings of the International Conference on Computational Advances in Bio and Medical Sciences (ICCABS), 2012, pp. 1–6.

[53] J.P. Walters, V. Chaudhary, B. Schmidt, Database searching with profile-hidden Markov models on reconfigurable and many-core architectures, in: B. Schmidt (Ed.), Bioinformatics—High Performance Parallel Computer Architectures, CRC Press, 2010, pp. 203–222.

[54] T. Rognes, E. Seeberg, Six-fold speed-up of Smith-Waterman sequence database searches using parallel processing on common microprocessors, Bioinformatics 16 (8) (2000) 699–706.

[55] M. Farrar, Striped Smith-Waterman speeds database searches six times over other SIMD implementations, Bioinformatics 23 (2) (2007) 156–161.

[56] National Center for Biotechnology Information, The NCBI Handbook, second ed. 2013, http://www.ncbi.nlm.nih.gov/books/NBK143764.

[57] The UniProt Consortium, UniProt: a hub for protein information, Nucl. Acids Res. 43 (D1) (2015) D204–D212.

[58] Khronos Group, OpenCL—The Open Standard for Parallel Programming of Heterogeneous Systems, https://www.khronos.org/opencl/ (accessed July 14, 2015).

Graph algorithms on GPUs

7

F. Busato, N. Bombieri
University of Verona, Verona, Italy

1 GRAPH REPRESENTATION FOR GPUs

The graph representation adopted when implementing a graph algorithm for graphics processing units (GPUs) strongly affects implementation efficiency and performance. The three most common representations are *adjacency matrices*, *adjacency lists*, and *egdes lists* [1,2]. They have different characteristics and each one finds the best application in different contexts (i.e., graph and algorithm characteristics).

As for the sequential implementations, the quality and efficiency of the graph representation can be measured over three properties: the involved memory footprint, the time required to determine whether a given edge is in the graph, and the time it takes to find the neighbors of a given vertex. For GPU implementations, such a measure also involves load balancing and the memory coalescing.

Given a graph $G = (V, E)$, where V is the set of vertices, E is the set of edges, and d_{max} is the largest diameter of the graph, Table 1 summarizes the main features of the data representations, which are discussed in detail in the next paragraphs.

1.1 ADJACENCY MATRICES

An adjacency matrix allows representing a graph with a $V \times V$ matrix $M = [f(i,j)]$ where each element $f(i,j)$ contains the attributes of the edge (i,j). If the edges do not have an attribute, the graph can be represented by a boolean matrix to save memory space (Fig. 1).

Advances in GPU Research and Practice. http://dx.doi.org/10.1016/B978-0-12-803738-6.00007-0

Table 1 Main Feature of Data Representations

	Space	$(u,v) \in E$	$(u,v) \in adj(v)$	Load Balancing	Mem. Coalescing
Adj matrices	$O(|V|^2)$	$O(1)$	$O(|V|)$	Yes	Yes
Adj lists	$O(|V|+|E|)$	$O(d_{max})$	$O(d_{max})$	Difficult	Difficult
Edges lists	$O(2|E|)$	$O(|E|)$	$O(|E|)$	Yes	Yes

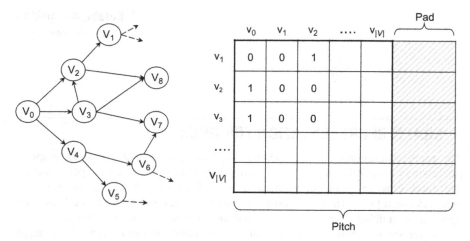

FIG. 1

Matrix representation of a graph in memory.

Common algorithms that use this representation are *all-pair shortest path* (APSP) and *transitive closure* [3–9]. If the graph is weighted, each value of $f(i,j)$ is defined as follows:

$$M[i,j] \begin{cases} 0 & \text{if } i = j \\ w(i,j) & \text{if } i \neq j \text{ and } (i,j) \in E \\ \infty & \text{if } i \neq j \text{ and } (i,j) \notin E \end{cases}$$

On GPUs, both directed and undirected graphs represented by an adjacency matrix take $O(|V|^2)$ memory space, because the whole matrix is stored in memory with a large continuous array. In GPU architectures, it is also important, for performance, to align the matrix with memory to improve coalescence of memory accesses. In this context, the Compute Unified Device Architecture (CUDA) language provides the function *cudaMallocPitch* [10] to pad the data allocation, with the aim of meeting the alignment requirements for memory coalescing. In this case the indexing changes are as follows:

$$M[i \cdot V + j] \rightarrow M[i \cdot pitch + j]$$

The $O(|V|^2)$ memory space required is the main limitation of the adjacency matrices. Even on recent GPUs, they allow handling of fairly small graphs. For example, on a GPU device with 4 GB of DRAM, graphs that can be represented through an adjacency matrix can have a maximum of only 32,768 vertices (which, for actual graph datasets, is considered restrictive). In general, adjacency matrices best represent small and dense graphs (i.e., $|E| \approx |V|^2$). In some cases, such as for the all-pairs shortest path problem, graphs larger than the GPU memory are partitioned and each part is processed independently [7–9].

1.2 ADJACENCY LISTS

Adjacency lists are the most common representation for sparse graphs, where the number of edges is typically a constant factor larger than $|V|$. Because the sequential implementation of adjacency lists relies on pointers, they are not suitable for GPUs. They are replaced, in GPU implementations, by the compressed sparse row (CSR) or the compressed row storage (CRS) sparse matrix format [11,12].

In general, an adjacency list consists of an array of vertices (ArrayV) and an array of edges (ArrayE), where each element in the vertex array stores the starting index (in the edge array) of the edges outgoing from each node. The edge array stores the destination vertices of each edge (Fig. 2). This allows visiting the neighbors of a vertex v by reading the edge array from ArrayV[v] to ArrayV[$v + 1$].

The attributes of the edges are in general stored in the edge array through an array of structures (AoS). For example, in a weighted graph, the destination and the weight of an edge can be stored in a structure with two integer values (*int2* in CUDA [13]). Such a data organization allows many scattered memory accesses to be avoided and, as a consequence, the algorithm performance to be improved.

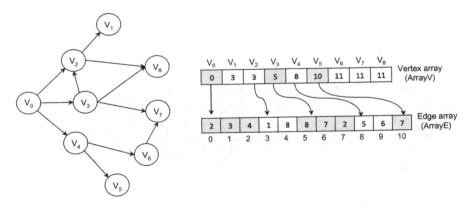

FIG. 2

Adjacency list representation of a weighted graph.

Undirected graphs represented with the CSR format take $O(|V| + 2|E|)$ space since each edge is stored twice. If the problem also requires the incoming edges, the same format is used to store the reverse graph where the vertex array stores the offsets of the incoming edges. The space required with the reverse graph is $O(2|V| + 2|E|)$.

The main issues of the CSR format are load balancing and memory coalescing because of the irregular structure of such a format. If the algorithm involves visiting each vertex at each iteration, the memory coalescing for the vertex array is simple to achieve, but on the other hand, it is difficult to achieve for the edge array. Achieving both load balancing and memory coalescing requires advanced and sophisticated implementation techniques (see Section 5).

For many graph algorithms, the adjacency list representation guarantees better performance than adjacency matrix and edge lists [14–18].

1.3 EDGE LISTS

The edge list representation of a graph, also called coordinate list (COO) sparse matrix [19], consists of two arrays of size $|E|$ that store the source and the destination of each edge (Fig. 3). To improve the memory coalescing, similarly to CSR, the source, the destination and other edge attributes (such as the edge weight) can be stored in a single structure (AoS) [20].

Storing some vertex attributes in external arrays is also necessary in many graph algorithms. For this reason, the edge list is sorted by the first vertex in each ordered pair such that adjacent threads are assigned to edges with the same source vertex. This improves coalescence of memory accesses for retrieval of the vertex attributes. In some cases, sorting the edge list in the lexicographic order may also improve coalescence of memory accesses for retrieving the attributes of the destination vertices [21]. The edge organization in a sorted list allows reducing the complexity (from $O(|E|)$ to $O(\log |E|)$) of verifying whether an edge is in the graph by means of a simple binary search [22].

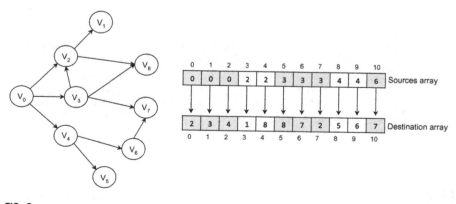

FIG. 3

Edges list representation of a weighted graph.

For undirected graphs, the edge list should not be replicated for the reverse graph. Processing the incoming edges can be done simply by reading the source-destination pairs in the inverse order, thus halving the number of memory accesses. With this strategy, the space required for the edge list representation is $O(2|E|)$.

The edge list representation is suitable in those algorithms that iterate over all edges. For example, it is used in the GPU implementation of algorithms such as *betweenness centrality* [21,23]. In general, this format does not guarantee performance comparable to the adjacency list, but it allows achieving both perfect load balancing and memory coalescing with a simple thread mapping. In graphs with a nonuniform distribution of vertex degrees, the COO format is generally more efficient than CSR [21,24].

2 GRAPH TRAVERSAL ALGORITHMS: THE BREADTH FIRST SEARCH (BFS)

The BFS is a core primitive for graph traversal and the basis for many higher-level graph analysis algorithms. It is used in several different contexts, such as image processing, state space searching, network analysis, graph partitioning, and automatic theorem proving. Given a graph $G(V, E)$, where V is the set of vertices and E is the set of edges, and a source vertex s, the BFS visit inspects every edge of E to find the minimum number of edges or the shortest path to reach every vertex of V from source s. Algorithm 1 summarizes the traditional sequential algorithm [1], where Q is an FIFO queue data structure that stores not-yet-visited vertices, Distance $[v]$ represents the distance of vertex v from the source vertex s (number of edges in the path), and Parent $[v]$ represents the parent vertex of v. An unvisited vertex v is denoted with Distance $[v]$ equal to ∞. The asymptotic time complexity of the sequential algorithm is $O(|V| + |E|)$.

ALGORITHM 1 SEQUENTIAL BFS ALGORITHM

for all verticies $v \in V(G)$ **do**
    Distance $[v] = \infty$
    Parent $[v] = -1$
end
Distance $[v_0] = 0$
Parent $[v_0] = v_0$
$Q \leftarrow \{v_0\}$
while $Q \neq \emptyset$ **do**
    $u = \text{DEQUEUE}(Q)$
    for all verticies $v \in adj\,[u]$ **do**
        if Distance $[v] = \infty$ **then**
            Distance $[v] = $ Distance $[u] + 1$
            Parent $[v] = u$
            $\text{ENQUEUE}(Q, v)$
    end
end

In the context of GPUs, the BFS algorithm is the only graph traversal method applied since it exposes a high level of parallelism. In contrast, the depth-first search traversal is never applied because of its intrinsic sequentiality.

2.1 THE FRONTIER-BASED PARALLEL IMPLEMENTATION OF BFS

The most efficient parallel implementations of BFS for GPUs exploit the concept of *frontier* [1]. They generate a breadth-first tree that has root *s* and contains all reachable vertices. The vertices in each *level* of the tree compose a *frontier (F)*. *Frontier propagation* checks every neighbor of a frontier vertex to see whether it has already been visited. If not, the neighbor is added into a new frontier.

The frontier propagation relies on two data structures, *F* and *F'*. *F* represents the actual frontier, which is read by the parallel threads to start the propagation step. *F'* is written by the threads to generate the frontier for the next BFS step. At each step, *F'* is filtered and swapped into *F* for the next iteration. Fig. 4 shows an example, in which starting from vertex "1," the BFS visit concludes in three steps.[1]

The filtering steps aim at guaranteeing correctness of the BFS visit as well as avoiding useless thread work and waste of resources. When a thread visits a neighbor already visited, that neighbor is eliminated from the frontier (e.g., vertex 3 visited by a thread from vertex 4 in step 2 of Fig. 4). When more threads visit the same neighbor in the same propagation step (e.g., vertex 9 visited by threads 3 and 4 in step 2), they generate *duplicate* vertices in the frontier. Duplicate vertices cause redundant work in the subsequent propagation steps (i.e., more threads visit the same path) and useless

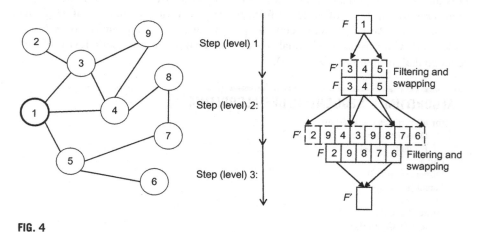

FIG. 4

Example of BFS visit starting from vertex "0."

---

[1]For the sake of clarity, the figure shows *F'* first written and then filtered. As explained in the following paragraphs, to reduce the global memory accesses, some implementations first filter the next frontier and then write the *F'* data [15,16,28].

occupancy of shared memory. The most efficient BFS implementations detect and eliminate duplicates by exploiting hash tables, Kepler 8-byte memory access mode, and warp shuffle instructions [15,16].

Several techniques have been proposed in literature to efficiently parallelize the BFS algorithm for GPUs. Harish and Narayanan [25] proposed the first approach, which relies on exploring all the graph vertices at each iteration (i.e., at each visiting level) to see whether the vertex belongs to the current frontier. This allows the algorithm to save GPU overhead by not maintaining the frontier queues. Nevertheless, the proposed approach on CSR representation, leads to a significant workload imbalance whenever the graph is not homogeneous in terms of vertex degree. In addition, with D as the graph diameter, the computational complexity of such a solution is $O(|V||D| + |E|)$, where $O(|V||D|)$ is spent to check the frontier vertices and $O(|E|)$ is spent to explore each graph edge. While this approach fits on dense graphs, in the worst case of sparse graphs (where $D = O(|V|)$), the algorithm has a complexity of $O(|V|^2)$. This implies that, for large graphs, such an implementation is slower than the sequential version.

A partial solution to the problem of workload imbalance was proposed in Ref. [18] by adopting the same graph representation. Instead of assigning a thread to a vertex, the authors propose thread groups (which they call *virtual warps*) to explore the array of vertices. The group size is typically 2, 4, 8, 16, or 32, and the number of blocks is inversely proportional to the virtual warp size. This leads to a limited speedup in case of low degree graphs, since many threads cannot be exploited at the kernel configuration time. Also, the virtual warp size is static and has to be properly set depending on each graph characteristics.

Ref. [26] presents an alternative solution based on matrices for sparse graphs. Each frontier propagation is transformed into a matrix-vector multiplication. Given the total number of multiplications D (which corresponds to the number of levels), the computational complexity of the algorithm is $O(|V| + |E||D|)$, where $O(|V|)$ is spent to initialize the vector, and $O(|E|)$ is spent for the multiplication at each level. In the worst case, that is, when $D = O(|V|)$, the algorithm complexity is $O(|V|^2)$.

Refs. [21,24] present alternative approaches based on *edge parallelism*. Instead of assigning one or more threads to a vertex, the thread computation is distributed to edges. As a consequence, the thread divergence is limited, and the workload is balanced even with high-degree graphs. The main drawback is the overhead introduced by the visit of all graph edges at each level. In many cases, the number of edges is much greater than the number of vertices. In these cases, the parallel work is not sufficient to improve the performance against vertex parallelism.

An efficient BFS implementation with computational complexity $O(|V| + |E|)$ is proposed in Ref. [17]. The algorithm exploits a single hierarchical queue shared across all thread blocks and an interblock synchronization [27] to save queue accesses in global memory. Nevertheless, the small frontier size requested to avoid global memory writes and the visit exclusively based on vertex parallelism limit the overall speedup. In addition, the generally high-degree vertices are handled through an expensive precomputation phase rather than at runtime.

Merrill et al. [16] present an algorithm implementation that achieves work complexity $O(|V| + |E|)$. They make use of parallel prefix-scan and three different approaches to deal with the workload imbalance: *vertex expansion and edge contraction*, *edge contraction and vertex expansion*, and *hybrid*. The algorithm also relies on a technique to reduce redundant work because of *duplicate* vertices on the frontiers.

Beamer et al. propose a central processing unit (CPU) multicore hybrid approach, which combines the frontier-based algorithm along with a bottom-up BFS algorithm. The bottom-up algorithm can greatly reduce the number of edges examined compared to common parallel algorithms. The bottom-up BFS traversal searches vertices of the next iteration (at distance $L + 1$) in the reverse direction by exploring the unvisted vertices of the graph. This approach requires only a thread per unvisted vertex that explores the neighbor until a previously visited vertex is found (at distance L). The bottom-up BFS is particularly efficient on low-diameter graphs where, at the ending iterations, a substantial fraction of neighbors are valid parents. In the context of GPUs, such a bottom-up approach for graph traversal was implemented by Wang et al. [28] in the Gunrock framework and by Hiragushi et al. [29].

ALGORITHM 2 OVERVIEW OF A PREFIX-SUM PROCEDURE IMPLEMENTED WITH SHUFFLE INSTRUCTIONS

EXCLUSIVEWARPPREFIXSUM

```
for (i = 1; i ≤ 16; i = i * 2) do
    n = __shfl_up(v, i, 32)
    if lane_id ≥ i then
        v += n
end
__shfl_up(v, 1, 32)
if lane_id = 0 then
    v = 0
```

2.2 BFS-4K

BFS-4K [15] is a parallel implementation of BFS for GPUs that exploits the more advanced features of GPU-based platforms (i.e., NVIDIA Kepler, Maxwell [30,31]) to improve the performance w.r.t. the sequential CPU implementations and to achieve an asymptotically optimal work complexity.

BFS-4K implements different techniques to deal with the potential workload imbalance and thread divergence caused by actual graph nonhomogeneity (e.g., number of vertices, edges, diameter, vertex degree), as follows:

- *Exclusive prefix-sum.* To improve data access time and thread concurrency during the propagation steps, the frontier data structures are stored in shared memory and handled by a *prefix-sum* procedure [32,33]. Such a procedure is implemented through warp shuffle instructions of the Kepler architecture. BFS-4K implements a two-level exclusive prefix-sum, that is, at warp-level and block-level. The first is implemented by using Kepler warp-shuffle instructions, which guarantee the result computation in log n steps. Algorithm 2 shows a high-level representation of such a prefix-sum procedure implemented with a warp shuffle instruction (i.e., __shfl_up()).

- *Dynamic virtual warps.* The *virtual warp* technique presented in Ref. [18] is applied to minimize the waste of GPU resources and to reduce the divergence during the neighbor inspection phase. The idea is to allocate a chunk of tasks to each warp and to execute different tasks as serial rather than assigning a different task to each thread. Multiple threads are used in a warp for explicit single instruction multiple data (SIMD) operations only, thus preventing branch-divergence altogether.

Differently from Ref. [18], BFS-4K implements a strategy to dynamically calibrate the warp size at each frontier propagation step. BFS-4K implements a *dynamic* virtual warp, whereby the warp size is calibrated at each frontier propagation step i, as

$$WarpSize_i = nearest\_pow2 \left(\frac{\#ResThreads}{|F_i|} \right) \in [K_1, 32]$$

where *#ResThreads* refers to the maximum number of resident threads.

- *Dynamic parallelism.* In the case of vertices with degrees much greater than average (e.g., scale-free networks or graphs with power-law distribution in general), BFS-4K applies the dynamic parallelism provided by the Kepler architecture instead of virtual warps. Dynamic parallelism implies an overhead that, if not properly used, may worsen the algorithm performance. BFS-4K checks, at runtime, the characteristics of the frontier to decide whether and how to apply this technique.

- *Edge-discover.* With the edge-discover technique, threads are assigned to edges rather than vertices to improve thread workload balancing during frontier propagation. The edge-discover technique makes intense use of warp shuffle instructions. BFS-4K checks, at each propagation step, the frontier configuration to apply this technique rather than dynamic virtual warps. BFS-4K implements thread assignment through a binary search based on warp shuffle instructions. The algorithm performs the following steps:

  1. Each warp thread reads a frontier vertex and saves the degree and the offset of the first edge.
  2. Each warp computes the warp shuffle prefix-sum on the vertices' degree.
  3. Each thread of the warp performs a warp shuffle binary search of the own warp id (i.e., $lane_{id} \in \{0, \ldots, 31\}$) on the prefix-sum results. The warp shuffle instructions guarantee the efficiency of the search steps (which are less than $\log_2(WarpSize)$ per warp).
  4. The threads of warp share, at the same time, the offset of the first edge with another warp shuffle operation.
  5. Finally, the threads inspect the edges and store possible new vertices on the local queue.

- *Single-block vs multiblock kernel.* BFS-4K relies on a two-kernel implementation. The two kernels are used alternately and combined with the preceding features presented during frontier propagation.
- *A duplicate detection and correction strategy.* This strategy is based on hash table and eight-bank access mode to sensibly reduce the memory accesses and improve the detection capability. BFS-4K implements a hash table in shared memory (i.e., one per streaming multiprocessor) to detect and correct duplicates and takes advantage of the eight-bank shared memory mode of Kepler to guarantee high performance of the table accesses. At each propagation step, each frontier thread invokes the `hash64` procedure depicted in Algorithm 3 to update the hash table with the visited vertex (v). Given the size of the hash table (*Hash_Table_Size*), each thread of a block calculates the address (h) in the table for v (row 2). The thread identifier (*thread$_{id}$*) and the visited vertex identifier (v) are merged into a single 64-bit word, to be saved in the calculated address (row 3). The merge operation (as well as the consequential split in row 5) is efficiently implemented through bitwise instructions. A duplicate vertex causes the update of the hash table in the same address by more threads. Thus each thread recovers the two values in the corresponding address (rows 4 and 5) and checks whether they have been updated (row 6) to notify a duplicate.

ALGORITHM 3 MAIN STEPS OF THE HASH TABLE MANAGING ALGORITHM

HASH64

```
1:    H_SZ : Hash_Table_Size
2:    h = hash(v)          → h ∈ [0, H_SZ]
3:    HashTable[h] = merge(v, thread_id)
4:    recover = HashTable[h];
5:    (v_R, thread_idR) = split(recover)
6:    return thread_id ≠ thread_idR ∧ v = v_R
```

- *Coalesced read/write memory accesses.* To reduce the overhead caused by the many accesses in global memory, BFS-4K implements a technique to induce coalescence among warp threads through warp shuffle.

BFS-4K exploits the features of the Kepler architecture, such as dynamic parallelism, warp-shuffle, and eight-bank access mode, to guarantee an efficient implementation of the previously listed characteristics. Table 2 summarizes the differences between the most representative state-of-the-art BFS implementations and BFS-4K, while Fig. 5 reports a representative comparison of speedups among the BFS implementations for GPUs presented in Section 2.1, BFS-4K, and the sequential counterpart.

Table 2 Comparison of the Most Representative State-of-the-Art BFS Implementations With BFS-4K

	Harish [25]	Virtual Warps [18]	Edge Parallelism [21]	Luo [17]	Garland [16]	BFS-4K [15]
Work complexity	$O(VD + E)$	$O(VD + E)$	$O(ED)$	$O(V + E)$	$O(V + E)$	$O(V + E)$
Space complexity	$O(3V + E)$	$O(2V + E)$	$O(2E)$	N/A	$\Omega(4V + 2E)$	$\Omega(4V + E)$
Type of parallelism	Vertices	Virtual warp	Edges	Vertices	Vertices, edges, CTA	Vertices, edges, dynamic virtual warp, dynamic parallelism
High-degree vertex management	No	Yes	Indifferent	No	Yes	Yes
Duplicate detection	No	No	No	No	Yes	Yes
Type of synchronization	Host-device	Host-device	Host-device	Host-device, interblock [27], thread barriers	Host-device, interblock [27]	Host-device, interblock [27], thread barriers

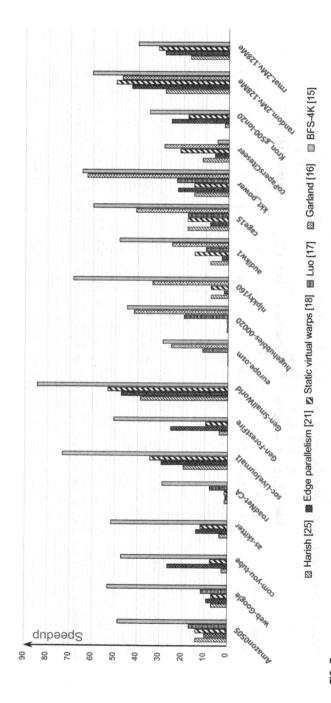

FIG. 5

Performance comparison (speedup) of BFS-4K with the most representative state-of-the-art implementations.

Harish [25]   Edge parallelism [21]   Static virtual warps [18]   Luo [17]   Garland [16]   BFS-4K [15]

The results show how BFS-4K outperforms all the other implementations in every graph. This is due to the fact that BFS-4K exploits the more advanced architecture characteristics (in particular, Kepler features) and that it allows the user to optimize the visiting strategy through different knobs.

3 THE SINGLE-SOURCE SHORTEST PATH (SSSP) PROBLEM

Given a weighted graph $G = (V, E)$, where V is the set of vertices and $E \subseteq (V \times V)$ is the set of edges, the SSSP problem consists of finding the shortest paths from a single source vertex to all other vertices [1]. Such a well-known and long-studied problem arises in many different domains, such as road networks, routing protocols, artificial intelligence, social networks, data mining, and VLSI chip layout.

The de facto reference approaches to SSSP are the Dijkstra [34] and Bellman-Ford [35,36] algorithms. The Dijkstra algorithm, by utilizing a priority queue where one vertex is processed at a time, is the most efficient, with a computational complexity almost linear to the number of vertices ($O(|V| \log |V| + |E|)$). Nevertheless, in several application domains where the modeled data maps to very large graphs involving millions of vertices, Dijkstra's sequential implementation becomes impractical. In addition, since the algorithm requires many iterations and each iteration is based on the ordering of previously computed results, it is poorly suited for parallelization.

On the other hand, the Bellman-Ford algorithm relies on an iterative process over all edge connections, which updates the vertices continuously until final distances converge. Even though it is less efficient than Dijkstra's ($O(|V||E|)$), it is well suited to parallelization [37].

In the context of parallel implementations for GPUs, where the energy and power consumption is becoming a constraint in addition to performance [38], an ideal solution to SSSP would provide both the performance of the Bellman-Ford algorithm and the work efficiency of the Dijkstra algorithm. In the last years, some work was done to analyze the spectrum between massive parallelism and efficiency, and different parallel solutions for GPUs have been proposed to implement parallel-friendly and work-efficient methods to solve SSSP [39]. Experimental results confirmed that these trade-off methods provide a fair speedup by doing much less work than traditional Bellman-Ford methods while adding only a modest amount of extra work over serial methods.

On the other hand, none of these solutions, as well as Dijkstra's implementations, work in graphs with negative weights [1]. The Bellman-Ford algorithm is the only solution that can also be applied in application domains where the modeled data maps on graphs with negative weights, such as power allocation in wireless sensor networks [40,41], systems biology [42], and regenerative braking energy for railway vehicles [43].

3.1 THE SSSP IMPLEMENTATIONS FOR GPUs

The Dijkstra and Bellman-Ford algorithms span a parallel versus efficiency spectrum. Dijkstra allows the most efficient ($O(V \log V + E)$) sequential implementations [44,45] but exposes no parallelism across vertices. Indeed, the solutions proposed to parallelize the Dijkstra algorithm for GPUs are shown to be asymptotically less efficient than the fastest CPU implementations [46,47]. On the other hand, at the cost of lower efficiency ($O(VE)$), the Bellman-Ford algorithm is shown to be more easily parallelizable for GPUs by providing speedups of up to two orders of magnitude with respect to the sequential counterpart [14,37].

Meyer and Sanders [48] propose the Δ-stepping algorithm, a trade-off between the two extremes of Dijkstra and Bellman-Ford. The algorithm involves a tunable parameter Δ, whereby setting $\Delta = 1$ yields a variant of the Dijkstra algorithm, while setting $\Delta = \infty$ yields the Bellman-Ford algorithm. By varying Δ in the range $[1, \infty]$, we get a spectrum of algorithms with varying degrees of processing time and parallelism.

Meyer and Sanders [48] show that a value of $\Delta = \Theta(1/d)$, where d is the degree, gives a good tradeoff between work-efficiency and parallelism. In the context of GPU, Davidson et al. [39] selects a similar heuristic, $\Delta = cw/d$, where d is the average degree in the graph, w is the average edge weight, and c is the warp width (32 on our GPUs).

Crobak et al. [49] and Chakaravarthy et al. [50] present two different solutions to efficiently expose parallelism of this algorithm on the massively multithreaded shared memory system IBM Blue Gene/Q.

Parallel SSSP algorithms for multicore CPUs were also proposed by Kelley and Schardl [51], who presented a parallel implementation of Gabow's scaling algorithm [52] that outperforms Dijkstra's on random graphs. Shun and Blelloch [53] presented a Bellman-Ford scalable parallel implementation for CPUs on a 40-core machine. Over the last ten years, several packages were developed for processing large graphs on parallel architectures, including the Parallel Boost Graph Library [54], Pregel [55], and Pegasus [56].

In the context of GPUs, Davidson et al. [39] propose three different work-efficient solutions for the SSSP problem. The first two, *Near-Far Pile* and *Workfront Sweep*, are the most representative state-of-the-art implementations. Workfront Sweep implements a queue-based Bellman-Ford algorithm that reduces redundant work because of duplicate vertices during the frontier propagation. Such a fast graph traversal method relies on the merge path algorithm [22], which equally assigns the outgoing edges of the frontier to the GPU threads at each algorithm iteration. Near-Far Pile refines the Workfront Sweep strategy by adopting two queues similarly to the Δ-Stepping algorithm. Davidson et al. [39] also propose the *bucketing* method to implement the Δ-Stepping algorithm. Δ-Stepping algorithm is not well suited for SIMD architectures as it requires dynamic data structures for buckets. However, the authors provide an algorithm implementation based on sorting that, at each step, emulates the bucket structure. The Bucketing and Near-Far Pile strategies greatly reduce the amount of redundant work with respect to the Workfront Sweep method, but at the same time, they introduce overhead for handling more complex data structure (i.e., frontier queue). These strategies are less efficient than the sequential implementation on graphs with large diameters because they suffer from thread underutilization caused by such unbalanced graphs.

ALGORITHM 4 SEQUENTIAL BELLMAN-FORD ALGORITHM

INITIALIZE(G, s)
for all edges $(u, v) \in E(G)$ **do**
    RELAX(u, v, w)
end

3.2 H-BF: AN EFFICIENT IMPLEMENTATION OF THE BELLMAN-FORD ALGORITHM

Given a graph $G(V, E)$, a source vertex s, and a weight function $w\colon E \rightarrow \mathbb{R}$, the Bellman-Ford algorithm visits G and finds the shortest path to reach every vertex of V from source s. Algorithm 4 summarizes the original sequential algorithm, where the *Relax* procedure of an edge (u, v) with weight w verifies whether, starting from u, it is possible to improve the approximate (*tentative*) distance to v (which we call $d(v)$) found in any previous algorithm iteration. The relax procedure can be summarized as follows:

EDGE RELAX:

if $d(u) + w < d(v)$ **then**
    $d(v) = d(u) + w$

The algorithm, whose asymptotic time complexity is $O(|V||E|)$, updates the distance value of each vertex continuously until final distances converge.

H-BF [57] is a parallel implementation of the Bellman-Ford algorithm based on frontier propagation. Differently from all the approaches in literature, H-BF implements several techniques to improve the algorithm performance and, at the same time, to reduce the useless work done for solving SSSP involved by the parallelization process. H-BF implements such techniques by exploiting the features of the most recent GPU architectures, such as dynamic parallelism, warp-shuffle, read-only cache, and 64-bit atomic instructions.

The complexity of an SSSP algorithm is strictly related to the number of *relax* operations. The Bellman-Ford algorithm performs a higher number of *relax* operations than Dijkstra or Δ-Stepping algorithms, while on the other hand, it provides simple and lightweight management of the data structures. The *relax* operation is the most expensive in the Bellman-Ford algorithm, and in particular, in a parallel implementation, each *relax* involves an atomic instruction for handling race conditions, which takes much more time than a common memory access.

To optimize the number of relax operations, H-BF implements the graph visit by exploiting the concept of *frontier*. For this problem, the frontier, F, is an FIFO queue that, at each algorithm iteration, contains *active vertices*—that is, all and only vertices whose tentative distance has been modified and which therefore must be considered for the relax procedure at the next iteration. Given a graph G and a source vertex s, the parallel frontier-based algorithm can be summarized in Algorithm 5, where *adj[u]* returns the neighbors of vertex u. Fig. 6 shows an example of the basic algorithm iterations starting from vertex "0," where F is the active vertex queue and D is the corresponding data structure containing the tentative distances. The example shows, for each algorithm iteration, the dequeue of each vertex form the frontier, the corresponding relax operations, that is, the distance updating for each vertex (if necessary), and the vertex enqueues in the new frontier. In the example, the algorithm converges in a total of five relax operations over five iterations.

ALGORITHM 5 FRONTIER-BASED BELLMAN-FORD ALGORITHM

INITIALIZE(G, s)
$F \leftarrow \{s\}$
while $F \neq \emptyset$ **do**
    $u \leftarrow$ DEQUEUE(F)
    for all vertices $v \in adj[u]$ **do**
        if $d(u) + w < d(v)$ **then**
            $d(v) = d(u) + w$
            ENQUEUE(F, v)
    end
end

The frontier structure is similar to that applied for implementing the parallel BFS presented in Section 2.1. The main difference from BFS is the number of times a vertex can be inserted in the queue. In BFS, a vertex can be inserted in such a queue only once, while, in the Bellman-Ford implementation, a vertex can be inserted $O(|E|)$ times in the worst case.

Fig. 7 summarizes the speedup of the different implementations with respect to the sequential frontier-based Bellman-Ford implementation. The results show how H-BF outperforms all the other implementations in every graph. The speedup on graphs with very high diameter (leftmost side of the figure) is quite low for every parallel implementation. This is due to the very low degree of parallelism for propagating the frontier in such graph typology. In these graphs, H-BF is the only parallel implementation that outperforms the Boost Dijkstra solution in *asia.osm*, and it preserves comparable performance in *USA-road.d-CAL*. On the other hand, in the literature, the sequential Boost Dijkstra implementation largely outperforms all the other parallel solutions.

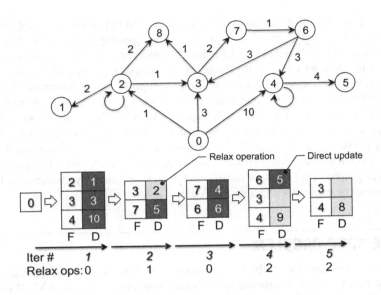

FIG. 6

Example of the basic algorithm iterations starting from vertex "0."

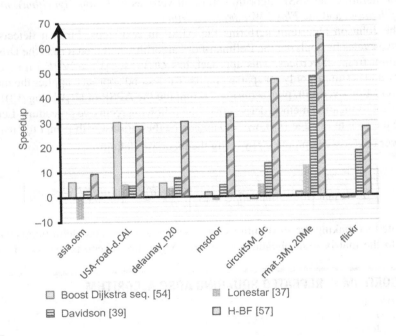

FIG. 7

Comparison of speedups.

H-BF provides the best performance (time and MTEPS) on the graphs on the rightmost side of Fig. 7. H-BF also provides high speedup in *rmat.3Mv.20Me* and *flickr*, which are largely unbalanced graphs. This underlines the effectiveness of H-BF to deal with such an unbalancing problem in traversing graphs. The optimization based on the *64-bit atomic* instruction strongly impacts the performance of graphs with small diameters. This is due to the fact that such graph visits are characterized by a rapid grow of the frontier, which implies a high number of duplicate vertices. The edge classification technique implemented in H-BF successfully applies to the majority of the graphs. In particular, *asia.osm* has a high number of vertices with an in-degree equal to one, while in *msdoor* and *circuit5M_dc* each vertex has a self-loop. Scale-free graphs (e.g., *rmat.3Mv.20Me* and *flickr*) are generally characterized by a high number of vertices with a low out-degree.

4 THE APSP PROBLEM

APSP is a fundamental problem in computer science that finds application in different fields such as transportation, robotics, network routing, and VLSI design. The problem is to find paths of minimum weight between all pairs of vertices in graphs with weighted edges. The common approaches to solving the APSP problem rely on iterating the SSSP algorithm from all vertices (*Johnson algorithm*), *matrix multiplication*, and the *Floyd-Warshall algorithm*.

The Johnson algorithm performs the APSP in two steps. First, it detects the negative cycles by applying the Bellman-Ford algorithm and then it runs the Dijsktra algorithm from all vertices. This approach has $O(|V|^2 \log |V| + |V||E|)$ time complexity and is suitable only for sparse graphs. The second approach applies the matrix multiplication over min, plus semiring to compute the APSP in $O(|V|^3 \log |V|)$. The matrix multiplication method derives from the following recursive procedure. Letting w_{ij} be the weight of edge (i,j), $w_{ii} = 0$ and d_{ij}^ℓ be the shortest path from i to j using ℓ or fewer edges, we compute d_{ij}^ℓ by using the recursive definition:

$$\begin{cases} d_{ij}^0 = w_{ij} \\ d_{ij}^\ell = \min\left\{d_{ij}^{\ell-1}, \min_{1\leq k\leq n} d_{ik}^{\ell-1} + w_{kj}\right\} \end{cases} \to d_{ij}^\ell = \min_{1\leq k\leq n}\left\{d_{ik}^{\ell-1} + w_{kj}\right\}$$

We note that making the substitutions min $\to$ + and + $\to$ ·, the definition is equivalent to the matrix multiplication procedure. Algorithm 6 reports the pseudocode.

ALGORITHM 6 REPEATED SQUARING APSP ALGORITHM

$D^0 = W$
for $L = 1$ to $\log V$ **do**
  for $i = 0$ to V **do**
    for $j = 0$ to V **do**
      $D^L[i,j] = \infty$
      for $k = 0$ to V **do**

$$D^L[i,j] = \min(D^{L-1}[i,j], D^{L-1}[i,k] + W[k,j])$$
        end
      end
    end
  end

Finally, the Floyd-Warshall algorithm, which is the standard approach for the APSP problem in the case of edges with negative weights, does not suffer from performance degradation for dense graphs. The algorithm has $O(|V|^3)$ time complexity and requires $O(|V|^2)$ memory space.

With $G = (V, E)$ being a weighted graph with an edge-weight function $w: E \rightarrow \mathbb{R}$ and $W = w(i,j)$ representing the weighted matrix, we have the pseudocode of the algorithm as shown in Algorithm 7.

ALGORITHM 7 FLOYD-WARSHALL

$D^0 = W$
for $k = 0$ to V **do**
  for $i = 0$ to V **do**
    for $j = 0$ to V **do**
      $D^k[i,j] = min(D^{k-1}[i,j], D^{k-1}[i,k] + D^{k-1}[k,j])$
    end
  end
end

4.1 THE APSP IMPLEMENTATIONS FOR GPUs

The first GPU solution for the APSP problem was proposed by Harish and Narayanan [25], who used their parallel SSSP algorithm from all vertices of the graph. Also Ortega et al. [58] resolved the APSP problem in the same way, by proposing a highly tunable GPU implementation of the Dijkstra algorithm.

The most important idea, which provided the basis for a subsequent efficient GPU implementations of the Floyd-Warshall algorithm was proposed by Venkataraman et al. [3] in the context of multicore CPUs. The proposed solution takes advantage of the cache utilization. It first partitions the graph matrix into multiple tiles that fit in cache, and then it iterates on each tile multiple times. In particular, such a blocked Floyd-Warshall algorithm comprises three main phases (Fig. 8).

1. The computation in each iteration starts from a tile in the diagonal of the matrix, from the upper-left to the lower-right. Each tile in the diagonal is independent of the rest of the matrix and can be processed in place.

FIG. 8

Blocked Floyd-Warshall algorithm. The *numbers* indicate the computation order of each tile.

2. In the second phase, all tiles that are in the same row and in the same column of the independent tiles are computed in parallel. All tiles in this phase are dependent only on itself and on the independent tiles.
3. In the third phase, all remaining tiles are dependent from itself and from the main row and the main column that were computed in the previous phase.

The blocked Floyd-Warshall algorithm was implemented for GPU architectures by Katz and Kider [4], who strongly exploited the shared memory as local cache. Lund et al. [5] improved such a GPU implementation by optimizing the use of registers and by taking advantage of memory coalescing. Buluç et al. [6] presented a recursive formulation of the APSP based on the Gaussian elimination (LU) and matrix multiplication with $O(|V|^3)$ complexity, which exposes a good memory locality.

Later, Harish et al. [59] revisited the APSP algorithm based on matrix multiplication, and they presented two improvements: *streaming blocks* and *lazy minimum evaluation*. The streaming block optimization describes a method to partition the adjacency matrix and to efficiently transfer each partition to the device through asynchronous read and write operations. The second optimization aims at decreasing the arithmetic computation by avoiding the minimum operation when one operand is set to infinite. The presented algorithm achieves a speedup from 5 to 10 over Katz and Kider algorithm. Nevertheless, it is slower than the Gaussian elimination method of Buluç et al. On the other hand, they showed that their algorithm is more scalable and that the optimization of the lazy minimum evaluation is not orthogonal to the Gaussian elimination method.

Tran et al. [9] proposed an alternative algorithm based on matrix multiplication and on the *repeated squaring* technique (Algorithm 6). It outperforms the base Floyd-Warshall algorithm when the graph matrix exceeds the GPU memory.

Matsumoto et al. [7] proposed a hybrid CPU-GPU based on OpenCL, which combines the blocked Floyd-Warshall algorithm for a coarse-grained partition of the graph matrix and the matrix multiplication as a main procedure.

Finally, Djidjev et al. [8] proposed an efficient implementation of APSP on multiple GPUs for graphs that have good *separators*.

5 LOAD BALANCING AND MEMORY ACCESSES: ISSUES AND MANAGEMENT TECHNIQUES

Load unbalancing and noncoalesced memory accesses are the main problems when implementing any graph algorithm for GPUs. The two are caused by the nonhomogeneity of real graphs. Different techniques have been presented in the literatures to decompose and map the graph algorithm workload to threads [15,16,18,25,60–62]. All these techniques differ in terms of the complexity and in terms of the overhead they introduce in an application's execution. The simplest solutions [18,25] apply best to very regular workloads, but they cause strong unbalancing and consequently loss of performance in irregular workloads. More complex solutions [15,16,60–62] apply best to irregular problems through semidynamic or dynamic workload-to-thread mappings. Nevertheless, the overhead introduced for such a mapping often worsens the overall performance of an application when run on regular problems.

In general, the techniques for decomposing and mapping a workload to GPU threads for graph applications rely on the *prefix-sum* data structure[2] [16]. Given a workload to be allocated (e.g., a set of graph vertices or edges) over GPU threads, prefix-sum calculates the offsets to be used by the threads to access the corresponding *work-units* (fine-grained mapping) or to block work-units, which we call *work-items* (coarse-grained mapping). All these decomposition and mapping techniques can be organized in three classes: *Static mapping*, *semidynamic mapping*, and *dynamic mapping*.

5.1 STATIC MAPPING TECHNIQUES

This class includes all the techniques that statistically assign each work-item (or blocks of work-units) to a corresponding GPU thread. This strategy allows to considerably reduce the overhead for calculating the work-item to thread mapping during the application execution, but on the other hand, it suffers from load unbalancing when the work-units are not regularly distributed over the work-items. The most important techniques are summarized in the following sections.

5.1.1 Work-items to threads

This approach represents the simplest and fastest mapping method by which each work-item is mapped to a single thread [25]. Fig. 9A shows an example in which eight items are assigned to a corresponding number of threads. For the sake of clarity, only four threads per warp are considered in the example, which underlines two levels of possible unbalancing of this technique. First, irregular (i.e., unbalanced) work-items mapped to threads of the same warp cause the warp threads to be in idle

---

[2]The prefix-sum array is generated, depending on the mapping technique, in a preprocessing phase [63], at run-time if the workload changes at every iteration [15,16], or it could already be part of the problem [64].

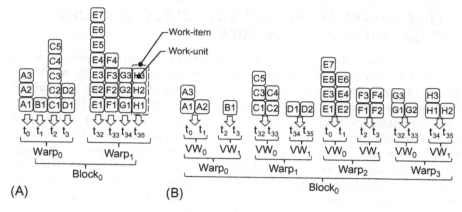

FIG. 9

Example of static mapping techniques: (A) work-items to threads and (B) virtual warps.

state (i.e., branch divergence). t_1, t_3, and t_0 of $warp_0$ in Fig. 9A are examples. Then irregular work-items cause whole warps to be in idle state (e.g., $warp_0$ w.r.t. $warp_1$ in Fig. 9A). In a third level of unbalancing, this technique can cause whole blocks of threads to be in idle state.

In addition, considering that work-units of different items are generally stored in nonadjacent addresses in global memory, this mapping strategy leads to sparse and noncoalesced memory accesses. As an example, threads t_0, t_1, t_2, and t_3 of $Warp_0$ concurrently access to the nonadjacent units A_1, B_1, C_1, and D_1, respectively. For all these reasons, this technique is suitable for applications running on very regular data structures, in which any more-advanced mapping strategies will run at runtime (as explained in the following paragraphs), leading to unjustified overhead.

5.1.2 Virtual warps

This technique consists of assigning chunks of work-units to groups of threads called *virtual warps*, where the virtual warps are equally sized and the threads of a virtual warp belong to the same warp [18]. Fig. 9B shows an example in which the chunks correspond to the work-items and, for the sake of clarity, the virtual warps have a size equal to two threads. Virtual warps allow the workload assigned to threads of the same group to be almost equal, and consequently it allows reducing branch divergence. In addition, this technique improves the coalescing of memory accesses since more threads of a virtual warp have access to adjacent addresses in global memory (e.g., t_0, t_1 of $Warp_2$ in Fig. 9B). These improvements are proportional to the virtual warp size. Increasing the warp size leads to reducing branch divergence and better coalescing the work-unit accesses in global memory. Nevertheless, virtual warps have several limitations. First, the maximum size of virtual warps is limited by the number of available threads in the device. Given the number of work-items and a virtual warp size, the required number of threads is expressed as follows:

$$\#RequiredThreads = \#workitems \cdot |VirtualWarp|$$

If such a number is greater than the available threads, the work-item processing is serialized with a consequent decrease of performance. Indeed, a wrong sizing of the virtual warps can impact the application performance. In addition, this technique provides good balancing among threads of the same warp, while it does not guarantee good balancing among different warps or among different blocks. Finally, another major limitation of such a static mapping approach is that the virtual warp size has to be fixed statically. This represents a major limitation when the number and size of the work-items change at runtime.

The algorithm run by each thread to access the corresponding work-units is summarized as in Algorithm 8, where VW_INDEX and LANE_OFFSET are the virtual warp index and offset for the thread (e.g., VW_0, and 0 for t_0 in Fig. 9B), INIT represents the starting work-unit id, and the *for* cycle represents the accesses of the thread to the assigned work-units (e.g., A_1, A_3 for t_0 and A_2 for t_1).

ALGORITHM 8 VIRTUAL WARP LOAD BALANCING

1:    VW_INDEX = TH_INDEX / |*VirtualWarp*|
2:    LANE_OFFSET = TH_INDEX % |*VirtualWarp*|
3:    INIT = *prefixsum*[VW_INDEX] + LANE_OFFSET
4:    **for** i = INIT **to** *prefixsum*[VW_INDEX+1] **do**
5:        Output[i] = VW_INDEX
6:        $i = i + |VirtualWarp|$
7:    **end**

5.2 SEMIDYNAMIC MAPPING TECHNIQUES

This class includes the techniques by which different mapping configurations are calculated statically, and at runtime, the application switches among them.

5.2.1 Dynamic virtual warps + dynamic parallelism

This technique was introduced in Ref. [15] and relies on two main strategies. First, it implements a virtual warp strategy in which the virtual warp size is calculated and set at runtime depending on the workload and work-item characteristics (i.e., size and number). At each iteration, the right size is chosen among a set of possible values, which spans from 1 to the maximum warp size (i.e., 32 threads for NVIDIA GPUs, 64 for AMD GPUs). For performance reasons, the range is reduced to a power of two values only. Considering that a virtual warp size equal to one has the drawbacks of the *work-item to thread* technique and that memory coalescence increases proportionally with the virtual warp size (see Section 5.1.2), sizes that are too small are excluded from the range a priori. The dynamic virtual warp strategy provides a fair balancing in irregular workloads. Nevertheless, it is inefficient in cases of few and very large work-items (e.g., in datasets representing scale-free networks or graphs with power-law distribution in general).

On the other hand, dynamic parallelism, which exploits the most advanced features of the GPU architectures (e.g., from NVIDIA Kepler on) [30], allows recursion to be implemented in the kernels and thus threads and thread blocks to be dynamically created and properly configured at runtime without requiring kernel returns. This approach allows fully addressing the work-item irregularity. Nevertheless, the overhead introduced by the dynamic kernel stack may override this feature's advantages if it is replicated unconditionally for all the work-items [15].

To overcome these limitations, dynamic virtual warps and dynamic parallelism are combined into a single mapping strategy and applied alternatively at runtime. The strategy applies dynamic parallelism to the work-items having size greater than a threshold, and it applies dynamic virtual warps to the others. It applies best to applications with few and strongly unbalanced work-items that may vary at runtime (e.g., applications for sparse graph traversal). This technique guarantees load balancing among threads of the same warps and among warps. It does not guarantee balancing among blocks.

5.2.2 CTA + warp + scan

In the context of graph traversal, Merrill et al. [16] proposed an alternative approach to the load balancing problem. Their algorithm consists of three steps:

1. All threads of a block access the corresponding work-item (through the work-item to thread strategy) and calculate the item sizes. The work-items with sizes greater than a threshold (CTA_{TH}) are nondeterministically ordered, and are one at a time (i) copied in the shared memory, and (ii) processed by all the threads of the block (called cooperative thread array [CTA]). The algorithm (see Algorithm 9) for such a first step, which is called *strip-mined gathering*) is run by each thread (Th_{ID}).

ALGORITHM 9 STRIP-MINED GATHERING ALGORITHM

```
1:    while any(Workloads[ThID] > CTATH) do
2:        if Workloads[ThID] > CTATH then
3:            SharedWinnerID = ThID
4:        sync
5:        if ThID = SharedWinnerID then
6:            SharedStart = prefixsum[ThID]
7:            SharedEnd = prefixsum[ThID + 1]
8:    end
```

```
 9:        sync
10:        INIT = SharedStart + Th_ID % |Th_SET|
11:        for i = INIT to SharedEnd do
12:            Output[i] = SharedWinnerID
13:            i = i + |Th_SET|
14:        end
15:    end
```

In the pseudocode, row 3 implements the nondeterministic ordering (based on iterative match/winning among threads), rows 5–8 calculate information on the work-item to be copied in shared memory, while rows 10–14 implement the item partitioning for the CTA. This phase introduces sensible overhead for the two CTA synchronizations, and rows 5–8 are run by one thread only.

2. In the second step, the strip-mined gathering is run with a lower threshold ($Warp_{TH}$) and at warp level. That is, it targets smaller work-items, and a cooperative thread array consists of threads of the same warp. This allows avoiding any synchronization among threads (as they are implicitly synchronized in SIMD—like fashion in the warp) and addressing work-items with sizes proportional to the warp size.

3. In the third step, the remaining *work-items* are processed by all block threads. The algorithm computes a block-wide *prefix-sum* on the work-items and stores the resulting prefix-sum array in the shared memory. Finally, all threads of the block have use of such an array in order to access the corresponding work-unit. If the array size exceeds the shared memory space, the algorithm iterates.

This strategy provides a perfect balancing among threads and warps. On the other hand, the strip-mined gathering procedure run at each iteration introduces a enough overhead to slow down an application's performance in the case of quite regular workloads. The strategy works well only in cases of very irregular workloads.

5.3 DYNAMIC MAPPING TECHNIQUES

Contrary to *static mapping*, the *dynamic mapping* approaches achieve perfect workload partition and balancing among threads at the cost of additional computation at runtime. The core of such a computation is the binary search over the prefix-sum array. The binary search aims at mapping work-units to the corresponding threads.

5.3.1 Direct search

Given the *exclusive prefix-sum* array of the work-unit addresses stored in global memory, each thread performs a binary search over the array to find the corresponding *work-item* index. This technique provides perfect balancing among threads (i.e., one work-unit is mapped to one thread), warps, and blocks of threads. Nevertheless, the large size of the prefix-sum array involves an arithmetic-intensive computation (i.e., *#threads × binarysearch()*) and all the accesses performed by the threads to solve the mapping very scattered. This often eludes the benefit of the provided perfect balancing.

5.3.2 Local warp search

To reduce both the binary search computation and the scattered accesses to the global memory, this technique first loads chunks of the prefix-sum array from the global memory to the shared memory. Each chunk consists of 32 elements, which are loaded by 32 warp threads through a coalesced memory access. Then each thread of the warp performs a lightweight binary search (i.e., maximum $\log_2 32$ steps) over the corresponding chunk in the shared memory.

In the context of graph traversal, this approach was further improved by exploiting data locality in registers [15]. Instead of working on shared memory, each warp thread stores the workload offsets in their own registers and then performs a binary search by using *Kepler* warp-shuffle instructions [30].

In general, the local warp search strategy provides a very fast work-units to threads mapping and guarantees coalesced accesses to both the prefix-sum array and the work-units in global memory. On the other hand, since the sum of work units included in each chunk of the prefix-sum array is greater than the warp size, the binary search on the shared memory (or registers for the enhanced version for Kepler) is repeated until all work-units are processed. This leads to more work-units being mapped to the same thread. Indeed, although this technique guarantees a fair balancing among threads of the same warp, it suffers from a work unbalance between different warps since the sum of work-units for each warp cannot be uniform in general. For the same reason, it does not guarantee balancing among blocks of threads.

5.3.3 Block search

To deal with the local warp search limitations, Davidson et al. [60] introduced the block search strategy through *cooperative blocks*. Instead of warps performing 32-element loads, in this strategy each block of threads loads a *maxi chunk* of prefix-sum elements from the global to the shared memory, where the maxi chunk is as large as the available space in shared memory for the block. The maxi chunk size is equal for all the blocks. Each maxi chunk is then partitioned by considering the amount of work-units included and the number of threads per block. Finally, each block thread performs only one binary search to find the corresponding slot. With the block search strategy, all the units included in a slot are mapped to the same thread. This leads to several advantages. First, all the threads of a block are perfectly balanced. The binary searches are performed in shared memory, and the overall amount of searches is sensibly reduced (i.e., they are equal to the block size). Nevertheless, this strategy does not guarantee balancing among different blocks. This is due to the fact that the maxi chunk size is equal for all the blocks, but the chunks can include a different amount of work-units. In addition, this strategy does not guarantee memory coalescing among threads when they access the assigned work-units. Finally, this strategy cannot exploit advanced features for intrawarp communication and synchronization among threads, for example, warp shuffle instructions.

5.3.4 Two-phase search

Davidson et al. [60], Green et al. [61], and Baxter [62] proposed three equivalent methods to deal with the interblock load unbalancing. All the methods rely on two phases: *partitioning* and *expansion*.

First, the whole prefix-sum array is partitioned into *balanced* chunks, that is, chunks that point to the same amount of work-units. Such an amount is fixed as the biggest multiple of the block size that fits in the shared memory. As an example, in blocks of 128 threads with 2 prefix-sum chunks pointing to $128 \times K$ units and 1300 slots in shared memory, K is set to 10. The chunk size may differ among blocks. The partition array, which aims at mapping all the threads of a block into the same chunk, is built as follows. One thread per block runs a binary search on the whole prefix-sum array in global memory by using its own global id times the block size ($TH_{global_{id}} \times blocksize$). This allows for finding the chunk boundaries. The number of binary searches in global memory for this phase is equal to the number of blocks. The new partition array, which contains all the chunk boundaries, is stored in global memory.

In the expansion phase, all the threads of each block load the corresponding chunks into the shared memory (similarly to the dynamic techniques presented in the previous paragraphs). Then each thread of each block runs a binary search in such a local partition to get the (first) assigned work-unit. Each thread sequentially accesses all the assigned work units in global memory. The number of binary searches for the second step is equal to the block size. Fig. 10 shows an example of an expansion phase, in which three threads (t_0, t_1, and t_2) of the same warp access the local chunk of a prefix-sum array to get the corresponding starting point of the assigned work-unit. Then they sequentially access the corresponding K assigned units ($A_1 - D_1$ for t_0, $D_2 - F_2$ for t_1, etc.) in global memory.

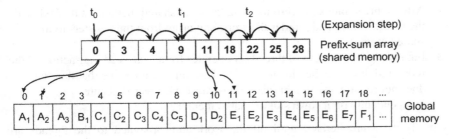

FIG. 10

Example of expansion phase in the two-phase strategy (10 work-units per thread).

In conclusion, the two-phase search strategy allows the workload among threads, warps, and blocks to be perfectly balanced at the cost of two series of binary searches. The first is run in global memory for the partitioning phase, while the second, which most affects the overall performance, is run in shared memory for the expansion phase.

The number of binary searches for partitioning is proportional to the K parameter. High values of K involve fewer and bigger chunks to be partitioned and consequently fewer steps for each binary search. Nevertheless, the main problem of such a dynamic mapping technique is that the partitioning phase leads to very scattered memory accesses of the threads to the corresponding work-units (see bottom of Fig. 10). Such a problem worsens by increasing the K value.

5.4 THE MULTIPHASE SEARCH TECHNIQUE

As an improvement of the dynamic load balancing techniques just presented, Ref. [65] proposes the *multiphase mapping* strategy, which aims at exploiting the balancing advantages of the two-phase algorithms while overcoming the limitations concerning the scattered memory accesses. This technique consists of two main contributions: coalesced expansion and iterated search.

5.5 COALESCED EXPANSION

The expansion phase consists of three subphases, by which the scattered accesses of threads to the global memory are reorganized into coalesced transactions. This is done in shared memory and by taking advantage of local registers. The technique works for both reading and writing accesses to the global memory as does the two-phase approach. For the sake of clarity, we consider *writing* accesses in the following steps:

1. Instead of sequentially writing on the work-units in global memory, each thread sequentially writes a small amount of work-units in the local registers. Fig. 11 shows an example. The amount of units is limited by the available number of free registers.
2. After a thread block synchronization, the local shared memory is flushed, and the threads move and reorder the work-unit array from the registers to the shared memory.
3. Finally, the entire warp of threads cooperates for a coalesced transaction of the reordered data into the global memory. It is important to note that this step does not require any synchronization because each warp executes independently on its own slot of shared memory.

Steps 2 and 3 are iterated until all the work-units assigned to the threads are processed. Even though these steps involve some extra computations with respect to the direct writings, the achieved coalesced accesses in global memory significantly improve the overall performance.

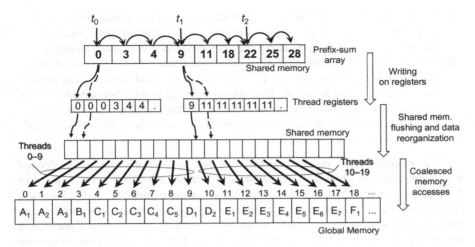

FIG. 11

Overview of the *coalesced expansion* optimization (10 work-units per thread).

5.6 ITERATED SEARCHES

The shared memory size and the size of thread blocks play an important role in the coalesced expansion phase. The bigger the block size, the shorter the partition array stored in shared memory. On the other hand, the bigger the block size, the greater the synchronization overhead among the block warps, and the more the binary search steps performed by each thread (see final considerations of the two-phase search in Section 5.3.4).

In particular, the overhead introduced to synchronize the threads after the writing on registers (see Step 1 of coalesced expansion) is the bottleneck of the expansion phase (each register writing step requires two barriers of thread). The iterated search optimization aims at reducing such an overhead as follows:

1. In the partition phase, the prefix-sum array is partitioned into balanced chunks. Differently from the two-phase search strategy, the size of such chunks is fixed as a multiple of the available space in shared memory as

$$Chunk_{size} = Block_{size} \times K \times IS$$

   where $Block_{size} \times K$ represents the biggest number of work-units (i.e., a multiple of the block size) that fit in shared memory (as in the two-phase algorithm), while IS represents the *iteration factor*. The number of threads required in this step decreases linearly with IS.
2. Each block of threads loads from global to shared memory a chunk of the prefix-sum, performs the function initialization, and synchronizes all threads.
3. Each thread of a block performs IS binary searches on such an extended chunk.

4. Each thread starts with the first step of the coalesced expansion, that is, it sequentially writes an amount of work-units in the local registers. Such an amount is equal to *IS* times larger than in the standard two-phase strategy.

5. The local shared memory is flushed, and each thread moves a portion of the extended work-unit array from the registers to the shared memory. The portion size is equal to $Block_{size} \times K$. Then the entire warp of threads cooperates for a coalesced transaction of the reordered data into the global memory, as in the coalesced expansion phase. This step iterates *IS* times, until all the data stored in the registers have been processed.

With respect to the standard partitioning and expansion strategy, the iterated search optimization reduces the number of synchronization points by a factor of $2 * IS$, avoids many block initializations, decreases the number of required threads, and maximizes the shared memory utilization during the loading of the prefix-sum values with many large consecutive intervals. Nevertheless, the required number of registers grows proportionally to the *IS* parameter. Considering that the maximum number of registers per thread is a fixed constraint for any GPU device (e.g., 32 for NVIDIA Kepler devices) and that exceeding such a constraint causes data to be *spilled* in L1 cache and then in L2 cache or global memory, values of *IS* that are too high may compromise the overall performance of the proposed approach.

Figs. 12–15 summarize and compare the performance of each technique over different graphs, each one having very different characteristics and structures. The results obtained with the *direct search* and *block search* techniques are much worse than the other techniques and, for the sake of clarity, are not reported in the figures.

In the first benchmark (Fig. 12), as expected, *work-items to threads* is the most efficient balancing technique. This is due to the very regular workload and the small

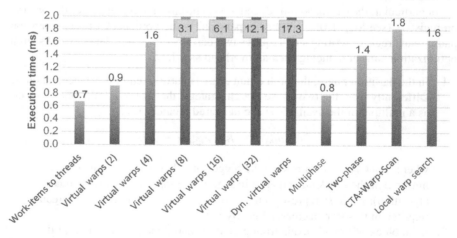

FIG. 12

Comparison of execution time on the great-britain_osm dataset.

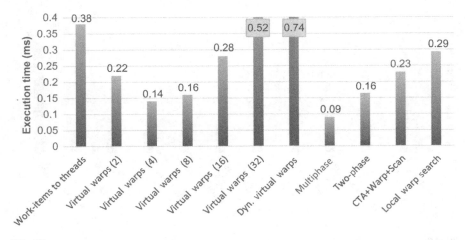

FIG. 13

Comparison of execution time on the web-NotreDame dataset.

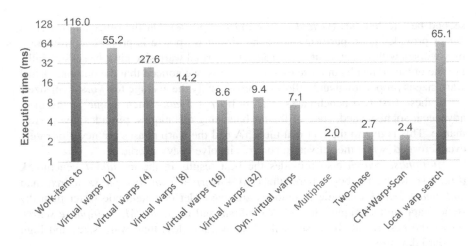

FIG. 14

Comparison of execution time on the Circuit5M dataset.

average work-item size. In this benchmark, any overhead for the dynamic item-to-thread mapping may compromise the overall algorithm performance. However, *multiphase search* is the second most efficient technique. This underlines the reduced overhead introduced by such a dynamic technique, which also applies well in cases of very regular workloads.

In the *web-NotreDame* benchmark (Fig. 13), *multiphase search* is the most efficient technique and provides almost twice the performance with respect to the

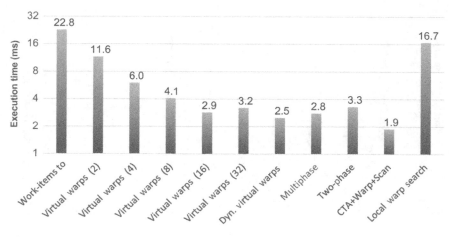

FIG. 15

Comparison of execution time on the kron_g500-logn20.

second best techniques (*virtual warps* and *two-phase*). On the other hand, *virtual warps* provides good performance if the virtual warp size is properly set, while it may worsen with sizes that are set wrong. The virtual warp size must be set statically. For the obtained results in these two benchmarks, we noticed that the optimal virtual warp size is proportional and follows approximately the average for work-item sizes.

In these first two benchmarks, *CTA + Warp + Scan*, which is one of the most advanced, sophisticated, state-of-the-art balancing techniques, provides low performance. This is due to the fact that the CTA and the warp phases are never or rarely ever activated, while the activation controls involve heavy overhead.

Multiphase search also provides the best results in the *circuit5M* benchmark (Fig. 14). In such a benchmark, the *CTA + Warp + Scan*, *two-phase search*, and *multiphase search* dynamic techniques are one order of magnitude faster than the static-mapping techniques. In *web-Notredame* and in *circuit5M*, *multiphase search* shows the best results because of the low average (less than warp size) and high standard deviation.

In the last benchmark, *kron_g500-logn20* (Fig. 15), *CTA + Warp + Scan* provides the best results because the CTA and warp phases are frequently activated and exploited. However, the performance of *multiphase* is comparable. *Dynamic virtual warps* and *virtual warps* provide a similar performance. Indeed, these two techniques are very efficient on high-average datasets because, with a thread group size of 32, they completely avoid the warp divergence. Finally, the *dynamic parallelism* feature provided by Kepler, implemented in the corresponding semidynamic technique, is the best application only when the work-item sizes and their average are very large. In any case, in all the analyzed data sets, all the dynamic load balancing techniques, and in particular the *multiphase search*, performed better without such a feature.

REFERENCES

[1] T. Cormen, C. Leiserson, R. Rivest, C. Stein, Introduction to Algorithms, MIT Press, Cambridge, MA, 2009.

[2] R. Sedgewick, K. Wayne, Algorithms 4th Edition, Addison-Wesley, Boston, MA, 2011.

[3] G. Venkataraman, S. Sahni, S. Mukhopadhyaya, A blocked all-pairs shortest-paths algorithm, J. Exp. Algorithmics 8 (2003) 2–2.

[4] G.J. Katz, J.T. Kider Jr, All-pairs shortest-paths for large graphs on the GPU, in: Proceedings of the 23rd ACM SIGGRAPH/EUROGRAPHICS Symposium on Graphics hardware, Eurographics Association, 2008, pp. 47–55.

[5] B. Lund, J.W. Smith, A multi-stage CUDA kernel for Floyd-Warshall, CoRRabs/1001.4108, (2010).

[6] A. Buluç, J.R. Gilbert, C. Budak, Solving path problems on the GPU, Parallel Comput. 36 (5) (2010) 241–253.

[7] K. Matsumoto, N. Nakasato, S.G. Sedukhin, Blocked all-pairs shortest paths algorithm for hybrid CPU-GPU system, in: 2011 IEEE 13th International Conference on High Performance Computing and Communications (HPCC), IEEE, 2011, pp. 145–152.

[8] H. Djidjev, S. Thulasidasan, G. Chapuis, R. Andonov, D. Lavenier, Efficient multi-GPU computation of all-pairs shortest paths, in: 2014 IEEE 28th International Parallel and Distributed Processing Symposium, IEEE, 2014, pp. 360–369.

[9] Q.-N. Tran, Designing efficient many-core parallel algorithms for all-pairs shortest-paths using CUDA, in: 2010 Seventh International Conference on Information Technology: New Generations (ITNG), IEEE, 2010, pp. 7–12.

[10] CUDA NVIDIA, CUDA API Reference Manual, 2015.

[11] N. Bell, M. Garland, Efficient sparse matrix-vector multiplication on CUDA, NVIDIA Technical Report NVR-2008-004, NVIDIA Corporation, 2008.

[12] N. Bell, M. Garland, Implementing sparse matrix-vector multiplication on throughput-oriented processors, in: Proceedings of the Conference on High Performance Computing Networking, Storage and Analysis, ACM, 2009, p. 18.

[13] CUDA NVIDIA, NVIDIA CUDA C Programming Guide, 2015.

[14] P. Harish, P.J. Narayanan, Accelerating large graph algorithms on the GPU using CUDA, in: High Performance Computing-HiPC 2007, Springer, 2007, pp. 197–208.

[15] F. Busato, N. Bombieri, BFS-4K: an efficient implementation of BFS for Kepler GPU architectures, IEEE Trans. Parallel Distrib. Syst. 26 (7) (2015) 1826–1838.

[16] D. Merrill, M. Garland, A. Grimshaw, Scalable GPU graph traversal, in: Proceedings of the 17th ACM SIGPLAN Symposium on Principles and Practice of Parallel Programming, PPoPP '12, 2012, pp. 117–128.

[17] L. Luo, M. Wong, W.-M. Hwu, An effective GPU implementation of breadth-first search, in: Proceedings of the 47th Design Automation Conference, DAC '10, 2010, pp. 52–55.

[18] S. Hong, S.K. Kim, T. Oguntebi, K. Olukotun, Accelerating CUDA graph algorithms at maximum warp, in: Proceedings of the 16th ACM Symposium on Principles and Practice of Parallel Programming, PPoPP '11, 2011, pp. 267–276.

[19] H.-V. Dang, B. Schmidt, The sliced COO format for sparse matrix-vector multiplication on CUDA-enabled GPUS, Procedia Comput. Sci. 9 (2012) 57–66.

[20] J. Siegel, J. Ributzka, X. Li, CUDA memory optimizations for large data-structures in the Gravit simulator, J. Algorithms Comput. Technol. 5 (2) (2011) 341–362.

[21] Y. Jia, V. Lu, J. Hoberock, M. Garland, J.C. Hart, Edge vs. Node Parallelism for Graph Centrality Metrics, GPU Computing Gems: Jade Edition, Elsevier, Waltham, MA, 2011, pp. 15–28.

[22] S. Odeh, O. Green, Z. Mwassi, O. Shmueli, Y. Birk, Merge path-parallel merging made simple, in: 2012 IEEE 26th International Parallel and Distributed Processing Symposium Workshops & PhD Forum (IPDPSW), IEEE, 2012, pp. 1611–1618.

[23] A. McLaughlin, D. Bader, et al., Revisiting edge and node parallelism for dynamic GPU graph analytics, in: Parallel & Distributed Processing Symposium Workshops (IPDPSW), 2014 IEEE International, IEEE, 2014, pp. 1396–1406.

[24] G. Singla, A. Tiwari, D.P. Singh, New approach for graph algorithms on GPU using CUDA, International Journal of Computer Applications, 72 (2013) 38–42.

[25] P. Harish, P.J. Narayanan, Accelerating large graph algorithms on the GPU using CUDA, in: Proceedings of the 14th International Conference on High Performance Computing, HiPC'07, 2007, pp. 197–208.

[26] S.M.Y. Deng, B.D. Wang, Taming irregular EDA applications on GPUs, in: Proc. of the IEEE International Conference on Computer-Aided Design (ICCAD'09), 2009, pp. 539–546.

[27] S. Xiao, W.C. Feng, Inter-block GPU communication via fast barrier synchronization, Tech. Rep., Dept. of Computer Science Virginia Tech, 2009.

[28] Y. Wang, A. Davidson, Y. Pan, Y. Wu, A. Riffel, J.D. Owens, Gunrock: a high-performance graph processing library on the GPU, in: Proceedings of the 20th ACM SIGPLAN Symposium on Principles and Practice of Parallel Programming, ACM, 2015, pp. 265–266.

[29] T. Hiragushi, D. Takahashi, Efficient hybrid breadth-first search on GPUs, in: Algorithms and Architectures for Parallel Processing, Springer, 2013 pp. 40–50.

[30] NVIDIA, Kepler GK110, www.nvidia.com/content/PDF/kepler/NV_DS_Tesla_KCompute_Arch_May_2012_LR.pdf.

[31] NVIDIA, Maxwell architecture, http://international.download.nvidia.com/geforce-com/international/pdfs/GeForce_GTX_980_Whitepaper_FINAL.PDF.

[32] Y. Dotsenko, N.K. Govindaraju, P.-P. Sloan, C. Boyd, J. Manferdelli, Fast scan algorithms on graphics processors, in: Proceedings of the 22nd Annual International Conference on Supercomputing, ICS '08, 2008, pp. 205–213.

[33] D. Merril, A. Grimshaw, Parallel scan for stream architectures, Tech. Rep. CS-200914, Department of Computer Science, University of Virginia, 2009.

[34] E.W. Dijkstra, A note on two problems in connection with graphs, Numerische Mathematik 1 (1) (1959) 269–271.

[35] R. Bellman, On a routing problem, Q. Appl. Math. 16 (1) (1958) 87–90.

[36] L.R. Ford, Network Flow Theory, Rand Corp., Santa Monica, CA, 1956.

[37] M. Burtscher, R. Nasre, K. Pingali, A quantitative study of irregular programs on GPUs, in: 2012 IEEE International Symposium on Workload Characterization (IISWC), IEEE, 2012, pp. 141–151.

[38] S. Hong, H. Kim, An integrated GPU power and performance model, in: Proceedings of the 37th Annual International Symposium on Computer Architecture, ISCA '10, 2010, pp. 280–289.

[39] A. Davidson, S. Baxter, M. Garland, J.D. Owens, Work-efficient parallel GPU methods for single-source shortest paths, in: Proceedings of the International Parallel and Distributed Processing Symposium, IPDPS, 2014, pp. 349–359.

[40] X. Zhang, F. Yan, L. Tao, D.K. Sung, Optimal candidate set for opportunistic routing in asynchronous wireless sensor networks, in: Proceedings—International Conference on Computer Communications and Networks, ICCCN, 2014, pp. 1–8.

[41] M. Saad, Joint optimal routing and power allocation for spectral efficiency in multihop wireless networks, IEEE Trans. Wireless Commun. 13 (5) (2014) 2530–2539.

[42] S. Klamt, A. von Kamp, Computing paths and cycles in biological interaction graphs, BMC Bioinformatics 10 (6) (2014) 1–11.

[43] S. Lu, P. Weston, S. Hillmansen, H.B. Gooi, C. Roberts, Increasing the regenerative braking energy for railway vehicles, IEEE Trans. Intell. Transp. Syst. 15 (181) (2009) 2506–2515.

[44] B.V. Cherkassky, A.V. Goldberg, T. Radzik, Shortest paths algorithms: theory and experimental evaluation, Math. Program. 73 (2) (1996) 129–174.

[45] F.B. Zhan, C.E. Noon, Shortest path algorithms: an evaluation using real road networks, Transp. Sci. 32 (1) (1998) 65–73.

[46] P.J. Martin, R. Torres, A. Gavilanes, CUDA solutions for the SSSP problem, in: Proceedings of the 9th International Conference on Computational Science: Part I, ICCS '09, 2009, pp. 904–913.

[47] H. Ortega-Arranz, Y. Torres, D.R. Llanos, A. Gonzalez-Escribano, A new GPU-based approach to the shortest path problem, in: Proceedings of the 2013 International Conference on High Performance Computing and Simulation, HPCS 2013, 2013, pp. 505–511.

[48] U. Meyer, P. Sanders, Δ-stepping: a parallelizable shortest path algorithm, J. Algorithms 49 (1) (2003) 114–152.

[49] J.R. Crobak, J.W. Berry, K. Madduri, D.A. Bader, Advanced shortest paths algorithms on a massively-multithreaded architecture, in: Parallel and Distributed Processing Symposium, 2007. IPDPS 2007. IEEE International, IEEE, 2007, pp. 1–8.

[50] V.T. Chakaravarthy, F. Checconi, F. Petrini, Y. Sabharwal, Scalable single source shortest path algorithms for massively parallel systems, in: Proceedings of the International Parallel and Distributed Processing Symposium, IPDPS, 2014, pp. 889–901.

[51] K. Kelley, T.B. Schardl, Parallel single-source shortest paths, MIT Computer Science and Artificial Intelligence Laboratory, 2010, pp. 1–7.

[52] H.N. Garbow, Scaling algorithms for network problems, J. Comput. Syst. Sci. 31 (2) (1985) 148–168.

[53] J. Shun, G.E. Blelloch, Ligra: a lightweight graph processing framework for shared memory, in: ACM SIGPLAN Notices, vol. 48, ACM, 2013, pp. 135–146.

[54] N. Edmonds, A. Breuer, D. Gregor, A. Lumsdaine, Single-source shortest paths with the parallel boost graph library, in: The Ninth DIMACS Implementation Challenge: The Shortest Path Problem, Piscataway, NJ, 2006, pp. 219–248.

[55] G. Malewicz, M.H. Austern, A.J.C. Bik, J.C. Dehnert, I. Horn, N. Leiser, G. Czajkowski, Pregel: a system for large-scale graph processing, in: Proceedings of the 2010 ACM SIGMOD International Conference on Management of data, ACM, 2010, pp. 135–146.

[56] E. Deelman, G. Singh, M.-H. Su, J. Blythe, Y. Gil, C. Kesselman, G. Mehta, K. Vahi, G.B. Berriman, J. Good, et al., Pegasus: a framework for mapping complex scientific workflows onto distributed systems, Sci. Program. 13 (3) (2005) 219–237.

[57] F. Busato, N. Bombieri, An efficient implementation of the Bellman-Ford algorithm for Kepler GPU architectures, IEEE Trans. Parallel Distrib. Syst. PP (99) (2015) 1–13.

[58] H. Ortega-Arranz, Y. Torres, D.R. Llanos, A. Gonzalez-Escribano, A tuned, concurrent-kernel approach to speed up the APSP problem, in: Proc. 13th Int. Conf. Comput. Math. Methods Sci. Eng.(CMMSE), Citeseer, 2013, pp. 1114–1125.

[59] P. Harish, V. Vineet, P.J. Narayanan, Large graph algorithms for massively multithreaded architectures, International Institute of Information Technology Hyderabad, Tech. Rep. IIIT/TR/2009/74, 2009.

[60] A. Davidson, S. Baxter, M. Garland, J.D. Owens, Work-efficient parallel GPU methods for single-source shortest paths, in: 2014 IEEE 28th International Parallel and Distributed Processing Symposium, IEEE, 2014, pp. 349–359.

[61] O. Green, R. McColl, D.A. Bader, GPU merge path: a GPU merging algorithm, in: Proceedings of the 26th ACM international conference on Supercomputing, ACM, 2012, pp. 331–340.

[62] Modern GPU Library, http://nvlabs.github.io/moderngpu/.

[63] K. Xu, Y. Wang, F. Wang, Y. Liao, Q. Zhang, H. Li, X. Zheng, Neural decoding using a parallel sequential Monte Carlo method on point processes with ensemble effect, BioMed Res. Int. 2014 (2014) 0–11.

[64] C. Yang, Y. Wang, J.D. Owens, Fast sparse matrix and sparse vector multiplication algorithm on the GPU, IPDPSW (2015).

[65] F. Busato, N. Bombieri, On the load balancing techniques for GPU applications based on prefix-scan, in: 2015 IEEE 9th International Symposium on Embedded Multicore/Many-core Systems-on-Chip (MCSoC), IEEE, 2015, pp. 88–95.

GPU alignment of two and three sequences

8

J. Li, S. Ranka, S. Sahni

University of Florida, Gainesville, FL, United States

1 INTRODUCTION

1.1 PAIRWISE ALIGNMENT

Sequence alignment is a fundamental bioinformatics problem. Algorithms for both *pairwise alignment* (ie, the alignment of two sequences) and the alignment of three sequences have been intensely researched deeply. In pairwise sequence alignment, we are given two sequences A and B and are to find their best alignment (either global or local). For DNA sequences, the alphabet for A and B is the 4 letter set $\{A, C, G, T\}$ and for protein sequences, the alphabet is the 20 letter set $\{A, C-I, K-N, P-T, VWY\}$. The best global and local alignments of the sequences A and B can be found in $O(|A| * |B|)$ time using the Needleman-Wunsch [1] and Smith-Waterman [2] dynamic programming algorithms. In this work, we consider only the local alignment problem, though our methods are readily extendable to the global alignment problem.

A variant of the pairwise sequence alignment problem asks for the best k, $k > 0$, alignments. In the *database alignment problem*, we are to find the best k alignments of a sequence A with the sequences in a database D. The database alignment problem can be solved by solving $|D|$ pairwise alignment problems with each pair comprising A and a distinct sequence from D. This solution requires $|D|$ applications of the Smith-Waterman algorithm.

When the sequences A and B are long or when the number of sequences in the database D is large, computational efficiency is often achieved by replacing the Smith-Waterman algorithm with a heuristic that trades accuracy for computational time. This is done, for example in the sequence alignment systems BLAST [3], FASTA [4], and Sim2 [5]. However, with the advent of low-cost parallel computers, there is renewed interest in developing computationally practical systems that do not sacrifice accuracy. Toward this end, several researchers have developed parallel versions of the Smith-Waterman algorithm that are suitable for graphics processing units (GPUs) [6–11]. The work of Khajej-Saeed et al. [9], Sriwardena and Ranasinghe [10], and Li et al. [12] is of particular relevance to us as this work specifically targets the alignment of two very long sequences, while the remaining research on GPU algorithms for sequence alignment focuses on the database alignment problem, and the developed algorithms and software are unable to handle very large sequences. For example, $CUDASW++2.0$ [8] cannot handle strings whose length is more than 70,000 on NVIDIA Tesla C2050 GPU.

As noted in Ref. [9], biological applications often have $|A|$ in the range 10^4 to 10^5 and $|B|$ in the range 10^7 to 10^{10}. We refer to instances of this size as very large. Ref. [9] modified the Smith-Waterman dynamic programming equations to obtain a set of equations that were more amenable to parallel implementation. However, this modification introduced significant computational overhead. Despite this overhead, their algorithm was able to achieve a computational rate of up to 0.7 GCUPS (billion cell updates per second) using a single NVIDIA Tesla C2050. The instance sizes they experimented with had $|A| * |B|$ up to 10^{11}. Although Ref. [10] developed their GPU algorithms for pairwise sequence alignment specifically for the global alignment version, their algorithms are easily adapted to the case of local alignment. While their adaptations do not have the overheads of those of Ref. [9] that result from modifying the recurrence equations so as to increase parallelism, their algorithm is slower than that of Ref. [9]. The pairwise sequence alignment algorithms developed by Ref. [12] are currently the fastest GPU algorithms for very long sequences. We elaborate on these later in this chapter and benchmark these algorithms against those of Refs. [9,10].

1.2 ALIGNMENT OF THREE SEQUENCES

In the three-sequence alignment problem, we are given three sequences, S_0, S_1, and S_2. We are to insert gaps into the sequences so that the resulting sequences are of the same length; in the resulting sequences, each character is said to be aligned with the gap or character in the corresponding position in each of the other sequences; and the alignment score is maximized. On a single-core CPU, the best alignment of the given three sequences (ie, the one with maximum score) can be found in $O(|S_0| * |S_1| * |S_3|)$ time using dynamic programming [13].

Several papers have been written on three-sequence alignment. We briefly mention a few here. Ref. [14] developed algorithms for the optimal alignment of three sequences using a constant gap weight. Ref. [15] developed algorithms to align three sequences using an affine gap penalty model. Ref. [16] reduced the memory requirement of these algorithms to be quadratic in the sequence length. Ref. [17] developed a faster three-sequence alignment algorithm using a speed-up technique based on Ukkonen's greedy algorithm [18]. Ref. [19] used a position-specific gap penalty model for three-sequence alignment. Ref. [20] proposed a divide-and-conquer algorithm for three-sequence alignment, and Ref. [21] proposed a parallel algorithm for three-sequence alignment.

Besides being of interest in its own right, three-sequence alignment has been proposed as a base step in the alignment of a larger number of sequences. For example, Ref. [22] reported improved accuracy when three-sequence alignment was used instead of pairwise sequence alignment in their progressive multiple sequence alignment program *aln3nn*. Three-sequence alignment also helps in the tree alignment problem [23].

Two GPU algorithms to align three sequences were developed by Ref. [24]. These are described later in this chapter.

2 GPU ARCHITECTURE

The GPU algorithms described later in this chapter target the NVIDIA Tesla C2050 GPU, which is also known as Fermi. The C2050 has 14 streaming multiprocessors (SMs) and each SM has 32 streaming processors (SPs) giving the C2050 a total of 448 SPs or cores. Fig. 1 shows the architecture of a C2050 SM. Although each SP of a C2050 has its own integer, single- and double-precision units, the 32 SPs of an SM share 4 single-precision transcendental function units. An SM has 64 KB of on-chip memory that can be "configured as 48 KB of shared memory with 16 KB of L1 cache (default setting) or as 16 KB of shared memory with 48 KB of L1 cache" [25]. Additionally, there are 32K 32-bit registers per SM and 3 GB of off-chip device/global memory that is shared by all 14 SMs. The peak performance of a C2050 is 1288 GFlops (or 1.288 TFlops) of single-precision operations, and 515 GFlops of double-precision operations and the power consumption is 238 W [26]. Once again, the peak of 1288 GFlops requires that MADDs and SF instructions be dual-issued. When there are MADDs alone, the peak single-precision rate is 1.03 GFlops.

In NVIDIA parlance, the compute capability of the C2050 is 2.0. The key challenge in deriving high performance on CUDA GPUs is to be able to effectively minimize the memory traffic between the SMs and the global memory of the GPU. Data that is used repeatedly should go to registers or shared memory, while data that is used less frequently but of larger size should go to device memory.

3 PAIRWISE ALIGNMENT

In this section, we describe the single-GPU parallelizations of the unmodified Smith-Waterman algorithm that were originally developed by us in Ref. [12]. These obtain a speedup of up to 17 relative to the single-GPU algorithm of Ref. [9] and a computational rate of 7.1 GCUPS. Our high-level parallelization strategy is similar to that used by Ref. [28,29] to arrive at parallel algorithms for local alignment and syntenic alignment on a cluster of workstations, respectively. Both divide the scoring matrix into as many strips as there are processors, and each processor computes the scoring matrix for its strip row wise. Ref. [28] did the traceback needed to determine the actual alignment serially using a single processor, while Ref. [29] did the traceback in parallel using a strategy similar to the one we used. The essential differences between our work and that of Refs. [28,29] are (a) our algorithms are optimized for a GPU rather than for a cluster, (b) we divide the scoring matrix into many more strips than

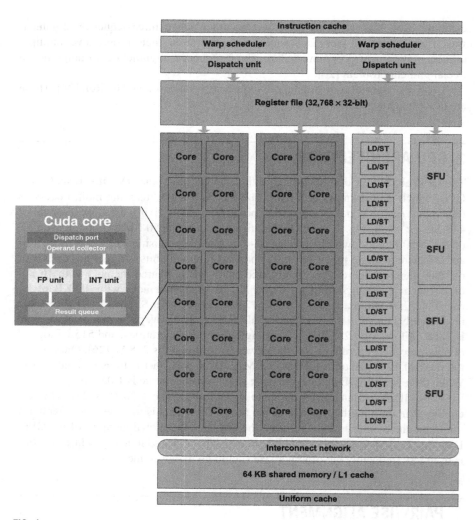

FIG. 1

Architecture of one SM of the NVIDIA Fermi [27].

the number of SMs in a GPU, and (c) the computation of a strip is done in parallel using many threads and the CUDA cores of an SM rather than serially.

3.1 SMITH-WATERMAN ALGORITHM

Let $A = a_1 a_2 \ldots a_m$ and $B = b_1 b_2 \ldots b_n$ be the two sequences that are to be locally aligned. Let $c(a_i, b_j)$ be the score for matching or aligning a_i and b_j, and let α

be the gap opening penalty and β the gap extension penalty. So the penalty for a gap of length k is $\alpha + k\beta$. Gotoh's [30] variant of the Smith-Waterman dynamic programming algorithm with an affine penalty function uses the following three recurrences:

$$H(i,j) = \max \begin{cases} H(i-1,j-1) + c(a_i, b_j) \\ E(i,j) \\ F(i,j) \\ 0 \end{cases}$$

$$E(i,j) = \max \begin{cases} E(i-1,j) - \beta \\ H(i-1,j) - \alpha - \beta \end{cases}$$

$$F(i,j) = \max \begin{cases} F(i,j-1) - \beta \\ H(i,j-1) - \alpha - \beta \end{cases}$$

$$\text{where } 1 \le i \le m, \ \ 1 \le j \le n$$

Here the score matrices H, E, and F have the following meaning:

1. $H(i,j)$ is the score of the best local alignment for $(a_1 \ldots a_i)$ and $(b_1 \ldots b_j)$.
2. $E(i,j)$ is the score of the best local alignment for $(a_1 \ldots a_i)$ and $(b_1 \ldots b_j)$ under the constraint that a_i is aligned to a gap.
3. $F(i,j)$ is the score of the best local alignment for $(a_1 \ldots a_i)$ and $(b_1 \ldots b_j)$ under the constraint that b_j is aligned to a gap.

The initial conditions are $H(0,0) = H(i,0) = H(0,j) = 0$; $E(0,0) = -\infty$; $E(i,0) = -\alpha - i\beta$; $E(0,j) = -\infty$; $F(0,0) = -\infty$; $F(i,0) = -\infty$; $F(0,j) = -\alpha - j\beta$; $1 \le i \le m$, $1 \le j \le n$. The pseudocode is shown in Algorithm 1.

ALGORITHM 1 SMITH-WATERMAN ALGORITHM

```
 1: function PAIRWISEALIGN(s1, s2)
 2:     score ← 0
 3:     m ← length of s1
 4:     n ← length of s2
 5:     H, E, F ← matrices of size (m + 1) * (n + 1)
 6:     H[0][0] ← 0
 7:     E[0][0] ← −∞
 8:     F[0][0] ← −∞
 9:     for i = 1 to m do
10:         H[i][0] ← 0
11:         E[i][0] ← −α − i * β
12:         F[i][0] ← −∞
13:     end for
14:     for i = 1 to n do
15:         H[0][i] ← 0
16:         E[0][i] ← −∞
17:         F[0][i] ← −α − i * β
```

```
18:        end for
19:      for i = 1 to m do
20:         for j = 1 to n do
21:             c ← substitution_score(s1[i − 1], s2[j − 1])
22:             newF ← max(H[i][j − 1] − α, F[i][j − 1] − β)
23:             newE ← max(H[i − 1][j] − α, E[i − 1][j] − β)
24:             newH ← max(max(H[i − 1][j − 1] + c, newE), max(newF, 0))
25:             E[i][j] ← newE
26:             F[i][j] ← newF
27:             H[i][j] ← newH
28:             score ← max(score, newH)
29:         end for
30:      end for
31:      return score
32: end function
```

As mentioned in the introduction, the GPU adaptations of Refs. [9,10] are most suited for the pairwise alignment of very long sequences. Ref. [9] enhanced parallelism by rewriting the recurrence equations. This rewrite eliminated the E terms and so their algorithm initially computed H values that differ from those computed by the original set of equations. Let H' be the computed H values. In a follow-up step, modified E values, E', were computed. The correct H values were then computed in a final step from H' and E'. Although the resulting three-step computation increased parallelism, it also increased I/O traffic between device memory and the SMs.

Ref. [10] proposed two GPU algorithms for global alignment using the Needleman-Wunsch dynamic programming algorithm [1]. These strategies can be readily deployed for local alignment using Gotoh's variant of the Smith-Waterman algorithm. Both of the strategies of Ref. [10] are based on the observation that for any (i,j), the H, E, and F values depend only on values in the positions immediately to the north, northwest, and west of (i,j) (Fig. 2). Consequently, it is possible to compute all H, E, and F values on the same antidiagonal, in parallel, once these values have been computed for the preceding two antidiagonals. The first algorithm, *Antidiagonal*, of Ref. [10] does precisely this. The GPU kernel computes H, E, and F values on a single antidiagonal using values stored in device/global memory for the preceding two antidiagonals. The host program sends the two strings A and B to device memory and then invokes the GPU kernel once for each of the $m + n - 1$ antidiagonals. Additional (but minor) speedup can be attained by recognizing that the computation for the first and last few antidiagonals can be done faster on the host CPU and invoking the GPU kernel only for sufficiently large antidiagonals. When we want to determine the score of only the best alignment, the device memory needed by *Antidiagonal* is $O(\min\{m, n\})$. However, when the best alignment also is to be reported, we need to save, for each (i,j), the direction (north, northwest, west) and the scoring matrices (H, E, F) that yielded the values for this position. $O(mn)$ memory is required to save this information. Following the

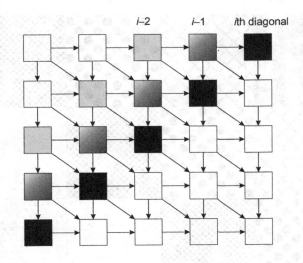

FIG. 2

Data dependency of Smith-Waterman algorithm.

computation of the H, E, and F values, a serial traceback is done to determine the best alignment.

The second GPU algorithm, *BlockedAntidiagonal*, of Ref. [10] partitions the H, E, and F values into $s \times s$ square blocks (Fig. 3) and employs a GPU kernel to compute the values for a block. The host program allocates blocks to SMs, and each SM computes the H, E, and F values for its assigned block using values computed earlier and stored in device memory for the blocks immediately to its north, northwest, and west. Hence *BlockedAntidiagonal* attempts to enhance performance by utilizing both block-level parallelism and parallelism within an antidiagonal of a block. More importantly, it seeks to reduce I/O traffic to device memory and to utilize shared memory. Notice that device I/O is now needed only at the start and end of a block computation. The block assignment strategy of Fig. 3 does the computation in blocked antidiagonal order with the host invoking the kernel for all blocks on the same antidiagonal. The total number of blocks is $O(mn/s^2)$, and the I/O traffic between global memory and the SMs is $O(mn)$. In contrast, the I/O traffic for *Antidiagonal* is $O(mn)$. Experimental results reported in Ref. [10] demonstrate that *BlockedAntidiagonal* is roughly two times faster than *Antidiagonal*. Their research shows that *BlockedAntidiagonal* exhibits near-optimal performance when the block size s is 8. The *BlockedAntidiagonal* strategy of Fig. 3 may be enhanced for the case when we are interested only in the score of the best alignment. In this enhancement, we write to global memory only the computed values for the bottom and right boundaries of each block. This reduces the global memory I/O traffic to $O(mn/s)$.

FIG. 3

Illustration of *BlockedAntidiagonal*.

3.2 COMPUTING THE SCORE OF THE BEST LOCAL ALIGNMENT

In our GPU adaptation, *StripedScore*, of the Smith-Waterman algorithm, we assume that $m \leq n$ (in case this is not so, simply swap the roles of A and B) and partition the scoring matrices H, E, and F into $\lceil n/s \rceil$ $m \times s$ strips (Fig. 4). Here s is the strip width. Let p be the number of SMs in the GPU (for the C2050, $p = 14$). The GPU kernel is written so that SM i computes the H, E, and F values for all strips j such that j mod $p = i$, $0 \leq j < \lceil n/s \rceil$, $0 \leq i < p$. Each SM works on its assigned strips serially from left to right. That is, if SM 0 is assigned strips 0, 14, 28, and 42 (this is the case, for example, when $q = 14$, $s = 8$, and $n = 440$), SM 0 first computes all H, E, and F values for strip 0, then for strip 14, then for strip 28, and finally for strip 42. When computing the values for a strip, the SM computes by antidiagonals confined to the strip with values along the same antidiagonal computed in parallel. The computed values for each antidiagonal are stored in shared memory. Each SM uses three one-dimensional arrays (preceding two antidiagonals and current antidiagonal) residing in shared memory and one for each of E and F and one for swapping purposes.

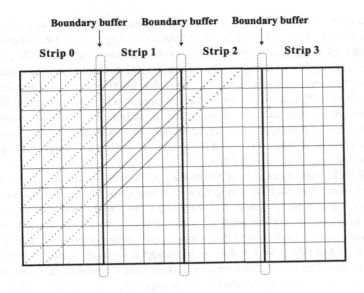

FIG. 4

Striped Smith-Waterman algorithm.

The size of each of these arrays is $O(\min\{m, s\})$. Additionally, each strip needs to communicate m H values and m F values to the strip immediately to its right. This communication is done via global memory. First, each strip accumulates, in a buffer, a threshold number, T, of H and F values needed by its right adjacent strip in shared memory. When this threshold is reached, the accumulated H and F values are written to global memory. The threshold T is chosen to optimize the total time. Each SM polls global memory to determine whether the next batch of H and F values it needs from its left adjacent strip are ready in global memory. If so, it reads this batch and computes the next T antidiagonals for its strip. If not, it waits in an idle state.

Our striped algorithm therefore requires $O(\min\{m, s\})$ shared memory per SM and $O(mn/s)$ global memory. The I/O traffic between global memory and the SMs is $O(mn/s)$. To derive the computational time requirements (exclusive of the time taken by the global memory I/O traffic), we assume that the threshold value T is $O(1)$. We note that the computation for the kth strip cannot begin until the top-right value of strip $k - 1$ has been computed. An SM with c processors takes $T_a = O(s^2/c)$ to compute the top-right value of the strip assigned to it and $O(ms/c)$ time to complete the computation for the entire strip. So SM $p - 1$ cannot start working on the first strip assigned to it until time $(p - 1)T_a$. When an SM can go from the computation of one strip to the computation of the next strip with no delay, the completion time of SM $p - 1$, and hence the time taken by the GPU to do all its assigned work (exclusive of the time taken by global memory I/O traffic), is $O((p - 1)T_a + \frac{ms}{c} * \frac{n}{ps})$ $= O(\frac{ps^2}{c} + \frac{mn}{pc})$. When an SM takes less time to complete the computation for a strip than it takes to compute the data needed to commence on the next strip assigned to the SM (approximately, $\frac{ms}{c} < pT_a$), an SM must wait $O(pT_a - \frac{ms}{c})$ time between the computation of successive strips assigned to it. So the time at which SM p finishes is $O((\frac{n}{s} - 1)T_a + \frac{ms}{c}) = O(\frac{(m+n)s}{c})$. We see that while computation time exclusive of global I/O time increases as s increases, and global I/O time decreases as s increases. Our experiments in Section 3.4 show that for large m and n, the reduction in global I/O memory traffic that comes from increasing the strip size s more than compensates for the increase in time spent on computational tasks. Although using a larger strip size s reduces overall time, the size of the available shared memory per SM limits the value of s that may be used in practice.

In our GPU implementation of *StripedScore*, the substitution matrix is stored in the shared memory of each SM using $23 \times 23 \times size\,of(int)$ bytes. Additionally, each SM has an output buffer of length 32 for writing values on the boundary of each strip to global memory. This buffer takes $32 \times size\,of(int)$ bytes. We also use 6 arrays of length $\min\{s, m\} + 2$ each to hold the H values on 3 adjacent antidiagonals, E values and F values, and new E or F values to be swapped with old values. Another 1200 bytes are reserved by the CUDA compiler to store built-in variables and pass function parameters. The shared memory cache was configured as 48 KB shared memory and 16 KB L1 cache. So, $\min(s, m)$ should be less than 1902. Since we are aligning very large sequences, we assume $s < m$. Hence $s < 1902$ for our implementation.

The following are some of the key differences between *BlockedAntidiagonal* and *StripedScore*:

1. *BlockedAntidiagonal* requires many kernel invocations from the host, while *StripedScore* requires just one kernel invocation. In other words, the synchronization of *BlockedAntidiagonal* is done on the host side, while in *StripedScore* the synchronization is done on the device side, which significantly reduces the overhead.

2. In *BlockedAntidiagonal* the assignment of blocks that are ready for computation to SMs is done by the GPU block scheduler, while in *StripedScore* the assignment of strips to SMs is programmed into the kernel code.

3. The I/O traffic of *StripedScore* is $O(mn/s)$, while that of *BlockedAntidiagonal* is $O(mn)$.

4. While for *BlockedAntidiagonal* near-optimal performance is achieved when $s = 8$, we envision much larger s values for *StripedScore*, which can be up to 1900. Consequently, there is greater opportunity for parallelism within a strip than within a block.

The preceding steps can lead to significant improvement in the overall performance.

3.3 COMPUTING THE BEST LOCAL ALIGNMENT

In this section, we describe three GPU algorithms for the case when we want to determine both the best alignment and its score.

3.3.1 StripedAlignment

With each position (u, v) of H, E, and F, we associate a start state, which is a triple (i, j, X), where (i, j) are the coordinates of the local start point of the optimal path to (u, v). This local start point is either a position in the current strip or a position on the right boundary of the strip immediately to the left of the current strip. X is one of H, F, and E and identifies whether the optimal path to (say) $H(u, v)$ begins at $H(i, j)$, $F(i, j)$, or $E(i, j)$. *StripedAlignment* is a three-phase algorithm. The first phase is an extension of *StripedScore* in which each strip stores, in global memory, not only the H and F values needed by the strip to its right but also the local start states of the optimal path to each boundary cell. For each boundary cell (u, v), three start states (one for each of $H(u, v)$, $F(u, v)$, and $E(u, v)$) are stored. So, for the four strips of Fig. 5, the boundary cells store, in global memory, the local start states of subpaths that end at the boundary cells $(*, 4)$, $(*, 8)$, $(*, 12)$, and $(*, 16)$. Additionally, we need to store the local start state and the end state for the overall best alignment. Since the highest H score is to $(8, 9)$ and the local start state for $H(8, 9)$ is $(7, 8, H)$, $(7, 8, H)$ is initially stored in registers and finally written along with $(8, 9, H)$ to global memory. In Phase 1, the local start states for the optimal paths to all boundary cells (not just the boundary cells through which the overall alignment path traverses) are written to global memory.

In Phase 2, we serially determine, for each strip, the start state and end state of the optimal alignment subpath that goes through this strip. Suppose for our example in Fig. 5, we determine that the optimal alignment path comprises a subpath

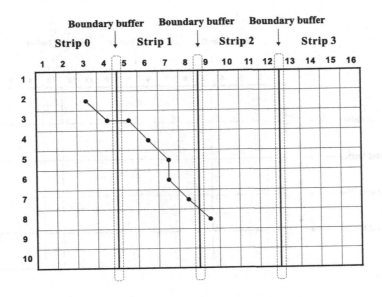

FIG. 5

Example for *StripedAlignment*.

from $(7, 8, H)$ to $(8, 9, H)$, another subpath from $(3, 4, F)$ to $(7, 8, H)$, and one from $(2, 3, H)$ to $(3, 4, F)$.

Finally, in Phase 3, the optimal subpath for each strip the optimal path goes through is computed by recomputing the H, E, and F values for the strips the optimal alignment path traverses. Using the saved boundary H and F values, it is possible to compute the subpaths for all strips in parallel.

3.3.2 ChunkedAlignment1

*ChunkedAlignment*1, like *StripedAlignment*, is a three-phase algorithm. In *ChunkedAlignment*1, each strip is partitioned into chunks of height h (Fig. 6). For each $h \times s$ chunk, we store, in global memory, the H, F, and local start states for positions on right vertical chunk boundaries (ie, vertical buffers, which are the same as boundary buffers in *StripedAlignment*) and the H and E values for horizontal buffers. The assignment of strips to SMs is the same as in *StripedScore* (and *StripedAlignment*).

In Phase 2, we use the data stored in global memory by the Phase 1 computation to determine the start and end states of the subpaths of the optimal alignment path within each strip. Finally, in Phase 3, the optimal subpaths are constructed by a computation within each strip through which the optimal alignment traverses. However, the computation with a strip can be limited to essential chunks, as shown by the shaded chunks in Fig. 6. The computation for these substrips can be done in parallel.

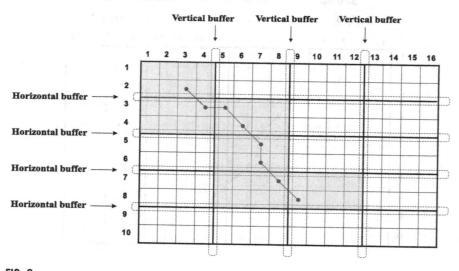

FIG. 6

Example for *ChunkedAlignment*.

There are two major differences between *StripedAlignment* and *Chunked Alignment*1:

1. *ChunkedAlignment*1 generates more I/O traffic than does *StripedAlignment* and also requires more global memory on account of storing horizontal buffer data. Assuming that the height and width of the chunk are nearly equal, the I/O traffic and the global memory requirement are roughly twice the amount for *StripedAlignment* for the same strip size as the width of the chunk.

2. Unlike *StripedAlignment*, the computation begins at the start point of a chunk rather than at the first row of the strip. In practice, this should reduce the amount of computation significantly.

3.3.3 ChunkedAlignment2

ChunkedAlignmment2 is a natural extension of *ChunkedAlignment*1. Phase 1 is modified to additionally store, for the horizontal buffers, the local start state (local to the chunk) of the optimal path that goes through that buffer. Similarly, for vertical buffers the start state local to the chunk (rather than local to the strip) is stored. In Phase 2, we use the data stored in global memory during Phase 1 to determine the chunks through which the optimal alignment path traverses as well as the start and end states of the subpath through these chunks. In Phase 3, the subpath within each chunk is computed by using data stored in Phase 1 and the knowledge of the subpath end states determined in Phase 2. As was the case for *StripedAlignment* and *ChunkedAlignment*1, the subpaths for all identified chunks can be computed in parallel.

Unlike *ChunkedAlignment*1, additional computations and I/O need to be performed in Phase 1. The advantage is that the computation for all the chunks can be performed in parallel in Phase 3. So, for a given data set, if a large number of chunks corresponding to the shortest path are present in a given strip, this work will be assigned to a single SP for *ChunkedAlignment*1 and will effectively be performed sequentially. However, these chunks can potentially be assigned to multiple SPs. For example, in Fig. 6, strip 2 has three chunks. These will be assigned to the same SP using *ChunkedAlignment*1, but can be assigned to three different SPs using *ChunkedAlignment*2. Thus the amount of parallelism available is significantly increased.

3.3.4 Memory requirements

The code of Ref. [9] to find the actual alignment stores three $m \times n$ matrices in global memory. Since each matrix element is a score, each is a 4-byte *int*, so the code of Ref. [9] needs $12mn$ bytes of global memory. The code of Ref. [10] when extended to affine cost functions also needs $12mn$ bytes of global memory. The global memory required by our methods is instance-dependent. For each position encountered in Phase 3, we store direction information for all three matrices. For H, six possibilities exist for one cell, which are *NEW* (this cell starts a new alignment), *DIAGONAL* (this cell comes from diagonal direction), *E_UP* (this cell comes from the above cell in matrix E), *H_UP* (this cell comes from the above cell in matrix H), *F_LEFT* (this cell comes from the left cell in matrix *F*), and *H_LEFT* (this cell comes from the left cell in matrix *H*). Three bits are enough to store this information for each cell. For *E*, two possibilities exist, *E_UP* and *H_UP*. One bit is enough for this information. For *F*, one bit is enough to distinguish *F_LEFT* and *H_LEFT*. So, in the worst-case scenario, *StripedAlignment* requires $5mn/8$ bytes of global memory while *ChunkedAlignment1* and *ChunkedAlignment2* require $5(ms + nh)/8$ bytes. Hence *StripedAlignment*, for example, can handle problems with an *mn* value about 19 times as large as that handled by Refs. [9,10]. Besides, when more memory space is required, Phase 3 can be split into multiple iterations. The same memory space required for one SM to compute part of the alignment within one strip can be reused in different iterations while computing for different strips.

3.4 EXPERIMENTAL RESULTS

In this section, we present experimental results for scoring and alignment, respectively. All of these experiments were conducted on a NVIDIA Tesla C2050 GPU.

StripedScore

First, we measured the running time of *StripedScore* as a function of strip width *s* (Table 1 and Fig. 7). *lenQuery* is the length of the query sequence, and *lenDB* is the length of the subject sequence. As predicted in the analysis of Section 3.2, for sufficiently large sequences, the running time decreases as *s* increases. However, if sequences are relatively small, when *s* increases, the running time decreases first and then increases.

Next we compared the relative performance of *StripedScore* with $s = 1900$, *PerotRecurrence* (the code of Ref. [9] modified to report the best score rather than the best 200 scores), *BlockedAntidiagonal* [10], *EnhancedBA* (our enhancement of *BlockedAntidiagonal* in which only the values on the right and bottom boundaries of each block are stored in global memory thus reducing global memory usage significantly), and *CUDASW++2.0* [8]. Table 2 and Fig. 8 give the runtime for these algorithms. As can be seen, *PerotRecurrence* takes 13–17 times the time taken by

Table 1 Running Time (ms) of *StripedScore* for Different *s* Values

lenQuery	5103	10,206	20,412	30,618	51,030
lenDB	7168	14,336	28,672	43,008	71,680
s = 64	67.2	260.2	1031.7	2316.7	6427.1
s = 128	36.2	132.9	518.9	1161.4	3216.0
s = 256	23.1	72.6	269.8	597.5	1645.2
s = 512	22.3	50.1	160.9	344.9	932.3
s = 1024	–	59.4	135.5	261.7	664.4
s = 1900	–	–	175.0	279.9	625.7

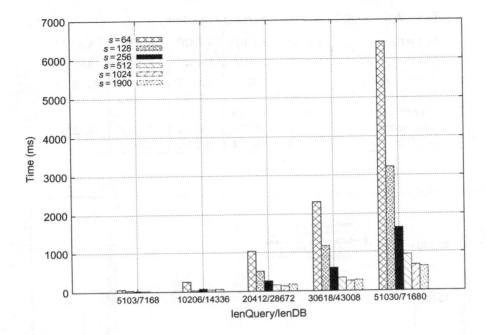

FIG. 7

Plot of running time (ms) of *StripedScore* for different *s* values.

StripedScore. The speedup ranges of *StripedScore* relative to *BlockedAntidiagonal*, *EnhancedBA*, and *CUDASW++2.0* are, respectively, 20–33, 2.8–9.3, and 7.7–22.8. *BlockedAntidiagonal* and *CUDASW++2.0* were unable to solve large instances because of the excessive memory they required.

StripedAlignment

For ease of coding, our implementation uses a *char* to store the direction information at each position encountered in Phase 3 rather than three bits as in the analysis of Section 3.3.4. We tested *StripedAlignment* with different *s* values, and the results are shown in Table 3 and Fig. 9. Using a similar analysis as used in Section 3.2, we determine the maximum strip size, which is limited by the amount of shared memory per SM, to be 410. The time for Phase 2 is negligible and is not reported separately. The time for all three phases generally decrease as *s* increases. For a really large *s*, the number of strips is comparable to or smaller than the number of SPs leading to idle time on some processors. Generally, choosing $s = 256$ gives the best overall performance for sequences of size up to 37,000. Choosing a larger *s* allows for larger sequences to be aligned (as I/O is inversely proportional to *s*).

We do not compare *StripedAlignment* with the algorithms of Refs. [8–10] for the following reasons (a) in Ref. [10], the traceback is done serially in the host CPU,

Table 2 Running Time (ms) of Scoring Algorithms

lenQuery	1×10^4	2×10^4	3×10^4	5×10^4	1×10^5
lenDB	1×10^4	2×10^4	3×10^4	5×10^4	1×10^5
PerotRecurrence	815.3	1917.7	3061.7	7014.9	20,437.3
StripedScore	48.4	113.0	216.3	449.8	1543.1
BlockedAntidiagonal	957.2	3719.9	–	–	–
EnhancedBA	137.4	527.0	1185.9	3438.6	14,327.4
CUDASW++2.0	374.5	1530.4	3404.0	10,259.1	–

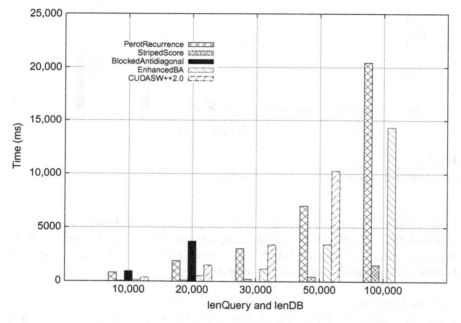

FIG. 8

Comparison of different scoring algorithms.

(b) *CUDASW++2.0* [8] does not have a traceback capability, and (c) the traceback of [9] is specifically designed for the benchmark suite SSCA#1 [31] and so aligns only multiple but small subsequences of length less than 128.

ChunkedAlignment1

There are two parameters in *ChunkedAlignment*1, *s* representing the width of one strip, and *h* representing the height of one chunk. Effectively, the scoring matrix is divided into blocks of size $h \times s$. The data in Tables 4 through 6 show that, as was the

Table 3 Running Time (ms) of *StripedAlignment* for Different *s* Values

lenQuery	10,430			15,533			20,860		
lenDB	**14,560**			**21,728**			**29,120**		
Phase	**1**	**3**	**Total**	**1**	**3**	**Total**	**1**	**3**	**Total**
$s = 64$	616.9	440.1	1066.4	1352.9	973.5	2343.5	2402.4	1745.1	4176.5
$s = 128$	328.6	298.9	633.5	707.4	650.2	1367.2	1245.4	1147.0	2408.1
$s = 256$	183.9	318.0	505.6	384.0	715.7	1104.5	670.4	1273.5	1952.6
$s = 410$	136.4	380.9	520.7	264.6	827.3	1096.0	484.2	1531.8	2020.9

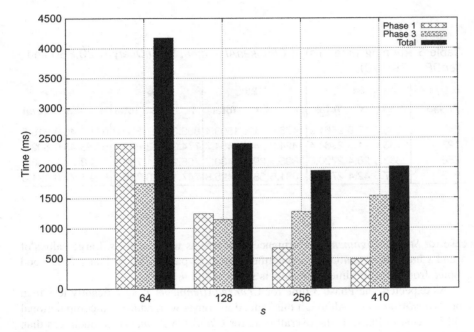

FIG. 9

Running time (ms) of *StripedAlignment* when *lenQuery* = 20,860 and *lenDB* = 29,120.

Table 4 Running Time (ms) of *ChunkedAlignment*1 (*lenQuery* = 10,430 and *lenDB* = 14,560)

h ↓ /s →	64			128			256			410		
Phase	**1**	**3**	**Total**	**1**	**3**	**Total**	**1**	**3**	**Total**	**1**	**3**	**Total**
64	728.5	8.9	742.3	390.0	10.8	404.7	220.1	11.6	235.3	159.2	21.1	183.7
128	702.7	10.7	718.0	376.9	12.5	393.1	212.8	13.0	229.2	154.5	23.8	181.5
256	689.4	14.6	708.7	368.7	15.5	387.9	208.3	15.7	227.4	152.2	30.0	185.4
512	682.9	20.1	707.7	364.8	19.0	387.6	205.5	20.7	229.7	151.0	38.4	192.5

Table 5 Running Time (ms) of *ChunkedAlignment*1 (*lenQuery* = 15,533 and *lenDB* = 21,728)

h ↓ /s →	64			128			256			410		
Phase	1	3	Total	1	3	Total	1	3	Total	1	3	Total
64	1596.6	13.1	1616.7	838.7	16.0	859.9	459.0	16.3	479.9	309.2	31.2	344.5
128	1540.4	15.9	1562.8	810.1	18.2	833.1	443.5	18.4	465.8	300.0	34.5	338.2
256	1511.3	21.6	1539.4	792.9	22.8	820.5	434.2	23.5	461.5	295.5	44.8	344.0
512	1497.0	30.3	1533.9	784.6	28.3	817.6	428.6	30.7	463.1	293.0	56.3	352.9

Table 6 Running Time (ms) of *ChunkedAlignment*1 (*lenQuery* = 20,860 and *lenDB* = 29,120)

h ↓ /s →	64			128			256			410		
Phase	1	3	Total	1	3	Total	1	3	Total	1	3	Total
64	2833.3	17.9	2861.2	1475.0	21.4	1503.4	803.8	21.7	830.9	571.2	40.3	616.5
128	2733.6	21.5	2764.4	1424.0	24.4	1454.7	774.3	24.3	803.4	553.3	45.0	602.7
256	2683.0	28.4	2720.6	1395.1	29.4	1430.7	756.2	29.1	789.9	544.8	57.2	606.0
512	2657.5	42.4	2709.2	1381.5	38.3	1425.8	747.1	43.8	795.3	539.1	77.9	621.0

case for *StripedAlignment*, performance improves as we increase s. Large values of h and s have the potential to reduce the amount of parallelism in Phase 3. A good choice from our experimental results is $s = 410$ and $h = 128$.

As expected, the Phase 3 time for *ChunkedAlignment*1 is significantly less than for *StripedAlignment*. Although this reduction comes with additional computational and I/O cost in Phase 1, the overall time for *ChunkedAlignment*1 is much less than for *StripedAlignment*. For sequences of size 20,860 and 29,120, the best time for *StripedAlignment* is 1952.6 ms, while that for *ChunkedAlignment*1 is 602.7 ms ($s = 410, h = 128$); the ratio is slightly more than 3.

The major advantage of *ChunkedAlignment*2 is better parallelism in Phase 3. However, the additional overhead in Phases 1 and 3 (in terms of I/O) result in performance that is slightly worse than that of *ChunkedAlignment*1, as shown in Tables 7–10 and Fig. 10. *ChunkedAlignment*2 is better than *ChunkedAlignment*1 only for strings in which, for the shortest distance, there are many chunks in one strip. For the strip sizes and the data sets that we used, we did not find this to be the case.

Since *StripedScore* is an order of magnitude faster than *PerotRecurrence* and *ChunkedAlignment*1 is not an order of magnitude slower than *StripedScore*, we conclude, without experiment, that *ChunkedAlignment*1 is faster than the code of Ref. [9] modified to find the best alignment.

Table 7 Running Time (ms) of *ChunkedAlignment*2 (*lenQuery* = 10,430 and *lenDB* = 14,560)

h ↓ /s →	64			128			256			410		
Phase	1	3	Total	1	3	Total	1	3	Total	1	3	Total
64	797.3	13.2	817.0	426.4	18.8	451.0	241.7	26.4	273.4	174.2	38.7	218.3
128	739.8	15.1	760.7	403.4	17.4	425.8	229.2	21.2	255.0	164.1	27.9	196.3
256	710.2	21.7	737.5	383.1	22.0	409.8	219.8	23.7	247.7	158.6	35.1	197.6
512	695.8	36.5	737.9	373.6	30.1	408.2	211.8	40.2	255.8	154.7	53.9	212.4

Table 8 Running Time (ms) of *ChunkedAlignment*2 (*lenQuery* = 15,533 and *lenDB* = 21,728)

h ↓ /s →	64			128			256			410		
Phase	1	3	Total	1	3	Total	1	3	Total	1	3	Total
64	1745.0	19.6	1774.2	916.8	28.0	952.8	504.2	39.5	550.9	338.4	56.3	401.9
128	1619.8	22.6	1650.5	866.2	26.2	898.9	477.2	32.3	515.2	317.7	40.5	364.8
256	1555.6	32.8	1595.9	823.7	32.5	862.0	457.7	34.5	497.2	308.2	51.9	364.8
512	1524.0	55.8	1587.4	802.9	44.0	852.5	441.2	58.2	504.0	300.2	81.5	386.0

Table 9 Running Time (ms) of *ChunkedAlignment*2 (*lenQuery* = 20,860 and *lenDB* = 29,120)

h ↓ /s →	64			128			256			410		
Phase	1	3	Total	1	3	Total	1	3	Total	1	3	Total
64	3105.7	1.6	3119.3	1612.1	37.6	1660.7	880.8	53.2	943.7	629.5	2.6	640.4
128	2886.5	1.7	2898.0	1521.3	35.0	1564.7	831.1	42.2	880.6	592.6	53.8	653.3
256	2762.9	43.6	2817.0	1449.4	43.7	1500.5	796.7	45.2	848.1	574.1	65.9	645.7
512	2706.2	73.6	2790.3	1413.3	58.1	1478.4	771.2	76.5	853.2	557.2	108.7	670.9

Table 10 Best Running Time (ms) of *ChunkedAlignment*1 and *ChunkedAlignment*2

lenQuery/lenDB	10,430/14,560			15,533/21,728			20,860/29,120		
Phase	1	3	Total	1	3	Total	1	3	Total
ChunkedAlignment1	154.5	23.8	181.5	300.0	34.5	338.2	553.3	45.0	602.7
ChunkedAlignment2	164.1	27.9	196.3	318.7	40.5	364.8	629.5	2.6	640.4

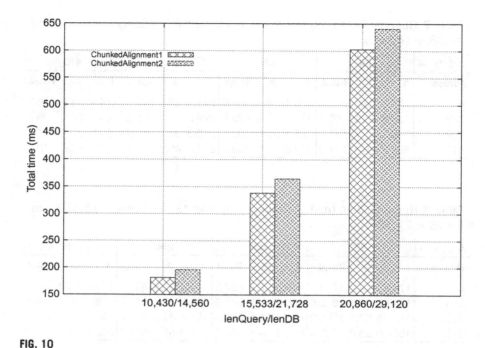

FIG. 10

Plot of best running time (ms) of *ChunkedAlignment*1 and *ChunkedAlignment*2.

4 ALIGNMENT OF THREE SEQUENCES

In this section, we describe two single-GPU algorithms for the optimal alignment of three sequences. These algorithms were originally presented by us in Ref. [24]. The first of these uses a layering approach, while the second uses a sloped approach. Experimental results using a NVIDIA GPU show that the sloped approach results in a faster algorithm and that this algorithm is an order of magnitude faster than a single-core alignment algorithm running on the host computer.

4.1 THREE-SEQUENCE ALIGNMENT ALGORITHM

The input to the three-sequence alignment problem is a set $\{S_0, S_1, S_2\}$ of three sequences and a substitution matrix *sub* such as BLOSUM [32] or PAM [33], which defines the score for character pairs xy. The output is a $3 \times l$ matrix M where $l \geq \max(|S_0|, |S_1|, |S_2|)$. Row i of M is S_i, $0 \leq i < 3$, with gaps possibly inserted at various positions and such that each column of M has at least one nongap character.

M defines an alignment whose score is

$$score(M) = \sum_{i=0}^{l-1} obj(M[0][i], M[1][i], M[2][i])$$

In this section, we define obj to be the sum-of-pairs function [13]:

$$
\begin{aligned}
obj(M[0][i], M[1][i], M[2][i]) = {} & sub[M[0][i]][M[1][i]] \\
& + sub[M[0][i]][M[2][i]] \\
& + sub[M[1][i]][M[2][i]]
\end{aligned}
$$

The alignment M is optimal if it maximizes $score(M)$. The dynamic programming algorithm to construct M first computes an $(|S_0| + 1) \times (|S_1| + 1) \times (|S_2| + 1)$ matrix H using the following recurrences [13]:

$$
H[i][j][k] = \max \begin{cases}
H[i-1][j-1][k-1] + obj(S_0[i-1], S_1[j-1], S_2[k-1]) \\
H[i-1][j-1][k] + obj(S_0[i-1], S_1[j-1], -) \\
H[i-1][j][k-1] + obj(S_0[i-1], -, S_2[k-1]) \\
H[i][j-1][k-1] + obj(-, S_1[j-1], S_2[k-1]) \\
H[i-1][j][k] + obj(S_0[i-1], -, -) \\
H[i][j-1][k] + obj(-, S_1[j-1], -) \\
H[i][j][k-1] + obj(-, -, S_2[k-1])
\end{cases}
$$

Here "$-$" denotes a GAP and β is the GAP penalty. The initial conditions are ($i > 0, j > 0, k > 0$):

$$H[0][0][0] = 0$$
$$H[i][0][0] = 2 \times i \times \beta$$
$$H[0][j][0] = 2 \times j \times \beta$$
$$H[0][0][k] = 2 \times k \times \beta$$

$$
H[i][j][0] = \max \begin{cases}
H[i-1][j-1][0] + obj(S_0[i-1], S_1[j-1], -) \\
H[i-1][j][0] + obj(S_0[i-1], -, -) \\
H[i][j-1][0] + obj(-, S_1[j-1], -)
\end{cases}
$$

$$
H[i][0][k] = \max \begin{cases}
H[i-1][0][k-1] + obj(S_0[i-1], -, S_2[k-1]) \\
H[i-1][0][k] + obj(S_0[i-1], -, -) \\
H[i][0][k-1] + obj(-, -, S_2[k-1])
\end{cases}
$$

$$
H[0][j][k] = \max \begin{cases}
H[0][j-1][k-1] + obj(-, S_1[j-1], S_2[k-1]) \\
H[0][j-1][k] + obj(-, S_1[j-1], -) \\
H[0][j][k-1] + obj(-, -, S_2[k-1])
\end{cases}
$$

The score of the optimal alignment is $H[|S_0|][|S_1|][|S_2|]$, and the corresponding alignment matrix M may be constructed using a backtrace process that starts at $H[|S_0|][|S_1|][|S_2|]$. The time required to compute the H values is $O(|S_0||S_1||S_2|)$. An additional $O(l)$ time is required to construct the optimal alignment matrix. The pseudocode to compute the optimal alignment score is shown in Algorithm 2.

ALGORITHM 2 THREE-SEQUENCE ALIGNMENT ALGORITHM

```
1:  function THREEALIGN(s1, s2, s3)
2:      len1 ← length of s1
3:      len2 ← length of s2
4:      len3 ← length of s3
5:      H ← matrix of size (len1 + 1) * (len2 + 1) * (len3 + 1)
6:      for i = 0 to len1 do
7:          H[i][0][0] ← 2 * i * β
8:      end for
9:      for j = 0 to len2 do
10:         H[0][j][0] = 2 * j * β
11:     end for
12:     for k = 0 to len3 do
13:         H[0][0][k] = 2 * k * β
14:     end for
15:     for i = 1 to len1 do
16:         for j = 1 to len2 do
17:             h1 ← H[i − 1][j − 1][0] + obj(s1[i − 1], s2[j − 1], GAP)
18:             h2 ← H[i − 1][j][0] + obj(s1[i − 1], GAP, GAP)
19:             h3 ← H[i][j − 1][0] + obj(GAP, s2[j − 1], GAP)
20:             H[i][j][0] ← max(h1, h2, h3)
21:         end for
22:     end for
23:     for i = 1 to len1 do
24:         for k = 1 to len3 do
25:             h1 ← H[i − 1][0][k − 1] + obj(s1[i − 1], GAP, s3[k − 1])
26:             h2 ← H[i − 1][0][k] + obj(s1[i − 1], GAP, GAP)
27:             h3 ← H[i][0][k − 1] + obj(GAP, GAP, s3[k − 1])
28:             H[i][0][k] ← max(h1, h2, h3)
29:         end for
30:     end for
31:     for j = 1 to len2 do
32:         for k = 1 to len3 do
33:             h1 ← H[0][j − 1][k − 1] + obj(GAP, s2[j − 1], s3[k − 1])
34:             h2 ← H[0][j − 1][k] + obj(GAP, s2[j − 1], GAP)
35:             h3 ← H[0][j][k − 1] + obj(GAP, GAP, s3[k − 1])
36:             H[0][j][k] ← max(h1, h2, h3)
37:         end for
38:     end for
```

ALGORITHM 3

```
39:    for i = 1 to len1 do
40:      for j = 1 to len2 do
41:        for k = 1 to len3 do
42:          h1 ← H[i − 1][j − 1][k − 1] + obj(s1[i − 1], s2[j − 1], s3[k − 1])
43:          h2 ← H[i − 1][j − 1][k] + obj(s1[i − 1], s2[j − 1], GAP)
44:          h3 ← H[i − 1][j][k − 1] + obj(s1[i − 1], GAP, s3[k − 1])
45:          h4 ← H[i][j − 1][k − 1] + obj(GAP, s2[j − 1], s3[k − 1])
46:          h5 ← H[i − 1][j][k] + obj(s1[i − 1], GAP, GAP)
47:          h6 ← H[i][j − 1][k] + obj(GAP, s2[j − 1], GAP)
48:          h7 ← H[i][j][k − 1] + obj(GAP, GAP, s3[k − 1])
49:          H[i][j][k] ← max(h1, h2, h3, h4, h5, h6, h7)
50:        end for
51:      end for
52:    end for
53:    return H[len1][len2][len3]
54: end function
```

4.2 COMPUTING THE SCORE OF THE BEST ALIGNMENT

4.2.1 Layered algorithm

GPU computational strategy

In this algorithm, which is called *LAYERED*, the three-dimensional matrix H is partitioned into $s \times s \times (|S_2| + 1)$ chunks (cuboids), as shown in Fig. 11, where s is an algorithm design parameter.

Let d be the number of chunks in the partitioning of H. These chunks form an $(|S_1| + 1)/s \times (|S_0| + 1)/s$ matrix whose elements may be numbered from 0 through $d − 1$ in antidiagonal (ie, top-right to bottom-left) order as in Fig. 11. Let p be the number of SMs in the GPU (for the C2050, $p = 14$). SM i of the GPU will compute the H values for all chunks j such that $j \mod p = i$, $0 \le j < c$, $0 \le i < p$.

Each SM works on its assigned chunks serially. For example, when $p = 3$ and $d = 12$, SM 0 is assigned chunks 0, 3, 6, and 9. This SM will first compute the H values for chunk 0, then for chunk 3, then for chunk 6, and finally for chunk 9. In general, SM i computes chunk i, followed by $i + p$ and so on.

The H values of a chunk are computed by the SM to which the chunk is assigned one layer at a time, where a layer is comprised of all H values in an $s \times s$ horizontal slice of the chunk. As can be seen, the total number of layers is $|S_2|+1$. Within a layer, the computations are done in antidiagonal order beginning with the antidiagonal that is composed of the top-left element of the layer (or slice). All values on the same antidiagonal of the layer are computed in parallel in a single instruction multiple data fashion. After one layer is computed, the SM moves to the next layer. After all layers are computed, the SM moves to the next chunk assigned to it. In order to achieve high performance, the computed H values for a layer are stored in the shared memory of the SM until the computation of the next layer is complete because the current layer's H values are needed to compute those of the next layer. At any time during the computation, only two layers of H values are kept in shared memory, and the memory space for these two layers is used in a round-robin fashion to save shared memory.

From the dynamic programming recurrence for H, we see that the H values in a chunk depend only on those on the shared boundary (east vertical face) of the chunks to its west and northwest and those on the shared boundary (south vertical face) of the chunks to its north and northwest. With respect to the $(|S_1| + 1)/s \times (|S_0| + 1)/s$ matrix of chunks, it is necessary for the SM that computes the H values for chunk (i, j) to communicate the computed H values on its east vertical face to the SM that will compute the chunks $(i, j + 1)$ and $(i + 1, j + 1)$ (the top-left corner of this matrix is indexed $(0, 0)$), and the values on its south vertical face to the SM that will compute the chunks $(i + 1, j)$ and $(i + 1, j + 1)$. The $s \times (|S_2| + 1)$ H values on each of these vertical faces are communicated to the appropriate SMs via the GPU's global memory. Each SM writes the H values on its east and south faces to global memory. When an SM completes the computation for its current layer, it polls the global memory to determine whether the boundary values needed for the next layer are ready. If so, it proceeds to the next layer. If not, it idles. In case there is not a next layer in the current chunk, the SM proceeds to its next assigned chunk.

Analysis

To run the layered algorithm, each SM requires $O(s^2)$ shared memory to store the values associated with a layer and $O(|S_0||S_1||S_2|/s)$ global memory to communicate the H values on its east and south faces. Since shared memory is very small on current GPUs, the available shared memory constrains the chunk size s. Because of the high cost of data transfer between SMs and global memory (relative to the cost

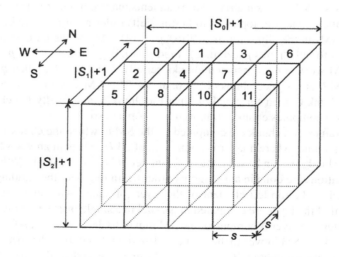

FIG. 11

The partitioning of the three-dimensional matrix H.

of arithmetic), the runtime performance of a GPU algorithm is often correlated to the volume of data transferred between the SMs and global memory. The layered algorithm transfers a total of $O(|S_0||S_1||S_2|/s)$ data between the GPU's global memory and the SMs.

The computational time (excluding time taken by the global memory I/O traffic) is computed by first noting that the c cores of an SM can do the computation for one layer in $O(s^2/c)$ time computing the H values on each antidiagonal of a layer in parallel. So the time to do the computation for one chunk is $O(s^2|S_2|/c)$. Since the computation for the ith chunk cannot begin until the first layers of its west, north, and northwest neighbor chunks have been computed, each SM, other than SM 0, experiences a startup delay. Because the antidiagonal from which the first chunk assigned to the last SM, SM $p - 1$, is $O(\sqrt{p})$, the startup delay for SM $p - 1$ is $O(\sqrt{p} * (s^2/c))$. When $|S_2|$ is sufficiently large (larger than $\lceil\sqrt{p}\rceil$), SMs experience (almost) no further delay in working on their assigned SMs. The number of chunks assigned to an SM is $O(|S_0||S_1|/(ps^2))$. So the total computation time (exclusive of global memory I/O time) is $O(|S_0||S_1||S_2|/(pc) + \sqrt{p} * (s^2/c))$.

While computation time exclusive of global I/O time increases as s increases (because the startup delay for SMs increases), global I/O time decreases as s increases. Our experiments show that for large $|S_0|$, $|S_1|$, and $|S_2|$, the reduction in global I/O memory traffic that comes from increasing s is substantially higher than the increase in time spent on computational tasks. Thus, within limits, choosing a large s will reduce the overall time requirements. As noted earlier, the value of s is, however, upper-bounded by the amount of shared memory per SM.

4.2.2 Sloped algorithm
GPU computational strategy

In this algorithm, which is called *SLOPED*, we partition H into $s \times s \times (|S_2| + 1)$ chunks and assign these chunks to SMs as in the layered algorithm. However, instead of computing the H values in a chunk by horizontal layers and within a layer by antidiagonals, the H values are computed by "sloped" planes composed of $H[i][j][k]s$ for which $q = i + j + k$ is the same. The first sloped plane has $q = 0$, the next has $q = 1$, and the last has $q = 2s + |S_2| - 2$. The computation for the plane $q + 1$ begins after that for the plane q completes. Within a plane q, the H values for all i, j, and k for which $i + j + k = q$ can be done in parallel. The number of parallel steps in the computation of a chunk is therefore $2s + |S_2| - 1$. In contrast, the layered algorithm cannot compute all H values in a chunk's layer in parallel. The computation of a layer is done by antidiagonals in $2s - 1$ steps with each step computing the values on one antidiagonal in parallel. The total number of parallel steps employed by the layered algorithm in the computation of a chunk is $(2s - 1) * (|S_2| + 1)$. Hence when both the layered and sloped algorithms use the same s, the sloped algorithm uses fewer steps with each step encompassing more work that can be done in parallel. Under these conditions, the sloped algorithm is expected to perform better than the layered algorithm. However, as noted earlier, the value of s is constrained by the amount of local SM memory available. As we presently show, the sloped algorithm requires more SM memory and so must use a smaller s.

Analysis

To compute the H values on a sloped plane q, we need the H values from the planes $q - 1$, $q - 2$, and $q - 3$. For efficient computation, we must therefore have adequate SM memory for four sloped planes. Because a sloped plane may have up to $(s + 1)^2$ H values, each SM must have sufficient memory to accommodate $4(s + 1)^2$ H values, which is twice the number of H values that the layered algorithm stores in the shared memory of an SM. The sloped algorithm generates the same amount of I/O traffic between the SMs and global memory as does the layered algorithm. The two algorithms also require the same amount of global memory.

Proceeding as for *LAYERED*, we see that the delay time for SM $p - 1$ is $O(\sqrt{p}(s^3/c))$ where $O(s^3/c)$ is the time taken to compute the small pyramid. The time to compute all the chunks assigned to an SM is $O(|S_0||S_1||S2|/(pc))$. So the total time (exclusive of global I/O traffic time) is $O(|S_0||S_1||S_2|/(pc) + \sqrt{p} * (s^3/c))$. Although the analysis shows the total time for *SLOPED* is larger than that for *LAYERED*, because of the larger delay to start SM $p - 1$ when S_0, S_1, and S_2 are large, the greater parallelism afforded by *SLOPED* coupled with the need for fewer synchronization steps dominates, and the measured runtime is smaller for *SLOPED*.

4.3 COMPUTING THE BEST ALIGNMENT

The layered and sloped algorithms may be extended to compute not only the score of the best alignment but also the best alignment. We describe three possible extensions for the layered algorithm. These extensions represent a tradeoff among conceptual and implementation simplicity, computational requirements for the traceback done to compute the best alignment from the scores, and the amount of parallelism. Identical extensions may be made to the sloped algorithm.

4.3.1 *LAYERED-BT*1

To compute the best alignment, we need to maintain additional information that can be used during the traceback. In particular, for each position (i, j, k) of H, we associate the coordinates (i_s, j_s, k_s) of the local start point of the optimal path to (i, j, k). This local start point is a position on the boundary of north, northwest, or west neighbor chunk of the chunk that contains the position (i, j, k). *LAYERED-BT*1 is a three-phase algorithm, as shown here:

1. Phase 1: This is an extension of *LAYERED* in which each chunk stores, in global memory, not only the H values needed by its neighboring chunks but also the local start point of the optimal path to each boundary cell.
2. Phase 2: For each chunk, we sequentially determine the start point and end point of the subpath of the best alignment that goes through this chunk. This is done by tracing the best path backward from position $(|S_0|, |S_1|, |S_2|)$ to position $(0, 0, 0)$ using the local start points of boundary cells computed in Phase 1. This traceback goes from the boundary of one chunk to the boundary of a neighbor chunk without actually entering any chunk.

3. Phase 3: The subpath of the best path within each chunk is computed by recomputing the *H* values for the chunks through which the best alignment path traverses. Note that Phase 2 determines which chunks the best path goes through. Using the saved boundary *H* values, it is possible to compute the subpaths for all chunks in parallel.

The global memory required by *LAYERED-BT*1 is more than that required by *LAYERED* because Phase 1 stores a 3D position with *H* value saved. Assuming 4 bytes for each coordinate of a 3D position and 4 bytes for an *H* value, *LAYERED-BT*1 requires 16 bytes per boundary cell, while *LAYERED* requires only 4. Additionally, in the Phase 3 computation, with every position in a chunk, we need to store which of the seven options on the right-hand side of the dynamic programming recurrence for *H* resulted in the max value. This can be done using 3 bits (or more realistically, 1 byte) per position in a chunk.

4.3.2 *LAYERED-BT2*

Although *LAYERED-BT*2 is also a three-phase algorithm, *LAYERED-BT*2 partitions each chunk into subchunks of height *h* (Fig. 12). The three phases are as follows:

1. Phase 1: Chunks are assigned to SMs as in *LAYERED*. In addition to the *H* and local start points stored in global memory by *LAYERED-BT*1, we store the *H* values of the positions on the bottom face of each subchunk.
2. Phase 2: Use the local start point data stored in global memory by the Phase 1 computation to determine the start and end points of the subpaths of the best alignment path within each chunk. This phase computes the same start and end points as computed in Phase 2 of *LAYERED-BT*1.
3. Phase 3: The subpath of the best path within each chunk is computed by recomputing the *H* values for the chunks through which the best alignment path traverses. For each chunk through which this path passes, the computation begins at the first layer of the topmost subchunk through which the path passes (Fig. 12, shaded subchunks are the subchunks through which the best alignment path passes). The computation for the different chunks through which the best alignment path passes can be done in parallel as in *LAYERED-BT*1.

The major differences between *LAYERED-BT*1 and *LAYERED-BT*2 are as follows:

1. Since *LAYERED-BT*2 saves *H* values on the bottom face of each subchunk in addition to data saved by *LAYERED-BT*1, it generates more I/O traffic than *LAYERED-BT*1 and also requires more global memory. The amount of additional I/O traffic and global memory required is $O(S_1||S_2||S_3|/h)$.
2. For each chunk through which the best alignment path passes, *LAYERED-BT*1 begins the Phase 3 computations at layer 1 of that chunk while *LAYERED-BT*2 begins this computation at the first layer of the topmost subchunk through which this path passes.

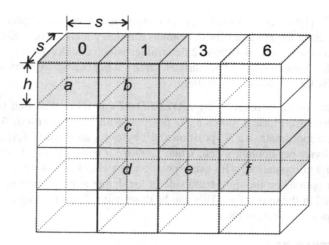

FIG. 12

Some of the chunks traversed by the optimal path.

4.3.3 *LAYERED-BT*3

For *LAYERED-BT*3, the local start points are defined to be positions on neighboring subchunks of the subchunk that contains the position (i, j, k) (rather than points on neighboring chunks of the chunk that contains (i, j, k)). Here are the three phases of *LAYERED-BT*3:

1. Phase 1: Chunks are assigned to SMs as in *LAYERED*. For each subchunk, we store in global memory, the H values on its south, east, and bottom faces as well as the local start point of the optimal path to each of the positions on these faces.
2. Phase 2: For each subchunk, we sequentially determine, the start point and end point (if any) of the subpath of the best alignment path that goes through this subchunk.
3. Phase 3: The subpath (if any) of the best path within each subchunk is computed by recomputing the H values for those subchunks through which the best alignment path traverses. Note that Phase 2 determines the subchunks through which the best path goes. Using the saved boundary H values, it is possible to compute the subpaths for all subchunks in parallel.

   *LAYERED-BT*3 has more global I/O traffic than *LAYERED-BT*2 in Phase 1 and also requires more global memory. Phase 2 of both algorithms do the same amount of work. We expect Phase 3 of *LAYERED-BT*3 to be faster than that of *LAYERED-BT*2 because of better load balancing resulting from the finer granularity of the per-subchunk work and the fact that there are more subchunks than chunks, which leads to more parallelism. For example, suppose one chunk has 50 subchunks through

Table 11 Running Time (s) for Different Instances

	(113, 166, 364)	(347, 349, 365)	(267, 439, 452)	(764, 771, 773)	(1399, 1404, 1406)
LAYERED	0.034	0.165	0.162	1.250	6.643
SLOPED	0.044	0.087	0.090	0.416	1.921
Scoring	0.570	3.610	4.270	37.500	–
Traceback	0.630	4.010	4.760	41.600	–

which the best alignment path passes and another chunk has only 1 such subchunk. Phase 3 of *LAYERED-BT*2 can use at most 2 SMs with 1 working on all 50 subchunks of the first chunk and the other working on the single subchunk of the second chunk. The workload over the two assigned SMs is unbalanced and the degree of parallelism is only two. Phase 3 of *LAYERED-BT*3, however, is able to use up to 51 SMs assigning 1 subchunk to each SM resulting in better workload balancing and a higher degree of parallelism.

4.4 EXPERIMENTAL RESULTS

We benchmarked the GPU three-sequence alignment algorithms against a single-core algorithm running on the host machine, which had an Intel i7-980x 3.33 GHz CPU and 12 GB DDR3 RAM.

4.4.1 Computing the score of the best alignment

We fixed $s = 67$ for *LAYERED* and $s = 47$ for *SLOPED* and experimented with real instances of different sizes. These two s values were determined from our experimental results that produced the least running time. The sequences used were retrieved from NCBI Entrez Gene [34], and their sizes are represented as a tuple $(|S_0|, |S_1|, |S_2|)$. The running time is shown in Table 11. The running time of the single-core scoring method and the single-core traceback method running on our host CPU is referred to as *Scoring* and *Traceback* in Table 11, respectively, for comparison purpose. As can be seen, *SLOPED* is about three times as fast as *LAYERED* for large instances and is up to 90 times as fast as the single-core CPU algorithm! In our tests speedup increases with instance size.

4.4.2 Computing the alignment

Because of memory limitations, our scoring algorithms can handle sequences whose size is up to approximately $(2500, 2500, 2500)$, while our alignment algorithms can handle sequences of size up to approximately $(1500, 1500, 1500)$. We used $s = 47$, $h = 40$ for layered algorithms and $s = 31$, $h = 100$ for the sloped algorithms that were determined by experiments to be the optimal values.

We tested our alignment algorithms, set with the preceding parameters, on the real instances used earlier for the scoring experiments. The measured runtimes are reported in Table 12 and Fig. 13 (*L*- for *LAYERED*, *S*- for *SLOPED*). We do not

Table 12 Running Time (s) of Traceback Methods for Real Instances

	(113, 166, 364)			(347, 349, 365)			(267, 439, 452)			(764, 771, 773)			(1399, 1404, 1406)		
	Phase 1	Phase 3	Total	Phase 1	Phase 3	Total	Phase 1	Phase 3	Total	Phase 1	Phase 3	Total	Phase 1	Phase 3	Total
L-BT1	0.062	0.012	0.076	0.298	0.042	0.342	0.348	0.035	0.386	2.814	0.121	2.941	14.994	0.277	15.300
L-BT2	0.062	0.005	0.069	0.298	0.010	0.310	0.347	0.010	0.359	2.813	0.014	2.834	14.982	0.021	15.036
L-BT3	0.062	0.005	0.069	0.298	0.010	0.310	0.347	0.009	0.360	2.812	0.016	2.836	14.977	0.023	15.040
S-BT1	0.013	0.002	0.030	0.064	0.005	0.111	0.077	0.006	0.125	0.583	0.021	0.736	3.513	0.058	3.850
S-BT2	0.014	0.002	0.032	0.067	0.002	0.114	0.080	0.002	0.127	0.606	0.003	0.748	3.648	0.005	3.946
S-BT3	0.014	0.002	0.032	0.067	0.002	0.114	0.080	0.002	0.127	0.604	0.004	0.747	3.636	0.006	3.939

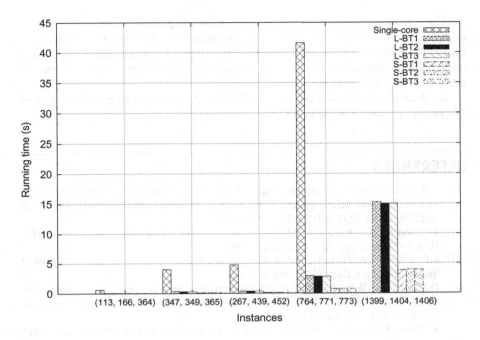

FIG. 13

Plot of running time (s) of traceback methods for real instances.

report the time for Phase 2 because it is negligible compared to that for the other phases. Although *BT*2 and *BT*3 reduce the runtime of the third phase, the overall time is dominated by that for Phase 1. Again, the *SLOPED* algorithms are about three times as fast as the *LAYERED* algorithms. The *SLOPED* algorithms provide a speedup between 21 and 56 relative to the single-core algorithm running on our host CPU.

5 CONCLUSION

GPUs are well suited to solve bioinformatics problems such as sequence alignment. However, performance is very dependent on the strategy used to map the underling serial algorithm to the GPU. For example, our GPU parallelizations of the unmodified Smith-Waterman algorithm for pairwise sequence alignment, *StripedScore*, achieves a speedup of 13–17 relative to the GPU algorithm of Ref. [9]. The speedup ranges relative to *BlockedAntidiagonal* [10] and *CUDASW++2.0* [8] are, respectively, 20–33 and 7.7–22.8. Our algorithms achieve a computational rate of 7.1 GCUPS on a single GPU.

The sloped scoring algorithm for three-sequence alignment, which is three times as fast as the layered algorithm, provides a speedup of up to 90 relative to a single-core algorithm running on our host CPU. The sloped alignment algorithm is also three times as fast as the layered one and provides a speedup between 21 and 56 relative to the single-core algorithm.

As demonstrated in this chapter, GPUs have the potential to provide orders of magnitude speedup over the host CPU.

REFERENCES

[1] S.B. Needleman, C.D. Wunsch, A general method applicable to the search for similarities in the amino acid sequence of two proteins, Mol. Biol. 48 (1970) 443–453, ISSN 0022-2836, doi:10.1016/0022-2836(70)90057-4.

[2] T.F. Smith, M.S. Waterman, Identification of common molecular subsequences, Mol. Biol. 147 (1981) 195–197, ISSN 0022-2836.

[3] S.F. Altschul, W. Gish, W. Miller, E.W. Myers, D.J. Lipman, Basic Local Alignment Search Tool, Mol. Biol. 215 (1990) 403–410.

[4] D.J. Lipman, W.R. Pearson, Rapid and sensitive protein similarity searches, Science 227 (1985) 1435–1441, doi:10.1126/science.2983426, http://www.sciencemag.org/content/227/4693/1435.full.pdf.

[5] K. Chao, J. Zhang, J. Ostell, W. Miller, A local alignment tool for very long DNA sequences, Comput. Appl. Biosci 11 (1995) 147–153.

[6] A. Khalafallah, H.F. Elbabb, O. Mahmoud, A. Elshamy, Optimizing Smith-Waterman algorithm on graphics processing unit, in: 2010 2nd International Conference on Computer Technology and Development (ICCTD), 2010, pp. 650–654, doi:10.1109/ICCTD.2010.5645976.

[7] S. Manavski, G. Valle, CUDA compatible GPU cards as efficient hardware accelerators for Smith-Waterman sequence alignment, BMC Bioinformatics 9 (2008) S10, ISSN 1471-2105, doi:10.1186/1471-2105-9-S2-S10.

[8] Y. Liu, B. Schmidt, D. Maskell, CUDASW++2.0: enhanced Smith-Waterman protein database search on CUDA-enabled GPUs based on SIMT and virtualized SIMD abstractions, BMC Res. Notes 3 (2010) 93, ISSN 1756-0500, doi:10.1186/1756-0500-3-93.

[9] A. Khajeh-Saeed, S. Poole, J. Blair Perot, Acceleration of the Smith-Waterman algorithm using single and multiple graphics processors, Comput. Phys. (2010) ISSN 00219991, doi:10.1016/j.jcp.2010.02.009.

[10] T.R.P. Siriwardena, D.N. Ranasinghe, Accelerating global sequence alignment using CUDA compatible multi-core GPU, in: ICIAFs 2010, 2010, pp. 201–206, doi:10.1109/ICIAFS.2010.5715660.

[11] L. Ligowski, W. Rudnicki, An efficient implementation of Smith-Waterman algorithm on GPU using CUDA, for massively parallel scanning of sequence databases, IPDPS 2009 (2009) 1–8 doi:http://doi.ieeecomputersociety.org/10.1109/IPDPS.2009.5160931.

[12] J. Li, S. Ranka, S. Sahni, Pairwise sequence alignment for very long sequences on GPUs, IEEE Int. Conf. Comput. Adv. Bio Med. Sci. (2012) 1–6, doi:http://doi.ieeecomputersociety.org/10.1109/ICCABS.2012.6182641.

[13] B. Schmidt, Bioinformatics: High Performance Parallel Computer Architectures, first ed., CRC Press, Inc., Boca Raton, FL, USA, 2010, ISBN 1439814880, 9781439814888.

[14] M. Murata, J.S. Richardson, J.L. Sussman, Simultaneous comparison of three protein sequences, Proc. Natl Acad. Sci. 82 (10) (1985) 3073–3077.

[15] O. Gotoh, Alignment of three biological sequences with an efficient traceback procedure, J. Theor. Biol. 121 (3) (1986) 327–337.

[16] X. Huang, Alignment of three sequences in quadratic space, ACM SIGAPP Appl. Comput. Rev. 1 (2) (1993) 7–11.

[17] D.R. Powell, L. Allison, T.I. Dix, Fast, optimal alignment of three sequences using linear gap costs, J. Theor. Biol. 207 (3) (2000) 325–336.

[18] E. Ukkonen, On approximate string matching, in: Foundations of Computation Theory, Springer, 1983, pp. 487–495.

[19] C.-L. Hung, C.-Y. Lin, Y.-C. Chung, C.Y. Tang, Introducing variable gap penalties into three-sequence alignment for protein sequences, in: 22nd International Conference on Advanced Information Networking and Applications-Workshops, 2008. AINAW 2008, IEEE, 2008, pp. 726–731.

[20] F. Yue, J. Tang, A divide-and-conquer implementation of three sequence alignment and ancestor inference, in: IEEE International Conference on Bioinformatics and Biomedicine, 2007. BIBM 2007, IEEE, 2007, pp. 143–150.

[21] C.Y. Lin, C.T. Huang, Y.-C. Chung, C.Y. Tang, Efficient parallel algorithm for optimal three-sequences alignment, in: International Conference on Parallel Processing, 2007. ICPP 2007, IEEE, 2007, pp. 14–14.

[22] M. Kruspe, P.F. Stadler, Progressive multiple sequence alignments from triplets, BMC Bioinformatics 8 (1) (2007) 254.

[23] A. Varón, W.C. Wheeler, et al., The tree alignment problem, BMC Bioinformatics 13 (2012) 293.

[24] J. Li, S. Ranka, S. Sahni, Optimal alignment of three sequences on a GPU, in: Proceedings of the 6th International Conference on Bioinformatics and Computational Biology, 2014.

[25] NVIDIA, CUDA Toolkit Documentation, 2009, http://docs.nvidia.com/cuda/#programming-guides.

[26] NVIDIA, TESLA C2050/C2070 GPU Computing Processor, 2010, http://www.nvidia.com/object/product_tesla_C2050_C2070_us.html.

[27] NVIDIA, NVIDIA Fermi Compute Architecture Whitepaper, 2009, http://www.nvidia.com/content/pdf/fermi_white_papers/nvidia_fermi_compute_architecture_whitepaper.pdf.

[28] A. Melo, M. Walter, R. Melo, M. Santana, R. Batista, Local DNA sequence alignment in a cluster of workstations: algorithms and tools, J. Braz. Comput. Soc. 10 (2004) 81–88, ISSN 0104-6500.

[29] N. Futamura, S. Aluru, X. Huang, Parallel syntenic alignments, in: Proceedings of the 9th International Conference on High Performance Computing, HiPC '02, Springer-Verlag, London, UK, ISBN 3-540-00303-7, 2002, pp. 420–430.

[30] O. Gotoh, An improved algorithm for matching biological sequences, Mol. Biol. 162 (1982) 705–708.

[31] D.A. Bader, K. Madduri, J.R. Gilbert, V. Shah, J. Kepner, T. Meuse, A. Krishnamurthy, Designing scalable synthetic compact applications for benchmarking high productivity computing systems, CTWatch Q 2 (4B) (2006) 41–51.

[32] S. Henikoff, J.G. Henikoff, Amino acid substitution matrices from protein blocks, Proc. Natl Acad. Sci. USA 89 (22) (1992) 10915–10919, ISSN 0027-8424, doi:10.1073/pnas.89.22.10915.

[33] M.O. Dayhoff, R.M. Schwartz, B.C. Orcutt, A model of evolutionary change in proteins, Atlas Protein Seq. Struct. 5 (Suppl 3) (1978) 345–351.

[34] D. Maglott, J. Ostell, K.D. Pruitt, T. Tatusova, Entrez gene: gene-centered information at NCBI, Nucl. Acids Res. 33 (suppl 1) (2005) D54–D58, doi:10.1093/nar/gki031.

Augmented Block Cimmino Distributed Algorithm for solving tridiagonal systems on GPU

9

Y.-C. Chen, C.-R. Lee

National Tsing Hua University, Hsinchu City, Taiwan

1 INTRODUCTION

A tridiagonal matrix has nonzero elements only on the main diagonal, the diagonal upon the main diagonal, and the diagonal below the main diagonal. This special structure appears often in scientific computing and computer graphics [1,2]. Because many of them require real-time execution, the solver must compute the result quickly as well as correctly. Many parallel algorithms for solving a tridiagonal system have been proposed [2–6]. These algorithms can give answers with superior accuracy and short execution time. Many applications or open-source tridiagonal matrix solvers are based on these algorithms, such as Alternating Direction Implicit [1] and cuSPARSE package [7].

The Augmented Block Cimmino Distributed (ABCD) method [8] is a new type of algorithm to solve linear systems. It partitions the matrix into block rows and constructs the augmented matrices to make each block row orthogonal. Although the augmentation increases the problem size, the orthogonalization makes the parallelization easy, since each augmented block row can be solved independently. Moreover, because of the orthogonal property, each block row can be solved stably without pivoting.

This chapter describes the implementation and performance optimization techniques of the ABCD algorithm for solving tridiagonal systems on a graphics processing unit (GPU). Although ABCD algorithm can be paralleled easily at the coarse-grained level, for multicore devices such as a GPU, fine-grained parallelization is more important. The major problem is that the operations in the block row solver are few, so the optimization of each step in the implementation is critical to the overall performance.

Advances in GPU Research and Practice. http://dx.doi.org/10.1016/B978-0-12-803738-6.00009-4

The rest of the chapter is organized as follows: Section 2 introduces the ABCD method for solving tridiagonal systems. Section 3 describes the details of GPU implementation and performance optimization techniques. Section 4 presents the experimental results. The conclusion is given in the last section.

2 ABCD SOLVER FOR TRIDIAGONAL SYSTEMS

The ABCD method is a redesigned block Cimmino algorithm, which is an iterative method for solving large linear least square problems. Let A be an $m \times n$ matrix and b an m vector. The linear least square problem is to solve x

$$\min_x \|b - Ax\|^2 = \min_x \sum_{i=1}^{m} \left(e_i^T b - e_i^T Ax \right)^2$$

where e_i is the ith column of an $m \times m$ identity matrix I. The preceding question can be written in the block form,

$$\min_x \|b - Ax\|^2 = \min_x \sum_{i=1}^{p} \left(E_i^T b - E_i^T Ax \right)^2$$

where E_i is the ith block column of the identity matrix. This is equivalent to partitioning the matrix A into p equal-sized row blocks, as well as the vector b. Fig. 1 shows a picture of the partition. If we let $b_i = Ei^T b$ and $A_i = E_i^T A$, the preceding equation becomes

$$\min_x \|b - Ax\|^2 = \min_x \sum_{i=1}^{p} (b_i - A_i x)^2$$

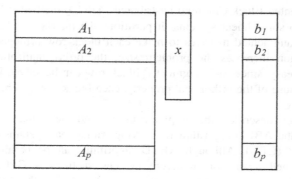

FIG. 1

Partition of the system.

The original block Cimmino method approximates the solution of each row block in parallel, and iteratively makes the approximations converge to the solution.

If each block row A_i is orthogonal to each other, which means $A_i^T A_j = O$ for $i \neq j$, the exact solution can be obtained in one iteration. Of course, most matrices do not possess such a property. However, we can augment the matrix so that the augmented matrix has this property. For instance, suppose the original matrix A has four row blocks, $A = (A_1 \; A_2 \; A_3 \; A_4)^T$, in which case, we can construct an augmented matrix

$$\hat{A} = \begin{pmatrix} \hat{A}_1 \\ \hat{A}_2 \\ \hat{A}_3 \\ \hat{A}_4 \end{pmatrix} = \begin{pmatrix} A_1 & A_1 & A_1 & A_1 & & & \\ A_2 & -A_2 & & & A_2 & A_2 & \\ A_3 & & -A_3 & & -A_3 & & A_3 \\ A_4 & & & -A_4 & & -A_4 & -A_4 \end{pmatrix}$$

in which $\hat{A}_i^T \hat{A}_j = O$ if $i \neq j$. In the preceding example, the matrix size is increased seven times by augmentation.

Augmentation could be small if a matrix has some special structures, such as tridiagonal matrices. Here is an example. Let A be a 9×9 tridiagonal matrix, and let $p = 3$, which means matrix A is partitioned into three row blocks.

$$A = \left(\begin{array}{ccc|ccc|ccc} a_1 & b_1 & & & & & & & \\ c_2 & a_2 & b_2 & & & & & & \\ & c_3 & a_3 & b_3 & & & & & \\ \hline & & c_4 & a_4 & b_4 & & & & \\ & & & c_5 & a_5 & b_5 & & & \\ & & & & c_6 & a_6 & b_6 & & \\ \hline & & & & & c_7 & a_7 & b_7 & \\ & & & & & & c_8 & a_8 & b_8 \\ & & & & & & & c_9 & a_9 \end{array} \right)$$

To make each block row orthogonal to each other, we can simply augment the matrix as follows:

$$\hat{A} = \left(\begin{array}{ccc|ccc} a_1 & b_1 & & & & \\ c_2 & a_2 & b_2 & & b_2 c_4 & \\ & c_3 & a_3 & b_3 & a_3 c_4 + b_3 a_4 & b_3 c_4 \\ \hline & & c_4 & a_4 & b_4 & -1 \\ & & & c_5 & a_5 & b_5 & -1 & b_5 c_7 \\ & & & & c_6 & a_6 & b_6 & a_6 c_7 + b_6 a_7 & b_6 c_8 \\ \hline & & & & & c_7 & a_7 & b_7 & -1 \\ & & & & & & c_8 & a_8 & b_8 & -1 \\ & & & & & & & c_9 & a_9 \end{array} \right)$$

Because only few elements are overlapped between consecutive row blocks in a tridiagonal matrix, only $2(p - 1)$ column augmentation should be added for p partitions.

Suppose $Ax = b$ is the original tridiagonal system to solve, where A is an $m \times m$ tridiagonal matrix, x is the unknown, and b is an m vector. The augmented system can be written as

$$\begin{pmatrix} A & C \\ O & I \end{pmatrix} \begin{pmatrix} x \\ y \end{pmatrix} = \begin{pmatrix} b \\ o \end{pmatrix}$$

The solution of x will be the same solution as the original problem. The only problem is that the augmented row block $(O\ I)$ is not orthogonal to other row blocks in $(A\ C)$, which makes parallelization difficult. This can be solved by projecting $(O\ I)$ to the orthogonal subspace of $(A\ C)$. Let $\bar{A} = (A\ C)$, and $\bar{A}_1, \bar{A}_2, \dots, \bar{A}_p$ be the block rows of $\bar{A}$. The oblique projector of $\bar{A}$ is

$$P = \sum_{i=1}^{p} \bar{A}_i^T \left(\bar{A}_i \bar{A}_i^T \right)^{-1} \bar{A}_i$$

Therefore we can construct the appending matrix

$$W = (B\ S) = (O\ I)(I - P) \tag{1}$$

and the augmented right-hand side

$$f = (B\ S)\begin{pmatrix} x \\ o \end{pmatrix} \tag{2}$$

The augmented system becomes

$$\begin{pmatrix} A & C \\ B & S \end{pmatrix} \begin{pmatrix} x \\ y \end{pmatrix} = \begin{pmatrix} b \\ f \end{pmatrix} \tag{3}$$

The solution of Eq. (3) is

$$\begin{pmatrix} x \\ y \end{pmatrix} = \left(\sum_{i=1}^{p} \bar{A}_i^T \left(\bar{A}_i \bar{A}_i^T \right)^{-1} \right) b + W^T \left(W W^T \right)^{-1} f \tag{4}$$

whose upper part x is the solution of the original system.

The ABCD method is summarized in Algorithm 1.

ALGORITHM 1 AUGMENTED BLOCK CIMMINO DISTRIBUTED METHOD

1. Determine partition size p and construct augmented matrix C.
2. Compute $u_i = \bar{A}_i^T \left(\bar{A}_i \bar{A}_i^T \right)^{-1} b_i,\ S_i = C_i^T \left(\bar{A}_i \bar{A}_i^T \right)^{-1} C_i, f_i = (O\ I)u_i$,
   and $W_i = \bar{A}_i^T (\bar{A}_i \bar{A}_i^T)^{-1} C_i$ for $i = 1, \dots, p$ in parallel.
3. Compute $u = \sum_{i=1}^{p} u_i,\ S = I - \sum_{i=1}^{p} S_i, f = -\sum_{i=1}^{p} f_i$,
   and $W = \begin{pmatrix} O \\ I \end{pmatrix} - \sum_{i=1}^{p} W_i$
4. Solve $Sz = f$ and compute $v = Wz$.
5. Return the upper part of $u + v$.

---

3 GPU IMPLEMENTATION AND OPTIMIZATION

Here we present the details of the GPU implementation of the ABCD method for solving tridiagonal systems and the performance optimization techniques.

3.1 QR METHOD AND GIVENS ROTATION

The major computation in Algorithm 1 is the calculation of

$$\bar{A}_i^T (\bar{A}_i \bar{A}_i^T)^{-1} \text{ and } (\bar{A}_i \bar{A}_i^T)^{-1} \tag{5}$$

where $\bar{A}_i$ is a block row of the augmented matrix. Each block row has three nonzero diagonal elements and few augmented elements. However, the calculation using Eq. (5) has some drawbacks. First, although the matrix is quite sparse, the direct calculation still iterates many times, especially the calculation of $(\bar{A}_i \bar{A}_i^T)^{-1}$. If $\bar{A}_i$ is an $k \times q$ matrix, $\bar{A}_i \bar{A}_i^T$ is an $k \times k$ matrix. Because $\bar{A}_i$ is almost a tridiagonal matrix, $\bar{A}_i \bar{A}_i^T$ will be a band matrix with five diagonals. Second, the direct calculation of oblique projector using Eq. (5) is numerically unstable [9, Chapter 14], even with some pivoting strategies. A better choice is the QR method.

The QR method first decomposes the matrix $\bar{A}_i^T$ into the product of an orthogonal matrix Q_i and an upper triangular matrix R_i, $\bar{A}_i^T = Q_i R_i$. Based on that, Eq. (5) can be simplified as

$$\bar{A}_i^T \left(\bar{A}_i \bar{A}_i^T\right)^{-1} = Q_i R_i \left(R_i^T Q_i^T Q_i R_i\right)^{-1} = Q_i R_i \left(R_i^T R_i\right)^{-1} = Q_i R_i^{-T} \tag{6}$$

and

$$\left(\bar{A}_i \bar{A}_i^T\right)^{-1} = \left(R_i^T Q_i^T Q_i R_i\right)^{-1} = R_i^{-1} R_i^{-T} \tag{7}$$

assuming $\bar{A}_i$ or R_i is of full rank. As can be seen, the formulas in Eqs. (6), (7) are much simpler and cleaner than that in Eq. (5).

There are several algorithms to carry out the QR decomposition [10, Chapter 5]. The most suitable one for matrix A_i^T is the Givens rotation, because A_i^T, a tridiagonal matrix, is very close to the upper triangular matrix R_i structurally, except for one subdiagonal and few augmented elements, and the Givens rotation method annihilates those nonzero elements one by one using rotation matrices. A rotation matrix for a two-vector $v = (a\ b)^T$ is

$$G = \begin{pmatrix} c & s \\ -s & c \end{pmatrix}$$

where $c = a/d$, $s = b/d$, and $d = \sqrt{a^2 + b^2}$. By premultiplying G to v, $Gv = (\sqrt{a^2 + b^2}\ 0)^T$. Note that G is a orthonormal matrix, and it preserves the length of the multiplicand, which means v and Gv have the same length.

Table 1 Operation Counts of Givens Rotation and Direct Multiplication

Equation	Givens Rotation	Direct Method
$u_i = \bar{A}_i^T (\bar{A}_i \bar{A}_i^T)^{-1} b_i$	$41k + 24$	$46k - 3$
$S_i = C_i^T (\bar{A}_i \bar{A}_i^T)^{-1} C_i$	$5k\ell + 20k - 6\ell + 6$	$9k\ell + 20k - 12\ell + 6$
$W_i = \bar{A}_i^T (\bar{A}_i \bar{A}_i^T)^{-1} C_i$	$2k\ell + 17k - 6$	$2k\ell + 6k + 14$

The QR decomposition by Givens rotation uses the diagonal and subdiagonal elements to create rotation matrices to brings zeros to the subdiagonal. The final Q matrix can be obtained by cumulating the rotation matrices.

Table 1 compares the operation counts of the Givens rotation and the direct method using Eq. (5). The size of $\bar{A}_i^T$ is $n \times k$, and the size of C_i is $\ell \times k$. The operation count of the direct method is based on the spare matrix multiplication and Gaussian elimination for band matrix. As can be seen, the operation count of Givens rotation is almost half in the computation of S_i, compared to that of the direct method.

3.2 SPARSE STORAGE FORMAT

Because A is tridiagonal, which is extremely sparse, a special storage format should be considered to reduce the used memory. A simple format of a tridiagonal matrix is to use three vectors to store the nonzero elements. In addition to that, we also need to consider the storage for intermediate results, such as the storage for matrix Q and matrix R.

Based on those requirements, we designed a $5n$ array as the major storage format, as shown in Fig. 2. Matrix A can be stored in the first three n vectors. Matrix R is also a tridiagonal matrix, whose nonzeros are all above the main diagonal. After the QR decomposition, matrix R can use the same space as matrix A's since A is no longer needed in the computation. Matrix Q is a block diagonal matrix. To store it may take too much space. Alternatively, we keep the Q matrix in the decomposed form and store the rotation matrices G_i. Since each G_i only has two parameters, we only need two elements to store each G_i. So the last two vectors are used to store the rotation matrix G_i. When the matrix Q is required in computation, such as Eq. (6), we multiply those G_i by the multiplicand directly.

3.3 COALESCED MEMORY ACCESS

We reformat the matrix storage to improve the performance on the GPU. As suggested in Ref. [11], the data accessed by threads within a block should be successively stored because threads in a thread-block read or store simultaneously. Successively stored data allows coalesced memory access on the GPU, which can

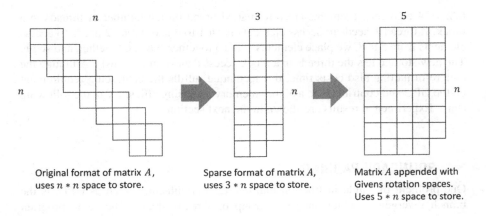

Original format of matrix A, uses $n * n$ space to store.

Sparse format of matrix A, uses $3 * n$ space to store.

Matrix A appended with Givens rotation spaces. Uses $5 * n$ space to store.

FIG. 2

Sparse storage format of matrix A.

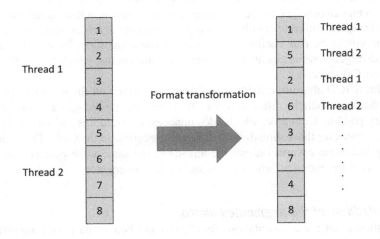

FIG. 3

Coalesced format transformation.

read/write 128 or more elements simultaneously, depending on the GPU hardware structure.

The original data storage format that stores the adjacent tridiagonal elements successively in memory cannot make coalesced memory access. Therefore we modify to the storage method so that the element k in the ith partition is before the element k in $i - 1$th partition and followed by the element k in the $i + 1$th partition.

Fig. 3 shows an example. There are eight elements, and each block has two threads. The number of partitions is two, which means that each thread controls

$8/2 = 4$ elements. Elements are reformatted based on the number of threads in a block. If thread 1 needs to access elements from 1 to 4 and thread 2 needs to access elements from 5 to 8, we place elements 1 and 5 together, 3 and 6 together, and so on. The new storage lets the threads in a block access data simultaneously. Although the data reformatting also costs time, this technique fulfills the coalescing requirement on the GPU and contributes to a higher memory accessing efficiency in the following steps. Experimental results are shown in the next section.

3.4 BOUNDARY PADDING

One problem of single instruction multiple data architecture, such as GPU, is the branch divergence, which means a group of threads sharing the same program counter have different execution paths. On a Compute Unified Device Architecture (CUDA) core, threads from a block are bundled into fixed-size warps for execution. Threads within a warp follow the same instruction synchronously. If a kernel function encounters an if-then-else statement that some threads evaluate to *true* while others to *false*, a branch divergence occurs. Because of the restriction that threads in a warp cannot diverge to different conditions, warp deactivates the *false* conditioned threads and proceeds to the *true* condition, and then reverses condition. In other words, the branch divergence serializes all the possible execution paths, which can really hurt a GPU's performance.

In the ABCD algorithm, the branch divergence occurs on the boundary process, which needs to handle different data. To solve the problem, we proposed the boundary padding technique, which adds unnecessary paddings and uses additional memory spaces for those threads with different execution on the GPU. The boundary padding technique ensures that all the threads in the same warp perform the same operations at any moment, which eliminates branch divergence.

3.4.1 Padding of the augmented matrix

Fig. 4 shows that the augmentations for the top and bottom partitions are different from those of the middle partitions, because they lack either $C_{i,j}$ or negative identity $-I$, which will lead to divergences. Our implementation adds zero elements to the top and bottom parts of the augmented matrix. Those zero elements have no actual influence on the final solution. The padding does not cost extra storage. Fig. 5 shows how those padding are stored in a compact format.

3.4.2 Padding for Givens rotation

During the rotation steps, the first partition of ABCD is different from other partitions. It rotates to middle and lower diagonal, while other partitions rotate to lower and below the lower diagonal, which leads to branches. To reduce the branches, we add redundant elements to the first partition. In other words, the first partition

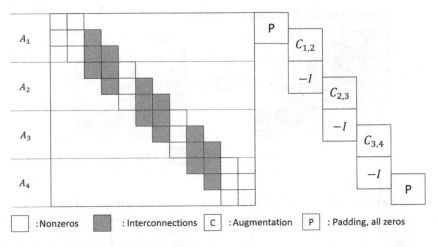

FIG. 4

Padding of augmented matrix C.

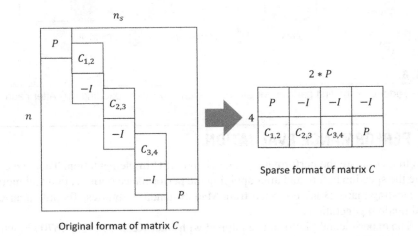

FIG. 5

The storage format of augmented matrix C.

will further rotate to the lower diagonal and the diagonal below the lower diagonal. This technique doubles the work of the first partition but unifies the work among all threads. In our experiment results, the total time of calculating the Givens rotations can be reduced to half of the original time. Fig. 6 shows the padding before and after the padding on the first partition.

Givens rotation applied on the first partition:

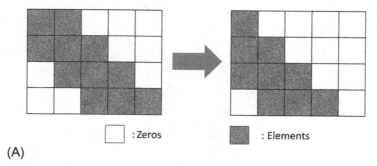

(A)

Add a column on left hand side and apply Givens rotation on first partition again:

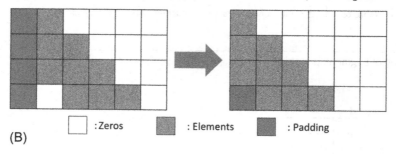

(B)

FIG. 6

The padding of the first partition for Givens rotation. (A) Before padding. (B) After padding.

4 PERFORMANCE EVALUATION

We first compare the performance of CPU and GPU implementation. Then we evaluate the speedup before and after applying the performance optimization techniques. The testing matrices are collected from Matlab standard libraries, Toeplitz matrices, and random generations.

The experimental platform is equipped with Intel Xeon CPU E5-2670 v2, which is of 2.50 GHz. The used GPU is NVIDIA Tesla K20m. The operating system is CentOS 6.4, and the NVIDIA Driver is 340.65.

4.1 COMPARISON WITH CPU IMPLEMENTATION

Fig. 7 shows the comparison between our implementations of the ABCD algorithm on the GPU and on CPU. The dataflow are the same for all the functions. The CPU version is implemented in C; the GPU version is implemented in CUDA. As shown in Table 2, the calculation of two implementations are similar if the matrix size is smaller than 2^{17} because we have to load data onto GPU memory before starting

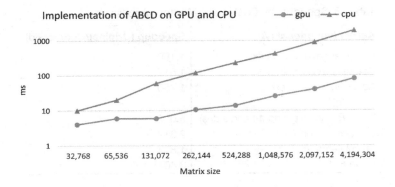

FIG. 7

Comparison of the execution time on the GPU and on the CPU.

Table 2 Performance Comparison of GPU and CPU Implementation

Matrix Size	GPU (ms)	CPU (ms)	Speedup (CPU Time/GPU Time)
32,768	4.0	10	2.50
65,536	5.9	20	3.39
131,072	5.9	60	10.17
262,144	10.6	120	11.32
524,288	13.8	230	16.66
1,048,576	26.1	430	16.47
2,097,152	40.8	910	22.30
4,194,304	82.0	1980	24.15

calculation. The overload caused by moving the data is large compared to calculation time. But the CPU calculation time nearly doubles when the dimension of the matrix doubles, while GPU calculation time increases only a little. The difference is because of GPU's architecture. If the dimension rises to 4 million, a 24.15 times speedup can be obtained by using GPU. The speedup of difference between a matrix size of 2 million and 4 million is small because we believe that GPU reaches the hardware limits.

4.2 SPEEDUP BY MEMORY COALESCING

Table 3 lists the speedups of different kernels made by the coalescing storage format, as described in Section 3.3. The matrix size is 4 million. The speedup is calculated by the ratio of the time without coalesced format and the time with coalesced format. Coalesced format can attribute to over five times speedup for solving R_i^{-1} with multiple right-hand sides.

Table 3 Speedup by Coalesced Memory Access

Kernel (Functionality)	Speedup (Original/Coalesced)
Assign augmented matrix	1.180
Create Givens rotation	1.519
Apply Givens rotation	1.750
Solve R_i^{-1}	1.959
Solve R_i^{-1} (multiple right-hand sides)	5.082
Calculate u and f	2.319
Calculate matrix S	1.873
Solve S^{-1}	3.464

There are many factors influencing the possible speedup. The major one is the size of memory accessed by the kernel. More memory accesses give a larger speedup. When the data size is small, its effectiveness is limited. As shown in Table 3, only a 1.15× speedup can be obtained for the task of assigning an augmented matrix. Another reason is the data access pattern. With the original data format, increasing the number of threads cannot accelerate the performance. But with a coalesced data format, doubling the number of threads reduces almost half of the execution time. This is because the bottleneck of the program using the original data format is memory access. More threads do not help to improve the performance. On the other hand, with a coalesced data format, the memory access is no longer the performance bottleneck. So other performance-tuning techniques can take effect. The other factors influencing the speedups include memory size, total number of threads, and the operations on the memory.

4.3 BOUNDARY PADDING

Although padding adds useless work to some threads, all threads can perform the same instructions simultaneously, which increases the overall performance.

Table 4 shows the speedup of the boundary padding technique. The speedup comes from two major factors. First, the boundary padding technique reduces the branch divergence because all the threads have the same execution path. Second, the boundary padding technique increases the coalesced memory access, since the memory access pattern is unified.

Table 4 Speedup by Boundary Padding

Kernel (Functionality)	Speedup (Times)
Add padding to the augmented matrix C	1.254
Add padding for Givens rotation (create rotation)	2.548
Add padding for Givens rotation (apply rotation)	1.898

The padding for a Givens rotation can not only improve the performance of creating the rotation matrix but also accelerate the kernel that applies the Givens rotations, as shown in the results in Table 4.

5 CONCLUSION AND FUTURE WORK

We present the GPU implementation of the ABCD algorithm, which provides a totally new aspect of parallel algorithm using augmentation. We focus on the problem of solving tridiagonal systems. Because of the special structure of tridiagonal matrices, two performance optimization techniques are proposed to accelerate the GPU implementation. The first is the memory coalesced data format, which significantly reduces the memory access time. The second one is the boundary padding, which adds useless data to unify the execution paths, and can effectively reduce the branches' divergence on the GPU. Experiments show that a speedup of more than 24 times can be obtained by using the GPU implementation.

Several future directions are worthy of investigation. First, the ABCD algorithm can be applied to general sparse matrices, but the matrix structure will be varied. How to handle the general sparse matrices effectively is a question. Second, here we only consider the parallelization on single-GPU platform. For better scalability, a multi-GPU platform or even heterogeneous platforms that hybrid various devices should be considered. How to design and optimize the algorithms is an interesting problem.

REFERENCES

[1] N. Sakharnykh, Efficient tridiagonal solvers for ADI methods and fluid simulation, in: GTC, 2010.
[2] R.W. Hockney, A fast direct solution of Poisson's equation using Fourier analysis, J. ACM 12 (1) (1965) 95–113, ISSN 0004-5411, doi:10.1145/321250.321259.
[3] H.S. Stone, An efficient parallel algorithm for the solution of a tridiagonal linear system of equations, J. ACM 20 (1) (1973) 27–38, ISSN 0004-5411, doi:10.1145/321738.321741.
[4] W. Gander, G.H. Golub, Cyclic reduction history and applications, in: Proceedings of the Workshop on Scientific Computing, 1997, pp. 10–12.
[5] E. Polizzi, A.H. Sameh, A parallel hybrid banded system solver: the SPIKE algorithm, Parallel Comput. 32 (2) (2006) 177–194.
[6] L.-W. Chang, J.A. Stratton, H.-S. Kim, W.W. Hwu, A scalable, numerically stable, high-performance tridiagonal solver using GPUs, in: 2012 International Conference for High Performance Computing, Networking, Storage and Analysis (SC), ISSN 2167-4329, 2012, pp. 1–11, doi:10.1109/SC.2012.12.
[7] CUDA toolkit, http://docs.nvidia.com/cuda/cusparse/.
[8] I.S. Duff, R. Guivarch, D. Ruiz, M. Zenadi, The augmented block Cimmino distributed method, SIAM J. Sci. Comput. 37 (3) (2015) A1248–A1269.

[9] N.J. Higham, Accuracy and Stability of Numerical Algorithms, second ed., Society for Industrial and Applied Mathematics, Philadelphia, PA, 2002, ISBN 0-89871-521-0, xxx+680 pp.
[10] G.H. Golub, C.F. Van Loan, Matrix Computations, third ed., Johns Hopkins University Press, Baltimore, MD, 1996, ISBN 0-8018-5414-8.
[11] CUDA C Programming Guide, http://docs.nvidia.com/cuda/cuda-c-programming-guide/index.html.

GPU computing applied to linear and mixed-integer programming

10

V. Boyer[1], D. El Baz[2], M.A. Salazar-Aguilar[1]

Graduate Program in Systems Engineering, Universidad Autónoma de Nuevo León, Mexico[1]
LAAS-CNRS, Université de Toulouse, CNRS, Toulouse, France[2]

1 INTRODUCTION

Graphics processing units (GPUs) are many-core parallel architectures that were originally designed for visualization purposes. Over the past decade, they evolved toward becoming powerful computing accelerators for high-performance computing (HPC).

The study of GPUs for HPC applications presents many advantages:

- GPUs are powerful accelerators featuring thousands of computing cores.
- GPUs are widely available and relatively cheap devices.
- GPUs accelerators require less energy than classical computing devices.

Tesla NVIDIA computing accelerators are currently based on Kepler and Maxwell architectures. The recent versions of Compute Unified Device Architecture (CUDA), such as CUDA 7.0, coupled with the Kepler and Maxwell architectures facilitate the dynamic use of GPUs. Moreover, data transfers can now happen via high-speed network directly from any GPU memory to any other GPU memory in any other cluster without involving the assistance of the CPU. At present efforts are placed on maximizing the GPU resources and fast data exchanges between host and device. In 2016 the PASCAL architecture should feature more memory, 1 TB/s memory bandwith, and twice as many flops as Maxwell. NVLink technology will also permit data to move 5–10 times faster between GPUs and CPUs than with current PCI-Express, making GPU computing accelerators very efficient devices for HPC. Looking at the GPU computing accelerators previously released (some of which are presented in Table 1, which also summarizes the characteristics of GPUs considered in this chapter), we can measure the progress accomplished during one decade.

Advances in GPU Research and Practice. http://dx.doi.org/10.1016/B978-0-12-803738-6.00010-0

Table 1 Overview of NVIDIA GPUs Quoted in the Chapter (see http://www.nvidia.com for More Details)

GPU	# Cores	Clock (GHz)	Memory (GB)
GeForce 7800 GTX	24	0.58	0.512
GeForce 8600 GTX	32	0.54	0.256
GeForce 9600 GT	64	0.65	0.512
GeForce GTX 260	192	1.4	0.9
GeForce GTX 280	240	1.296	1
GeForce GTX 285	240	1.476	1
GeForce GTX 295	240	1.24	1
GeForce GTX 480	480	1.4	1.536
Tesla C1060	240	1.3	4
T10 (Tesla S1070)	240	1.44	4
C2050	448	1.15	3
K20X	2688	0.732	6

GPUs have been widely applied to signal processing and linear algebra. The interest in GPU computing is now widespread. Almost all domains in science and engineering are interested, for example, astrophysics, seismic studies, the oil industry, and the nuclear industry (e.g., see [1]). Most of the time GPU accelerators lead to dramatic improvements in the computation time required to solve complex practical problems. It was quite natural for the operations research (OR) community, whose field of interest has prolific difficult problems, to be interested in GPU computing.

Some works have attempted to survey contributions on a specific topic in the OR field. Brodtkorb et al. [2] and Schulz et al. [3] deal with routing problems. Van Luong [4] considers metaheuristics on GPUs. More generally, Alba et al. [5] study parallel metaheuristics.

In this chapter, we present an overview of the research contributions for GPU computing applied to OR. Each section contains a short introduction and useful references for the algorithm implementations. The chapter is directed toward researchers, engineers, and students working in the field of OR who are interested in the use of GPU to accelerate their optimization algorithms. This work will also help readers identify new areas for research in this field.

The organization of this chapter is as follows: Section 2 introduces the field of OR. The primary optimization algorithms implemented via GPU computing in the domain of OR are described in Section 3. Section 4 presents relevant metaheuristics that have been developed with GPU computing. Finally, some conclusions and future research lines are discussed in Section 5.

2 OPERATIONS RESEARCH IN PRACTICE

OR can be described as the application of scientific and especially mathematical methods to the study and analysis of problems involving complex systems. It has been used intensively in business, industry, and government realms. Many new analytical methods have evolved, such as mathematical programming, simulation, game theory, queuing theory, network analysis, decision analysis, and multicriteria analysis, these methods have a powerful application to practical problems with the appropriate logical structure.

Most of the problems OR tackles are messy and complex, often entailing considerable uncertainty. OR can use advanced quantitative methods, modeling, problem structuring, simulation, and other analytical techniques to examine assumptions, facilitate an in-depth understanding, and determine practical actions.

Many decisions currently are formulated as mathematical programs that require the maximization or minimization of an objective function subject to a set of constraints. A general representation of an optimization problem is

$$\max f(x) \tag{1}$$
$$\text{s.t.} \quad x \in \mathcal{D} \tag{2}$$

where $x = (x_1, x_2, \ldots, x_n)$, $n \in \mathbb{N}$, is the vector of decision variables, Eq. (1) is the objective function, and Eq. (2) imposes that x belongs to a defined domain $\mathcal{D}$. A solution x^* is said to be feasible when $x^* \in \mathcal{D}$ and x^* is optimal when $\forall x \in \mathcal{D}$, $f(x^*) \geq f(x)$.

When the problem is linear, the objective function is linear, and the domain $\mathcal{D}$ can be described by a set of linear equations. In this case, it exists $p = (p_1, p_2, ..., p_n)$ called the vector of profits such that $f(x) = p^T \cdot x$, and there exist a matrix $A \in \mathbb{R}^n \times \mathbb{R}^m$, $m \in \mathbb{N}$, and a vector $b \in \mathbb{R}^m$ such that $x \in \mathcal{D} \Leftrightarrow Ax = b$. Hence a linear program has the following general form:

$$\max p^T x \tag{3}$$
$$\text{s.t.} \quad Ax = b \tag{4}$$

The relationships among the objective function, constraints, and decision variables determine how hard it is to solve and the solution methods that can be used for optimization. There are different classes of linear optimization problems according to the nature of the variable x: linear programming (LP) (x is continuous), mixed-integer programming (a part of the decision variables in x should be integer), combinatorial problem (the decision variables can take only 0–1 values), and so on. No single method or algorithm works best on all classes of problems.

LP problems are generally solved with the simplex algorithm and its variants (see [6]). A basis solution is defined such that $x = (x_B, x_H)$ and $A \cdot x = A_B x_B + A_H x_H$, where $A_B = \mathbb{R}^n \times \mathbb{R}^n$ and $det(A_B) \neq 0$. In this case, it is $x_B = A_B^{-1} b$ and $x_H = 0$.

The principle of the simplex algorithm is to build at each iteration a new basis solution that improves the current objective value $p^T x$ by swapping one variable in x_B with one in x_H, until no further improvement is possible.

Mixed-integer programming and combinatorial problems are generally much harder to solve because, in the worst-case scenario, all possible solutions for x should be explored in order to prove optimality. The Branch-and-Bound (B&B) algorithm is designed to explore these solutions in a smart way by building an exploration tree where each branch corresponds to a subspace of solutions. For instance, in combinatorial optimization, two branches can be generated by fixing a variable to 0 and 1. During the exploration, the encountered feasible solution is used to eliminate branches in the tree through bounding techniques. They consist of evaluating the best solution that can be found in a subspace (relaxing the integrality of the variables and solving the resulting linear subproblem with the simplex is commonly used).

Metaheuristics are designed to tackle complex optimization problems where other optimization methods failed to provide a good feasible solution in a convenient processing time. These methods are now recognized as one of the most practical approaches for solving many complex problems, and this is particularly true for many real-world problems that are combinatorial in nature (see [7]). Simulated Annealing (SA), Tabu Search (TS), Scatter Search (SS), Genetic Algorithms (GAs), Variable Neighborhood Search (VNS), Greedy Randomized Adaptive Search Procedure (GRASP), Adaptive Large Neighborhood Search (ALNS), and Ant Colony Optimization (ACO) are some of the most widely used metaheuristics.

The purpose of a metaheuristic is to find an optimal or near optimal solution without a guarantee of optimality in order to save processing time. These algorithms generally start from a feasible solution obtained through a constructive method and then try to improve it by exploring one or more defined neighborhoods. A neighborhood is composed of all solutions that are obtained by applying a specific change (move) in the current solution. So the goal of the exploration is to find better solutions than the current one. This process can be repeated until a stopping criterion is reached. In order to reinforce the search process, sometimes multiple initial solutions are generated and explored in parallel, such as GA and ACO, and information is exchanged between these solutions in order to improve the convergency of the approach.

The solutions for real-world problems represented as mathematical programs (optimization problems) are often hindered by size. In mathematical programming, size is determined by the number of variables, the number and complexity of the constraints, and objective functions. Hence the methods for solving optimization problems tend to be complex and require considerable numerical effort. By developing specialized solution algorithms to take advantage of the problem structure, significant gains in computational efficiency and a reduction in computer memory requirements may be achieved. Hence, practitioners and researchers have concentrated their efforts on developing optimization algorithms that exploit the capabilities of GPU computing.

In the literature related to GPU computing applied to OR, two main classes of optimization problems have been studied: LP problems and mixed-integer programming problems. For solving linear optimization problems, the simplex method is by far one of the most widely used exact methods, and for mixed-integer optimization problems the B&B method is the most common exact method. For solving different mixed-integer optimization problems metaheuristics like TS, GA, ACO, and SA have been proposed by using GPU computing, and their high performance is remarkable with respect to their sequential implementation.

3 EXACT OPTIMIZATION ALGORITHMS

In this section, the GPU implementation of exact optimization methods is presented. These methods are essentially the simplex, the dynamic programming, and the B&B algorithms (see [8]). Because these algorithms should follow a strict scheme to guarantee optimality, and tend to have a tree structure, their implementation on GPUs is particularly challenging. Research in this area mainly focuses on data arrangement for coalesced memory accesses or on speeding part of the algorithm on GPUs.

3.1 THE SIMPLEX METHOD

Originally designed by Dantzig [9], the simplex algorithm and its variants (see [6]) are largely used to solve LP problems. Basically, from an initial feasible solution, the simplex algorithm tries, at each iteration, to build an improved solution while preserving feasibility until optimality is reached. Although this algorithm is designed to solve LPs, it is also used to solve the linear relaxation of mixed-integer problems (MIPs) in many heuristics and exact approaches like the B&B. Furthermore, it is known that in algorithms like the B&B, the major part of the processing time is spent in solving these linear relaxations. Hence, faster simplex algorithms benefit to all fields of OR. Table 2 summarizes the contributions related to GPU implementations of simplex algorithms that can be found in the literature.

The first GPU implementation of a simplex algorithm, that is, the revised simplex method, was proposed by Greeff [17] in 2005. Most of the GPU computing drawbacks encountered by Greeff at that time have been addressed since then, with the development of the GPU architecture and CUDA. However, in this early work, a speedup of 11.5 was achieved as compared with an identical CPU implementation.

Simplex algorithm, like the revised simplex algorithm, involves many operations on matrices, and many authors have tried to take advantage of recent advances in LP. Indeed, some well-known tools like BLAS (Basic Linear Algebra Subprograms) or MATLAB have some of their matrix operations, such as inversions or multiplication, implemented in GPU. Spampinato and Elster [16], with cuBLAS (https://developer.nvidia.com/cublas), achieved a speedup of 2.5 for problems with 2000 variables

Table 2 Linear Programming and GPUs

Algorithm	Reference
The Simplex Tableau	[10,11]
The Two-Phase Simplex	[12]
The Revised Simplex	[13]
	[14]
	[15]
	[16]
	[17]
The Interior Point Method	[18]
The Exterior Point Method	[13]

and 2000 constraints when comparing their GPU implementation on a NVIDIA GeForce GTX 280 GPU to the ATLAS-based solver [19] on an Intel Core 2 Quad 2.83 GHz processor. Ploskas and Samaras [14] proposed an implementation based on MATLAB and CUDA environments and reported a speedup of 5.5 with an Intel Core i7 3.4 GHz and a NVIDIA Quadro 6000 with instances of up to 5000 variables and 5000 constraints.

In order to improve the efficiency of their approach, Ploskas and Samaras [14] did a complete study on the basis update for the revised simplex method. They proposed a GPU implementation of the Product Form of the Inverse (PFI) from Dantzig and Orchard-Hays [20] and of Modification of the PFI (MPFI) from Benhamadou [21]. Both approaches tend to reduce the computation effort of the matrices operations. Their results showed that PFI is slightly better than MPFI.

Ploskas and Samaras [13] presented a comparison of GPU implementations of the revised simplex and the exterior point method. In the exterior point method, the simplex algorithm can explore infeasible regions in order to improve the convergence of the algorithm. They also used the MATLAB environment for their implementation and compared their results to the MATLAB large-scale linprog built-in function. All the main phases of both algorithms are performed on GPUs. The experimental tests carried out with some instances of the netlib benchmark and a NVIDIA Quadro 6000 show that the exterior point method outperforms the revised simplex method with a maximum speedup of 181 on dense LPs and 20 on the sparse ones.

Bieling et al. [15] proposed some algorithm optimizations for the revised simplex used by Ploskas and Samaras [13]. They used the steepest-edge heuristic from Goldfarb and Reid [22] to select the entering variables and an arbitrary bound process in order to select the leaving variables. The authors compared their results to the GLPK solver (http://www.gnu.org/software/glpk/) and reported a reduction in computation time by a factor of 18 for instances with 8000 variables and 2700 constraints on a system with an Intel Core 2 Duo E8400 3.0 GHz processor and a NVIDIA GeForce 9600 GT GPU.

Like Bieling et al. [15] showed, sometimes controlling all the implementation of the algorithm can lead to better performance. The simplex tableau algorithm is very appealing in this context. Indeed, in this case, data are organized in a table structure that fits particularly well to the GPU architecture. Lalami et al. [10,11] and Meyer et al. [12] proposed two implementations of this algorithm, on one GPU and on multi-GPUs, and they reported that both algorithms reached a significant speedup.

Lalami et al. [11] used the algorithm of Garfinkel and Nemhauser [23], which improved the algorithm of Dantzig by reducing the number of operations and the memory occupancy. They extended this implementation to the multi-GPU context in Lalami et al. [11]. They adopted a horizontal decomposition where the constraints, that is, the lines in the tableau, are distributed on the different GPUs. Hence, each GPU updates only a part of the tableau, and the work of each GPU is managed by a distinct CPU thread. For their experimental tests, they used a server with an Intel Xeon E5640 2.66 GHz CPU and two NVIDIA C2050 GPUs, and instances with up to 27,000 variables and 27,000 constraints. They observed a maximum speedup of 12.5 with a single GPU and 24.5 with two GPUs.

Meyer et al. [12] proposed a multi-GPU implementation of the two-phase simplex. The authors consider a vertical decomposition of the simplex tableau, that is, the variables are distributed among the GPUs, in order to have less communications between GPUs. Like in Lalami et al. [10,11], they considered the implementation of the pivoting phase and the selection of the entering and leaving variables. They used a system with two Intel Xeon X5570 2.93 GHz processors and four NVIDIA Tesla S1070. They solved instances with up to 25,000 variables and 5000 constraints and showed that their approach outperforms the open-source solver CLP (https://projects.coin-or.org/Clp) of the COIN-OR project.

Jung and O'Leary [18] studied the implementation of the interior point method. They proposed a mixed precision hybrid algorithm using a primal-dual interior point method. The algorithm is based on a rectangular-packed matrix storage scheme and uses the GPU for computationally intensive tasks such as matrix assembly, Cholesky factorization, and forward and backward substitution. However, computational tests showed that the proposed approach does not clearly outperform the sequential version on CPU because of the data transfer cost and communication latency. To the best of our knowledge, it is the only interior point method that has been proposed in the literature even though it is one of the most effective for sequential implementations.

3.2 DYNAMIC PROGRAMMING

The Dynamic Programming algorithm was introduced by Bellman [24]. The main idea of this algorithm is to solve complex problems by decomposing them into smaller problems that are iteratively solved. This algorithm has a natural parallel structure. An overview of the literature dealing with the implementation of Dynamic Programming on GPUs can be found in Table 3. As we can see, only Knapsack

Table 3 Dynamic Programming on GPUs

Algorithm	Problem	Reference
Dense Dynamic Programming	Knapsack	[25,26]
Dense Dynamic Programming	Multi-Choice Knapsack	[27]

Problems (KP) have been studied so far. We provide more details on these contributions in the following section.

3.2.1 Knapsack problems

The KP (see [28]) is one of the most studied problems in OR. It consists of selecting a set of items that are associated with a profit and a weight. The objective is to maximize the sum of the profits of the chosen items without exceeding the capacity of the knapsack. In this context, the dynamic algorithm starts to explore the possible solutions with a capacity equal to zero and increases the capacity of the knapsack by one unit at each iteration until the maximum capacity is reached.

Boyer et al. [25] proposed a hybrid dense dynamic programming algorithm on a GPU. Data were organized in a table where the columns represented the items and the raws, represent the capacity of the knapsack in increasing order. At each iteration, a raw was filled based on information provided by the previous one. The authors also proposed a data compression technique in order to deal with the high memory requirements of the approach. This technique permits one to reduce the memory occupancy needed to reconstruct the optimal solution and the amount of data transferred between the host and the device. Computational experiments were carried out on a system with an Intel Xeon 3.0 GHz and a NVIDIA GTX 260 GPU, and randomly generated correlated problems with up to 100,000 variables were considered. A reduction in computation time by a factor of 26 was reported, and the reduction in memory occupancy appeared to be more efficient when the size of the problem increased, while the overhead did not exceed 3% of the overall processing time.

Boyer et al. [26] extended their approach whereby a multi-GPU hybrid implementation of the dense dynamic programming method was proposed. The solution presented is based on multithreading and the concurrent implementation of kernels on GPUs: each kernel is associated with a given GPU and managed by a CPU thread; the context of each host thread is maintained all along the application, that is, host threads are not killed at the end of each dynamic programming step. This technique also tends to reduce data exchanges between the host and the devices. A load balancing procedure was also implemented in order to maintain efficiency of the parallel algorithm. Computational experiments, carried out on a machine with an Intel Xeon 3 GHz processor and a Tesla S1070 computing system, showed a speedup of 14 with one GPU and 28 with two GPUs, without any data compression techniques. Strongly correlated problems with up to 100,000 variables were considered.

3.2.2 Multiple-choice knapsack problem

Suri et al. [27] studied a variant of the KP, called the multiple-choice KP (see [28]). In this case, the items are grouped in subsets and exactly one item of each subset is selected without exceeding the capacity of the knapsack. Their dynamic programming algorithm is similar to the one of Boyer et al. [25,26]; however, in order to ensure high processor utilization, multiple cells of the table are computing by one GPU thread.

They reported an important speedup of 220 as compared to a sequential implementation of the algorithm and a speedup of 4 compared to a CPU multicore one. Furthermore, they showed that their implementation outperformed the one of Boyer et al. [25,26] on randomly generated instances of the multichoice KP. For their experimental tests, they used two Intel Xeon E5520 CPUs and a NVIDIA Tesla M2050. However, no information was given on the memory occupancy of their algorithm.

3.3 BRANCH-AND-BOUND

The B&B algorithm was been designed to explore in a smart way the solution space of an MIP. In the original problem, the B&B generated new nodes that corresponded with subproblems obtained by fixing variables or adding constraints. Each node generated in a similar way other nodes and so on until the optimality condition was reached. The tree structure of the B&B is irregular and generally leads to branching performance issues with a GPU; thus implementing this algorithm on a GPU is in many cases a challenge.

To the best of our knowledge, as shown in Table 4, three types of problems were solved by a B&B GPU implementation: KP, Flow-shop Scheduling Problems (FSP) (see [29]), and a Traveling Salesman Problem (TSP) (see [30]). Two parallel approaches have been proposed:

- either MIP is entirely solved on GPU(s) through a specific or adapted parallel algorithm
- or GPUs are used to accelerate only the most time-consuming activities or parts of codes.

3.3.1 Knapsack problem

Boukedjar et al. [31], Lalami et al. [32], and Lalami [33] studied the GPU implementation of the B&B algorithm for KPs. In this algorithm, the nodes are first generated sequentially on the host. When their number reached a threshold, the GPU is then used to explore the nodes in parallel, that is, one node per GPU thread. Almost all the phases of the algorithm are implemented on the device, that is, bounds computation, generation of the new nodes, and updates of the best lower bound found via atomic

Table 4 Branch-and-Bound on a GPU

Algorithm	Problem	Reference
Branch-and-Bound	Knapsack	[31]
		[32]
		[33]
Branch-and-Bound	Flow-Shop Scheduling	[34]
		[35,36]
		[37]
Branch-and-Bound	Traveling Salesman	[38]

operations. Parallel bounds comparison and identification of nonpromising nodes are also performed on the GPU. At each step, a concatenation of the list of nodes is performed on the CPU. An Intel Xeon E5640 2.66 GHz processor and a NVIDIA C2050 GPU were used for the computational tests. The authors reported a speedup of 52 in Lalami [33] for strongly correlated problems with 1000 variables.

3.3.2 Flow-shop scheduling problem

The solution of the FSP via parallel B&B methods using GPU was studied by Melab et al. [37], Chakroun et al. [34], and Chakroun et al. [35]. In this problem, a set of jobs has to be scheduled on a set of available machines. In Melab et al. [37] and Chakroun et al. [35], the authors identified that 99% of the time spent by the B&B algorithm is in the bounding process. Hence they focused their efforts on parallelizing this operator on a GPU, and eliminating, selecting, and branching were carried out by the CPU. Indeed, at each step in the tree exploration of the B&B, a pool of subproblems is selected and sent to the GPU which performs, in parallel, the evaluation of their lower bound through the algorithm proposed by Lageweg et al. [39].

Furthermore, in order to avoid divergent threads in a warp resulting from conditional branches, the authors proposed a branch refactoring which involves rewriting the conditional instructions so that threads of the same warp execute an uniform code (see Table 5).

Computational experiments were carried out on a system with an Intel Xeon E5520 2.27 GHz and a NVIDIA C2050 computing system. Some instances of FSP proposed by Taillard [40] and a maximum speedup factor of 77 was observed for instances with 200 jobs on 20 machines as compared to a sequential version. This approach was extended in Chakroun et al. [34] to the multi-GPU case where a maximum speedup of 105 was reported with two Tesla T10.

Finally, Chakroun et al. [36] considered a complete hybrid CPU-GPU implementation to solve the FSP, where CPU cores and GPU cores cooperate in parallel for the exploration of the nodes. Based on the results obtained in their previous work, they added the branching and the pruning operator on the GPU to the bounding operator. Two approaches were then considered: first, a concurrent exploration of the B&B tree, where a pool of subproblems is partitioned between the CPU cores; second, a

Table 5 Branch Refactoring From Chakroun et al. [35]

Original Condition	Branch Refactoring
if $(x \neq 0)$ $a = b$;	int coef = __ cos $f(x)$;
else $a = c$;	$a = (1 - coef) \times b + coef \times c$;
if $(x > y)$ $a = b$;	int coef = min(1, __ exp $f(x - y - 1)$);
(x and y are integers)	$a = coef \times b + (1 - coef) \times a$;

cooperative exploration of the B&B tree, where CPU threads handle a part of the pool of the subproblems to explore on the GPU, which allows interleaving and overlapping data transfer through asynchronous operations. The pool of subproblems to explore is determined dynamically with a heuristic according to the instance being solved and the GPU configuration.

With an Intel Xeon E5520 2.27 GHz and a NVIDIA C2050, on the instances of Taillard [40], they achieved an acceleration of 160 with the cooperative approach. Indeed, the cooperative approach appeared to be 36% faster than the concurrent one. From these results, the authors recommended to using the GPU cores for the tree exploration and the CPU cores for the preparation and the transfer of data.

3.3.3 Traveling salesman problem
Carneiro et al. [38] considered the solution of the TSP on a GPU. The TSP consists of finding the shortest route that a salesman will follow to visit all his customers. At each step of their B&B algorithm, a pool of pending subproblems is sent to the GPU. A GPU thread processed the exploration of the resulting subtree through a depth-first strategy with backtracking. This strategy permitted them to generate only one child at each iteration, and the complete exploration of the subspace of solution is ensured through the backtracking process. The process is repeated until all pending subproblems are solved. Hence, in this approach, the GPU explores in parallel different portions of the solution space. As compared to an equivalent sequential implementation, Carneiro et al. [38] reported a maximum speedup of 11 on a system with an Intel Core i5 750 2.66 GHz and a NVIDIA GeForce GTS 450. The authors used randomly generated instances of an asymmetric TSP for up to 16 cities.

4 METAHEURISTICS
A metaheuristic is formally defined as an iterative generation process that guides a subordinate heuristic by logically combining different concepts for exploring and exploiting the search space, learning strategies are used to structure information in order to find efficiently near-optimal solutions (see [41]).

GPU implementations of metaheuristics have received particular attention from practitioners and researchers. Unlike exact optimization procedures, metaheuristics allow high flexibility on their design and implementation, and they are usually easier to implement. However, they are approximate methods that sacrifice the guarantee of finding optimal solutions for the sake of getting good solutions in a short computation time. In this chapter, we discuss the most relevant metaheuristics (GA, ACO, TS, among others) that have been implemented under a GPU architecture.

4.1 GENETIC ALGORITHMS

As shown in Table 6, GAs and their variants on GPUs have been proposed in the literature for the solution of complex optimization problems. GAs try to imitate the natural process of selection. GAs are based on three main operators:

- Selection (a subset of the population is selected in order to generate the new generation)
- Crossover (a pair of parents are recombined in order to produce a child)
- Mutation (the initial gene of an individual is partially or entirely altered in order to provide diversification)

At the beginning of the algorithm, a population is created. Each individual in the population represents a solution of the problem to solve. At each iteration, a subset of the individuals are selected according to a fitness function, and a new population is created through the crossing operator. The mutation operator is then applied in order to bring diversity into the search space.

4.1.1 The traveling salesman problem

Li et al. [47] and Chen et al. CDJN2011 proposed a Fine-Grained Parallel GA on a GPU in order to solve the well-known TSP. In the approach of Li et al. [47], a tour is assigned to a block of GPU threads, and each thread within this block is associated to a city. All the operators are treated on the GPU. In particular, they use

Table 6 Genetic Algorithms on GPU

Algorithm	Problem	Reference
Cellular Genetic Algorithm	Independent Tasks Scheduling	[42,43]
Systolic Genetic Search	Knapsack	[44]
Island-Based Genetic Algorithm	Flow-Shop Scheduling	[45]
Genetic Algorithm	Traveling Salesman	[46]
Immune Algorithm	Traveling Salesman	[47]

a partially mapped crossover method (see [48]), and the selection of the parents is done via an *adjacency-partnership method*; however, no details have been provided on this process. The tournament selection was preferred to the classic roulette-wheel selection. On a GeForce 9600GT, they reported an acceleration between 2.42 and 11.5, on instances with up to 226 cities.

Chen et al. [46] used an order crossover operator where parents exchange their sequence orders in a portion of their chromosome, which prevents a city from appearing more than once in a solution. Furthermore, they implemented the *2-opt mutation operator*, which seems to be particularly adapted to the TSP. They also used a simple selection process, that preserves the best chromosome. Because of the need for synchronization at each step of their GA, they carried out experimental tests with only one block on a Tesla C2050. Indeed, we recall that within the same block during a kernel call, threads can be synchronized, which is not possible with threads belonging to different blocks. However, it is possible to synchronize all the blocks through multiple kernel calls. Although they did not explore all the capability of computation of their GPU, they showed that their parallel GA on the GPU outperforms the sequential one on an Intel Xeon E5504.

4.1.2 Scheduling problems

Pinel et al. [42] proposed a fine-grained parallel GA for a scheduling problem, that is, the Independent Tasks Scheduling Problem. In this variant of the FSP, no precedence relation is considered between the tasks. The proposed algorithm, called GraphCell, starts by building a good feasible solution using the Min-Min heuristic from Ibarra and Kim [49], and this solution is added to the initial population of a Cellular GA (see [50]). The two main steps of this algorithm are conducted in parallel on the GPU, that is, the search for the best machine assignment for each task and the update of the solution.

In the Cellular GA, the population is arranged in a 2D grid, and only individuals close to each others are allowed to interact. This approach, whereby one individual is managed by one thread, reduces the communications involved. Computational tests carried out by Pinel et al. [42] with a Tesla C2050 on randomly generated instances with up to 65,536 tasks and 2048 machines showed the following:

- The Min-Min heuristic on GPUs outperformed the parallel implementation on CPUs (two Intel Xeon E5440 processors with 2×4 cores).
- The Cellular GA was able to improve, in the first generation, up to 3% the initial solution provided by the Min-Min heuristic.

In Zajíček and Šucha [45], a parallel island-based GA is implemented on a GPU for the solution of the FSP. In this variant of the GA, the population is divided in multiple subpopulations isolated on an island in order to preserve genetic diversity. These populations could share genetic information through an operator of migration. Zajíček and Šucha performed evaluations, mutations, and crossovers of individuals in subpopulations in parallel and independently from other populations, and they reported a speedup of 110 on a Tesla C1060.

4.1.3 Knapsack problems

Pedemonte et al. [44] proposed a Systolic Genetic Search (SGS) for the solution of the KP using GPU. The population is arranged in a 2D toroidal grid of cells, and at each iteration, solutions transit horizontally and vertically in a determined direction within the grid. This communication scheme is based on the model of systolic computation from Kung [51] and Kung and Leiserson [52], that is, the synchronous circulation of data through a grid of processing units.

Cells are in charge of the crossover and mutation operators, the fitness function evaluation, and the selection operator. The authors associated a block of GPU threads with a cell of the grid.

Experiments were carried out on a system with a GeForce GTX 480 GPU. Problems without correlation and up to 1000 variables were considered. Experimental results showed that the SGS method produced solutions of very good quality and that the reduction in computation time ranged from 5.09 to 35.7 according to the size of the tested instances.

4.2 ANT COLONY OPTIMIZATION

In this section, we focus on ant colony approaches that have been receiving a particular attention in the literature for the solution of routing problems. As we can see in Table 7, to the best of our knowledge, no other class of problems has been addressed in the literature on GPUs with ant colony.

ACO (see [53]) is an other population-based metaheuristic for solving complex optimization problems. This algorithm mimics the behavior of ants searching for a path from their colony to a point of interest (food). It comprises two main operators; that is, the constructive operator and the pheromone update operator. Artificial ants are used to construct solutions by considering pheromone trails that reflect the search procedure.

The first implementation of the ACO was due to Catala et al. [61] for the solution of the orienteering problem (OP), also known as the selective TSP (see [62]). In this variant of the TSP, the visits are optional, and each customer has a positive score that is collected by the salesman if and only if the customer is visited. Hence the OP consists of finding a route that maximizes the total collected score within a time limit.

The authors proposed to arrange the path followed by each ant in a 2D table where each row is associated with an ant, and a column represents the position of a node in the ant's path. The attraction between a pair of nodes (or pheromones) is stored also in a table. In order to build the paths for the ants, the authors used a *selection by projection* based on the principle of an orthographic camera clipping a space to determine, in parallel, the next node to visit. The results obtained showed that their

Table 7 Ant Colony Algorithms on GPU

Algorithm	Problem	Reference
Ant Colony Optimization	Transit Stop Inspection and Maintenance Scheduling	[54]
Ant Colony Optimization	Traveling Salesman	[55]
Max-Min Ant System	Traveling Salesman	[56]
Ant Colony Optimization	Traveling Salesman	[57]
Max-Min Ant System	Traveling Salesman	[58]
Max-Min Ant System	Traveling Salesman	[59]
Max-Min Ant System	Traveling Salesman	[60]
Ant Colony Optimization	Orienteering	[61]

approach, implemented on a single GeForce 6600 GT GPU, is competitive with a parallel ACO running on a GRID with up to 32 nodes.

Cecilia et al. [57] studied different strategies for the GPU implementation of the constructive operator and the pheromone update operator involved in the ACO. Each ant is associated with a block of threads, and each block thread represents a set of nodes (customers) to visit. Hence the parallelism in the tour constructor phase is improved and warp divergence is reduced. They also proposed to use a scatter-to-gather transformation (see [63]) for the pheromone update, in place of built-in atomic operations. Their results obtained with a C1060 GPU with instances with up to 2396 nodes showed a speedup of 25.

Uchida et al. [55] proposed an extensive study on strategies to accelerate the ACO on a GPU. In particular, they studied different selection methods for the construction operator to determine randomly the next city to visit. In their implementation a thread is associated to a city which computes its fitness value. Then a random number is generated and a city is selected based on a roulette-wheel scheme. The proposed methods differ in how to avoid selecting a node already visited by using the prefix-sum algorithm (see [64]), eliminating them through a compression method or by stochastic trial. They also studied the update of the pheromones through the shared memory in order to avoid uncoalesced memory access. The computational tests carried out with a GTX580 and a set of benchmark instances from the TSPLIB (see [65]) showed that the efficiency of the proposed approaches depends on the number of visited cities, so they proposed a hybrid approach. A maximum speedup of 22 was reported.

The solution of the transit stop inspection and maintenance scheduling problem was presented by Kallioras et al. [54]. In this problem, the transit stops need to be grouped in districts, and the visits, of the transit stops, for each vehicle within a district need be scheduled. They proposed a hybrid CPU-GPU implementation where the length of the ant's path, the pheromone update, addition, and comparison operations are performed on the GPU. The implementation was not detailed in the paper, and they reported a speedup of 21 with a GTX 660M.

Reference was also made to You [66] and Li et al. [67] who also studied the GPU implementation of ACO on a GPU. However, very few details on the implementation are provided in their published article.

4.2.1 Max-min ant system

The max-min ant system (MMAS) (see [68]) is a variant of the ACO. It adds the following features to the classic ACO:

- Only the best ants are allowed to update the pheromone trails.
- Pheromone trail values are bounded to avoid premature convergences.
- It can be combined with a local search algorithm.

Jiening et al. [60] and Bai et al. [59] proposed the first implementations of the MMAS on a GPU for the solution of TSP. In Jiening et al. [60], only the tour construction stage is processed on a GPU, while in Bai et al. [59], the pheromone update on a GPU was also studied. In these works, the reported speedup did not exceed 2.

Fu et al. [58] used the Jacket toolbox, which connects MATLAB with GPU, for their implementation of MMAS on a GPU. Ants share only one pseudorandom number matrix, one pheromone matrix, one tabu matrix, and one probability matrix in order to reduce communication between the CPU and GPU. Furthermore, they presented a variation of the traditional roulette-wheel selection, that is, the *All-In-Roulette*, which appears to be more adapted to the GPU architecture. With their approach, they achieved a speedup of 30 with a Tesla C1060 GPU, and computational tests were carried out on a system with an Intel i7 3.3 GHz processor and a NVIDIA Tesla C1060 GPU, based on benchmark instances, with up to 1002 cities. They also showed that the solution obtained was close to the one provided by their sequential algorithm.

More recently, Delévacq et al. [56] presented an MMAS for the parallel ant and the multiple colony approaches. In this paper, the authors discussed extensively the drawbacks encountered in such an implementation and proposed solutions based on previous works. In particular, they used the Linear Congruential Generator as proposed by Yu et al. [69] and a GPU 3-opt local search to improve solution quality. Furthermore, the authors compared different GPU implementations where ants were associated with one GPU thread or with one GPU block of threads, also when considering multiple colonies distributed among the GPU block. In experiments conducted with two GPUs of a NVIDIA Fermi C2050 server, on benchmark instances with up to 2396 cities, showed not only a maximum speedup of 24 but also preservation of the quality of the reported solution. These results were obtained when multiple colonies were considered combined with a local search strategy.

4.3 TABU SEARCH

As we can see in Table 8, TS approaches have also been used extensively for the solution of scheduling problems. TS, created by Glover [70,71], uses local

Table 8 Tabu Search on GPU

Algorithm	Problem	Reference
Tabu Search	Resource Constrained Project Scheduling	[72,73]
Tabu Search	Permutation Flow-Shop Scheduling	[74]
Tabu Search	Traveling Salesman Problem/Flow-Shop Scheduling	[75]

search approaches to find a good solution for a problem. From an initial solution, it iteratively selects a new solution from a defined neighborhood. The neighborhood is updated according to the information provided by the new solution. Furthermore, in order to filter the search space, a tabu list is maintained, which corresponds to forbidden moves, such as the set of solutions explored in the previous iterations of the procedure.

The first reported GPU implementation of a TS algorithm was due to Janiak et al. [75] in 2008. This paper deals with the solution of the TSP and the Permutation Flow-Shop Scheduling Problem (PFSP), in which the sequence of operations at each machine should be the same. The authors defined a neighborhood on swap move, that is, by interchanging the position of two customers or two jobs in the current solution. A table of two dimensions is created on the GPU, which computes in each cell of coordinates (i,j) the new solution that results from swapping position i with j. All possible swap moves are then covered, and the CPU selects the best solution from the neighborhood according to the tabu list, which contains forbidden swap moves from previous iterations. This new solution is used to generate the new neighborhood, and so on, until the maximum number of iterations is reached. They used commercial GPUs (GeForce 7300 GT, GeForce 8600 GT, and GeForce 8800 GT) for their experimental tests and, with randomly generated instances, achieved a speedup of 4 with the PFSP and almost no speedup with the TSP.

Based on the results of Janiak et al. [75], who showed that 90% of the processing time is spent in the evaluation function, Czapiński and Barnes [74] designed an improved parallelization of TS for the PFSP. They used a limited parallelization of evaluations as proposed by Bożejko [76]. They proposed to reorder the way a solution is coded in the GPU to ensure a coalesced memory access. Furthermore, the evaluation of the starting time of each job on each machine is done through the use of the shared memory, in an iterative manner in order not to saturate this memory. The matrix of processing time of the jobs on each machine is also stored on the constant memory for faster memory access. Czapiński and Barnes [74] reached a maximum speedup of 89 with a Tesla C1060, based on instances from the literature, and showed that their implementation outperformed the one by Janiak et al. [75].

Bukata et al. [72] and Bukata and Šucha [73] subsequently presented a parallel TS method for the Resource Constrained Project Scheduling Problem (RCPSP). In this variant of the FSP, in order to be executed, each job uses a renewable resource that is available in limited quantity. The used resource of a job is released at the end of its execution. Swap moves are used to define a new neighborhood; however, at each iteration, preprocessing is done to eliminate unfeasible swaps, that is, swaps that violated the precedence constraints on the jobs. Moreover, only a subset of the swaps is performed in order to limit the neighborhood size. The tabu list is represented by a 2D table where position (i,j) contains the value *false* if swapping position i with position j is permitted, or *true* otherwise. The authors also proposed some algorithmic optimization in order to update the starting time of each job and the resources consumed after a swap.

Bukata et al. [72] proposed to concurrently run a TS in each GPU block that manages its own incumbent solution. A list of incumbent solutions is maintained on the global memory that each block accesses through atomic operations. Hence blocks could cooperate through the exchange of solutions, and a diversification technique is processed when a solution is not improved after a certain number of iterations. Experiments were carried out on a server with a GTX 650, with a benchmark from the literature of up to 600 projects and 120 activities. The results were compared with a sequential and a parallel CPU version of their algorithm. They showed that the GPU version achieved a speedup of almost 2 compared to the parallel one without degrading the solution quality.

4.4 OTHER METAHEURISTICS

In addition to the metaheuristics presented in the previous sections, which have been widely studied by different authors, other metaheuristics have received less attention in the literature on GPU computing. In this section, we present these approaches. Table 9 gives an overview of the literature that is detailed in this section.

4.4.1 Deep greedy switching

The deep greedy switching (DGS) heuristic (see [81]) starts from a random initial solution and moves to better solutions by considering a neighborhood resulting from a restricted *2-exchange* approach. This algorithm was implemented on a GPU by Roverso et al. [80] for the solution of the Linear Sum Assignment Problem. This problem consists of assigning a set of jobs to a set of agents. An agent can perform

Table 9 Other Metaheuristics on GPU

Algorithm	Problem	Reference
Constructive Heuristic	Nurse Rerostering	[77]
Multiobjective Local Search	Multiobjective Flow-Shop Scheduling	[78,79]
Deep Greedy Switching	Linear Sum Assignment	[80]

only one job, and when it is performed, a specific profit is collected. The objective is to maximize the sum of the collected profits.

The authors focused on the neighborhood exploration, which is generated by swapping jobs between agents (*2-exchange operator*). Hence the evaluation of the new solution obtained after a swap was processed in parallel on the GPU. Computational experiments were carried out on a system with a NVIDIA GTX 295 GPU with randomly generated instances of up to 9744 jobs. The authors reported a reduction of computation time by a factor of 27.

4.4.2 Multiobjective local search
Luong et al. [78] and Luong [79] studied the implementation on GPUs of a multiobjective local search for the multiobjective FSP. The neighborhood exploration is done on GPU, and they consider different algorithms for the Pareto frontier estimation: an aggregated TS, where the objectives are aggregated in order to obtain a monoobjective problem, along with a Pareto Local Search Algorithms from Paquete and Stützle [82]. Furthermore, in order to overcome the noncoalesced accesses to the memory, they propose to use the texture memory of the GPU.

They carried out their experimental tests on problems ranging from 20 jobs and 10 machines to 200 jobs and 20 machines. They considered three objectives: the makespan, total tardiness, and number of jobs delayed with regard to their due date. With a GTX 480, they observed a maximum speedup of 16 times with the aggregated TS and 15.7 times with the Pareto local search algorithm.

4.4.3 Constructive heuristic
Zdeněk et al. [77] presented an implementation of the Constructive Heuristic of Moz and Pato [83], who proposed this heuristic to initialize their GA for the solution of the Nurse Rerostering Problem. This Constructive Heuristic proceeded as follows: from an original roster, a randomly ordered shift list is generated; then the current roster is cleared, and the shifts are assigned back to the modified roster one by one according to certain rules. In their heterogeneous model, the GPU is used to do the shift assignment, and the rest of the algorithm is performed on the CPU. Furthermore, multiple randomly ordered shift lists are generated in order to explore in parallel multiple shift reassignments and to take advantage of the GPU.

Experimental tests were carried out with a GTX 650, based on the instances from Moz and Pato [83]; up to 32 nurses with a planning horizon of 28 days were considered. They achieved a maximum speedup of 2.51 with an optimality gap between 4% and 18%.

5 CONCLUSIONS

The domain of OR is ripe with difficult problems. In this chapter, we concentrated on GPU computing in the OR field. In particular, we surveyed the major contributions to integer programming and LP. In many cases, significant reduction in computing time was observed for OR problems. Nevertheless, it is difficult to establish a quantitative comparison between the different approaches quoted in this chapter because the reported results were obtained via different GPUs architectures. Therefore it is not possible to identify the best implementation for a given algorithm. Metrics that facilitate comparisons between the various parallel algorithms have not been designed and commonly accepted. Issues related to the quality of solutions must also to be taken into account.

As shown in this chapter, most of the classic OR algorithms have been implemented on GPUs. Exact methods have received less attention than metaheuristics, essentially because of their lack of flexibility. In order to achieve consequent speedup, the operators of the different metaheuristics have to be adapted to fit into the GPU architecture. We note for instance that important acceleration in GA and ACO were achieved by modifying the roulette-wheel selection. Also, the coding solutions and the way they are stored in the GPU memory play major roles in the performance of the algorithms. The main drawbacks of implementation come from the fact that we try to fit algorithms that are sequential by nature into a parallel architecture. Dedicated parallel OR algorithms need to be designed.

Because many applications include OR problems, the future of GPU computing seems very promising. New features such as dynamic parallelism (i.e., the possibility for GPU threads to automatically spawn new threads) simplify parallel programming and seem particularly suited to integer programming applications. The new NVIDIA Pascal architecture should feature more memory, 1 TB/s memory bandwidth, and twice as much FLOPS as the current Maxwell architecture. NVLink technology should also permit data to move 5–10 times faster than PCI-Express technology.

CUDA updates and OpenCL updates (or the recent OpenACC http://www.openacc-standard.org/) always tend to facilitate programming and improve efficiency of accelerators by hiding programming difficulties. We note in particular that OpenACC is a set of high-level programs that enables C/C++ and Fortran programmers to use highly parallel processors with much of the convenience of OpenMP.

In the future OR industrial codes will be able to benefit from accelerators like GPUs that are widely available and to propose attractive and fast solutions to customers. Nevertheless, an important challenge remains in the exact solution of industrial problems of significant size via GPUs.

ACKNOWLEDGMENTS

Dr Didier El Baz thanks NVIDIA Corporation for support. Dr Vincent Boyer and Dr M. Angélica Salazar-Aguilar thank the Program for Teachers Improvement (PROMEP) for support under the grant PROMEP/103.5/13/6644.

CONFLICTS OF INTEREST

The authors declare that they have no conflicts of interest.

REFERENCES

[1] H. Nguyen, GPU GEMS 3, Addison Wesley Professional, Santa Clara, CA, 2008.

[2] A.R. Brodtkorb, T.R. Hagen, C. Schulz, G. Hasle, GPU computing in discrete optimization. Part I: introduction to the GPU, EURO J. Transp. Logist. 2 (2013) 129–157.

[3] C. Schulz, G. Hasle, A.R. Brodtkorb, T.R. Hagen, GPU computing in discrete optimization. Part II: survey focused on routing problems, EURO J. Transp. Logist. 2 (2013) 159–186.

[4] T. Van Luong, Métaheuristiques parallèles Sur GPU, Ph.D. thesis, Université Lille 1—Sciences et Technologies, 2011.

[5] E. Alba, G. Luque, S. Nesmachnow, Parallel metaheuristics: recent advances and new trends, Int. Trans. Oper. Res. 20 (1) (2013) 1–48, ISSN 1475-3995.

[6] A. Schrijver, Theory of Integer and Linear Programming, Wiley, Chichester, 1986.

[7] S. Ólafsson, Chapter 21 metaheuristics, in: S.G. Henderson, B.L. Nelson (Eds.), Simulation, Handbooks in Operations Research and Management Science, vol. 13, Elsevier, 2006 pp. 633–654.

[8] W.L. Winston, J.B. Goldberg, Operations Research: Applications and Algorithms, vol. 3, Duxbury Press, Boston, 2004.

[9] G.B. Dantzig, Maximization of a linear function of variables subject to linear inequalities, in: Activity Analysis of Production and Allocation, Wiley and Chapman-Hall, 1951, pp. 339–347.

[10] M.E. Lalami, V. Boyer, D. El Baz, Efficient implementation of the simplex method on a CPU-GPU system, in: 25th IEEE International Parallel and Distributed Processing Symposium, Workshops and PhD Forum (IPDPSW), Workshop PCO'11, ISSN 1530-2075, 2011, pp. 1999–2006.

[11] M.E. Lalami, D. El Baz, V. Boyer, Multi GPU implementation of the simplex algorithm, in: 13th IEEE International Conference on High Performance Computing and Communications (HPCC 2011), 2011, pp. 179–186.

[12] X. Meyer, P. Albuquerque, B. Chopard, A multi-GPU implementation and performance model for the standard simplex method, in: Euro-Par 2011, 2011, pp. 312–319.

[13] N. Ploskas, N. Samaras, Efficient GPU-based implementations of simplex type algorithms, Appl. Math. Comput. 250 (2015) 552–570.

[14] P. Nikolaos, S. Nikolaos, A computational comparison of basis updating schemes for the simplex algorithm on a CPU-GPU system, Am. J. Oper. Res. 3 (2013) 497.

[15] J. Bieling, P. Peschlow, P. Martini, An efficient GPU implementation of the revised simplex method, in: 24th IEEE International Parallel Distributed Processing Symposium, Workshops and PhD Forum (IPDPSW 2010), 2010, pp. 1–8.

[16] D.G. Spampinato, A.C. Elster, Linear optimization on modern GPUs, in: 2009 IEEE International Parallel and Distributed Processing Symposium (IPDPS), ISSN 1530-2075, 2009, pp. 1–8.

[17] G. Greeff, The revised simplex algorithm on a GPU, Univ. of Stellenbosch, Tech. Rep., 2005.

[18] J.H. Jung, D.P. O'Leary, Implementing an interior point method for linear programs on a CPU-GPU system, Electron. Trans. Numer. Anal. 28 (2008) 174–189.

[19] R.C. Whaley, J. Dongarra, Automatically tuned linear algebra software, in: Ninth SIAM Conference on Parallel Processing for Scientific Computing, 1999, pp. 1–27.

[20] G.B. Dantzig, W. Orchard-Hays, The product form for the inverse in the simplex method, Math. Tables Other Aids Comput. 8 (1954) 64–67.

[21] M. Benhamadou, On the simplex algorithm "revised form", Adv. Eng. Software 33 (11) (2002) 769–777.

[22] D. Goldfarb, J.K. Reid, A practicable steepest-edge simplex algorithm, Math. Program. 12 (1) (1977) 361–371.

[23] R.S. Garfinkel, G.L. Nemhauser, Integer Programming, vol. 4, Wiley, New York, 1972.

[24] R. Bellman, Dynamic Programming, Princeton University Press, Princeton, NJ, 1957.

[25] V. Boyer, D. El Baz, M. Elkihel, Dense dynamic programming on multi GPU, in: 19th International Conference on Parallel, Distributed and network-based Processing (PDP 2011), ISSN 1066-6192, 2011, pp. 545–551.

[26] V. Boyer, D. El Baz, M. Elkihel, Solving knapsack problems on GPU, Comput. Oper. Res. 39 (1) (2012) 42–47, ISSN 0305-0548.

[27] B. Suri, U.D. Bordoloi, P. Eles, A scalable GPU-based approach to accelerate the multiple-choice knapsack problem, in: Design, Automation Test in Europe Conference Exhibition (DATE), ISSN 1530-1591, 2012, pp. 1126–1129.

[28] S. Martello, P. Toth, Knapsack Problems: Algorithms and Computer Implementations, John Wiley & Sons, Inc., Chichester, UK, 1990.

[29] M.L. Pinedo, Scheduling: Theory, Algorithms, and Systems, Springer Science & Business Media, New York, 2012.

[30] G. Reinelt, The Traveling Salesman: Computational Solutions for TSP Applications, Springer-Verlag, Berlin, 1994.

[31] A. Boukedjar, M.E. Lalami, D. El Baz, Parallel branch and bound on a CPU-GPU system, in: 20th International Conference on Parallel, Distributed and Network-Based Processing (PDP 2012), ISSN 1066-6192, 2012, pp. 392–398.

[32] M.E. Lalami, D. El Baz, GPU implementation of the branch and bound method for knapsack problems, in: 26th IEEE International Parallel and Distributed Processing Symposium, Workshops and PhD Forum (IPDPSW), Workshop PCO'12, 2012, pp. 1769–1777.

[33] M.E. Lalami, Contribution à la résolution de problèmes d'optimisation combinatoire: méthodes séquentielles et parallèles, Ph.D. Thesis, Université Paul Sabatier, Toulouse, 2012.

[34] I. Chakroun, N. Melab, An adaptative multi-GPU based Branch-and-Bound. A case study: the flow-shop scheduling problem, in: IEEE 14th International Conference on High Performance Computing and Communication and 2012 IEEE 9th International Conference on Embedded Software and Systems (HPCC-ICESS), 2012, pp. 389–395.

[35] I. Chakroun, M. Mezmaz, N. Melab, A. Bendjoudi, Reducing thread divergence in a GPU-accelerated branch-and-bound algorithm, Concurr. Comput. 25 (8) (2012) 1121–1136.

[36] I. Chakroun, N. Melab, M. Mezmaz, D. Tuyttens, Combining multi-core and GPU computing for solving combinatorial optimization problems, J. Parallel Distrib. Comput. 73 (12) (2013) 1563–1577.

[37] N. Melab, I. Chakroun, M. Mezmaz, D. Tuyttens, A GPU-accelerated Branch-and-Bound algorithm for the flow-shop scheduling problem, in: 2012 IEEE International Conference on Cluster Computing (CLUSTER), 2012, pp. 10–17.

[38] T. Carneiro, A.E. Muritiba, M. Negreiros, G.A.L. de Campos, A new parallel schema for Branch-and-Bound algorithms using GPGPU, in: 2011 23rd International Symposium on Computer Architecture and High Performance Computing (SBAC-PAD), IEEE, 2011, pp. 41–47.

[39] B. Lageweg, J. Lenstra, A.R. Kan, A general bounding scheme for the permutation flow-shop problem, Oper. Res. 26 (1) (1978) 53–67.

[40] E. Taillard, Benchmark for basic scheduling problems, J. Oper. Res. 64 (1993) 278–285.

[41] I.H. Osman, G. Laporte, Metaheuristics: a bibliography, Ann. Oper. Res. 63 (5) (1996) 511–623.

[42] F. Pinel, B. Dorronsoro, P. Bouvry, Solving very large instances of the scheduling of independent tasks problem on the GPU, J. Parallel Distrib. Comput. 73 (1) (2013) 101–110, ISSN 0743-7315.

[43] F. Pinel, B. Dorronsoro, P. Bouvry, A new cellular genetic algorithm to solve the scheduling problem designed for the GPU, in: Metaheuristics Conference (META), 2010.

[44] M. Pedemonte, E. Alba, F. Luna, Towards the design of systolic genetic search, in: 26th IEEE International Parallel and Distributed Processing Symposium, Workshops and PhD Forum (IPDPSW 2012), Workshop PCO'12, 2012, pp. 1778–1786.

[45] T. Zajíček, P. Šucha, Accelerating a flow Shop scheduling algorithm on the GPU, in: Workshop on Models and Algorithms for Planning and Scheduling Problems (MAPSP), 2011.

[46] S. Chen, S. Davis, H. Jiang, A. Novobilski, CUDA-based genetic algorithm on traveling salesman problem, in: R. Lee (Ed.), Computers and Information Science, Springer, Berlin, Heidelberg, 2011, pp. 241–252.

[47] J. Li, L. Zhang, L. Liu, A parallel immune algorithm based on fine-grained model with GPU-acceleration, in: 2009 Fourth International Conference on Innovative Computing, Information and Control (ICICIC), 2009, pp. 683–686.

[48] S.N. Sivanandam, S.N. Deepa, Introduction to Genetic Algorithms, Springer, New York, 2007.

[49] O.H. Ibarra, C.E. Kim, Heuristic algorithms for scheduling independent tasks on nonidentical processors, J. ACM 24 (2) (1977) 280–289, ISSN 0004-5411.

[50] E. Alba, B. Dorronsoro, Cellular Genetic Algorithms, vol. 42, Springer, New York, 2008.

[51] H. Kung, Why systolic architectures?, IEEE Comput. 15 (1) (1982) 37–46.

[52] H. Kung, C.E. Leiserson, Systolic Arrays (for VLSI), in: Sparse Matrix Proceedings, 1978, pp. 256–282.

[53] M. Dorigo, M. Birattari, T. Stützle, Ant colony optimization, IEEE Comput. Intell. Mag. 1 (4) (2006) 28–39.

[54] N.A. Kallioras, K. Kepaptsoglou, N.D. Lagaros, Transit stop inspection and maintenance scheduling: a GPU accelerated metaheuristics approach, Transp. Res. C Emerg. Technol. 55 (2015) 246–260.

[55] A. Uchida, Y. Ito, K. Nakano, Accelerating ant colony optimisation for the travelling salesman problem on the GPU, Int. J. Parallel Emergent Distrib. Syst. 29 (4) (2014) 401–420.

[56] A. Delévacq, P. Delisle, M. Gravel, M. Krajecki, Parallel ant colony optimization on graphics processing units, J. Parallel Distrib. Comput. 73 (1) (2013) 52–61.

[57] J.M. Cecilia, J.M. Garcia, M. Ujaldon, A. Nisbet, M. Amos, Parallelization strategies for ant colony optimisation on GPUs, in: 25th IEEE International Parallel and Distributed Processing Symposium, Workshops and PhD Forum (IPDPSW 2011), ISSN 1530-2075, 2011, pp. 339–346.

[58] J. Fu, L. Lei, G. Zhou, A parallel Ant Colony Optimization algorithm with GPU-acceleration based on All-In-Roulette selection, in: Third International Workshop on Advanced Computational Intelligence (IWACI 2010), 2010, pp. 260–264.

[59] H. Bai, D. Ouyang, X. Li, L. He, H. Yu, MAX-MIN Ant System on GPU with CUDA, in: Fourth International Conference on Innovative Computing, Information and Control (ICICIC 2009), 2009, pp. 801–804.

[60] W. Jiening, D. Jiankang, Z. Chunfeng, Implementation of Ant Colony algorithm based on GPU, in: Sixth International Conference on Computer Graphics, Imaging and Visualization, 2009 (CGIV '09), 2009, pp. 50–53.

[61] A. Catala, J. Jaen, J.A. Modioli, Strategies for accelerating ant colony optimization algorithms on graphical processing units, in: 2007 IEEE Congress on Evolutionary Computation (CEC 2007), 2007, pp. 492–500.

[62] G. Laporte, S. Martello, The selective travelling salesman problem, Discret. Appl. Math. 26 (2) (1990) 193–207.

[63] T. Scavo, Scatter-to-gather transformation for scalability, 2010, https://hub.vscse.org/resources/223.

[64] M. Harris, S. Sengupta, J.D. Owens, Parallel prefix sum (scan) with CUDA, GPU Gems 3 (39) (2007) 851–876.

[65] G. Reinelt, TSPLIB—a traveling salesman problem library, ORSA J. Comput. 3 (4) (1991) 376–384.

[66] Y.S. You, Parallel ant system for traveling salesman problem on GPUs, in: Eleventh Annual Conference on Genetic and Evolutionary Computation, 2009, pp. 1–2.

[67] J. Li, X. Hu, Z. Pang, K. Qian, A parallel ant colony optimization algorithm based on fine-grained model with GPU-acceleration, Int. J. Innov. Comput. Inf. Control 5 (11) (2009) 3707–3716.

[68] T. Stützle, H.H. Hoos, MAX-MIN ant system, Futur. Gener. Comput. Syst. 16 (8) (2000) 889–914.

[69] Q. Yu, C. Chen, Z. Pan, Parallel genetic algorithms on programmable graphics hardware, in: Advances in Natural Computation, Springer, 2005 pp. 1051–1059.

[70] F. Glover, Tabu Search—part I, ORSA J. Comput. 1 (3) (1989) 190–206.

[71] F. Glover, Tabu Search—part II, ORSA J. Comput. 2 (1) (1990) 4–32.

[72] L. Bukata, P. Šůcha, Z. Hanzálek, Solving the resource constrained project scheduling problem using the parallel Tabu Search designed for the {CUDA} platform, J. Parallel Distrib. Comput. 77 (2015) 58–68.

[73] L. Bukata, P. Šucha, A GPU algorithm design for resource constrained scheduling problem, in: 21st Conference on Parallel, Distributed and Networked-Based Processing (PDP), 2013, pp. 367–374.

[74] M. Czapiński, S. Barnes, Tabu Search with two approaches to parallel flow shop evaluation on CUDA platform, J. Parallel Distrib. Comput. 71 (2011) 802–811.

[75] A. Janiak, W. Janiak, M. Lichtenstein, Tabu Search on GPU, J. Univ. Comput. Sci. 14 (14) (2008) 2416–2427.

[76] W. Bożejko, Solving the flow shop problem by parallel programming, J. Parallel Distrib. Comput. 69 (5) (2009) 470–481.

[77] B. Zdeněk, D. Jan, Š. Přemysl, H. Zdeněk, An acceleration of the algorithm for the nurse rerostering problem on a graphics processing unit, Lect. Notes Manag. Sci. 5 (2013) 101–110.

[78] T.V. Luong, N. Melab, E.G. Talbi, GPU-based approaches for multiobjective local search algorithms. A case study: the flowshop scheduling problem, Evol. Comput. Comb. Optim. 6622 (2011) 155–166.

[79] T.V. Luong, Métaheuristiques parallèles sur GPU, Ph.D. Thesis, Université Lille 1, 2011.

[80] R. Roverso, A. Naiem, M. El-Beltagy, S. El-Ansary, S. Haridi, A GPU-enabled solver for time-constrained linear sum assignment problems, in: 7th International Conference on Informatics and Systems (INFOS), 2011, pp. 1–6.

[81] A. Naiem, M. El-Beltagy, Deep greedy switching: a fast and simple approach for linear assignment problems, in: 7th International Conference of Numerical Analysis and Applied Mathematics, 2009.

[82] L. Paquete, T. Stützle, Stochastic local search algorithms for multiobjective combinatorial optimization: a review, Tech. Rep., Institut de Recherches Interdisciplinaires et de Développements en Intelligence Artificielle, 2006.

[83] M. Moz, M.V. Pato, A genetic algorithm approach to a nurse rerostering problem, Comput. Oper. Res. 34 (3) (2007) 667–691.

GPU-accelerated shortest paths computations for planar graphs

11

G. Chapuis[1], H. Djidjev[1], D. Lavenier[2], R. Andonov[3]

LANL, Los Alamos, NM, United States[1] CNRS, Rennes, France[2] University of Rennes 1, Rennes, France[3]

1 INTRODUCTION

1.1 MOTIVATION

Computing shortest paths or distances in a graph is a central problem in many domains ranging from bioinformatics and the analysis of large interaction graphs to network routing. Shortest paths or distances are a first step to obtaining graph measures that are useful to the understanding of a given network. Such measures include graph diameter, the largest distance between any two vertices in the graph; the excentricity of a given vertex, the greatest distance between this vertex and any other vertex in the graph; and the betweenness centrality of a given vertex or edge, the number of shortest paths in the graph going through this vertex or edge. Betweenness centrality is especially important as it can be used to determine the importance of a node or edge in a graph. In a road network, for instance, betweenness centrality can assess the impact of removing a road intersection in the network.

Once computed, shortest paths in a graph will allow for faster computation of these measures relevant to network analyses. To this end, one can compute and store some or all of these shortest paths in order to obtain graph measures that are needed for their analyses, in most cases, in linear time complexity.

Graphics processing units (GPUs) have proven to be an efficient alternative to CPUs for the general-purpose computation of problems that fit the GPU paradigm. Shortest path algorithms that create the lowest time complexity can be implemented on the GPU at the cost of implementing complex data structures that may not perform optimally on a GPU. Other approaches exist that offer higher time complexity but fit ideally the GPU paradigm. The algorithms we describe in this chapter are similar in structure to a matrix multiplication, which is an ideal candidate for computation on GPUs, while offering a time complexity comparable to the best-known algorithms for shortest paths. Additionally, these proposed algorithms present a high level of

Advances in GPU Research and Practice. http://dx.doi.org/10.1016/B978-0-12-803738-6.00011-2

coarse-grained parallelism and can be distributed efficiently across cluster nodes. Our implementations allow the computation of all shortest paths in real and artificially generated planar graphs with millions of vertices in minutes and can answer shortest path queries on these graphs in a quarter of a millisecond.

1.2 SHORTEST PATH PROBLEMS

The Single-Source Shortest Path (SSSP) problem consists of finding the shortest paths between a given vertex v and all other vertices in the graph. Algorithms such as Breadth-First-Search (BFS) for unweighted graphs or Dijkstra [1] solve this problem. The All-Pairs Shortest Path (APSP) problem consists of finding the shortest path between all pairs of vertices in the graph. To solve this second problem, one can use the Floyd-Warshall algorithm [2] or apply the Dijkstra algorithm to each vertex in the graph.

The Single-Pair Shortest Path (SPSP) problem consists of finding the shortest path between a single pair of vertices. This problem is mostly solved using Dijkstra, though in this case a single result is kept and other shortest paths are discarded.

We will use the following notations in the rest of this chapter. A graph $G(V, E)$ is composed of a set V or vertices and a set E of edges between these vertices. Let $e(v_1, v_2)$ denote the presence of an edge between vertices v_1 and v_2. Each edge e in E has a weight $w(e)$—for unweighted graphs, edges can be assigned the same arbitrary weight. Let $dist_G(v_1, v_2)$ denote the length of the shortest path between vertices v_1 and v_2 in the graph—that is, the sum of the weights of the edges composing the shortest path. For instance, if $e(v_1, v_2) \in E$ and there exists no shorter path between v_1 and v_2 in the graph, we have that $dist_G(v_1, v_2) = w(e(v_1, v_2))$. Let $\overline{dist}(v_1, v_2)$ denote the distance of the shortest path known so far in the graph between v_1 and v_2. The inequality $dist_G(v_1, v_2) \leq \overline{dist}(v_1, v_2)$ therefore always holds. Further notations will be introduced in the following sections where necessary.

1.3 FLOYD-WARSHALL'S APSP

The Floyd-Warshall algorithm presents a systematic approach to solving the APSP problem. For every vertex k in a given graph and every pair of vertices (i, j), the algorithm attempts to improve the shortest known path between i and j by going through k (see Algorithm 1).

ALGORITHM 1 FLOYD-WARSHALL'S ALGORITHM. THIS VERSION COMPUTES THE SHORTEST DISTANCES WITHOUT SAVING THE SHORTEST PATHS

```
INPUT: A graph G(V,E).
OUTPUT: Shortest distances between all
        pairs of vertices in V stored
        in dist.
```

```
function Floyd-Warshall(G)
    // Initialization
    for vertices (i,j) in VxV do
        if e(i,j) is in E then
            dist[i,j] = w(e(i,j))
        else
            dist[i,j] = infinity
        end if
    end for

    // Shortest paths computations
    for vertex k in V do
        for vertices (i,j) in VxV do
            new_dist = dist[i,k]+dist[k,j]
            if new_dist < dist[i,j] then
                dist[i,j] = new_dist
            end if
        end for
    end for
    return dist
end function
```

This approach to the APSP problem presents several advantages. First, the structure of the algorithm is identical to a matrix multiplication where the dot product—with $(+, *)$ operations—is replaced by a *tropical* product—with $(\min, +)$ operations. This similarity with a matrix multiplication includes regular data access patterns and thus a certain level of cache-friendliness. The total number of operations solely depends on the number of vertices in the graph; two graphs with the same number of vertices will require the same number of operations and should execute in roughly the same time on similar machines. This predictability is useful when balancing workloads between different computational units.

The main drawback of this approach, however, is its $O(n^3)$ complexity, where $n = |V|$. This approach and its cubic complexity make runtimes prohibitively high for large sparse graphs.

1.4 DIJKSTRA'S SSSP

Unlike Floyd-Warshall, the Dijkstra algorithm exploits the sparsity of a graph to reduce its complexity. The algorithm explores outgoing edges of the graph from the source vertex starting with the lowest weighted edge and incrementally builds the shortest paths to all other vertices (see Algorithm 2). Dijkstra's algorithm can be used to solve all three presented shortest path problems so long as no negative edge weights exist in the graph. In Algorithm 2, we present the SSSP problem-solving variant of Dijkstra. In order to solve the APSP problem, we simply need to apply the same algorithm using every vertex in the graph as the source vertex. To solve the SPSP problem, we can use the same algorithm and stop the exploration once the target vertex is reached.

Whether it is useful in practice to stop the computation once the target vertex is reached is debatable. In the worst case where the target node is found last, checking at every iteration whether the target vertex is reached will definitely increase the runtime. For the optimal case on a large graph (the target vertex is the closest neighbor of the source vertex), checking whether the target vertex is reached should be faster. The usefulness of such a check on the average case is hardware-dependent, and problem-dependent as well. Different architectures will not tolerate identically the extra comparison and branches induced by the additional check.

ALGORITHM 2 DIJKSTRA'S ALGORITHM. THIS VERSION COMPUTES THE SHORTEST DISTANCES WITHOUT SAVING THE SHORTEST PATHS

INPUT: A graph G(V,E) and a source vertex s.
OUTPUT: Shortest distances between s and all
        vertices in V stored in dist.

```
function Dijkstra(G, s)
    // Initialization
    dist[s] = 0
    for vertex v in G do
        if v != s then
            dist[v] = infinity
        end if
        add v to Q
    end for

    // Shortest paths computations
    while Q is not empty do
        u = vertex in Q with min dist[u]
        remove u from Q
        for neighbor v of u do
            new_dist = dist[u]+w(u, v)
            if new_dist < dist[v] then
                dist[v] = new_dist
            end if
        end for
    end while
    return dist
end function
```

This second approach trades regular data access patterns and workload predictibility for lower complexity when the graph is sparse. The complexity of this algorithm for the SSSP problem is in $O(|E| + |V| \log(|V|))$, when using a Fibonacci heap for the queue. For solving the APSP problem, this complexity becomes $O(|V||E| + |V|^2 \log |V|)$; when the graph is sparse, it is a clear improvement over Floyd-Warshall's algorithm, but for a complete graph, the complexity is the same as Floyd-Warshall's. When solving the SPSP problem, we can gain a factor 2 on average over SSSP's complexity, which results in the same complexity in big O notation. It is also important to note that, unlike Floyd-Warshall's, this algorithm will not work for graphs with negative edges.

1.5 IMPLEMENTATION CHALLENGES IN A DISTRIBUTED GPU ENVIRONMENT

When considering a GPU implementation, the regularity of data accesses of Floyd-Warshall's algorithm is a great advantage. The high latency of global fetches and small caches of GPUs require a high level of cache-friendliness for an implementation to reach a high efficiency. Moreover, when considering a distributed implementation, the fact that the complexity of the algorithm is only a function of the number of vertices means that balancing workloads between physical nodes is trivial. Namely, two subgraphs with the same number of vertices will be computed in the same time regardless of the two graph's internal structures, thus making an efficient, static load balancing scheme easy to implement.

Dijkstra's algorithm, on the other hand, is difficult to implement efficiently on a GPU. The performance of the algorithm relies on a complicated data structure for the queue. This data structure will necessarily have irregular data access patterns, which will hinder the performance on a GPU. Furthermore, the fact that the complexity of the approach depends on the internal structure of the input graph means that load balancing has to be a dynamic process computed at runtime. Despite these drawbacks, the lower complexity for sparse graphs allows Dijkstra implementations to scale much better with larger graphs.

When it comes to solving the APSP problem on a cluster of GPUs, both the Dijkstra and Floyd-Warshall approaches have advantages and drawbacks. Although a Floyd-Warshall approach is slower, the regularity of its memory accesses—identical to those of a matrix multiplication—makes it an ideal candidate for an implementation on a highly vectorized hardware such as GPUs. Additionally, the complexity of the approach is independent of the internal structure of the graph and solely depends on the number of vertices; this particular property allows workloads to be easily balanced between multiple processing units.

Dijkstra's approach, on the other hand, is much faster for sparse graphs but requires complex data structures that are difficult to implement efficiently on a GPU.

In order to target executions on a distributed GPU environment, we would ideally like the regular workloads and access patterns of Floyd-Warshall's algorithm and the better complexity for sparse graphs of Dijkstra's.

2 RELATED WORK

The development of parallel solvers for the APSP problem is an active field of research. Harish and Narayanan [3] proposed GPU implementations of both the Dijkstra and Floyd-Warshall algorithms to solve the APSP problem and compared them to parallel CPU implementations. Both approaches, however, require that the whole graph fit in a single GPU's memory. Given the limited, though gradually increasing, amount of memory available on GPUs compared to their CPU counterpart, this limitation prevents large graphs from being computed. They reported solving APSP for a 100k vertex graph in approximately 22 min on a single GPU. Katz et al. [4] proposed a cache-efficient parallel, blocked version of the Floyd-Warshall algorithm for solving the APSP problem on GPUs. While Ref. [4] mentions graphs that are larger than what would fit onto a GPU's on-board memory, the largest graph instances described in the paper are still only approximately 10k vertices.

Buluç et al. [5] proposed a blocked-recursive Floyd-Warshall approach. Their implementation, running on a single GPU, shows a speedup of 17–45 when compared to a multicore CPU implementation and outperform both GPU implementations from Ref. [3]. Their blocked-recursive implementation also requires that the entire graph fit in the GPU's global memory; therefore they only report timings for graphs with up to 8k vertices. Okuyama et al. [6] proposed an improvement over the GPU implementation of Dijkstra for APSP from Ref. [3] by caching data in on-chip memory and exhibiting a higher level of parallelism. Their approach showed a speedup of 2.8–13 over Dijkstra's SSSP-based method of Ref. [3]. Matsumoto et al. [7] also proposed a blocked Floyd-Warshall algorithm that they implemented for simultaneous computations on a single GPU and a multicore CPU. Their implementation handles graphs with up to 32k vertices and achieves near peak performance. Only Ortega-Arranz et al. [8] report solving APSP on large graphs, up to 1024k vertices. Using an SSSP-based Dijkstra approach, their implementation runs on a multicore CPU and up to two GPUs simultaneously and computes the complete APSP problem on a 1024k vertex graph in less than 4.5 h. Recent experimental work on parallel algorithms for solving just the SSSP problem for large graph instances using a Δ-stepping approach [9] is described in Ref. [10].

Concerning the SPSP problem, many sequential algorithms exist. Dijkstra's algorithm [1] finds the distances between a source vertex v and all other vertices of the graph in $O(|E|\log|V|)$ time, where $|V|$ and $|E|$ are the numbers of the vertices and edges of the graph, respectively. The same approach can be used to find efficiently the distance between a single pair of vertices. This algorithm is nearly optimal (within a logarithmic factor), but has irregular structure, which makes it hard to implement efficiently in parallel. Floyd-Warshall's algorithm [2,11], on the other hand, finds the distances between all pairs of vertices of the graph in $O(|V|^3)$ time, which is efficient for dense ($|E| = \Theta(|V|^2)$) graphs, has a regular structure good for parallel implementation, but is inefficient for sparse ($|E| = O(|V|)$) graphs such as planar graphs. The query version of the single pair problem consists of constructing a data structure that will allow for quickly answering any subsequent distance query.

A distance query asks, given an arbitrary pair of vertices v, w, to compute $dist_g(v, w)$. There is an obvious trade-off between the size of the data structure and the time for answering a query. For instance, Dijkstra's algorithm gives a use solution of the query version of the SP problem with (small) $O(|V| + |E|)$ space (for storing the input graph), but large $O(|E| \log |V|)$ query time (for running Dijkstra's algorithm with the first query vertex as the source). On the other end of the spectrum, Floyd-Warshall's algorithm can be used to construct a (large) $O(|V|^2)$ data structure (the distance matrix) in $O(|V|^3)$ preprocessing time, allowing (short) $O(1)$ query time (retrieving the distance from the data base).

However, for very large graphs, the $O(|V|^2)$ space requirement and the $O(|V|^3)$ time needed to create the data structure are impractical. We are interested in an algorithm that needs significantly less than $O(|V|^2)$ space, but will answer queries in sublinear time. Our SPSP algorithm will make use of the structure of planar graphs for increased efficiency, as most road networks are planar or near-planar, and will also be highly parallelizable, making use of the features available in modern high-performance clusters and specialized processors such as GPUs.

The query version for shortest path queries in planar graphs was proposed in Ref. [12] and different aspects of the problem were later studied by multiple authors, for example, Refs. [13,14]. Here we present the first distributed implementation for solving the problem and the first one that is designed to make use of the potential for parallelism offered by GPUs.

3 PARTITIONED APPROACHES

In this section, we describe three algorithms for shortest path computations suitable for GPU acceleration as well as their associated implementations. The first two algorithms target the APSP problem. Of these two algorithms, the first one allows the computation of shortest paths for graphs with negative edges. The second of these two algorithms trades the ability of working with negative edges for a better parallel scalability and improved memory distribution. The third algorithm targets the SPSP query problem.

This section is organized as follows: we first describe the graph partitioning procedure, common to all three algorithms, and then we describe our two APSP algorithms and our SPSP algorithm. The following section describes two GPU primitives for the computation of shortest paths that are extensively used in our implementations.

The input graph, respectively, intermediate and final results, can easily be represented as an n by n distance matrix D, where $D[i][j]$ can, respectively, contain the input distance from vertex i to vertex j, the shortest distance discovered so far from i to j and eventually, the shortest distance in the graph from i to j. For very large graphs, however, such a representation cannot be kept on a single machine's memory as the n by n requirement would rapidly exceed the available memory with increasing values of n.

3.1 GRAPH PARTITIONING

As a first step to our three algorithms, the input graph G is divided into k components of roughly the same size. The decomposition is done by identifying a set of edges (a cut set) whose removal from G results into a disconnected graph of k parts we call components. The set of all components is called a partition. Note that, although by the standard definition in graph theory, a component is connected, this is not a requirement in our case (although in the typical case, our components will be connected). A requirement is that every vertex in G belongs to exactly one component of the partition. Moreover, in order for the resulting shortest path algorithms to be efficient, the cut set of edges should be small. Not all classes of graphs have such partitions, but some important classes do. These include the class of planar graphs, the class of graphs of low genus (that can be drawn on a sphere with a small number of "handles" [15]), some geometric graphs, and graphs corresponding to networks with good community structure. The algorithms described in the chapter will work efficiently only for graphs of these classes.

In our implementations, this partitioning step is performed by a k-way partitioning routine from the METIS library [16]. The result is a partition of the graph into k parts, where the number of incident edges—edges between vertices of different components—is minimized. Because this problem belongs to the NP-hard class, METIS uses a heuristic approach to quickly obtain a satisfying approximate solution. This call to the METIS library represents a negligible portion of the total runtimes of our approaches.

Once a partition is obtained, a reordering of the vertices is performed so that vertices from the same component are given consecutive indices. Boundary vertices, that is, vertices directly connected to other components, are given the lowest indices of their component. Fig. 1 shows a distance matrix representation of the graph after such a reordering of the vertices.

We can distinguish two types of submatrices: diagonal submatrices, which contain the shortest distances known so far (at this point only initial distances in the graph) between vertices of the same component (Fig. 2), and nondiagonal submatrices, which contain the shortest distances known so far between vertices of

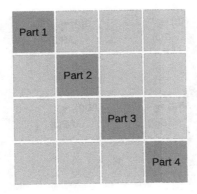

FIG. 1

Distance matrix representation of the input graph after reordering of the vertices. Vertices from the same components have contiguous indices. The matrices on the diagonal correspond to distances between vertices from the same component.

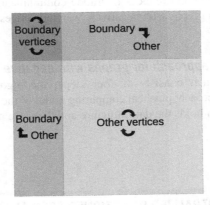

FIG. 2

Diagonal submatrix in the distance matrix representation of the graph. Boundary vertices have the lowest indices of their component.

different components (Fig. 3). Note that for the case of an undirected graph, the lower and upper triangles of the distance matrix are identical.

3.2 ALL-PAIRS SHORTEST PATH ALGORITHMS

We describe here two algorithms and their respective implementations for the APSP problem. The first approach is a centralized master/slave approach. The second

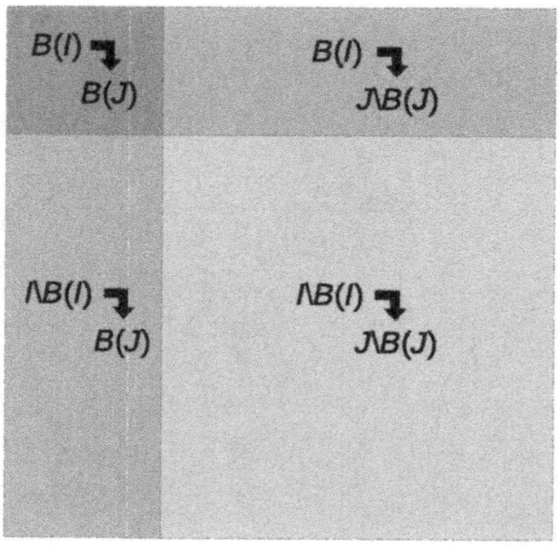

FIG. 3

Nondiagonal submatrix in the distance matrix representation of the graph. This submatrix contains the distances between components i and j. The *arrows* assume $i < j$.

approach is decentralized and reduces internode communication at the expense of the ability to work with graphs with negatively weighted edges.

3.2.1 A centralized approach for graphs with negative weights

The centralized approach consists of four steps; the algorithm is detailed in Algorithm 3. In this approach, physical computing nodes of the cluster are composed of a master node, which holds the data structure and the slave nodes, which are used for computations.

ALGORITHM 3 CENTRALIZED PARTITIONED APSP ALGORITHM

```
INPUT: A graph G(V,E) and a number of
       components k.
OUTPUT: Shortest distances between all
        pairs of vertices in V.

function partitionedAPSP_master(G, k)
    if num_vertices(G) < MIN_SIZE then
        Floyd_Warshall(G)
        output_distances(G)
    else
        // Step 1
```

```
        partition(G,k)
        // Step 2
        for component c in G do
            requestFloydWarshall(c)
        end for
        // Step 3
        BG = extract_boundary_graph(G)
        partitionedAPSP_master(BG, f(k))
        for component c in G do
            requestFloydWarshall(c)
            output_distances(c)
        end for
        // Step 4
        for components (c1 ,c2) in G do
            requestFloydWarshall(c1,c2)
            output_distances(c1,c2)
        end for
    end if
end function
```

The first step is to partition the input graph into k components of roughly the same number of vertices (see Section 3.1). This partitioning step is executed on the master node only. Once a partition is obtained, the second step consists of computing the shortest distances within each of the components of the partition. For this purpose, relevant diagonal submatrices of a hypothetical distance matrix for the entire graph are created and sent by the master node to slave nodes. Slave nodes receive diagonal submatrices and send them to their GPUs for computation and send results back to the master node.

Shortest distances are computed using a block-recursive Floyd-Warshall implementation described in Section 3.4.1. Using Floyd-Warshall for these computations ensures that slaves receive the same amount of work—since components have roughly the same number of vertices—thus guaranteeing a good balance between physical nodes of the cluster. This second step provides k similar tasks and requires $2k$ data transfers to and from the master node (Fig. 4). Shortest distances computed at this point may not be actual shortest distances in the graph as the actual shortest path may go through vertices from other components.

Once the master has received shortest distances for each component, the boundary graph is extracted. The boundary graph contains the subgraph induced by boundary vertices plus edges between all pairs of boundary vertices from the same component weighted with distances computed at the previous step. Boundary vertices are vertices connected to other components of the initial graph. This subgraph contains

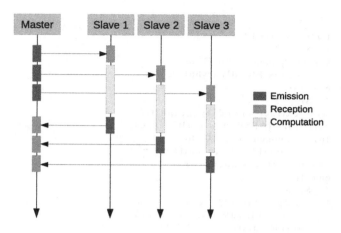

FIG. 4

Slave/master communication in our centralized approach.

original edges of the initial input graph and virtual edges consisting of relevant distances computed in Step 2 (Fig. 5).

The APSP distances for the boundary graph are then computed recursively using the same algorithm. The number k of components is reduced—using a strictly decreasing function f—at each recursion step as boundary graphs become denser with the addition of virtual edges. Recursion stops when the boundary graph becomes small enough to be computed using Floyd-Warshall on a single GPU in a reasonable time. At this point, distances between boundary vertices are accurate, but distances between two arbitrary vertices of the same component may not be accurate. Diagonal submatrices computed at Step 2 are updated with new values from the boundary graph and shortest distances are computed once more using Floyd-Warshall.

At the end of Step 3, shortest distances between boundary vertices and vertices of the same component are accurate and can be output to disk. Shortest distances between nonboundary vertices from different components remain to be computed. Those values correspond to nondiagonal submatrices of the distance matrix for the entire graph. The shortest distance from vertex i from component I to vertex j from component J is the sum of three already computed distances: $\overline{dist}(i, b_I)$, the distance from i to a boundary vertex b_I from component I, $\overline{dist}(b_I, b_J)$, the distance from b_I to a boundary vertex b_J from component J, and $\overline{dist}(b_J, j)$. It remains to identify boundary vertices b_I and b_J.

Values for $\overline{dist}(i, b_I)$ and $\overline{dist}(b_J, j)$ belong to diagonal submatrices I and J, respectively, and $\overline{dist}(b_I, b_J)$ belongs to the boundary graph. Computing the shortest distances of a nondiagonal submatrix (I, J) thus requires distances from nonboundary vertices of component I to boundary vertices of component I, distances from

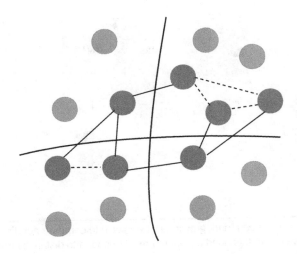

FIG. 5

The boundary graph is composed of vertices (in *green* [dark gray in print version]) connected to other components and original edges between them plus virtual edges (*dashed lines*).

boundary vertices of component I to boundary vertices of component J, and distance from boundary vertices of component J to nonboundary vertices of component J (Fig. 6). The shortest distances in any nondiagonal submatrix are the product of the three submatrices in green (dark gray in print version) in Fig. 6. All required distances have already been computed at this point and are available on the master node. There are $k^2 - k$ nondiagonal submatrices to compute; these computations are distributed by the master node to slave nodes.

This centralized algorithm and its implementation provide a high degree of balanced task parallelism. All computations are done using a variant of Floyd-Warshall; this algorithm can thus solve APSP for graphs with negative edge weights. Nevertheless, the master/slave approach induces a large amount of communication between nodes. Because all communications include the master node, sending work to slave nodes and processing results can rapidly become a bottleneck. Moreover, diagonal submatrices and distance matrices for boundary graphs are all stored on the master node. For large graph instances, this centralized memory scheme can also require more memory than is available on the master node.

3.2.2 A decentralized approach for better scaling and improved memory distribution

The objective of this decentralized approach is to solve the communication bottleneck and memory usage issues of the centralized approach. In this version, each physical node of the cluster is a worker node. The optimal number of components k can

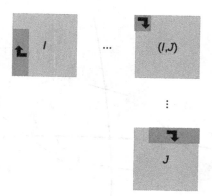

FIG. 6

Required distances (in *green* [dark gray in print version]) to compute nondiagonal submatrix (*I*, *J*). Values in this nondiagonal matrix correspond to distances from component *I* to component *J*.

be computed as a function of the number of vertices *n* and the number of cluster nodes *p*. Each worker is statically attributed the same number of components and is responsible for the computations of shortest distances from vertices in these components and storing these intermediate results. For simplicity, we set $k = p$; each worker is thus assigned a single component of the graph.

ALGORITHM 4 DECENTRALIZED PARTITIONED APSP ALGORITHM. HERE WE ASSUME FOR SIMPLICITY THAT $K = P$

```
INPUT: A graph G(V,E) and a number of
    components k.
OUTPUT: Shortest distances between all
    pairs of vertices in V.

// Executed on all nodes
function partitionedAPSP(G, k)
    // Step 1
    partition(G,k)
    // Step 2
    component my_c =
        get_component(g, my_rank)
    FloydWarshall(my_c)
    exchange_distances_from/to_boundaries()
    // Step 3
    BG = extract_boundary_graph(G)
    for BoundaryVertex v in my_c do
        Dijkstra(BG,v)
```

```
        end for
        output_distances(BG)
        FloydWarshall(my_c)
        output_distances(my_c)
        exchange_distances_from/to_boundaries()
        // Step 4
        for component c in G do
            if c != my_c then
                FloydWarshall(my_c,c)
                output_distances(my_c,c)
            end if
        end for
    end function
```

The decentralized algorithm is also composed of four steps (see Algorithm 4). The first step is to obtain a partition of the graph as in the centralized version; this time, however, each worker computes the partition and holds the initial representation of the input graph. The second step also consists of computing the shortest distances within each of the components. Each worker computes shortest distances in the components it is attributed. Resulting diagonal matrices are then exchanged between all workers so that each node has a copy of all diagonal matrices. Compared to the centralized approach, the maximum number of communications at each node for this step is reduced. In the centralized approach, $2k$ transfers were required; in this case, each worker is involved in k transfers. Fig. 7 shows the communication pattern for this second step of the algorithm. This figure assumes a hardware broadcast capability of the network; if unavailable, broadcast operations are usually implemented using a tree-based approach, which executes a broadcast from a node to all other nodes in $\log(p)$ transfers, where p is the number of receiving nodes.

For Step 3, each worker extracts a dense representation of the boundary graph containing initial edges from the input graph and virtual edges from diagonal submatrices. Each worker is then responsible for computing distances from boundary vertices of its components to all other boundary vertices. For this task, Dijkstra's algorithm is better suited than Floyd-Warshall; in this case, Dijkstra is called to solve the SSSP problem in the boundary graph using each boundary vertex as the source vertex. Because it is impossible to know exactly how long each Dijkstra call will take to run based simply on the number of vertices in the graph, workloads across different nodes may be imbalanced for this step; this imbalance is tolerated since this approach for computing the boundary graph does not require communication between nodes.

The absence of recursion means that we need to store only a single distance matrix for the boundary graph, which greatly reduces memory usage. Moreover, this memory usage for the distance matrix of the boundary graph is distributed across all

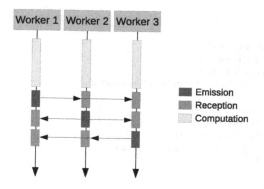

FIG. 7

Communication pattern in our decentralized approach.

available nodes. Once the boundary graph is computed, each worker updates diagonal submatrices for the components it is in charge of and computes Floyd-Warshall on these diagonal submatrices. These diagonal submatrices are again broadcast to all other nodes.

Step 4 still consists of computing distances between vertices from different components. Each worker is responsible for computing distances from vertices of its own components to all other vertices; in the distance matrix representation, these distances correspond to nondiagonal submatrices located on the same rows as diagonal submatrices each worker is responsible for. Because all workers hold a copy of every diagonal submatrix, this step does not require any internode communication. Computations are by construction balanced between nodes as components have roughly the same number of vertices, and the complexity of the Floyd-Warshall algorithm, used at this step, depends only on the number of vertices.

Compared to the centralized version, this decentralized approach reduces the number of internode communications and improves memory usage distribution. Communications are limited to a total of $2k$ broadcast operations for diagonal submatrices. Memory usage on each node is limited to diagonal submatrices and stripes of the distance matrix for the boundary graph. These improvements allow this decentralized implementation to scale better with increasing numbers of nodes. The use of Dijkstra for Step 3, however, prevents the presence of negative edges in the input graph.

3.3 SINGLE-PAIR SHORTEST PATH QUERY ALGORITHM

We derive from our previous algorithm a new approach to solve the SPSP query problem. This problem consists of answering multiple distance queries between two vertices in the graph. To solve this problem, one can decide to precompute some shortest distances to decrease the time it takes to answer a query; the precomputation of such shortest distances is later on referred to as preprocessing mode, while answering queries is referred to as query mode. An approach to solving this problem is thus a trade-off between the time it take to preprocess the graph, the amount of memory required to store preprocessed distances, and the time it takes to answer each query.

Dijkstra can easily be used to address this problem. To answer a query for the shortest distance from vertex u to vertex v in graph G, we can call Dijkstra using u as the source vertex, return the result for vertex v, and discard other vertices. In this configuration, preprocessing is nonexistent. Using Dijkstra to solve this problem is therefore optimal for preprocessing time and memory usage, but query times can be prohibitive for large graphs.

Another approach to solve this problem would be to use Floyd-Warshall. The algorithm can be applied to the entire graph; queries can subsequently be answered by a simple lookup in the results. This solution is optimal for query times—$O(1)$ time complexity—but requires memory usage in $O(n^2)$ and preprocessing time in $O(n^3)$.

3.3.1 Preprocessing mode

Our proposed approach for the preprocessing mode is similar to the first steps of our decentralized approach (see Section 3.2.2). Once the graph is partitioned, we distributedly precompute shortest distances within each component—these distances are not actual shortest distances in the initial graph as they do not take into account potentially shorter paths leaving the component. We then distributedly precompute actual shortest distances between boundary vertices (see Algorithm 5).

ALGORITHM 5 PREPROCESSING MODE OF OUR SPSP QUERY ALGORITHM

```
INPUT: A graph G(V,E) and a number of
    components k.
OUTPUT: Preprocessed shortest distances.

// Executed on all nodes
function preprocessing(G, k)
    // Step 1
    partition(G,k)
    // Step 2
    component my_c =
        get_component(g, my_rank)
    FloydWarshall(my_c)
    exchange_distances_from/to_boundaries()
```

```
// Step 3
BG = extract_boundary_graph(G)
for BoundaryVertex v in my_c do
    Dijkstra(BG,v)
end for
end function
```

Unlike in our decentralized approach to APSP, we do not recompute shortest distances within components using shortest distances between boundary vertices.

3.3.2 Query mode

Once distances within components and between boundary vertices are computed, queries can be answered rapidly. For a query between vertices u and v of components U and V, respectively, the cluster node that holds the precomputed distances for U is in charge of answering the query; we later refer to this node as the answering node. The node holding precomputed distances for V, if different from the answering node, provides the answering node with the precomputed distances from boundary vertices of V to v.

The answering node then computes the tropical product of the distances from u to the boundary vertices of U and distances from boundary vertices of U to boundary vertices of V. The answering node then computes the tropical product of the previous results with the distances from boundary vertices of V to v. The result of this second product is a single distance. If $U \neq V$, this distance is the shortest between u and v in the graph and can be returned. On the other hand, if $U = V$, this distance corresponds to the distance of the shortest path between u and v that leaves the component. It may be that the shortest distance found in Step 2 of the preprocessing mode—the shortest distance between u and v within the component —is smaller; the minimum of these two values is therefore returned (see Algorithm 6).

ALGORITHM 6 QUERY MODE OF OUR SPSP QUERY ALGORITHM

```
INPUT: A graph G(V,E) with preprocessed
    shortest distances, a source
    vertex u and a target vertex v.
OUTPUT: Shortest distance between u and
    v in G.

// Executed on all nodes
function query(G, u, v)
```

```
    if u is in my_components then
        if v is not in my_components then
            request(component(v))
        end if
        // Compute shortest distance btw.
        // two components
        tmp =
            tropical_product(u_to_boundaries,
                boundaries_to_boundaries)
        min_dist = tropical_product(tmp,
            boundaries_to_v)
        if component(u)==component(v) then
            // u and v belong to the same
            // component, a shorter distance
            // may already be known
            min_dist =
                min(min_dist, precomputed(u,v))
        end if
        return min_dist
    else if v is in my_components then
        send(component(v))
    end if
end function
```

The two products required to answer a query do not generate enough computations to efficiently exploit a GPU (see Fig. 8). Instead, the answering node uses its available cores to compute them.

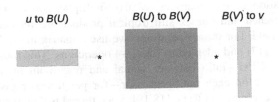

FIG. 8

Illustration of the two tropical products performed to answer a query. The first and third matrices are only a single column and row, respectively, and do not provide enough parallelism to exploit a GPU.

3.4 FAST SHORTEST PATH PRIMITIVES ON GPU

Two types of matrix multiplication-like operations are used extensively in all three algorithms previously described. What we later on refer to as an in situ tropical product, consists of computing the tropical product—product with (min, +) operators—of a matrix by itself and writing the results on the input matrix. The product of two matrices to produce a third distinct matrix is later on referred to as an ex situ tropical product. Floyd-Warshall's algorithm computes the in situ tropical product and induces data dependencies. Namely, iterations of the outermost loop need to be done sequentially, thus reducing the amount of available parallelism. This particular operation is used in all three algorithms. The ex situ product is used in both APSP solving algorithms and exhibits a higher degree of parallelism as no data dependencies exist.

3.4.1 In situ tropical product

To compute the in situ tropical product, we use the block-recursive approach from Ref. [5]. In this approach, the input matrix is recursively split into four submatrices of the same size. Recursion stops early for large nondiagonal submatrices, which can be directly computed using the fast ex situ tropical product method described in Section 3.4.2 as they present no data dependency. Diagonal submatrices, however, are recursively split until they reach a blocking factor and then are processed iteratively using Floyd-Warshall's algorithm. This method allows large nondiagonal submatrices to be extracted and computed in parallel, as opposed to block iterative approaches where all submatrices are the same size. This specificity is a great advantage when computing on GPUs, because larger matrices allow the GPUs to reach a higher percentage of the peak bandwidth.

3.4.2 Ex situ tropical product

The ex situ tropical product presents no data dependency and can thus be treated as the multiplication of two matrices. Matrix multiplication on GPUs has been extensively researched and our ex situ tropical product greatly benefits from the advances in that field. For these operations, we use a matrix multiplication routine derived from Ref. [17] and adapted to (min, +) operations. This routine trades high occupancy of the GPU—ratio between actual and maximum number of threads running concurrently on each multiprocessor—for per thread register and shared memory space, as explained in Refs. [18,19]. Each thread is then responsible for the computation of multiple results and has access to more registers. Data items stored in registers can then be reused multiple time without having to pay the high latency of global memory accesses.

4 COMPUTATIONAL COMPLEXITY ANALYSIS

In this section, we assess the computation complexities of our APSP and SSST algorithms. Our time analysis does not take into account the fine-grained parallelism that the GPU architecture provides.

Let us denote by n and m the number of the vertices and edges of G, by n_b and m_b the number of vertices and edges of BG, and by $\hat{n}$ and $\hat{b}$ the maxima over the number of vertices and the number of boundary vertices belonging to any component of the partition, respectively. We also assume that G is planar and has bounded maximum vertex degree. For such G, there exists a partition of its vertices into k parts such that $\hat{n} = O(n/k)$ vertices and $\hat{b} = O(\sqrt{n/k})$ [20]. We assume hereafter that the partition that is found in Step 1 of the algorithms has such properties. Moreover, since G is planar, then $m = O(n)$. We can further estimate

$$n_b \leq k\hat{b} = O(\sqrt{kn})$$

and

$$m_b = O(n_b) + k\hat{b}^2 = O(\sqrt{kn}) + O(n) = O(n)$$

In the last equality, $O(n_b)$ is the number of edges joining vertices of BG from different components of the partition, and $k\hat{b}^2$ is a bound on the edges joining vertices from the same component. We will use the preceding bounds in the analysis of the individual algorithms.

4.1 ANALYSIS OF THE CENTRALIZED APSP

We assume we have a master node and p slave nodes. Step 1 is sequential and takes $O(n \log m) = O(n \log n)$ time.

Step 2 involves transferring the subgraphs by the master node to all slaves (sequentially), computation by the slaves (in parallel), and sending back the computed distance matrices to the master. Hence the time for Step 2 is

$$O(n + m) + kO(\hat{n}^3)/p + kO(\hat{n}^2) = O(n + k(n/k)^3/p + k(n/k)^2)$$
$$= O(n^3/(k^2p) + n^2/k), \quad \text{for } p \leq k \tag{1}$$

and the work (number of operations) is

$$O(n + m) + kO(\hat{n}^3) + kO(\hat{n}^2) = O(n^3/k^2)$$

Step 3 consists of computing APSP for BG and repeating Step 2 for the updated components. To simplify the analysis, we will assume the value of MIN_SIZE in Algorithm 3 was chosen to be no less than n_b, so Floyd-Warshall is used on BG. A more accurate analysis that takes into account the recursion and results in a slightly better bound is given in Ref. [21]. Then the time for Step 3 (taking into account the time for Step 2) is

$$O(n_b^3/p) + O(n^3/k^2/p + n^2/k) = O((kn)^{3/2}/p + n^3/k^2/p + n^2/k)$$
$$= O((n^{3/2}k^{3/2} + n^3/k^2)/p + n^2/k) \qquad (2)$$

and the work is

$$O(n^{3/2}k^{3/2} + n^3/k^2)$$

Step 4 consists of $k^2 - k$ independent tasks, each involving the multiplication of three matrices with dimensions $n/k \times \sqrt{n/k}$, $\sqrt{n/k} \times \sqrt{n/k}$, and $\sqrt{n/k} \times n/k$. Multiplying the first and second matrix involves

$$O((n/k)\sqrt{n/k}\sqrt{n/k}) = O((n/k)^2)$$

computations and results in a matrix of dimensions $n/k \times \sqrt{n/k}$. Multiplying that matrix with the third one takes

$$O((n/k)\sqrt{n/k}(n/k)) = O((n/k)^{5/2})$$

computations, which dominates the first term. Finally, the amount of data transferred from a master node to a slave for one task is

$$n/k + 2(n/k)^{3/2} = O((n/k)^{3/2})$$

Hence the time and work for Step 4 are

$$O(k^2((n/k)^{5/2}/p + (n/k)^{3/2})) = O(n^{5/2}/(k^{1/2}p) + n^{3/2}k^{1/2}), \quad \text{for } p \le k^2 \qquad (3)$$

and

$$O(n^{5/2}/k^{1/2})$$

respectively. Summing up the corresponding expressions for the time and work for Steps 1–4, we find that the time for the algorithm is

$$O\left(\frac{n^2}{k} + \frac{n^3}{pk^2} + n^{3/2}k^{3/2} + \frac{n^{5/2}}{pk^{1/2}}\right)$$

if $p \le k$, or

$$O\left(\frac{n^2}{k} + \frac{n^3}{k^3} + n^{3/2}k^{3/2} + \frac{n^{5/2}}{pk^{1/2}}\right)$$

if $k < p \le k^2$, and the work is

$$O\left(\frac{n^3}{k^2} + n^{3/2}k^{3/2} + \frac{n^{5/2}}{k^{1/2}}\right)$$

The work is minimized (in terms of the big-O notation) when

$$n^{3/2}k^{3/2} = n^{5/2}/k^{1/2}$$

or $k = n^{1/2}$. For that value of k, the work is $O(n^{9/4})$, or sightly worse than the optimal $O(n^2)$. The time is minimized for $p = k^2$, for which value of p it is

$$O\left(\frac{n^2}{k} + \frac{n^3}{k^3} + n^{3/2}k^{3/2} + \frac{n^{5/2}}{k^{5/2}}\right) = O\left(\frac{n^2}{k} + \frac{n^3}{k^3} + n^{3/2}k^{3/2}\right)$$

since $k \leq n$. The last expression is minimized for $k = n^{1/3}$ resulting in time complexity $O(n^2)$ for $p = n^{2/3}$.

4.2 ANALYSIS OF THE DECENTRALIZED APSP

We will analyze only the time bound; the work bounds follow easily from the time calculations. We assume that there are p processors. Step 1 is the same as in the centralized version, and Step 2 involves the same computations, but the communication cost is different. At the end of the computation, each node sends the computed distances between boundary vertices to all other nodes. The amount of data sent from a node is

$$\hat{b}^2 = O\left(\sqrt{n/k}^2\right) = O(n/k)$$

and since there are k transfers, the transfer time is $O(n)$. Combining this bound with Eq. (1), we get for the time of Step 2 the bound

$$= O(n^3/(k^2p) + n) \tag{4}$$

for $p \leq k$.

Step 3 involves running Dijkstra on BG for each vertex of BG. Running one instance of Dijkstra takes time

$$O(m_b \log n_b) = O\left(n \log\left(\sqrt{kn}\right)\right) = O(n \log n)$$

There are n_b instances, so using p processors running Dijkstra takes time

$$n_b/p\, O(n \log n) = O\left(\sqrt{kn}/p\, n \log n\right)$$
$$= O(n^{3/2}k^{1/2} \log n/p) \tag{5}$$

The rest of Step 3 includes the same computation as Step 2, plus transferring computed distances from/to boundary vertices to/from other vertices of the component. There are k total transfers, so the total number of distances transferred is no more than

$$k\hat{b}\hat{n} = kO\left(\sqrt{n/k}\right)O(n/k) = O(n^{3/2}/k^{1/2}) \tag{6}$$

By combining Eqs. (4)–(6), we get for the time of Step 3 the bound

$$O(n^{3/2}k^{1/2}\log n/p + n^3/(k^2 p) + n + n^{3/2}/k^{1/2}) \tag{7}$$

The computation time for Step 4 is the same as the computation time for that step in the centralized version, except that there is no data transfer time. Hence the time for Step 4 is

$$O\left(\frac{n^{5/2}}{pk^{1/2}}\right), \quad \text{for } p \le k^2 \tag{8}$$

Adding Eqs. (4), (5), (8), we get for the total time of the decentralized algorithm the bound

$$O\left(n + \frac{n^{3/2}}{k^{1/2}} + \frac{n^3}{pk^2} + \frac{n^{3/2}k^{1/2}\log n}{p} + \frac{n^{5/2}}{pk^{1/2}}\right) \tag{9}$$

An analysis of the expression (9) shows that it is minimized if we choose $p = k$, and the resulting function is decreasing on k and tends to $O(n \log n)$ as k tends to n.

4.3 ANALYSIS OF THE SSST QUERY ALGORITHM

We first analyze the preprocessing phase. The preprocessing algorithm is identical to Steps 1–3 of the APSP decentralized algorithm, except that in Step 3 the distances within each component are not recomputed. Hence the preprocessing time bound can be found by adding expressions (4), (5), getting the bound

$$O(n^3/(k^2 p) + n + n^{3/2}k^{1/2}\log n/p)$$

This value is minimized for $k = O(n^{3/5})$, giving a time bound of

$$O(n^{9/5}\log n/p)$$

For the query algorithm, most of the time goes for computing the two tropical products. Computing the vector `tmp` involves multiplying two matrices of size $1 \times b_1$ and $b_1 \times b_2$, where $b_1, b_2 \le \hat{b}$. Therefore time for this operation is

$$O(b_1 b_2) = O(\hat{b}^2) = O(n/k)$$

Finding `min_dist` involves computing of the tropical product of two vectors of sizes $1 \times b_2$ and $b_2 \times 1$, taking time $O(b_2) = O((n/k)^{1/2})$. Hence the time for the query algorithm is $O(n/k)$. Using the value $k = O(n^{3/5})$ chosen for the preprocessing algorithm, we get a bound for the query algorithm

$$O(n/k) = O(n/n^{3/5}) = O(n^{2/5})$$

Note that for the query algorithm analysis we assume that a single processor is used.

When considering a GPU implementation, several properties of an algorithm can greatly simplify the work of the programmer, while improving the efficiency of the computations performed on the GPU. These properties include simplicity of used data structures, strict locality of data accesses, and branchlessness. As stated in our introduction, Floyd-Warshall's algorithm possesses all these qualities for an efficient GPU implementation but suffers from a cubic complexity, while Dijkstra's algorithm presents a lower complexity by taking advantage of the sparsity of the graph but exhibits none of the aforementioned properties. Partitioning a sparse graph allows us to reduce the complexity of our approaches, while keeping (in most cases) the required properties of Floyd-Warshall's algorithm for an efficient GPU implementation.

5 EXPERIMENTS AND RESULTS

In this section, we present results for all three of our algorithms. These results were obtained on a cluster of more than 300 computer nodes each equipped with 2 NVIDIA C2090 GPUs, a 16-core Intel(R) Xeon(R) CPU E5-2670 0 @ 2.60 GHz and 32 GB of RAM. These results were initially presented in Refs. [21–23].

5.1 PARTITIONED APSP WITH REAL EDGE WEIGHTS

We proceeded to compare our centralized APSP implementation with real (positive as well as negative) edge weights to two parallel Dijkstra implementations. It is important to note that, unlike Dijkstra-based approaches, our implementation allows graphs with negative edge weights, but no negative cycles.

The benchmark used for these comparisons consists of generated random graphs with increasing numbers of vertices, ranging from 1024 to 1024k. These graphs, generated using the LEDA library [24], were made planar to ensure good partitioning properties.

The centralized implementation was able to process instances up to $512k$ vertices without exceeding the 32 GB of main memory available per node on our cluster. For the $1024k$ vertex instance, memory usage exceeded the limit; to reduce memory usage, temporary results were output to disk and retrieved when necessary. We later refer to our implementation without using external memory as "Part. APSP no EM" and our implementation using external memory as "Part. APSP EM."

The GPU Dijkstra implementation from Ref. [8] is, to the best of our knowledge, the only implementation that was reported to solve APSP for graphs with up to $1024k$ vertices; we later refer to this implementation as "GPU Dijkstra." In Ref. [8], SSSP computations for each vertex of the graph were executed in parallel on a single computer using two GPUs and a multicore CPU. To allow for a fair comparison, we restricted computations of both implementations to using only two GPUs. Both implementations thus ran on a single cluster node and did not require internode communication.

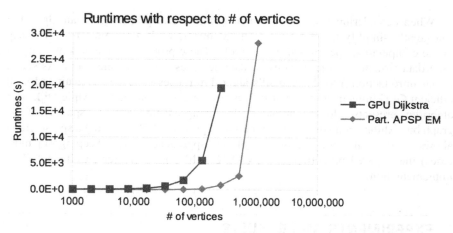

FIG. 9

Evolution of runtimes with respect to the number of vertices. Two implementations are compared: our implementation using external memory and the GPU Dijkstra implementation from Ref. [8]. Computations were run using two GPUs on a single cluster node.

Fig. 9 shows the runtimes for GPU Dijkstra and Part. APSP EM for graphs with numbers of vertices ranging from 1024 to 1024k using only two GPUs. The GPU Dikstra implementation could not compute the last two instances—512k and 1024k vertices—within the 10-h limit enforced on the cluster. Our approach significantly outperformed GPU Dijkstra for the instances where both implementations could run. Fig. 10 shows the evolution of the speedup of our method without using external memory with respect to the number of GPUs used for the computations. Speedups were computed using the runtime with a single GPU as a reference. Computations were done for the 512k vertex instance using the Part. APSP no I/O implementation. Our centralized implementation scales, almost optimally, were up to approximately 31 GPUs; however, almost no benefit was gained from using more than about 63 GPUs. For a large number of slave nodes, the master node was unable to process workload requests quickly enough to allow for an optimal parallel execution. Fig. 11 shows a comparison between our two implementations—centralized with and without using external memory—and a distributed Dijkstra approach (later referred to as CPU Dijkstra) for graphs ranging from 1024 to 1024k vertices. The distributed Dijkstra approach was implemented by dynamically distributing SSSP computations for each vertex of the graph over every core of every available cluster node. The Dijkstra-based implementation used is that of the Boost C++ library [25]. This experiment is not intended to be a direct comparison of the performances of two GPUs to a multicore CPU. Instead, we intend to show that our approach is competitive with a distributed Dijkstra approach given a fixed number of

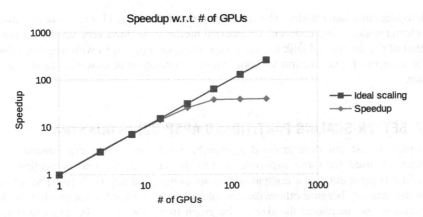

FIG. 10

Evolution of speedups with respect to the number of GPUs. The ideal scaling line is given as a reference.

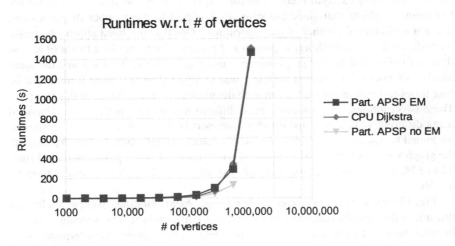

FIG. 11

Evolution of runtimes with respect to the number of vertices. Three implementations are compared: our two implementations, with and without using external memory, and a distributed Dijkstra implementation referred to as CPU Dijkstra. All computations were run on 64 cluster nodes.

heterogeneous cluster nodes. The runtimes presented in Fig. 11 were obtained using 64 cluster nodes. Our version using external memory obtained very similar runtimes as that of the distributed Dijkstra version, while allowing graphs with negative edges to be computed. Our version without external memory was, however, significantly faster.

5.2 BETTER-SCALING PARTITIONED APSP USING DIJKSTRA

In order to test our decentralized approach, we designed two experiments. The benchmark used for these experiments was the same as the one in Section 5.1. The first experiment was a comparison to our centralized approach to APSP (using external memory because otherwise it would not work for the largest graphs). In this experiment, we increased the size of the graph from $64k$ to $1024k$. The graph size was doubled between two instances, and the number of nodes p was multiplied by 4—the number of nodes used ranged from 1 for the $64k$ vertex instance to 256 for the $1024k$ vertex instance. Similarly, the number of components k was multiplied by 4 between two instances and set to $k = 4 * p$. For each instance, the total runtime was broken down into runtimes for every step of the algorithm. It is important to note that the decentralized approach no longer works with graphs with negative edges because it uses Dijkstra internally to compute the boundary graph.

Fig. 12 shows the results for this first experiment. Even though the master/slave version was using external memory in this experiment, it was not sufficient for the last instance. (Note that since the value of k is tied to the number of processors, it is not optimized for either of the algorithms.) Our decentralized approach clearly outperformed our master/slave approach and improved runtimes by a factor of almost three for the second largest graph instance using the same values for k and the same number of nodes. The largest instance was completed in less than 6 min, that is, four times faster than our fastest run with the master/slave approach for this instance. These two runtimes are, however, more difficult to compare as they were obtained using different values for k and different numbers of nodes. In a second experiment, we aimed to assess the scalability of our decentralized approach. In this experiment, the graph size was fixed to $512k$ vertices, and number of nodes p was increased from 32 to 128. The number of components k was set to $k = 2 * p$; k thus ranges from 64 to 256.

Fig. 13 shows the results for this second experiment. Runtimes were again broken down into the runtimes for the various steps of our approach. The speedups—given in black here and with values taken on the right y-axis—should be interpreted with caution because the value for k varies between two instances and has an impact on the overall complexity of the approach. Nevertheless, this decentralized approach clearly benefits from using up to 256 GPUs simultaneously. Though not clearly interpretable, this extended scalability is a definite improvement over our master/slave approach, which drew almost no benefit from using more than 63 GPUs.

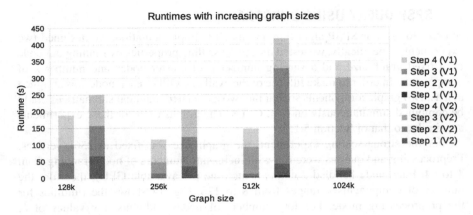

FIG. 12

Evolution of runtimes with increasing graph sizes. The decentralized version (in red [light gray in print]) is compared to the centralized approach (in blue [dark gray in print]). A breakdown of the runtime between the different steps of the algorithm is given.

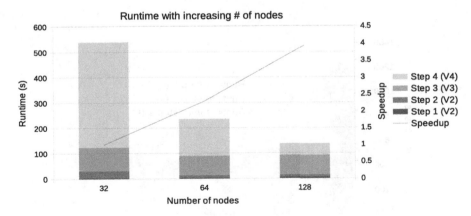

FIG. 13

Evolution of runtimes with increasing numbers of nodes. Speedups (in *black*) are computed using the runtime for 32 nodes as the basis and should be read on the right *y*-axis.

5.3 SPSP QUERY USING DIJKSTRA

In order to test our SPSP algorithm and its GPU implementation, we designed two experiments. Specifically, we tested the strong scaling properties by running our code on a fixed graph size and a varying number p of cluster nodes and number k of components. In order to make full use of the available GPUs, each node was assigned at least two graph components so that the two associated diagonal submatrices could be computed simultaneously on both GPUs. The graphs used for these experiments are similar to that of Section 5.1.

For the strong-scaling experiment, the graph size was fixed at $256k$ vertices. Preprocessing and queries were run with increasing numbers of nodes ranging from 4 to 64. Each node handled 2 components (one per available GPU); therefore the number of components k ranges from 8 to 128. Fig. 14 shows the runtimes for the preprocessing mode. For low numbers of nodes and thus low values of k, preprocessing time was dominated by Step 2—the computation of the shortest distances within each component—since lower k values mean larger components. For higher numbers of nodes and thus higher values of k, preprocessing time became dominated by Step 3 (the computation of the boundary graph) as more components mean higher numbers of incident edges and thus larger boundary graphs.

Note that while the figure seems to show supralinear speedup, that is not the case (and similarly for the memory usage). The reason is that, when increasing the number of processors p, the number k of parts is increased as well (since it is tied to p in this implementation), so the complexity of the algorithm was altered; in this case, it is reduced.

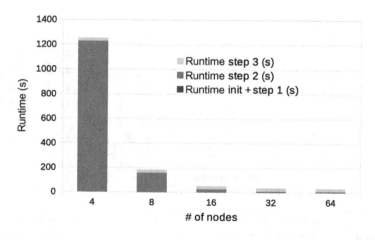

FIG. 14

Preprocessing runtimes for a fixed graph size of $256k$ vertices and increasing number of nodes.

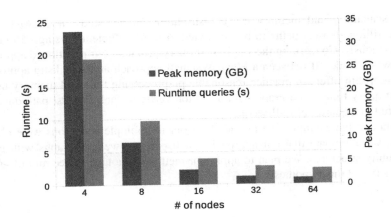

FIG. 15

Peak memories and runtimes for 10k queries for a fixed graph size of 256k vertices and increasing number of parts/processors.

Fig. 15 shows the query times and peak memory usage per node. The runtimes are given for 10,000 queries from random sources to random targets. Note that in the query mode only fine-grained (node-level) parallelism is used, while multiple nodes are still needed for distributed storage and, optionally, to handle multiple queries in parallel (not implemented in the current version). For the memory usage, the optimal value for k, theoretically expected to be $\sqrt{n}$—or 512 for this instance—was not reached in this experiment since k only goes up to 128. We can, however, see that peak memory usage per node is still dropping with increasing values of k up to 128. The query times in the figure vary from about 2 ms per query for $k = 8$ to 0.25 ms for $k = 128$. Compared with the Boost library implementation of Dijkstra's algorithm, our implementation answers queries on the largest instances about 1000 times faster.

5.4 DISCUSSION AND PERSPECTIVES

Our implementations showed that partitioned approaches perform shortest paths computations on large planar graphs efficiently on GPU clusters. Partitioning the input graph provides a way to gain the benefits of a Floyd-Warshall approach (i.e., simple data structures, regular memory accesses, and predictable workloads) while getting close to the optimal complexity of a Dijkstra approach. Such a divide-and-conquer approach also exhibits a high level of parallelism, enabling implementations to scale up efficiently on large distributed supermachines.

Our centralized partitioned algorithm for APSP allows large graphs to be treated in a reasonable time, while allowing negative edges in the graphs. Trading the ability of working with negative edges, our decentralized implementation for APSP offers better scalability and memory usage distribution. In our study, it allowed more than a trillion shortest paths to be computed in 6 min efficiently using 256 GPUs simultaneously. Concerning the single-pair query problem, our partitioned approach again was a trade-off between a Floyd-Warshall approach and a Dijkstra approach. This algorithm offers in practice reasonable preprocessing time and memory usage for fast query time. On a graph with a million vertices, each shortest path query is answered in a quarter of millisecond.

Although the examples we provided for our three implementations were planar graphs, we anticipate that our approaches will perform well on graphs with good community structures. We plan to apply our methods to a larger spectrum of graph families to test this hypothesis.

REFERENCES

[1] E.W. Dijkstra, A note on two problems in connexion with graphs, Numerische Mathematik 1 (1) (1959) 269–271.

[2] S. Warshall, A theorem on Boolean matrices, J. ACM 9 (1) (1962) 11–12.

[3] P. Harish, P. Narayanan, Accelerating large graph algorithms on the GPU using CUDA, in: High performance computing-HiPC 2007, Springer, 2007, pp. 197–208.

[4] G.J. Katz, J.T. Kider, Jr, All-pairs shortest-paths for large graphs on the GPU, in: Proceedings of the 23rd ACM SIGGRAPH/EUROGRAPHICS symposium on Graphics hardware, GH '08, Eurographics Association, Aire-la-Ville, Switzerland, Switzerland, ISBN 978-3-905674-09-5, 2008, pp. 47–55.

[5] A. Buluç, J.R. Gilbert, C. Budak, Solving path problems on the GPU, Parallel Comput. 36 (5) (2010) 241–253.

[6] T. Okuyama, F. Ino, K. Hagihara, A task parallel algorithm for finding all-pairs shortest paths using the GPU, Int. J. High Perform. Comput. Netw. 7 (2) (2012) 87–98.

[7] K. Matsumoto, N. Nakasato, S.G. Sedukhin, Blocked united algorithm for the all-pairs shortest paths problem on hybrid CPU-GPU systems, IEICE Trans. Inf. Syst. 95 (12) (2012) 2759–2768.

[8] E. Jeannot, J. Žilinskas, The All-pair shortest-path problem in shared-memory heterogeneous systems, in high-performance computing on complex environments, John Wiley & Sons, Inc., Hoboken, NJ, USA, (2014). doi:10.1002/9781118711897.ch15.

[9] U. Meyer, P. Sanders, Delta-stepping: a parallelizable shortest path algorithm, J. Algorithms 49 (1) (2003) 114–152, http://dblp.uni-trier.de/db/journals/jal/jal49.html#MeyerS03.

[10] K. Madduri, D.A. Bader, J.W. Berry, J.R. Crobak, An experimental study of a parallel shortest path algorithm for solving large-scale graph instances, in: ALENEX, vol. 7, SIAM, 2007, pp. 23–35, http://dblp.uni-trier.de/db/conf/alenex/alenex2007.html#MadduriBBC07.

[11] R.W. Floyd, Algorithm 97: shortest path, Commun. ACM 5 (6) (1962) 345.

[12] H. Djidjev, Efficient algorithms for shortest path queries in planar digraphs, in: F. d'Amore, P. Franciosa, A. Marchetti-Spaccamela (Eds.), Graph-Theoretic Concepts in Computer Science, Lecture Notes in Computer Science, vol. 1197, Springer, Berlin, Heidelberg, ISBN 978-3-540-62559-9, 1997, pp. 151–165.

[13] D.Z. Chen, J. Xu, Shortest path queries in planar graphs, in: Proceedings of the Thirty-Second Annual ACM Symposium on Theory of Computing, STOC '00, ACM, New York, NY, USA, ISBN 1-58113-184-4, 2000, pp. 469–478.

[14] S. Mozes, C. Sommer, Exact distance oracles for planar graphs, in: Proc. of the 23rd Annual ACM-SIAM Symposium on Discrete Algorithms, 2012, pp. 209–222.

[15] J.L. Gross, T.W. Tucker, Topological Graph Theory, Wiley-Interscience, New York, NY, USA, 1987, ISBN 0-471-04926-3.

[16] G. Karypis, V. Kumar, Multilevel k-way partitioning scheme for irregular graphs, J. Parallel Distrib. Comput. 48 (1) (1998) 96–129.

[17] V. Volkov, J.W. Demmel, Benchmarking GPUs to tune dense linear algebra, in: SC '08: Proceedings of the 2008 ACM/IEEE conference on Supercomputing, IEEE Press, Piscataway, NJ, USA, ISBN 978-1-4244-2835-9, 2008, pp. 1–11, doi:10.1145/1413370.1413402.

[18] V. Volkov, Better performance at lower occupancy, in: Proceedings of the GPU Technology Conference, GTC, vol. 10, 2010.

[19] V. Volkov, Use registers and multiple outputs per thread on GPU, in: 6th International Workshop on Parallel Matrix Algorithms and Applications (PMAA 2010), 2010.

[20] G.N. Frederickson, Fast algorithms for shortest paths in planar graphs, with applications, SIAM J. Comput. 16 (6) (1987) 1004–1022.

[21] H. Djidjev, G. Chapuis, R. Andonov, S. Thulasidasan, D. Lavenier, All-pairs shortest path algorithms for planar graph for GPU-accelerated clusters. J. Parallel Distrib. Comput. (85) (2015) 91–103.

[22] G. Chapuis, H. Djidjev, Shortest-path queries in planar graphs on GPU-accelerated architectures, arXiv preprint arXiv:1503.07192, 2015.

[23] H. Djidjev, S. Thulasidasan, G. Chapuis, R. Andonov, D. Lavenier, Efficient multi-GPU computation of all-pairs shortest paths, in: 2014 IEEE 28th International Parallel and Distributed Processing Symposium, Phoenix, AZ, USA, May 19–23, 2014, 2014, pp. 360–369, doi:10.1109/IPDPS.2014.46.

[24] K. Mehlhorn, S. Näher, LEDA: a platform for combinatorial and geometric computing, Commun. ACM 38 (1) (1995) 96–102, ISSN 0001-0782, doi:10.1145/204865.204889.

[25] B. Dawes, D. Abrahams, R. Rivera, Boost C++ libraries, vol. 35, 2009, p. 36, http://www.boost.org.

ABOUT THE AUTHORS

Guillaume Chapuis is a postdoctoral research associate with the Information Sciences Group (CCS3) at Los Alamos National Laboratory, New Mexico, United States. He holds a PhD in Computer Science from ENS Cachan (France) and a Computer Engineering degree from INSA Rennes (France). His research interests include parallel discrete event simulation, graph theory, high performance computing, general-purpose graphics processing units, and bioinformatics.

Hristo Djidjev is a scientist at Los Alamos National Laboratory. His research interests include combinatorial optimization, graph partitioning, shortest path computations, high-performance computing, and software-hardware codesign. He is an Adjunct Professor at Carleton University and Editor of *Parallel Processing Letters*.

Dominique Lavenier is a senior CNRS (French National Center for Scientific Research) researcher. He is currently leading the GenScale bioinformatics team at IRISA/INRIA, Rennes. He was the recipient of the "Médaille de Bronze" of the French Council for Research CNRS in 1992, and received the French Cray Prize (1996) in algorithm, architecture, and microelectronics. From August 1999 to August 2000, he worked in the Nonproliferation and International Security Division at the Los Alamos National Laboratory, Los Alamos, NM, United States. His research interests include HPC, parallel architecture, GPU computing bioinformatics, structural biology, and the management of genomic data coming from next generation sequencing technologies.

Rumen Andonov is currently Professor of Computer Science at the University of Rennes 1 and is a member of the IRISA/INRIA GenScale bioinformatics team. His research interests include combinatorial optimization, parallel algorithms, and high-performance computing for bioinformatics applications, with particular emphasis on structural bioinformatics.

GPU sorting algorithms

12

M. Gopi

University of California, Irvine, CA, United States

1 INTRODUCTION

Modern graphics processing units (GPUs) are no longer tied to their graphics ancestery but have proven themselves to be the most successful desktop supercomputing architecture for general-purpose computing. Once thought to be for video games, today's GPUs find their place in solving varied problems in varied areas from astrophysics and arts to seismology and surgery [1]. In this chapter we discuss a few classical solutions and implementation techniques related to fundamental problems in sorting algorithms. We specifically focus on NVidia's GPU architecture and CUDA programming language. Nevertheless, OpenCL versions of the same algorithms, that are applicable to generic parallel computation architectures, have also been proposed and developed by researchers.

1.1 GPU ARCHITECTURE

The CUDA programming model is a parallel programming model that provides an abstract view of how processes can be run on underlying GPU architectures. The evolution of GPU architecture and the CUDA programming language have been quite parallel and interdependent. Although the CUDA programming model has stabilized over time, the architecture is still evolving in its capabilities and functionality. GPU architecture has also grown in terms of the number of transistors and number of computing units over years, while still supporting the CUDA programming model.

Until 2000 GPU architectures supported fixed pipeline functionality tightly coupled with graphics pipeline. Separate silicon real estate was dedicated to each state of the pipeline. Around 2001 programmability for 2D operations (pixel shaders) and 3D operations (vertex shaders) were introduced. Then from approximately 2006 through 2008 all these operations were combined to be executed by a shared and common computational unit using a much higher-level programmable feature.

Advances in GPU Research and Practice. http://dx.doi.org/10.1016/B978-0-12-803738-6.00012-4

This programmability was introduced as the CUDA programming model. Since then the CUDA programming model has been used to implement many algorithms and applications other than graphics, and this explosion of use and permeability of CUDA with hitherto unknown applications has catapulted the GPU's near ubiquitous use in many domains of science and technology. Since then all the GPUs designed are CUDA-capable. It should be noted that before CUDA was released, there were attempts to create high-level languages and template libraries such as Glift [2] and Scout [3]. But such efforts tapered down with the introduction of CUDA, and more effort was spent on refining CUDA and building libraries using its constructs.

One of the conceptual differences between CPU and GPU is that CPU is defined for minimum latency so that context switch time is minimum, while GPU is primarily designed for maximum throughput through fine grain pipelining (and hence more latency than CPU). In other words, in the CPU design, there is plenty of cache memory and control logic to reduce the time taken to bring the data to the ALU and thus reduce the wait and latency. On the other hand, GPU has a lot of ALUs and may wait for the data to be fetched from external DRAM to its local cache. The fundamental optimization of GPU programming hence focuses on hiding this latency by providing enough work for the ALUs while the data is fetched from DRAM.

The two main components of the GPU board that go into the PCI express bus in the PC are the global memory (around 12 GB currently) and the actual streaming multiprocessor (SM) chip along with associated circuitry. The basic GPU processing flow consists of three steps: (1) moving data from the host's (main CPU, memory, etc.) main memory to the device's (GPU board) global memory, (2) CPU issuing instructions to GPU while the data for this computation is taken from the GPU's global memory and the results are put back in that global memory, and finally (3) transferring the results from the GPU's global memory back to the host's main memory through the PCI express bus.

In the latest GPU architectures starting from Kepler, it is possible to communicate between multiple GPUs directly from one GPU's global memory to another's through MPI calls, without going through the intermediate host's memory. Furthermore, not all jobs that the GPU is doing need to be instructed by the CPU—the GPUs can launch their own jobs. The latter feature is also called CUDA dynamic parallelism and can be useful in several ways: It would reduce the communication required between GPU and CPU through the slow PCI bus; it can be used to program recursive parallel algorithms and dynamic load balancing; features like adaptive hierarchical spatial subdivision and computational fluid dynamic grid simulation can effectively be done for efficient and accurate simulation. Conceptually, dynamic parallelism moves GPU from being a coprocessor to being an autonomous, dynamic parallel processor.

Each multiprocessing chip has many processors. Each processor can handle thousands of threads of processes. Each basic hardware unit that handles one thread is called a core, also called a CUDA core. For example, the Kepler SM chip has 15 processors, and each processor can manage 2048 threads—it has 2048 CUDA cores. Each of these 15 processors has plenty of registers (over 64K 32-bit registers) and also shared memory (around 48K) that are accessible to all the threads running in a processor. The threads running in the same processor can cooperate and share data using the registers and shared memory.

1.2 CUDA PROGRAMMING MODEL

CUDA is basically an extension of C++. The goal of the CUDA design is to let the programmer focus on parallel algorithms rather than on the underlying multiprocessor architecture. It is both a programming model and a memory model. A typical CUDA application has a mixture of serial code and parallel code. The serial segments of the code run on the host (CPU), while the parallel code, also called kernels, runs on the device (GPU) across multiple processing elements. While the parallel code is running on the GPU, the serial code can continue to work on the CPU.

A kernel is a piece of code for one thread. Many instances of the kernel are executed in parallel with potentially different data for each thread under the single instruction multiple data (SIMD) model. All the threads that run in the same processor are grouped together and are called a block. Each block runs on different processor in the multiprocessor chip, and potentially at different times. A group of these blocks is called a grid. In other words, a grid consists of all the instances of the kernel partitioned as thread blocks. The hardware takes care of scheduling these thread blocks on each of the cores in the processor, and there is no cost associated with switching between threads. When the number of blocks exceed the number of available processors, multiple thread blocks may be scheduled to the same streaming processor and in any arbitrary order. Hence there is no simple way to communicate between threads in different blocks because they may be separated both in space (different processors) and time. The goal of efficient CUDA code is to make sure that the task is partitioned into sufficiently fine-grained threads such that the latency of data transfer from the DRAM to the multiprocessor chip is well hidden through overlap of the computation tasks of the threads.

Each block has a unique id, and each thread within a block also has a unique id. They are referred using the built-in variables threadIdx and blockIdx. These IDs can be 1D, 2D, or 3D entities. The number of threads within a block can be read back from the variable blockDim, and the number of blocks in a grid are stored in the variable gridDim. The linear id of a thread among all the threads spawned by the kernel is given by blockDim.x * blockIdx.x + threadIdx.x. The .x refers to the first dimension of the three dimensions assuming that the other two dimensions each have the value 1, thus representing just a linear array of 1D threads. (Note that the maximum number of the block index value is 64K. So if you need more than 64K blocks, you may need to fold that vector into a 2D array of blocks in which the index of each dimension can go upto 64K.) The 3D representation of block and thread indices is just to give flexibility in representation that might implicitly align with the problem description. For example, a kernel operating on each element of a dense matrix might need to refer to each thread using a 2D index. Linearization of the index of a thread in a 2D array of threads is done as follows:

```
int iy = blockDim.y*bloxkIdx.y + threadIdx.y;
int ix = blockDim.x*blockIdx.x + threadIdx.x;
int idx = iy*w + ix;
```

Kepler architecture can keep track of 2048 threads or 64 warps (number of threads that can run in simultaneous lock step), or 16 blocks per stream processor. In other words, each block should have at least 128 threads to keep the GPU "compute-busy." It is good to have a number of threads per block that is a multiple of 32 since that is the warp size. For each device, there are 14 stream processors. So we need to have at least 224 blocks to keep the GPU busy, and typically we will have 1000 or more blocks in a grid. This will also make the code ready for future GPUs.

1.3 CUDA MEMORY MODEL

The memory hierarchy used by CUDA is supported by the SM and GPU architectures. Within each processor inside the chip, we noted that there are registers that are accessible per thread and that this space is valid until that thread is alive. If a thread uses more registers than are available, the system automatically uses "Local memory" which is actually the off-chip memory on the GPU card (device). So, although the data can be transparently fetched from the local memory as though it were in the register, the latency of this data fetch is as high as the data fetched from the global memory, for the simple reason that "local" memory is just a part of allocated global memory. The "shared" memory is an on-chip memory like registers, but are allocated per-block, and the data in the shared memory is valid until the block is being executed by the processor. Global memory, as mentioned earlier, is off-chip, but on the GPU card. This memory is accessible to all threads of all kernels, as well as the host (CPU). Data sharing between threads in different blocks of the same kernel or even different kernels can be done using the global memory. The host (CPU) memory, which is the slowest from the GPU perspective, is not directly accessible by CUDA threads, but the data has to be explicitly transferred from the host memory to the device memory (global memory). However, CUDA 6 introduces unified memory by which the data in the host memory can be directly indexed from the GPU side without explicitly transferring data between the host and the device. Finally, communication between different GPUs has to go through the PCI express bus and through the host memory. This is clearly the most expensive mode of communication. However, the latest NVLink, a power-efficient, high-speed bus between the CPU and the GPU and between multiple GPUs, allows much higher transfer speeds than those achievable by using PCI Express.

1.4 COMPUTATION MODELS FOR GPUs

The performance prediction model for the CUDA GPGPU platform [4] encompasses the various facets of the GPU architecture, such as scheduling, memory hierarchy, and pipelining. This work demonstrates the effects of various memory access strategies and can also be used to analyze pseudocode for a CUDA kernel to estimate a performance. Time taken by a program P is given by

$$T(P) = \sum_{i=1}^{i=r} T(K_i)$$

where r is the number of kernels K_i in the program, and $T(K_i)$ is the time taken by that kernel. Let each block consist of N_w warps and each warp consist of N_t threads, and let threads in each warp execute in parallel, and let $N_B(K)$ be the number of blocks of kernel K assigned to each multiprocessor in sequence. Let N_c be the number of cores in an SM in GPU, and D be the depth of the pipeline that has the effect of executing D threads in parallel. Then the number of cycles required for kernel K is given by

$$C(K) = N_B(K) \cdot N_w(K) \cdot N_t(K) \cdot C_T(K) \cdot \frac{1}{N_c \cdot D}$$

where $C_T(K)$ represents the maximum number of cycles required by any thread T in kernel K. If R is the clock rate of the GPU core, time taken by each kernel is given by

$$T(K) = \frac{C(K)}{R}$$

Contemporary to the preceding work is Ref. [5], which details an analytical model for a GPU architecture with memory-level and thread-level parallelism awareness. This model estimates the execution time of highly parallel programs using the estimate of number of parallel memory requests (aka memory warp parallelism) by considering the number of running threads and memory bandwidth. Based on the degree of memory warp parallelism, the model estimates the cost of memory requests, thereby estimating the overall execution time of a program.

Following the preceding works, the K-model [6] was suggested. This model requires the program to be divided into parallel complexity units and serial complexity units for the computation of the complexity of the program.

Memory modeling for GPUs is more fundamental for performance modeling. Nakano [7] first introduced the discrete memory machine (DMM) and the unified memory machine (UMM), to capture the essential features of the shared memory and the global memory, respectively, of NVIDIA GPUs. These models are good for a single SM on the GPU. Later these models were integrated and extended to hierarchical memory machine (HMM) [8], which consists of multiple DMMs and a single UMM, and that also reflects the architecture of GPUs more accurately. A few fundamental algorithms, including sum of n numbers and convolution, and their complexity analysis on HMM is presented in Ref. [8].

As mentioned earlier, the speedup achieved by a GPU depends on how effectively the memory-access latency can be hidden through low-overhead context switching among a large number of threads. If the number of threads were infinite, the Parallel

RAM (PRAM) model predicts the performance of such machines well. In Ref. [9], the authors try to analyze situations when this is not always possible since only finite number of threads can run at the same time. A new model called the Threaded Many-core Memory model is introduced, which is designed to capture the important characteristics of these highly threaded, many-core machines and has been shown to capture some fine aspects of the algorithm specific to many-core architectures. Most recently Ref. [10] proposed a new model called AGPU that abstracts the essence of current GPU architectures such as global and shared memory, memory coalescing, and bank conflicts, and also show the use of the proposed model in I/O optimal sorting.

2 GENERIC PROGRAMMING STRATEGIES FOR GPU

One of the primary goals of code optimization is latency hiding. When one thread is waiting on a data fetch, the GPU can switch to another waiting thread without any overhead. In other words, if we have many threads waiting to be executed, as many as the system can support, then we can effectively hide latency automatically. The number of such concurrent threads running with respect to the maximum allowed is referred to as *occupancy*, which is one of the parameters that should be maximized to achieve good latency hiding. On the other hand, a large number of threads will reduce the number of registers available to each thread, which may reduce the performance. Thus both (a) spawning enough number of threads to hide latency and at the same time (b) reducing the number of registers required per thread so that all threads can be accommodated without having to use the shared memory are required to improve performance. The next level of memory hierarchy is the shared memory, which is typically divided into 32 banks of memory units. Each memory bank is supposed to be accessed by one thread in the warp so that all threads can be serviced in parallel. If more than one thread accesses the same bank, it introduces bank conflict, which can be serviced only sequentially, thus affecting the performance. Hence the allocation of memory, especially while using matrices, and the elements assigned to each thread have to be carefully designed to avoid bank conflicts. The third level in the memory hierarchy is the global memory in GPU that transfers data as only complete words or quad words (32 bytes or 128 bytes), even if only a portion of the word is requested by a thread. Hence it is important for multiple threads in the same warp to access contiguous data so that every word that is transferred is used completely.

As defined earlier, a *warp* is a 32-thread group that is executed simultaneously in an SIMD fashion. Code coherency within the warps will improve performance. For example, both parts of a branch instruction have to be executed or waited on by all the threads in a warp. This is called thread divergence. One technique, especially in processors that allow dynamic parallelism, is to spawn new kernels within each path of the branch so that the number of instructions on each path are minimized and, at the same time, so that no branch will be in each of those kernels. Since threads of the same kernel will be grouped, newly spawned threads would have no branching operation or no thread would wait on other threads, thus maximizing the parallelism achieved.

GPUs have not only high degree of data parallelism but also very good task parallelism. Current GPUs support up to 16 concurrent kernel launches (32 for processors that support CUDA 3.5 and above). Copying of data to/from CPU and GPU can also be done at the same time. In other words, if properly scheduled, we can simultaneously copy data from the CPU to the GPU, execute 16 different kernels, and copy data from the GPU back to the CPU using CUDA *streams*. A good GPU implementation will have the following three characteristics [11]: coalesced memory access and effective use of the memory hierarchy; minimizing thread divergence within a warp; and reducing scattered reads and writes. Further optimizing strategies are detailed in Ref. [12].

3 SORTING ALGORITHMS

Sorting algorithm is a typical stream processing algorithm that is difficult to implement in a GPU with a performance comparable to that of multicore CPUs because of irregular and global data dependencies. The difference between CPU and GPU performances with respect to such streaming algorithms may lie in fine-grained hardware synchronizations and writable shared memory architectures.

3.1 BITONIC SORT

Bitonic Sort is an algorithm designed by Ken Batcher for parallel sorting. A bitonic sequence is a sequence with $x_0 \leq \cdots \leq x_k \geq \cdots \geq x_{n-1}$ or a circular shift of such a sequence. Given a bitonic sequence, a bitonic merge algorithm recursively splits the sequence and merges them again to produce a single sorted sequence (see Algorithms 1–3).

ALGORITHM 1 BITONIC MERGE

function BITONICMERGE(*direction*, *x*)
▷ Assume input x is bitonic, and sorted list is returned   ▷ *direction* is TRUE for ascending and FALSE for descending orders
  if len(x) == 1 **then return** x
  else BITONICSPLIT(*direction*, *x*)
     Half1 ← BITONICMERGE(*direction*, *x*[0 : *len*(*x*)/2])
     Half2 ← BITONICMERGE(*direction*, *x*[*len*(*x*)/2 : *len*(*x*)])
  return Half1 + Half2   ▷ Return sorted list
  end if
end function

ALGORITHM 2 BITONIC SPLIT

function BITONICSPLIT(*direction*, *x*)
    HalfLength ← len(x)/2
    for i=0; i<HalfLength; i++ **do**
        if (x[i] > x[i+HalfLength]) == *direction* **then**
            SWAP(x[i], x[i + HalfLength])
        end if
    end for
end function

The actual bitonic sorting function is a simple recursion with a minor twist: the input list is divided into two lists; then each list is sorted in a different order and merged using BitonicMerge in the required order.

ALGORITHM 3 BITONIC SORT

function BITONICSORT(*direction*, *x*)
    if len(x) ≤ 1 **then return** x
    else
        FirHalf ← BITONICSORT(TRUE, x[0:len(x)/2])   ▷ ↑ half
        SecHalf ← BITONICSORT(FALSE, x[len(x)/2:len(x)])   ▷ ↓ half
        return BITONICMERGE(*direction*, FirHalf + SecHalf)
    end if
end function

Based on the classic paper on optimal bitonic sorting on shared memory parallel architectures proposed by Bilardi and Nicolau [13], Greß and Zachmann [14] propose an optimal parallel sorting on stream processors. Another implementation of bitonic sort was proposed by Ref. [15]. An elegant, simple implementation of bitonic sort is described in Ref. [16] and is reproduced with comments in Algorithm 4, in which each element of the list is handled by a thread.

ALGORITHM 4 GPU BITONIC SORT

function GPUBITONICSORT

    shared[tid] = values[tid];   ▷ Copy input to shared memory
    __syncthreads();
    for int k = 2; k ≤ NUM; k *= 2 **do**   ▷ Parallel Bitonic Sort
        for int j = k / 2; j>0; j /= 2 **do**   ▷ Bitonic merge
            int exch = tid XOR j;   ▷ Find the index of the compare element

```
        if exch > tid then                          ▷ Only one of the two threads work
            if (tid AND k) == 0 then                ▷ One half ascending
                if shared[tid] > shared[exch] then
                Swap(shared[tid], shared[exch])
                    end if
                else                                ▷ Other descending
                    if shared[tid] < shared[exch] then
                    Swap(shared[tid], shared[exch]);
                        end if
                    end if
                end if
                __syncthreads();
            end for
        end for
        values[tid] = shared[tid];                  ▷ Write result
    end function
```

The GPU implementation of the bitonic sort algorithm presented in Ref. [17] reduces communication and synchronization by letting one thread process compare/exchange operations of more than one consecutive step (refer to Fig. 1). Data allocation to the threads makes sure that the consecutive compare/exchange operations work on the same data elements so that the data in the register is retained and used without any communication until multiple steps of compare/exchange operations that use that data are finished. A formal analysis and limitations of this interesting approach is presented in Ref. [18].

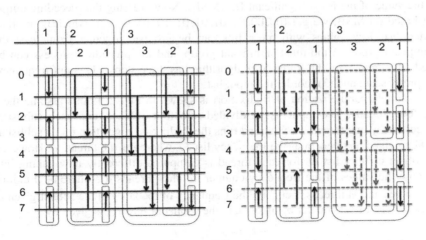

FIG. 1

Bitonic Sort algorithm: Data dependency (*left*) and the thread allocation (*right*) [17].

3.2 RADIX SORT

Radix Sort is a counting sort as opposed to a comparison sort. When n-bit keys are sorted, 2^n unique key values are possible, and hence a list of 2^n counters called the *frequency counters* F are allocated one for each key. Note that the counters are implicitly ordered based on their values. The input list is scanned once, and each counter is incremented according to the number of times its corresponding key appears in the list. Then another set of 2^n counters called the *offset counter* O is initialized in which each counter o counts the number of keys in the list that is less than the key corresponding to the counter o. Counter list O is computed from F using an algorithm called *prefix sum*, which is the sum of all values in the preceding counters. Each counter in the list O gives the starting location in the final sorted list from which its corresponding key should be placed, while its corresponding counter in the list F gives the number of times that key is repeated in the final sorted list.

Consider an example list of 2 bit numbers: $(1, 0, 1, 2, 1, 3, 0, 3, 1, 2)$. Since the keys are all 2-bit keys, the frequency and offset counts are of size 4. The frequency of occurrence of $(0, 1, 2, 3)$ are $F = (2, 4, 2, 2)$. Prefix sum of F is given by $O = (0, 2, 6, 8)$. In other words, in the sorted list, 0 starts at location 0, 1 starts at location 2, 2 at 6, and 3 at 8, and the number of times these numbers have to be repeated is given by the list F. Hence the sorted list is $(0, 0, 1, 1, 1, 1, 2, 2, 3, 3)$.

In order to reduce the size of the counters, the preceding algorithm can be repeated (with minor change) once for each bit, starting from the least significant bit. The change involves not using F to repeat the key values in the sorted list but using the input list to copy the actual value. For example, rewriting the given list using bits $(01, 00, 01, 10, 01, 11, 00, 11, 01, 10)$ and ordering using the least significant bit, we get $(00, 10, 00, 10, 01, 01, 01, 11, 11, 01)$. Note that if two numbers have the same Least Significant Bit (LSB), their order does not change in the output list, irrespective of the value of the Most Significant Bit (MSB). Now ordering the preceding output list based on MSB, we get $(00, 00, 01, 01, 01, 01, 10, 10, 11, 11)$, which is the final sorted list. Key values with more bits can be grouped together from least the significant group to the most significant group, and the preceding process can be used. To summarize, the Radix Sort algorithm has three steps: (1) count frequency; (2) prefix scan; and (3) reorder the input list.

A simple parallelization of Radix Sort is shown in Fig. 2. Let us assume there are four threads. The input list is divided into four sublists, and each sublist is processed by one thread. Each thread runs the Radix Sort algorithm on its sublist as just explained and generates the frequency list F_i, where i is the thread id. However, the offset counter list O_i for each thread is computed differently now, taking into account the values of the frequency counter in other threads. Let there be n unique key values and m threads. Let f_i^j be the frequency of the key j in the sublist given to thread i. The offset counter o_t^k of key k in the sublist of thread t is given by

$$o_t^k = \sum_{j<0}^{j=k-1} \sum_{i=0}^{i=m-1} f_i^j + \sum_{i=0}^{i=t-1} f_i^k$$

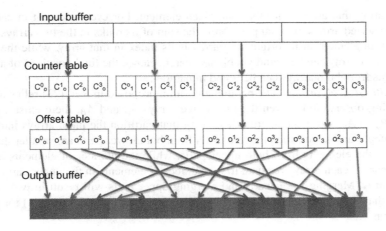

FIG. 2

Parallel Radix Sort.

Once the offset counter values are computed for each thread, the reordering step proceeds as before in ordering the input list into the global sorted output list using the local offset counter value for each thread. More details of this simple algorithm can be found in Ref. [19]. Other implementations include Ref. [20].

One of the fastest Radix Sort implementations on GPU was proposed in Refs. [21, 22]. They use a variety of programming techniques to gain maximum parallelism in GPUs, including metaprogramming—using the compiler's preprocessing features to expand and generate code based on architectural configurations, which provides the implementation with generality over targeted problems and generations of programming GPU hardware. This work is one of the most pragmatic takes on sorting algorithms with the implementation of *early exit* optimization that detects and reduces computation on low-degree binning problems where sorting would be superfluous.

3.3 MERGE SORT

The Merge Sort implementation presented in Ref. [23] can be executed in machines with multiple GPUs. The algorithm is divided into two phases. In the first phase, each GPU sorts its own sublist, and in the second phase, the sorted sublists from multiple GPUs are merged. Single GPU sorting Phase 1 has two steps: (1) The input array is divided into multiple chunks of m records each. Then any well-known sorting algorithm that can efficiently sort the small lists (chunks) is used. (2) $\log_2 \frac{n}{m}$ pairwise list mergings are performed with $\frac{n}{m}$ sorted lists like the usual merge sort. For this step, an implementation based on the parallel merge sort proposed by Ref. [24] is used, which is based on finding the ranks of the elements—the number of elements in the array that are smaller than the given element. For every element in each of the two sorted arrays, its final position is the sum of its ranks in the two arrays. The rank of an element in its originating array is its index in that array, while the rank in the other array can be found via binary search. Hence the final positions of all the elements from both arrays can be found in parallel.

Multi-GPU algorithm: The parallel algorithm proposed in Ref. [23] relies on the following observation. Given the two sorted arrays A_α and A_β, there exist a pivot point P_α in A_α and its counterpart P_β in A_β that partition the input arrays into two parts, upper and lower, such that elements from both lower parts are smaller than or equal to the elements from both upper parts, while the number of elements in the lower part of each array are equal to the number of elements in the upper part of the other array. Merging lower parts and merging upper parts will result in two sorted arrays that, when concatenated, provide one sorted array (see Algorithm 5) for pivot selection.

ALGORITHM 5 PARALLEL MERGE SORT PIVOT SELECTION

```
function PIVOT SELECTION(array a, array b)
    pivot = len(a)/2;
    stride = pivot/2;
    while stride > 0 do
        if a[len(a) - pivot - 1] < b[pivot] then
            if a[len(a) - pivot - 2] < b[pivot+1] & a[len(a) - pivot] < b[pivot-1] then return pivot
            else pivot = pivot - stride;
            end if
        else pivot = pivot + stride;
        end if
        stride = stride/2;
    end while
    return pivot
end function
```

The guarantee of the preceding observation that $A_{\alpha,upper}$ and $A_{\beta,lower}$ will have the same number of elements enables an efficient inter-GPU merge operation with a simple swap of consecutive records ($A_{\beta,lower}$ and $A_{\alpha,upper}$) between GPUs with no new memory allocations or memory overflow, while keeping the data evenly distributed across GPUs. When multiple candidate pivots exist, the smaller pivot P is used in order to minimize the amount of data to swap. Fig. 3 illustrates the algorithm with four GPUs and hence two (log 4) merge stages. The first iteration (Steps 1 through 3 in the figure) uses only pairs of GPUs, and the algorithm proceeds as previously explained. At the end of the iteration, each GPU will have a sorted list with the property that $A_0 \leq A_1$ and $A_2 \leq A_3$. Subsequent iterations need to find pivots and transfer data between two or more GPUs. Because pivots can fall in any of the GPUs, two or four GPUs (in case of a four GPU system) will have

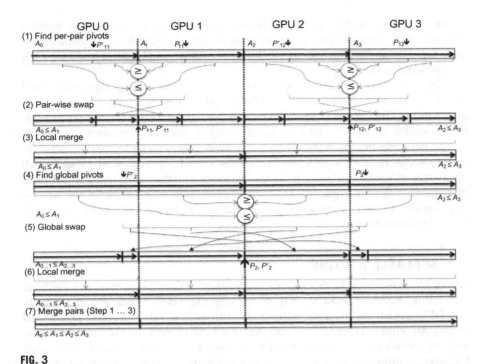

FIG. 3

GPU Parallel Merge Sort Algorithm [23]

to swap some of the records with their peers. After swapping records, previously established array relationships between A_0, A_1 and A_2, A_3 do not hold, but now the relationship $A_{0...1} \leq A_{2...3}$ holds. Earlier steps are recursively followed to ensure $A_0 \leq A_1 \leq A_2 \leq A_3$. This same procedure can be repeated as many times as necessary to perform a merge sort using an arbitrary number of GPUs.

3.4 OTHER SORTING ALGORITHMS

Quicksort: Quicksort is a recursive comparison sort in which a pivot is chosen and the input list is divided into two sublists: one with elements smaller than the pivot and the other with elements greater than the pivot. Each sublist is again recursively sorted with its own pivot (usually the second element in the list). Finally, all these sorted lists are just appended together to get the final sorted list. The GPU implementation of Quicksort was not considered efficient because of noncoalesced memory access requirements. In Ref. [25], the Quicksort algorithm is slightly modified to first compute the number of items in the two sublists using parallel prefix-sum (similar to parallel Radix Sort), and this information is used for efficient allocation of memory for each thread for dividing the input list into two sublists. Each sublist is again iteratively processed in parallel until the size of the list reaches a minimum number, after which the list is directly sorted since the overhead of Quicksort on small lists is quite high. Other implementations of Quicksort with an emphasis on load balancing is considered in Ref. [26].

Warpsort: Ref. [27] introduces a new GPU-specific sorting algorithm called *warpsort* that is a combination of bitonic sort and merge sort. This algorithm makes use of GPU warps (32 parallel threads executed in single instruction multiple thread mode) for fast barrier-free bitonic sorts by assigning independent bitonic sorting networks to each warp. At the same time, care is taken to provide sufficient homogeneous parallel comparisons to all the threads in a warp to avoid branch divergence in the bitonic sort. In the second stage of merge sort, independent pairs of sequences to be merged are assigned to each warp making use of the barrier-free bitonic network, maintaining coalesced global memory access to eliminate bandwidth bottlenecks.

3.5 SCALABLE SORTING

As we have discussed in this chapter, very efficient GPU algorithms are available for sorting. Some of these algorithms are targeting smaller data sets and usually one GPU device or one computing node with several GPU devices. Distributed sorting algorithms tailored for large datasets tend to fully utilize available node memory, which typically exceeds GPU memory size several times. Hence out-of-GPU-core sorting algorithms that handle GUP memory must be designed. A truly scalable large-scale sorting with 1024 nodes of supercomputer and over 4000 Nvidia K20x GPUs was proposed by Ref. [28] that reported sorting over 4 TB of 64-bit integer data. This is still a preliminary work that directly reimplemented an existing algorithm, HykSort [29]. Fig. 4 has four basic steps: local sorting of smaller chunks of data, selecting splitters, transferring and distributing data between processors, and finally merging the sorted data. In the GPU implementation, only the local sorting is offloaded to GPU, and the rest are done on the host. Since the GPU implementation of merging (Merge Path [30]) is slower than the CPU implementation, because of the data transfer bottleneck between the host the GPU, the merge part of the distributed algorithm is executed by the host in Ref. [28]. In the future, with improved communication using faster bus and NVLinks between GPU-Host and between GPUs, we can expect GPU execution of merging will also be more efficient than the CPU implementation. Further optimization of the implementation or even drastically new implementation that takes into account complete latency hiding and memory management for very large data sets in highly parallel GPU systems is still an open problem.

3.6 SORTING ALGORITHMS FOR LARGE DATA SETS

Sorting in databases. Ref. [31] presents one of the earliest GPU-based external sorting algorithms with hybrid in-GPU memory and cross-GPU sorting to handle

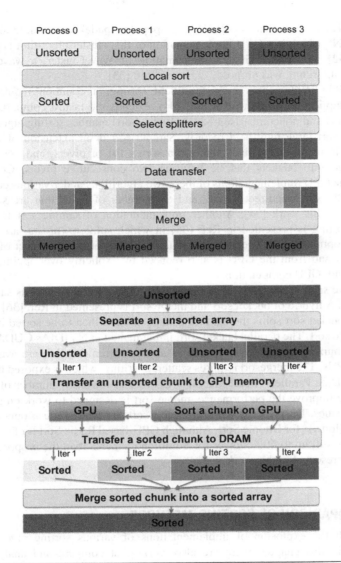

FIG. 4

Top: The general data flow of splitter-merger-based parallel algorithms. *Bottom*: The data flow of the sorting algorithm presented in Ref. [28].

very large databases (60 GB). This algorithm also uses bitonic sort as the basis for the sorting algorithm and presents a scalable approach to sort massive databases using efficient large data partitions. Clustering algorithms are fundamental tools in data mining. Clustering can be considered as a coarser version of sorting in higher dimensions. Density-Based Spatial Clustering of Applications with Noise

(DBSCAN) and its variant VDBSCAN are popular spatial data mining algorithms. VDBSCAN* which is a GPU implementation of this cluster algorithm is presented in Ref. [32]. A parallel GPU implementation of WaveCluster, a wavelet-based clustering algorithm, was proposed earlier in Ref. [33].

The GPU implementation of multifield sorting, a common requirement in database application, presented in Ref. [34], extends the fastest comparison-based (sample sort) and noncomparison-based (Radix Sort) number sorting algorithms on a GPU to sort large multifield records. Sample sort is an extension of Quicksort in which, instead of one pivot, there is a sorted list of pivots, and the input list is presorted into buckets that lie between two consecutive pivots. Comparison between the GPU implementations of these two algorithms under various conditions, including the direct/indirect sorting and the number of fields that are sorted, are discussed in this work [34]. Another implementation of sample sort for parallel external sorting is presented in Ref. [35] in which splitters (pivots) are carefully chosen to optimize GPU memory utilization. The performance impact of memory transfers to and from the GPU is also reduced by explicitly overlapping memory transfers with GPU computation.

We have seen a combination of bitonic and merge sorts, as well as sample and merge sort. A hybrid of bucket sort and merge sort is presented in Ref. [36]. Initially, a parallel bucket sort splits the list into enough sublists then to be sorted in parallel using merge sort. The parallel bucket sort, implemented in NVIDIAs CUDA, utilizes the synchronization mechanisms, such as atomic increment, that are available on modern GPUs. The mergesort requires scattered writing, which is exposed by CUDA and ATI's Data Parallel Virtual Machine. In order to lower the number of memory fetches and improve the performance, merge sort is designed to work on groups of four float values. The presented GPU algorithm sorts on $n \log n$ time as opposed to the standard $n(\log n)^2$ for Bitonic Sort. Although GPU-based Radix Sort is of complexity $n \log n$, it is still up to 40% slower for 8 million elements than the proposed hybrid algorithm presented in this work.

3.7 COMPARISON OF SORTING METHODS

Along with the explosion of implementations of various sorting algorithms as explained in this chapter, there are also works that compare and analyze these algorithms and implementations, both theoretically and empirically. One such work is Ref. [37] in which the authors introduce a new computational model, which they call the *K-model* designed to consider all the important features of many-core architectures (including memory hierarchies such as the registers, shared memory, and main memory [host memory]) and to map the Bitonic Sort network in an optimal way in this model with the space complexity of $\Theta(1)l$. According to K-model, the authors show that mapping with the bitonic sorting network improves the following main aspects of many-core architectures: the utilization of processors, and the on-chip/off-chip memory bandwidth utilization. Different algorithms (Quicksort and Radisort) for sorting integers on stream multiprocessors are both experimentally and theoretically (on the *K-model*) compared, and their viability on large data sets are discussed.

Parallel sorting [38] and its earlier version of the work [39] make an extensive experimental analysis using parallel implementations of three popular sorting algorithms: Odd-Even sort, rank sort, and Bitonic Sort, on CPU and different GPU architectures. The work also presents an implementation of a new parallel algorithm: Min-Max butterfly network, for finding minimum and maximum in large data sets. Implementation of these algorithms have exploited data parallelism using OpenCL specification.

REFERENCES

[1] D.P. Luebke, Graphics hardware & GPU computing: past, present, and future, in: Proceedings of the Graphics Interface 2009 Conference, May 25–27, 2009, Kelowna, British Columbia, Canada, 2009, 6 pp., http://dx.doi.org/10.1145/1555880.1555888.

[2] A.E. Lefohn, S. Sengupta, J. Kniss, R. Strzodka, J.D. Owens, Glift: generic, efficient, random-access GPU data structures, ACM Trans. Graph. 25 (1) (2006) 60–99, http://dx.doi.org/10.1145/1122501.1122505.

[3] P. McCormick, J. Inman, J. Ahrens, J. Mohd-Yusof, G. Roth, S. Cummins, Scout: a data-parallel programming language for graphics processors, Parallel Comput. 33 (10–11) (2007) 648–662, ISSN 0167-8191, http://dx.doi.org/10.1016/j.parco.2007.09.001.

[4] K. Kothapalli, R. Mukherjee, M.S. Rehman, S. Patidar, P.J. Narayanan, K. Srinathan, A performance prediction model for the CUDA GPGPU platform, in: 2009 International Conference on High Performance Computing (HiPC), 2009, pp. 463–472, http://dx.doi.org/10.1109/HIPC.2009.5433179.

[5] S. Hong, H. Kim, An analytical model for a GPU architecture with memory-level and thread-level parallelism awareness, SIGARCH Comput. Archit. News 37 (3) (2009) 152–163, ISSN 0163-5964, http://dx.doi.org/10.1145/1555815.1555775.

[6] G. Capannini, F. Silvestri, R. Baraglia, K-model: a new computational model for stream processors, in: 2010 12th IEEE International Conference on High Performance Computing and Communications (HPCC), Sep., 2010, pp. 239–246, http://dx.doi.org/10.1109/HPCC.2010.22.

[7] K. Nakano, Simple memory machine models for GPUs, in: Parallel and Distributed Processing Symposium Workshops PhD Forum (IPDPSW), 2012 IEEE 26th International, 2012, pp. 794–803, http://dx.doi.org/10.1109/IPDPSW.2012.98.

[8] K. Nakano, The hierarchical memory machine model for GPUs, in: 2013 IEEE 27th International Parallel and Distributed Processing Symposium Workshops PhD Forum (IPDPSW), 2013, pp. 591–600, http://dx.doi.org/10.1109/IPDPSW.2013.17.

[9] L. Ma, K. Agrawal, R.D. Chamberlain, A memory access model for highly-threaded many-core architectures, Future Gener. Comput. Syst. 30 (2014) 202–215, ISSN 0167-739X, http://dx.doi.org/10.1016/j.future.2013.06.020, http://www.sciencedirect.com/science/article/pii/S0167739X13001349.

[10] A. Koike, K. Sadakane, A novel computational model for GPUs with application to I/O optimal sorting algorithms, in: 2014 IEEE International Parallel & Distributed Processing Symposium Workshops, Phoenix, AZ, USA, May 19–23, 2014, 2014, pp. 614–623, http://dx.doi.org/10.1109/IPDPSW.2014.72.

[11] Y. Wang, A.A. Davidson, Y. Pan, Y. Wu, A. Riffel, J.D. Owens, Gunrock: a high-performance graph processing library on the GPU, in: Proceedings of the 20th ACM SIGPLAN Symposium on Principles and Practice of Parallel Programming, PPoPP 2015, San Francisco, CA, USA, February 7–11, 2015, 2015, pp. 265–266, http://dx.doi.org/10.1145/2688500.2688538.

[12] A.R. Brodtkorb, T.R. Hagen, M.L. Sætra, Graphics processing unit (GPU) programming strategies and trends in GPU computing, J. Parallel Distrib. Comput. 73 (1) (2013) 4–13, http://dx.doi.org/10.1016/j.jpdc.2012.04.003.

[13] G. Bilardi, A. Nicolau, Adaptive bitonic sorting: an optimal parallel algorithm for shared memory machines, SIAM J. Comput. 18 (2) (1988) 216–228.

[14] A. Greß, G. Zachmann, GPU-ABiSort: optimal parallel sorting on stream architectures, in: 20th International Parallel and Distributed Processing Symposium (IPDPS 2006), Proceedings, April 25–29, 2006, Rhodes Island, Greece, 2006, http://dx.doi.org/10.1109/IPDPS.2006.1639284.

[15] S. White, N. Verosky, T. Newhall, A CUDA-MPI hybrid bitonic sorting algorithm for GPU clusters, in: 41st International Conference on Parallel Processing Workshops, ICPPW 2012, Pittsburgh, PA, USA, September 10–13, 2012, 2012, pp. 588–589, http://dx.doi.org/10.1109/ICPPW.2012.82.

[16] https://graphics.cg.uni-saarland.de/fileadmin/cguds/courses/ws1213/pp_cuda/slides/06_-_Sorting_in_Parallel.pdf.

[17] H. Peters, O. Schulz-Hildebrandt, N. Luttenberger, Fast in-place sorting with CUDA based on bitonic sort, in: PPAM: 8th International Conference on Parallel Processing and Applied Mathematics, Wroclaw, Poland, September 13–16, 2009—Conference Proceedings, 2009, pp. 1–10.

[18] H. Peters, O. Schulz-Hildebrandt, N. Luttenberger, Fast in-place, comparison-based sorting with CUDA: a study with bitonic sort, Concurr. Comput. Pract. Exper. 23 (7) (2011) 681–693, ISSN 1532-0626, http://dx.doi.org/10.1002/cpe.1686.

[19] http://www.heterogeneouscompute.org/wordpress/wp-content/uploads/2011/06/Radix Sort.pdf.

[20] L.K. Ha, J.H. Krüger, C.T. Silva, Fast four-way parallel radix sorting on GPUs, Comput. Graph. Forum 28 (8) (2009) 2368–2378, http://dx.doi.org/10.1111/j.1467-8659.2009.01542.x.

[21] D. Merrill, A.S. Grimshaw, High performance and scalable radix sorting: a case study of implementing dynamic parallelism for GPU computing, Parallel Process. Lett. 21 (2) (2011) 245–272, http://dx.doi.org/10.1142/S0129626411000187.

[22] D.G. Merrill, A.S. Grimshaw, Revisiting sorting for GPGPU stream architectures, in: Proceedings of the 19th International Conference on Parallel Architectures and Compilation Techniques, ACM, 2010, pp. 545–546.

[23] I. Tanasic, L. Vilanova, M. Jordà, J. Cabezas, I. Gelado, N. Navarro, W.W. Hwu, Comparison based sorting for systems with multiple GPUs, in: Proceedings of the 6th Workshop on General Purpose Processor Using Graphics Processing Units, GPGPU-6, Houston, Texas, USA, March 16, 2013, 2013, pp. 1–11, http://dx.doi.org/10.1145/2458523.2458524.

[24] N. Satish, M. Harris, M. Garland, Designing efficient sorting algorithms for manycore GPUs, in: 23rd IEEE International Symposium on Parallel and Distributed Processing, IPDPS 2009, Rome, Italy, May 23–29, 2009, 2009, pp. 1–10, http://dx.doi.org/10.1109/IPDPS.2009.5161005.

[25] D. Cederman, P. Tsigas, GPU-Quicksort: a practical Quicksort algorithm for graphics processors, ACM J. Exp. Algorithmics 14 (2009), http://dx.doi.org/10.1145/1498698.1564500.

[26] D. Cederman, P. Tsigas, On sorting and load balancing on GPUs, SIGARCH Comput. Archit. News 36 (5) (2008) 11–18, http://dx.doi.org/10.1145/1556444.1556447.

[27] X. Ye, D. Fan, W. Lin, N. Yuan, P. Ienne, High performance comparison-based sorting algorithm on many-core GPUs, in: 24th IEEE International Symposium on Parallel and Distributed Processing, IPDPS 2010, Atlanta, Georgia, USA, April 19–23, 2010—Conference Proceedings, 2010, pp. 1–10, http://dx.doi.org/10.1109/IPDPS.2010.5470445.

[28] H. Shamoto, K. Shirahata, A. Drozd, H. Sato, S. Matsuoka, Large-scale distributed sorting for GPU-based heterogeneous supercomputers, in: 2014 IEEE International Conference on Big Data, Big Data 2014, Washington, DC, USA, October 27–30, 2014, pp. 510–518, http://dx.doi.org/10.1109/BigData.2014.7004268.

[29] H. Sundar, D. Malhotra, G. Biros, HykSort: a new variant of hypercube Quicksort on distributed memory architectures, in: Proceedings of the 27th International ACM Conference on International Conference on Supercomputing, ICS '13, ACM, New York, NY, USA, ISBN 978-1-4503-2130-3, 2013, pp. 293–302, http://dx.doi.org/10.1145/2464996.2465442.

[30] O. Green, R. McColl, D.A. Bader, GPU merge path: a GPU merging algorithm, in: Proceedings of the 26th ACM International Conference on Supercomputing, ICS '12, ACM, New York, NY, USA, ISBN 978-1-4503-1316-2, 2012, pp. 331–340, http://dx.doi.org/10.1145/2304576.2304621.

[31] N.K. Govindaraju, J. Gray, R. Kumar, D. Manocha, GPUTeraSort: high performance graphics co-processor sorting for large database management, in: Proceedings of the ACM SIGMOD International Conference on Management of Data, Chicago, Illinois, USA, June 27–29, 2006, 2006, pp. 325–336, http://dx.doi.org/10.1145/1142473.1142511.

[32] C.R. Valencio, G.P. Daniel, C.A. de Medeiros, A.M. Cansian, L.C. Baida, F. Ferrari, VDBSCAN+: performance optimization based on GPU parallelism, in: 2013 International Conference on Parallel and Distributed Computing, Applications and Technologies (PDCAT), 2013, pp. 23–28, http://dx.doi.org/10.1109/PDCAT.2013.11.

[33] A.A. Yildirim, C. Özdogan, Parallel wavelet-based clustering algorithm on GPUs using CUDA, in: First World Conference on Information Technology, WCIT 2010, Istanbul, Turkey, October 6–10, 2010, 2011, pp. 396–400, http://dx.doi.org/10.1016/j.procs.2010.12.066.

[34] S. Bandyopadhyay, S. Sahni, Sorting large multifield records on a GPU, in: 17th IEEE International Conference on Parallel and Distributed Systems, ICPADS 2011, Tainan, Taiwan, December 7–9, 2011, 2011, pp. 149–156, http://dx.doi.org/10.1109/ICPADS.2011.124.

[35] H. Peters, O. Schulz-Hildebrandt, N. Luttenberger, Parallel external sorting for CUDA-enabled GPUs with load balancing and low transfer overhead, in: 24th IEEE International Symposium on Parallel and Distributed Processing, IPDPS 2010, Atlanta, Georgia, USA, April 19–23, 2010—Workshop Proceedings, 2010, pp. 1–8, http://dx.doi.org/10.1109/IPDPSW.2010.5470833.

[36] E. Sintorn, U. Assarsson, Fast parallel GPU-sorting using a hybrid algorithm, J. Parallel Distrib. Comput. 68 (10) (2008) 1381–1388, http://dx.doi.org/10.1016/j.jpdc.2008.05.012.

[37] G. Capannini, F. Silvestri, R. Baraglia, Sorting on GPUs for large scale datasets: a thorough comparison, Inf. Process. Manag. 48 (5) (2012) 903–917, http://dx.doi.org/10.1016/j.ipm.2010.11.010.

[38] B. Jan, B. Montrucchio, C. Ragusa, F.G. Khan, O. Khan, Fast parallel sorting algorithms on GPUs, Int. J. Distrib. Parallel Syst. 3 (6) (2012) 107–118.

[39] F.G. Khan, O.U. Khan, B. Montrucchio, P. Giaccone, Analysis of fast parallel sorting algorithms for GPU architectures', in: 2011 Frontiers of Information Technology, FIT 2011, Islamabad, Pakistan, December 19–21, 2011, pp. 173–178, http://dx.doi.org/10.1109/FIT.2011.39.

MPC: An effective floating-point compression algorithm for GPUs[a]

13

A. Yang, J. Coplin, H. Mukka, F. Hesaaraki, M. Burtscher

Texas State University, San Marcos, TX, United States

1 INTRODUCTION

High-performance computing (HPC) applications often process and transfer large amounts of floating-point data. For example, many simulations exchange data between compute nodes and with mass-storage devices after every time step. Most HPC programs retrieve and store large data sets, some of which may have to be sent to other locations for additional processing, analysis, or visualization. Moreover, scientific programs often save checkpoints at regular intervals.

Compression can reduce the amount of data that needs to be transmitted and/or stored. However, if the overhead lowers the effective throughput, compression will not be used in the performance-centric HPC domain. Hence the challenge is to maximize the compression ratio (CR) while meeting or exceeding the available transfer bandwidth. In other words, the compression and decompression have to be done in real time. Furthermore, the compression should be lossless and single pass. Intermediate program results that are exchanged between compute nodes, for example, generally cannot be lossy. A single-pass algorithm is needed so that the data can be compressed and decompressed in a streaming fashion as they are being generated and consumed, respectively.

Some compression algorithms are asymmetric, meaning that compression takes much longer than decompression. This is useful in situations where data are compressed once and decompressed many times. However, this is not the case for checkpoints, which are almost never read, nor for intermediate program results that are compressed to boost the transmission speed between compute nodes, between

---

[a]This chapter is a modified version of our IEEE Cluster 2015 publication [1]. The chapter contains more results as well as updated results from a new implementation that is up to 2.5 times faster than the one described in the conference paper.

Advances in GPU Research and Practice. http://dx.doi.org/10.1016/B978-0-12-803738-6.00013-6

accelerators and hosts, or between compute nodes and storage devices. Thus we focus on symmetric algorithms in this chapter.

Massively parallel compute graphics processing units (GPUs) are quickly spreading in HPC environments to accelerate calculations as GPUs not only provide much higher peak performance than multicore CPUs but also are more cost- and energy-efficient. However, utilizing GPUs for data compression is difficult because compression algorithms typically compress data based on information from previously processed words. This makes compression and decompression data-dependent operations that are difficult to parallelize. Thus most of the relatively few parallel compression approaches from the literature simply break the data up into chunks that are compressed independently using a serial algorithm. However, this technique is not suitable for massively parallel hardware. First, the data would have to be broken up into hundreds of thousands of small chunks, at least one per thread, thus possibly losing much of the history needed to compress the data well. Second and more importantly, well-performing serial compression algorithms generally require a large amount of internal state (e.g., predictor tables or dictionaries), making it infeasible to run tens of thousands of them in parallel. As a consequence, the research community does not yet possess a good understanding of how to design effective compression algorithms for massively parallel machines.

At a high level, most data compression algorithms comprise two main steps, a data model and a coder. Roughly speaking, the goal of the model is to predict the data. The residual (i.e., the difference) between each actual value and its predicted value will be close to zero if the model is accurate for the given data. This residual sequence of values is then compressed with the coder by mapping the residuals in such a way that frequently encountered values or patterns produce shorter output than infrequently encountered data. The reverse operations are performed to decompress the data. For instance, an inverse model takes the residual sequence as input and regenerates the original values as output.

To systematically search for effective and massive parallelism-friendly compression algorithms, we synthesized a large number of compressors and their corresponding decompressors using the following approach. We started with a detailed study of previously proposed floating-point compression algorithms [2–14]. Short overviews of these algorithms as well as additional related work are available elsewhere [1]. We then broke each algorithm down into their constituent parts, rejected all parts that could not be parallelized well, and generalized the remaining parts as much as possible. This yielded a number of algorithmic components for building data models and coders. We then implemented each component using a common interface, that is, each component can be given a block of data as input, which it transforms into an output block of data. This makes it possible to chain the components, allowing us to generate a vast number of compression-algorithm candidates from a given set of components. Note that each component comes with an inverse that performs the opposite transformation. Thus, for any chain of components, which represents a compression algorithm, we can synthesize the matching decompressor. Fig. 1 illustrates this approach on the example of the four components named LNV6s, BIT,

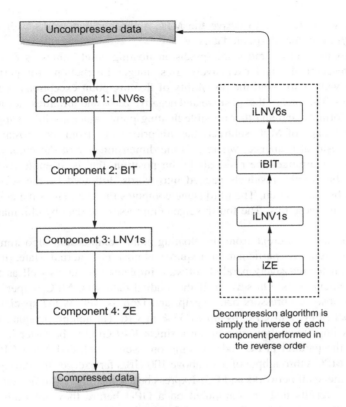

FIG. 1

The four chained components that make up the 6D MPC compression algorithm along with the corresponding four inverse components that make up the decompression algorithm.

LNV1s, and ZE that make up the 6D version of our Massively Parallel Compression (MPC) algorithm.

We used exhaustive search to determine the most effective compression algorithms that can be built from the available components. Limiting the components to those that can exploit massively parallel hardware guarantees that all of the compressors and decompressors synthesized in this way are, by design, GPU-friendly.

Because floating-point computations are prevalent on highly parallel machines and floating-point data tend to be difficult to compress, we decided to target this domain. In particular, we implemented 24 highly parallel components in the Compute Unified Device Architecture (CUDA) C++ programming language for GPUs and employed our approach on single- and double-precision versions of 13 real-world data sets. Based on a detailed analysis and generalization of the best four-stage compression algorithms we found for each data set as well as the best overall algorithm, we were able to derive the MPC algorithm that works well on many different types of floating-point data.

MPC treats double- and single-precision floating-point values as 8- or 4-byte integers, respectively, and exclusively uses integer instructions for performance reasons as well as to avoid the possibility of floating-point exceptions or rounding inaccuracies. This means that positive and negative zeros and infinities, not-a-number (NaN), denormals, and all other possible floating-point values are fully supported.

The first stage of MPC subtracts the nth prior value from the current value to produce a residual sequence, where n is the dimensionality of the input data. The second stage rearranges the residuals by bit position, that is, it emits all the most significant bits of the residuals packed into words, followed by the second-most significant bits, and so on. The third stage computes the residual of the consecutive words holding these bits. The fourth stage compresses the data by eliminating zero words.

MPC is quite different from the floating-point compression algorithms in the current literature. In particular, it requires almost no internal state, making it suitable both for massively parallel software implementations as well as for hardware implementations. On several of the studied data sets, MPC outperforms the general-purpose compressors bzip2, gzip, and lzop as well as the special-purpose compressors pFPC and GFC by up to 33% in CR. Throughput evaluations show our CUDA implementation running on a single K40 GPU to be faster in all cases than even the parallel pFPC code running on twenty high-end Xeon CPU cores. Moreover, MPC's throughput of at or above 100 GB/s far exceeds the throughputs of current-of-the-shelf networks and PCI-Express buses, making real-time compression possible for results that are computed on a GPU before they are transferred to the host or the network interface card (NIC), and making real-time decompression possible for compressed data that are streamed to the GPU from the CPU or the NIC. The performance-optimized CUDA implementation of MPC is available at http://cs.txstate.edu/~burtscher/research/MPC/.

This chapter makes the following key contributions:

- It presents the lossless MPC compression algorithm for single- and double-precision floating-point data that is suitable for massively parallel execution.
- It systematically evaluates millions of component combinations to determine well-performing compression algorithms within the given search space.
- It analyzes the chains of components that work well to gain insight into the design of effective parallel compression algorithms and to predict how to adapt them to other data sets.
- It describes previously unknown algorithms that compress several real-world scientific numeric data sets significantly better than prior work.
- It demonstrates that, in spite of substantial constraints, MPC's CRs rival those of the best CPU-based compressors while yielding much higher throughputs and energy efficiency than (multicore) CPU-based compressors.

2 METHODOLOGY

2.1 SYSTEM AND COMPILERS

We evaluated the CPU compressors on a system with dual 10-core Xeon E5-2687W v3 processors running at 3.1 GHz and 128 GB of main memory. The operating system was CentOS 6.7. We used the gcc compiler version 4.4.7 with "-O3 -pthread -march=native" for the CPU implementations.

For GPU compressors, we used a Kepler-based Tesla K40c GPU. It had 15 streaming multiprocessors with a total of 2880 CUDA cores running at 745 MHz and 12 GB of global memory. We also used a Maxwell-based GeForce GTX Titan X GPU. It had 24 streaming multiprocessors with a total of 3072 CUDA cores running at 1 GHz and 12 GB of global memory. We used nvcc version 7.0 with the "-O3 -arch=sm_35" flags to compile the GPU codes for the K40 and "-O3 -arch=sm_52" to compile the GPU codes for the Titan X.

2.2 MEASURING THROUGHPUT AND ENERGY

For all special-purpose floating-point compressors, the timing measurements were performed by adding code to read a timer before and after the compression and decompression code sections and recording the difference. For the general-purpose compressors, we measured the runtime of compression and decompression when reading the input from a disk cache in main memory and writing the output to /dev/null. In the case of GPU code, we excluded the time to transfer the data to or from the GPU as we assumed the data to have been produced or transferred there with or without compression. Each experiment was conducted three times, and the median throughput was reported. Note that the three measured throughputs were very similar in all cases. The decompressed results were always compared to the original data to verify that every bit was identical.

For measuring energy on the CPU, we used a custom power measurement tool based on the PAPI framework [15]. PAPI makes use of the Running Average Power Limit (RAPL) functionality of certain Intel processors, which in turn measures Model Specific Registers to calculate the energy consumption of a processor in real time. Our power tool simply made calls to the PAPI framework to start the energy measurements, to run the code to be measured, and then to stop the measurements and output the result. Doing so incurred negligible overhead.

For measuring energy on the GPU, we used the K20 Power Tool, which also works for the K40c GPU we used in our experiments [16]. To measure the energy consumption of the GPU, the K20 Power Tool uses power samples from the GPU's internal power sensor and the "active" runtime. The power tool defines this as the amount of time the GPU is drawing power above the idle level. Fig. 2 illustrates this.

Because of how the GPU draws power and how the built-in power sensor samples, only readings above a certain threshold (the dashed line at 55 W in this case) reflect when the GPU is actually executing the program [16]. Measurements below the threshold are either the idle power (less than about 26 W) or the "tail power" due

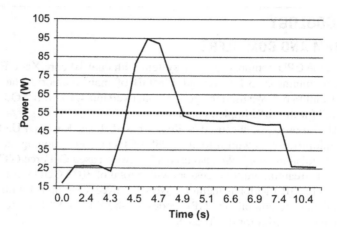

FIG. 2

Sample power profile.

to the driver keeping the GPU active for a time before powering it down. Using the active runtime ignores any execution time that may take place on the CPU. The power threshold is dynamically adjusted to maximize accuracy for different GPU settings.

2.3 DATA SETS

We used the 13 FPC data sets for our evaluation [3]. Each data set consisted of a binary sequence of IEEE 754 double-precision floating-point values. They included MPI messages (msg), numeric results (num), and observational data (obs).

MPI messages: These five data sets contain the numeric messages sent by a node in a parallel system running NAS Parallel Benchmark (NPB) and ASCI Purple applications.

- msg_bt: NPB computational fluid dynamics pseudo-application bt
- msg_lu: NPB computational fluid dynamics pseudo-application lu
- msg_sp: NPB computational fluid dynamics pseudo-application sp
- msg_sppm: ASCI Purple solver sppm
- msg_sweep3d: ASCI Purple solver sweep3d

Numeric simulations: These four data sets are the result of numeric simulations.

- num_brain: Simulation of the velocity field of a human brain during a head impact
- num_comet: Simulation of the comet Shoemaker-Levy 9 entering Jupiter's atmosphere

- num_control: Control vector output between two minimization steps in weather-satellite data assimilation
- num_plasma: Simulated plasma temperature evolution of a wire array z-pinch experiment

Observational data: These four data sets comprise measurements from scientific instruments.

- obs_error: Data values specifying brightness temperature errors of a weather satellite
- obs_info: Latitude and longitude information of the observation points of a weather satellite
- obs_spitzer: Data from the Spitzer Space Telescope showing a slight darkening as an extrasolar planet disappears behinds its star
- obs_temp: Data from a weather satellite denoting how much the observed temperature differs from the actual contiguous analysis temperature field

Table 1 provides pertinent information about each data set. The first two data columns list the size in megabytes and in millions of double-precision values. The middle column shows the percentage of values that are unique. The fourth column displays the first-order entropy of the values in bits. The last column expresses the randomness of each data set in percent, that is, it reflects how close the first-order entropy is to that of a truly random data set with the same number of unique values. For the single-precision experiments, we simply converted the double-precision data sets.

Table 1 Information About the Double-Precision Data Sets

	Size (MB)	Doubles (Millions)	Unique Values (%)	First-Order Entropy (Bits)	Randomness (%)
msg_bt	254.0	33.30	92.9	23.67	95.1
msg_lu	185.1	24.26	99.2	24.47	99.8
msg_sp	276.7	36.26	98.9	25.03	99.7
msg_sppm	266.1	34.87	10.2	11.24	51.6
msg_sweep3d	119.9	15.72	89.8	23.41	98.6
num_brain	135.3	17.73	94.9	23.97	99.9
num_comet	102.4	13.42	88.9	22.04	93.8
num_control	152.1	19.94	98.5	24.14	99.6
num_plasma	33.5	4.39	0.3	13.65	99.4
obs_error	59.3	7.77	18.0	17.80	87.2
obs_info	18.1	2.37	23.9	18.07	94.5
obs_spitzer	189.0	24.77	5.7	17.36	85.0
obs_temp	38.1	4.99	100.0	22.25	100.0

2.4 ALGORITHMIC COMPONENTS

We tested the following algorithmic components in our experiments. They are generalizations or approximations of components extracted from previously proposed compression algorithms. Each component takes a block of data as input, transforms it, and outputs the transformed block.

The input data are broken down into fixed-size chunks. Each chunk is assigned to a thread block for parallel processing. We chose 1024-element chunks to match the maximum number of threads per thread block in our GPUs.

The **NUL** component simply outputs the input block. The **INV** component flips all the bits. The **BIT** component breaks a block of data into chunks and then emits the most significant bit of each word in the chunk, followed by the second most significant bits, and so on. The **DIMn** component also breaks the blocks into chunks and then rearranges the values in each chunk such that the values from each dimension are grouped together. For example, DIM2 emits all the values from the even positions first and then all the values from the odd positions. We tested the dimensions n = 2, 3, 4, 5, 8, 16, and 32. The **LNVns** component uses the nth prior value in the same chunk as a prediction of the current value, subtracts the prediction from the current value, and emits the residual. The **LNVnx** component is identical except it XORs the prediction with the current value to form the residual. In both cases, we tested n = 1, 2, 3, 5, 6, and 8. Note that all of the preceding components transform the data blocks without changing their size. The following two components are the only ones that can actually reduce the length of a data block. The **ZE** component outputs a bitmap for each chunk that specifies which values in the chunk are zero. The bitmap is followed by the nonzero values. The **RLE** component performs run-length encoding, that is, it replaces repeating values by a count and a single copy of the value. Each component has a corresponding inverse that performs the opposite transformation for decompression.

Because it may be more effective to operate at byte rather than word granularity, we also included the singleton pseudo component "|", which we call the cut, that converts a block of words into a block of bytes through type casting (i.e., no computation is necessary). As a result, we need three versions of each component and its inverse, one for double-precision values (8-byte words), one for single-precision values (4-byte words), and one for byte values. Each component operates on an integer representation of the floating-point data, that is, the bit pattern representing the floating-point value is copied verbatim into an appropriately sized integer variable.

We chose this limited number of components because we only included components that we could implement in a massively parallel manner. Nevertheless, as the results in the next section show, very effective compression algorithms can be created from these components. In other words, the sophistication and effectiveness of the ultimate algorithm is the result of the clever combination of components, not the capability of each individual component. This is akin to how complex programs can be expressed through a suitable sequence of very simple machine instructions.

To derive MPC, we investigated all four-stage compression algorithms that can be built from the preceding components. Because of the presence of the NUL component, this includes all one-, two-, and three-stage algorithms as well. Note that only the first three stages can contain any 1 of the 24 components just described. The last stage must contain a component that can reduce the amount of data, that is, either ZE or RLE. The cut can be before the first component, in which case the data is exclusively treated as a sequence of bytes; after the last component, in which case the data is exclusively treated as a sequence of words; or between components, in which case the data is initially treated as words and then as bytes. The 5 possible locations for the cut, the 24 possible components in each of the first three stages, and the 2 possible components in the last stage result in $5 * 24 * 24 * 24 * 2 = 138,240$ possible compression algorithms with four stages.

3 EXPERIMENTAL RESULTS

3.1 SYNTHESIS ANALYSIS AND DERIVATION OF MPC

Table 2 shows the four chained components and the location of the cut that the exhaustive search found to work best for each data set as well as across all 13 data sets, which is denoted as "Best." For Best, the CR is the harmonic mean over the data sets.

Table 2 Best Four-Stage Algorithm for Each Data Set, for All Single-Precision Data Sets, and for All Double-Precision Data Sets

		Double Precision		Single Precision
		Four-Stage Algorithm		**Four-Stage Algorithm**
Data Set	**CR**	**With Cut**	**CR**	**With Cut**
msg_bt	1.143	LNVls BIT LNVls ZE |	1.233	DIM5 ZE LNV6x | ZE
msg_lu	1.244	LNVSs | DIM8 BIT RLE	1.588	LNVSs LNVSs LNV5x | ZE
msg_sp	1.192	DIM3 LNV5x BIT ZE |	1.362	DIM3 LNV5x BIT ZE |
msg_sppm	3.359	DIM5 INV6x ZE | ZE	4.828	RLE DIMS LNV6s ZE |
msg_sweep3d	1.293	LNVls DIM32 | DIM8 RLE	1.545	LNVls DIM32 | DIM4 RLE
num_brain	1.182	LNVls BIT LNVls ZE |	1.344	LNVls BIT LNVls ZE |
num_comet	1.267	LNVls BIT LNVls ZE |	1.199	LNVls | DIM4 BIT RLE
num_control	1.106	LNVls BIT LNVls ZE |	1.122	LNVls BIT LNVls ZE |
num_plasma	1.454	LNV2s LNV2s LNV2x | ZE	1.978	LNV2s LNV2s LNV2x | ZE
obs_error	1.210	LNVlx ZE INVls ZE |	1.289	LNV6S BIT LNVls ZE |
obs_info	1.245	LNV2s | DIM8 BIT RLE	1.477	LNV8s DIM2 | DIM4 RLE
obs_spitzer	1.231	ZE BIT LNVls ZE |	1.080	ZE BIT LNVls ZE |
obs_temp	1.101	LNV8s BIT LNVls ZE |	1.126	BIT INVlx DIM32 | RLE
Best	1.214	LNV6s BIT LNVls ZE |	1.265	LNV6s BIT LNVls ZE |

3.1.1 Observations about individual algorithms

The individual best algorithms are truly the best within the search space, that is, the next best algorithms compress successively worse (by a fraction of a percent). Hence it is not the case that an entire set of algorithms performs equally well.

Whereas the last component (ignoring the cut) has to be ZE or RLE, ZE is chosen more often. This indicates that the earlier components manage to transform the data in a way that generates zeros but not many zeros in a row, which RLE would be better able to compress.

Interestingly, in most cases, the first three stages do not include a ZE or RLE component, that is, they do not change the length of the data stream but transform it to make the final stage more effective. Clearly, these noncompressing transformations are very important, emphasizing that the best overall algorithm is generally not the one that maximally compresses the data in every stage. This also demonstrates that chaining whole compression algorithms, as proposed in some related work, is unlikely to yield the most effective algorithms.

There were several instances of DIM8 right after the cut in the double-precision algorithms and of DIM4 right after the cut in the single-precision algorithms. This utilization of the DIM component differs from the anticipated usage. Instead of employing it for multidimensional data sets, these algorithms use DIM to separate the different byte positions from each 4- or 8-byte word. Note that the frequently used BIT component serves a similar purpose but at a finer granularity. This repurposing of the DIM component shows that automatic synthesis is able to devise algorithms that the authors of the components may not have foreseen.

The very frequent occurrence of BIT indicates that the individual bits of floating-point values tend to correlate more strongly across values than within values. This might be expected as, for example, the top exponent bits of consecutive values are likely to be the same.

Another interesting observation is that the cut was often at the end, that is, it is not used. This means that the entire algorithm operates at word granularity, including the Best algorithm, and that there is no benefit from switching to byte granularity. This is good news because it simplifies and speeds up the implementation as only word-granular components are needed. NUL and INV are also not needed. Clearly, inverting all the bits is unnecessary and algorithms with fewer than four components (i.e., that include NUL) compress less well.

The LNV predictor component is obviously very important. Every listed algorithm includes it, and most of them include two such components. LNV comes in two versions, one that uses integer subtraction to form the residual and the other that uses XOR (i.e., bitwise subtraction). Subtraction is much more frequent, which is noteworthy as the current literature seems undecided as to which method to prefer.

In many cases, the single-precision algorithm is the same as the corresponding double-precision algorithm, especially when excluding the aforementioned DIM4 versus DIM8 difference immediately after the cut. This similarity is perhaps expected since the data sets contain the same values (albeit in different formats). However, in about half the cases, the algorithms are different, sometimes substantially (e.g., on msg_bt) and yield significantly different CRs. This implies that the bits that are dropped when converting from double- to single-precision benefit more from different compression algorithms than the remaining bits. Hence it would probably be advantageous if distinct algorithms were used for compressing the bits or bytes at different positions within the floating-point words.

3.1.2 Observations about the Best algorithm

Focusing on the Best algorithm, which is the algorithm shown in Fig. 1, we find that the single- and double-precision data sets result in the same algorithm that maximizes the harmonic-mean CR. Hence the following discussion applies to both formats. The most frequent pattern of components in the individual algorithms is "LNV*s BIT LNV1s ZE," where the star represents a digit. Consequently, it is not surprising that the Best algorithm also follows this pattern. It is interesting, however, that Best uses a "6" in the starred position even though, with one exception, none of the individual algorithms do. We believe that the exhaustive search selected a 6 because 6 is the least common multiple of 1, 2, and 3, all of which occur more often than 6. In other words, the first component tries to predict each value using a similar prior value, which is best done when looking back n positions, where n is the least common multiple of the dimensionality of the various data sets. Hence it is possible that a larger n will work better, but we only tested up to $n = 8$.

With this in mind, we can now explain the operation of the Best algorithm. The job of the LNV6s component is to predict each value using a similar prior value to obtain a residual sequence with many small values. Because not all bit positions are equally predictable (e.g., the most significant exponent bits are more likely than the other bits to be predicted correctly and to therefore be zero in the residual sequence), it is beneficial to group bits from the same bit position together, which is what the BIT component does. The resulting sequence of values apparently contains consecutive "words" that are identical, which the LNV1s component turns into zeros. The ZE component then eliminates these zeros.

3.1.3 Derivation of the MPC algorithm

With this insight, a good compression algorithm for floating-point data can be derived by adapting the first component to the dimensionality of the data set and keeping the other three components fixed. We named the resulting algorithm MPC for "Massively Parallel Compressor." It is based on the aforementioned "LNV*s BIT LNV1s ZE" pattern but uses the data-set dimensionality in the starred location. Note that we obtained the same pattern when using cross-validation, that is, when excluding one of the inputs so as not to train and test on the same input. MPC is identical to the best algorithm the exhaustive search found for several of the studied data sets. Even better, in cases where the actual dimensionality is above eight, MPC yields CRs exceeding those of the Best algorithm (cf. the Best results in Table 2 vs the MPC results in Tables 3 and 4), which validates our generalization of the Best algorithm.

3.2 COMPRESSION RATIOS

Tables 3 and 4 show the CRs on the double- and single-precision data sets, respectively, for the general-purpose compressors pbzip2 [17], pigz [18], and lzop [19], the special-purpose floating-point compressors pFPC [20] and GFC [21] (they only support double precision), and for MPC. The highest CR for each data set is highlighted in the tables. Because we wanted to maximize the CR, we selected the command-line flags that result in the highest CR where possible. For lzop we used –c6, as this is the highest compression level before the runtime becomes intractable. For pigz and pbzip2, we used –c9 –p20. For GFC and MPC, we specified the data-set dimensionality on the command line. GFC and MPC are parallel GPU implementations. pFPC, pbzip2, and pigz are parallel CPU implementations. The remaining compressor, lzop, is a serial CPU implementation.

All of the tested algorithms except lzop and GFC compressed at least one data set best. MPC delivered the highest CR on six double-precision and eight single-precision data sets. This was a rather surprising result given that MPC is "handicapped" by being constrained to only utilize GPU-friendly components that retain almost no internal state.

MPC proved to be superior to lzop and GFC, both of which it outperformed on most of the tested data sets in terms of CR. Moreover, GFC and pFPC did not support single-precision data. pFPC and pbzip2 outperformed MPC on average. However, this was the case only because of two data sets, msg_sppm and num_plasma, on which they yielded much higher CRs than MPC.

Most of the double-precision data sets were less compressible than the single-precision data sets. This was expected as the least significant mantissa bits tend to be the most random in floating-point values and many of those bits are dropped when converting from double to single precision.

3.3 COMPRESSION AND DECOMPRESSION SPEED

Tables 5 and 7 list the double- and single-precision throughputs in gigabytes per second on the 13 data sets for all tested compressors. Tables 6 and 8 list the same information, but for decompression. As stated before, GFC and pFPC do not support single-precision data. For the GPU-based compressors, we show results for both the K40, which has a compute capability of 3.5, and the Titan X, which has a compute capability of 5.2.

lzop is the fastest CPU-based algorithm at compression and decompression, but it is still 28 times slower than MPC. Thus MPC not only compresses better than lzop but also greatly outperforms it in throughput.

pFPC, the overall best implementation in terms of CR (on the double-precision data), is roughly 18 times slower when running on 20 CPU cores than MPC. GFC is the fastest tested implementation (on the double-precision data sets). It is roughly 1.5–2 times faster than MPC, which is expected as GFC is essentially a two-component algorithm whereas MPC has four. However, GFC compresses

Table 3 Compression Ratios on the Double-Precision Data Sets

	msg_bt	msg_lu	msg_sp	msg_sppm	msg_sweep3d	num_brain	num_comet	num_control	num_plasma	obs_error	obs_info	obs_spitzer	obs_temp	harmean
Izop	1.049	1.000	1.000	4.935	1.017	1.000	1.072	1.011	1.031	1.258	1.000	1.030	1.000	1.102
pigz	1.131	1.057	1.111	**7.483**	1.093	1.064	1.160	1.057	1.608	**1.447**	1.157	1.228	1.035	1.240
pbzip2	1.088	1.018	1.055	6.920	1.292	1.043	1.173	1.029	**5.787**	1.335	1.217	**1.745**	1.023	1.320
pFPC	**1.250**	1.144	**1.240**	4.702	**1.643**	1.144	1.146	1.037	4.740	1.313	1.192	1.013	1.005	**1.326**
GFC	1.200	1.148	1.203	3.521	1.219	1.091	1.094	1.013	1.128	1.237	1.148	1.013	1.039	1.185
MPC	1.210	**1.215**	1.211	3.015	1.290	**1.185**	**1.270**	**1.108**	1.167	1.183	**1.217**	1.187	**1.103**	1.251

Bold values denote the best value in each column.

Table 4 Compression Ratios on the Single-Precision Data Sets

	msg_bt	msg_lu	msg_sp	msg_sppm	msg_sweep3d	num_brain	num_comet	num_control	num_plasma	obs_error	obs_info	obs_spitzer	obs_temp	harmean
Izop	1.044	1.000	1.000	6.608	1.017	1.000	1.077	1.013	1.000	1.165	1.000	1.003	1.000	1.096
pigz	1.185	1.095	1.209	**9.635**	1.159	1.128	1.151	1.082	1.386	**1.468**	1.211	1.185	1.079	1.271
pbzip2	1.129	1.041	1.141	8.732	**2.361**	1.113	1.117	1.043	**8.647**	1.338	1.327	**1.391**	1.049	**1.398**
MPC	**1.339**	**1.444**	**1.389**	3.843	1.537	**1.347**	**1.181**	**1.124**	1.348	1.301	**1.440**	1.049	**1.117**	1.354

Bold values denote the best value in each column.

Table 5 Double-Precision Compression Throughput in Gigabytes per Second

	msg_bt	msg_lu	msg_sp	msg_sppm	msg_sweep3d	num_brain	num_comet	num_control	num_plasma	obs_error	obs_info	obs_spitzer	obs_temp	Average
lzop	0.573	0.629	0.624	0.391	0.623	0.626	0.561	0.624	0.435	0.200	0.576	0.215	0.595	0.513
Pigz	0.168	0.184	0.133	0.096	0.181	0.174	0.140	0.187	0.223	0.104	0.160	0.123	0.175	0.157
pbzip2	0.040	0.047	0.038	0.028	0.038	0.043	0.046	0.035	0.009	0.041	0.029	0.052	0.031	0.037
pFPC	0.637	0.570	0.666	0.844	0.555	0.514	0.467	0.506	0.268	0.348	0.149	0.556	0.255	0.487
GFC_35	**42.20**	**30.75**	**45.96**	**44.20**	**19.92**	**22.47**	17.01	**25.27**	5.559	9.848	2.999	**31.39**	6.327	**23.38**
GFC_52	38.63	28.34	40.75	40.73	18.35	20.71	15.67	23.29	5.123	9.075	2.764	27.84	5.830	21.32
MPC_35	13.46	13.70	13.63	13.54	13.39	13.40	13.43	13.60	13.23	13.40	12.79	13.59	13.12	13.40
MPC_52	18.47	18.41	18.61	18.74	18.61	18.48	**18.49**	18.23	**17.79**	**18.16**	**16.86**	18.65	**17.57**	18.23

Bold values denote the best value in each column.

Table 6 Double-Precision Decompression Throughput in Gigabytes per Second

	msg_bt	msg_lu	msg_sp	msg_sppm	msg_sweep3d	num_brain	num_comet	num_control	num_plasma	obs_error	obs_info	obs_spitzer	obs_temp	Average
lzop	0.674	0.810	0.811	0.523	0.771	0.805	0.687	0.804	0.580	0.435	0.689	0.442	0.759	0.676
Pigz	0.084	0.082	0.075	0.228	0.081	0.081	0.087	0.089	0.108	0.097	0.085	0.074	0.087	0.097
pbzip2	0.145	0.125	0.138	0.383	0.121	0.116	0.125	0.122	0.152	0.110	0.063	0.148	0.089	0.141
pFPC	1.108	1.013	1.172	2.112	1.101	0.951	0.848	0.875	0.760	0.773	0.402	0.935	0.562	0.970
GFC_35	53.67	39.11	58.45	56.21	25.33	28.58	21.63	32.14	7.070	12.52	3.814	39.93	8.046	29.73
GFC_52	**58.07**	**42.32**	**63.07**	**60.82**	**27.41**	**30.92**	**23.40**	**34.77**	7.650	13.55	4.127	**43.20**	8.706	**32.16**
MPC_35	19.25	19.06	19.31	19.09	18.87	18.87	18.94	18.73	**18.10**	**18.85**	**17.40**	18.76	**18.21**	18.72
MPC_52	18.93	18.80	18.93	18.84	18.55	18.57	18.60	18.47	17.77	18.49	17.03	18.43	17.93	18.41

Bold values denote the best value in each column.

Table 7 Single-Precision Compression Throughput in Gigabytes per Second

	msg_bt	msg_lu	msg_sp	msg_sppm	msg_sweep3d	num_brain	num_comet	num_control	num_plasma	obs_error	obs_info	obs_spitzer	obs_temp	Average
lzop	0.482	0.619	0.614	0.509	0.581	0.612	0.507	0.601	0.561	0.166	0.520	0.318	0.566	0.512
Pigz	0.160	0.171	0.142	0.477	0.161	0.152	0.134	0.176	0.168	0.053	0.130	0.087	0.146	0.166
pbzip2	0.050	0.034	0.038	0.019	0.013	0.042	0.041	0.036	0.009	0.042	0.025	0.048	0.030	0.033
MPC_35	13.25	13.20	13.17	13.22	13.17	13.17	12.93	13.05	12.43	12.71	11.83	13.17	12.67	12.92
MPC_52	**18.97**	**18.80**	**18.76**	**19.03**	**18.55**	**18.75**	**18.39**	**18.79**	**17.51**	**18.07**	**16.13**	**18.96**	**17.62**	**18.33**

Bold values denote the best value in each column.

Table 8 Single-Precision Decompression Throughput in Gigabytes per Second

	msg_bt	msg_lu	msg_sp	msg_sppm	msg_sweep3d	num_brain	num_comet	num_control	num_plasma	obs_error	obs_info	obs_spitzer	obs_temp	Average
lzop	0.653	0.812	0.801	0.503	0.768	0.787	0.656	0.794	0.701	0.333	0.597	0.555	0.705	0.667
pigz	0.082	0.082	0.073	0.240	0.079	0.079	0.088	0.085	0.085	0.089	0.081	0.070	0.081	0.093
pbzip2	0.128	0.112	0.131	0.408	0.137	0.109	0.110	0.108	0.097	0.089	0.047	0.117	0.060	0.127
MPC_35	**18.85**	**18.41**	**18.59**	**18.98**	**17.25**	**18.73**	**18.22**	**18.56**	**17.48**	**17.75**	**15.94**	**18.77**	**17.61**	**18.09**
MPC_52	18.57	18.17	18.36	18.72	17.13	18.45	17.87	18.35	17.34	17.68	15.83	18.55	17.44	17.88

Bold values denote the best value in each column.

relatively poorly. Importantly, the single- and double-precision compression and decompression throughput of MPC matches or exceeds that of the PCI-Express v3.0 bus linking the GPU to the CPU in our system, making real-time operation possible.

3.4 COMPRESSION AND DECOMPRESSION ENERGY

Tables 9 and 11 show the energy efficiency when compressing each of the 13 double- and single-precision inputs. Tables 10 and 12 show the same information, but for decompression. As stated before, pFPC does not support single-precision data. Also, the K20 Power Tool does not currently support measuring energy on the Titan X. Thus we provide energy measurements only for MPC_35.

We can clearly see that MPC dominates the CPU compressors in terms of energy efficiency. For the CPU compressors, lzop is best for double- and single-precision compression as well as single-precision decompression, while pFPC is best for double-precision decompression.

Data compression on the GPU is between 1.8 to over 80 times more energy efficient than even the most energy efficient of the tested CPU compressors. Furthermore, it appears that decompression is more energy efficient on average than compression for lzop, pbzip2, and pFPC. For pigz and MPC, compression is more efficient than decompression, though on average, MPC decompression is still over 25 times more energy efficient than CPU decompression.

3.5 COMPONENT COUNT

Fig. 3 illustrates by how much the CR is affected when changing the number of chained components on the double-precision data sets. The bars marked "Best" refer to the single algorithm that yields the highest harmonic-mean CR over all 13 data sets. The other bars refer to the best algorithm found for each individual data set. We used exhaustive search for up to four-component algorithms. Because the runtime of exhaustive search is exponential in the number of components, we had to use a different approach for algorithms with more than four stages. In particular, we chose a genetic algorithm to find good (though not generally the best) algorithms in those vast search spaces. The single-precision results are not shown as they are qualitatively similar.

Except on two data sets, a single-component suffices to reach roughly 80–90% of the CR achieved with four components. Moreover, the increase in CR when going from one to two stages is generally larger than going from two to three stages, which in turn is larger than going from three to four stages, and so on. For example, looking at the harmonic mean, going from one to two stages, the CR improves by 8.9%; going from two to three stages, it improves by 8.4%, then by 4.8%, 2.3%, and 0.7%; and going from six to seven stages, the harmonic mean does not improve any more at all (which is in part because of the genetic algorithm not finding better solutions). In other words, the improvements start to flatten out, that is, algorithms with large numbers of stages do not yield much higher CRs and are slower than the

Table 9 Double-Precision Energy Efficiency in Words Compressed per Micro-Joule

	msg_bt	msg_lu	msg_sp	msg_sppm	msg_sweep3d	num_brain	num_comet	num_control	num_plasma	obs_error	obs_info	obs_spitzer	obs_temp	Average
lzop	0.755	0.827	0.820	0.516	0.817	0.822	0.737	0.820	0.569	0.266	0.748	0.285	0.777	0.674
Pigz	0.165	0.180	0.132	0.101	0.178	0.170	0.142	0.183	0.222	0.105	0.162	0.122	0.173	0.157
pbzip2	0.040	0.045	0.039	0.026	0.038	0.042	0.046	0.036	0.008	0.042	0.030	0.051	0.032	0.037
pFPC	0.597	0.532	0.631	0.876	0.562	0.487	0.432	0.456	0.282	0.342	0.152	0.519	0.246	0.470
MPC_35	**44.53**	**30.37**	**46.54**	**56.14**	**53.56**	**52.80**	**117.67**	**52.10**	**4.134**	**3.942**	**6.379**	**43.46**	**4.840**	**39.73**

Bold values denote the best value in each column.

Table 10 Double-Precision Energy Efficiency in Words Decompressed per Micro-Joule

	msg_bt	msg_lu	msg_sp	msg_sppm	msg_sweep3d	num_brain	num_comet	num_control	num_plasma	obs_error	obs_info	obs_spitzer	obs_temp	Average
lzop	0.887	1.061	1.064	0.697	1.014	1.054	0.906	1.053	0.753	0.576	0.903	0.586	0.992	0.888
pigz	0.108	0.105	0.097	0.292	0.104	0.105	0.111	0.113	0.138	0.125	0.109	0.095	0.111	0.124
pbzip2	0.134	0.116	0.128	0.348	0.114	0.109	0.119	0.114	0.146	0.106	0.067	0.136	0.088	0.133
pFPC	1.190	1.086	1.267	2.249	1.200	1.019	0.909	0.932	0.820	0.835	0.445	1.003	0.613	1.044
MPC_35	**43.64**	**31.80**	**47.52**	**45.70**	**20.60**	**23.23**	**17.58**	**26.13**	**5.748**	**10.18**	**3.101**	**32.46**	**6.541**	**24.17**

Bold values denote the best value in each column.

Table 11 Single-Precision Energy Efficiency in Words Compressed per Micro-Joule

	msg_bt	msg_lu	msg_sp	msg_sppm	msg_sweep3d	num_brain	num_comet	num_control	num_plasma	obs_error	obs_info	obs_spitzer	obs_temp	Average
lzop	1.273	1.621	1.605	1.328	1.520	1.605	1.336	1.572	1.450	0.438	1.383	0.841	1.490	1.343
Pigz	0.317	0.339	0.282	0.973	0.319	0.300	0.289	0.346	0.341	0.112	0.270	0.175	0.294	0.335
pbzip2	0.097	0.070	0.076	0.037	0.026	0.085	0.084	0.074	0.017	0.085	0.057	0.094	0.064	0.067
MPC_35	**50.94**	**165.1**	**51.53**	**84.31**	**119.36**	**90.32**	**107.7**	**93.18**	**6.239**	**7.929**	**3.620**	**79.42**	**3.206**	**66.37**

Bold values denote the best value in each column.

Table 12 Single-Precision Energy Efficiency in Words Decompressed per Micro-Joule

	msg_bt	msg_lu	msg_sp	msg_sppm	msg_sweep3d	num_brain	num_comet	num_control	num_plasma	obs_error	obs_info	obs_spitzer	obs_temp	Average
lzop	1.708	1.621	1.605	1.328	1.520	1.605	1.336	1.572	1.450	0.438	1.383	0.841	1.490	1.377
pigz	0.210	0.339	0.282	0.973	0.319	0.300	0.289	0.346	0.341	0.112	0.270	0.175	0.294	0.327
pbzi p2	0.242	0.070	0.076	0.037	0.026	0.085	0.084	0.074	0.017	0.085	0.057	0.094	0.064	0.078
MPC_3S	**49.43**	**109.7**	**45.83**	**82.37**	**10.37**	**10.46**	**19.92**	**135.6**	**7.269**	**8.488**	**2.082**	**65.69**	**2.772**	**42.31**

Bold values denote the best value in each column.

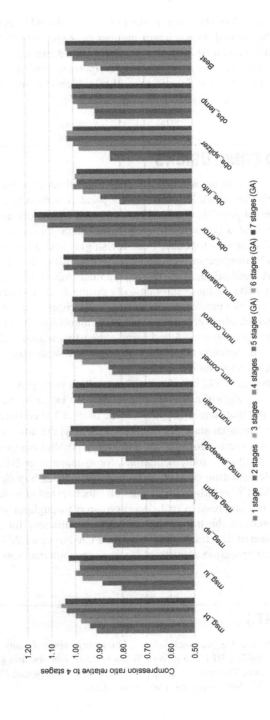

FIG. 3

Best exhaustive-search-based double-precision CRs with 1, 2, 3, and 4 stages and best genetic-algorithm-based CRs with 5, 6, and 7 stages relative to the best CRs with four stages; the y-axis starts at 0.5 and the cut-off bar for msg_sppm reaches 0.4.

chosen four-stage algorithms. Note that, due to the presence of the NUL component, the algorithms that can be created with a larger number of stages represent a strict superset of the algorithms that can be created with fewer stages. As a consequence, the exhaustive-search results in Fig. 3 monotonically increase with more stages. However, this is not the case for the genetic algorithm, which does not guarantee finding the best solution in the search space.

4 SUMMARY AND CONCLUSIONS

The goal of this work is to determine whether effective algorithms exist for floating-point data compression that are suitable for massively parallel architectures. To this end, we evaluated millions of possible combinations of 24 GPU-friendly algorithmic components to find the best algorithm for each tested data set as well as the best algorithm for all 13 data sets together, both for single- and double-precision representations. This study resulted in well-performing algorithms that have never before been described. A detailed analysis thereof yielded important insights that helped us understand why and how these automatically synthesized algorithms work. This, in turn, enabled us to make predictions as to which algorithms will likely work well on other data sets, which ultimately led to our MPC algorithm. It constitutes a generalization of the best algorithms we found using exhaustive search and requires only two generally known parameters about the input data: the word size (single- or double-precision) and the dimensionality.

It rivals the CRs of the best CPU-based algorithms, which is surprising because MPC is limited to using only algorithmic components that can be easily parallelized and that do not use much internal state. In contrast, some of the CPU compressors we tested utilize megabytes of internal state per thread. We believe the almost stateless operation of MPC make it a great algorithm for any highly parallel compute device as well as for FPGAs and hardware implementations, for instance in an NIC.

Our open-source implementation of MPC, which is available at http://cs.txstate. edu/~burtscher/research/MPC/, greatly outperforms all other tested algorithms that compress similarly well in compression and decompression throughput as well as in energy efficiency. Moreover, the throughput of MPC is sufficient for real-time compression/decompression of data transmitted over the PCIe bus or a LAN. Clearly, highly parallel, effective compression algorithms for floating-point data sets do exist.

ACKNOWLEDGMENTS

This work was supported by the US National Science Foundation under Grants 1141022, 1217231, 1406304, and 1438963, a REP grant from Texas State University, and grants and gifts from NVIDIA Corporation. The authors acknowledge the Texas Advanced Computing Center for providing some of the HPC resources used in this study.

REFERENCES

[1]   A. Yang, H. Mukka, F. Hesaaraki, M. Burtscher, MPC: a massively parallel compression algorithm for scientific data, in: IEEE Cluster Conference, September, 2015.

[2]   A. Balevic, Parallel variable-length encoding on GPGPUs, in: International Conference on Parallel Processing, Springer-Verlag, 2009, pp. 26–35.

[3]   A. Balevic, L. Rockstroh, M. Wroblewski, S. Simon, Using arithmetic coding for reduction of resulting simulation data size on massively parallel GPGPUs, in: 15th European PVM/MPI Users' Group Meeting, Springer Verlag, 2008, pp. 295–302.

[4]   T. Bicer, J. Yiny, D. Chiuz, G. Agrawal, K. Schuchardt, Integrating online compression to accelerate large-scale data analytics applications, in: International Parallel and Distributed Processing Symposium, 2013.

[5]   M. Burtscher, P. Ratanaworabhan, FPC: a high-speed compressor for double-precision floating-point data, IEEE Trans. Comput. 58 (1) (2009) 18–31.

[6]   M. Burtscher, P. Ratanaworabhan, pFPC: a parallel compressor for floating-point data, in: Data Compression Conference, 2009, pp. 43–52.

[7]   D. Chen, Y.J. Chiang, N. Memon, X. Wu, Lossless geometry compression for steady-state and time-varying irregular grids, in: IEEE Symposium on Visualization, 2006, pp. 275–282.

[8]   R. Filgueira, D.E. Singh, A. Calderón, J. Carretero, CoMPI: enhancing MPI-based applications performance and scalability using run-time compression, in: EUROPVM/MPI, 2009.

[9]   R. Filgueira, D.E. Singh, J. Carretero, A. Calderón, F. Garcia, Adaptive-CoMPI: enhancing MPI-based applications's performance and scalability by using adaptive compression, Int. J. High Perform. Comput. Appl. 25 (1) (2011) 93–114.

[10] P. Lindstrom, M. Isenburg, Fast and efficient compression of floating-point data, IEEE Trans. Vis. Comput. Graph. 12 (5) (2006) 1245–1250.

[11] M.A. O'Neil, M. Burtscher, Floating-point data compression at 75 Gb/s on a GPU, in: Workshop on General Purpose Processing Using GPUs, 2011.

[12] A. Ozsoy, M. Swany, CULZSS: LZSS lossless data compression on CUDA, in: IEEE International Conference on Cluster Computing, 2011, pp. 403–411.

[13] R. Patel, Y. Zhang, J. Mak, A. Davidson, J. Owens, Parallel lossless data compression on the GPU, Innov. Parallel Comput. (2012) 1–9.

[14] E.R. Schendel, Y. Jin, N. Shah, J. Chen, C.S. Chang, S.H. Ku, S. Ethier, S. Klasky, R. Latham, R.B. Ross, N.F. Samatova, ISOBAR preconditioner for effective and high-throughput lossless data compression, in: 28th Annual IEEE International Conference on Data Engineering (ICDE), 2012, pp. 138–149.

[15] http://icl.cs.utk.edu/papi/.

[16] M. Burtscher, I. Zecena, Z. Zong, Measuring GPU power with the K20 built-in sensor, in: Seventh Workshop on General Purpose Processing on Graphics Processing Units, March, 2014.

[17] http://www.bzip.org/.

[18] http://www.gzip.org/.

[19] http://www.lzop.org/.

[20] http://users.ices.utexas.edu/~burtscher/research/pFPC/.

[21] http://cs.txstate.edu/~burtscher/research/GFC/.

Adaptive sparse matrix representation for efficient matrix-vector multiplication

14

P. Zardoshti[1,2], F. Khunjush[1,2], H. Sarbazi-Azad[2,3]

Shiraz University, Shiraz, Iran[1] Institute for Research in Fundamental Sciences (IPM), Tehran, Iran[2] Sharif University of Technology, Tehran, Iran[3]

1 INTRODUCTION

The prevalence of parallel architectures has introduced several challenges from a design-level perspective to an application level [1]. Dealing with these challenges requires new paradigms from circuit design techniques to writing applications for these architectures. Introducing the common application categories [1], which have profound impact on various scientific fields, can be considered as a guide toward the goal of dealing with fundamental problems in parallel environments. Among these applications, sparse matrix-vector multiplication (SpMV) is a fundamental building block for numerous computational hungry applications such as image processing, data mining, structural mechanics, and web page ranking algorithms employed by search engines [2].

Over the past decade, graphics processing units (GPUs) have gained an important place in the field of high-performance computing (HPC) because of their low cost and massive parallel processing powers. A GPU provides tremendous computational power and very high memory bandwidth. It is also very well suited for dense matrix computations; however, several challenges are faced in achieving high performance for sparse matrix computations, which is a well-established class of problems in the parallel computing community [1]. Sparsity patterns vary greatly from one matrix to another, because they can represent random graphs, electronic circuits, social interactions, discretization of partial differential equations (PDEs) on structured or unstructured grids, and a range of other problems. Therefore processing all types of matrices with a fixed format might lead to performance degradation in most cases. On the other hand, architectural parameters greatly impact application performance. For example, improper selection of these parameters adversely affects the performance.

In this chapter, we study the parameterization of the SpMV in order to determine the best data representation to execute on GPUs, depending on properties of different matrices and architectural parameters. Furthermore, we illustrate how auto-tuning can be used to produce efficient implementations across a diverse set of current GPU architectures. In Section 2, we give an overview of the SpMV and different formats, followed by a description of the GPU architecture that used in this study in Section 3. This is followed, in Section 4, by optimization principles for SpMV that have a key effect on the performance of sparse matrix computation. We present our design of an auto-tuner system in Section 5. Finally, we present performance results followed by conclusions in Sections 6 and 7.

2 SPARSE MATRIX-VECTOR MULTIPLICATION

SpMV is one of the key operations in many scientific computations and is used heavily kernels in various domains of scientific, medical, and engineering studies, including iterative solvers for linear systems of equations, image processing, solving PDEs, and PageRank computation for ranking web pages [2]. SpMV performs the operation $y \leftarrow y + Ax$, where A is a sparse matrix, and x and y are dense vectors. Sparse kernels suffer from memory storage overhead, as well as irregular structure of sparse matrices. Many studies have been on how to optimize and improve the performance of sparse computations on different platforms [3–34]. Because the performance of sparse matrix computations depends on its representation format [3], many researchers proposed various formats to store and represent these matrices [4–16,32]. For example, Fig. 1 illustrates the performance of SpMV with *nd24k* input matrix using different formats. As can be seen, the difference among speedups can be up to $45\times$. Achieving good performance requires selecting proper storage formats by exploiting properties of both the sparse matrix (during runtime) and the underlying machine architecture. However, because there are many different applications with diverse requirements, a unique representation is not suitable for all sparse matrices, as revealed by experimental results [3,4]. Table 1 shows various matrices used in different applications along with the format that works best for each matrix. This section describes seven state-of-the-art sparse matrix formats. Fig. 2 shows the basic representation formats of sparse matrix.

Diagonal format (DIA) uses two arrays to store nonzero elements: DiaVal array stores nonzero values, and DiaOffset records the diameter offsets with respect to the main diameter. The diagonal format is a proper scheme for matrices deriving from the application of stencils to regular grids, a common discretization method because of the nonzero elements in these matrices are distributed in a diametrical way [3]. However, most sparse matrices do not have a diametrical structure, which hinders wide use of this format.

Compressed Sparse Row (CSR) format is probably the most widely used format for storing general sparse matrices [3,4]. In this format, the input matrix is represented by the following components: CsrVal, which contains nonzero values; ColIdx, which holds the column index of nonzero elements; CsrPtr, which shows the first nonzero element in each row. It includes $N+1$ elements, N being the number

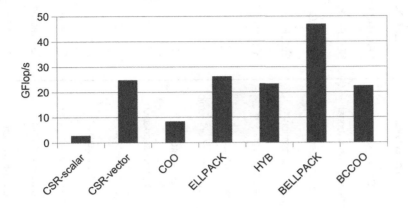

FIG. 1

Performance achieved by different formats for nd24k matrix on Kepler K20X.

of rows in the matrix. The number of nonzero elements in row i can be computed from the variance of i and $i + 1$ arrays in `CsrPtr`.

CSR (scalar) format assigns one thread to process each row. By doing so, the memory access pattern is not coalescent, which leads to performance degradation. The modified version of the CSR format, CSR (vector), is also proposed in Ref. [4]. In this format one warp is allocated to process each row to achieve the memory access contiguously.

ELLPACK format first shifts the nonzero elements of the matrix to the left then pads each row with zeros, if needed. In order to store a sparse matrix, ELLPACK uses two arrays: `EllVal`, which stores nonzero elements, and `ColIdx`, which holds the index of nonzero columns. The ELL format is recommended for vector structures. ELLPACK works well for matrices in which the maximum number of nonzero elements in all rows is not substantially different from the average. However, when the number of nonzeros varies largely between rows, the performance is degraded because of the redundant memory usage and the redundant computation. The ELLPACK format is suitable for matrices with a regular structure.

Coordinate format (COO) is the simplest way to store a sparse matrix. COO keeps a matrix using three arrays: `CooVal`, `RowIdx`, and `ColIdx`, which contain the nonzero data values, the row index of the elements corresponding to CooVal, and the column index of the elements corresponding to `CooVal`, respectively. All kinds of sparse matrices can be stored in the COO format. In order to implement this format on GPUs, atomic operation is used to collect intrathread results.

Hybrid format (HYB) uses the syntax of COO and ELL representations [4]. In this type, the input matrix is partitioned into two parts based on a parameter, K. The first part of the matrix is stored in the ELLPACK format, and the second part is represented in the COO format. If a row has less than k nonzero elements in the first part, it is padded with zeros. This format is suitable for unstructured sparse matrices.

Table 1 Matrices

Name	Spyplot	DimRow	%NNZ	Avg.	Max.	Description	Best Format
Dense		2000	100	2000	2000	Dense	BCCOO
pdb1HYS		36,417	33	119.3	204	Protein data bank 1HY2S	BELLPACK
consph		83,334	9	72.1	81	Concentric spheres	BELLPACK
cantilever		62,451	10	64.1	78	Cantilever	BELLPACK
pwtk		217,918	2	53.4	180	Pressurized wind tunnel	BELLPACK
rma10		46,835	11	50.6	145	3D CFD of Charleston Harbor	BELLPACK
QCD		49,152	8	39.0	39	Quark propagation	BELLPACK
shipsec1		140,874	2	55.4	102	Ship section	BELLPACK
mac-econ-fwd500		206,500	0.3	6.1	44	Macroeconomics model	HYB
mc2depi		525,825	0.07	3.9	4	2D Markov model of epidemic	ELLPACK
cop20k_A		121,192	2	21.6	81	Accelerator	BCCOO
scircuit		170,998	0.3	5.6	353	Motorola circuit simulation	BCCOO
webbase-1M		1,000,005	0.03	3.1	4700	Web connectivity	HYB
atmosmodd		1,270,432	0.05	6.9	7	CFD problem	DIA
cage14		1,505,785	0.12	18	41	directed weighted graph	ELLPACK
crankseg_2		63,838	35	221	3423	structural problem	CSR(vector)
ldoor		952,203	0.4	48.9	77	structural problem	ELLPACK
nd24k		72,000	55	308	520	ND problem set	BELLPACK
F1		343,791	2	39.5	435	FEM-AUDI engine	CSR (vector)
shallow-water1		81,920	0.4	4	4	CFD problem	ELLPACK

$$A = \begin{bmatrix} 4 & 9 & 0 & 0 \\ 0 & 2 & 7 & 0 \\ 3 & 0 & 8 & 5 \\ 0 & 1 & 0 & 6 \end{bmatrix}$$

(A)

$$EllVal = \begin{bmatrix} 4 & 9 & * \\ 2 & 7 & * \\ 3 & 8 & 5 \\ 1 & 6 & * \end{bmatrix} \quad Colldx = \begin{bmatrix} 0 & 1 & * \\ 1 & 2 & * \\ 0 & 2 & 3 \\ 1 & 3 & * \end{bmatrix}$$

(B)

$$DiaVal = \begin{bmatrix} * & 4 & 9 \\ * & 2 & 7 \\ 3 & 8 & 5 \\ 1 & 6 & * \end{bmatrix} \quad DiaOffset = [-2 \quad 0 \quad 1]$$

(C)

$CsrVal = [4 \quad 9 \quad 2 \quad 7 \quad 3 \quad 8 \quad 5 \quad 1 \quad 6]$
$Colldx = [0 \quad 1 \quad 1 \quad 2 \quad 0 \quad 2 \quad 3 \quad 1 \quad 3]$
$CsrPtr = [0 \quad 2 \quad 4 \quad 7 \quad 9]$

(D)

$CooVal = [4 \quad 9 \quad 2 \quad 7 \quad 3 \quad 8 \quad 5 \quad 1 \quad 6]$
$Rowldx = [0 \quad 0 \quad 1 \quad 1 \quad 2 \quad 2 \quad 2 \quad 3 \quad 3]$
$Colldx = [0 \quad 1 \quad 1 \quad 2 \quad 0 \quad 2 \quad 3 \quad 1 \quad 3]$

(E)

FIG. 2

Sparse matrix representations. (A) Example matrix. (B) ELLPACK (ELL) format. (C) Diagonal (DIA) format. (D) Compressed Sparse Row (CSR) format. (E) Coordinate (COO) format.

BELLPACK format [9] compresses the sparse matrix by small dense entry blocks and then reorders the row of blocks according to the number of blocks per row. Finally, in order to reduce the required padding relative to conventional ELLPACK storage, the rows of matrices are partitioned into submatrices, each stored using the ELLPACK scheme. BELLPACK assigns one thread block per block row of the matrix and within a row block; warps are assigned to consecutive register-block rows.

BCCOO format [13] partitions a matrix into a number of subblocks to reduce the size of arrays. The implementation of BCCOO uses three arrays: `value` contains the nonzero entries and the other two arrays, `col_index` and `BitFlag`, contain the corresponding row and column indices for each nonzero element. In order to avoid load imbalance problems, each thread processes the same number of nonzero blocks in a BCCOO scheme.

3 GPU ARCHITECTURE AND PROGRAMMING MODEL

GPUs have evolved over the past few years, and increasing demands for HPC across many fields of science make GPUs available for general-purpose computing. GPUs have several thousand threads that operate in groups across large amounts of data in parallel to hide long latency operations.

3.1 HARDWARE ARCHITECTURES

The GPU architecture consists of several hundred simple cores called streaming processors (SPs), which are grouped in a set of streaming multiprocessors (SMs). Each SM executes instructions in a single-instruction multiple-threads (SIMT) mode and supports a multithreading execution mechanism. GPUs are capable of utilizing large amounts of memory bandwidth. To further increase usable bandwidth, modern GPUs also contain a series of on-chip caches. In modern GPU architecture, each thread has its own private register. For memory, a thread has its own memory space, which is called the local memory. A block also has its own 64 KB on-chip memory that can be configured as shared memory and L1 cache. All threads in a block can access the same shared memory and L1 cache, while threads in other blocks cannot. The L2 cache is the primary point of data unification between the SM units, servicing all load, store, and texture requests and providing efficient, high-speed data sharing across the GPU. The entire kernel also has a global memory. All threads in a block can access the global memory space. Also, all threads can access read-only constant memory and texture memory spaces [35].

NVIDIA GeForce GTX 480

The NVIDIA GPU is based on the GF100 processor architecture with 480 cores. It works with a clock frequency of 1.4 GHz, and has 1.5 GB DRAM with a 177 GB/s bandwidth. This GPU consists of 15 SMs. Each SM has a memory space that can be configured as 48K of shared memory with 16K of L1 cache, or as 16K of shared memory with 48K of L1 cache [35].

NVIDIA Tesla K20X

There are 2688 cores with a clock frequency of 0.73 GHz in the Kepler GK110 architecture. It has 6 GB DRAM with 250 GB/s bandwidth. Kepler allows additional flexibility in configuring the memory space of SMs by permitting a 32K/32K split between allocation of shared memory and L1 cache [36]. Table 2 summarizes the specifications of these architectures.

Table 2 Architectural Summary of Evaluated Platforms

Architecture	GTX 480 GeForce	Tesla K20X
Model	GF100	GK100
Core	480	2688
Clock (GHz)	1.4	0.73
DP Peak (GFlop/s)	168	1310
SP Peak (GFlop/s)	1345	3950
Memory bandwidth (GB/s)	177.4	250

3.2 PROGRAMMING MODEL

Compute Unified Device Architecture (CUDA) introduced by NVIDIA provides a simple model for programming GPUs. CUDA source code has a mixture of both *host code* that runs on the CPUs and *device code* that runs on the GPUs. The GPU-related part of an application, called kernel, is processed by thousands of threads that are grouped into blocks, and these blocks form a grid. Threads within a block may synchronize freely at barriers, but separate blocks may not directly synchronize with each other. The SM executes threads in groups of 32 parallel threads called warps. Each warp is scheduled by a warp scheduler for execution, and full efficiency is achieved when all the threads within a warp agree on their execution path without any branch divergences.

3.3 MATRICES

The performance of the SpMV depends strongly on the features of the matrices. Most important properties of a sparse matrix include the number of rows and columns (*DimRow*), the number of nonzero elements (*NNZ*), the average number of nonzero elements in each row (*AvgNNZ*), and the maximum number of nonzeros in the row (*MaxNNZ*). We consider a variety of matrices with different behaviors and characterizations that exist in real applications. Table 3 summarizes the matrix benchmark set that we chose from the UF sparse matrix collection [37].

4 OPTIMIZATION PRINCIPLES FOR SpMV

This section describes the principle of performance optimizations based on the architectures and SpMV outlined in pervious sections. In most cases, improperly choosing architectural parameters can significantly affect the performance. However, it is not clear which architectural parameters have the greatest impact on performance. We studied the potential impact of various parameter selections that are appropriate for different representations in order to reach high performance. To understand

Table 3 The Best Register Configuration Achieved for Each Format

Formats	Register (Single-Double)
DIA	14–16
ELLPACK	15–16
COO	14–16
CSR (scalar)	16–20
CSR (vector)	24–34

the behavior of sparse matrix applications in various situations, we studied their performance under different representations and parameters. We identified that the performances of SpMV applications benefit from the effective selection of parameters such as block size, number of registers, and memory hierarchy.

4.1 BLOCK SIZE

The first parameter that has considerable effect on the performance is block size. Defining the precise number of threads inside a block plays a key role in reaching higher performance. Choosing the value of a block size from high to low can affect the occupancy favorably or adversely, respectively. According to the CUDA architecture, there are hard upper limits on the size of a thread block and active thread blocks on a single multiprocessor in GPUs (i.e., SMs). For example, each SM in Kepler architecture can have 2048 simultaneously active threads, or 64 warps. These may come from 2 thread blocks of 32 warps with 100% occupancy or 2 thread blocks of 24 warps with 75% occupancy. In addition to the previously mentioned limitations, the number of active blocks in an SM depends on other resource limitations, such as register file and shared memory. To illustrate the importance of choosing parameter values for sparse matrix representations, the results of experiments with different parameter selections are shown in Fig. 3. This figure shows the speedup due to block size on the DIA format when using various block sizes with the *atmosmodd* matrix.

Regarding the performance of the DIA format in Fig. 3, we can see that the number of threads inside a block is crucial to the performance of SpMV on a GPU 512 resident threads per block deliver an average of 2× speedup over the 64-thread scenario. It is because the number of resident threads per SM (64×16, 1024 threads, 50% occupancy, in contrast to 514×4, 2048 threads, 100% occupancy in Tesla K20X and 648, 512 threads, 33% occupancy, in contrast to 51×23, 15×36 threads, 100% occupancy in GTX480) heavily influence the performance of DIA format.

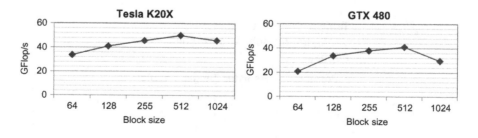

FIG. 3

The performance achieved by DIA format with different blocks sizes for *atmosmodd*.

4.2 REGISTER

The number of allocated registers for each thread is another factor that affects the performance. Occupancy rate depends on the amount of register memory each thread requires. Increasing the register usage may consequently decrease the SM's occupancy and utilization. Register memory access is very fast, but the number of available registers per block are limited. For example, the maximum and minimum hardware limits for compute capability 3.x are 255 and 16 registers per thread, respectively. The limit of registers per thread are specified by the *-maxrregcount* flag at compile time to increase the number of concurrently running threads and to improve thread-level parallelism in running kernels on GPUs. Some kernels use less than 16 registers in the single-precision mode, such as DIA. Reducing the register usage can lead to higher performance. However, it may cause spilling registers into L2 cache. Spilling occurs if the register count is exceeded, which in turn leads to an increase in reading/writing from/to L2 cache, which is expensive. Experiments are used to determine the optimum balance of spilling versus occupancy. As shown in Fig. 4, varying the number of registers assigned to each thread has changed the performance of the COO format for the *pdb1HYS* input matrix. The optimized kernels use enough extra registers to maintain the utilization of SMs, which combined with more efficient memory accesses, results in a speedup of 1.33× compared to the initial kernel configuration. Table 3 shows the best register configuration achieved for each format.

4.3 MEMORY

Most highly multithreaded applications such as SpMV are memory-bounded, and their performance depends strongly on efficient use of the memory subsystem. Therefore information about the interaction of SpMV applications with the memory system is crucial for tuning the performance. The capability to configure the shared memory and L1 cache provides opportunities to select appropriate configurations for a given representation or an input matrix. The patterns of the global memory accesses

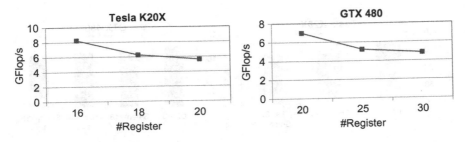

FIG. 4

The performance achieved by COO format with different register file sizes for *pdb1HYS* matrix.

govern the amount of local memory needed to allocate as L1 cache. For example, in applications with regular memory access patterns, increasing the size of the shared memory can improve the performance; however, in cases with more frequent or unpredictable accesses to larger regions of DRAM, L1 cache size has a strong impact on the performance [38]. In addition to L1 cache and shared memory, the read-only texture memory can also be utilized. It provides more effective bandwidth by reducing memory traffic and increases the performance compared to accessing the global memory. For example, The vector x can be kept in the texture memory, which improves performance through improving the utilization of memory bandwidth in GPUs [4,35,36]. The impact of different configurations of memory on bandwidth are illustrated in Fig. 5. For this case, the ELLPACK kernel is launched for *nd24k* matrix. The memory configuration of GTX 480 also contains additional options in which the L1 cache has been disabled in order to analyze how the performance is changed. As shown in this figure, the achieved bandwidth for *nd24k* matrix increases when the L1 cache size grows. We further improve kernels by storing the vector x in the texture memory to enhance the cache hit rates when accessing the vector. In addition, the elements of this vector are reused during the execution, and the locality of accesses to a location is high, which results in performance improvement.

5 PLATFORM (ADAPTIVE RUNTIME SYSTEM)

In this section, we discuss the details of an adaptive runtime system, which is proposed to automatically choose the optimum storage scheme for an input sparse matrix. We consider both GPU architectural parameters and characteristics of sparse matrices to optimize the SpMV performance and to select the best format. To that end, after determining which parameters to vary and evaluating the amount of those values, all kernels were configured with these final values. Our auto-tuner consists of two phases, namely a training phase and a processing phase. In the training phase, the auto-tuner chooses a subsample from an input sparse matrix and converts it to all basic representations. In the processing phase, we assess the performance of each

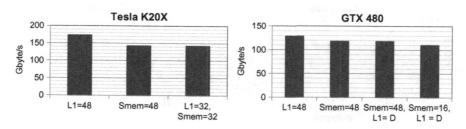

FIG. 5

Bandwidth achieved by ELLPACK format with different configuration memory for the *nd24k* matrix.

format to identify the best one. A flowchart of this process is shown in Ref. [39]. It should be mentioned that we used basic formats that are frequently used for storing sparse matrices and some other formats that are derived from them, such as HYB [4]. Furthermore, there is a possibility to consider new formats in our auto-tuner. For example, we added HYB, BELLPACK [9], and BCCOO formats [13] to our auto-tuner.

The training phase involves the generation of samples from matrices. It should be noted that completely running SpMV applications using each representation format is a tremendously time-consuming process. For this reason, our auto-tuner uses a small portion of the input matrix to test the performance of all schemes. To ensure that the chosen submatrix is the appropriate metric to find the best format, we divide an input matrix into five submatrices, and all kernels execute 10% of each submatrix to choose the suitable storage scheme for an input submatrix. In most matrices, the best format for all submatrices has the same storage format. It must be noted that there is a discrepancy between some submatrices of the matrix that chose the ELLPACK or HYB format as the best format. The submatrices with a small standard deviation value selected the ELLPACK format, and the submatrices with a disparity between *MaxNNZ* and *AvgNNZ* in their structure, chose the HYB storage scheme. This mismatch can be ignored because there is no notable difference between these submatrices from a performance point of view. Therefore, in this system, we use the first portion of matrices in an initial stage. The auto-tuner configures the kernels of formats by using the information that is extracted from the parameter extraction stage. This approach allows us to evaluate sparse matrices while preserving the execution time across changing formats.

The processing phase executes the input application for five iterations with different representation formats. The first five iterations help to ensure stability in an application's behavior and are adequate for predicting the appropriate representation format. The auto-tuner framework inspects the behavior of applications by collecting a number of performance metrics such as computing power and bandwidth. It is worth mentioning that the results of this phase depend on the input matrix characteristics, such as distribution of nonzero elements. According to the results of the previous stage, the auto-tuner picks the storage format that yields the best performance to run the rest of the application. One of the outstanding features of our runtime system is its scalability through which users can add new storage formats to the proposed system. Furthermore, the auto-tuner is portable and can be extended to different GPU architectures (e.g., Maxwell).

6 RESULTS AND ANALYSIS

In this section, we present and analyze the performance and bandwidth of SpMV for each of the two architectures. Because the elements of matrices are floating-point numbers and all benchmarks are run on the same ISA, GFlop/s is a proper metric to measure and compare the performance. It is worth mentioning that these metrics were widely used in previous studies. In addition, in all kernels, we assume that matrices and vectors reside in the GPU's device memory, eliminating the need for any PCIe transfers. This is a reasonable assumption for any local iterative sparse solver.

6.1 PARAMETERS SETTING EXPERIMENTS

Block size

We searched the block size space through different configurations for the optimal value of the number of threads inside a block. The same experiment was conducted when using all formats. The total size of a block was limited to 2048 and 1536 threads in GK110 and Fermi architectures, respectively. Fig. 6 shows the performance of the basic format for different input matrices. As shown in this figure, the optimal value for the COO format is 128 threads per block. The best block size for CSR (scalar) format is 64 threads. In this format, a thread processes each row, and each row has a different number of nonzero elements, which causes some threads to make extra calculations, while others will stay idle. Therefore a simple thread-per-row decomposition strategy when matrices have different *NNZ* per rows is a challenge for parallelism in GPUs. The BCCOO format has shown the best performance when using 256 threads per block. Moreover, CUDA provides a barrier synchronization mechanism for the threads in the same block. Therefore, by increasing the size of a block, more active threads can cooperate [35]. On the other hand, there is no native way to synchronize all threads from all blocks, and the synchronization overhead leads to a reduction in performance. That is why, 512 threads per block yield the best performance for ELLPACK, BELLPACK, CSR (vector), and DIA formats. These formats benefit from more active threads with a minimum number of blocks. Using smaller blocks reduces their performance because of the significant interblock synchronization overhead. The best configurations achieved in this stage will be used when running the applications in our adaptive environment.

Register

The primary limitation is the maximum number of threads on SMs, primarily imposed by the number of 32-bit registers that can be allocated across all the threads inside an SM. The register limit constrains the number of active blocks and the amount of parallelism among threads because only 65,536 (32,768 for compute capability 2.x) registers are available for each SM, and the maximum number of registers that can be accessed by a thread are 255 in the GK110 architecture and 64 in the Fermi architecture. Considering the restrictions on the number of registers, the measure of occupancy of CSR (vector) on GTX480 is shown in Table 4. During compilation, the NVCC compiler allocates 27 and 33 registers to each thread of the CSR (vector) kernel for single- and double-precision computations, respectively. It should be noted that double-precision operations require more registers. However, all allocated registers are rarely used, and a poor choice will lead to a poor performance. Therefore reducing the number of registers can dramatically improve the performance for some matrices by increasing the number of standby registers, and consequently more active threads will be accessible inside a block. To illustrate the effect of the register file, Fig. 7 shows the performance of SpMV using basic formats.

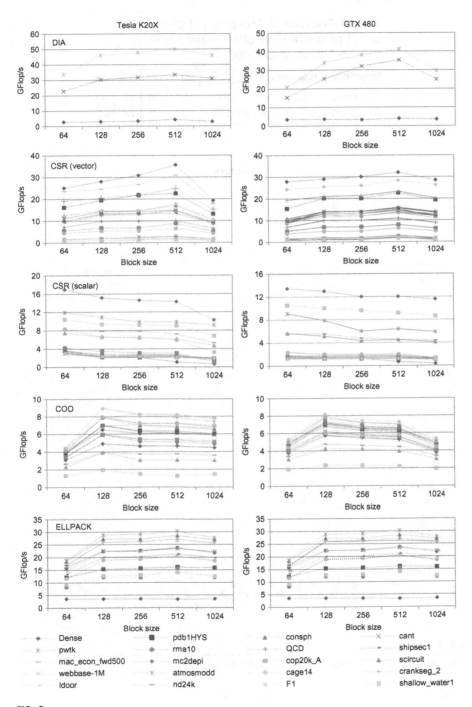

FIG. 6

The impact of different block sizes on SpMV performance.

Table 4 The Rate of Occupancy of CSR (Vector) Based on the Number of Allocated Registers to Each Thread on GTX480

Number of Registers	20	25	30	35
Occupancy for single-precision (%)	100	66	66	66
Occupancy for double-precision (%)	100	66	66	33

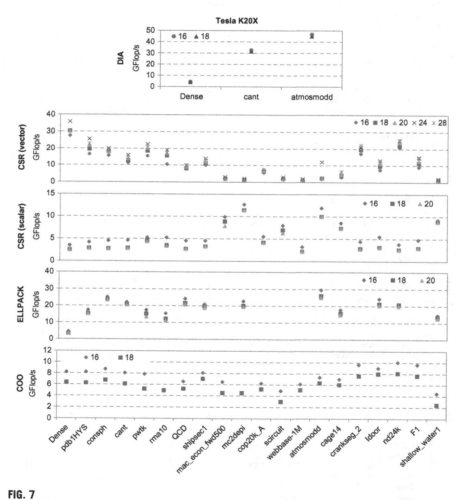

FIG. 7

The effect of register on performance on basic formats.

Reducing the number of registers delivers better performance except for *ndk24* and *crankseg_2* input matrices. Threads need more registers to compute rows of these matrices because of their structure and distribution of nonzero elements. Moreover, other matrices do not require many registers, and register spilling does not degraded the performance significantly.

Memory

Memory optimization is a key factor in improving the performance of memory-bound irregular applications such as SpMV. In this section, we evaluated all possible configurations of L1 cache size and set associativity to investigate the cache size effects on SpMV performance. Figs. 8 and 9 present the results, and as can be seen, the memory access patterns of sparse matrices govern the performance of these types of applications. To compare the performance based on the cache size, we conclude that a small L1 cache size generates huge cache capacity misses. Touching a small fraction of a large block of data implies that a large fraction is not accessed. Therefore buffering a large amount of data into the shared memory of GPUs suffers from high miss rates and increases the data transfer time by performing many address calculations and memory operations. On the other hand, using a data cache that brings only a cache line (i.e., 128B) is more beneficial because the L1 cache latency is much lower than shared memory latency. Results show that increasing cache size leads to the overall performance improvement in sparse matrix operations. Furthermore, we exploit the read-only texture memory for the multiplied vector x to improve the cache hit rate for accessing its elements. For example, cache hit rates for *cantilever* and *atmosmodd* matrices are equal to 99% (calculated by Nvidia Visual profiler [40]). We observe a better performance, and the access pattern of matrices is a good match for the texture cache. In addition, because of the regular accesses to the *Dense* matrix, there is no performance improvement.

6.2 ADAPTIVE RUNTIME SYSTEM

We present and analyze the results of our auto-tuner on each of the two architectures. The last group of bars represents the achieved average performance. Having selected the best parameters for each representation in the previous sections, we measured the performance of our system when using these parameters to run the entire application. The last bar of each matrix shows the performance of the adaptive system. Our framework takes advantage of optimized SpMV implementations and obtains the maximum speed up of $2.1\times$ (single-precision) and $1.6\times$ (double-precision), as well as determining the optimal formats as shown in Figs. 10 and 11. We discuss only the results of GTX480 in this section; refer to the original reference studies for additional details [39].

In order to evaluate the accuracy of our system, we conducted several experiments with different matrices. Figs. 10 and 11 show the performance of SpMV computation

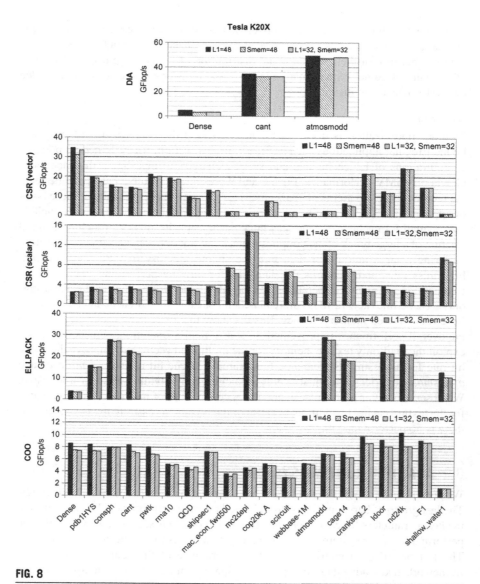

FIG. 8

The impact of different memory configurations on basic format.

for various sparse matrices on GTX 480. The *atmosmodd* matrix has a strictly diagonal structure and a symmetric nonzero pattern. The data reuse is improved by a contiguous access pattern of rows to vector *x*. As a result of these properties, the DIA format is well suited for this matrix. CSR (vector) delivers better performance for *F1*

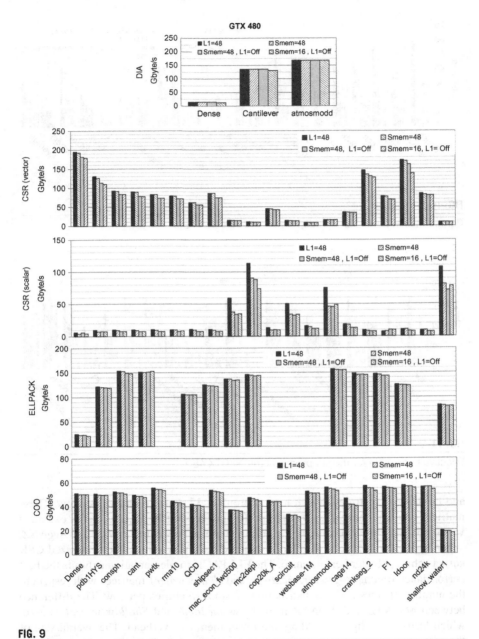

FIG. 9

Bandwidth results for matrices with different memory configuration on basic formats.

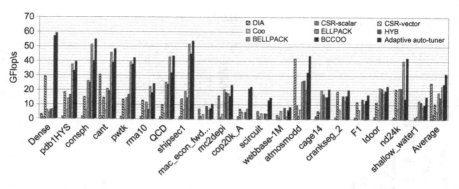

FIG. 10

Computational power for the adaptive scheme on GTX 480.

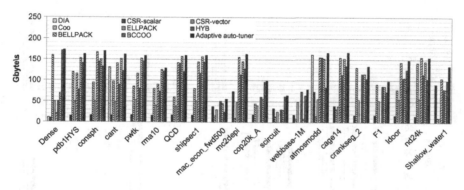

FIG. 11

Effective bandwidth for the adaptive scheme on GTX 480.

and *crankseg-2* matrices, which have more than 32 nonzero entries per row. These matrices could not have a satisfactory performance using the ELL format or extended version of this format because of the great difference between *MaxNNZ* and *AvgNNZ*. When applied to matrices with large standard deviation values, the vectorized CSR kernel achieves better performance. The ELLPACK implementation exhibits the best performance for *cage14*, *ldoor*, *mc2depi*, and *shallw water1* matrices with respect to the number of rows and the distribution of nonzero entries per row. The difference between *MaxNNZ* and *AvgNNZ* in matrices *mc2depi* and *Shallow water1* is zero, which leads to negligible padding and lower memory overhead. The overall size of the portion of memory required is reduced because of the lower amount of padding. In addition, it helps loading more useful data in the cache and improves data reuse in the cache. Although the BELLPACK format is also proper for *cage14* and *ldoor*, it takes too much time to convert them to this format; for example, *cage14* takes 7474.02 s to convert to BELLPACK format.

Matrices such as *mac_econ_fwd500* and *webbase-1M* with less than five nonzero entries per row could not benefit from CSR (vector) because several threads will be idle when a row is much shorter than the warp. Moreover, the great difference between *MaxNNZ* and *AvgNNz* values result in the ELL implementation that is not suitable for these matrices. The hybrid format achieves good performance for these kinds of sparsity patterns and solves the problem with the robustness of COO. However, the performance of the HYB format would be low for small matrices because of the overhead introduced by requiring three different kernels to compute SpMV. Indeed, the performance of block-based formats is determined by input matrices whose structure is a block structure (i.e., *Dense matrix*). Matrices from scientific problems whose structures contain mixed block structures such as *cop20K_A* and *Scircuit* reach the best performance by the BCCOO format. The performance of BCCOO is reduced substantially as a result of using matrices that are derived from the graph. It should be mentioned that the BCCOO format supports only single-precision floating-point formats [34] and suffers from the significant overhead associated with generating the data structure. BELLPACK works best for other matrices with a small dense block substructure. In addition, padding matrices with explicit zeroes result in a considerable memory overhead and performance degradation in unstructured matrices.

We compare the results of the proposed auto-tuner and the methods introduced by Bell and Garland [4] and Neelima et al. [19] (see Zardoshti [39] for more information). By comparison, we see some mismatches in results that are derived for two reasons. First, we use a wider range of formats in our auto-tuner, which leads to expanding the search space of the auto-tuner and improves the overall performance of SpMV. On the other hand, the method of Neelima et al. [19] just analyzes the basic formats in their static model, and it is difficult to extend the model to include new formats. Consequently, predicting a suitable format based on the structure of a matrix may not always be accurate, especially for sparsity patterns. More precisely, the static model shows that the COO implementation delivers the best performance for *mac_econ_fwd500*, while the HYB format provides better performance.

7 SUMMARY

We presented a novel solution to select the best storage format for SpMV, which is easy to state and to analyze. The diversity of architectural designs and input matrix characteristics means that a complex combination of architecture- and matrix-specific techniques are essential to achieve this level of performance. We designed and implemented an adaptive GPU-based SpMV system. First, we thoroughly analyzed the factors that impact the performance of SpMV algorithms using basic sparse matrix representation formats. All optimized implementations delivered substantially better performance. Second, based on these experiments, we proposed an adaptive runtime system that adapts to the behavior of the running application by profiling a small portion of the input matrix. Experimental results revealed that the proposed runtime system adapts well to the behavior of different applications by selecting the appropriate representation for each input sparse matrix. The preliminary results exhibited that the runtime system improves the performance of SpMV by $2.1\times$ for single-precision and $1.6\times$ for double-precision formats, on average.

REFERENCES

[1] K. Asanovic, et al., The landscape of parallel computing research: a view from Berkeley, Vol. 2, Tech. Rep. UCB/EECS-2006-183, EECS Department, University of California, Berkeley, 2006.

[2] L. Page, S. Brin, R. Motwani, T. Winograd, The PageRank Citation Ranking: Bringing Order to the Web, Technical Report SIDL-WP-1999-0120, Stanford University, 1999.

[3] Y. Saad, Iterative Methods for Sparse Linear Systems, 2nd ed., Society for Industrial and Applied Mathematics, Philadelphia, PA, USA, 2003.

[4] N. Bell, M. Garland, Implementing sparse matrix-vector multiplication on throughput-oriented processors, in: Proceedings of the Conference on High Performance Computing Networking, Storage and Analysis, ACM, 2009.

[5] M.M. Baskaran, R. Bordawekar, Optimizing sparse matrix-vector multiplication on GPUs using compile-time and run-time strategies, IBM Research Report RC24704 (W0812-047), 2008.

[6] M.M. Baskaran, R. Bordawekar, Sparse matrix-vector multiplication toolkit for graphics processing units, http://www.alphaworks.ibm.com/tech/spmv4gpu.

[7] A. Monakov, A. Lokhmotov, A. Avetisyan, Automatically tuning sparse matrix-vector multiplication for GPU architectures, in: High Performance Embedded Architectures and Compilers, Springer, Berlin, Heidelberg, 2010, pp. 111–125.

[8] A. Monakov, Specialized sparse matrix formats and SpMV kernel tuning for GPUs, in: Proceedings of the GPU Technology Conference (GTC), May, 2012.

[9] J.W. Choi, A. Singh, R.W. Vuduc, Model-driven autotuning of sparse matrix-vector multiply on GPUs, ACM SIGPLAN Not. 45 (5) (2010) 115–126.

[10] D. Grewe, A. Lokhmotov, Automatically generating and tuning GPU code for sparse matrix-vector multiplication from a high-level representation, in: Proceedings of the Fourth Workshop on General Purpose Processing on Graphics Processing Units, ACM, 2011.

[11] I. Reguly, M. Giles, Efficient sparse matrix-vector multiplication on cache-based GPUs, in: Innovative Parallel Computing (InPar), 2012, IEEE, 2012.

[12] F. Vázquez, J.J. Fernández, E.M. Garzón, A new approach for sparse matrix vector product on NVIDIA GPUs, Concurr. Comput. Pract. Exp. 23 (8) (2011) 815–826.

[13] S. Yan, et al., yaSpMV: yet another SpMV framework on GPUs, ACM SIGPLAN Not. 49 (8) (2014) 107–118.

[14] A. Ashari, et al., An efficient two-dimensional blocking strategy for sparse matrix-vector multiplication on GPUs, in: Proceedings of the 28th ACM International Conference on Supercomputing, ACM, 2014.

[15] C. Zheng, et al., BiELL: a bisection ELLPACK-based storage format for optimizing SpMV on GPUs, J. Parallel Distrib. Comput. 74 (7) (2014) 2639–2647.

[16] C.C. Yan, et al., Memory bandwidth optimization of SpMV on GPGPUs, Front. Comput. Sci. 9 (3) (2015) 431–441.

[17] P. Guo, L. Wang, Accurate cross-architecture performance modeling for sparse matrix-vector multiplication (SpMV) on GPUs, Concurr. Comput. Pract. Exp. 27 (13) (2014) 32381–3294.

[18] K. Li, W. Yang, K. Li, Performance analysis and optimization for SpMV on GPU using probabilistic modeling, IEEE Trans. Parallel Distrib. Syst. 26 (1) (2015) 196–205.

[19] B. Neelima, G.R.M. Reddy, P.S. Raghavendra, Predicting an optimal sparse matrix format for SpMV computation on GPU, in: 2014 IEEE International Conference on Parallel & Distributed Processing Symposium Workshops (IPDPSW), IEEE, 2014.

[20] N. Sedaghati, T. Mu, L.N. Pouchet, S. Parthasarathy, P. Sadayappan, Automatic selection of sparse matrix representation on GPUs, in: Proceedings of the 29th ACM International Conference on Supercomputing, ACM, 2015.

[21] R.W. Vuduc, Automatic performance tuning of sparse matrix kernels, Dissertation.

[22] S. Williams, et al., Optimization of sparse matrix-vector multiplication on emerging multicore platforms, Parallel Comput. 35 (3) (2009) 178–194.

[23] S.W. Williams, Auto-tuning performance on multicore computers, ProQuest, 2008.

[24] R.W. Vuduc, J.W. Demmel, K. A. Yelick, OSKI: a library of automatically tuned sparse matrix kernels, J. Phys. Conf. Ser. 16 (1) (2005) 521–530.

[25] J. Bilmes, et al., Optimizing matrix multiply using PHiPAC: a portable, high-performance, ANSI C coding methodology, in: Proceedings of the 11th International Conference on Supercomputing, ACM, 1997.

[26] R.C. Whaley, J.J. Dongarra, Automatically tuned linear algebra software, in: Proceedings of the 1998 ACM/IEEE Conference on Supercomputing, IEEE Computer Society, 1998.

[27] E.J. Im, K.A. Yelick, R.W. Vuduc, Sparsity: optimization framework for sparse matrix kernels, Int. J. High Perform. Comput. Appl. 18 (1) (2004) 135–158.

[28] J. Li, et al., SMAT: an input adaptive auto-tuner for sparse matrix-vector multiplication, ACM SIGPLAN Not. 48 (6) (2013) 117–126.

[29] R.W. Vuduc, H.J. Moon, High performance computing and communications, in: Fast Sparse Matrix-Vector Multiplication by Exploiting Variable Block Structure, Springer, Berlin/Heidelberg, 2005, pp. 807–816.

[30] A.T. Ogielski, W. Aiello, Sparse matrix computations on parallel processor arrays, SIAM J. Sci. Comput. 14 (3) (1993) 519–530.

[31] B.C. Lee, et al., Performance models for evaluation and automatic tuning of symmetric sparse matrix-vector multiply, in: International Conference on Parallel Processing 2004 (ICPP 2004), IEEE, 2004.

[32] E.J. Im, K.A. Yelick, Optimizing the Performance of Sparse Matrix-Vector Multiplication, University of California, Berkeley, 2000.

[33] K. Kourtis, et al., CSX: an extended compression format for SpMV on shared memory systems, ACM SIGPLAN Not. 46 (8) (2011) 247–256.

[34] W. Liu, B. Vinter, Csr5: an efficient storage format for cross-platform sparse matrix-vector multiplication, in: Proceedings of the 29th ACM International Conference on Supercomputing, ACM, 2015.

[35] NVIDIA, NVIDIA CUDA C Programming Guide, 2013.

[36] NVIDA, Whitepaper NVIDIAs Next Generation CUDA Compute Architecture: Kepler GK110/210, 2014.

[37] T.A. Davis, Y. Hu, The University of Florida sparse matrix collection, ACM Trans. Math. Softw. (TOMS) 38 (1) (2011) 1.

[38] NVIDIA Corporation, Tuning CUDA Applications for Kepler, 2014.

[39] P. Zardoshti, F. Khunjush, H. Sarbazi-Azad, Adaptive sparse matrix representation for efficient matrix-vector multiplication, J. Supercomput. (2015) http://dx.doi.org/10.1007/s11227-015-1571-0.

[40] NVIDIA, Compute Visual Profiler User Guide, 2013.

Architecture
and performance

A framework for accelerating bottlenecks in GPU execution with assist warps

15

N. Vijaykumar[1], G. Pekhimenko[1], A. Jog[2], S. Ghose[1], A. Bhowmick[1], R. Ausavarungnirun[1], C. Das[2], M. Kandemir[2], T.C. Mowry[1], O. Mutlu[1]

Carnegie Mellon University, Pittsburgh, PA, United States[1] Pennsylvania State University, State College, PA, United States[2]

1 INTRODUCTION

Modern graphics processing units (GPUs) play an important role in delivering high performance and energy efficiency for many classes of applications and different computational platforms. GPUs employ fine-grained multithreading to hide the high memory access latencies with thousands of concurrently running threads [1]. GPUs are well provisioned with different resources (e.g., SIMD-like computational units, large register files) to support the execution of a large number of these hardware contexts. Ideally, if the demand for all types of resources is properly balanced, all these resources should be fully utilized by the application. Unfortunately, this balance is very difficult to achieve in practice.

As a result, bottlenecks in program execution, for example, limitations in memory or computational bandwidth, lead to long stalls and idle periods in the shader pipelines of modern GPUs [2–5]. Alleviating these bottlenecks with optimizations implemented in dedicated hardware requires significant engineering cost and effort. Fortunately, the resulting underutilization of on-chip computational and memory resources from these imbalances in application requirements offers some new opportunities. For example, we can use these resources for efficient integration of *hardware-generated threads* that perform useful work to accelerate the execution of the primary threads. Similar *helper threading* ideas have been proposed in the context of general-purpose processors [6–12] either to extend the pipeline with more contexts or to use spare hardware contexts to precompute useful information that aids main code execution (to aid branch prediction, prefetching, etc.).

We believe that the general idea of helper threading can lead to even more powerful optimizations and new opportunities in the context of modern GPUs than in CPUs because (1) the abundance of on-chip resources in a GPU obviates the need

Advances in GPU Research and Practice. http://dx.doi.org/10.1016/B978-0-12-803738-6.00015-X

for idle hardware contexts [9,13] or the addition of more storage (registers, rename tables, etc.) and compute units (CUs) [6,14] required to handle more contexts and (2) the relative simplicity of the GPU pipeline avoids the complexities of handling register renaming, speculative execution, precise interrupts, etc. [7]. However, GPUs that execute and manage thousands of thread contexts at the same time pose new challenges for employing helper threading, which must be addressed carefully. First, the numerous regular program threads executing in parallel could require an equal or larger number of helper threads that need to be managed at low cost. Second, the compute and memory resources are dynamically partitioned between threads in GPUs, and resource allocation for helper threads should be cognizant of resource interference and overhead. Third, lock-step execution and complex scheduling—which are characteristic of GPU architectures—exacerbate the complexity of fine-grained management of helper threads.

In this chapter, we describe a new, flexible framework for bottleneck acceleration in GPUs via helper threading (called Core-Assisted Bottleneck Acceleration or CABA), which exploits the aforementioned new opportunities while effectively handling the new challenges. CABA performs acceleration by generating special warps—*assist warps*—that can execute code to speed up application execution and system tasks. To simplify the support of the numerous assist threads with CABA, we manage their execution at the granularity of a *warp* and use a centralized mechanism to track the progress of each *assist warp* throughout its execution. To reduce the overhead of providing and managing new contexts for each generated thread, as well as to simplify scheduling and data communication, an assist warp *shares the same context* as the regular warp it assists. Hence the regular warps are overprovisioned with *available registers* to enable each of them to host its own assist warp.

Use of CABA for compression

We illustrate an important use case for the CABA framework: alleviating the memory bandwidth bottleneck by enabling *flexible data compression* in the memory hierarchy. The basic idea is to have assist warps that (1) compress cache blocks before they are written to memory, and (2) decompress cache blocks before they are placed into the cache.

CABA-based compression/decompression provides several benefits over a purely hardware-based implementation of data compression for memory. First, CABA primarily employs hardware that is already available on-chip but is otherwise underutilized. In contrast, hardware-only compression implementations require *dedicated logic* for specific algorithms. Each new algorithm (or a modification of an existing one) requires engineering effort and incurs hardware cost. Second, different applications tend to have distinct data patterns [15] that are more efficiently compressed with different compression algorithms. CABA offers versatility in algorithm choice as we find that many existing hardware-based compression algorithms (e.g., base-delta-immediate [BDI] compression [15], frequent pattern compression [FPC] [16], and C-Pack [17]) can be implemented using different assist warps with the CABA framework. Third, not all applications benefit from data compression.

Some applications are constrained by other bottlenecks (e.g., oversubscription of computational resources) or may operate on data that is not easily compressible. As a result, the benefits of compression may not outweigh the cost in terms of additional latency and energy spent on compressing and decompressing data. In these cases, compression can be easily disabled by CABA, and the CABA framework can be used in other ways to alleviate the current bottleneck.

Other uses of CABA

The generality of CABA enables its use in alleviating other bottlenecks with different optimizations. We discuss two examples: (1) using assist warps to perform *memoization* to eliminate redundant computations that have the same or similar inputs [18–20], by storing the results of frequently performed computations in the main memory hierarchy (i.e., by converting the computational problem into a storage problem) and (2) using the idle memory pipeline to perform opportunistic *prefetching* to better overlap computation with memory access. Assist warps offer a hardware/software interface to implement hybrid prefetching algorithms [21] with varying degrees of complexity. We also briefly discuss other uses of CABA for (1) redundant multithreading, (2) speculative precomputation, (3) handling interrupts, and (4) profiling and instrumentation.

Contributions

The chapter makes the following contributions:

- It introduces the CABA framework, which can mitigate different bottlenecks in modern GPUs by using underutilized system resources for *assist warp* execution.
- It provides a detailed description of how our framework can be used to enable effective and flexible data compression in GPU memory hierarchies.
- It comprehensively evaluates the use of CABA for data compression to alleviate the memory bandwidth bottleneck. Our evaluations across a wide variety of applications from Mars [22], CUDA [23], Lonestar [24], and Rodinia [25] benchmark suites show that CABA-based compression on average (1) reduces memory bandwidth by $2.1\times$, (2) improves performance by 41.7%, and (3) reduces overall system energy by 22.2%.
- It discusses at least six other use cases of CABA that can improve application performance and system management, showing that CABA is a primary general framework for taking advantage of underutilized resources in modern GPU engines.

2 BACKGROUND

A GPU consists of multiple simple cores, also called streaming multiprocessors (SMs) in NVIDIA terminology or CUs in AMD terminology. Our example architecture (shown in Fig. 1) consists of 15 cores each with an single instruction

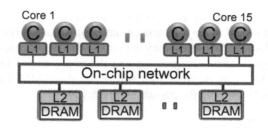

FIG. 1

Baseline GPU architecture.

Figure reproduced from Ref. [28].

multiple thread (SIMT) width of 32, and 6 memory controllers (MCs). Each core is associated with a private L1 data cache and read-only texture and constant caches along with a low latency, programmer-managed shared memory. The cores and MCs are connected via a crossbar and every MC is associated with a slice of the shared L2 cache. This architecture is similar to many modern GPU architectures, including NVIDIA Fermi [26] and AMD Radeon [27].

A typical GPU application consists of many kernels. Each kernel is divided into groups of threads, called thread-blocks (or cooperative thread arrays [CTAs]). After a kernel is launched and its necessary data are copied to the GPU memory, the thread-block scheduler schedules available CTAs onto all the available cores [29]. Once the CTAs are launched onto the cores, the warps associated with the CTAs are scheduled onto the cores' SIMT pipelines. Each core is capable of concurrently executing many warps, where a warp is typically defined as a group of threads that are executed in lockstep. In modern GPUs, a warp can contain 32 threads [26], for example. The maximum number of warps that can be launched on a core depends on the available core resources (available shared memory, register file size, etc.). For example, in a modern GPU as many as 64 warps (i.e., 2048 threads) can be present on a single GPU core.

For more details on the internals of modern GPU architectures, we refer the reader to Refs. [30,31].

3 MOTIVATION

We observe that different bottlenecks and imbalances during program execution leave resources unutilized within the GPU cores. We motivate our proposal, CABA, by examining these inefficiencies. CABA leverages these inefficiencies as an opportunity to perform useful work.

Unutilized compute resources

A GPU core employs fine-grained multithreading [32,33] of *warps*, that is, groups of threads executing the same instruction, to hide long memory and arithmetic logic unit (ALU) operation latencies. If the number of available warps is insufficient to cover these long latencies, the core stalls or becomes idle. To understand the key sources of inefficiency in GPU cores, we conduct an experiment where we show the breakdown of the applications' execution time spent on either useful work (*active cycles*) or stalling because of one of four reasons: *compute, memory, data dependence stalls*, and *idle cycles*. We also vary the amount of available off-chip memory bandwidth: (i) half (1/2 × BW), (ii) equal to (1 × BW), and (iii) double (2 × BW), the peak memory bandwidth of our baseline GPU architecture. Section 6 details our baseline architecture and methodology.

Fig. 2 shows the percentage of total issue cycles, divided into five components (as already described). The first two components—*memory and compute stalls*—are attributed to the main memory and ALU-pipeline structural stalls. These stalls are because of backed up pipelines due to oversubscribed resources that prevent warps from being issued to the respective pipelines. The third component (*data dependence stalls*) is due to data dependence stalls. These stalls prevent warps from issuing new instruction(s) when the previous instruction(s) from the same warp are stalled on long-latency operations (usually memory load operations). In some applications (e.g., dmr), special-function-unit (SFU) ALU operations that may take tens of cycles to finish are also the source of data dependence stalls. The fourth component, *idle cycles*, refers to idle cycles when either all the available warps are issued to the pipelines and not ready to execute their next instruction or the instruction buffers (IBs) are flushed due to a mispredicted branch. All these components are sources of inefficiency that cause the cores to be underutilized. The last component, *active cycles*, indicates the fraction of cycles during which at least one warp was successfully issued to the pipelines.

We make two observations from Fig. 2. First, *compute, memory*, and *data dependence stalls* are the major sources of underutilization in many GPU applications. We distinguish applications based on their primary bottleneck as either *memory* or *compute bound*. We observe that a majority of the applications in our workload pool (17 out of 27 studied) are *memory bound*, and bottlenecked by the off-chip memory bandwidth.

Second, for the *memory-bound* applications, we observe that the *memory* and *data dependence* stalls constitute a significant fraction (61%) of the total issue cycles on our baseline GPU architecture (1 × BW). This fraction goes down to 51% when the peak memory bandwidth is doubled (2 × BW) and increases significantly when the peak bandwidth is halved (1/2 × BW), indicating that limited off-chip memory bandwidth is a critical performance bottleneck for *memory-bound* applications. Some applications, for example, *BFS*, are limited by the interconnect bandwidth. In contrast, the *compute-bound* applications are primarily bottlenecked by stalls in the ALU pipelines. An increase or decrease in the off-chip bandwidth has little effect on the performance of these applications.

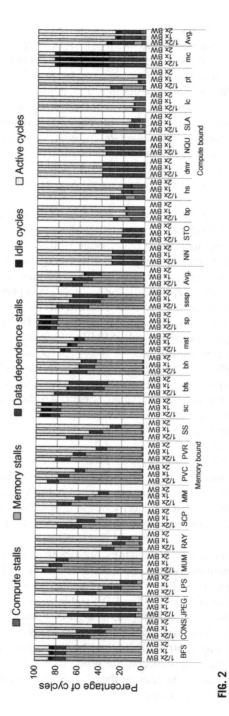

FIG. 2

Breakdown of total issue cycles for 27 representative CUDA applications. See Section 6 for methodology.

Figure reproduced from Ref. [28]

Unutilized on-chip memory

The *occupancy* of any GPU SM, that is, the number of threads running concurrently, is limited by a number of factors: (1) the available registers and shared memory, (2) the hard limit on the number of threads and thread-blocks per core, and (3) the number of thread-blocks in the application kernel. The limiting resource from the preceding leaves the other resources underutilized. This is because it is challenging, in practice, to achieve a perfect balance in utilization of all the preceding factors for different workloads with varying characteristics. Very often, the factor determining the occupancy is the thread or thread-block limit imposed by the architecture. In this case, many registers are left unallocated to any thread-block. Also, the number of available registers may not be a multiple of those required by each thread-block. The remaining registers are not enough to schedule an entire extra thread-block, which leaves a significant fraction of the register file and shared memory unallocated and unutilized by the thread-blocks. Fig. 3 shows the fraction of statically unallocated registers in a 128 KB register file (per SM) with a 1536 thread, 8 thread-block occupancy limit, for different applications. We observe that on average 24% of the register file remains unallocated. This phenomenon has previously been observed and analyzed in detail in Refs. [34–38]. We observe a similar trend with the usage of shared memory (not graphed).

Our goal

We aim to exploit the underutilization of compute resources, registers, and on-chip shared memory as an opportunity to enable different optimizations to accelerate various bottlenecks in GPU program execution. To achieve this goal, we want to enable efficient helper threading for GPUs to dynamically generate threads in

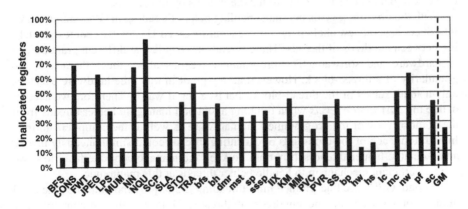

FIG. 3

Fraction of statically unallocated registers.

Figure reproduced from Ref. [28].

hardware that use the available on-chip resources for various purposes. In the next section, we present the detailed design of our CABA framework that enables the generation and management of these threads.

4 THE CABA FRAMEWORK

In order to understand the major design choices behind the CABA framework, we first present our major design goals and describe the key challenges in applying helper threading to GPUs. We then show the detailed design, hardware changes, and operation of CABA. Finally, we briefly describe potential applications of our proposed framework. Section 5 goes into a detailed design of one application of the framework.

4.1 GOALS AND CHALLENGES

The purpose of CABA is to leverage underutilized GPU resources for useful computation. To this end, we need to efficiently execute subroutines that perform optimizations to accelerate bottlenecks in application execution. The key difference between CABA's *assisted execution* and regular execution is that CABA must be *low overhead* and, therefore, helper threads need to be treated differently from regular threads. The *low overhead* goal imposes several key requirements in designing a framework to enable helper threading. First, we should be able to easily manage helper threads—to enable, trigger, and kill threads when required. Second, helper threads need to be flexible enough to adapt to the runtime behavior of the regular program. Third, a helper thread needs to be able to communicate with the original thread. Finally, we need a flexible interface to specify new subroutines, with the framework being generic enough to handle various optimizations.

With the preceding goals in mind, enabling helper threading in GPU architectures introduces several new challenges. First, execution on GPUs involves context switching between hundreds of threads. These threads are handled at different granularities in hardware and software. The programmer reasons about these threads at the granularity of a thread-block. However, at any point in time, the hardware executes only a small subset of the thread-block, that is, a set of warps. Therefore we need to define the *abstraction levels* when thinking about and managing helper threads from the point of view of the programmer, the hardware as well as the compiler/runtime. In addition, each of the thousands of executing threads could simultaneously invoke an associated helper thread subroutine. To keep the management overhead low, we need an efficient mechanism to handle helper threads at this magnitude.

Second, GPUs use fine-grained multithreading [32,33] to time multiplex the fixed number of CUs among the hundreds of threads. Similarly, the on-chip memory resources (i.e., the register file and shared memory) are statically partitioned between the different threads at compile time. Helper threads require their own registers and compute cycles to execute. A straightforward approach is to dedicate a few registers and CUs just for helper thread execution, but this option is both expensive and wasteful. In fact, our primary motivation is to utilize *existing idle resources* for helper thread execution. In order to do this, we aim to enable sharing of the existing resources between primary threads and helper threads at low cost, while minimizing the interference to primary thread execution. In the remainder of this section, we describe the design of our low-overhead CABA framework.

4.2 DESIGN OF THE CABA FRAMEWORK

We choose to implement CABA using a hardware/software co-design, as pure hardware or pure software approaches pose certain challenges that we will describe. There are two alternatives for a fully software-based approach to using helper threads. The first alternative, treating each helper thread as independent kernel code, has high overhead, since we are now treating the helper threads essentially as regular threads. This would reduce the primary thread occupancy in each SM (there is a hard limit on the number of threads and blocks that an SM can support). It would also complicate the data communication between the primary and helper threads, since no simple interface exists for interkernel communication. The second alternative, embedding the helper thread code within the primary thread kernel itself, offers little flexibility in adapting to runtime requirements, since such helper threads cannot be triggered or squashed independently of the primary thread.

On the other hand, a pure hardware solution would make register allocation for the assist warps and the data communication between the helper threads and primary threads more difficult. Registers are allocated to each thread-block by the compiler and are then mapped to the sections of the hardware register file at runtime. Mapping registers for helper threads and enabling data communication between those registers and the primary thread registers would be nontrivial. Furthermore, a fully hardware approach would make it challenging to offer the programmer a flexible interface.

Hardware support enables simpler fine-grained management of helper threads that is aware of micro-architectural events and runtime program behavior. Compiler/runtime support enables simpler context management for helper threads and more flexible programming interfaces. Thus, to get the best of both worlds, we propose a *hardware/software cooperative approach*, where the hardware manages the scheduling and execution of helper thread subroutines, while the compiler performs the allocation of shared resources (e.g., register file and shared memory) for the helper threads, and the programmer or the microarchitect provides the helper threads themselves.

4.2.1 Hardware-based management of threads

To use the available on-chip resources the same way that thread-blocks do during program execution, we dynamically insert sequences of instructions into the execution stream. We track and manage these instructions at the granularity of a warp and refer to them as *assist warps*. An assist warp is a set of instructions issued into the core pipelines. Each instruction is executed in lock step across all the SIMT lanes, just like any regular instruction, with an active mask to disable lanes as necessary. The assist warp does *not* own a separate context (e.g., registers, local memory), and instead shares both a context and a warp ID with the regular warp that invoked it. In other words, each assist warp is coupled with a *parent warp*. In this sense, it is different from a regular warp and does not reduce the number of threads that can be scheduled on a single SM. Data sharing between the two warps becomes simpler, since the assist warps share the register file with the parent warp. Ideally, an assist warp consumes resources and issue cycles that would otherwise be idle. We describe the structures required to support hardware-based management of assist warps in Section 4.3.

4.2.2 Register file/shared memory allocation

Each helper thread subroutine requires a different number of registers depending on the actions it performs. These registers have a short lifetime, with no values being preserved between different invocations of an assist warp. To limit the register requirements for assist warps, we impose the restriction that only one instance of each helper thread routine can be active for each thread. All instances of the same helper thread for each parent thread use the same registers, and the registers are allocated to the helper threads statically by the compiler. One of the factors that determines the runtime SM occupancy is the number of registers required by a thread-block (i.e., per-block register requirement). For each helper thread subroutine that is enabled, we add its register requirement to the per-block register requirement, to ensure the availability of registers for both the parent threads as well as every assist warp. The registers that remain unallocated after allocation among the parent thread-blocks should suffice to support the assist warps. If not, register-heavy assist warps may limit the parent thread-block occupancy in SMs or increase the number of register spills in the parent warps. Shared memory resources are partitioned in a similar manner and allocated to each assist warp as or if needed.

4.2.3 Programmer/developer interface

The assist warp subroutine can be written in two ways. First, it can be supplied and annotated by the programmer/developer using CUDA extensions with PTX instructions and then compiled with regular program code. Second, the assist warp subroutines can be written by the microarchitect in the internal GPU instruction format. These helper thread subroutines can then be enabled or disabled by the application programmer. This approach is similar to that proposed in prior work (e.g., [6]). It offers the advantage of potentially being highly optimized for energy and performance while having flexibility in implementing optimizations that are not easy to map using existing GPU PTX instructions. The instructions for the helper thread subroutine are stored in an on-chip buffer (described in Section 4.3).

Along with the helper thread subroutines, the programmer also provides: (1) the *priority* of the assist warps to enable the warp scheduler to make informed decisions,

(2) the trigger conditions for each assist warp, and (3) the live-in and live-out variables for data communication with the parent warps.

Assist warps can be scheduled with different priority levels in relation to parent warps by the warp scheduler. Some assist warps may perform a function that is required for correct execution of the program and are *blocking*. At this end of the spectrum, the *high priority* assist warps are treated by the scheduler as always taking higher precedence over the parent warp execution. Assist warps should be given a high priority only when they are required for correctness. *Low priority* assist warps, on the other hand, are scheduled for execution only when computational resources are available, that is, during idle cycles. There is no guarantee that these assist warps will execute or complete.

The programmer also provides the conditions or events that need to be satisfied for the deployment of the assist warp. This includes a specific point within the original program and/or a set of other microarchitectural events that could serve as a *trigger* for starting the execution of an assist warp.

4.3 MAIN HARDWARE ADDITIONS

Fig. 4 shows a high-level block diagram of the GPU pipeline [39]. To support assist warp execution, we add three new components: (1) an Assist Warp Store (AWS) to hold the assist warp code, (2) an Assist Warp Controller (AWC) to perform the

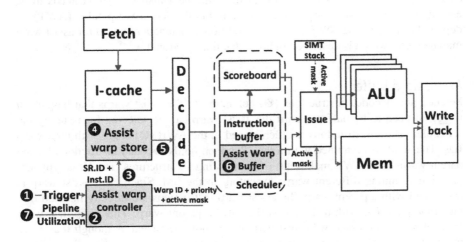

FIG. 4

CABA framework flow within a typical GPU pipeline [39]. The *shaded blocks* are the components introduced for the framework.

Figure reproduced from Ref. [28]

deployment, tracking, and management of assist warps, and (3) an Assist Warp Buffer (AWB) to stage instructions from triggered assist warps for execution.

Assist warp store

Different assist warp subroutines are possible based on the purpose of the optimization. These code sequences for different types of assist warps need to be stored on-chip. An on-chip storage structure called the AWS (❹) is preloaded with these instructions before application execution. It is indexed using the subroutine index (SR.ID) along with the instruction ID (Inst.ID).

Assist warp controller

The AWC (❷) is responsible for the triggering, tracking, and management of assist warp execution. It stores a mapping between trigger events and a SR.ID in the AWS, as specified by the programmer. The AWC monitors for such events, and when they take place, triggers the fetch, decode, and execution of instructions from the AWS for the respective assist warp.

Deploying all the instructions within an assist warp, back-to-back, at the trigger point may require increased fetch/decode bandwidth and buffer space after decoding [7]. To avoid this, at each cycle, only a few instructions from an assist warp, at most equal to the available decode/issue bandwidth, are decoded and staged for execution. Within the AWC, we simply track the next instruction that needs to be executed for each assist warp, and this is stored in the Assist Warp Table (AWT), as depicted in Fig. 5. The AWT also tracks additional metadata required for assist warp management, which is described in more detail in Section 4.4.

Assist warp buffer

Fetched and decoded instructions (❷) belonging to the assist warps that have been triggered need to be buffered until the assist warp can be selected for issue by the scheduler. These instructions are then staged in the AWB (❻) along with their warp IDs. The AWB is contained within the *IB*, which holds decoded instructions for the parent warps. The AWB makes use of the existing IB structures. The IB is typically partitioned among different warps executing in the SM. Since each assist warp is associated with a parent warp, the assist warp instructions are directly inserted into the *same partition* within the IB as that of the parent warp. This simplifies warp scheduling, as the assist warp instructions can now be issued as though they were parent warp instructions with the same warp ID. In addition, using the existing partitions avoids the cost of separate dedicated instruction buffering for assist warps. We do, however, provision a small additional partition with two entries within the IB, to hold nonblocking *low priority* assist warps that are scheduled only during idle cycles. This additional partition allows the scheduler to distinguish *low priority* assist warp instructions from the parent warp and *high priority* assist warp instructions, which are given precedence during scheduling, allowing them to make progress.

4.4 THE MECHANISM

Trigger and deployment

An assist warp is triggered (❶) by the AWC (❷) based on a specific set of architectural events and/or a triggering instruction (e.g., a load instruction). When an assist warp is triggered, its specific instance is placed into the Assist Warp Table (AWT) within the AWC (Fig. 5). Every cycle, the AWC selects an assist warp to deploy in a round-robin fashion. The AWS is indexed (❸) based on the SR.ID—which selects the instruction sequence to be executed by the assist warp, and the Inst.ID—which is a pointer to the next instruction to be executed within the subroutine (Fig. 5). The selected instruction is entered (❹) into the AWB, (❺) and at this point, the instruction enters the active pool with other active warps for scheduling. The Inst.ID for the assist warp is updated in the AWT to point to the next instruction in the subroutine. When the end of the subroutine is reached, the entry within the AWT is freed.

Execution

Assist warp instructions, when selected for issue by the scheduler, are executed in much the same way as any other instructions. The scoreboard tracks the dependencies between instructions within an assist warp in the same way as any warp, and instructions from different assist warps are interleaved in execution in order to hide latencies. We also provide an active mask (stored as a part of the AWT), which allows for statically disabling/enabling different lanes within a warp. This is useful to provide flexibility in lock-step instruction execution when we do not need all threads within a warp to execute a specific assist warp subroutine.

Dynamic feedback and throttling

Assist warps, if not properly controlled, may stall application execution. This can happen for several reasons. First, assist warps take up issue cycles, and only a limited number of instructions can be issued per clock cycle. Second, assist warps require structural resources: the ALU units and resources in the load-store pipelines (if the assist warps consist of computational and memory instructions, respectively). We may, hence, need to throttle assist warps to ensure that their performance benefits

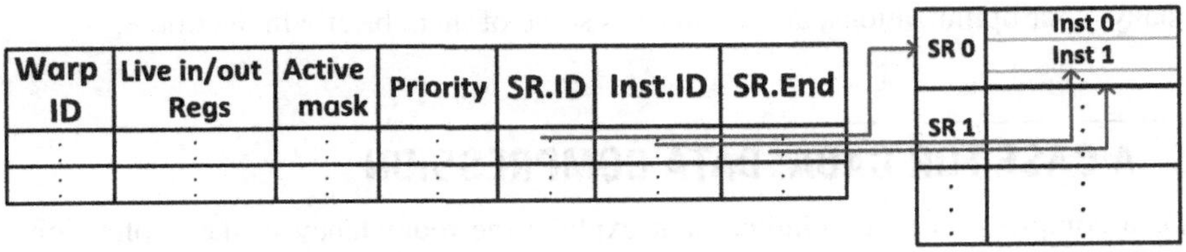

Warp ID	Live in/out Regs	Active mask	Priority	SR.ID	Inst.ID	SR.End
:	:	:	:	:	:	:
:	:	:	:	:	:	:

SR 0	Inst 0
	Inst 1
SR 1	:
:	:
:	:

FIG. 5

Fetch Logic: Assist Warp Table (contained in the AWC) and the AWS.

Figure reproduced from Ref. [28]

outweigh the overhead. This requires mechanisms to appropriately balance and manage the aggressiveness of assist warps at runtime.

The overhead associated with assist warps can be controlled in different ways. First, the programmer can statically specify the priority of the assist warp. Depending on the criticality of the assist warps in making forward progress, the assist warps can be issued either in idle cycles or with varying levels of priority in relation to the parent warps. For example, warps performing *decompression* are given a high priority, whereas warps performing *compression* are given a low priority. Low priority assist warps are inserted into the dedicated partition in the IB and are scheduled only during idle cycles. This priority is statically defined by the programmer. Second, the AWC can control the number of times the assist warps are deployed into the AWB. The AWC monitors the utilization of the functional units (❼) and idleness of the cores to decide when to throttle assist warp deployment.

Communication and control

An assist warp may need to communicate data and status with its parent warp. For example, memory addresses from the parent warp need to be communicated to assist warps performing decompression or prefetching. The IDs of the registers containing the live-in data for each assist warp are saved in the AWT when an assist warp is triggered. Similarly, if an assist warp needs to report results to its parent warp (e.g., in the case of memoization), the register IDs are also stored in the AWT. When the assist warps execute, *MOVE* instructions are first executed to copy the live-in data from the parent warp registers to the assist warp registers. Live-out data are communicated to the parent warp in a similar fashion, at the end of assist warp execution.

Assist warps may need to be *killed* when they are not required (e.g., if the data does not require decompression) or when they are no longer beneficial. In this case, the entries in the AWT and AWB are simply flushed for the assist warp.

4.5 APPLICATIONS OF THE CABA FRAMEWORK

We envision multiple applications for the CABA framework, for example, data compression [15–17,40], memoization [18–20], and data prefetching [41–45]. In Section 5, we provide a detailed case study on enabling data compression with the framework, as well as discuss various tradeoffs. We believe CABA can be useful for many other optimizations, and we discuss some of them briefly in Section 8.

5 A CASE FOR CABA: DATA COMPRESSION

Data compression is a technique that exploits the redundancy in the application's data to reduce capacity and bandwidth requirements for many modern systems by saving and transmitting data in a more compact form. Hardware-based data compression has been explored in the context of on-chip caches [15–17,40,46–50], interconnect [51], and main memory [52–58] as a means to save storage capacity as well as memory bandwidth. In modern GPUs, memory bandwidth is a key limiter to system performance in many workloads (see Section 3). As such, data compression is a promising technique to help alleviate this bottleneck. Compressing data enable less data to be transferred from/to DRAM and the interconnect.

In bandwidth-constrained workloads, idle compute pipelines offer an opportunity to employ CABA to enable data compression in GPUs. We can use assist warps to (1) decompress data, before loading it into the caches and registers, and (2) compress data, before writing it back to memory. Since assist warps execute instructions, CABA offers some flexibility in the compression algorithms that can be employed. Compression algorithms that can be mapped to the general GPU execution model can be flexibly implemented with the CABA framework.

5.1 MAPPING COMPRESSION ALGORITHMS INTO ASSIST WARPS

In order to employ CABA to enable data compression, we need to map compression algorithms into instructions that can be executed within the GPU cores. For a compression algorithm to be amenable for implementation with CABA, it ideally needs to be (1) reasonably parallelizable and (2) simple (for low latency). Decompressing data involves reading the encoding associated with each cache line that defines how to decompress it and then triggering the corresponding decompression subroutine in CABA. Compressing data, on the other hand, involves testing different encodings and saving data in the compressed format.

We perform compression at the granularity of a cache line. The data needs to be decompressed before it is used by any program thread. In order to utilize the full SIMD width of the GPU pipeline, we want to decompress/compress all the words in the cache line in parallel. With CABA, helper thread routines are managed at the warp granularity, enabling fine-grained triggering of assist warps to perform compression/decompression when required. However, the SIMT execution model in a GPU imposes some challenges: (1) threads within a warp operate in lock step, and (2) threads operate as independent entities, that is, they do not easily communicate with each other.

In this section, we discuss the architectural changes and algorithm adaptations required to address these challenges and provide a detailed implementation and evaluation of *data compression* within the CABA framework using the *BDI compression* algorithm [15]. Section 5.1.3 discusses implementing other compression algorithms.

5.1.1 Algorithm overview

BDI compression is a simple compression algorithm that was originally proposed in the context of caches [15]. It is based on the observation that many cache lines contain data with low dynamic range. BDI exploits this observation to represent a cache line with low dynamic range using a common *base* (or multiple bases) and an array of *deltas* (where a delta is the difference of each value within the cache line and the common base). Since the *deltas* require fewer bytes than the values themselves, the

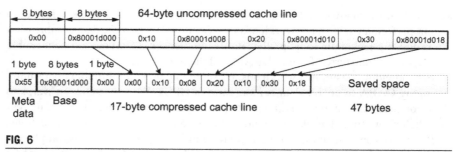

FIG. 6

Cache line from *PVC* compressed with BDI.

Figure reproduced from Ref. [28].

combined size after compression can be much smaller. Fig. 6 shows the compression of an example 64-byte cache line from the *PageViewCount (PVC)* application using BDI. As Fig. 6 indicates, in this case, the cache line can be represented using two bases (an 8-byte base value, 0x8001D000, and an implicit 0 value base) and an array of eight 1-byte differences from these bases. As a result, the entire cache line data can be represented using 17 bytes instead of 64 bytes (1-byte metadata, 8-byte base, and eight 1-byte deltas), saving 47 bytes of the originally used space.

Our example implementation of the BDI compression algorithm [15] views a cache line as a set of fixed-size values, that is, eight 8-byte, sixteen 4-byte, or thirty-two 2-byte values for a 64-byte cache line. For the size of the deltas, it considers three options: 1, 2, and 4 bytes. The key characteristic of BDI, which makes it a desirable compression algorithm to use with the CABA framework, is its fast parallel decompression that can be efficiently mapped into instructions that can be executed on GPU hardware. Decompression is simply a masked vector addition of the deltas to the appropriate bases [15].

5.1.2 Mapping BDI to CABA

In order to implement BDI with the CABA framework, we need to map the BDI compression/decompression algorithms into GPU instruction subroutines (stored in the AWS and deployed as assist warps).

Decompression

To decompress the data compressed with BDI, we need a simple addition of deltas to the appropriate bases. The CABA decompression subroutine first loads the words within the compressed cache line into assist warp registers and then performs the base-delta additions in parallel, employing the wide ALU pipeline.[1] The subroutine then writes back the uncompressed cache line to the cache. It skips the addition for

---

[1] Multiple instructions are required if the number of deltas exceeds the width of the ALU pipeline. We use a 32-wide pipeline.

the lanes with an implicit base of zero by updating the active lane mask based on the cache line encoding. We store a separate subroutine for each possible BDI encoding that loads the appropriate bytes in the cache line as the base and the deltas. The high-level algorithm for decompression is presented in Algorithm 1.

ALGORITHM 1 BDI: DECOMPRESSION

1: load *base, deltas*
2: *uncompressed_data = base + deltas*
3: store *uncompressed_data*

Compression

To compress data, the CABA compression subroutine tests several possible encodings (each representing a different size of base and deltas) in order to achieve a high compression ratio. The first few bytes (2–8 depending on the encoding tested) of the cache line are always used as the base. Each possible encoding is tested to check whether the cache line can be successfully encoded with it. In order to perform compression at a warp granularity, we need to check whether all of the words at every SIMD lane were successfully compressed. In other words, if any one word cannot be compressed, that encoding cannot be used across the warp. We can perform this check by adding a global predicate register, which stores the logical AND of the per-lane predicate registers. We observe that applications with homogeneous data structures can typically use the same encoding for most of their cache lines [15]. We use this observation to reduce the number of encodings we test to just one in many cases. All necessary operations are done in parallel using the full width of the GPU SIMD pipeline. The high-level algorithm for compression is presented in Algorithm 2.

ALGORITHM 2 BDI: COMPRESSION

1: **for** *each base_size* **do**
2:     load *base, values*
3:     **for** *each delta_size* **do**
4:        *deltas = abs(values - base)*
5:        **if** *size(deltas) <= delta_size* **then**
6:           store *base, deltas*
7:           **exit**
8:        **end if**
9:     **end for**
10: **end for**

5.1.3 Implementing other algorithms

The BDI compression algorithm is naturally amenable toward implementation using assist warps because of its data-parallel nature and simplicity. The CABA framework can also be used to realize other algorithms. The challenge in implementing algorithms like FPC [59] and C-Pack [17], which have variable-length compressed words, is primarily in the placement of compressed words within the compressed cache lines. In BDI, the compressed words are in *fixed* locations within the cache line, and for each encoding, all the compressed words are of the same size and can, therefore, be processed in parallel. In contrast, C-Pack may employ multiple dictionary values as opposed to just one base in BDI. In order to realize algorithms with *variable length words* and *dictionary values* with assist warps, we leverage the coalescing/address generation logic [60,61] already available in the GPU cores. We make two minor modifications to these algorithms [17,59] to adapt them for use with CABA. First, similar to prior works [17,54,59], we observe that few encodings are sufficient to capture almost all the data redundancy. In addition, the impact of any loss in compressibility because of fewer encodings is minimal as the benefits of bandwidth compression are at multiples of a only single DRAM burst (e.g., 32B for GDDR5 [62]). We exploit this to reduce the number of supported encodings. Second, we place all the metadata containing the compression encoding at the *head* of the cache line to be able to determine how to decompress the entire line *upfront*. In the case of C-Pack, we place the dictionary entries after the metadata.

We note that it can be challenging to implement complex algorithms efficiently with the simple computational logic available in GPU cores. Fortunately, SFUs [63, 64] are already in the GPU SMs, used to perform efficient computations of elementary mathematical functions. SFUs could potentially be extended to implement primitives that enable the fast iterative comparisons performed frequently in some compression algorithms. This would enable more efficient execution of the described algorithms, as well as implementation of more complex compression algorithms, using CABA. We leave the exploration of an SFU-based approach to future work.

We now present a detailed overview of mapping the FPC and C-Pack algorithms into assist warps.

5.1.4 Implementing the FPC algorithm

For FPC, the cache line is treated as a set of fixed-size words, and each word within the cache line is compressed into a simple prefix or encoding and a compressed word if it matches a set of frequent patterns, for example, narrow values, zeros, or repeated bytes. The word is left uncompressed if it does not fit any pattern. We refer the reader to the original work [59] for a more detailed description of the original algorithm.

The challenge in mapping assist warps to the FPC decompression algorithm is in the serial sequence in which each word within a cache line is decompressed. This is because, in the original proposed version, each compressed word can have a different size. To determine the location of a specific compressed word, it is necessary to have decompressed the previous word. We make some modifications to the algorithm in order to parallelize the decompression across different lanes in the GPU cores. First, we move the word prefixes (metadata) for each word to the front of the cache line, so we know *upfront* how to decompress the rest of the cache line. Unlike with BDI, each word within the cache line has a different encoding and hence a different compressed word length and encoding pattern. This is problematic because statically storing the sequence of decompression instructions for every combination of patterns for all the words in a cache line would require very large instruction storage. In order to mitigate this issue, we break each cache line into a number of segments. Each segment is compressed independently, and all the words within each segment are compressed using the *same encoding*, whereas different segments may have different encodings. This creates a trade-off between simplicity/parallelizability versus compressibility. Consistent with previous works [59], we find that this does not significantly impact compressibility.

Decompression
The high-level algorithm we use for decompression is presented in Algorithm 3. Each segment within the compressed cache line is loaded in series. Each of the segments is decompressed in parallel—this is possible because all the compressed words within the segment have the same encoding. The decompressed segment is then stored before moving on to the next segment. The location of the next compressed segment is computed based on the size of the previous segment.

ALGORITHM 3 FPC: DECOMPRESSION

1: **for** *each segment* **do**
2:     load *compressed words*
3:     *pattern specific decompression (sign extension/zero value)*
4:     store *decompressed words*
5:     *segment-base-address = segment-base-address + segment-size*
6: **end for**

Compression
Similar to the BDI implementation, we loop through and test different encodings for each segment. We also compute the address offset for each segment at each iteration to store the compressed words in the appropriate location in the compressed cache line. Algorithm 4 presents the high-level FPC compression algorithm we use.

Implementing the C-Pack algorithm
C-Pack [17] is a dictionary-based compression algorithm where frequent "dictionary" values are saved at the beginning of the cache line. The rest of the cache line contains encodings for each word that may indicate zero values, narrow values, full or partial matches into the dictionary or simply that the word is uncompressible.

ALGORITHM 4 FPC: COMPRESSION

```
 1: load words
 2: for each segment do
 3:     for each encoding do
 4:         test encoding
 5:         if compressible then
 6:             segment-base-address = segment-base-address + segment-size
 7:             store compressed words
 8:             break
 9:         end if
10:     end for
11: end for
```

In our implementation, we reduce the number of possible encodings to partial matches (only last byte mismatch), full word match, zero value, and zero extend (only last byte), and we limit the number of dictionary values to 4. This enables fixed compressed word size within the cache line. A fixed compressed word size enables compression and decompression of different words within the cache line in parallel. If the number of required dictionary values or uncompressed words exceeds 4, the line is left decompressed. This is, as in BDI and FPC, a trade-off between simplicity and compressibility. In our experiments, we find that it does not significantly impact the compression ratio—primarily because of the 32B minimum data size and granularity of compression.

Decompression

As described, to enable parallel decompression, we place the encodings and dictionary values at the head of the line. We also limit the number of encodings to enable quick decompression. We implement C-Pack decompression as a series of instructions (one per encoding used) to load all the registers with the appropriate dictionary values. We define the active lane mask based on the encoding (similar to the mechanism used in BDI) for each load instruction to ensure the correct word is loaded into each lane's register. Algorithm 5 provides the high-level algorithm for C-Pack decompression.

ALGORITHM 5 C-PACK: DECOMPRESSION

```
 1: add base-address + index-into-dictionary
 2: load compressed words
 3: for each encoding do
 4:     pattern specific decompression      ▷ Mismatch byte load for zero extend or partial match
 5: end for
 6: Store uncompressed words
```

Compression

Compressing data with C-Pack involves determining the dictionary values that will be used to compress the rest of the line. In our implementation, we serially add each word from the beginning of the cache line to be a dictionary value if it was not already covered by a previous dictionary value. For each dictionary value, we test whether the rest of the words within the cache line are compressible. The next dictionary value is determined using the predicate register to determine the next uncompressed word, as in BDI. After four iterations (dictionary values), if all the words within the line are not compressible, the cache line is left uncompressed. Similar to BDI, the global predicate register is used to determine the compressibility of all of the lanes after four or fewer iterations. Algorithm 6 provides the high-level algorithm for C-Pack compression.

ALGORITHM 6 C-PACK: COMPRESSION

1: load *words*
2: **for** each dictionary value (including zero) **do**   ▷ To a maximum of four
3:     *test match/partial match*
4:     **if** *compressible* **then**
5:         Store *encoding and mismatching byte*
6:         **break**
7:     **end if**
8: **end for**
9: **if** *all lanes are compressible* **then**
10:     Store *compressed cache line*
11: **end if**

5.2 WALKTHROUGH OF CABA-BASED COMPRESSION

We show the detailed operation of CABA-based compression and decompression mechanisms in Fig. 7. We assume a baseline GPU architecture with three levels in the memory hierarchy—two levels of caches (private L1s and a shared L2) and main memory. Different levels can potentially store compressed data. In this section and in our evaluations, we assume that only the L2 cache and main memory contain compressed data. Note that there is no capacity benefit in the baseline mechanism because compressed cache lines still occupy the full uncompressed slot, that is, we only evaluate the bandwidth-saving benefits of compression in GPUs.

5.2.1 The decompression mechanism

Load instructions that access global memory data in the compressed form trigger the appropriate assist warp to decompress the data before it is used. The subroutines to decompress data are stored in the AWS. The AWS is indexed by the compression

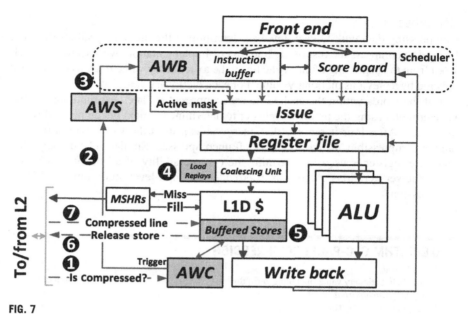

FIG. 7

Walkthrough of CABA-based compression.

Figure reproduced from Ref. [28].

encoding at the head of the cache line and by a bit indicating whether the instruction is a load (decompression is required) or a store (compression is required). Each decompression assist warp is given *high priority* and, hence, stalls the progress of its parent warp until it completes its execution. This ensures that the parent warp correctly gets the decompressed value.

L1 access
We store data in L1 in the uncompressed form. An L1 hit does not require an assist warp for decompression.

L2/memory access
Global memory data cached in L2/DRAM could potentially be compressed. A bit indicating whether the cache line is compressed is returned to the core along with the cache line (**❶**). If the data are uncompressed, the line is inserted into the L1 cache and the writeback phase resumes normally. If the data are compressed, the compressed cache line is inserted into the L1 cache. The encoding of the compressed cache line and the warp ID are relayed to the AWC, which then triggers the AWS (**❷**) to deploy the appropriate assist warp (**❸**) to decompress the line. During regular execution, the load information for each thread is buffered in the coalescing/load-store unit [60,61]

until all the data are fetched. We continue to buffer this load information (❹) until the line is decompressed.

After the CABA decompression subroutine ends execution, the original load that triggered decompression is resumed (❹).

5.2.2 The compression mechanism

The assist warps to perform compression are triggered by store instructions. When data are written to a cache line (i.e., by a store), the cache line can be written back to main memory either in the compressed or uncompressed form. Compression is off the critical path, and the warps to perform compression can be scheduled when the required resources are available.

Pending stores are buffered in a few dedicated sets within the L1 cache or in available shared memory (❺). In the case of an overflow in this buffer space (❺), the stores are released to the lower levels of the memory system in the uncompressed form (❻). Upon detecting the availability of resources to perform the data compression, the AWC triggers the deployment of the assist warp that performs compression (❷) into the AWB (❸), with *low priority*. The scheduler is then free to schedule the instructions from the compression subroutine. Since compression is not on the critical path of execution, keeping such instructions as low priority ensures that the main program is not unnecessarily delayed.

L1 access

On a hit in the L1 cache, the cache line is already available in the uncompressed form. Depending on the availability of resources, the cache line can be scheduled for compression or simply written to the L2 and main memory uncompressed, when evicted.

L2/memory access

Data in memory is compressed at the granularity of a full cache line, but stores can be at granularities smaller than the size of the cache line. This poses some additional difficulty if the destination cache line for a store is already compressed in main memory. Partial writes into a compressed cache line would require the cache line to be decompressed first then updated with the new data and written back to main memory. The common case—where the cache line that is being written to is uncompressed initially—can be easily handled. However, in the worst case, the cache line being partially written to is already in the compressed form in memory. We now describe the mechanism to handle both these cases.

Initially, to reduce the store latency, we assume that the cache line is uncompressed and issue a store to the lower levels of the memory hierarchy, while buffering a copy in L1. If the cache line is found in L2/memory in the uncompressed form (❶), the assumption was correct. The store then proceeds normally, and the buffered stores are evicted from L1. If the assumption is incorrect, the cache line is retrieved (❼) and decompressed before the store is retransmitted to the lower levels of the memory hierarchy.

5.3 REALIZING DATA COMPRESSION

Supporting data compression requires additional support from the main MC and the runtime system, as we describe here.

5.3.1 Initial setup and profiling

Data compression with CABA requires a one-time data setup before the data are transferred to the GPU. We assume initial software-based data preparation where the input data are stored in CPU memory in the compressed form with an appropriate compression algorithm before transferring the data to GPU memory. Transferring data in the compressed form can also reduce PCIe bandwidth usage.[2]

Memory-bandwidth-limited GPU applications are the best candidates for employing data compression using CABA. The compiler (or the runtime profiler) is required to identify those applications that are most likely to benefit from this framework. For applications where memory bandwidth is not a bottleneck, data compression is simply disabled.

5.3.2 Memory controller changes

Data compression reduces off-chip bandwidth requirements by transferring the same data in fewer DRAM bursts. The MC needs to know whether the cache line data are compressed and how many bursts (1–4 bursts in GDDR5 [62]) are needed to transfer the data from DRAM to the MC. Similar to prior work [55,65], we require metadata information for every cache line that keeps track of how many bursts are needed to transfer the data. Similar to prior work [65], we simply reserve 8 MB of GPU DRAM space for the metadata (~0.2% of all available memory). Unfortunately, this simple design would require an additional access for the metadata for every access to DRAM effectively doubling the required bandwidth. To avoid this, a simple *metadata (MD) cache* that keeps frequently accessed metadata on chip (near the MC) is required. Note that this metadata cache is similar to other metadata storage and caches proposed for various purposes in the MC, for example, [55,66–70]. Our experiments show that a small 8 KB four-way associative MD cache is sufficient to provide a hit rate of 85% on average (more than 99% for many applications) across all applications in our workload pool.[3] Hence, in the common case, a second access to DRAM to fetch compression-related metadata can be avoided.

---

[2]This requires changes to the DMA engine to recognize compressed lines.

[3]For applications where MD cache miss rate is low, we observe that MD cache misses are usually also TLB misses. Hence most of the overhead of MD cache misses in these applications is outweighed by the cost of page table lookups.

6 METHODOLOGY

We model the CABA framework in GPGPU-Sim 3.2.1 [71]. Table 1 provides the major parameters of the simulated system. We use GPUWattch [72] to model GPU power and CACTI [73] to evaluate the power/energy overhead associated with the MD cache (see Section 5.3.2) and the additional components (AWS and AWC) of the CABA framework. We implement BDI [15] using the Synopses Design Compiler with 65 nm library (to evaluate the energy overhead of compression/decompression for the dedicated hardware design for comparison to CABA), and then we use ITRS projections [74] to scale our results to the 32 nm technology node.

Evaluated applications

We use a number of CUDA applications derived from CUDA SDK (*BFS, CONS, JPEG, LPS, MUM, RAY, SLA, TRA*) [23], Rodinia (*hs, nw*) [25], Mars (*KM, MM, PVC, PVR, SS*) [22], and lonestar (*bfs, bh, mst, sp, sssp*) [24] suites. We run all applications to completion or for 1 billion instructions (whichever comes first). CABA-based data compression is beneficial mainly for memory-bandwidth-limited applications. In computation-resource-limited applications, data compression is not only unrewarding, but it can also cause significant performance degradation due to the computational overhead associated with assist warps. We rely on static profiling to identify memory-bandwidth-limited applications and disable CABA-based compression for the others. In our evaluation (see Section 7), we demonstrate detailed results for applications that exhibit some compressibility in memory bandwidth (at least 10%). Applications without compressible data (e.g., sc, SCP) do not gain any performance from the CABA framework, and we verified that these applications do not incur any performance degradation (because the assist warps are *not* triggered for them).

Evaluated metrics

We present instructions per cycle (*IPC*) as the primary performance metric. We also use *average bandwidth utilization*, defined as the fraction of total DRAM cycles that

Table 1 Major Parameters of the Simulated Systems

System overview	15 SMs, 32 threads/warp, 6 memory channels
Shader core config.	1.4 GHz, GTO scheduler [75], 2 schedulers/SM
Resources/SM	48 warps/SM, 32,768 registers, 32 KB shared memory
L1 cache	16 KB, 4-way associative, LRU replacement policy
L2 cache	768 KB, 16-way associative, LRU replacement policy
Interconnect	1 crossbar/direction (15 SMs, 6 MCs), 1.4 GHz
Memory model	177.4 GB/s BW, 6 GDDR5 MCs, FR-FCFS scheduling, 16 banks/MC
GDDR5 timing [62]	$t_{CL} = 12$, $t_{RP} = 12$, $t_{RC} = 40$, $t_{RAS} = 28$, $t_{RCD} = 12$, $t_{RRD} = 6$, $t_{CLDR} = 5$, $t_{WR} = 12$

the DRAM data bus is busy, and *compression ratio*, defined as the ratio of the number of DRAM bursts required to transfer data in the compressed versus the uncompressed form. As reported in prior work [15], we use decompression/compression latencies of 1/5 cycles for the hardware implementation of BDI.

7 RESULTS

To evaluate the effectiveness of using CABA to employ data compression, we compare five different designs: (1) *Base*—the baseline system with no compression, (2) *HW-BDI-Mem*—hardware-based *memory bandwidth compression* with dedicated logic (data are stored compressed in main memory but uncompressed in the last-level cache, similar to prior works [55,65]), (3) *HW-BDI*—hardware-based *interconnect and memory bandwidth compression* (data are stored uncompressed only in the L1 cache), (4) *CABA-BDI*—CABA framework (see Section 4) with all associated overhead of performing compression (for both interconnect and memory bandwidth), and (5) *Ideal-BDI*—compression (for both interconnect and memory) with no latency/power overhead for compression or decompression. This section provides our major results and analyses.

7.1 EFFECT ON PERFORMANCE AND BANDWIDTH UTILIZATION

Figs. 8 and 9 show, respectively, the normalized performance (vs *Base*) and the memory bandwidth utilization of the five designs. We make three major observations.

First, all compressed designs are effective in providing high performance improvement over the baseline. Our approach (CABA-BDI) provides a 41.7% average improvement, which is only 2.8% less than the ideal case (Ideal-BDI) with none of the overhead associated with CABA. CABA-BDI's performance is 9.9% better than the previous [65] hardware-based memory bandwidth compression design (HW-BDI-Mem), and *only* 1.6% worse than the purely hardware-based design (HW-BDI) that

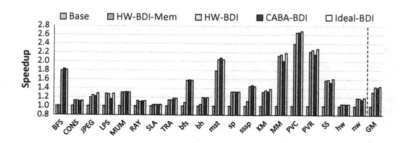

FIG. 8

Normalized performance.

Figure reproduced from Ref. [28].

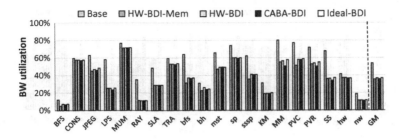

FIG. 9

Memory bandwidth utilization.

performs both interconnect and memory bandwidth compression. We conclude that our framework is effective at enabling the benefits of compression without requiring specialized hardware compression and decompression logic.

Second, performance benefits, in many workloads, correlate with the reduction in memory bandwidth utilization. For a fixed amount of data, compression reduces the bandwidth utilization, and thus increases the effective available bandwidth. Fig. 9 shows that CABA-based compression (1) reduces the average memory bandwidth utilization from 53.6% to 35.6% and (2) is effective at alleviating the memory bandwidth bottleneck in most workloads. In some applications (e.g., *bfs* and *mst*), designs that compress *both* the on-chip interconnect and the memory bandwidth, that is, CABA-BDI and HW-BDI, perform better than the design that compresses only the memory bandwidth (HW-BDI-Mem). Hence CABA seamlessly enables the mitigation of the interconnect bandwidth bottleneck as well, since data compression/decompression is flexibly performed at the cores.

Third, for some applications, CABA-BDI performs slightly (within 3%) better than Ideal-BDI and HW-BDI. The reason for this counter intuitive result is the effect of warp oversubscription [75–78]. In these cases, too many warps execute in parallel, polluting the last level cache. CABA-BDI sometimes reduces pollution as a side effect of performing more computation in assist warps, which slows down the progress of the parent warps.

We conclude that the CABA framework can effectively enable data compression to reduce both on-chip interconnect and off-chip memory-bandwidth utilization, thereby improving the performance of modern GPGPU applications.

7.2 EFFECT ON ENERGY

Compression decreases energy consumption in two ways: (1) by reducing bus energy consumption, (2) by reducing execution time. Fig. 10 shows the normalized energy consumption of the five systems. We model the static and dynamic energy of the cores, caches, DRAM, and all buses (both on-chip and off-chip), as well as the energy

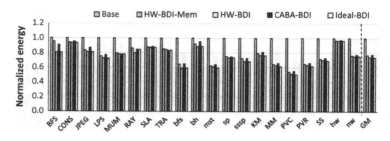

FIG. 10

Normalized energy consumption.

Figure reproduced from Ref. [28].

overhead related to compression: metadata (MD) cache and compression/decompression logic. We make two major observations.

First, CABA-BDI reduces energy consumption by as much as 22.2% over the baseline. This is especially noticeable for memory-bandwidth-limited applications, for example, *PVC*, *mst*. This is a result of two factors: (1) the reduction in the amount of data transferred between the LLC and DRAM (as a result of which we observe a 29.5% average reduction in DRAM power) and (2) the reduction in total execution time. This observation agrees with several prior works on bandwidth compression [55,56]. We conclude that the CABA framework is capable of reducing the overall system energy, primarily by decreasing the off-chip memory traffic.

Second, CABA-BDI's energy consumption is only 3.6% more than that of the HW-BDI design, which uses dedicated logic for memory-bandwidth compression. It is also only 4.0% more than that of the Ideal-BDI design, which has no compression-related overhead. CABA-BDI consumes more energy because it schedules and executes assist warps, utilizing on-chip register files, memory and computation units, which is less energy-efficient than using dedicated logic for compression. However, as results indicate, this additional energy cost is small compared to the performance gains of CABA (recall, 41.7% over Base), and may be amortized by using CABA for other purposes as well (see Section 8).

Power consumption

CABA-BDI increases the system power consumption by 2.9% over the baseline (not graphed), mainly due to the additional hardware and higher utilization of the compute pipelines. However, the power overhead enables energy savings by reducing bandwidth use and can be amortized across other uses of CABA (see Section 8).

Energy-delay product

Fig. 11 shows the product of the normalized energy consumption and normalized execution time for the evaluated GPU workloads. This metric simultaneously

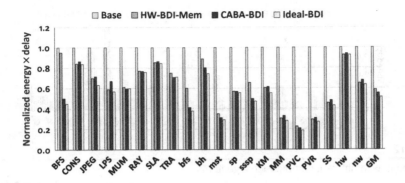

FIG. 11

Energy-Delay product.

captures two metrics of interest—energy dissipation and execution delay (inverse of performance). An optimal feature would simultaneously incur low energy overhead while also reducing the execution delay. This metric is useful in capturing the efficiencies of different architectural designs and features which may expend differing amounts of energy while producing the same performance speedup or vice-versa. Hence a lower Energy-Delay product is more desirable. We observe that CABA-BDI has a 45% lower Energy-Delay product than the baseline. This reduction comes from energy savings from reduced data transfers as well as lower execution time. On average, CABA-BDI is within only 4% of Ideal-BDI, which incurs none of the energy and performance overhead of the CABA framework.

7.3 EFFECT OF ENABLING DIFFERENT COMPRESSION ALGORITHMS

The CABA framework is *not limited to a single compression algorithm* and can be effectively used to employ other hardware-based compression algorithms (e.g., FPC [16] and C-Pack [17]). The effectiveness of other algorithms depends on two key factors: (1) how efficiently the algorithm maps to GPU instructions and (2) how compressible the data are with the algorithm. We map the FPC and C-Pack algorithms to the CABA framework and evaluate the framework's efficacy.

Fig. 12 shows the normalized speedup with four versions of our design: *CABA-FPC*, *CABA-BDI*, *CABA-C-Pack*, and *CABA-BestOfAll* with the FPC, BDI, and C-Pack compression algorithms. CABA-BestOfAll is an idealized design that selects and uses the best of all three algorithms in terms of compression ratio for *each cache line*, assuming no selection overhead. We make three major observations.

First, CABA significantly improves performance with any compression algorithm (20.7% with FPC, 35.2% with C-Pack). Similar to CABA-BDI, the applications that benefit the most are those that are both memory-bandwidth-sensitive (Fig. 9) and

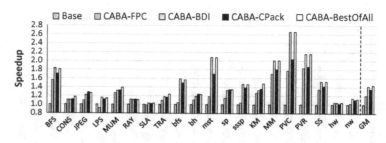

FIG. 12

Speedup with different compression algorithms.

Figure reproduced from Ref. [28].

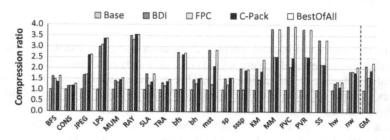

FIG. 13

Compression ratio of algorithms with CABA.

Figure reproduced from Ref. [28].

compressible (Fig. 13). We conclude that our proposed framework, CABA, is general and flexible enough to successfully enable different compression algorithms.

Second, applications benefit differently from each algorithm. For example, *LPS*, *JPEG*, *MUM*, and *nw* have higher compression ratios with FPC or C-Pack; whereas *MM*, *PVC*, and *PVR* compress better with BDI. This indicates the necessity of having *flexible data compression* with different algorithms within the same system. Implementing multiple compression algorithms completely in hardware is expensive as it adds significant area overhead, whereas CABA can flexibly enable the use of different algorithms via its general assist warp framework.

Third, the design with the best of three compression algorithms, CABA-BestOfAll, can sometimes improve performance more than each individual design with just one compression algorithm (e.g., for *MUM* and *KM*). This happens because, even within an application, different cache lines compress better with different algorithms. At the same time, different compression-related overhead of different algorithms can cause one to have higher performance than another even though the latter may have a higher compression ratio. For example, CABA-BDI provides higher performance on *LPS* than CABA-FPC, even though BDI has a lower compression ratio than FPC for *LPS*, because BDI's compression/decompression latencies are much lower than FPC's. Hence a mechanism that selects the best compression algorithm based on *both* compression ratio and the relative cost of compression/decompression is desirable to get the best multiple compression algorithm. The CABA framework can flexibly enable the implementation of such a mechanism, whose design we leave for future work.

7.4 SENSITIVITY TO PEAK MAIN MEMORY BANDWIDTH

As described in Section 3, main memory (off-chip) bandwidth is a major bottleneck in GPU applications. In order to confirm that CABA works for different designs with varying amounts of available memory bandwidth, we conduct an experiment where CABA-BDI is used in three systems with $0.5\times$, $1\times$, and $2\times$ amount of bandwidth of the baseline.

Fig. 14 shows the results of this experiment. We observe that, as expected, each CABA design (**-CABA*) significantly outperforms the corresponding baseline designs with the same amount of bandwidth. The performance improvement of CABA is often equivalent to the doubling the off-chip memory bandwidth. We conclude that CABA-based bandwidth compression, on average, offers almost all the performance benefit of doubling the available off-chip bandwidth with only modest complexity to support assist warps.

7.5 SELECTIVE CACHE COMPRESSION WITH CABA

In addition to reducing bandwidth consumption, data compression can also increase the *effective capacity* of on-chip caches. While compressed caches can be beneficial—as higher effective cache capacity leads to lower miss rates—supporting cache compression requires several changes in the cache design [15–17,46,50].

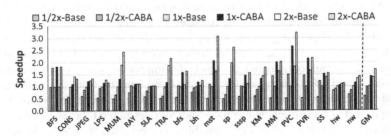

FIG. 14

Sensitivity of CABA to memory bandwidth.

Figure reproduced from Ref. [28].

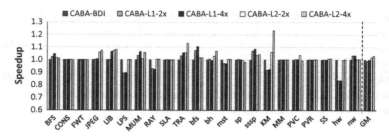

FIG. 15

Speedup of cache compression with CABA.

Fig. 15 shows the effect of four cache compression designs using CABA-BDI (applied to both L1 and L2 caches with $2\times$ or $4\times$ the number of tags of the baseline[4]) on performance. We make two major observations. First, several applications from our workload pool are not only bandwidth sensitive but also cache capacity sensitive. For example, *bfs* and *sssp* significantly benefit from L1 cache compression, while *TRA* and *KM* benefit from L2 compression. Second, L1 cache compression can severely degrade the performance of some applications, for example, *hw* and *LPS*. The reason for this is the overhead of decompression, which can be especially high for L1 caches as they are accessed very frequently. This overhead can be easily avoided by disabling compression at any level of the memory hierarchy.

7.6 OTHER OPTIMIZATIONS

We also consider several other optimizations of the CABA framework for data compression: (1) avoiding the overhead of decompression in L2 by storing data in the uncompressed form and (2) optimized load of *only useful* data.

Uncompressed L2

The CABA framework allows us to store compressed data selectively at different levels of the memory hierarchy. We consider an optimization where we avoid the overhead of decompressing data in L2 by storing data in uncompressed form. This provides another trade-off between the savings in on-chip traffic (when data in L2 is compressed—default option) and savings in decompression latency (when data in L2 is uncompressed). Fig. 16 depicts the performance benefits from this optimization. Several applications in our workload pool (e.g., *RAY*) benefit from storing data uncompressed as these applications have high hit rates in the L2 cache. We conclude that offering the choice of enabling or disabling compression at different levels of the

---

[4]The number of tags limits the effective compressed cache size [15,16].

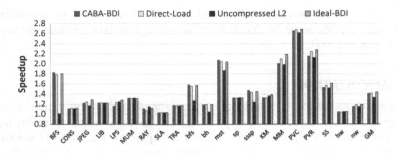

FIG. 16

Effect of different optimizations (uncompressed data in L2 and direct load) on applications' performance.

memory hierarchy can provide higher levels of the software stack (e.g., applications, compilers, runtime system, system software) with an additional performance knob.

Uncoalesced requests

Accesses by scalar threads from the same warp are coalesced into fewer memory transactions [79]. If the requests from different threads within a warp span two or more cache lines, multiple lines have to be retrieved and decompressed before the warp can proceed its execution. Uncoalesced requests can significantly increase the number of assist warps that need to be executed. An alternative to decompressing each cache line (when only a few bytes from each line may be required) is to enhance the coalescing unit to supply only the correct *deltas* from within each compressed cache line. The logic that maps bytes within a cache line to the appropriate registers will need to be enhanced to take into account the encoding of the compressed line to determine the size of the *base* and the *deltas*. As a result, we do not decompress the entire cache lines and extract only the data that is needed. In this case, the cache line is not inserted into the L1D cache in the uncompressed form, and hence every line needs to be decompressed even if it is found in the L1D cache.[5] *Direct-load* in Fig. 16 depicts the performance impact from this optimization. The overall performance improvement is 2.5% on average across all applications (as high as 4.6% for *MM*).

8 OTHER USES OF THE CABA FRAMEWORK

The CABA framework can be employed in various ways to alleviate system bottlenecks and increase system performance and energy efficiency. In this section,

---

[5]This optimization also benefits cache lines that might *not* have many uncoalesced accesses, but have poor data reuse in the L1D.

we discuss two other potential applications of CABA, focusing on two: *memoization* and *prefetching*. We leave the detailed evaluations and analysis of these use cases of CABA to future work.

8.1 MEMOIZATION

Hardware memoization is a technique used to avoid redundant computations by reusing the results of previous computations that have the same or similar inputs. Prior work [19,80,81] observed redundancy in inputs to data in GPU workloads. In applications limited by available compute resources, memoization offers an opportunity to trade-off computation for storage, thereby enabling potentially higher energy efficiency and performance. In order to realize memoization in hardware, a look-up table (LUT) is required to dynamically cache the results of computations as well as the corresponding inputs. The granularity of computational reuse can be at the level of fragments [19], basic blocks or functions [18,20,82–84], or long-latency instructions [85]. The CABA framework provides a natural way to implement such an optimization. The availability of on-chip memory lends itself to use as the LUT. In order to cache previous results in on-chip memory, look-up tags (similar to those proposed in Ref. [34]) are required to index correct results. With applications tolerant of approximate results (e.g., image processing, machine learning, fragment rendering kernels), the computational inputs can be hashed to reduce the size of the LUT. Register values, texture/constant memory or global memory sections that are not subject to change are potential inputs. An assist warp can be employed to perform memoization in the following ways: (1) compute the hashed value for a look-up at predefined trigger points, (2) use the load/store pipeline to save these inputs in available shared memory, and (3) eliminate redundant computations by loading the previously computed results in the case of a hit in the LUT.

8.2 PREFETCHING

Prefetching has been explored in the context of GPUs [3,4,36,86–89] with the goal of reducing effective memory latency. With memory-latency-bound applications, the load/store pipelines can be employed by the CABA framework to perform opportunistic prefetching into GPU caches. The CABA framework can potentially enable the effective use of prefetching in GPUs for several reasons. First, even simple prefetchers such as the stream [42,43,90] or stride [44,45] prefetchers are nontrivial to implement in GPUs since access patterns need to be tracked and trained at the fine granularity of warps [87,89]. CABA could enable fine-grained book keeping by using spare registers and assist warps to save metadata for each warp. The computational units could then be used to continuously compute strides in access patterns both within and across warps. Second, it has been demonstrated that software prefetching and helper threads [13,36,91,92,92–97] are very effective in performing prefetching for irregular access patterns. Assist warps offer the hardware/software interface to implement application-specific prefetching algorithms with varying degrees of complexity without the additional overhead of various hardware implementations. Third, in bandwidth-constrained GPU systems, uncontrolled prefetching could potentially flood the off-chip buses, delaying demand requests. CABA can enable flexible prefetch throttling (e.g., [90,98,99]) by scheduling assist warps that perform prefetching, *only* when the memory pipelines are idle or underutilized. Fourth, prefetching with CABA entails using load or prefetch instructions, which not only enables prefetching to the hardware-managed caches, but also could simplify the usage of unutilized shared memory or register files as prefetch buffers.

8.3 OTHER USES

Redundant multithreading

Reliability of GPUs is a key concern, especially today when they are popularly employed in many supercomputing systems. Ensuring hardware protection with dedicated resources can be expensive [100]. Redundant multithreading [101–104] is an approach where redundant threads are used to replicate program execution. The results are compared at different points in execution to detect and potentially correct errors. The CABA framework can be extended to redundantly execute portions of the original program via the use of such approaches to increase the reliability of GPU architectures.

Speculative precomputation

In CPUs, speculative multithreading [105–107] has been proposed to speculatively parallelize serial code and verify the correctness later. Assist warps can be employed in GPU architectures to speculatively preexecute sections of code during idle cycles to further improve parallelism in the program execution. Applications tolerant to approximate results could particularly be amenable to this optimization [108].

Handling interrupts and exceptions

Current GPUs do not implement support for interrupt handling except for some support for timer interrupts used for application time-slicing [26]. CABA offers a natural mechanism for associating architectural events with subroutines to be executed in throughput-oriented architectures where thousands of threads could be active at any given time. Interrupts and exceptions can be handled by special assist warps, without requiring complex context switching or heavy-weight kernel support.

Profiling and instrumentation

Profiling and binary instrumentation tools like Pin [109] and Valgrind [110] proved to be very useful for development, performance analysis, and debugging on modern CPU systems. At the same time, there is a lack[6] of tools with same/similar

---

[6] With the exception of one recent work [111].

capabilities for modern GPUs. This significantly limits software development and debugging for modern GPU systems. The CABA framework can potentially enable easy and efficient development of such tools, as it is flexible enough to invoke user-defined code on specific architectural events (e.g., cache misses, control divergence).

9 RELATED WORK

To our knowledge, this chapter is the first to (1) propose a flexible and general framework for employing idle GPU resources for useful computation that can aid regular program execution, and (2) use the general concept of *helper threading* to perform memory and interconnect bandwidth compression. We demonstrate the benefits of our new framework by using it to implement multiple compression algorithms on a throughput-oriented GPU architecture to alleviate the memory-bandwidth bottleneck. In this section, we discuss related works in helper threading, memory-bandwidth optimizations, and memory compression.

Helper threading

Previous works [6–9,11–13,91–97,112–116] demonstrated the use of *helper threads* in the context of simultaneous multithreading (SMT) and multicore and single-core processors, primarily to speed up single-thread execution by using idle SMT contexts, idle cores in CPUs, or idle cycles during which the main program is stalled on a single thread context. These works typically use helper threads (generated by the software, the hardware, or cooperatively) to precompute useful information that aids the execution of the primary thread (e.g., by prefetching, branch outcome precomputation, cache management). No previous work discussed the use of helper threads for memory/interconnect bandwidth compression or cache compression.

These works primarily use helper threads to capture data flow and precompute useful information to aid in the execution of the primary thread. In these prior works, helper threads are either generated with the help of the compiler [113–115] or completely in hardware [9,96,97]. These threads are used to perform prefetching in Refs. [6,13,91,92,92–97,117] which the helper threads predict future load addresses by doing some computation and then prefetch the corresponding data. Simultaneous subordinate multithreading [6] employs hardware generated helper threads to improve branch prediction accuracy and cache management. Speculative multi-threading [105–107,118] involves executing different sections of the serial program in parallel and then later verifying the runtime correctness. Assisted execution [8,12] is an execution paradigm where tightly coupled *nanothreads* are generated using *nanotrap handlers* and execute routines to enable optimizations like prefetching. In slipstream processors [92], one thread runs ahead of the program and executes a reduced version of the program. In runahead execution [96,97], the main thread is executed speculatively solely for prefetching purposes when the program is stalled because of a cache miss.

While our work was inspired by these prior studies of helper threading in latency-oriented architectures (CPUs), developing a framework for helper threading (or *assist warps*) in throughput-oriented architectures (GPUs) enables new opportunities and poses new challenges, both being due to the massive parallelism and resources present in a throughput-oriented architecture (as discussed in Section 1). Our CABA framework exploits these new opportunities and addresses these new challenges, including (1) low-cost management of a large number of assist warps that could be running concurrently with regular program warps, (2) means of state/context management and scheduling for assist warps to maximize effectiveness and minimize interference, and (3) different possible applications of the concept of assist warps in a throughput-oriented architecture.

In the GPU domain, CudaDMA [119] is a recent proposal that aims to ease programmability by decoupling execution and memory transfers with specialized DMA warps. This work does *not* provide a general and flexible hardware-based framework for using GPU cores to run warps that aid the main program.

Memory latency and bandwidth optimizations in GPUs

Many prior works focus on optimizing for memory bandwidth and memory latency in GPUs. Jog et al. [3] aim to improve memory latency tolerance by coordinating prefetching and warp scheduling policies. Lakshminarayana et al. [36] reduce effective latency in graph applications by using spare registers to store prefetched data. In OWL [4,76], intelligent scheduling is used to improve DRAM bank-level parallelism and bandwidth utilization, and Rhu et al. [120] propose a locality-aware memory to improve memory throughput. Kayiran et al. [76] propose GPU throttling techniques to reduce memory contention in heterogeneous systems. Ausavarangniran et al. [78] leverage heterogeneity in warp behavior to design more intelligent policies at the cache and MC. These works do not consider data compression and are orthogonal to our proposed framework.

Compression

Several prior works [47,50,53,55–58,65,121] study memory and cache compression with several different compression algorithms [15–17,40,47,49], in the context of CPUs or GPUs.

Alameldeen et al. [121] investigated the possibility of bandwidth compression with FPC [59]. The authors show that significant decrease in pin bandwidth demand can be achieved with FPC-based bandwidth compression design. Sathish et al. [65] examine the GPU-oriented memory link compression using C-Pack [17] compression algorithm. The authors make the observation that GPU memory (GDDR3 [122]) indeed allows transfer of data in small bursts and propose to store data in compressed form in memory, but without capacity benefits. Thuresson et al. [53] consider a CPU-oriented design where a compressor/decompressor logic is located on the both ends of the main memory link. Pekhimenko et al. [55] propose linearly compressed pages (LCP) with the primary goal of compressing main memory to increase capacity.

Our work is the first to demonstrate how one can adapt some of these algorithms for use in a general helper threading framework for GPUs. As such, compression/decompression using our new framework is more flexible since it does not require a specialized hardware implementation for any algorithm and instead utilizes the existing GPU core resources to perform compression and decompression. Finally, as discussed in Section 8, our CABA framework is applicable beyond compression and can be used for other purposes.

10 CONCLUSION

This chapter makes a case for the CABA framework, which employs *assist warps* to alleviate different bottlenecks in GPU execution. CABA is based on the key observation that various imbalances and bottlenecks in GPU execution leave on-chip resources (i.e., computational units, register files) and on-chip memory (underutilized). CABA takes advantage of these idle resources and employs them to perform useful work that can aid the execution of the main program and the system.

We provide a detailed design and analysis of how CABA can be used to perform flexible data compression in GPUs to mitigate the memory bandwidth bottleneck. Our extensive evaluations across a variety of workloads and system configurations show that the use of CABA for memory compression significantly improves system performance (by 41.7% on average on a set of bandwidth-sensitive GPU applications) by reducing the memory-bandwidth requirements of both the on-chip and the off-chip buses.

We conclude that CABA is a general substrate that can alleviate the memory-bandwidth bottleneck in modern GPU systems by enabling flexible implementations of data compression algorithms. We believe CABA is a general framework that can have a wide set of use cases to mitigate many different system bottlenecks in throughput-oriented architectures, and we hope that future work explores both new uses of CABA and more efficient implementations of it.

ACKNOWLEDGMENTS

We thank the reviewers for their valuable suggestions. We thank the members of the SAFARI group for their feedback and the stimulating research environment they provide. Special thanks to Evgeny Bolotin and Kevin Hsieh for their feedback during various stages of this project. We acknowledge the support of our industrial partners: Facebook, Google, IBM, Intel, Microsoft, Nvidia, Qualcomm, VMware, and Samsung. This research was partially supported by NSF (grants 0953246, 1065112, 1205618, 1212962, 1213052, 1302225, 1302557, 1317560, 1320478, 1320531, 1409095, 1409723, 1423172, 1439021, 1439057), the Intel Science and Technology Center for Cloud Computing, and the Semiconductor Research Corporation. Gennady Pekhimenko is supported in part by a Microsoft Research Fellowship and a Nvidia Graduate Fellowship. Rachata Ausavarungnirun is supported in part by the Royal Thai Government scholarship. This article is a revised and extended version of our previous ISCA 2015 paper [28].

REFERENCES

[1] S.W. Keckler, et al., GPUs and the future of parallel computing, in: IEEE Micro, 2011.

[2] V. Narasiman, et al., Improving GPU performance via large warps and two-level warp scheduling, in: MICRO, 2011.

[3] A. Jog, et al., Orchestrated scheduling and prefetching for GPGPUs, in: ISCA, 2013.

[4] A. Jog, et al., OWL: cooperative thread array aware scheduling techniques for improving GPGPU performance, in: ASPLOS, 2013.

[5] A. Sethia, et al., Equalizer: dynamic tuning of GPU resources for efficient execution, in: MICRO, 2014.

[6] R.S. Chappell, et al., Simultaneous subordinate microthreading (SSMT), in: ISCA, 1999.

[7] R.S. Chappell, et al., Microarchitectural support for precomputation microthreads, in: MICRO, 2002.

[8] M. Dubois, et al., Assisted execution, Tech. Rep., USC, 1998.

[9] J.D. Collins, et al., Dynamic speculative precomputation, in: MICRO, 2001.

[10] A. Roth, et al., Speculative data-driven multithreading, in: HPCA, 2001.

[11] C. Zilles, et al., Execution-based prediction using speculative slices, in: ISCA, 2001.

[12] M. Dubois, Fighting the memory wall with assisted execution, in: CF, 2004.

[13] J.D. Collins, et al., Speculative precomputation: long-range prefetching of delinquent loads, in: ISCA, 2001.

[14] A. Moshovos, et al., Slice-processors: an implementation of operation-based prediction, in: ICS, 2001.

[15] G. Pekhimenko, et al., Base-Delta-Immediate compression: practical data compression for on-chip caches, in: PACT, 2012.

[16] A. Alameldeen, et al., Adaptive cache compression for high-performance processors, in: ISCA, 2004.

[17] X. Chen, et al., C-Pack: a high-performance microprocessor cache compression algorithm, in: IEEE Trans. on VLSI Systems, 2010.

[18] A. Sodani, et al., Dynamic instruction reuse, in: ISCA, 1997.

[19] J. Arnau, et al., Eliminating redundant fragment shader executions on a mobile GPU via hardware memoization, in: ISCA, 2014.

[20] D.A. Connors, et al., Compiler-directed dynamic computation reuse: rationale and initial results, in: MICRO, 1999.

[21] E. Ebrahimi, et al., Techniques for bandwidth-efficient prefetching of linked data structures in hybrid prefetching systems, in: HPCA, 2009.

[22] B. He, et al., Mars: a MapReduce framework on graphics processors, in: PACT, 2008.

[23] NVIDIA, CUDA C/C++ SDK code samples, 2011, http://developer.nvidia.com/cuda-cc-sdk-code-samples.

[24] M. Burtscher, et al., A quantitative study of irregular programs on GPUs, in: IISWC, 2012.

[25] S. Che, et al., Rodinia: a benchmark suite for heterogeneous computing, in: IISWC, 2009.

[26] NVIDIA, Fermi: NVIDIA's next generation CUDA compute architecture, 2011.

[27] AMD, Radeon GPUs, http://www.amd.com/us/products/desktop/graphics/amd-radeon-hd-6000/Pages/amd-radeon-hd-6000.aspx.

[28] N. Vijaykumar, et al., A case for Core-Assisted Bottleneck Acceleration in GPUs: enabling flexible data compression with assist warps, in: ISCA, 2015.

[29] A. Bakhoda, G.L. Yuan, W.W.L. Fung, H. Wong, T.M. Aamodt, Analyzing CUDA workloads using a detailed GPU simulator, in: ISPASS, 2009.

[30] D.B. Kirk, W. Hwu, Programming massively parallel processors: a hands-on approach, Morgan Kaufmann, 2010.

[31] J.L. Hennessey, D.A. Patterson, Computer architecture, a quantitative approach, Morgan Kaufmann, 2010.

[32] B. Smith, A pipelined, shared resource MIMD computer, in: Advance Computer Architecture, 1986.

[33] J.E. Thornton, Parallel operation in the control data 6600, in: Proceedings of the AFIPS FJCC, 1964.

[34] M. Gebhart, et al., Unifying primary cache, scratch, and register file memories in a throughput processor, in: MICRO, 2012.

[35] M. Abdel-Majeed, et al., Warped register file: a power efficient register file for GPGPUs, in: HPCA, 2013.

[36] N. Lakshminarayana, et al., Spare register aware prefetching for graph algorithms on GPUs, in: HPCA, 2014.

[37] M. Gebhart, et al., Energy-efficient mechanisms for managing thread context in throughput processors, in: ISCA, 2011.

[38] M. Gebhart, et al., A compile-time managed multi-level register file hierarchy, in: MICRO, 2011.

[39] GPGPU-Sim v3.2.1, GPGPU-Sim Manual, http://gpgpu-sim.org/manual/index.php5/GPGPU-Sim_3.x_Manual.

[40] J. Yang, et al., Frequent value compression in data caches, in: MICRO, 2000.

[41] S. Srinath, et al., Feedback directed prefetching: improving the performance and bandwidth-efficiency of hardware prefetchers, in: HPCA, 2007.

[42] N. Jouppi, Improving direct-mapped cache performance by the addition of a small fully-associative cache and prefetch buffers, in: ISCA, 1990.

[43] S. Palacharla, et al., Evaluating stream buffers as a secondary cache replacement, in: ISCA, 1994.

[44] J. Baer, et al., Effective hardware-based data prefetching for high-performance processors, in: IEEE Trans. Comput., 1995.

[45] J.W.C. Fu, et al., Stride directed prefetching in scalar processors, in: MICRO, 1992.

[46] S. Sardashti, et al., Decoupled compressed cache: exploiting spatial locality for energy-optimized compressed caching, in: MICRO, 2013.

[47] A. Arelakis, et al., SC2: a statistical compression cache scheme, in: ISCA, 2014.

[48] J. Dusser, et al., Zero-content augmented caches, in: ICS, 2009.

[49] M. Islam, et al., Zero-value caches: cancelling loads that return zero, in: PACT, 2009.

[50] G. Pekhimenko, et al., Exploiting compressed block size as an indicator of future reuse, in: HPCA, 2015.

[51] R. Das, et al., Performance and power optimization through data compression in network-on-chip architectures, in: HPCA, 2008.

[52] B. Abali, et al., Memory expansion technology (MXT): software support and performance, in: IBM J.R.D., 2001.

[53] M. Thuresson, et al., Memory-link compression schemes: a value locality perspective, in: IEEE Trans. Comput., 2008.

[54] M. Ekman, et al., A robust main-memory compression scheme, in: ISCA-32, 2005.

[55] G. Pekhimenko, et al., Linearly compressed pages: a low complexity, low latency main memory compression framework, in: MICRO, 2013.

[56] A. Shafiee, et al., MemZip: exploring unconventional benefits from memory compression, in: HPCA, 2014.

[57] G. Pekhimenko, et al., Toggle-aware compression for GPUs, in: IEEE CAL, 2015.

[58] G. Pekhimenko, et al., A case for toggle-aware compression in GPUs, in: HPCA, 2016.

[59] A. Alameldeen, et al., Frequent pattern compression: a significance-based compression scheme for L2 caches, Tech. Rep., University of Wisconsin, 2004.

[60] B.S. Nordquist, et al., Apparatus, system, and method for coalescing parallel memory requests, 2009, US Patent 7,492,368.

[61] L. Nyland, et al., Systems and methods for coalescing memory accesses of parallel threads, 2011, US Patent 8,086,806.

[62] Hynix., Hynix GDDR5 SGRAM Part H5GQ1H24AFR Revision 1.0.

[63] E. Lindholm, et al., Nvidia Tesla: a unified graphics and computing architecture, in: IEEE Micro, 2008.

[64] D. De Caro, et al., High-performance special function unit for programmable 3-D graphics processors, Trans. Cir. Sys. Part I 56 (9) (2009) 1968–1978.

[65] V. Sathish, et al., Lossless and Lossy memory I/O link compression for improving performance of GPGPU workloads, in: PACT, 2012.

[66] V. Seshadri, et al., Page overlays: an enhanced virtual memory framework to enable fine-grained memory management, in: ISCA, 2015.

[67] J. Meza, et al., Enabling efficient and scalable hybrid memories, in: IEEE CAL, 2012.

[68] M. Qureshi, et al., Fundamental latency trade-off in architecting DRAM caches: outperforming impractical SRAM-tags with a simple and practical design, in: MICRO, 2012.

[69] M. Ghosh, et al., Smart refresh: an enhanced memory controller design for reducing energy in conventional and 3D die-stacked DRAMs, in: MICRO, 2007.

[70] J. Liu, et al., RAIDR: retention-aware intelligent DRAM refresh, in: ISCA, 2012.

[71] A. Bakhoda, et al., Analyzing CUDA workloads using a detailed GPU simulator, in: ISPASS, 2009.

[72] J. Leng, et al., GPUWattch: enabling energy optimizations in GPGPUs, in: ISCA, 2013.

[73] S. Thoziyoor, et al., CACTI 5.1, Tech. Rep. HPL-2008-20, HP Laboratories, 2008.

[74] ITRS, International Technology Roadmap for Semiconductors, 2011, http://www.itrs.net.

[75] T.G. Rogers, et al., Cache-conscious wavefront scheduling, in: MICRO, 2012.

[76] O. Kayiran, et al., Neither more nor less: optimizing thread-level parallelism for GPGPUs, in: PACT, 2013.

[77] O. Kayiran, et al., Managing GPU concurrency in heterogeneous architectures, in: MICRO, 2014.

[78] R. Ausavarangnirun, et al., Exploiting inter-warp heterogeneity to improve GPGPU performance, in: PACT, 2014.

[79] NVIDIA, Programming Guide, http://docs.nvidia.com/cuda/cuda-c-programming-guide/index.html#axzz3DAGrtrOq.

[80] C. Alvarez, et al., Fuzzy memoization for floating-point multimedia applications, IEEE Trans. Comput. 54 (7) (2005) 922–927.

[81] M. Samadi, et al., SAGE: self-tuning approximation for graphics engines, in: MICRO, 2013.

[82] C. Alvarez, et al., On the potential of tolerant region reuse for multimedia applications, in: ICS, 2001.

[83] J. Huang, et al., Exploiting basic block value locality with block reuse, in: HPCA, 1999.

[84] C. Alvarez, et al., Dynamic tolerance region computing for multimedia, IEEE Trans. Comput. 61 (5) (2012) 650–665.

[85] D. Citron, et al., Accelerating multi-media processing by implementing memoing in multiplication and division units, in: ASPLOS, 1998.

[86] J. Meng, et al., Dynamic warp subdivision for integrated branch and memory divergence tolerance, in: ISCA, 2010.

[87] J. Lee, et al., Many-thread aware prefetching mechanisms for GPGPU applications, in: MICRO, 2010.

[88] J. Arnau, et al., Boosting mobile GPU performance with a decoupled access/execute fragment processor, in: ISCA, 2012.

[89] A. Sethia, et al., APOGEE: adaptive prefetching on GPUs for energy efficiency, in: PACT, 2013.

[90] S. Srinath, et al., Feedback directed prefetching: improving the performance and bandwidth-efficiency of hardware prefetchers, in: HPCA, 2007.

[91] J.A. Brown, et al., Speculative precomputation on chip multiprocessors, in: MTEAC, 2001.

[92] K.Z. Ibrahim, et al., Slipstream execution mode for CMP-based multiprocessors, in: HPCA, 2003.

[93] C. Luk, Tolerating memory latency through software-controlled pre-execution in simultaneous multithreading processors, in: ISCA, 2001.

[94] K. Sundaramoorthy, et al., Slipstream processors: improving both performance and fault tolerance, in: ASPLOS, 2000.

[95] T.M. Aamodt, et al., Hardware support for prescient instruction prefetch, in: HPCA, 2004.

[96] O. Mutlu, et al., Techniques for efficient processing in runahead execution engines, in: ISCA, 2005.

[97] O. Mutlu, et al., Runahead execution: an alternative to very large instruction windows for out-of-order processors, in: HPCA, 2003.

[98] E. Ebrahimi, et al., Coordinated control of multiple prefetchers in multi-core systems, in: MICRO, 2009.

[99] E. Ebrahimi, et al., Prefetch-aware shared resource management for multi-core systems, in: ISCA, 2011.

[100] Y. Luo, et al., Characterizing application memory error vulnerability to optimize data center cost via heterogeneous-reliability memory, in: DSN, 2014.

[101] J. Wadden, et al., Real-world design and evaluation of compiler-managed GPU redundant multithreading, in: ISCA '14, 2014.

[102] S. Mukherjee, et al., Detailed design and evaluation of redundant multithreading alternatives, in: ISCA.

[103] M. Qureshi, et al., Microarchitecture-based introspection: a technique for transient-fault tolerance in microprocessors, in: DSN, 2005.

[104] C. Wang, et al., Compiler-managed software-based redundant multi-threading for transient fault detection, in: CGO, 2007.

[105] P. Marcuello, et al., Speculative multithreaded processors, in: ICS, 1998.

[106] C.G. Quinones, et al., Mitosis compiler: an infrastructure for speculative threading based on pre-computation slices, in: PLDI, 2005.

[107] G.S. Sohi, et al., Multiscalar processors, in: ISCA, 1995.

[108] A. Yazdanbakhsh, et al., Mitigating the memory bottleneck with approximate load value prediction, in: IEEE Date and Test, 2016.

[109] C. Luk, et al., Pin: building customized program analysis tools with dynamic instrumentation, in: PLDI, 2005.

[110] N. Nethercote, et al., Valgrind: a framework for heavyweight dynamic binary instrumentation, in: PLDI, 2007.

[111] M. Stephenson, et al., Flexible software profiling of GPU architectures, in: ISCA, 2015.

[112] M. Kamruzzaman, et al., Inter-core prefetching for multicore processors using migrating helper threads, in: ASPLOS, 2011.

[113] D. Kim, et al., Design and evaluation of compiler algorithms for pre-execution, in: ASPLOS, 2002.

[114] W. Zhang, et al., Accelerating and adapting precomputation threads for efficient prefetching, in: HPCA, 2007.

[115] J. Lu, et al., Dynamic helper threaded prefetching on the Sun UltraSPARC CMP processor, in: MICRO, 2005.

[116] C. Zilles, et al., The use of multithreading for exception handling, in: MICRO, 1999.

[117] D. Kim, et al., Physical experimentation with prefetching helper threads on Intel's hyper-threaded processors, in: CGO, 2004.

[118] V. Krishnan, J. Torrellas, A chip-multiprocessor architecture with speculative multithreading, IEEE Trans. Comput. 48 (9) (1999) 866–880.

[119] M. Bauer, et al., CudaDMA: optimizing GPU memory bandwidth via warp specialization, in: SC, 2011.

[120] M. Rhu, M. Sullivan, J. Leng, M. Erez, A locality-aware memory hierarchy for energy-efficient GPU architectures, in: MICRO, 2013.

[121] A. Alameldeen, et al., Interactions between compression and prefetching in chip multiprocessors, in: HPCA, 2007.

[122] Hynix, 512M (16mx32) GDDR3 SDRAM hy5rs123235fp.

Accelerating GPU accelerators through neural algorithmic transformation

16

A. Yazdanbakhsh[1], J. Park[1], H. Sharma[1], P. Lotfi-Kamran[2], H. Esmaeilzadeh[1]

Georgia Institute of Technology, Atlanta, GA, United States[1] Institute for Research in Fundamental Sciences (IPM), Tehran, Iran[2]

1 INTRODUCTION

Historically, the improvement in processor performance was driven by two phenomena: Moore's law [1] and Dennard scaling [2]. Technology scaling, which refers to the technology of shrinking transistor dimensions, provided processor designers with transistor density that doubled every 2 years (Moore's law). Moreover, the reduction in the supply voltage enabled processor designers to operate twice the number of transistors that technology offers, without an increase in power consumption (Dennard scaling). Taking advantage of Moore's law and Dennard scaling, computer architects improved the processing power by constantly increasing the complexity and frequency of processors. Decades of technology scaling allowed powerful processors with deep and aggressive Out-of-Order pipelines and high clock frequency to emerge.

Unfortunately, improving the performance of processors with the historical approach is no longer viable. As physical restrictions slow down the reduction of the supply voltage, Dennard scaling has effectively stopped [3]. While Moore's law is still valid and the number of transistors increases by a factor of 2 every 2 years, the failure of Dennard scaling makes power and energy the primary constraints of processors. As such, it is no longer desirable to increase the clock frequency of processors or increase the complexity of the processor pipeline to improve performance, as these approaches are not energy efficient [4].

The diminishing returns from technology scaling [5–7] have coincided with an overwhelming increase in the rate of data generation. Expert analyses showed that in 2011, the amount of generated data surpassed 1.8 trillion GB, and the estimates indicate that consumers will generate 50× this staggering figure in 2020 [8]. On one hand, processing the ever-growing amount of generated data requires significant and

Advances in GPU Research and Practice. http://dx.doi.org/10.1016/B978-0-12-803738-6.00016-1

continual boost of processors' performance. On the other hand, we have reached the limits of an historical style of improving performance.

To overcome these challenges, both the semiconductor industry and the research community are exploring new avenues in computer architecture design. Two of the promising approaches are acceleration and approximation. Among programmable accelerators, graphics processing units (GPUs) offer significant performance and energy efficiency gains. While GPUs were originally designed to accelerate graphics functions, now they are being used to execute a wide range of applications, including recognition, learning, gaming, data analytics, weather prediction, molecular dynamics, multimedia, scientific computing, and much more. The availability of programming models for GPUs and the advances in their microarchitecture have played a significant role in their widespread adoption. Many companies, such as Microsoft, Google, and Amazon, use GPUs to accelerate their enterprise services. As GPUs play a major role in accelerating many classes of data-intensive applications, improving GPUs performance and energy efficiency is imperative to cope with the ever-increasing rate of data generation.

Many of the applications that execute on GPUs are amenable to imprecise execution [9–12]. This means that some variation in output of these applications is acceptable and some degradation in the output quality is tolerable. This characteristic of many GPU applications provides a unique opportunity to devise approximation techniques that trade small losses in the quality of the results for significant gains in performance and energy efficiency.

Many approximation techniques target approximable code. Approximable code is a segment of code that if approximated will not lead to catastrophic failures in execution (e.g., segmentation fault), and its approximation may lead only to graceful degradation of an application's output quality. Among approximation techniques that target approximable code, neural acceleration, which provided significant gains for CPUs [13–17] is a good candidate for GPUs [18,19]. Neural acceleration relies on an automated algorithmic transformation that converts an approximable segment of code to a neural network. A neural network is a family of models inspired by the brain and is used to approximate functions. There are algorithms to determine a good neural network for approximation of a given function. The transformation of a segment of code to a neural network is called the neural transformation [13]. The compiler automatically performs the neural transformation and replaces the approximable segment with an invocation of a neural hardware that mimics the behavior of that segment of code.

To demonstrate the potential benefits of neural acceleration in GPUs, we first study its applicability using a diverse set of representative GPU applications. Fig. 1 shows the breakdown of application runtime and energy dissipation between neurally approximable regions and the regions that cannot be neurally approximated. (The details of the breakdown methodology is discussed in Section 2. Section 6.1 presents our experimental methodology.) The neurally approximable segments are the ones that can be approximated by a neural network. Applications spend 56% of their runtime and 59% of their energy in neurally approximable regions on average. Some applications such as inversek2j and newton-raph spend more than 93% of their runtime and energy in neurally approximable regions. These results demonstrate

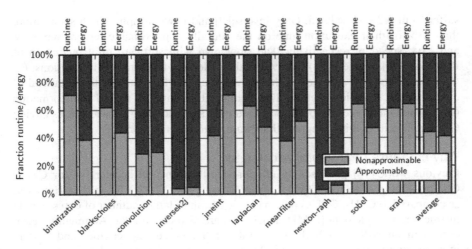

FIG. 1

Runtime and energy breakdown between neurally approximable regions and the regions that cannot be approximated.

that a significant fraction of time and energy of these GPU applications are spent on regions where neural accelerators can be applied to. Consequently, there is a significant potential for using neural acceleration on GPU processors.

Why hardware acceleration?

As previous work [20] suggested, it may be desirable to apply neural transformation with no hardware modifications and replace the approximable region with an efficient software implementation of the neural network that mimics the region. We explored this possibility and the results are shown in Fig. 2. On average, the applications

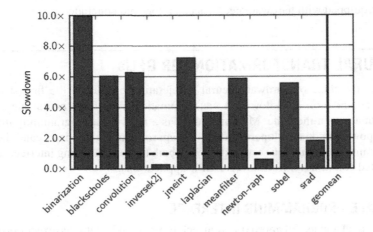

FIG. 2

Slowdown with software-only neural transformation due to the lack of hardware support for the neural acceleration.

suffer from 3.2× slowdown. Only inversek2j and newton-raph, which spend more than 93% of their execution time on the neurally approximable region, see 3.6× and 1.6× speedup, respectively. The slowdown with software implementation of neural network is due to (1) the overhead of fetching/decoding the instructions, (2) the cost of frequent accesses to the memory/register file, and (3) the overhead of executing the sigmoid function. The significant potential of neural transformation (Fig. 1) and the slowdown of the software-only approach (Fig. 2) necessities having GPU architectures with integrated hardware neural accelerators.

Why not reuse CPU neural accelerators?

Previous work [13] proposes an efficient hardware neural accelerator for CPUs. One possibility is to use CPU neural processing unit (NPU) for GPUs. However, as compared to CPUs, GPUs contain (1) significantly larger number of cores (single instruction multiple data [SIMD] lanes) that are also (2) simpler. Augmenting each core with an NPU that harbors several parallel processing engines and buffers imposes significant area overhead. Area overhead of integrating NPUs to a GPU while reusing SIMD lanes' multiply-add units is 31.2%. Moreover, neural networks are structurally parallel. As such, replacing a code segment with neural networks adds structured parallelism to the thread. In the CPU case, NPU's multiple multiply-add units exploit this added parallelism to reduce the thread execution time. GPUs, on the other hand, already exploit data-level parallelism and leverage many-thread execution to hide thread execution time. It has been shown that the added parallelism is not the main source of benefits from neural acceleration in GPUs [18,19]. Consequently, neural acceleration in GPUs leads to a significantly different hardware design as compared to that of CPUs.

In the rest of this chapter, we first introduce the programming interface, compilation workflow, and ISA extension for the support of neural acceleration in GPUs. Then we explain the hardware extensions and modifications necessary to enable neural execution of threads in GPUs. Finally, we present the evaluation results of a GPU equipped with hardware neural accelerators and conclude.

2 NEURAL TRANSFORMATION FOR GPUs

To take advantage of hardware neural acceleration on GPUs, the first step is to have a compilation workflow that can automatically perform neural algorithmic transformation on the code. Moreover, there is a need for a programming interface that empowers code developers to delineate approximable regions as candidates for neural transformation. The section describes both the programming interface and the automated compilation workflow for GPU applications.

2.1 SAFE PROGRAMMING INTERFACE

Any practical and useful approximation technique should guarantee execution safety. The safety guarantees prevent catastrophic failures such as out-of-bound memory accesses from happening due to approximation. In other words, approximation should never affect critical data and operations. The criticality of data and operations is a semantic property of a program and can be identified only by programmers. Therefore a programming language for approximate computation must offer ways for programmers to specify where approximation is safe. This requirement is commensurate with prior work on safe approximate programming languages, such as EnerJ [21], Rely [22], FlexJava [23], and Axilog [24]. For this goal, we extend the Compute Unified Device Architecture (CUDA) programming language with a pair of *#pragma* annotations that enable marking the beginning and the end of a safe-to-approximate region of a GPU application. The following example illustrates these annotations.

```
#pragma(begin_approx , "min max")
mi = __min(r, __min(g, b));
ma = __max(r, __max(g, b));
result = ((ma + mi) > 127 * 2) ? 255 : 0;
#pragma(end_approx "min max")
```

The preceding segment of code is approximable and is marked as a candidate for neural transformation by a programmer. The #pragma(begin_approx, "min_max") indicates the segment's beginning and associates a name ("min_max") to it. The #pragma(end_approx, "min_max") indicates the end of a segment that was named "min_max."

It is worth mentioning that, in addition to what is presented in this section, there are other approaches for safe programming interfaces, such as EnerJ [21] that require annotating approximate data declarations. We chose to use *#pragma* to identify a segment of approximable code due to the lower annotation overhead, simplicity, and compatibility with the current CUDA compilers. However, the workflow presented in this chapter can also leverage other models if they are extended to CUDA.

2.2 COMPILATION WORKFLOW

As discussed, the main idea of neural algorithmic transformation is to learn the behavior of a code segment using a neural network and then to replace the segment with an invocation of an efficient neural hardware [13,18,19]. To have this algorithmic transformation, the compiler needs to (1) identify the inputs and outputs of the segment of code; (2) collect the training data by observing (logging) the inputs and outputs; (3) find and train a neural network that mimics and approximates the observed behavior; and finally (4) replace that segment of code with instructions that configure and control the neural hardware. These steps are shown in Fig. 3. The compilation workflow is similar to the one described in Ref. [13] that targets CPU acceleration. However, the four steps have been specialized for GPU applications. Moreover, step (1) is done automatically to further automate the transformation.

1. *Input/output identification.* To find and train a neural network that mimics a code segment, the compiler needs to collect the input-output pairs that represent the

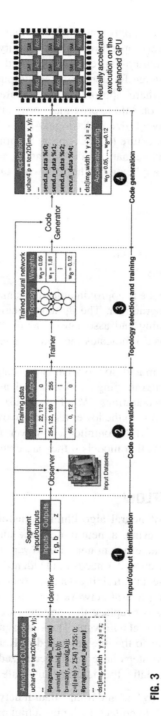

FIG. 3

Overview of the compilation workflow for neural acceleration in GPU throughput processors.

functionality of the code segment. To this end, a compiler first needs to identify the inputs and outputs of the delineated segment. The compiler uses a combination of live variable analysis and Mod/Ref analysis [25] to automatically identify the inputs and outputs of the annotated segment. The inputs are the intersection of live variables in the beginning of the code segment and the set of variables that are referenced within the segment. The outputs are the intersection of live variables at the end of the code segment and the set of variables that are modified within the segment. In the previous example, this analysis identifies r, g, and b as the inputs to the segment and *result* as the output.

2. *Code observation.* After identifying the inputs and outputs of the segment, the compiler instructs these inputs and outputs to log their values in a file as the program runs. The compiler then runs the program with a series of representative input data sets (such as the ones from a program test suite) and logs the pairs of input-output values. The collected set of input-output values constitutes the training data that captures the behavior of the segment. The training data will be used in the next step to find and train a neural network for the code segment.

3. *Topology selection and training.* In this step, the compiler needs to both find a topology for the neural network and train it. While searching for a topology for the neural network, the objective is to strike a balance between the network's accuracy and its overhead. Theoretically, a larger, more complex network offers higher accuracy potentials but is likely to be slower and less energy efficient than a smaller network. The accuracy of neural networks does not improve beyond a certain point even if they are enlarged. To pick a good topology, the compiler considers a search space for the neural topology and selects the smallest network that offers comparable accuracy to the largest network in the space. The neural network of choice in this study is multilayer perceptron (MLP) that consists of a fully connected set of neurons organized into layers: the input layer, any number of hidden layers, and the output layer. The number of neurons in the input and output layers is fixed and corresponds to the number of inputs and outputs to the code segment. The goal is to find the number of hidden layers and the number of neurons in each hidden layer.

As the space of all possible topologies is infinitely large we restrict the search space to neural networks with at most two hidden layers. The number of neurons per hidden layer is also restricted to the powers of 2, up to 32 neurons. These choices limit the search space to 30 possible topologies. The maximum number of hidden layers and the maximum number of neurons per hidden layer are compilation options and can be changed. All possible neural networks are trained independently in parallel. To pick the best fitting neural network topology, the input-output pairs obtained in step (2) are partitioned into a training data set (usually two-thirds of the pairs) and a selection data set (the remaining pairs). The training data sets are used to train a neural network (i.e., determine the weights of the connections) for a given topology, and the selection data sets are used to select the final neural network topology based on the observed application quality loss (the smallest topology that offers the lowest quality loss will be selected). Note that we use completely separate data sets to measure the final quality loss in Section 6.

For training the neural network using the training data sets, we use the standard backpropagation [26] algorithm. Our compiler performs 10-fold cross-validation for training each neural network. The output from this phase consists of a neural network topology—specifying the number of layers and the number of neurons in each layer—along with the weight of each connection that are determined by the training algorithm.

4. *Code generation.* After identifying the best neural network and having the weights for the connections, the compiler replaces the code segment with special instructions that send the inputs to the neural accelerator (we will talk about the details of the neural accelerator later in this chapter) and retrieve the results. The compiler also generates the configuration of the neural accelerator. The configuration includes the weights and the schedule of the operations within the accelerator. The configuration of the neural network is loaded into the integrated neural accelerators at the beginning when the program is loaded for the execution.

3 INSTRUCTION-SET-ARCHITECTURE DESIGN

To enable neural acceleration, the instruction-set architecture of a GPU should have three instructions: (1) an instruction for sending the inputs to the neural accelerator; (2) an instruction for receiving outputs from the neural accelerator; and finally (3) an instruction for sending the accelerator configuration and the weights. For this purpose, we extend the Parallel Thread Execution (PTX) ISA, which is used in Nvidia's CUDA programming environment with the following three instructions:

1. *send.n_data %r.* This instruction sends the value of register %r to the neural accelerator. The instruction also informs the accelerator that the value is an input and not a configuration.
2. *recv.n_data %r.* This instruction retrieves a value from the accelerator and writes it to the register %r.
3. *send.n_cfg %r.* This instruction sends the value of register %r to the accelerator. The instruction also informs the accelerator that the value is for setting the configuration of the neural accelerator.

We use PTX ISA version 4.2. PTX 4.2 supports vector instructions that can read or write two or four registers. We take advantage of this feature and introduce two vector versions for each of our instructions. The *send.n_data.v2 {%r0, %r1}* sends two register values to the accelerator and a single *send.n_data.v4 {%r0, %r1, %r2, %r3}* sends the value of four registers to the neural accelerator. The latter instruction can replace four scalar *send.n_data %r* instructions. The vector versions for *recv.n_data* and *send.n_cfg* have similar semantics. These vector instructions reduce the number of instructions that should be fetched and decoded for communication with the neural accelerator. The reduction in the number of instructions lowers the overhead of invoking the accelerator and provides more opportunities for speedup and energy-efficiency gains.

These instructions will be executed in a single instruction, multiple threads (SIMT) mode similar to other GPU instructions. GPU applications typically consist of kernels, and GPU threads execute the same kernel code. The neural transformation approximates segments of these kernels. This means that each corresponding thread will contain the aforementioned instructions to communicate with the neural accelerator. Moreover, the neural network that approximates a segment of the kernel is the same for all threads. Each thread applies different input data only to the same neural network. GPU threads are grouped into cooperative thread arrays (a unit of thread blocks). The threads in different thread blocks are independent and can be executed in any order. The thread-block scheduler maps thread blocks to GPU processing cores called the streaming multiprocessors (SMs). An SM divides threads of a thread block into smaller groups called warps, which typically consists of 32 threads. All the threads within a warp execute the same instruction in lock step. The lock-step execution implies that the *send.n_data*, *recv.n_data*, and *send.n_cfg* instructions execute at the same time in all the threads of a warp, just like other instructions. This means that executing each of these instructions, conceptually, communicates data with 32 parallel neural accelerators per SM.

The GPU-specific challenge is designing a hardware neural accelerator that can be replicated 32 times within each individual SM without imposing extensive hardware overhead. A typical GPU architecture, such as Fermi [27], contains 15 SMs, each with warp size of 32. To support hardware neural acceleration for this GPU architecture, 480 neural accelerators need to be integrated. The next section describes the design of a neural accelerator that efficiently scales to such large numbers.

4 NEURAL ACCELERATOR: DESIGN AND INTEGRATION

For the purpose of describing the design of the neural accelerator and its integration into the GPU architecture, we consider a GPU processor based on the Nvidia Fermi. Fermi's SMs contain 32 double-clocked SIMD lanes that execute 2 half warps (16 threads) simultaneously, where all of the threads of a warp execute in lockstep. Ideally, for preserving the data-level parallelism across the threads and making sure that the default SIMT execution model does not hinder, every SM should be augmented with 32 neural accelerators. Therefore the main objective is to design a neural accelerator that is capable of being replicated 32 times within each SM and that offers low hardware overhead. These two requirements fundamentally change the design space of the neural accelerator designed for GPUs from prior work that aims at accelerating CPU cores with only one accelerator.

A naive approach is to add and replicate the previously proposed CPU neural accelerator [13] to each SM. These CPU-specific accelerators harbor multiple

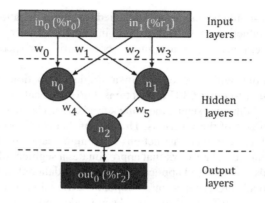

FIG. 4

Neural network replacing a segment of a GPU code.

processing engines and contain a significant amount of buffering for weights and control. Such a design not only imposes significant hardware overhead but also is overkill for data-parallel GPU architectures as the results in Section 6.3 show. Instead, we present the design of a neural accelerator that is tightly integrated in every SIMD lane of GPU SMs [18,19].

The neural algorithmic transformation takes advantage of MLPs to approximate CUDA code segments. As Fig. 4 depicts, an MLP consists of a network of neurons arranged in multiple layers. Each neuron in a layer is connected to all of the neurons in the next layer. Each neuron input is associated with a weight that is obtained in the training process. All neurons are identical, and each neuron computes its output (y) based on $y = sigmoid(sum\_of(w_i \times x_i))$, where x_i is a neuron input and w_i is the input's associated weight. As a result, all the computations of a neural network are a set of multiply-add operations followed by the nonlinear sigmoid operation. A neural accelerator needs to support only these two operations.

4.1 INTEGRATING THE NEURAL ACCELERATOR TO GPUs

Every SM has 32 SIMD lanes, divided into two 16-lane groups that execute two half-warps simultaneously. There is an arithmetic logic unit (ALU) in each lane that supports a floating-point multiply-and-add operation. The neural accelerators that enhance the lanes for neural computation reuse these ALUs. The integration of neural accelerators to SIMD lanes is done in a way to leverage the existing SIMT execution model in order to minimize the hardware overhead for the weights and control. In the rest of this chapter, we refer to the SIMD lanes with neural computation capabilities as neurally enhanced SIMD lanes.

Fig. 5 shows a neutrally enhanced SM. The components that are included to support neural computation are numbered and highlighted in green (dark gray in

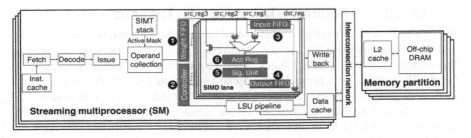

FIG. 5

SM pipeline after integrating the neural accelerator within SIMD lanes. The added hardware is highlighted in *green* (*dark gray* in print version).

print version). The first component is a Weight FIFO (First-In-First-Out) (1). The Weight FIFO is a circular buffer that stores the neural network's weights. Because an identical neural network approximates the approximable segment of all threads in a warp, only one Weight FIFO per actively executing warp is needed. The single Weight FIFO is shared across all SIMD lanes that execute the warp. For the Fermi architecture, the Weight FIFO has two read ports corresponding to the two warps that are executing simultaneously (i.e., 1 Weight FIFO port per 16 SIMD lanes that execute a half warp). Each port supplies a weight to 16 ALUs. The second component is the Controller (2) that controls the execution of the neural network across the SIMD lanes. Again, the Controller is shared across 16 SIMD lanes that execute a half warp (2 controllers per SM). The Controller follows the SIMT pattern of execution for neural computation and enables the ALUs to perform the same computation of the same neuron on different input data across all threads in a warp.

Moreover, every SIMD lane is augmented with an Input FIFO (3) and an Output FIFO (4). The Input FIFO stores the inputs of the neural computation. The Output FIFO stores the output of the neurons including the final output of the neural computation. These two FIFOs are small structures that are replicated in each SIMD lane. Every SIMD lane also harbors a Sigmoid Unit (5) that contains a read-only look-up table. The look-up table implements the nonlinear sigmoid function and is synthesized as combinational logic to reduce the area overhead. Finally, the Acc Reg (6), which is the accumulator register in each of the SIMD lanes, retains the partial results of the sum of products (Sum_of ($w_i \times x_i$)) before passing it to the Sigmoid Unit.

One of the advantages of the presented design is that it restricts all major modifications and changes to the execution part of the SIMD lanes (pipelines). There is no need to change any other part of the SM except for adding support for decoding the ISA extensions that communicate data to the accelerator (i.e., input and output buffers). Scheduling and issuing the added instructions are similar to arithmetic instructions and do not require specific changes.

4.2 EXECUTING NEURALLY TRANSFORMED THREADS

Fig. 6 shows how a neutrally transformed warp, which contains normal precise and special approximate (i.e., *send.n_data/recv.n_data*) instructions, is executed on the neutrally enhanced SIMD lanes. The second simultaneously executing warp (similarly contains both normal and special instructions) is not shown for clarity. In the first phase of the execution (1), SIMD lanes execute the precise instructions as usual before reaching the first *send.n_data* instruction. In the second phase of execution (2), SIMD lanes execute the two *send.n_data* instructions to copy the neural-network inputs from the register file to the input buffers. These instructions also cause SIMD lanes to switch to the neural mode. In the third phase of execution (3), the neurally enhanced SIMD lanes (or the neural accelerators) perform the neural computation and store the results in their output buffers.

At the same time, the SM issues the *recv.n_data* instruction. As the output of the neural network is not ready yet, the SM stops issuing the following instructions and waits for the neurally enhanced SIMD lanes to finish computing the neural-network output. In the fourth phase of execution (4) and once the neural-network output is ready, the *recv.n_data* instruction copies the results of the neural computation from the output buffers to the register file and then, in the fifth phase of execution (5), normal execution resumes. Because there is no control divergence or memory access in the neural mode, this design does not switch the running warp with another warp in the neural mode to avoid the significant overhead of dedicated input/output buffers or control logic per active warp (SMs support 48 ready-to-execute warps in the Fermi architecture).

4.3 ORCHESTRATING NEURALLY ENHANCED SIMD LANES

For the purpose of efficient execution of neural networks on the neurally enhanced SIMD lanes, the compiler should create a static schedule for the neural computation and arrange the weights in proper order in the FIFO. This schedule and the preordered weights are encoded in the program binary and are preloaded to the Weight FIFO (Fig. 5(1)) when the program loads for execution. The compiler generates the schedule of the execution using the following steps:

1. The computations for the neurons in each layer are independent on the output of the neurons in the previous layer. As a result, the compiler assigns a unique order to the neurons starting from the first hidden layer down to the output layer. This unique order determines the order of the execution of the neurons. In Fig. 4 n_0, n_1, and n_2 show this order.
2. Having the order of the neurons, the compiler generates the order of the multiply-and-add operations for each neuron. The multiply-and-add operations are followed by a sigmoid operation. This schedule is shown in Fig. 7 for the neural network in Fig. 4. The phase (3) of Fig. 6 illustrates how the neurally enhanced SIMD lanes execute this schedule in SIMT mode while sharing the weights and control.

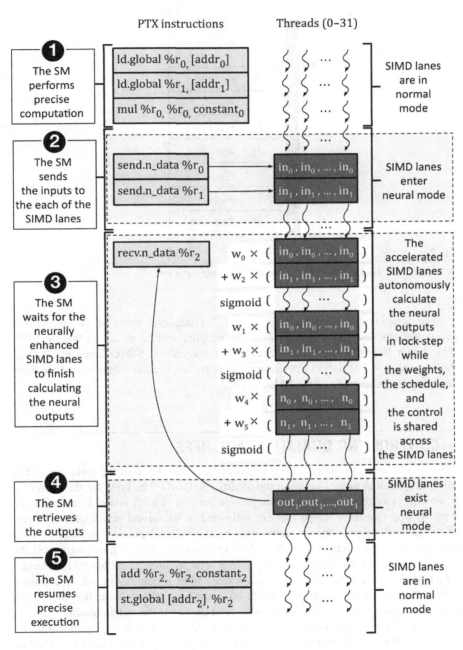

FIG. 6

Accelerated execution on the enhanced SM.

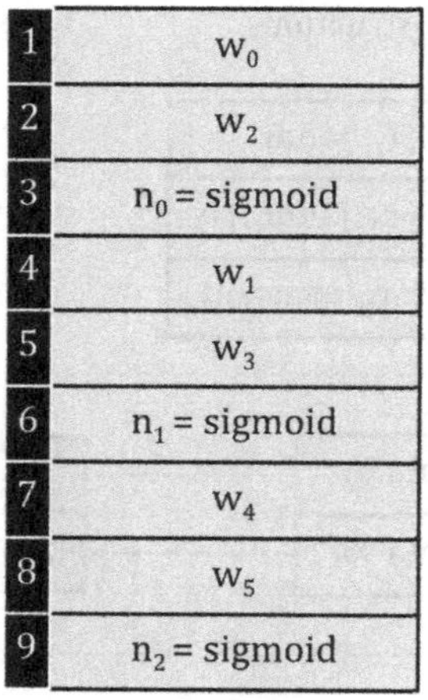

1	w_0
2	w_2
3	n_0 = sigmoid
4	w_1
5	w_3
6	n_1 = sigmoid
7	w_4
8	w_5
9	n_2 = sigmoid

FIG. 7

Schedule for the accelerated execution of the neural network.

The schedule that is presented in Fig. 7 constitutes most of the accelerator configurations and the order in which the weights will be stored in Weight FIFO ((1) shown in Fig. 5). For each accelerator invocation, SIMD lanes go through these weights in lockstep and perform the neural computation autonomously without engaging the other parts of the SM.

5 CONTROLLING QUALITY TRADE-OFFS

All approximation techniques need to expose a quality knob to the compiler and/or runtime system in order to control the quality trade-offs. The knob for the presented neural accelerator is the accelerator invocation rate, which is the fraction of the neurally approximable warps that are offloaded to the neural accelerator. The rest of the neurally approximable warps execute the original precise segment of code and generate exact outputs. Without having a quality-control mechanism, all the warps that contain the approximable segment will go through the neural accelerator which translates into a 100% invocation rate. With a quality-control mechanism, only a fraction of the warps will go through the accelerator. Naturally, the higher the invocation rate, the higher the benefits, and the lower the output quality.

For a given quality target, the compiler predetermines the invocation rate by examining the output quality loss on a held-out evaluation input data set. Starting from 100% invocation rate, the compiler gradually reduces the invocation rate until the quality loss is less than the quality target. During runtime, a quality monitor, similar to the one proposed in SAGE [9], stochastically checks the output quality of the running application and adjusts the invocation rate to make sure that output quality remains below the quality target.

For the purpose of controlling the quality loss, the benefits of using a more sophisticated approach has been investigated [18,19]. The more sophisticated approach uses another neural network to filter out those invocations of the accelerator that result in significant quality degradation. The empirical study suggested that the simpler approach of reducing the invocation rate provides similar benefits.

6 EVALUATION

In this section, we present benefits of the proposed architecture across different bandwidth and accelerator settings [18,19]. We use a diverse set of applications, cycle-accurate simulation, logic synthesis, and consistent detailed energy modeling.

6.1 APPLICATIONS AND NEURAL TRANSFORMATION

Applications

As Table 1 shows, we use a diverse set of approximable GPU applications from the Nvidia SDK [28] and Rodinia [29] benchmark suites to evaluate the integration of the presented neural accelerators within GPU architectures. Moreover, three more applications are added to the mix from different sources [30–32]. As shown in Table 1, the benchmarks are taken from finance, machine learning, image processing, vision, medical imaging, robotics, 3D gaming, and numerical analysis. No benchmark is rejected due to its performance, energy, or quality shortcomings.

Annotations

As mentioned in Section 2.1, we annotate the CUDA source code of each application using the *#pragma* directives. We take advantage of these directives to delineate a region within a CUDA kernel that has a fixed number of inputs/outputs and is safe to be approximated. Although it is possible and might also boost the benefits to annotate multiple regions, for the study in this chapter, we annotate only one easy-to-identify region that is frequently executed. We did not make any algorithmic changes to enable neural acceleration.

Table 1 shows the number of function calls, conditionals, and loops of the approximable region of each benchmark. Table 1 illustrates that the approximable regions exhibit a rich and diverse control-flow behavior. As an example, the approximable region in *inversk2j* has three loops and five conditionals. Other regions similarly have several loops/conditionals and function calls. Among these applications, the approximable region in *jmeint* has the most complicated control flow with 37 *if/else* statements. The approximable regions are also diverse in size and vary from small (*binarization* with 27 PTX instructions) to large (*jmeint* with 2250 PTX instructions).

Table 1 Applications, Accelerated Regions, Training and Evaluation Data Sets, Quality Metrics, and Approximating Neural Networks

	Description	Source	Domain	Quality Metric	# of Function Calls	# of Function oops	# of Ifs/Elses	# of PTX Insts.	Training Input Set	Evaluation Input Set	Digital NPU	
											Neural Network Topology	Quality Loss
binarization	Image binarization	Nvidia SDK	Image Processing	Image diff	1	0	1	27	Three 512 × 512 pixel images	Twenty 2048×2048 pixel images	3 -> 4 -> 2 -> 1	8.23%
blackscholes	Option pricing	Nvidia SDK	Finance	Avg. rel. error	2	0	0	96	8192 options	262,144 options	6 -> 8 -> 1	4.35%
convolution	Data filtering operation	Nvidia SDK	Machine learning	Avg. rel. error	0	2	2	886	8192 data points	262,144 data points	17 -> 2 -> 1	5.25%
inversek2j	Inverse kinematics for 2-joint arm	CUDA-based kinematics	Robotics	Avg. rel. error	0	3	5	132	8192 2D coordinates	262,144 2D coordinates	2 -> 16 -> 3	8.73%
jmeint	Triangle intersection detection	jMonkey game	3D Gaming	Miss rate	4	0	37	2250	8192 3D coordinates	262,144 3D coordinates	18 -> 8 -> 2	17.32%
laplacian	Image sharpening filter	Nvidia SDK	Image processing	Image diff	0	2	1	51	Three 512 × 512 pixel images	Twenty 2048×2048 pixel images	9 -> 2 -> 1	6.01%
meanfilter	Image smoothing filter	Nvidia SDK	Machine vision	Image diff	0	2	1	35	Three 512 × 512 pixel images	Twenty 2048×2048 pixel images	7 -> 4 -> 1	7.06%
newton-raph	Newton-Raphson equation solver	Likelihood estimators	Numerical analysis	Avg. rel. error	2	2	1	44	8192 cubic equations	262,144 cubic equations	5 -> 2 -> 1	3.08%
sobel	Edge detection	Nvidia SDK	Image processing	Image diff	2	2	1	86	Three 512 × 512 pixel images	Twenty 2048×2048 pixel images	9 -> 4 -> 1	5.45%
srad	Speckle reducing anisotropic diffusion	Rodinia	Medical imaging	Image diff	0	0	0	110	Three 512 × 512 pixel images	Twenty 2048×2048 pixel images	5 -> 4 -> 1	7.43%

Evaluation/training data sets

Table 1 shows the data sets that are used for the benchmarks. The data sets for measuring the quality, performance, and energy are completely disjointed from the ones that are used for training the neural networks. The training inputs are typical representative inputs (such as sample images) that can be found in application test suites. As an example, we use the image of *lena*, *peppers*, and *mandrill* for applications that operate on image data. Since the chosen regions are frequently executed, even a single application input provides a large amount of training data. For instance, a 512×512 pixel image generates 262,144 training data elements in *sobel*.

Neural networks

The "Neural Network Topology" column in Table 1 shows the topology of the neural network that replaces the approximable region of code. As an example, the topology of the neural network for the *blackscholes* benchmark is $6 \rightarrow 8 \rightarrow 1$. With this topology, the neural network has six inputs, one hidden layer with eight neurons, and one output neuron. The compiler automatically picks the topology. For training the chosen neural network, we use the 10-fold cross validation technique. As indicated by the topologies of the benchmarks, different applications require different topologies. Consequently, the SM architecture should be reconfigurable and can accommodate different topologies.

Quality

We use application-specific quality metrics, shown in Table 1, to assess the quality of each application's output after neural acceleration. In all cases, we compare the output of the original precise application to the output of the neurally accelerated application. For *blackscholes*, *inversek2j*, *newton-raph*, and *srad* which generate numeric outputs, we measure the average relative error. For *jmeint* which determines whether two 3D triangles intersect, we report the misclassification rate. For *convolution*, *binarization*, *laplacian*, *meanfilter*, and *sobel* which produce image outputs, we use the average root-mean-square image difference. In Table 1, the "quality loss" column reports the whole-application quality degradation based on the preceding metrics. This loss includes the accumulated errors due to repeated execution of the approximated region. The quality loss in Table 1 represents the case where all dynamic threads with safe-to-approximate regions are neurally accelerated (i.e., 100% invocation rate).

Even with a 100% invocation rate, the quality loss with neural acceleration is less than 10% except in the case of *jmeint*. The *jmeint* application's control flow is very complex, and the neural network is not capable of capturing all the corner cases to achieve below 10% quality degradation. These results are commensurate with prior work on CPU-based neural acceleration [14,16]. Prior works on GPU approximation such as SAGE [9] and Paraprox [10] report similar quality losses in the default setting. EnerJ [21] and Truffle [33] show less than 10% loss for some applications and even 80% loss of quality for others. Green [34] and loop perforation

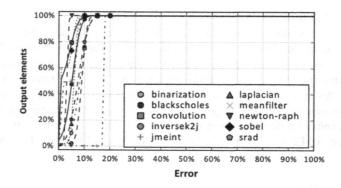

FIG. 8

Cumulative distribution function (CDF) plot of the applications' output quality loss. A point (x, y) indicates that y fraction of the output elements shows quality loss less than or equal to x.

[35] show less than a 10% error for some applications and more than 20% for others. Later in this section, we discuss how to use the invocation rate to control the quality trade-offs, and achieve an even lower loss of quality when desired.

To better illustrate the nature of quality loss in GPU applications, Fig. 8 shows the cumulative distribution function (CDF) plot of the final quality loss with respect to the elements of the output. The output of an application is a collection of elements—an image consists of pixels; a vector consists of scalars; and so on. The quality-loss CDF shows that, across all benchmarks, only very few output elements show a large loss; the majority of output elements (from 78% to 100%) show a quality loss of less than 10%.

6.2 EXPERIMENTAL SETUP

Cycle-accurate simulations

GPGPU-Sim version 3.2.2 [38] is used for cycle-accurate simulation. The simulator is modified to include the ISA extensions and the extra microarchitectural modifications necessary for the integration of neural accelerators within GPUs. The overhead of ISA extensions for communication with the accelerator are modeled. For baseline simulations that do not include any approximation or acceleration, the unmodified GPGPU-Sim is used. We use one of the GPGPU-Sim's default configurations that closely models the Nvidia GTX 480 chipset with Fermi architecture. Table 2 summarizes the microarchitectural parameters of the chipset. We run the applications to completion. We use NVCC 4.2 with -O3 to enable aggressive compiler optimizations. Moreover, we optimize the number of thread blocks and number of threads-per-block of each kernel for the simulated hardware.

Table 2 GPU Microarchitectural Parameters

System overview: No. of SMs: 15, warp size: 32 threads/warp; Shader core config: 1.4 GHz, GTO scheduler [36], 2 schedulers/SM; Resources/SM: No. of warps: 48 warps/SM, No. of registers: 32,768; Interconnect: 1 crossbar/direction (15 SMs, 6 MCs), 700 MHz; L1 data cache: 16 KB, 128B line, 4-way, LRU; Shared memory: 48 KB, 32 banks; L2 unified cache: 768 KB, 128B line, 16-way, LRU; Memory: 6 GDDR5 memory controllers, 924 MHz, FR-FCFS [37]; Bandwidth: 177.4 GB/s.

Energy modeling and overhead

For the purpose of measuring the GPU energy usage, we use GPUWattch [39], which is integrated with GPGPU-Sim. To measure the neural accelerator energy usage, we benefit from an event log that is generated during the cycle-accurate simulation. The energy evaluations are based on a 40 nm process node with 1.4 GHz clock frequency. Neural acceleration requires the following changes to the SM and SIMD lanes and are modeled using McPAT [40] and CACTI 6.5 [41]. In each SM, we add a 2 KB dual-port weight FIFO. The input/output FIFOs are 256 bytes per SIMD lane. The sigmoid look-up table which is added to each SIMD lane contains 2048 32-bit entries. Because GPUWattch uses McPAT and CACTI, we benefit from a unified and consistent framework for energy measurement.

6.3 EXPERIMENTAL RESULTS

Performance and energy benefits

Fig. 9 shows the whole application speedup when all the invocations of the approximable region are accelerated with the neural accelerator. The remaining part (i.e., the nonapproximable region) is executed normally. The results are normalized to the baseline where the entire application is executed on the GPU with no acceleration.

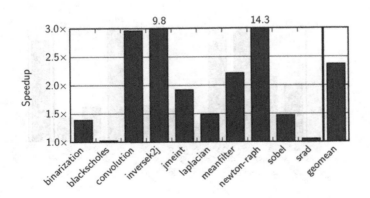

FIG. 9

NGPU whole application speedup.

The highest speedup is observed for *newton-raph* (14.3×) and *inversek2j* (9.8×), where the bulk of execution time is spent on approximable parts (see Fig. 1). The lowest speedup is observed for *blackscholes* and *srad* (about 2% and 5%) which are bandwidth-hungry applications. While a considerable fraction of the execution time in *blackscholes* and *srad* is spent in the approximate regions (see Fig. 1), the speedup of accelerating these two applications is modest. This is because these applications use most of the off-chip bandwidth, even when they run on a GPU without any acceleration. Because of bandwidth limitation, neural acceleration cannot reduce the execution time as most of the time is spent on loading data from memory. We study the effect of increasing the off-chip bandwidth on these two applications and show that with reasonable improvement in bandwidth, even these benchmarks observe significant benefits. On average, the evaluated applications see a 2.4× speedup through neural acceleration.

Fig. 10 shows the energy reduction for each benchmark as compared to the baseline where the whole benchmark is executed on a GPU without acceleration. Similar to the speedup, the highest energy saving is achieved for *inversek2j* (18.9×) and *newton-raph* (14.8×), where the bulk of the energy is consumed for the execution of approximable parts (see Fig. 1). The lowest energy saving is obtained on *jmeint* (30%) as for this application the fraction of energy consumed on approximable parts is relatively small (see Fig. 1). Unlike the speedup, we see that all applications including those that are bandwidth-hungry benefit from neural acceleration to reduce the energy usage. On average, the evaluated applications see a 2.8× reduction in energy usage.

The quality loss when all the invocations of the approximable region are executed on neural accelerators (i.e., the highest quality loss) is shown in Table 1 (labeled "quality loss"). We study the effects of the quality-control mechanism on trading performance and energy savings for better quality later in this section.

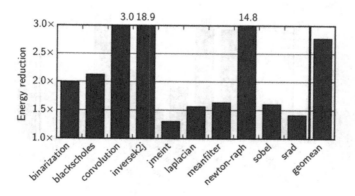

FIG. 10

NGPU whole application energy reduction.

Area overhead

To estimate the area overhead, we synthesize the sigmoid unit using Synopsys Design Compiler and NanGate 45 nm Open Cell library, targeting the same frequency as the SMs. We extract the area of the buffers and FIFOs from CACTI. Overall, the added hardware requires about 0.27 mm^2. We estimate the area of the SMs by inspecting the die photo of GTX 480 that implements the Fermi architecture. Each SM is about 22 mm^2, and the die area is 529 mm^2 with 15 SMs. The area overhead per SM is approximately 1.2%, and the total area overhead is 0.77%. The low area overhead is because the described architecture uses the same ALUs that are already available in each SIMD lane, shares the weight buffer across the SIMD lanes, and implements the sigmoid unit as a read-only look-up table, enabling the synthesis tool to optimize its area. This low area overhead confirms the scalability of the mentioned design.

Opportunity for further improvements

To explore the opportunity for further improving the execution time by making the neural accelerator faster, see Fig. 11, which shows the time breakdown of approximable and nonapproximable regions of applications when applications run on GPU (no acceleration) and neurally accelerated GPU (NGPU), normalized to the case where the application runs on GPU (no acceleration). As Fig. 11 shows, NGPU is effective at significantly reducing the time that is spent on the approximable region for all but two applications: *blackscholes* and *srad*. These two applications use most of the bandwidth of the GPU and, consequently, do not benefit from the accelerators due to the bandwidth wall. The rest of the applications significantly

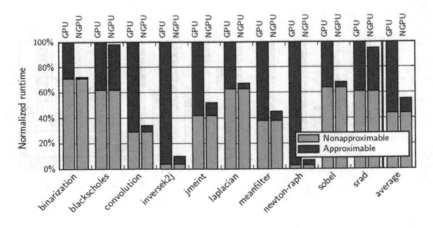

FIG. 11

Breakdown of runtime between nonapproximable and approximable regions normalized to the runtime of the GPU. For each application, the *first (second) bar* shows the normalized value when the application is executed on the GPU (NGPU).

benefit from the accelerators. On some applications (e.g., *binarization*, *laplacian*, *sobel*), the execution time of the approximable region on NGPU is significantly smaller than the execution time of the nonapproximable region. Hence no further improvement is possible with faster accelerators. For the rest of the applications, the execution time of the approximable region on NGPU, although considerably reduced, is comparable to and sometimes exceeds (e.g., *inversek2j*) the execution time of the nonapproximable region. For such applications, there is a potential to further reduce the execution time with faster accelerators.

We similarly study the opportunity to further reduce the energy usage with more energy-efficient accelerators. Fig. 12 shows the energy breakdown between approximable and nonapproximable regions when applications run on GPU and NGPU, normalized to the case where applications run on GPU. The results in Fig. 12 clearly show that neural accelerators are effective at reducing the energy usage of applications when executing the approximable region. For many of the applications, the energy that is consumed for running the approximable region is modest as compared to the energy that is consumed for running the nonapproximable region (e.g., *blackscholes*, *convolution*, *jmeint*). For these applications, a more energy-efficient neural accelerator may not bring further energy savings. However, there are some applications, such as *binarization*, *laplacian*, and *sobel*, for which the fraction of energy that is consumed on neural accelerators is comparable to the fraction of energy consumed on nonapproximable regions. For these applications, further energy saving is possible with a more energy-efficient implementation of neural accelerators (e.g., analog neural accelerators [14]).

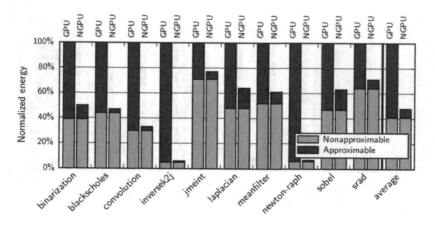

FIG. 12

Breakdown of energy consumption between nonapproximable and approximable regions normalized to the energy consumption of the GPU. For each application, the *first (second) bar* shows the normalized value when the application is executed on the GPU (NGPU).

Sensitivity to accelerator speed

To study the effects of an accelerator's speed on the performance gains, in this section we vary the latency of neural accelerators and measure the overall speedup. Fig. 13 shows the results of this experiment. We decrease the delay of the default accelerators by a factor of 2 and 4 and also include an ideal neural accelerator with zero latency. Moreover, we show the speedup numbers when the latency of the default accelerators increases by a factor of 2, 4, 8, and 16. Unlike Fig. 11 that suggests having faster accelerators results in performance improvement for some applications, Fig. 13 shows virtually no speedup benefits as a result of making neural accelerators faster beyond what they offer in the default design. Even making the neural accelerators slower by a factor of 2 does not considerably change the speedup numbers. Slowing down the neural accelerators by a factor of 4, many applications show a loss in a performance (e.g., *laplacian*).

To illustrate the previously mentioned behavior, Fig. 14 shows the bandwidth usage of GPU and NGPU across all applications. While on the baseline GPU, only two applications require more than 50% of the off-chip bandwidth (i.e., *blackscholes* and *srad*), on NGPU, many applications need more than 50% of the off-chip bandwidth (e.g., *inversek2j*, *jmeint*, *newton-raph*). Because applications run faster with neural accelerators, the rate at which they access data increases The high rate of accessing data puts pressure on off-chip bandwidth. This phenomenon shifts the bottleneck of execution from computation to data delivery. With the default accelerators, computation is no longer the major bottleneck. Consequently, speeding up thread execution beyond a certain point has a marginal effect on the overall execution time. Even increasing the accelerator speed by a factor of 2 (e.g., by adding more multiply-and-add units) has a marginal effect on the execution time. This insight has been leveraged for the simplification of the accelerator design and the reuse of available ALUs in the SMs as described is Section 4.1.

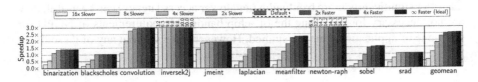

FIG. 13

Sensitivity of the application's total speedup to the neural accelerator delay. Each *bar* indicates the application's total speedup when
the neural accelerator delay is altered by different factors. The default delay for neural accelerator varies from one application to
an other and depends on the neural network topology trained for that application. The ideal case (∞ faster) shows the total
application speedup when the neural accelerator has zero delay.

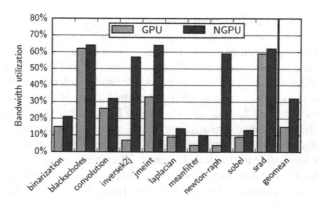

FIG. 14

Memory bandwidth consumption when the applications are executed on GPU (*first bar*) and NGPU (*second bar*).

Sensitivity to off-chip bandwidth

To study the effect of off-chip bandwidth on the benefits of NGPU, we increase the off-chip bandwidth up to 8× and report the performance numbers. Fig. 15 shows the speedup of NGPU with 2×, 4×, and 8× bandwidth over the baseline NGPU (i.e., 1× bandwidth) across all benchmarks. Because NGPU is bandwidth-limited for many applications (see Fig. 14), we expect a considerable improvement in performance as the off-chip bandwidth increases. Indeed, Fig. 15 shows that bandwidth-hungry applications (i.e., *blackscholes*, *inversek2j*, *jmeint*, and *srad*) show a speedup of 1.5× when we double the off-chip bandwidth. After doubling the off-chip bandwidth, no application remains bandwidth-limited. As a result, increasing the off-chip bandwidth to 4× and 8× has little effect on performance. It may be possible to achieve the 2× extra bandwidth using data compression [42] with few changes to the architecture of existing GPUs. Although technologies like 3D DRAM that offer significantly more bandwidth (and lower access latency) can be useful, they are not necessary for providing the off-chip bandwidth requirements of NGPU for the range of applications that we studied. However, even without any of these likely

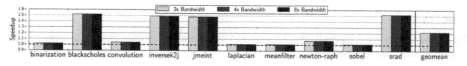

FIG. 15

The total application speedup with NGPU for different off-chip memory communication bandwidths normalized to the execution with NGPU with default bandwidth. The default bandwidth is 177.4 GB/s.

technological advances (compression or 3D stacking), the NGPU provides significant benefits across most of the applications.

Controlling quality trade-offs

To illustrate the effect of the quality-control mechanism, Fig. 16 shows the energy-delay product of NGPU normalized to the energy-delay product of the baseline GPU (without acceleration) when the output quality loss changes from 0% (i.e., no acceleration) to 10%. The quality-control mechanism enables navigating the trade-off between the quality loss and the gains. All applications show declines in benefits when the invocation rate decreases (i.e., output quality improves). Because of the Amdahl's Law effect, the applications that spend more than 90% of their execution in the approximable region (*inversek2j* and *newton-raph*) show larger declines in benefits when the invocation rate decreases. However, even with a 2.5% quality loss, the average speedup is 1.9× and the energy savings is 2.1×.

Comparison with prior CPU neural acceleration

Prior work [13] has explored improving CPU performance and energy efficiency with NPUs. As NPUs offer considerably higher performance and energy efficiency with CPUs, we compare NGPU to CPU + NPU and GPU + NPU. For the evaluation, we use a MARSSx86 cycle-accurate simulator for the single-core CPU simulations with a configuration that resembles Intel Nehalem (3.4 GHz with 0.9 V at 45 nm) and is the same as the setup used in the most recent NPU work [14].

Fig. 17 shows the application speedup and Fig. 18 shows the application energy reduction with CPU, GPU, GPU + NPU, and NGPU over CPU + NPU. Even without using neural acceleration, a GPU provides significant performance and efficiency benefits over NPU-accelerated CPU by leveraging data-level parallelism. A GPU

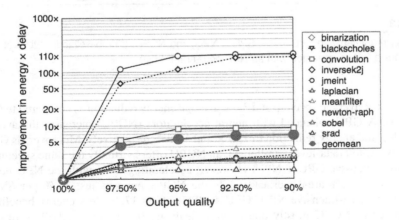

FIG. 16

Energy × delay benefits versus output quality (log scale).

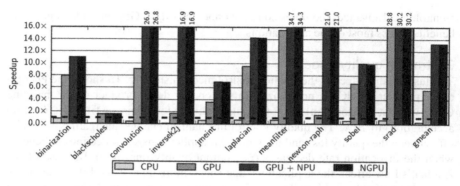

FIG. 17

Speedup with CPU, GPU, GPU + NPU, and NGPU. (The baseline is CPU + NPU, which is a CPU augmented with an NPU accelerator [13]).

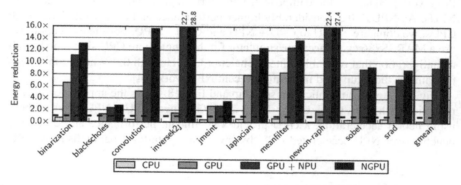

FIG. 18

Energy reduction with CPU, GPU, GPU + NPU, and NGPU. (The baseline is CPU + NPU, which is a CPU augmented with an NPU accelerator [13]).

offers 5.6× average speedup and 3.9× average energy reduction as compared to CPU + NPU. A GPU enhanced with neural accelerators (NGPU) increases the average speedup and energy reduction to 13.2× and 10.8×, respectively. Moreover, as GPUs already exploit data-level parallelism, an NGPU offers virtually the same speedup as the area-intensive GPU + NPU. However, accelerating GPU with the NPU design imposes a 31.2% area overhead while the NGPU imposes just 1.2% per SM. A GPU with area-intensive NPU (GPU + NPU) offers 17.4% less energy benefits as compared to NGPU mostly due to more leakage. In summary, NGPU offers the highest level of performance and energy efficiency across the examined benchmarks with the modest area overhead of approximately 1.2% per SM.

7 RELATED WORK

Recent work explored a variety of approximation techniques that include: (a) approximate storage designs [43,44] that trade quality of data for reduced energy [43] and longer lifetime [44], (b) voltage over-scaling [33,45,46], (c) loop perforation [35,47,48], (d) loop early termination [34], (e) computation substitution [9,12,34,49], (f) memoization [10,11,50], (g) limited fault recovery [47,51–55], (h) precision scaling [21,56], (i) approximate circuit synthesis [24,57–62], and (j) neural acceleration [13–19].

What has been presented in this chapter falls in the last category with the focus being the integration of neural accelerators into GPU throughput processors [18,19]. Some recent work on neural acceleration focuses on single-threaded CPU code acceleration by either loosely coupled neural accelerators [15–17,63,64] or tightly coupled ones [13,14]. Grigorian et al. study the effects of eliminating control-flow divergence by converting SIMD code to software neural networks with no hardware support [2]. However, these pieces of work do not explore tight integration of neural hardware in throughput processors and do not study the interplay of data-parallel execution and hardware neural acceleration. Prior to this work, the benefits, limits, and challenges of integrating hardware neural acceleration within GPUs for many-thread data-parallel applications was unexplored.

There are several other approximation techniques in the literature that can or have been applied to GPU architectures. Loop perforation [35] periodically skips loop iteration for gains in performance and energy efficiency. Green [34] terminates loops early or substitute compute-intensive functions with simpler, lower quality versions that are provided by the programmer. Relax [51] is a compiler/architecture system for suppressing hardware fault recovery in approximable regions of code, exposing these errors to the application. Fuzzy memoization foregoes invoking a floating-point unit if the inputs are in the neighborhood of previously seen inputs. The result of the previous calculation is reused as an approximate result. Arnau et al. use hardware memoization to reduce redundant computation in GPUs [11]. Sartori et al. propose a technique that mitigates branch divergence by forcing the divergent threads to execute the most popular path [12]. In case of memory divergence, they force all the threads to access the most commonly demanded memory block. SAGE [9] and Paraprox [1] perform compile-time static code transformations on GPU kernels that include data compression, profile-directed memoization, thread fusion, and atomic operation optimization. Our quality-control mechanism takes inspiration from the quality control in these two pieces of work.

In contrast, in this chapter, we describe a hardware approximation technique that integrates neural accelerators within the pipeline of the GPU cores. In our design, we aim at minimizing the pipeline modifications and utilizing existing hardware components. Specifically, this work explores the interplay between data parallelism and neural acceleration and studies its limits, challenges, and benefits.

8 CONCLUSION

Many of the emerging applications that can benefit from GPU acceleration are amenable to inexact computation. We exploited this opportunity by integrating an approximate form of acceleration, neural acceleration, within GPU architectures. The NGPU architecture provides significant performance and energy-efficiency benefits while providing reasonably low hardware overhead (1.2% area overhead per SM). The quality-control knob and mechanism also provided a way to navigate the trade-off between the quality and the benefits in efficiency and performance. Even with as low as only a 2.5% quality loss, the NGPU architecture provides average speedup of $1.9\times$ and average energy savings of $2.1\times$. These benefits are more than $10\times$ in several cases. These results suggest that hardware neural acceleration for GPU throughput processors can be a viable approach to significantly improve their performance and efficiency.

REFERENCES

[1] G.E. Moore, Cramming more components onto integrated circuits, Electronics 38 (8) (1965) 114–117.

[2] R.H. Dennard, F.H. Gaensslen, H.-N. Yu, V.L. Rideout, E. Bassous, A.R. Leblanc, Design of ion-implanted MOSFET's with very small physical dimensions, IEEE J. Solid-State Circuits 9 (5) (1974) 256–268.

[3] R.H. Dennard, J. Cai, A. Kumar, A perspective on today's scaling challenges and possible future directions, Solid-State Electron. 51 (4) (2007) 518–525.

[4] F.J. Pollack, New microarchitecture challenges in the coming generations of CMOS process technologies, (keynote address)(abstract only), in: Proceedings of the 32nd Annual ACM/IEEE International Symposium on Microarchitecture, November, 1999, p. 2.

[5] H. Esmaeilzadeh, E. Blem, R. St. Amant, K. Sankaralingam, D. Burger, Dark silicon and the end of multicore scaling, in: Proceedings of the 38th Annual International Symposium on Computer Architecture, June, 2011, pp. 365–376.

[6] N. Hardavellas, M. Ferdman, B. Falsafi, A. Ailamaki, Toward dark silicon in servers, IEEE Micro 31 (4) (2011) 6–15.

[7] G. Venkatesh, J. Sampson, N. Goulding, S. Garcia, V. Bryksin, J. Lugo-Martinez, S. Swanson, M.B. Taylor, Conservation cores: reducing the energy of mature computations, in: Proceedings of the Architectural Support for Programming Languages and Operating Systems, March, 2010, pp. 205–218.

[8] J. Gantz, D. Reinsel, Extracting value from chaos, 2016, http://www.emc.com.

[9] M. Samadi, J. Lee, D.A. Jamshidi, A. Hormati, S. Mahlke, SAGE: self-tuning approximation for graphics engines, in: Proceedings of the 46th Annual IEEE/ACM International Symposium on Microarchitecture, December, 2013, pp. 13–24.

[10] M. Samadi, D.A. Jamshidi, J. Lee, S. Mahlke, Paraprox: pattern-based approximation for data parallel applications, in: Proceedings of the 19th International Conference on Architectural Support for Programming Languages and Operating Systems, March, 2014, pp. 35–50.

[11] J.M. Arnau, J.M. Parcerisa, P. Xekalakis, Eliminating redundant fragment shader executions on a mobile GPU via hardware memoization, in: Proceeding of the 41st Annual International Symposium on Computer Architecuture, June, 2014, pp. 529–540.

[12] J. Sartori, R. Kumar, Branch and data herding: reducing control and memory divergence for error-tolerant GPU applications, IEEE Trans. Multimedia 15 (2) (2013) 279–290.

[13] H. Esmaeilzadeh, A. Sampson, L. Ceze, D. Burger, Neural acceleration for general-purpose approximate programs, in: Proceedings of the 45th Annual IEEE/ACM International Symposium on Microarchitecture, December, 2012, pp. 449–460.

[14] R. St. Amant, A. Yazdanbakhsh, J. Park, B. Thwaites, H. Esmaeilzadeh, A. Hassibi, L. Ceze, D. Burger, General-purpose code acceleration with limited-precision analog computation, in: Proceeding of the 41st Annual International Symposium on Computer Architecture, June, 2014, pp. 505–516.

[15] B. Grigorian, N. Farahpour, G. Reinman, BRAINIAC: bringing reliable accuracy into neurally-implemented approximate computing, in: Proceeding of the IEEE 21st International Symposium on High Performance Computer Architecture, 2015, pp. 615–626.

[16] T. Moreau, M. Wyse, J. Nelson, A. Sampson, H. Esmaeilzadeh, L. Ceze, M. Oskin, SNNAP: approximate computing on programmable SoCs via neural acceleration, in: Proceeding of the IEEE 21st International Symposium on High Performance Computer Architecture, February, 2015, pp. 603–614.

[17] L. McAfee, K. Olukotun, EMEURO: a framework for generating multi-purpose accelerators via deep learning, in: Proceedings of the 13th Annual IEEE/ACM International Symposium on Code Generation and Optimization, February, 2015, pp. 125–135.

[18] A. Yazdanbakhsh, J. Park, H. Sharma, P. Lotfi-Kamran, H. Esmaeilzadeh, Neural acceleration for GPU throughput processors, in: Proceedings of the 48th Annual IEEE/ACM International Symposium on Microarchitecture, December, 2015, pp. 482–493.

[19] A. Yazdanbakhsh, J. Park, H. Sharma, P. Lotfi-Kamran, H. Esmaeilzadeh, Neural acceleration for GPU throughput processors, in: GT-CS-15-05, 2015.

[20] B. Grigorian, G. Reinman, Accelerating divergent applications on SIMD architectures using neural networks, in: Proceedings of the 32nd IEEE International Conference on Computer Design, October, 2014, pp. 317–323.

[21] A. Sampson, W. Dietl, E. Fortuna, D. Gnanapragasam, L. Ceze, D. Grossman, EnerJ: approximate data types for safe and general low-power computation, in: Proceedings of the 32nd ACM Conference on Programming Language Design and Implementation, June, 2011, pp. 164–174.

[22] M. Carbin, S. Misailovic, M.C. Rinard, Verifying quantitative reliability for programs that execute on unreliable hardware, in: Proceedings of the 2013 ACM International Conference on Object Oriented Programming Systems Languages and Applications, October, 2013, pp. 33–52.

[23] J. Park, H. Esmaeilzadeh, X. Zhang, M. Naik, W. Harris, FlexJava: language support for safe and modular approximate programming, in: Proceedings of the 10th Joint Meeting on Foundations of Software Engineering, August–September, 2015, pp. 745–757.

[24] A. Yazdanbakhsh, D. Mahajan, B. Thwaites, J. Park, A. Nagendrakumar, S. Sethuraman, K. Ramkrishnan, N. Ravindran, R. Jariwala, A. Rahimi, H. Esmaeilzadeh, K. Bazargan, Axilog: language support for approximate hardware design, in: Proceedings of the Conference on Design, Automation and Test in Europe, March, 2015, pp. 812–817.

[25] J.P. Banning, An efficient way to find the side effects of procedure calls and the aliases of variables, in: Proceedings of the 6th ACM Symposium on Principles of Programming Languages, January, 1979, pp. 29–41.

[26] D.E. Rumelhart, G.E. Hinton, R.J. Williams, Learning internal representations by error propagation, in: Parallel Distributed Processing: Explorations in the Microstructure of Cognition, Vol. 1, 1986, pp. 318–362.

[27] Whitepaper: NVIDIA Fermi, 2016, http://www.nvidia.com.

[28] NVIDIA corporation, NVIDIA CUDA SDK code samples, 2016, http://www.nvidia.com.

[29] S. Che, M. Boyer, J. Meng, D. Tarjan, J.W. Sheaffer, S.H. Lee, K. Skadron, Rodinia: a benchmark suite for heterogeneous computing, in: IEEE International Symposium on Workload Characterization, October, 2009, pp. 44–54.

[30] jMonkeyEngine 2015, http://jmonkeyengine.org.

[31] O.A. Aguilar, J.C. Huegel, Inverse kinematics solution for robotic manipulators using a CUDA-based parallel genetic algorithm, in: Proceedings of the 10th Mexican International Conference on Advances in Artificial Intelligence—Vol. I, December, 2011, pp. 490–503.

[32] M. Creel, M. Zubair, A high performance implementation of likelihood estimators on GPUs, in: Proceedings of the SC Companion: High Performance Computing, Networking, Storage and Analysis, November, 2012, pp. 1147–1153.

[33] H. Esmaeilzadeh, A. Sampson, L. Ceze, D. Burger, Architecture support for disciplined approximate programming, in: Proceedings of the 17th International Conference on Architectural Support for Programming Languages and Operating Systems, March, 2012, pp. 301–312.

[34] W. Baek, T.M. Chilimbi, Green: a framework for supporting energy-conscious programming using controlled approximation, in: Proceedings of the 31st ACM SIGPLAN Conference on Programming Language Design and Implementation, June, 2010, pp. 198–209.

[35] S. Sidiroglou-Douskos, S. Misailovic, H. Hoffmann, M. Rinard, Managing performance vs. accuracy trade-offs with loop perforation, in: Proceedings of the 19th ACM SIGSOFT Symposium and the 13th European Conference on Foundations of Software Engineering, September, 2011, pp. 124–134.

[36] T.G. Rogers, M. O'Connor, T.M. Aamodt, Cache-conscious wavefront scheduling, in: Proceedings of the 45th Annual IEEE/ACM International Symposium on Microarchitecture, December, 2012, pp. 72–83.

[37] S. Rixner, W.J. Dally, U.J. Kapasi, P. Mattson, J.D. Owens, Memory access scheduling, in: Proceedings of the 27th Annual International Symposium on Computer Architecture, June, 2000, pp. 128–138.

[38] A. Bakhoda, G. Yuan, W. Fung, H. Wong, T. Aamodt, Analyzing CUDA workloads using a detailed GPU simulator, in: Proceedings of the IEEE International Symposium on Performance Analysis of Systems and Software, April, 2009, pp. 163–174.

[39] J. Leng, T. Hetherington, A. El-Tantawy, S. Gilani, N.S. Kim, T.M. Aamodt, V.J. Reddi, GPUWattch: enabling energy optimizations in GPGPUs, in: Proceedings of the 40th Annual International Symposium on Computer Architecture, June, 2013, pp. 487–498.

[40] S. Li, J.H. Ahn, R.D. Strong, J.B. Brockman, D.M. Tullsen, N.P. Jouppi, McPAT: an integrated power, area, and timing modeling framework for multicore and manycore architectures, in: Proceedings of the 42nd Annual IEEE/ACM International Symposium on Microarchitecture, December, 2009, pp. 469–480.

[41] N. Muralimanohar, R. Balasubramanian, N. Jouppi, Optimizing NUCA organizations and wiring alternatives for large caches with CACTI 6.0, in: Proceedings of the 40th Annual IEEE/ACM International Symposium on Microarchitecture, December, 2007, pp. 3–14.

[42] N. Vijaykumar, G. Pekhimenko, A. Jog, A. Bhowmick, R. Ausavarungnirun, C. Das, M. Kandemir, T.C. Mowry, O. Mutlu, A case for core-assisted bottleneck acceleration in GPUs: enabling efficient data compression, in: Proceedings of the 42nd Annual International Symposium on Computer Architecture, June, 2015, pp. 41–53.

[43] S. Liu, K. Pattabiraman, T. Moscibroda, B.G. Zorn, Flikker: saving refresh-power in mobile devices through critical data partitioning, in: Proceedings of the Sixteenth International Conference on Architectural Support for Programming Languages and Operating Systems, March, 2011, pp. 213–224.

[44] A. Sampson, J. Nelson, K. Strauss, L. Ceze, Approximate storage in solid-state memories, in: Proceedings of the 46th Annual IEEE/ACM International Symposium on Microarchitecture, December, 2013, pp. 25–36.

[45] L.N. Chakrapani, B.E.S. Akgul, S. Cheemalavagu, P. Korkmaz, K.V. Palem, B. Seshasayee, Ultra-efficient (embedded) SOC architectures based on probabilistic CMOS (PCMOS) technology, in: Proceedings of the Conference on Design, Automation and Test in Europe, March, 2006, pp. 1110–1115.

[46] L. Leem, H. Cho, J. Bau, Q.A. Jacobson, S. Mitra, ERSA: error resilient system architecture for probabilistic applications, in: Proceedings of the Conference on Design, Automation and Test in Europe, March, 2010, pp. 1560–1565.

[47] S. Misailovic, S. Sidiroglou, H. Hoffman, M. Rinard, Quality of service profiling, in: Proceedings of the 32nd ACM/IEEE International Conference on Software Engineering—Vol. 1, May, 2010, pp. 25–34.

[48] M. Rinard, H. Hoffmann, S. Misailovic, S. Sidiroglou, Patterns and statistical analysis for understanding reduced resource computing, in: Proceedings of the ACM International Conference on Object Oriented Programming Systems Languages and Applications, October, 2010, pp. 806–821.

[49] J. Ansel, C. Chan, Y.L. Wong, M. Olszewski, Q. Zhao, A. Edelman, S. Amarasinghe, Petabricks: a language and compiler for algorithmic choice, in: Proceedings of the 30th ACM SIGPLAN Conference on Programming Language Design and Implementation, June, 2009, pp. 38–49.

[50] C. Alvarez, J. Corbal, M. Valero, Fuzzy memoization for floating-point multimedia applications, IEEE Trans. Comput. 54 (7) (2005) 922–927.

[51] M. de Kruijf, S. Nomura, K. Sankaralingam, Relax: an architectural framework for software recovery of hardware faults, in: Proceedings of the 37th Annual International Symposium on Computer Architecture, June, 2010, pp. 497–508.

[52] X. Li, D. Yeung, Application-level correctness and its impact on fault tolerance, in: Proceedings of the 13th International Symposium on High Performance Computer Architecture, February, 2007, pp. 181–192.

[53] X. Li, D. Yeung, Exploiting application-level correctness for low-cost fault tolerance, J. Instr. Level Parallel. 10 (2008) 1–28.

[54] M. de Kruijf, K. Sankaralingam, Exploring the synergy of emerging workloads and silicon reliability trends, in: Workshop on Silicon Errors in Logic-System Effects, March, 2009.

[55] Y. Fang, H. Li, X. Li, A fault criticality evaluation framework of digital systems for error tolerant video applications, in: Proceedings of the Asian Test Symposium, November, 2011, pp. 329–334.

[56] S. Venkataramani, V.K. Chippa, S.T. Chakradhar, K. Roy, A. Raghunathan, Quality programmable vector processors for approximate computing, in: Proceedings of the 46th Annual IEEE/ACM International Symposium on Microarchitecture, December, 2013, pp. 1–12.

[57] A. Ranjan, A. Raha, S. Venkataramani, K. Roy, A. Raghunathan, ASLAN: synthesis of approximate sequential circuits, in: Proceedings of the Conference on Design, Automation and Test in Europe, March, 2014, pp. 364:1–364:6.

[58] S. Venkataramani, A. Sabne, V. Kozhikkottu, K. Roy, A. Raghunathan, SALSA: systematic logic synthesis of approximate circuits, in: Proceedings of the 49th ACM/EDAC/IEEE Design Automation Conference, June, 2012, pp. 796–801.

[59] J. Miao, A. Gerstlauer, M. Orshansky, Approximate logic synthesis under general error magnitude and frequency constraints, in: Proceedings of the International Conference on Computer-Aided Design, November, 2013, pp. 779–786.

[60] K. Nepal, Y. Li, R.I. Bahar, S. Reda, ABACUS: a technique for automated behavioral synthesis of approximate computing circuits, in: Proceedings of the Conference on Design, Automation and Test in Europe, March, 2014, pp. 361:1–361:6.

[61] A. Lingamneni, C. Enz, K. Palem, C. Piguet, Synthesizing parsimonious inexact circuits through probabilistic design techniques, ACM Trans. Embed. Comput. 12 (2) (2013) 93:1–93:26.

[62] A. Lingamneni, K.K. Muntimadugu, C. Enz, R.M. Karp, K.V. Palem, C. Piguet, Algorithmic methodologies for ultra-efficient inexact architectures for sustaining technology scaling, in: Proceedings of the 9th Conference on Computing Frontiers, May, 2012, pp. 3–12.

[63] B. Belhadj, A. Joubert, Z. Li, R. Heliot, O. Temam, Continuous real-world inputs can open up alternative accelerator designs, in: Proceedings of the 40th Annual International Symposium on Computer Architecture, June, 2013, pp. 1–12.

[64] Z. Du, A. Lingamneni, Y. Chen, K. Palem, O. Temam, C. Wu, Leveraging the error resilience of machine-learning applications for designing highly energy efficient accelerators, in: 19th Asia and South Pacific Design Automation Conference, January, 2014, pp. 201–206.

The need for heterogeneous network-on-chip architectures with GPGPUs: A case study with photonic interconnects

17

N. Mansoor, A. Ganguly, S.L. Alarcon
Rochester Institute of Technology, Rochester, NY, United States

1 INTRODUCTION

Future computers will have heterogeneous components in order to serve the needs of different types of applications [1]. Modern and future multi- and many-core chips will integrate hundreds of cores on a single die. To serve the demands of heterogeneity in the applications, these cores need to be custom logic central processing units (CPUs), memory, general-purpose graphics processing units (GPGPUs), and reconfigurable fabrics like field programmable gate arrays [2]. In such systems, applications will be mapped to the appropriate type of core where they will be executed in the most efficient manner with respect to either performance or energy efficiency or any other metric of interest. The interconnection fabric for such massive multicore chips is envisioned to be an on-chip network commonly referred to as a network-on-chip (NoC). In an NoC, data between two cores are packetized and transmitted over a fabric comprising switches and links. However, the heterogeneous cores in future multicore chips also will require different interconnection frameworks to enable the heterogeneous communication demands between them. It was demonstrated in Ref. [3] that, even in a regular tile-based multicore chip interconnected with a regular mesh-based NoC with homogeneous traffic distributions between the cores, some links and switches handle a higher volume of traffic than others. On the other hand different applications benefit differently from higher bandwidth resources in the interconnection fabric [4].

With the advent of novel and emerging interconnect paradigms such as photonic links new opportunities open up to enable heterogeneous interconnection bandwidth

Advances in GPU Research and Practice. http://dx.doi.org/10.1016/B978-0-12-803738-6.00017-3

allocation for the various types of cores on the die [5,6,10,11]. Typically to increase the data rate on on-chip photonic interconnects dense wavelength division multiplexing (DWDM) is adopted. The bandwidth of a link is proportional to the number of wavelengths reserved for any pair of communicating cores. Hence the pairs that need a higher bandwidth will be allocated a higher number of wavelength channels to increase the allocated bandwidth. Adopting this basic principle while designing photonic NoCs will enable a dynamic and heterogeneous interconnection framework for modern and future heterogeneous multicore chips.

In this chapter we investigate the impact of bandwidth allocation on the performance and energy consumption of GPGPU-based cores that will partially make up the fabric of future many-core chips. Through this study, we establish the motivation and the need for the design of heterogeneous NoCs potentially with emerging interconnect paradigms like photonic interconnects.

2 BACKGROUND

In this section we discuss the background work related to the understanding of traffic demands on heterogeneous multicore chips.

2.1 CHARACTERIZATION OF TRAFFIC DEMANDS OF HETEROGENEOUS MULTICORE CHIPS

In recent years, research has been done to characterize the utilization of NoC links and switches. In Ref. [3] it is shown that in a mesh-based NoC links and switch buffers in certain portions of the NoC are utilized more than others depicting a spatial variation in the utilization of network components. Consequently, dedicated high-performance components in these highly utilized areas can improve performance of the NoC. To reduce the energy consumption of the interconnects in the chip multiprocessor (CMP), authors in Ref. [7] proposed a heterogeneous interconnect architecture by using wired interconnects of different power and latency values for the partial and ordinary reply messages from memory to cores. Consequently, using a high-power and low-latency interconnect for the time-critical partial reply messages and low-power interconnects for ordinary reply messages reduces the power consumption in an NoC. In Ref. [4] it is shown that different applications have different sensitivities to bandwidth and latency of NoC links. Consequently, providing high-bandwidth links for bandwidth-sensitive applications and low-latency links for latency-sensitive ones are shown to result in best improvements in performance. In Ref. [8] QoS is used as a means to ensure appropriate resources to high-bandwidth or sensitive data. On the other hand, in Ref. [2] large-scale heterogeneous systems-on-chips consisting of GPGPU, CPU cores, custom logic, and programmable fabrics are envisioned. Simply reserving various levels of QoS is neither enough nor scalable for such widely varying types of cores demanding different characteristics from the NoC fabric. Consequently, heterogeneous NoC architectures consisting of links with different characteristics are required for such systems. Authors in Ref. [9], proposed a checkerboard-based NoC for many-core accelerators, providing better performance per unit area using full and half routers to exploit the GPU communication pattern.

2.2 RECENT PHOTONIC NoC ARCHITECTURES

Recent literature has explored photonic NoCs from tile-based architectures to crossbar-based high-radix ones [5,6,10,11]. It is argued in Ref. [1] that crossbar-based photonic NoC architectures scale better with number of cores in terms of reliability and performance. Among many variations of crossbar photonic crossbar architectures, the Firefly architecture can provide an energy efficient communication platform for many-core chips [6]. Being a reservation-based crossbar architecture the Firefly renders itself suitable for the design of a dynamic heterogeneous photonic NoC for modern and future heterogeneous computers-on-chips. To enable a photonic NoC, several different silicon-photonic components are required. Several research groups are involved in the design, fabrication, and verification of these devices. Here we summarize some of the recent advances in that direction.

2.3 WAVEGUIDES, LASER SOURCES, AND OPTICAL COUPLERS

In photonic NoCs, silicon waveguides are used to carry the optical signals across the chip. Such waveguides are fabricated using Si core and SiO_2 cladding with low transmission loss and good light confinement [6]. In order to provide a higher aggregate bandwidth for such waveguides, DWDM mechanism is adopted where multiple wavelengths are transmitted through the same waveguide with minimum interference between each wavelength. These wavelengths are generated using off-chip laser sources [12]. The optical signals generated by these laser sources are coupled with the waveguide using optical couplers [13].

2.4 MICRORING RESONATOR (MRR)

MRRs play a very important role in on-chip optical data transmission. MRRs can be used as both optical modulators and optical filters [13]. MRRs consist of an optical waveguide that is looped back on itself and a coupling mechanism to access the loop. When the resonance condition is met for the MRR, the light from a straight waveguide is trapped inside the ring, which then can be coupled into other waveguides. The resonance of a ring resonator depends on both the geometry of the resonator (e.g., circumference of the ring) and the index of refraction. In order to use the MRRs as optical modulators, an electric field is applied over the ring that changes the index of refraction of the ring. However, the resonance of an MRR is sensitive to temperature variation. Hence a thermal tuning is required for the MRRs to be able to resonate for a particular wavelength.

2.5 PHOTO DETECTOR

The photo detectors convert the optical power in the waveguides to electrical current, which is then sensed by a receiver and translated to ones and zeros.

However, photo detectors are wideband devices, and optical filters are used to perform the wavelength selection in DWDM. Then this filtered signal is fed to the photo detectors to demodulate the optical data back into an electrical domain. CMOS-compatible pure Germanium or GeSi are used to fabricate these photo detectors [13]. We envision using photonic interconnection-based NoCs using these devices, thus allowing wavelength division multiplexing (WDM) to be an enabler for heterogeneous communication fabrics for future many-core chips.

3 THE NEED FOR HETEROGENEOUS INTERCONNECTIONS

A new trend in CMP design is to incorporate graphics processing unit (GPU) cores, making them heterogeneous. The memory bandwidth requirements of CPU cores is for several benchmark applications are well studied [14]. GPU cores have a higher bandwidth requirement than CPU cores, as they tend to generate significantly more memory requests. In order to achieve good performance, there must be sufficient bandwidth between the GPU shader cores and the main memory to service these memory requests in a timely manner. However, designing for the highest possible bandwidth will lead to high-energy costs. The communication requirements of GPU cores must be determined in order to choose a proper interconnect. In this chapter we evaluate the bandwidth requirement for GPU cores with various standard GPU applications. We assumed a photonic interconnect model between the GPU and the memory shader to model the interaction, while keeping in mind that photonic interconnects is one of the potential high-bandwidth and low-energy on-chip interconnect paradigms.

3.1 PHOTONIC INTERCONNECT ARCHITECTURE MODEL

In this chapter, we envision a CMP in which the cores communicate via photonic interconnects. A photonic NoC can provide high bandwidth more efficiently than electronic interconnects, especially over long distances [15]. In a photonic NoC, multiple bits can be encoded into a beam of light by using WDM [15]. The bandwidth of these photonic interconnects can be modified by varying the number of wavelengths used. Increasing the number of wavelengths increases the bandwidth, but also increases the power consumption. Hence to gain the best performance, applications that benefit from increased bandwidth should be the only ones to use the high bandwidth photonic interconnects.

Our photonic network model consists of a single photonic waveguide. A waveguide is capable of transmitting up to 64 different wavelengths using WDM [11]. The modulators for each wavelength can operate at 10 Gbps [5]. Therefore a single waveguide can provide a bandwidth of 640 Gbps. We modeled a configuration with an equivalent bandwidth to represent the photonic interconnect in GPGPU-Sim [16] to evaluate the traffic exchange between the GPGPU and the memory unit. Here are the calculations for determining the flit size at 700 GHz to provide this equivalent bandwidth:

$$BW_{\text{photonic}} = f_{\text{tuning}} n_{\text{wavelength}}. \tag{1}$$

Here, f_{tuning} and n_{tuning} are the bandwidth per tuned frequency channel and the number of wavelength channels, respectively. Assuming a typical photonic on-chip waveguide with 64 channels and 10 Gbps bandwidth per channel, the total aggregate BW turns out to be 640 Gbps. We assume that this aggregate BW is shared between 8 communicating pairs of GPGPU and memory units resulting in a BW of 80 Gbps per pair. The memory clock being 700 MHz the flit width which is the number of bits, β that can be transmitted over the photonic link in one cycle is

$$\beta = \frac{BW_{\text{pair}}}{f_{\text{memory}}}. \tag{2}$$

This gives a flit width of approximately 128B. For comparison, we assumed a baseline photonic interconnect that matches the state-of-the-art wired BW of 179.2 Gbps (32B × 700 MHz). This can be modeled as a photonic interconnect with 18 wavelength channels, providing a comparable aggregate wavelength.

In addition to the bandwidth the energy consumption in data transfer between the GPU and the memory unit needs to be modeled. Photonic interconnects are demonstrated to be ultra-low power. The energy consumption of the various components is shown in Table 1. In a photonic interconnect, energy is needed to power the light source as well as heat the modulators to tune them. The following formulas were used to calculate power consumption for our photonic interconnects:

$$E_{\text{cycle}_{\text{wavelength}}} = E_{\text{launch}} + E_{\text{modulate}} + E_{\text{tuning}} \frac{n_{\text{wavelength}}}{2}. \tag{3}$$

Here E_{launch} and E_{modulate} are the energy required to launch and to modulate a single bit, respectively. E_{tuning} is the energy required to tune the modulators and demodulators to a particular frequency. The value of the tuning energy computed in Eq. (3) is the average for all the wavelengths. The total energy consumption per cycle, E_{cycle} is

$$E_{\text{cycle}} = E_{\text{cycle}_{\text{wavelength}}} n_{\text{wavelength}}. \tag{4}$$

Table 1 Energy Dissipation of Photonic Components

Component	Energy per Cycle (pJ)
Modulator/demodulator per bit	0.04 [17]
Tuning per nm	0.24 [17]
Laser launch	0.15 [18]

Consequently, the energy per flit is

$$E_{\text{flit}} = E_{\text{cycle}} \frac{\beta}{BW_{\text{photonic}}} f_{\text{clk}}, \tag{5}$$

where f_{clk} is the frequency of the interconnect clock. This gives the total photonic interconnect energy as

$$E_{\text{photonic}} = E_{\text{flit}} n_{\text{cycles}} R_{\text{flit}}. \tag{6}$$

The resulting power consumption of the photonic interconnect is therefore

$$P_{\text{photonic}} = E_{\text{photonic}} \frac{f_{\text{clk}}}{n_{\text{cycles}}}. \tag{7}$$

Using this model of the photonic interconnect between the GPGPU and the memory, we evaluate the impact of increasing interconnect bandwidth on various GPGPU applications.

4 CHARACTERIZATION OF GPGPU PERFORMANCE

In this section we show the detailed analyses of Compute Unified Device Architecture (CUDA) [19] and Rodinia [20] GPU benchmarks, followed by a policy for selecting bandwidth to differentiate the application that will have an improved performance from the ones that will not. Then we present a case study for a photonic NoC with dynamic bandwidth-allocation capabilities to demonstrate how the heterogeneous system performance can be improved using such a policy over static allocation.

4.1 METHODOLOGY

In order to characterize the potential GPU bandwidth requirements GPGPU-Sim [16] is used for the following experiments. Table 2 summarizes the baseline GPGPU-Sim configuration that is used for the experiments. This configuration came packaged with the simulator. It is supposed to model a NVIDIA GTX 480 GPU, which is a Fermi architecture. This configuration is set up such that it has 15 processing clusters and 1 core per cluster. There is a one-to-one mapping of single-instruction multiple-threads (SIMT) cores to SIMT core clusters instead of having multiple SIMT cores within each cluster. The only parameter that was changed was the flit size to make it directly proportional to the available bandwidth.

Table 2 Baseline GPGPU-SIM Configuration

Parameter	Value
Processing clusters	15
Cores per cluster	1
Memory controllers	6
DRAM chips per MC	2
Core clock rate	
Interconnect clock rate	700 MHz
L2 cache clock rate	
DRAM clock rate	924 MHz
Warps per cycle	48
Interconnect topology	Butterfly
Flit size	32B

4.2 SPEEDUP ANALYSIS WITH VARYING BANDWIDTH

In order to understand the impact of bandwidth on GPU applications, we evaluate different GPU benchmarks for Instruction Per Cycle (IPC) with different flit sizes. We used CUDA [19] and Rodinia [20] GPU benchmarks for this evaluation. The normalized IPC (i.e., IPC for flit size 1024B/IPC for flit size 32B) of these benchmarks is shown in Fig. 1. The increased flit size represents an increased bandwidth for GPU-memory communication. The figure shows that an increased bandwidth for GPU-memory communication improves performance (i.e., normalized IPC > 1) for some benchmarks. However, in several cases the performance is unaffected (i.e., normalized IPC = 1). Among all the benchmarks used in this study, we can observe that *BFS*, *cfd*, and *Kmeans* experienced the highest performance gain with increased bandwidth, as their speedup is 1.63, 1.59, and 1.28, respectively. However, most of the benchmarks used in this study show a change in performance of less than 4%. From these studies, we can see that bandwidth sensitive applications such as *BFS*, *cfd*, and *Kmeans* will have an improved performance if high bandwidth is provided for GPU-memory communication. On the other hand, higher GPU-memory bandwidth has no significant effect on the performance such as some applications. Hence we conclude that higher bandwidth is a necessary but not sufficient condition for optimal performance. If a GPU were designed to have the highest desirable bandwidth, it would use more power and performance would not improve for all applications. Hence, to meet the optimal performance gain with a provided power margin, a dynamic bandwidth allocation (DBA) is required.

We also evaluate these benchmarks with various flit sizes to determine the optimal bandwidth where the interconnect bandwidth is not a bottleneck for the performance. Fig. 2 shows the plot for speedup versus flit size for *BFS*, *MUM*, *b + tree*, *bfs*, *cfd*, and *Kmeans* benchmarks. For this study, we vary the flit size from 32B to 1024B. In Fig. 2

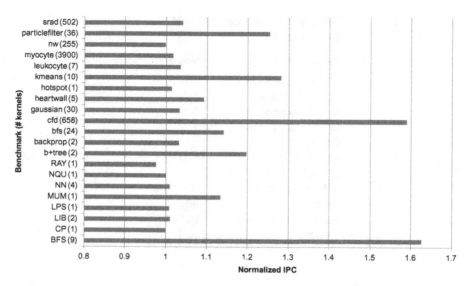

FIG. 1

Normalized IPC (IPC 1024B flit size/IPC 32B flit size) for CUDA SDK (*upper case*) and Rodinia (*lower case*) benchmark applications.

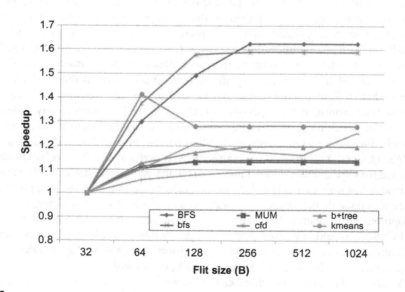

FIG. 2

Flit size versus speedup for selected benchmarks.

it can be seen that the selected benchmarks reached a performance plateau around 128B. In addition, detailed analysis shows that across all benchmarks, this statistic stays relatively constant beyond 128B flit size. Hence overprovisioning bandwidth on a GPU beyond this point will be a waste of resources, because the power consumption will increase, and there will be little to no improvement in performance.

4.3 DETAILED ANALYSIS

In this section we present a detailed study to find a statistic that can indicate how increasing bandwidth affects performance. For this study, we look at different metrics (e.g., interconnect stalls, DRAM stalls, etc.) other than the IPC. The goal is to find a way to predict how applications behave when the bandwidth increases without actually having to simulate them with multiple bandwidths. Initially, we looked at the number of memory accesses for each benchmark. Intuitively, it makes sense that a benchmark with more memory accesses will benefit from having a higher bandwidth. However, this is not true for all the benchmarks we used in this study. Some of the benchmarks that showed no improvement had numbers of memory accesses comparable to those that did improve. For each benchmark, we compared the number of DRAM and interconnect stalls at each bandwidth to the baseline. From this study, we see that among the benchmarks that performed better with higher bandwidth, the number of DRAM and interconnect stalls decreased as the bandwidth increased. However, for some other benchmarks, the decrease in interconnect stalls was counteracted by an increase in DRAM stalls. Presumably, the increased bandwidth allows data from DRAM to be sent back to the shader cores faster. This means that blocks are not stalled on memory accesses as long, which in turn means that they generate memory requests at a higher rate, resulting in more DRAM stalls. This increase in the number of DRAM stalls effectively canceled the benefit of having fewer interconnect stalls. In some other cases, such as in the case of leukocytes, both the DRAM and interconnect stalls decreased, but bad memory locality resulted in an increase in the L2 miss rate. The increase in cache misses means that more memory accesses is required, which would negate some of the benefit of the reduction in stalls. All of these observations are results of increasing the bandwidth and therefore not useful in making a prediction as to how bandwidth will affect performance.

From the results of our study, we can see that a good indicator of when a benchmark will benefit from a higher bandwidth was the rate at which stalls were occurring when compared to the number of execution cycles. The idea for this was adapted from Ref. [21], which showed that there was a correlation between speedup and the memory injection rate when using a perfect NoC (zero latency and infinite bandwidth). Figs. 3 and 4 show the detailed analysis for two of the benchmarks, *BFS* and *leukocyte*. In Fig. 3, *leukocyte* is a good example of the behaviors just described. Congestion in the memory controller for the shader core interconnect causes stalls, which leads to a lower memory injection rate and lower performance. Increasing the bandwidth of the interconnect helps alleviate the congestion and reduce the number of stalls.

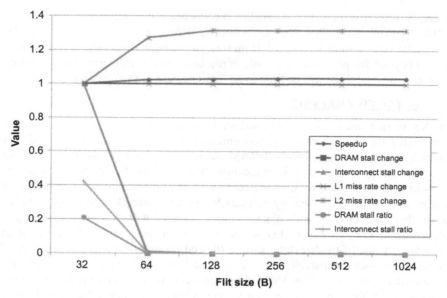

FIG. 3

Memory statistics for leukocyte benchmark.

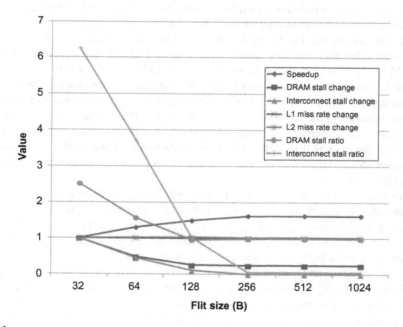

FIG. 4

Memory statistics for BFS benchmark.

4.4 BANDWIDTH SELECTION POLICY

Based on our study in the previous section, we discuss a bandwidth selection policy that indicates the benchmarks that will have an improvement in performance with increased bandwidth. From the study we observe that, if the stall rate per number of cycles for 32B flit size is greater than 0.95, then there is an improvement in performance with an increase in bandwidth for most of the benchmarks. Hence we use this stall rate value as a threshold for differentiating the benchmarks that will have an improved performance with increased bandwidth from the ones that will have no effect in performance. We also evaluate this policy for different benchmarks. We compare the speedups with bandwidth choices made using the policy mentioned above against the optimal bandwidth choice yielding the highest performance. This speedup comparison for different benchmarks is illustrated in Fig. 5. The average increase in performance when using the optimal choices as opposed to the policy choices was only 1.37%. Most of this increase in performance is because the policy inaccurately predicted the *particlefilter* benchmark, which has an interconnect stall ratio of 0.42, and the performance bottleneck was due to other metrics. However, the increase in power consumption for the optimal bandwidth choice was much greater than the increase in performance. The average power consumption of the benchmarks using the optimal bandwidth choices was 12.5% greater than the average power consumption when using our policy's bandwidth choices.

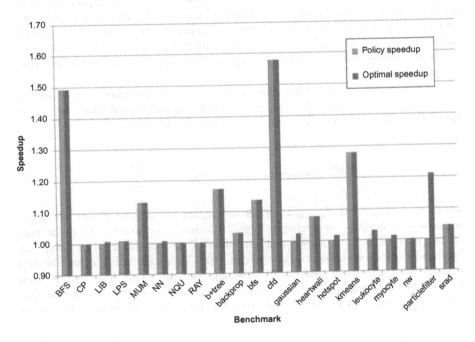

FIG. 5

Comparison of bandwidth selection policy and optimal choice.

We also compared the selected and optimal bandwidths using the photonic interconnect with the wired interconnect to illustrate the benefit of using photonic interconnect for DBA. The wired interconnect can provide only the high bandwidth and not the energy efficiency, making it less flexible than the photonic interconnect. The average performance of the wired interconnect was approximately equal to that of the photonic interconnect with optimal bandwidth choices. However, the wired interconnect with the lengths that we chose (46 and 16.25 mm) consumed significantly more power than the photonic interconnect. We additionally showed a 5.5 mm wired interconnect, which had a power consumption approximately equal to the photonic interconnect when using high bandwidth. For a wire with a capacitance of C_{wire}, length of l_{wire}, and a flit size S_{flit} the dynamic power of the wired interconnect can be calculated using following equation:

$$P_{wired} = 0.5 C_{wire} \times l_{wire} \times \text{flit rate} \times V_{DD}^2 \times f_{clk} \times S_{flit} \qquad (8)$$

Fig. 6 shows the power consumption for each benchmark with each of the different interconnects. From the figure, it can be seen that the 46 mm wire has $9.79\times$ higher power compared to the photonic interconnect with our selection policy and $8.70\times$ higher power than the photonic interconnect with optimal choices. For the wired interconnect with a length of 16.25 mm the power is $3.46\times$ and $3.07\times$ higher compared to our selection policy and optimal bandwidth selection, respectively. Even the 5.5 mm interconnect used 17% more power than our chosen policy interconnect and 4% more than the optimal photonic interconnect. On average, the electronic interconnects used 4.56 mJ/mm of wire, meaning that a wire length of less than 4.7 mm will consume the same or less average power as a photonic interconnect using our policy.

We also evaluated these different interconnects for energy-delay-product (EDP) a common metric to measure the trade-off between performance and energy consumption. The EDP for an interconnect technology was calculated as

$$EDP = E_{interconnect} n_{cycles} = P_{interconnect} \frac{n_{cycles}^2}{f_{clk}} \qquad (9)$$

where $E_{interconnect}$ and $P_{interconnect}$ refer to the energy and the power of the interconnect technology, respectively. Fig. 7 illustrates the average EDP for each of the interconnects. It shows that the photonic interconnect, when using our bandwidth selection policy, has the lowest EDP. This means that it has the best balance of performance and energy consumption. Intuitively, this makes sense because the photonic interconnect with our policy choices offers nearly identical performance and uses on the order of 10% less power than the optimal bandwidth choice case.

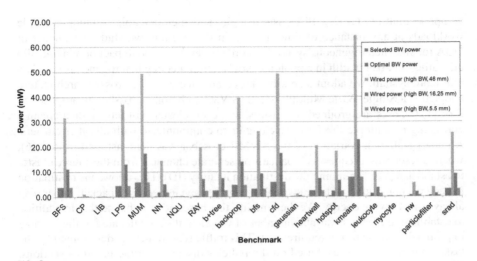

FIG. 6

Power consumption for each benchmark with different interconnect types.

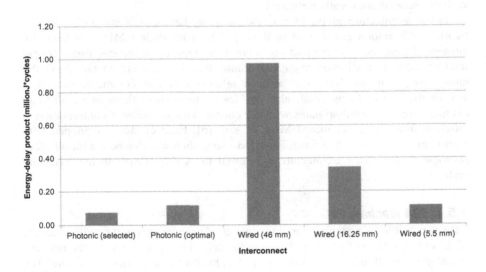

FIG. 7

Average energy-delay-product for each interconnect.

4.5 CASE STUDY WITH DBA IN A HETEROGENEOUS MULTICORE CHIP WITH A PHOTONIC NoC

In the previous sections, we discussed how individual GPU benchmarks can benefit from dynamic bandwidth. However, modern and future heterogeneous systems will comprise multiple GPU, CPU, custom logic, and memory units running multiple workloads at any instance of time. Hence, in this section, we study the impact of DBA for such heterogeneous systems. In order to evaluate the impact of dynamically allocating link bandwidth in a photonic NoC interconnecting heterogeneous core in a multicore system, we adopt a crossbar-based architecture. The crossbar architecture adopted is a Single-Write Multiple-Read (SWMR) photonic crossbar as proposed in Ref. [11]. Cores are grouped in clusters, and each cluster will have a data channel consisting of multiple DWDM wavelengths to communicate with all other clusters. An energy-efficient variation of the SWMR crossbar was demonstrated in Ref. [6], where a reservation request is broadcast on separate channels from the source cluster to establish a path containing the destination identity (ID). This allows the destination to keep the demodulators to be switched on only when it receives a packet, rather than always, thus saving energy. We then modify this baseline crossbar so that in addition to establishing a path, a variable number of wavelengths are allocated to the channel in proportion to the traffic requirement. This traffic requirement is determined by the task running on the cores, based on the policies discussed in the previous sections. Hence this bandwidth allocation happens only when there is a change in the task mapping on the chip and not on a per-packet basis. Therefore the overhead associated with this scheme are greatly mitigated.

In this architecture adopted for a case study, we have considered a hierarchical, hybrid configuration crossbar as in Refs. [6,22]. The whole CMP is divided into clusters of four cores. These four cores are interconnected using traditional copper interconnects in an all-to-all manner. Because the cores in a cluster are physically close, using wireline links can achieve reliable and fast communication. The size of the cluster being small also enables us to connect them in an all-to-all manner avoiding multihop paths within a cluster. This intracluster configuration is different from the concentrated Mesh in Ref. [6]. Each cluster is equipped with a photonic router, which is interconnected using photonic channels with all other photonic routers. This architecture is referred to as *d-HetPNoC* in the following sections.

4.5.1 DBA mechanism

DBA is possible by assigning variable number of wavelengths to the write channels of the clusters. When there is a change in the task allocation on a core, the network reconfigures itself and allocates necessary bandwidth to the cluster of the core. The total aggregate data bandwidth depends on the total number of DWDM wavelengths in all the data waveguides. Because this aggregate bandwidth budget has to be shared between all the clusters a token-based distributed mechanism to request and acquire wavelength channels in each photonic router is used in Ref. [22].

4.5.2 Performance evaluation of the d-HetPNoC

Applications mapped on the cores can demand high or low bandwidths with other clusters. For our experiments, we considered four different possible bandwidths for the photonic channels. In this part, we considered electro-optic modulators and demodulators operating at 12.5 Gbps on a single wavelength carrier channel as demonstrated in Ref. [17]. Hence the minimum channel bandwidth we considered is 12.5 Gbps, which can be realized with a single wavelength. Higher speed channels with 2, 4, and 8 wavelengths having 25, 50, and 100 Gbps bandwidths, respectively, were considered. These values represent the actual memory-interaction bandwidths required by various processing cores (e.g., CPU, GPGPU, custom logic) [2]. We experimented with varying number of clusters, requiring the four categories of bandwidths, as shown in Table 3, to study the effect of increasing skew in the traffic patterns. Traffic patterns with increasing skew demanded a higher frequency of communication for high bandwidth applications than the low bandwidth ones. We also evaluated the DBA-enabled *d-HetPNoC* with a uniform-random traffic pattern where all communication required the same uniform bandwidth, and all cores communicated with all other cores with equal data rate. The performance and energy consumption of the *d-HetPNoC* was compared to that of the baseline Firefly architecture to demonstrate the advantages over a uniform bandwidth allocation.

The NoC architectures were characterized using a cycle-accurate simulator that models the progress of the data flits accurately per clock cycle, accounting for those flits that reach the destination as well as those that are dropped. The simulation parameters are listed in Table 4. The network switches were synthesized from an RTL-level design using 65 nm standard cell libraries from CMP [23], using Synopsys. The delays and energy dissipation on the wired links were obtained through Cadence simulations taking into account the specific lengths of each link based on the established connections following the topology of the NoCs. The power dissipation of the photonic components such as modulators, demodulators, and laser sources were as shown in Table 1. The maximum number of wavelengths that can be accommodated in a single waveguide is considered to be 64 as in Ref. [6].

The normalized bandwidth for *d-HetPNoC* architecture with respect to Firefly PNoC for the different traffic patterns is shown in Fig. 8. The bandwidth was measured as the average number of bits successfully arriving at all the cores per second. As can be seen, with uniform traffic, the *d-HetPNoC* and the baseline crossbar-based Firefly performed similarly because both architectures provide the exact same bandwidth between all pairs of clusters. This is because, in a uniform-random traffic, all communication channels require the same bandwidth resulting

Table 3 Bandwidth Characteristics for Different Skewed Traffic Scenarios

Application	Frequency				Traffic
	100 Gbps	50 Gbps	25 Gbps	12.5 Gbps	
	50%	25%	12.5%	12.5%	Skewed1
	75%	12.5%	6.25%	6.25%	Skewed2
	90%	5%	2.5%	2.5%	Skewed3

Table 4 Simulation Parameters [22]

System size	Number of cores, 64
	Number of clusters, 16
	Cluster size, 4 cores
Die area	20 × 20 mm
Clock frequency	2.5 GHz
Simulation cycle	10,000 with 1000 reset cycle
Packet property	Packet size, 64 flits
	Packet size 32 bit (same as wire width)
Router memory	VC per port, 16
	Buffer depth per VC, 64 flits
Switching	Wormhole-based packet switching
Photonic data bandwidth (total 64 available wavelengths)	Firefly PNOC, 4 wavelengths per channel × 16 channels
	Heterogeneous PNoC, maximum channel bandwidth of 8 wavelengths

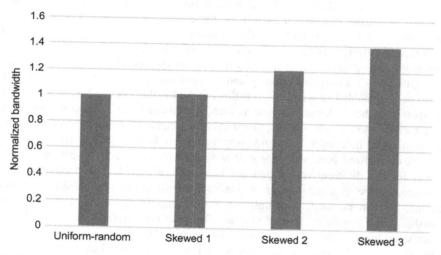

FIG. 8

Normalized bandwidth for *d-HetPNoC* with Firefly PNoC for uniform-random and skewed traffic patterns.

in the same configuration for both Firefly and the *d-HetPNoC*. This equality exists despite the fact that the *d-HetPNoC* has to send additional information about which wavelengths to use to the destinations in the reservation flit along with the destination ID and packet size. The size of each *wavelength identifier* is 6 bits, which denote the binary encoded wavelength number (out of 64 per waveguide). A waveguide number is not needed, as a single waveguide is sufficient to accommodate all 64 wavelengths for the data channels used in our experiments, as listed in Table 4. Because a cluster may need a maximum of eight wavelength identifiers to be sent to the destination, it will take 60 ps using a single waveguide to send the reservation flit. Consequently, this information can be sent in less than a single clock cycle, which is assumed to be 400 ps, along with the rest of reservation flit, as in Firefly, requiring no additional timing overhead. We assumed a clock period of 400 ps as a representative of the fastest system clocks in the 65 nm node that was used to synthesize all the NoC components.

Next, we discuss the impact of increasing heterogeneity or skew in the traffic exchanges. As the skew in traffic increases, the communication between the high-bandwidth applications also increases. In Firefly architecture, the uniformly assigned bandwidth is insufficient for the high-bandwidth applications. This insufficient bandwidth causes packets from frequently communicating high-bandwidth applications to wait longer in the photonic routers. This is in turn congests the photonic routers resulting in a degraded performance. Conversely, the *d-HetPNoC* provides sufficient bandwidth for these high-bandwidth applications, reducing the waiting time for the packets in the photonic routers. Hence even with an increase in the frequency of communication between the high-bandwidth applications, the photonic routers do not suffer from congestion as much as in the case of Firefly. Consequently, the *d-HetPNoC* architecture performs better than the basic Firefly architecture with an increased skew in the traffic as shown by the increased normalized bandwidth for the *d-HetPNoC* architecture.

The normalized packet energy of the *d-HetPNoC* architecture with respect to Firefly PNoC is shown in Fig. 9. Packet energy is the energy dissipated in transferring one packet completely from source to destination at network saturation. The Firefly architecture has the same packet energy as the *d-HetPNoC* for the uniform-random traffic, as they are practically the same architecture in this case. However, with increased skew in traffic, the packet energy also increases as the congestion in the photonic routers increases. On the other hand, for the *d-HetPNoC*, the packet energy increases less with an increase in skew of the traffic because of more efficient utilization of the available bandwidth. Consequently, the gain in packet energy for the *d-HetPNoC* increases with increasing skewness in traffic compared to the baseline Firefly architecture, as shown by the decrease in normalized packet energy in Fig. 9. In the next section, we evaluate our proposed *d-HetPNoC* with specific traffic cases.

4.5.3 Case studies with synthetic and real application-based traffic patterns

In this section, we present case studies for both the architectures with synthetic and real application-based traffic patterns. For the synthetic traffic patterns, we consider hotspot traffic coupled with the skewed communication pattern. In this case, a core is determined to be the hotspot core, and all cores send a certain percentage of all traffic

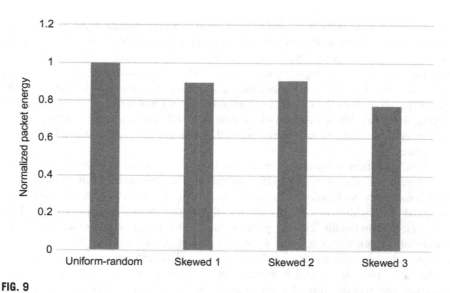

FIG. 9

Normalized packet energy for *d-HetPNoC* with Firefly PNoC for uniform-random and skewed traffic patterns.

to the hotspot. The rest of the traffic is distributed following the skewed traffic types outlined in Table 3. For our case study, the skewed hotspot1 and skewed hotspot2 traffic patterns generate 10% of the total traffic to the hotspot core, and the other 90% utilize the skewed 2 and skewed 3 traffic patterns mentioned in Table 3. The skewed hotspot3 and skewed hotspot4 reveal 20% of traffic to the hotspot coupled with skewed 2 and skewed 3 traffic patterns, respectively. These kinds of patterns capture the high-frequency communication with some central authority in the CMP like a scheduler or controller via the hotspot pattern as well as skewed core to memory interactions.

For the real application-based traffic, parallel GPU applications such as *MUM*, *BFS*, *CP*, *RAY*, and *LPS* are mapped to 20, 4, 4, 4, and 16 cores, respectively. These cores are considered to be GPUs occupying 12 clusters. The remaining four clusters are considered to have memory cores, which contain the data for the applications mapped to the GPU cores. Then the bandwidth requirement is determined using actual core-to-memory interactions from profiling these applications in GPGPU-Sim [16], using GPU-memory bandwidth of 128B flit size at 700 MHz. The peak bandwidth per core and packet energy values for these traffic patterns are shown in Fig. 10. In all the cases, the peak bandwidth per core of the *d-HetPNoC* is better than the Firefly architecture. This is because of the insufficient bandwidth allocation in the Firefly architecture for the high-bandwidth communications. However, the degradation in energy and bandwidth is less for the *d-HetPNoC* because it can

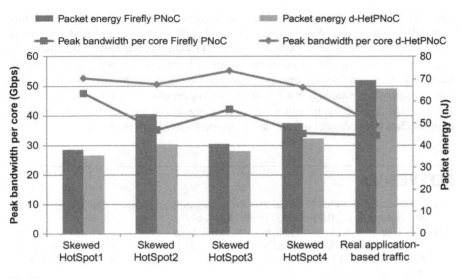

Packet energy Firefly PNoC **Packet energy d-HetPNoC**

Peak bandwidth per core Firefly PNoC **Peak bandwidth per core d-HetPNoC**

FIG. 10

Comparative performance for Firefly PNoC and *d-HetPNoC* with synthetic and real application-based traffic.

allocate high bandwidth to communication channels that need it, unlike the baseline Firefly. The same trend is observed regardless of the actual percentage traffic at the hotspot.

In real application-based traffic, the interactions between the memory clusters and some of the core clusters require higher bandwidth. This results in a lower peak bandwidth for Firefly compared to the *d-HetPNoC* because Firefly cannot provide the high bandwidth to clusters that need it.

5 CONCLUSION

A dynamic NoC architecture is required to cater to the varying bandwidth needs of the applications running on CMPs. Such architecture is also required for future CMPs that integrate heterogeneous cores such as custom logic, GPGPUs, programmable fabrics, and memory. In this chapter we discussed and demonstrated the needs of a heterogeneous interconnection fabric for future many-core chips that will integrate GPGPU cores to accelerate massively parallel threads. Our investigations conclude that some GPU tasks benefit from a higher bandwidth allocation between the GPU cores and its memory shader, and yet others do not. This difference in behavior can be argued to motivate the need for a DBA in the NoC fabric that is responsible for core-to-core communication in modern multi- and many-core chips. As a case study, we experimented with the design of a heterogeneous photonic NoC architecture with DBA, which can allocate different bandwidths between different clusters of cores based on an application's demands. Through system-level simulation, we demonstrated that the test architecture helps not only in achieving higher performance but also in achieving energy efficiency for the same overall data bandwidth. Consequently, we establish that for future heterogeneous many-core chips, the need for a dynamic NoC architecture with emerging interconnect paradigms such as photonic links are beneficial from an energy-performance perspective.

REFERENCES

[1] I. Ekmecic, I. Tartalja, V. Milutinovic, A survey of heterogeneous computing: concepts and systems, Proc. IEEE 84 (8) (1996) 1127–1144.

[2] E.S. Chung, P.A. Milder, J.C. Hoe, K. Mai, Single-chip heterogeneous computing: does the future include custom logic, FPGAs, and GPGPUs?, in: Proceedings of the 43rd Annual IEEE/ACM International Symposium on Microarchitecture (MICRO'10), December, 2010, pp. 225–236.

[3] A. Mishra, N. Vijaykrishnan, C.R. Das, A case for heterogeneous on-chip interconnects for CMPs, in: Proceedings of International Symposium Computer Architecture (ISCA'11), 2011, pp. 389–400.

[4] A.K. Mishra, O. Mutlu, C.R. Das, A heterogeneous multiple network-on-chip design: an application-aware approach, in: Proceedings of the 50th Annual Design Automation Conference (DAC'13), ACM, New York, NY, USA, 2013.

[5] A. Shacham, Photonic network-on-chip for future generations of chip multi-processors, IEEE Trans. Comput. 57 (9) (2008) 1246–1260.

[6] Y. Pan, et al., Firefly: illuminating future network-on-chip with nanophotonics, in: Proceedings of 36th Annual ACM International Symposium on Computer architecture (ISCA'09), 2009, pp. 429–440.

[7] A. Flores, J.L. Aragon, M.E. Acacio, Heterogeneous inter-connects for energy-efficient message management in CMPs, IEEE Trans. Comput. 59 (1) (2010) 16–28.

[8] B. Grot, J. Hestness, S. Keckler, O. Mutlu, Kilo-NoC: a heterogeneous network-on-chip architecture for scalability and service guarantees, in: Proceedings of International Symposium Computer Architecture (ISCA'11), 2011, pp. 401–412.

[9] A. Bakhoda, J. Kim, T.M. Aamodt, Throughput-effective on-chip networks for manycore accelerators, in: Proceedings of 43rd Annual IEEE/ACM International Symposium on Microarchitecture (MICRO'43), Atlanta, GA, USA, 2010, pp. 421–432.

[10] A. Joshi, et al., Silicon-photonic clos network for global on-chip communication, in: Proceedings of the 3rd International Symposium on Networks-on-Chip (NOCS), May 2009, pp. 124–133.

[11] D. Vantrease, et al., Corona: system implications of emerging nanophotonic technology, in: Proceedings of IEEE International Symposium on Computer Architecture (ISCA'08), 2008, pp. 153–164.

[12] Y. Xie, et al., Crosstalk noise and bit error rate analysis for optical network-on-chip, in: Proceedings of the 47th ACM/IEEE Design Automation Conference (DAC'10), 2010, pp. 657–660.

[13] C. Li, M. Browning, P.V. Gratz, S. Palermo, LumiNOC: a power-efficient, high-performance, photonic network-on-chip for future parallel architectures, in: Proceedings of the 21st International Conference on Parallel Architectures and Compilation Techniques (PACT'12), ACM, 2012, pp. 421–422.

[14] Spec CPU Benchmark, 2015, https://www.spec.org/cpu/.

[15] C. Nitta, M. Farrens, V. Akella, On-Chip Photonic Interconnects: A Computer Architect's Perspective, in: Synthesis Lectures on Computer Architecture, 8(5) (2014) 1–111.

[16] A. Bakhoda, G.L. Yuan, W. Fung, H. Wong, T. Aamodt, Analyzing CUDA workloads using a detailed GPU simulator, in: Proceedings of the IEEE International Symposium on Performance Analysis of Systems and Software (ISPASS'09), Boston, MA, USA, 2009, pp. 163–174.

[17] P. Dong, et al., Tunable high speed silicon microring modulator, in: Proceedings of the Conference on Lasers and Electro-Optics (CLEO) and Quantum Electronics and Laser Science Conference (QELS), May 2010, pp. 1–2.

[18] K. Preston, et al., Performance guidelines for WDM interconnects based on silicon microring resonators, in: Proceedings Of Laser and Electro-Optics (CLEO), 2011, pp. 1–2.

[19] CUDA Toolkit Documentation, 2015, http://docs.nvidia.com/cuda/cuda-samples/.

[20] S. Che, et al., Rodinia: a benchmark suite for heterogeneous computing, in: Proceedings of the IEEE International Symposium on Workload Characterization (IISWC), Washington, DC, USA, 2009, pp. 44–54.

[21] A. Bakhoda, J. Kim, T.M. Aamodt, Throughput-effective on-chip networks for manycore accelerators, in: MICRO 2010, December, 2010.

[22] A. Shah, N. Mansoor, B. Johnstone, A. Ganguly, S.A. Lopez, Heterogeneous photonic network-on-chip with dynamic bandwidth allocation, in: Proceedings of the 27th IEEE International System-on-Chip Conference (SOCC14), 2014, pp. 249–254.

[23] Circuits MultiProjects, 2015, http://cmp.imag.fr.

Accurately modeling GPGPU frequency scaling with the CRISP performance model

18

R. Nath, D. Tullsen

University of California, San Diego, La Jolla, CA, United States

1 INTRODUCTION

Dynamic voltage and frequency scaling (DVFS) [1] is employed in modern architectures to allow the system to adjust the frequency and supply voltage to particular components within the computer. DVFS has shown the potential for significant power and energy savings in many system components, including processor cores [2,3], memory system [4–6], last level cache [7], and interconnect [8–10]. DVFS scales voltage and frequency for energy and power savings, but can also address other problems such as temperature [11], reliability [12], and variability [13]. However, in all cases it trades off performance for other gains, so properly setting DVFS to maximize particular goals can only be done with the assistance of an accurate estimate of the performance of the system at alternate frequency settings. In addition, we must be able to predict performance in a way that both tracks the dynamic behavior of the application over time and minimizes the measurement and computation overhead of the predictive model.

This chapter describes the CRItical Stalled Path (CRISP) performance predictor for general-purpose computation on graphics processing units (GPGPUs) under varying core frequency. Existing analytical models that account for frequency change target only CPU performance, and do not effectively capture the execution characteristics of a GPU.

While extensive research has been done on DVFS performance modeling for CPU cores, there is little guidance in the literature for GPU and GPGPU settings, despite the fact that modern GPUs have extensive support for DVFS [14–17]. In fact, the potential for DVFS on GPUs is high for at least two reasons. First, the maximum power consumption in a GPGPU is often higher than CPUs, for example, 250 W for the NVIDIA GTX480. Second, while the range of DVFS settings in modern CPUs

Advances in GPU Research and Practice. http://dx.doi.org/10.1016/B978-0-12-803738-6.00018-5

is shrinking, that is not yet the case for GPUs, which have ranges such as 0.5–1.0 V (NVIDIA Fermi [18]).

This work presents a performance model that closely tracks GPGPU performance on a wide variety of workloads and that significantly outperforms existing models that are tuned to the CPU. The improvement is a result of key differences between CPU execution and GPU execution that are not handled by those models. We describe those differences and show how CRISP correctly accounts for them in its runtime model.

Existing CPU DVFS performance models fall into one of a few categories. Most are empirical and use statistical [19–23] or machine learning methods [24,25], or assume a simple linear relationship [26–32] between performance and frequency. Abe et al. [14] target GPUs, but with a regression-based offline statistical model that is neither targeted for nor conducive to runtime analysis.

Recent research presents new performance counter architectures [33–35] to model the impact of frequency scaling on CPU workloads. These analytical models (eg, leading load [33] and critical path [34]) divide a CPU program into two disjoint segments representing the nonpipelined (T_{Memory}) and pipelined (T_{Compute}) portion of the computation. They make two assumptions: (a) the memory portion of the computation never scales with frequency and (b) cores never stall for store operations. Though these assumptions are reasonably valid in CPUs, they start to fail as we move to massively parallel architecture like GPGPUs. No existing runtime analytical models for GPGPUs handle the effect of voltage-frequency changes.

A program running on a GPGPU, typically referred to as a kernel, will have a high degree of thread-level parallelism. The single instruction multiple thread (SIMT) parallelism in GPGPUs allows a significant portion of the computation to be overlapped with memory latency, which can make the memory portion of the computation elastic to core clock frequency and thus breaks the first assumption of the prior models.

Figs. 1 and 2 show this phenomenon on CPU and GPGPU kernels at different core clock frequencies. A CPU program will typically have little memory-overlapped computation, because it runs one or few threads, and has limited storage for unretired instructions. Thus, in this illustrative example, the memory-bound region remains memory bound unless the clock frequency is scaled by extreme amounts. On a GPGPU, however, due to very high amounts of thread and SIMT parallelism, the memory-overlapped computation can be quite significant, and thus a small reduction in frequency may convert the region, or even the entire kernel, from memory bound to compute bound.

Though memory/computation overlap has been used for program optimization, modeling frequency scaling in the presence of abundant parallelism and high memory/computation overlap is a new, complex problem. Moreover, due to the wide single instruction multiple data (SIMD) vector units in GPGPU streaming multiprocessors (SMs) and homogeneity of computation in SIMT scheduling, GPGPU SMs often stall due to stores.

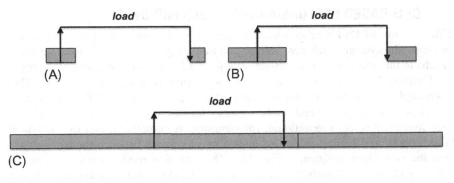

FIG. 1

Performance of CPU program under DVFS. (A) Clock frequency f. (B) Clock frequency $f/2$. (C) Clock frequency $f/10$.

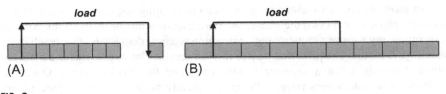

FIG. 2

Performance of GPGPU program under DVFS. (A) Clock frequency f. (B) Clock frequency $f/2$.

The CRISP predictor accounts for these differences, plus others. It provides accuracy within 4% when scaling from 700 to 400 MHz and 8% when scaling all the way to 100 MHz. It reduces the maximum error by a factor of 3.6 compared to prior models. Additionally, when used to direct GPU DVFS settings, it enables nearly double the gains of prior models (10.7% energy delay product [EDP] gain vs 5.7% with critical path and 6.2% with leading load). We also show CRISP effectively used to reduce energy delay squared product (ED^2P), or to reduce energy while maintaining a performance constraint.

2 MOTIVATION AND RELATED WORK

Our model of GPGPU performance in the presence of DVFS builds on prior work on modeling CPU DVFS. Since there are no analytical DVFS models for GPGPUs, we will describe some of the prior work in the CPU domain and the shortcomings of those models when applied to GPUs. We also describe recent GPU-specific performance models at the end of this section.

2.1 CPU-BASED PERFORMANCE MODELS FOR DVFS

Effective use of DVFS relies on some kind of prediction of the performance and power of the system at different voltage and frequency settings. An inaccurate model results in the selection of nonoptimal settings and lost performance and/or energy.

Existing DVFS performance models are primarily aimed at the CPU. They each exploit some kind of linear model, based on the fact that CPU computation scales with frequency speed while memory latency does not. These models fall into four classes: (a) proportional, (b) sampling, (c) empirical, and (d) analytical. The proportional scaling model assumes a linear relation between the performance and the core clock frequency (Fig. 3A). The sampling model better accounts for memory effects by identifying a scaling factor (ie, slope) for each application from two different voltage-frequency operating points. For example in Fig. 3B, we have two different slopes for two applications. The empirical model approximates that slope by counting aggregate performance counter events, such as the number of memory accesses. This model cannot distinguish between applications with low or high memory-level parallelism (MLP) [33].

An analytical model views a program as an alternating sequence of compute and memory phases. In a compute phase, the core executes useful instructions without generating any memory requests (eg, instruction fetches, data loads) that reach main memory. A memory request that misses the last level cache might trigger a memory phase, but only when a resource is exhausted and the pipeline stalls. Once the instruction or data access returns, the core typically begins a new compute phase. In all the current analytical models, the execution time (T) of a program at a voltage-frequency setting with cycle time t is expressed as

$$T(t) = T_{\text{Compute}}(t) + T_{\text{Memory}}. \tag{1}$$

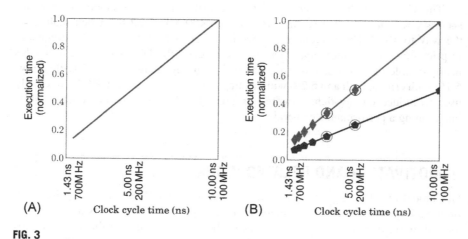

FIG. 3

Very basic DVFS performance models. (A) Proportionate. (B) Sampling.

They strictly assume that the pipeline portion of the execution time (T_{Compute}) scales with the frequency, while the nonpipeline portion (T_{Memory}) does not. The execution time at an unexplored voltage-frequency setting of v_2, f_2 can be estimated from the measurement in the current settings v_1, f_1 by

$$T(v_2, f_2) = T_{\text{Compute}}(v_1, f_1) \times \frac{f1}{f2} + T_{\text{Memory}}. \tag{2}$$

The accuracy of these models relies heavily on accurate classification of cycles into compute or memory phase cycles, and this is the primary way in which these models differ. We describe them next.

Stall time

Stall time [35] estimates the nonpipeline phase (T_{Memory}) as the number of cycles the core is unable to retire any instructions due to outstanding last level cache misses. It ignores computation performed during the miss before the pipeline stall. Since the scaling of this portion of computation can be hidden under memory latency, stall time overpredicts execution time.

Miss model

The Miss model [35] includes reorder buffer (ROB) fill time inside the memory phase. It identifies all the stand-alone misses, but only the first miss in a group of overlapped misses as a contributor to T_{Memory}. In particular, it ignores misses that occur within the memory latency of an initial miss. The resulting miss count is then multiplied by a fixed memory latency to compute T_{Memory}. This approach loses accuracy due to its fixed latency assumption and also ignores stall cycles due to instruction cache misses.

Leading load

Leading load [33,36] recognizes both front-end stalls due to instruction cache misses and back-end stalls due to load misses. Their model counts the cycles when an instruction cache miss occurs in the last level cache. It adopts a similar approach to the miss model to address MLP for data loads. However, to account for variable memory latency, it counts the actual number of cycles a contributor load is outstanding.

Critical path

Critical path [34] computes T_{Memory} as the longest serial chain of memory requests that stalls the processor. The proposed counter architecture maintains a global critical path counter (CRIT) and a critical path time stamp register (τ_i) for each outstanding load i. When a miss occurs in the last level cache (instruction or data), the snapshot of the global critical path counter is copied into the load's time stamp register. Once the load i returns from memory, the global critical path counter is updated with the maximum of CRIT and $\tau_i + L_i$, where L_i is the memory latency for load i.

Example

Fig. 4 provides an example of a CPU program that has one stand-alone load miss (A at cycle 0) and two overlapped load misses (B at cycle 12 and C at cycle 14). At clock frequency f, the core stalls between cycles 1–7 and 15–25 for the loads to complete. The total execution time of the program at clock frequency f is 33 units (18 units stalls + 15 units computation). As we scale down the frequency to $\frac{f}{2}$, the compute cycles (0, 8–14, 26–32) scale by a factor of 2. However, the expansion of compute cycles at 0 and 14 are hidden by the loads A and C, respectively. Thus the execution time at frequency $\frac{f}{2}$ becomes 46 units.

For each performance model, we identify the cycles classified as the nonpipelined (does not scale with the frequency of the pipeline) portion of computation. Leading load (LEAD) computes T_{Memory} as the sum of A and B's latencies ($7 + 8 = 15$). Miss model (MISS) identifies two contributor misses (A and B) and reports T_{Memory} to be 16 (8×2). Among two dependent load paths (A + B with length $8 + 7 = 15$, A + C with length $8 + 12 = 20$), critical path (CRIT) selects A + C as the longest chain of dependent memory requests and computes the critical path as 20. Stall time (STALL) counts the 18 cycles of load-related stalls.

We plug in the value of T_{Memory} in Eq. (2) and predict the execution time at clock frequency $\frac{f}{2}$. The predicted execution time by the different models is shown in Fig. 4. Note that the models also differ in their counting of $T_{Compute}$. Critical path (CRIT) outperforms the other models in this example. Although these models show reasonable accuracy in CPUs, optimization techniques like software and hardware prefetching may introduce significant overlap between computation and memory load latency, and thus invalidate the nonelasticity assumption of the memory component. In that case, the CRISP model should also provide significant improvement for CPU performance prediction.

2.2 DVFS IN GPGPUs

To explore the applicability of DVFS in GPGPUs, we simulate a NVIDIA Fermi architecture using GPGPU-Sim [37] and run nine kernels from the Rodinia [38] benchmark suite at different core clock frequencies—from 700 MHz (baseline) to 100 MHz (minimum). The performance curve in Fig. 5 shows the increase in runtime as we scale down the core frequency, that is, increase clock cycle time (x-axis). We make two major observations from this graph. First, like CPUs, there is significant opportunity for DVFS in GPUs—we see this because two of the kernels (cfd and km) are memory bound and insensitive to frequency changes (they have a flat slope in this graph), while three others (*ge*, *lm*, and *hw*) are only partially sensitive. For the memory-bound kernels, it is possible to reduce clock frequency and thus save energy without any performance overhead.

Our second observation is that the linear assumption of all prior models does not strictly hold because the partially sensitive kernels (eg, *lm* and *hw*) seem to follow two different slopes, depending on the frequency range. At high frequency, they follow

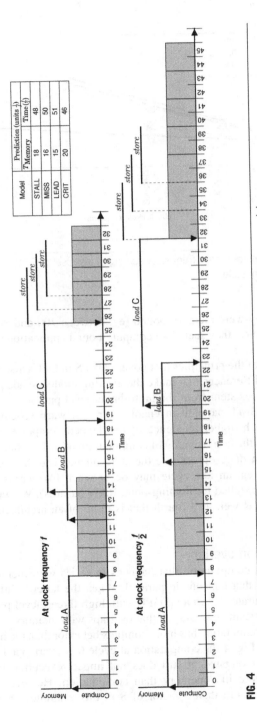

FIG. 4

T_{Memory} computation for a CPU program running at frequency f with different linear performance models.

Model	Prediction (units $\frac{1}{f}$)	
	T_{Memory}	Time ($\frac{1}{f}$)
STALL	18	48
MISS	16	50
LEAD	15	51
CRIT	20	46

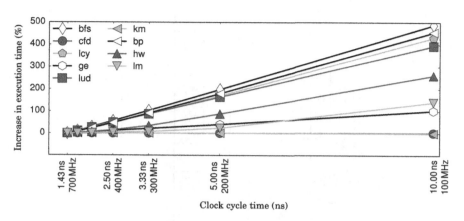

FIG. 5

Performance impact of core clock frequency scaling in a subset of GPGPU kernels from the Rodinia benchmark suite.

a flat slope, as if they were memory bound (eg, between 700 and 300 MHz in *lm*), but at lower frequencies, they scale like compute-bound applications (eg, below 300 MHz in *lm*).

So while several of the principles that govern DVFS in CPUs also apply to GPUs, we identify several differences that make the existing models inadequate for GPUs. All of these differences stem from the high thread-level parallelism in GPU cores, resulting from the SIMT parallelism enabled through warp scheduling. The first difference is the much higher incidence of overlapped computation and memory access. The second is the homogeneity of computation in SIMT scheduling, resulting in the easy saturation of resources like the store queue. The third is the difficulty of classifying stalls (eg, an idle cycle may occur when five warps are stalled for memory and three are stalled for floating-point RAW hazards). We will discuss each of these differences, as well as a fourth that is more of an architectural detail and easily handled.

Memory/computation overlap

Existing models treat computation that happens in series with memory access the same as computation that happens in parallel. When the latter is infrequent, those models are fairly accurate, but in a GPGPU with high thread-level parallelism, it is common to find significant computation that overlaps with memory.

This overlapped computation has more complex behavior than the nonoverlapped. In the top timeline in Fig. 4 the computation at cycle 0 is overlapped with memory, so even though it is elongated, it still does not impact execution time, thus that computation looks more like memory than computation. However, if we extend the clock enough (ie, more than a factor of 8 in this example), that computation completely covers the memory latency and then begins to impact total execution time, now looking like computation again. This phenomenon exactly explains the two-slope behavior exhibited by *hw* and *lm* in Fig. 5.

To examine this phenomenon more closely, we use the "load micro kernel" in Fig. 6 and run it for both single-threaded and many-threaded configurations. The cumulative distribution function shown in Fig. 7A shows that the single-threaded version has nearly zero computation-memory overlap. However, for the many-threaded version, more than 60% of loads have at least 50% of their cycles that are overlapped with computation. When we use the current performance models to predict the execution time of the many-threaded load kernel, the best ones (STALL,

```
loads(float *A, int N){
    int tid  = threadIdx.x;
    float sum = 0;
    for(int j=0;j<N;j++){
            sum+= j * A[j];
    }
    if( tid == -1 ) {
        A[tid] = sum;
    }
}
```

FIG. 6

Load micro kernel.

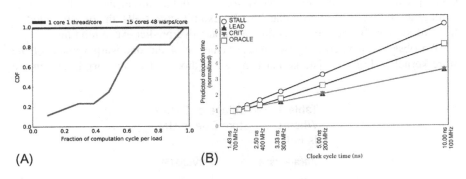

(A)   (B)

FIG. 7

Execution time prediction of load micro kernel under DVFS. (A) Fraction of load cycles overlapped with computation. (B) Prediction.

```
stores(float *A,int N){
    int tid=threadIdx.x;
    for(int j=0;j<N;j++){
        A[j*tid]=0;
    }
}
```

FIG. 8

Store micro kernel.

CRIT) underpredict execution time severely by ignoring the scaling of overlapped computation (Fig. 7B).

Store stalls

A core (CPU or GPU) will stall for a store only when the store queue fills, forcing it to stall and wait for one of the stores to complete. While this is a rare occurrence in CPUs, in a GPU with SIMT parallelism, it is common for all of the threads to execute stores at once, easily flooding the store queue, resulting in memory stalls that do not scale with frequency.

The "store micro kernel" in Fig. 8 initializes an array with constant values. In this code, the SIMD store instruction may fork into 32 individual stores, which can overload the load-store queue (LSQ) unit very quickly. As we increase the amount of parallelism by increasing the number of threads and warps, the percentage of cycles when the LSQ is full increases (Table 1) sharply. The prediction accuracy of the existing analytical models also decreases as we increase parallelism. As illustrated in Fig. 9A, the single-threaded configuration of the store micro kernel is fully compute bound with a very steep slope. Since there is no store-related stall, LEAD and CRIT predict execution time correctly for this configuration. However, for other configurations (Fig. 9B and C) that actually exhibit store stalls, the existing models treat the store stalls the same as computation and overpredict execution time.

We observe an interesting two-phase behavior of the one-warp version of the store kernel in Fig. 9B. The kernel behaves as though it is memory bound in the

Table 1 Percentage of Cycles When Load-Store Queue Unit Is Full

Parallelism	Cycle (%)
1 Thread × 1 core	0
1 Warp × 1 core	66
8 Warps × 15 cores	96

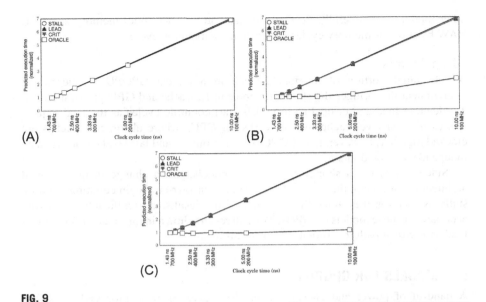

FIG. 9

Execution time prediction of store micro kernel under DVFS. (A) 1 Core 1 thread. (B) 1 Core 1 warp. (C) 15 Core many warps.

high-frequency range and compute bound in the low-frequency range. As we decrease the core clock frequency, the stalls also decrease because of the LSQ being full. In fact, the store-related stall cycles act as idle cycles that can be converted to computation in a lower frequency. Once the frequency is low enough that all of the store stalls disappear (are covered by computation), the kernel then exhibits fully compute-bound behavior.

Complex stall classification

Identifying the cause of a stall cycle is difficult in the presence of high thread-level parallelism. For example, if several threads are stalled waiting for memory, but a few others are stalled waiting for floating-point operations to complete, is this a computation or memory phase? Prior works (which start counting memory cycles only after the pipeline stalls) would categorize this as computation because the pipeline is not yet fully stalled for memory, and the ongoing floating-point operations will scale with frequency.

Consider what happens when, as described earlier, the overlapped computation is scaled to the point where it completely covers the memory latency and now starts to interfere with other computation. The originally idle cycles (eg, between dependent floating-point ops) will not contribute to extending execution time, but rather will now be interleaved with the other computation. Only the cycles where the pipeline was actually issuing instructions will impact execution time. Thus, unlike other models, we generally treat mixed-cause idle cycles (both memory and CPU RAW hazards) as memory cycles rather than computation cycles.

L1 cache miss

A substantial portion of memory latency in a typical GPGPU is due to the interconnect that bridges the streaming cores to L2 cache and GPU global memory. The leading load and critical path models start counting cycles as the load request misses the last level cache, which works for CPUs where all on-chip caches are clocked together; however, in our GPU the interconnect and last level cache are in an independent clock domain.

Since this is not a shortcoming in the models, just a change in the assumed architecture, we adapt these models (as well as our own) to begin counting memory stalls as soon as they miss the L1 cache. This results in significantly improved accuracy for those models on GPUs. Thus all results shown in this chapter for leading load and critical path incorporate that improvement.

2.3 MODELS FOR GPGPUs

A handful of power and energy models have recently been proposed for GPG-PUs [18]. However, very few of these models involve performance predictions. Dao et al. [39] propose linear and machine-learning-based models to estimate the runtime of kernels based on workload distribution. The integrated GPU power and performance (IPP) [40] model predicts the optimum number of cores for a GPGPU kernel to reduce power. However, they do not address the effect of clock frequency on GPU performance. Moreover, they ignore cache misses [41], which is critical for a DVFS model. Song et al. [42] contribute a similar model for a distributed system with GPGPU accelerators. Chen et al. [43] track NBTI-induced threshold voltage shift in GPGPU cores and determine the optimum number of cores by extending IPP. Equalizer [44] maintains performance counters to classify kernels as compute-intensive, memory-intensive, or cache-sensitive, using those classifications to change thread counts or P-States. However, because they have no actual model to predict performance, it still amounts to a sampling-based search for the right DVFS state.

None of these models address the effect of core clock frequency on kernel performance. CRISP is unique in that it is the first runtime analytical model, *either for CPUs or GPGPUs*, to model the nonlinear effect of frequency on performance—this effect can be seen in either system, but is just more prevalent on GPGPUs.

The only GPU analytical model that accounts for frequency is an empirical model [45] that builds a unique nonlinear performance model for each workload—this is intended to be used offline and is not practical for an online implementation. Abe et al. [14,15] also present an offline solution. They use a multiple linear regression-based approach with higher average prediction error (40%). Their maximum error is more than 100%.

3 GPGPU DVFS PERFORMANCE MODEL

This section describes the CRISP performance predictor, a novel analytical model for predicting the performance impact of DVFS in modern many-core architectures like GPGPUs.

3.1 CRITICAL STALLED PATH

Our model interprets computation in a GPGPU as a collection of three distinct phases: load outstanding, pure compute, and store stall (Fig. 10). The core remains in a pure compute phase in the absence of an outstanding load or any store-related stall. Once a fetch or load miss occurs in one of the level 1 caches (constant, data, instruction, texture), the core enters a load outstanding phase and stays there as long as a miss is outstanding. During this phase, the core may schedule instructions or stall due to control, data, or structural hazards. The store stall phase represents the idle cycles due to store operations, in the explicit case where the pipeline is stalled due to store queue saturation.

We split the total computation time into two disjoint segments: a load critical path (LCP) and a compute/store path (CSP).

$$T(t) = T_{\text{LCP}}(t) + T_{\text{CSP}}(t). \tag{3}$$

This division allows us to separately analyze (1) loads and the computation that competes with loads to become performance-critical versus (2) computation that never overlaps loads and is exposed regardless of the behavior of the loads. Store stalls fall into the latter category because any cycle that stalls in the presence of both loads and stores is counted as a load stall.

The LCP is the length of the longest sequence of dependent memory loads (possibly overlapped with computation) from parallel warps. Thus it does not necessarily include all loads, which enables it to account for MLP by not counting loads that occur in parallel, similar to Ref. [33,34]. Meanwhile, we form the CSP as a summation of nonoverlapped compute phases, store stall phases, and computation

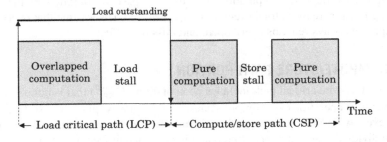

FIG. 10

Critical stalled path: abstract view.

overlapped only by loads not deemed part of the critical path. Since the two segments in Eq. (3) scale differently with core clock frequency, we develop separate models for each.

3.2 LCP PORTION

SMs have high thread-level parallelism. The maximum number of concurrently running warps per SM varies from 24 to 64 depending on the compute capability of the device (eg, 48 in the NVIDIA Fermi architecture). This enables the SM to hide significant amounts of memory latency, resulting in heavy overlap between load latency and useful computation. However, it often does not hide all of it, due to lack of parallelism (either caused by low inherent parallelism or restricted parallelism due to resource constraints) or poor locality.

We represent the LCP as a combination of memory-related overlapped stalls ($T_{LCP}^{\overline{Stall}}$) and overlapped computations ($T_{LCP}^{\overline{Comp}}$). Prior CPU-based models' assumption of T_{Memory}'s inelasticity creates a larger inaccuracy in GPGPUs than it does for CPUs because of the magnitude of $T_{LCP}^{\overline{Comp}}$, which scales linearly with frequency. The expansion of overlapped computation stays hidden under T_{Memory} as long as the frequency scaling factor is less than the ratio between T_{Memory} and the overlapped computation. As the frequency is scaled further, the LCP can be dominated by the length of the scaled overlapped computation. Thus we define the LCP portion of the model as

$$T_{LCP}(t) = \max \left(T_{Memory}, \frac{f_1}{f_2} \times T_{LCP}^{\overline{Comp}} \right). \tag{4}$$

We describe details on parameterizing this equation from hardware events in Sections 3.5 and 3.6. Fig. 11 shows the normalized execution time of the *lm* kernel for seven different frequencies. As expected, we see the load stalls decreasing with lower frequency, but without increasing total execution time for small changes in frequency. As the frequency is decreased further, the overlapped computation increases, with much of it turning into nonoverlapped computation (as some of the original overlapped computation now extends past the duration of the load), resulting in an increase in total execution time. Prior models assume that overlapped computation always remains overlapped, and miss this effect.

3.3 COMPUTE/STORE PATH PORTION

The compute/store critical path includes computation (T_{CSP}^{Comp}) that is not overlapped with memory operations and simply scales with frequency, plus store stalls (T_{CSP}^{Stall}). SMs have a wide SIMD unit (eg, 32 in Fermi). A SIMD store instruction may result in 32 individual scalar memory store operations if uncoalesced (eg, A[tid * 64] = 0). As a result, the LSQ may overflow very quickly during a store-dominant phase in the running kernel. Eventually, the level 1 cache runs out of miss status holding

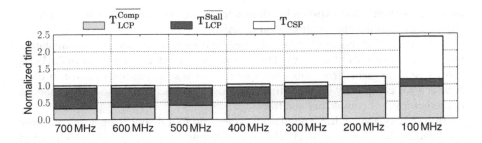

FIG. 11

Runtime of the *lm* kernel at different frequencies.

register (MSHR) entries, and the instruction scheduler stalls due to the scarcity of free entries in the LSQ or MSHR. We observe this phenomenon in several of our application kernels, as well as microbenchmarks we used to fine-tune our models. Again, this is a rare case for CPUs, but easily generated on an SIMD core. Although the store stalls are memory delays, they do not remain static as frequency changes. As frequency slows, the rate (as seen by the memory hierarchy) of the store generation slows, making it easier for the LSQ and the memory hierarchy to keep up. A simple model (meaning one that requires minimal hardware to track) that works extremely well empirically assumes that the frequency of stores decreases in response to the slowdown of nonoverlapped computation (recall, the overlapped computation may also generate stores, but those stores do not contribute to the stall being considered here). Thus we express the CSP by the following equation in the presence of DVFS.

$$T_{\text{CSP}}(t) = \max\left(T_{\text{CSP}}^{\text{Comp}} + T_{\text{CSP}}^{\text{Stall}}, \frac{f_1}{f_2} \times T_{\text{CSP}}^{\text{Comp}}\right). \tag{5}$$

We see this phenomenon, but only slightly, in Fig. 11, but much more clearly in Fig. 12, which shows one particular store-bound kernel in *cfd*. As frequency

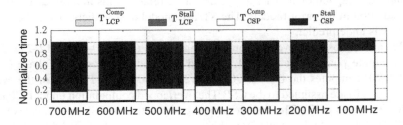

FIG. 12

Runtime of the *cfd* kernel at different frequencies.

decreases, computation expands but does not actually increase total execution time; it only decreases the contribution of store stalls.

We assume that the stretched overlapped computation and the pure computation will serialize at a lower frequency. This is a simplification, and a portion of CRISP's prediction error stems from this assumption. This was a conscious choice to trade accuracy for complexity, because tracking those dependencies between instructions is another level of complexity and tracking.

In summary, then, CRISP divides all cycles into four distinct categories: (1) *pure computation*, which is completely elastic with frequency, (2) *load stall*, which as part of the LCP is inelastic with frequency, (3) *overlapped computation*, which is elastic, but potentially hidden by the LCP, and (4) *store stall*, which tends to disappear as the pure computation stretches.

3.4 EXAMPLE

We illustrate the mechanism of our model in Fig. 13 where loads and computations are from all the concurrently running warps in a single SM. The total execution time of the program at clock frequency f is 31 units (5 units stall + 26 units computation). As we scale down the frequency to $\frac{f}{2}$, all the compute cycles scale by a factor of 2. Because of the scaling of overlapped computation under load A (cycles 0–6) at clock frequency $\frac{f}{2}$, the compute cycle 8 cannot begin before time unit 14. Similarly, the instruction at compute cycle 28 cannot be issued until time unit 50 because the expansion of overlapped computation under load C (cycles 14–23) pushes it further. Meanwhile, as the computation at cycle 28 expands due to frequency scaling, it overlaps with the subsequent store stalls.

For each of the prior performance models, we identify the cycles classified as the nonpipelined portion of computation (T_{Memory}). Leading load (LEAD) computes T_{Memory} as the sum of A, B, and D's latencies ($8 + 5 + 5 = 18$). Miss model (MISS) identifies three contributor misses (A, B, and D) and reports T_{Memory} to be 24 (8×3). Among two dependent load paths (A + B + D with length $8 + 5 + 5 = 18$, A + C with length $8 + 12 = 20$), CRISP computes the LCP as 20 (for the longest path A + C). The stall cycles computed by STALL are 4. We plug in the value of T_{Memory} in Eq. (2) and predict the execution time at clock frequency $\frac{f}{2}$. As expected, the presence of overlapped computation under T_{Memory} and store-related stalls introduces an error in the prediction of the prior models. The STALL model overpredicts, while the rest of the models underpredict.

Our model observes two load outstanding phases (cycles 0–7 and 12–27), three pure compute phases (cycles 8–11, 28, and 30), and one store stall phase (cycle 29). CRISP computes the LCP as 20 (8 + 12 for load A–C). The rest of the cycles ($11 = 31 - 20$) are assigned to the CSP. The overlapped computation under LCP is 17 (cycles 0–6 and 14–23). The nonoverlapped computation in CSP is 10 (cycles 8–13, 26–28, and 30). Note that cycle 29 is the only store stall cycle. CRISP computes the scaled LCP as max (17×2, 20) = 34 and CSP as max (10×2, 11) = 20. Finally,

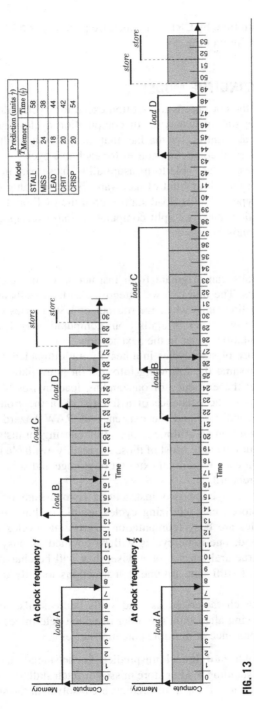

Model	Prediction (units $\frac{1}{f}$)	
	T_{Memory}	Time ($\frac{1}{f}$)
STALL	4	58
MISS	24	38
LEAD	18	44
CRIT	20	42
CRISP	20	54

At clock frequency f

At clock frequency $\frac{f}{2}$

FIG. 13

T_{Memory} computation for a GPU program running at frequency f with different linear performance models.

the predicted execution time by CRISP at clock frequency $\frac{f}{2}$ is 54 (34 + 20), which matches the actual execution time (54).

3.5 PARAMETERIZING THE MODEL

To utilize our model, the core needs to partition execution cycles along some fairly subtle distinctions, separating two types of computation cycles and two types of memory stalls, while accounting for the fact that, in a heavily multithreaded core, there are often a plethora of competing causes for each idle cycle.

Despite these issues, we are able to measure all of these parameters with some simple rules and a very small amount of hardware. First, we categorize each cycle as either one of two types of stalls (load stalls within the LCP or store stalls within the CSP) or computation. Next we split computation into overlapped computation (within the LCP) or nonoverlapped.

Identifying stalls

Memory hierarchy stalls can originate from instruction cache fetch misses, load misses, or store misses. The first two we categorize as load stalls and the last one only manifests in pipeline stalls when we run out of LSQ entries or MSHRs. We initially separate these two types of stalls from computation cycles and then will break down the computation cycles in the next section.

Identifying the cause of stall cycles in a heavily multithreaded core is less than straightforward. We assume the following information is available in the pipeline or L1 cache interface: the existence of outstanding load misses, the existence of outstanding store misses, the existence of a fetch stall in the front-end pipeline, MSHR or LSQ full condition, and the existence of RAW hazard on a memory operation, a RAW hazard on an arithmetic operation causing an instruction to stall, or an arithmetic structural hazard. Most of those are readily available in any pipeline, but the last three might each require an extra bit of storage and some minimal logic added to the GPU scoreboard.

Because our GPU can issue two instructions (two arithmetic or one arithmetic and one load/store), characterizing cycles as idle or busy is already a bit fuzzy. Two-issue cycles are busy (computation), zero-issue cycles are considered idle. On the other hand, one-issue cycles will be counted as busy if there is an arithmetic RAW or structural hazard; otherwise, they will be characterized as idle since there is a lack of sufficient arithmetic instructions to fully utilize the issue bandwidth.

Idle cycles will be characterized as load stalls, store stalls, or computation, according to the following algorithm, the order of which determines the characterization of stalls in the presence of multiple potential causes:

(A) If there is a control hazard (branch mispredict), cache/shared memory bank conflict, or no outstanding load or store misses or fetch stall, this cycle is counted as computation. Branch mispredicts are resolved at the speed of the pipeline, as are L1 cache and shared memory bank conflicts (L1 cache and shared memory run on the same clock as the pipeline).

(B) Else, if there is an outstanding load miss, then if there is a RAW hazard on the load/store unit, this cycle is a load stall. Otherwise, if there is an arithmetic RAW or structural hazard, then this cycle is computation. If neither is the case and the MSHR or LSQ are full, then this is a load stall. Finally, if there is a fetch stall in the front end, then it is a load stall.

(C) Else (no outstanding load miss), then if the MSHR or LSQ are full, this indicates a store stall.

(D) All other stalls must be solely due to arithmetic dependencies and are classified as computation.

Classifying computation

After identifying the total cycles of computation, we divide those into two groups: the pure computation that is part of the CSP and the overlapped computation that is overlapped by the LCP. The former includes both computation that does not overlap loads and computation that overlaps loads that are not part of the critical path. The reason for dividing computation into these sets is that the compute/store computation is always exposed (execution time is sensitive to their latency) while the latter become exposed only when they exceed the load stalls. We describe the mechanism to compute the computation under the LCP here, but revisit the need to precisely track the critical path in Section 3.4.

In order to track the computation that is overlapped by the LCP, we need to track the critical path using a mechanism similar to the critical path model [34]. This is done using a counter to track the global longest critical path (the current T_{Memory} up to this point), as well as counters for each outstanding load that record the critical path length when they started, so that we can decide when they finish if they extend the global longest critical path. However, we instead measure something we call the *adjusted LCP*, which adds load stalls as one-cycle additions to the running global longest critical path. In this way, when the longest critical path is calculated, its length will include both the critical path load latencies and the stalls that lie between the critical loads—the noncritical load stalls. That adjusted LCP is the $T_{\text{LCP}}(t)$ from Eq. (3), which is also the "LCP" from Fig. 10 and includes all load stalls (either as part of the critical load latencies or the noncritical stalls) as well as all overlapped computation. As a result, we can solve for the overlapped computation simply by subtracting the total load stalls from the adjusted LCP; this is possible because we also record the total load stalls in a counter.

In the top timeline in Fig. 13, the original critical path computation will count 8 (latency of A) + 12 (latency of C) = 20 cycles as the LCP, but our adjusted LCP will also pick up the stall at cycle 27 and will calculate 21 as our adjusted LCP. At the same time, we count 4 total load stall cycles. Subtracting 4 from 21 gives us 17 cycles of load-critical overlapped computation, which is exactly the number of computation cycles under the two critical path loads (A and C).

3.6 HARDWARE MECHANISM AND OVERHEAD

We now describe the hardware mechanisms that enable CRISP. It maintains three counters: adjusted LCP (T_{Memory}), load stall ($T_{\text{LCP}}^{\overline{\text{Stall}}}$), and store stall ($T_{\text{CSP}}^{\text{Stall}}$). The rest of the terms in Eqs. (3), (4) can be computed from these three counters and total time by simple subtraction. Like the original critical path (CRIT) model, it also maintains a critical path time stamp register (ts_i) for each outstanding miss (i) in the L1 caches (one per MSHR). Table 2 shows the total hardware overhead for these counters, 99% of which is inherited from CRIT. We discuss the software overhead in Section 5.

At the beginning of each kernel execution, the counters are set to zero. Once a load request i (instruction, data, constant, or texture) misses in the level 1 cache, CRISP copies T_{Memory} into the pending load's time stamp register (ts_i). When the load i's data is serviced from the L2 cache or memory after L_i cycles, T_{Memory} is updated with the maximum of T_{Memory} and $ts_i + L_i$. In the occurrence of a load stall, CRISP increments T_{Memory} and $T_{\text{LCP}}^{\overline{\text{Stall}}}$. For each nonoverlapped (store) stall, CRISP increments $T_{\text{CSP}}^{\text{Stall}}$.

An unoptimized implementation of the logic that detects load and store stall needs just 12 logic gates and is never on the critical path. Most of the signals used in the cycle classification logic are already available in current pipelines. To detect different kinds of hazards, we alter the GPU scoreboard, which requires 1 bit per warp in the GPU hardware scheduler and minimal logic.

4 METHODOLOGY

CRISP, like other existing online analytical models, requires specific changes in hardware. As a result, we rely on simulation (specifically, the GPGPU-Sim [37] simulator) to evaluate the benefit of our novel performance model, as in prior work (CRIT [34], LEAD [33,36]). The GPGPU configuration used in our experiment (Table 3) is very similar to the NVIDIA GTX 480 Fermi architecture (in Section 5.4,

Table 2 Hardware Storage Overhead per SM of CRISP

CRISP Component	Count	Overhead (Bytes)	
		per Element	Total
Adjusted LCP	1	4	4
Time stamp registers	164	4	656
Overlapped stall	1	4	4
Nonoverlapped stall	1	4	4
Total storage overhead (bytes)		CRISP	668
		CRIT	660
		LEAD	18
		STALL	4

Table 3 GPGPU Configuration

SM		Memory		Cache							Clock Frequency	
				Feature	L1				L2		Domain	MHz
					Inst	Data	Const	Text				
Register	32K	Size	2 GB	Size (KB)	2	16	8	12	786		SM	700
SP unit	32	Partition	6	Set	4	32	64	4	64		L2 cache	700
SFU unit	16	Subpartition	12	Assoc	4	4	2	24	8		Memory	1848
LD/ST unit	16	Scheduling	FRFCFS	MSHR	2	32	2	128	32		Interconnect	700
Max CTA	8	Queue size	16	Line size	128	128	64	128	128			
Warp size	32	Bus width	4	Replacement	LRU	LRU	LRU	LRU	LRU			
Max warp	48	Burst length	8	Write policy	RO	LWBGWT	RO	RO	WB			
Max thread	1536	Controller	6	WA policy	NWA	NWA	NWA	NWA	WA			
Two warp scheduler												
Greedy then oldest												

Notes: LWBGWT, local write back global write through; RO, read only; WA, write allocate.

we also evaluate a Tesla C2050). To evaluate the energy savings realized by CRISP, we update the original GPGPU-Sim with online DVFS capability. All the 15 SMs in our configured architecture share a single voltage domain with a nominal clock frequency of 700 MHz. We define six other performance states (P-State) for the SMs, ranging from 100 to 600 MHz with a step size of 100 MHz [18]. Similar to GPUWattch [18], we select the voltage for each P-State from 0.55 to 1.0 V. We rely on a fast-responding on-chip global DVFS regulator that can switch between P-States in 100 ns [18,46–48]. We account for this switching overhead for each P-State transition in our energy savings result.

We extend the GPUWattch [18] power simulator in GPGPU-Sim to estimate accurate power consumption in the presence of online DVFS. For each power calculation interval of GPUWattch, we collect the dynamic power at the nominal voltage-frequency (700 MHz, 1 V) setting and scale it for the current voltage-frequency ($P_{Dynamic} \propto v^2 f$). We use GPUSimpow [49] to estimate the static power of individual clock domains at nominal frequency, which is between 23% to 63% for the Rodinia benchmark suite. The static power in other P-States are estimated using voltage scaling ($P_{Static} \propto v$) [50].

We use the Rodinia [38] benchmark suite in our experiments. To initially assess the accuracy of different models, we run the first important kernel of each Rodinia benchmark for 4.8 million instructions—we exclude *nw* because the runtime of each kernel is smaller than a single reasonable DVFS interval. The 4.8 million-instruction execution of each kernel at nominal frequency translates into at least 10 μs execution time (ranging from 10 to 600 μs). We find that 10 μs is the minimum DVFS interval for which the switching overhead (100 ns) of the on-chip regulator is negligible (≤1%). Meanwhile, to evaluate the energy savings, we run the benchmarks for at least 1 billion instructions (except for *myc*, which we ran long enough to get 4286 full kernel executions). For some benchmarks, we ran for up to 9 billion instructions if that allowed us to run to completion. Eight of the benchmarks finish execution within that allotment. For presentation purposes, we divide the benchmarks into two groups. The benchmarks (bp, hw, hs, and patf) with at least 75% computation cycles are classified as compute bound. The rest of the benchmarks are memory-bound.

In Section 5.2, we demonstrate an application of our performance model in an online energy saving framework. In order to make decisions about DVFS settings to optimize EDP or similar metrics, we need both a performance model and an energy model. The energy model we use assumes that the phase of the next interval will be computationally similar to the current interval [34], which is typically a safe assumption for GPUs.

At each decision interval (10 μs), the DVFS controller uses the power model to find the static and dynamic power of the SMs at the current settings (v_c, f_c). It also collects static and dynamic power consumed by the rest of the components, including memory, interconnect, and level 2 cache. For each of the possible voltage-frequency settings (v, f), it predicts (a) static power of the SMs using voltage scaling, (b) dynamic power of the SMs using voltage and frequency scaling, and (c) execution time $T(f)$ using the underlying DVFS performance model (leading load, stall time, critical path, or critical stalled path). The static and dynamic power of the rest of the system are assumed to remain unchanged since we do not apply DVFS to those domains.

The controller computes the total static energy consumption at each frequency f as a product of total static power $P_{Static}(v,f)$ and $T(f)$. Meanwhile, the total dynamic energy consumption at frequency f is computed as $P_{Dynamic}(f) \times T(f_c)$. The static and dynamic energy components are added together to estimate the predicted energy $E(f)$ at P-State (v,f). Finally, the controller computes ED^2P (v,f) as $E(f) \times T(f)^2$ and makes a transition to the P-State with the predicted minimum ED^2P. For the EDP operating setting, the controller orchestrates DVFS in similar fashion, with minimum EDP as the goal.

We measure the online software overhead at 109 cycles per decision interval by running the actual code on a CPU. Note that the same software could also run on an SM. This overhead is included in our modeled performance overhead, in addition to the 1% P-State switching overhead. It should be noted that we do not have any overhead for measurement because we do the measurement in the hardware using performance counters, except for reading the counters that are part of our software overhead.

In our results, we average performance-counter statistics across all SMs in the power domain to drive our performance model. However, our experiments (not shown here) demonstrate that we could instead sample a single core with no significant loss in effectiveness.

5 RESULTS

This section examines the quality of the CRISP predictor in two ways. First, it evaluates the accuracy of the model in predicting kernel runtimes at different frequencies, compared to the prior state of the art. Second, it uses the predictor in a runtime algorithm to predict the optimal DVFS settings and measures the potential gains in energy efficiency. In each case we compare against leading load (LEAD), critical path (CRIT), and stall time (STALL). We also explore the performance of a computationally simpler version of CRISP. Last, we examine the generality of CRISP.

5.1 EXECUTION TIME PREDICTION

We simulate the first instance of a key kernel of each Rodinia [38] benchmark at all seven P-States and collect the execution time information at each frequency. We also save the performance model counter data at the nominal frequency (700 MHz) to drive the various performance models. We show the breakdown of the classifications computed by CRISP in Fig. 14; this raw data on each benchmark is useful in understanding some of the sources of prediction error. This data shows several interesting facts—(1) the benchmarks are diverse, (2) while the LCP often

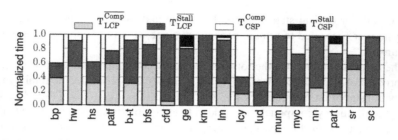

FIG. 14

Breakdown of execution time.

covers the majority of the execution time, the overlapped portion is often quite large, and (3) three of the kernels have noticeable nonoverlapped store stalls (T_{CSP}^{Stall}).

Based on the measured runtime and performance counter data at 700 MHz frequency, the performance models predict the execution time at six other frequencies (100–600 MHz). Fig. 15 shows the prediction error of each of the models for three target frequencies: 100, 400, and 600 MHz. We also highlight the mean absolute percentage error (MAPE) at these target frequencies in the rightmost graph of Fig. 15. The summarized average absolute percentage errors of the models across all six target frequencies for each benchmark are reported in Fig. 17.

STALL always overpredicts the execution time, conservatively treating all stalls as completely inelastic. The inaccuracy of STALL can be as high as 288%. Both LEAD and CRIT suffer from underprediction (65% or more for *bfs*) and overprediction (109% or more for *ge*). The accuracy of CRISP also varies, but the maximum prediction error (30%) is reduced by a factor of 3.6 compared to the maximum error (109%) with the best of the existing models.

We see that both LEAD and CRIT are more prone to underpredicting the memory-bound kernels (those on the right side of the graph); this comes from their inability to detect when the kernels transition to computation-bound and become more sensitive to frequency. The major exception is *ge*, where they both fail to account for the store-related stalls and heavily over-predict execution time.

We also note from these results that as we try to predict the performance with a high scaling factor (from 700 to 100 MHz), the error of the prior techniques becomes superlinear—that is, they become proportionally more inaccurate the further you depart from the base frequency. The leading load paper acknowledges this. A big factor in this superlinear error is that the greater the change in frequency, the more likely it is that the load stalls are completely covered and the kernel transitions to a compute-bound scaling factor. This explains why the CRISP results do not appear to share the superlinear error, in general. To illustrate this, we show the predicted execution time for the *lm* kernel as we scale the frequency from 700 to 100 MHz (Fig. 16). CRIT measures T_{Memory} as 0.88, while LEAD estimates it as 0.80. We measure the LCP length of *lm* to be 0.93 of which 34% are overlapped computations;

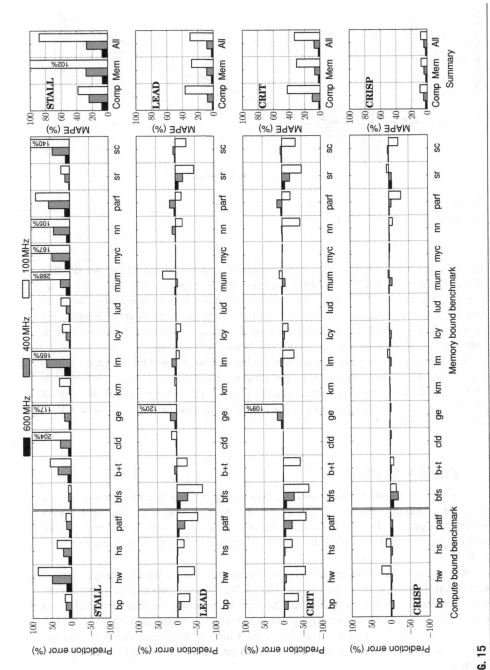

FIG. 15

Execution time prediction error for different target frequencies with baseline frequency of 700 MHz.

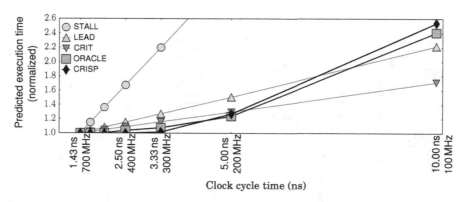

FIG. 16

Execution time prediction for *lm*.

thus we expect the LCP to be completely covered at about 233 MHz. We see that above this frequency CRIT is fairly accurate, but diverges widely after this point. Beyond this point, CRISP treats the kernel as completely compute-bound, while at 100 MHz CRIT is still assuming 52% of the execution time is spent waiting for memory. In contrast, CRISP closely follows the actual runtimes (ORACLE) both at memory-bound frequencies and at compute-bound frequencies.

We observe a similar phenomenon in the kernels *hw*, *hs*, and *bfs*. In each of these cases, CRISP successfully captures the piecewise linear behavior of performance under frequency scaling. As summarized in Fig. 17, the average prediction error of CRISP across all the benchmarks is 4% versus 11% with LEAD, 11% with CRIT, and 35% with STALL.

5.2 ENERGY SAVINGS

An online performance model, and the underlying architecture to compute it, is a tool. An expected application of such a tool would be to evaluate multiple DVFS settings to optimize for particular performance and energy goals. In this section, we will evaluate the utility of CRISP in minimizing two widely used metrics: EDP and ED^2P.

We compute the savings relative to the default mode, which always runs at maximum SM clock frequency (700 MHz, 1 V). We run two similar experiments with our simple DVFS controller (see Section 4) targeting (a) minimum EDP and (b) the minimum ED^2P operating point. During both experiments, the controller uses the program's behavior during the current interval to predict the next interval. We do the same for each of the other studied predictors—all use the same power predictor.

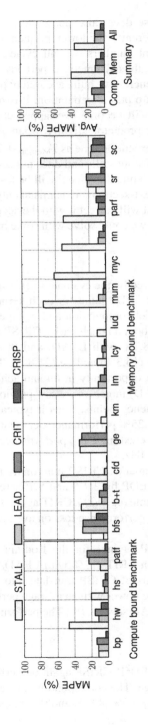

FIG. 17

Mean absolute percentage error averaged across all target frequencies with baseline frequency of 700 MHz.

Using CRISP for this purpose does raise one concern. All of the models are asymmetric (ie, will predict differently for lower frequency A->B than for higher frequency B->A) due to different numbers of stall cycles, different loads on the critical path, and so on. However, the asymmetry is perhaps more clear with CRISP. While predicting for lower frequencies, we quite accurately predict when overlapped computation will be converted into pure computation; it is more difficult to predict which pure computation cycles will become overlapped computations at a higher frequency. We thus modify our predictor slightly when predicting for a higher frequency. We calculate the new execution time as $T_{\text{Memory}} + T_{\text{CSP}}^{\text{Stall}} + T_{\text{CSP}}^{\text{Comp}} \times \frac{f_c}{f}$. This ignores the possible expansion of store stalls and does not account for conversion of pure computation to overlapped. While this model will be less accurate, in a running system with DVFS (as in the next section), if it mistakenly forces a change to a higher frequency, the next interval will correct it with the accurate model. While this could cause ping-ponging, which we could solve with some hysteresis, we found this unnecessary.

Optimizing for EDP

Fig. 18 shows EDP savings achieved by the evaluated performance models when the controller is seeking the minimum EDP point for each kernel. We included all the runtime overhead—software model computation and voltage switching overhead—in this result. For the 14 memory-bound benchmarks, CRISP reduces EDP by 13.9% compared to 8.9% with CRIT, 8.7% with LEAD, and 0% with STALL. CRISP achieves high savings in both *lm* (15.3%) and *ge* (21.8%). The other three models fail to realize any energy savings opportunity in *lm* and achieve very little savings (5% with CRIT and 1% with LEAD) in *ge*. As we saw previously in Fig. 16, CRISP accurately models *lm* at all frequency points. Thus it typically chooses to run this kernel at 300 MHz, resulting in 1.25% performance degradation but 16.4% reduced energy. CRIT and LEAD both overestimate the performance cost at this frequency and instead choose to run at 700 MHz.

For the compute-bound benchmarks, CRISP marginally reduces EDP by 0.5%, while LEAD and CRIT increase EDP by 2.7% and 5.7%, respectively. Because of the underprediction of execution time (eg, *patf*), CRIT aggressively reduces the clock frequency and experiences 13.3% performance loss on average (33% in *patf*) for the compute bound benchmarks.

In summary, the average EDP savings for the Rodinia benchmark suite with CRISP is 10.7% versus 5.7% with CRIT, 6.2% with LEAD, and 0% with STALL. The selected EDP operating points of CRISP translate into 12.9% energy savings and 15.5% reduction in the average power with an average performance loss of 3.4%. CRIT saves 10.6% energy and LEAD saves 8.1%. The performance loss is 6.3% with CRIT and 2.9% with LEAD.

Optimizing for ED²P

When attempting to optimize for ED²P, CRISP again outperforms the other models by reducing ED²P 9.0% on average. The corresponding average savings realized by CRIT, LEAD, and STALL are only 3.5%, 4.9%, and 0%, respectively. Fig. 19 shows

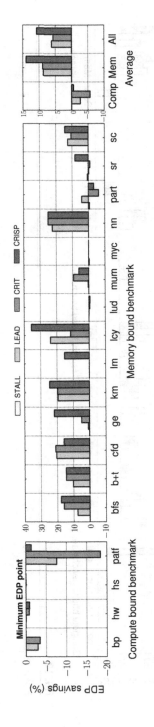

FIG. 18

EDP reduction while optimized for EDP.

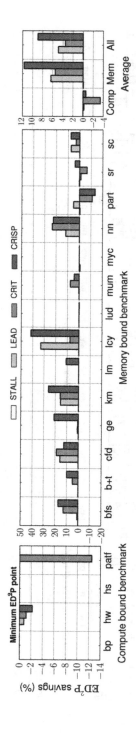

FIG. 19

ED^{2}P reduction while optimized for ED^{2}P.

that the savings with CRISP is much higher (11.7%) for memory-bound benchmarks compared to CRIT (5.5%), LEAD (6.4%), and STALL (0%).

CRISP achieves its highest ED^2P savings of 42% for *lcy*, by running the primary kernel at 500 MHz most of the time. CRIT and LEAD underpredict the energy saving opportunity and keep the frequency at 700 MHz for 50% and 41% of the duration of this kernel, respectively. As we analyze the execution trace, we find that 67% of cycles inside the LCP for that kernel are computation, thus are not handled accurately by the other models.

5.3 SIMPLIFIED CRISP MODEL

CRISP can be simplified to estimate the LCP length as the total number of load outstanding cycles, without regard for which stall cycles, and in particular, which computation are under the critical path. We simply treat all computation cycles that are overlapped by a load as though they were on the critical path. This approximated version of CRISP (CRISP-L) requires three counters, and thus removes 98% of the storage overhead of CRISP (all the time-stamp registers).

CRISP-L demonstrates competitive prediction accuracy (4.66% on average in Fig. 20) as CRISP (4.48% on average) does for the experiment in Section 5.1. However, when used in an EDP controller, CRISP-L suffers relative to CRISP, but still realizes far better (8.38%) EDP savings than CRIT (5.65%) and LEAD (6.16%). The inclusion of more compute cycles in LCP tends to create underpredictions of execution time, resulting in more aggressive frequency scaling. CRISP-L experiences more (6.28%) performance loss than CRISP (3.44%).

5.4 GENERALITY OF CRISP

All of the results so far were for a NVIDIA GTX 480 GPU. To demonstrate that the CRISP model is more general, we replicated the same experiments for a modeled

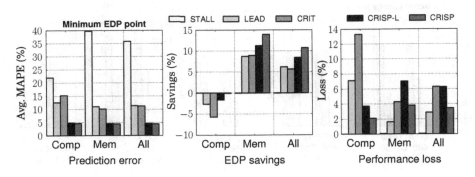

FIG. 20

Accuracy, benefit, and drawback of CRISP-L.

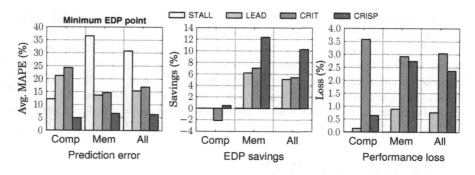

FIG. 21

Effectiveness of CRISP on NVIDIA Tesla C2050.

Tesla C2050 GPU. The Tesla differs in available clock frequency settings, number of cores, DRAM queue size, and in the topology of the interconnect. Results for predictor accuracy and effectiveness were consistent with the prior results. In this section, we show in particular the result for the EDP-optimized controller. Fig. 21 shows that the mean absolute percentage prediction error of CRISP (6.2%) is much lower than LEAD (16.9%) and CRIT (15.4%). Meanwhile, CRISP realizes 10.3% EDP savings, which is 5% more than the best of the prior models.

We also experimented with another DVFS controller goal; this one seeks to minimize energy while keeping the performance overhead under 1%. Fig. 22 shows the energy, EDP, ED^2P, average power savings, and the performance loss for GTX480 and Tesla C2050. In Tesla C2050, CRISP achieves 9.3% energy savings, which is 4% more than CRIT.

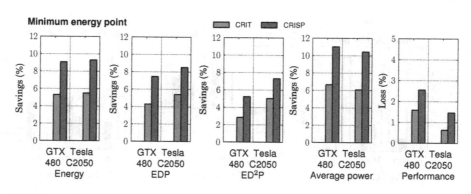

FIG. 22

Effectiveness of CRISP while optimizing for energy.

6 CONCLUSION

We introduce the CRISP performance model to enable effective DVFS control in GPGPUs. Existing DVFS models targeting CPUs do not capture key GPGPU execution characteristics, causing them to miss energy savings opportunities or causing unintended performance loss. CRISP effectively handles the impact of highly overlapped memory and computation in a system with high thread-level parallelism, and also captures the effect of frequent memory store-based stalls.

ACKNOWLEDGMENTS

This work was supported in part by NSF grants CCF-1219059 and CCF-1302682.

REFERENCES

[1] P. Macken, M. Degrauwe, M. Van Paemel, H. Oguey, A voltage reduction technique for digital systems, in: IEEE Int. Solid-State Circuits Conf., 1990.

[2] D. Snowdon, S. Ruocco, G. Heiser, Power management and dynamic voltage scaling: myths and facts, in: Power Aware Real-time Computing, 2005.

[3] S. Herbert, D. Marculescu, Analysis of dynamic voltage/frequency scaling in chip-multiprocessors, in: ISLPED, 2007.

[4] H. David, C. Fallin, E. Gorbatov, U. Hanebutte, O. Mutlu, Memory power management via dynamic voltage/frequency scaling, in: Proceedings of the 8th International Conference on Autonomic Computing (ICAC), 2011.

[5] Q. Deng, D. Meisner, A. Bhattacharjee, T. Wenisch, R. Bianchini, MultiScale: memory system DVFS with multiple memory controllers, in: International Symposium on Low Power Electronics and Design (ISLPED), 2012.

[6] Q. Deng, D. Meisner, L. Ramos, T. Wenisch, R. Bianchini, Memscale: active low-power modes for main memory, in: ACM SIGPLAN, 2011.

[7] X. Chen, Z. Xu, H. Kim, P. Gratz, J. Hu, M. Kishinevskyy, U. Ograsy, In-network monitoring and control policy for DVFS of CMP networks-on-chip and last level caches, in: NOCS, 2012.

[8] X. Chen, Z. Xu, H. Kim, P.V. Gratz, J. Hu, M. Kishinevsky, U. Ogras, R. Ayoub, Dynamic voltage and frequency scaling for shared resources in multicore processor designs, in: DAC, 2013.

[9] G. Liang, A. Jantsch, Adaptive power management for the on-chip communication network, in: Euromicro Conference on Digital System Design, 2006.

[10] A. Mishra, R. Das, S. Eachempati, R. Iyer, N. Vijaykrishnan, C. Das, A case for dynamic frequency tuning in on-chip networks, in: International Symposium on Microarchitecture (MICRO), 2009.

[11] D. Brooks, M. Martonosi, Dynamic thermal management for highperformance micro-processors, in: High-Performance Computer Architecture (HPCA), 2001.

[12] R. Teodorescu, J. Torrellas, Variation-aware application scheduling and power management for chip multiprocessors, in: Proc. 35th Ann. Int'l Symp. Computer Architecture (ISCA), 2008.

[13] D. Ernst, N.S. Kim, S. Das, S. Lee, D. Blaauw, T. Austin, T. Mudge,, K. Flautner, Razor: a low-power pipeline based on circuit-level timing speculation, in: International Symposium on Microarchitecture (MICRO), 2003.

[14] Y. Abe, H. Sasaki, S. Kato, K. Inoue, M. Edahiro, M. Peres, Power and performance characterization and modeling of GPU-accelerated systems, in: IEEE International Parallel and Distributed Processing Symposium (IPDPS), 2014.

[15] Y. Abe, H. Sasaki, S. Kato, K. Inoue, M. Edahiro, M. Peres, Power and performance analysis of GPU-accelerated systems, in: Proceedings of the USENIX Conference on Power-Aware Computing and Systems (HotPower), 2012.

[16] X. Mei, L.S. Yung, K. Zhao, X. Chu, A measurement study of GPU DVFS on energy conservation, in: Proceedings of the Workshop on Power-Aware Computing and Systems (HotPower), 2013.

[17] Nvidia GPU Boost, http://www.geforce.com/hardware/technology/gpu-boost-2/technology.

[18] J. Leng, T. Hetherington, A. ElTantawy, S. Gilani, N.S. Kim, T.M. Aamodt, V.J. Reddi, GPUWattch: enabling energy optimizations in GPGPUs, in: ISCA, 2013.

[19] K. Choi, R. Soma, M. Pedram, Fine-grained dynamic voltage and frequency scaling for precise energy and performance trade-off based on the ratio of off-chip access to on-chip computation times, in: DATE, 2004.

[20] G. Contreras, M. Martonosi, Power prediction for Intel XScale processors using performance monitoring unit events, in: ISLPED, 2005.

[21] M. Curtis-Maury, J. Dzierwa, C.D. Antonopoulos, D.S. Nikolopoulos, Online power-performance adaptation of multithreaded programs using hardware event-based prediction, in: Int. Conf. Supercomputing, 2006.

[22] M. Curtis-Maury, A. Shah, F. Blagojevic, D.S. Nikolopoulos, B.R. de Supinski, M. Schulz, Prediction models for multi-dimensional power-performance optimization on many cores, in: PACT, 2008.

[23] J. Carter, H. Hanson, K. Rajamani, F. Rawson, T. Rosedahl, M. Ware, Dynamic voltage and frequency scaling (DVFS) control for simultaneous multi-threading (SMT) processors, US Patent US20110113270A1, 2011.

[24] G. Dhiman, T.S. Rosing, Dynamic voltage frequency scaling for multi-tasking systems using online learning, in: ISLPED, 2007.

[25] M. Moeng, R. Melhem, Applying statistical machine learning to multicore voltage and frequency scaling, in: Int. Conf. Computing Frontiers, 2010.

[26] C.J. Hughes, J. Srinivasan, S.V. Adve, Saving energy with architectural and frequency adaptations for multimedia applications, in: MICRO, 2001.

[27] C. Isci, A. Buyuktosunoglu, C.Y. Cher, P. Bose, M. Martonosi, An analysis of efficient multi-core global power management policies: maximizing performance for a given power budget, in: MICRO, 2006.

[28] F. Xie, M. Martonosi, S. Malik, Efficient behavior-driven runtime dynamic voltage scaling policies, in: CODES+ISSS, 2005.

[29] D.C. Snowdon, S.M. Petters, G. Heiser, Accurate on-line prediction of processor and memory energy usage under voltage scaling, in: EMSOFT, 2007.

[30] C. Isci, A. Buyuktosunoglu, M. Martonosi, Long-term workload phases: duration predictions and applications to DVFS, in: IEEE Micro, 2005.

[31] A. Weissel, F. Bellosa, Process cruise control: event-driven clock scaling for dynamic power management, in: Intl Conf. Compilers, Architecture and Synthesis for Embedded Systems (CASES), 2002.

[32] C. Poellabauer, L. Singleton, K. Schwan, Feedback-based dynamic voltage and frequency scaling for memory-bound real-time applications, in: IEEE Real-Time Embedded Technology and Applications Symp. (RTAS), 2005.

[33] S. Eyerman, L. Eeckhout, A counter architecture for online DVFS profitability estimation, in: IEEE Trans. Comput., 2010.

[34] R. Miftakhutdinov, E. Ebrahimi, Y.N. Patt, Predicting performance impact of DVFS for realistic memory systems, in: International Symposium on Microarchitecture (Micro), 2012.

[35] G. Keramidas, V. Spiliopoulos, S. Kaxiras, Interval-based models for run-time DVFS orchestration in superscalar processors, in: ACM Int. Conf. Computing Frontiers (CF10), 2010.

[36] B. Rountree, D.K. Lowenthal, M. Schulz, B.R. de Supinski, Practical performance prediction under dynamic voltage frequency scaling, in: Int. Green Computing Conf. and Workshops, 2011.

[37] A. Bakhoda, G. Yuan, W. Fung, H. Wong, T. Aamodt, Analyzing CUDA workloads using a detailed GPU simulator, in: IEEE ISPASS, 2009.

[38] S. Che, J. Sheaffer, M. Boyer, L. Szafaryn, L. Wang, K. Skadron, A characterization of the Rodinia benchmark suite with comparison to contemporary CMP workloads, in: Proceedings of the IEEE International Symposium on Workload Characterization, 2010.

[39] T.T. Dao, J. Kim, S. Seo, B. Egger, J. Lee, A performance model for GPUs with caches, in: IEEE Transactions on Parallel and Distributed Systems, 2014.

[40] S. Hong, H. Kim, An integrated GPU power and performance model, in: Proc. 37th Ann. Int'l Symp. Computer Architecture (ISCA), 2010.

[41] S. Hong, H. Kim, An analytical model for a GPU architecture with memory-level and thread-level parallelism awareness, in: ISCA, 2009.

[42] S. Song, C. Su, B. Rountree, K. Cameron, A simplified and accurate model of power-performance efficiency on emergent GPU architectures, in: IEEE 27th International Symposium on Parallel and Distributed Processing, 2013.

[43] X. Chen, Y. Wang, Y. Liang, Y. Xie, H. Yang, Run-time technique for simultaneous aging and power optimization in GPGPUs, in: Proceedings of the 51st Annual Design Automation Conference, 2014.

[44] A. Sethia, S. Mahlke, Equalizer: dynamic tuning of GPU resources for efficient execution, in: MICRO, 2014.

[45] J. Issa, S. Figueira, A performance estimation model for GPU-based systems, in: 2nd International Conference on Advances in Computational Tools for Engineering Applications (ACTEA), 2012.

[46] W. Kim, M. Gupta, G.Y. Wei, D. Brooks, System level analysis of fast, per-core DVFS using on-chip switching regulators, in: High-Performance Computer Architecture (HPCA), 2008.

[47] L. Clark, E. Hoffman, J. Miller, M. Biyani, Y. Liao, S. Strazdus, M. Morrow, K. Velarde, M. Yarch, An embedded 32-b microprocessor core for low-power and high-performance applications, IEEE J. Solid-State Circuits 36 (2001) 1599–1608.

[48] T. Fischer, J. Desai, B. Doyle, S. Naffziger, B. Patella, A 90-nm variable frequency clock system for a power-managed Itanium architecture processor, IEEE J. Solid-State Circuits 10 (2006) 218–228.

[49] J. Lucas, S. Lal, M. Andersch, M.A. Mesa, B. Juurlink, How a single chip causes massive power bills GPUSimPow: a GPGPU power simulator, in: Proceedings of the IEEE International Symposium on Performance Analysis of Systems and Software, 2013.

[50] J.A. Butts, G.S. Sohi, A static power model for architects, in: International Symposium on Microarchitecture (MICRO), 2000.

Power and reliability

Energy and power considerations of GPUs

19

J. Coplin, M. Burtscher

Texas State University, San Marcos, TX, United States

1 INTRODUCTION

GPU-based accelerators are widely used in high-performance computing (HPC) and are quickly spreading in PCs and even handheld devices as they often provide higher performance and better energy efficiency than multicore CPUs. For example, in HPC environments, large energy consumption and the required cooling due to the resulting heat dissipation are major cost factors. To reach exascale computing, a 50-fold improvement in performance per watt is needed by some estimates [1]. Moreover, in all types of handheld devices, such as tablets and smartphones, battery life is a key concern.

For these and other reasons, power-aware and energy-efficient computing has become increasingly important. Although many hardware optimizations for reducing power have been proposed or are already in use, software techniques are lagging behind, particularly techniques that target accelerators like GPUs. To be able to optimize the power and energy efficiency of GPU code, it is essential to have a good understanding of the power-draw and energy-consumption behavior of programs on the one hand and of software techniques to manipulate performance, power, and energy on the other hand. Hence this chapter comprises two parts, one on power profiling and the other on improving GPU power and energy using various approaches that an end user can apply.

There are many challenges to studying energy efficiency and power draw on GPUs, not the least of which is trying to accurately measure the power draw. Current GPU-internal power sensors are set to sample at under 100 Hz, so the small-scale power behavior of programs may not be observable. In contrast, some external power sensors sample at rates many times that of internal sensors but may mix in the power from other hardware components and make it more difficult to correlate the measurements with the activities of the GPU code.

It is well known that code optimizations can improve GPU performance a great deal, but their impact on energy and power is less clear. Some studies report a one-to-one correspondence between runtime and energy [2–4]. These studies tend to focus on regular programs and primarily vary the program inputs, not the code itself. However, there are software techniques that improve energy or power substantially more than runtime. This chapter illustrates, on several compute- and memory-bound as well as regular and irregular codes, by how much source-code optimizations, changes in algorithms and their implementations, and GPU clock-frequency adjustments can help make GPUs more energy-efficient.

1.1 COMPUTE- AND MEMORY-BOUND CODES ON GPUS

A piece of code is said to be compute-bound when its performance is primarily limited by the computational throughput of the processing elements. Compute-bound code typically does a great deal of processing on each piece of data it accesses in the main memory. In contrast, the performance of memory-bound code is primarily limited by the data-transfer throughput of the memory system. Memory-bound code does relatively little processing on each piece of data it reads from the main memory.

1.2 REGULAR AND IRREGULAR CODES ON GPUS

By regular and irregular programs, we are referring to the behavior of the control flow and/or memory-access patterns of the code. In regular code, most of the control flow and the memory references are not data-dependent. Matrix-vector multiplication is a good example. Based only on the input size and the data-structure starting addresses, but without knowing any values of the input data, we can determine the dynamic behavior of the program on an in-order processor, that is, the memory reference stream and the conditional branch decisions. In irregular code, the input values determine the program's runtime behavior, which therefore cannot be statically predicted and may be different for different inputs. For instance, in a binary search tree implementation, the values and the order in which they are processed affect the shape of the search tree and the order in which it is built.

Irregular algorithms tend to arise from the use of complex data structures such as trees and graphs. For instance, in graph applications, memory-access patterns are usually data-dependent since the connectivity of the graph and the values on nodes and edges may determine which nodes and edges are touched by a given computation. This information is usually not known at compile time and may change dynamically even after the input graph is available, leading to uncoalesced memory accesses and bank conflicts. Similarly, the control flow is usually irregular because branch decisions differ for nodes with different degrees or labels, leading to branch divergence and load imbalance. As a consequence, the power draw of irregular GPU applications can change over time in a seemingly erratic manner.

2 EVALUATION METHODOLOGY

2.1 BENCHMARK PROGRAMS

In order to study GPU performance, energy, and power, we utilize programs from the LonestarGPU v2.0 [5], Parboil [6], Rodinia v3.0 [7], and SHOC v1.1.2 [8] benchmark suites as well as a few programs from the CUDA SDK v6.0 [9]. Each program and the used inputs are explained in the "Appendix" section.

2.2 SYSTEM, COMPILER, AND POWER MEASUREMENT

We performed all measurements presented in this chapter on a Nvidia Tesla K20c GPU, which has 5 GB of global memory and 13 streaming multiprocessors with a total of 2496 processing elements. The programs were compiled with nvcc version 7.0.27 and the "-O3 -arch=sm_35" optimization flags. The power measurements were obtained using the K20Power tool [10]. Throughout this chapter, we use the term "active runtime" to refer to the time during which the GPU is actively computing, which is in contrast to the application runtime that includes the CPU portions of the Compute Unified Device Architecture (CUDA) programs. The K20Power tool defines the active runtime as the time during which the GPU is drawing power above the idle level. Fig. 1 illustrates this procedure.

Because of how the GPU draws power and how the built-in power sensor samples, only readings above a certain threshold (the dashed line in Fig. 1 at 55 W in this case) correspond to when the GPU is actually executing the program [10]. Measurements below the threshold are either the idle power (less than about 26 W) or the "tail power" due to the driver keeping the GPU active for a while before powering it down. The power threshold is dynamically adjusted by the K20Power tool to maximize accuracy for different GPU frequency settings.

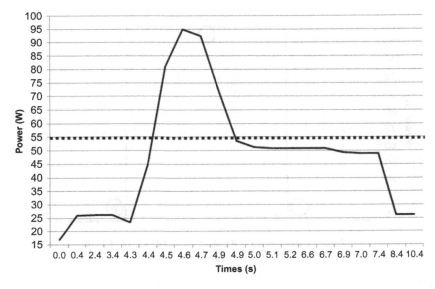

FIG. 1

Sample power profile.

3 POWER PROFILING OF REGULAR AND IRREGULAR PROGRAMS

3.1 IDEALIZED POWER PROFILE

Fig. 2 illustrates the shape of an idealized power profile as we would expect when running a regular kernel. At point 1, the GPU receives work and begins executing, which ramps up the power draw. The power remains constant throughout execution (2). All cores finish at point 3, thus returning the GPU to its idle power draw (about 17 W in this example), which completes the expected rectangular power profile. This profile and its shape can be fully captured with just two values, the active runtime and the average power draw.

3.2 POWER PROFILES OF REGULAR CODES

Fig. 3 shows the actual power profiles of three regular programs. Even though the power does not ramp up and down instantaneously and the active power is not quite constant, the profiles resemble the expected rectangular shape. In particular, the power ramps up quickly when the code is launched, stays level during execution, and then drops off. Note that the power peaks at different levels depending on the program that is run and how much it exercises the GPU hardware.

Once a kernel finishes running, the power does not return to idle immediately. Instead, the GPU driver steps down the power in a delayed manner as it first

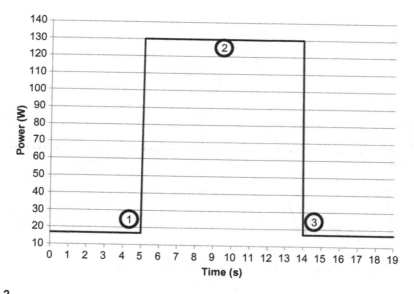

FIG. 2

Expected power profile.

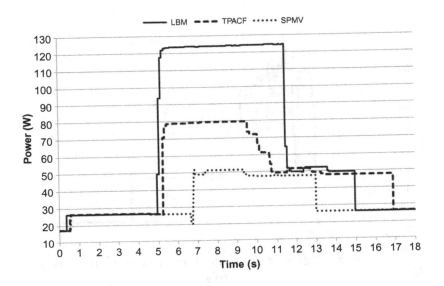

FIG. 3

Power profiles of three regular codes.

waits for a while in case another kernel is launched. The reason for the seemingly sloped (as opposed to instant) step downs is that the GPU samples the power sensor less frequently at lower power levels. Since the power sensor's primary purpose is to prevent the GPU from damaging itself by drawing too much power, the GPU automatically reduces the sampling frequency when the power is low as there is little chance of burning out.

3.3 POWER PROFILES OF IRREGULAR CODES

Fig. 4A and B shows the power profiles of seven irregular programs. Interestingly, the profiles of breadth-first search (BFS) and single-source shortest paths (SSSP) are very similar to the profiles of the regular codes shown in the previous section. These two programs also reach the highest power levels. This is because both implementations are topology-driven, meaning that all vertices are visited in each iteration, regardless of whether there is new work to be done or not. This approach is easy to implement as it essentially "regularizes" the code but may result in useless computations, poor performance, and unnecessary energy consumption. This is why BFS and SSSP behave like regular codes, as do their power profiles. NSP belongs to the same category because it also processes all vertices in each iteration.

In contrast, Delaunay mesh refinement (DMR), minimum spanning tree (MST), and points to analysis (PTA) exhibit many spikes in their profiles, which reflects the irregular nature of these programs. Due to dynamically changing data dependencies

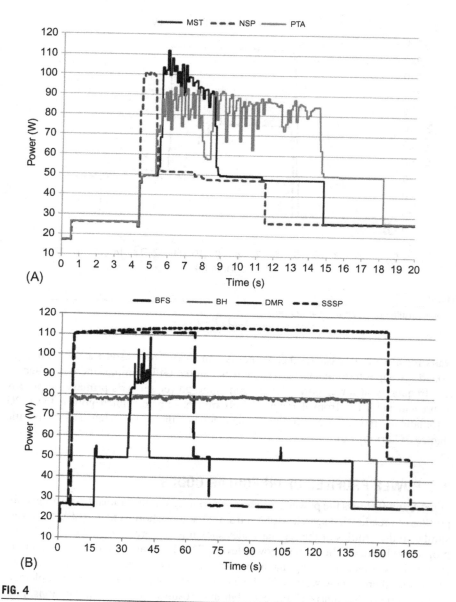

FIG. 4

(A) Power profiles of MST, NSP, and PTA. (B) Power profiles of BFS, BH, DMR, and SSSP.

and data parallelism, their power draw fluctuates widely and rapidly. Clearly, the profiles of these three codes are very different from those of regular programs. Moreover, they are different from each other, highlighting that there is no such thing as a standard power profile for irregular codes.

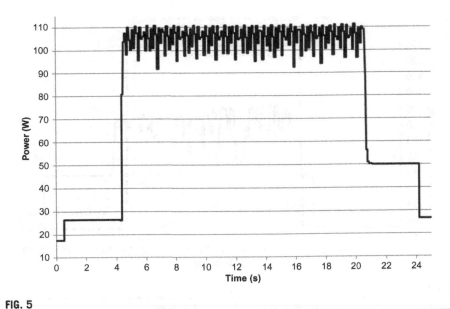

FIG. 5

Power profile of BH with 100k bodies and 100 time steps.

Barnes-Hut (BH) is more subtle in its irregularity. Its profile appears relatively regular except the active power level is unstable and wobbles constantly. For each time step, this program calls a series of kernels with different degrees of irregularity. Since the BH profile shown in Fig. 4B was obtained with 10,000 time steps (and 10,000 bodies), the true irregularity is largely masked by the short runtimes of each kernel. Fig. 5 shows the profile of the same BH code but with 100k bodies and only 100 time steps, which makes the repeated invocation of the different kernels much more evident. The power draw fluctuates by about 15 W while the program is executing. However, the irregularity within each kernel is still not visible. Note that the active power is over 100 W most of the time in Fig. 5, whereas the same program reaches only about 80 W in Fig. 4B. This is because running BH with 10,000 bodies does not fully load the GPU, and the 10,000 time steps result in many brief pauses between kernels, which lowers the power draw.

3.4 COMPARING EXPECTED, REGULAR, AND IRREGULAR PROFILES

Fig. 6 shows the expected power profile overlaid with a regular (Lattice-Boltzmann method [LBM]) profile and an irregular (PTA) profile of roughly the same active runtime. While the expected and regular profiles have a similar shape, the irregular power profile clearly does not. Whether because of load imbalance, irregular memory-access patterns, or unpredictable control flow, the irregular code's power draw fluctuates substantially. The active power draw of the PTA code averages 82 W

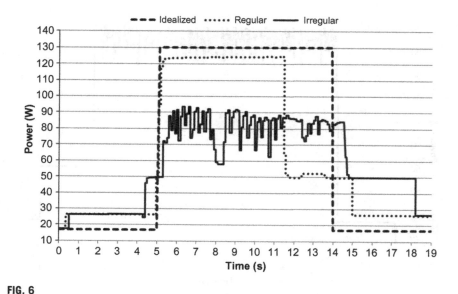

FIG. 6

Comparison of expected, regular, and irregular power profiles.

but reaches as high as 93 W and as low as 57 W, which is a fluctuation of over 60%. As a consequence, the power behavior of many irregular programs cannot accurately be captured by averages. Instead, the entire profile, that is, the power as a function of time, needs to be considered. As a side note, using the maximum power of an irregular code is also not necessarily viable because, while overestimation is generally safe, it can lead to gross overestimation.

4 AFFECTING POWER AND ENERGY ON GPUS

4.1 ALGORITHM IMPLEMENTATION

Changing the implementation of certain algorithms can have a profound impact on both the active runtime and the power draw. Fig. 7A illustrates this on the example of BFS, for which the LonestarGPU suite includes multiple versions. We profiled each version on the same USA roadmap input, that is, all five implementations compute the same result.

The default BFS implementation is topology-driven and therefore quite regular in its behavior but inefficient. *wla*, the next faster version, is still topology-driven but includes an optimization to skip vertices where no recomputation is needed. This results in a shorter runtime but also substantial load imbalance, which is why the active power is so low. *Atomic* maintains local worklists of updated nodes in shared memory, which makes it even faster but results in a somewhat irregular power profile due to overflows in the small worklists. The remaining implementations are data-driven

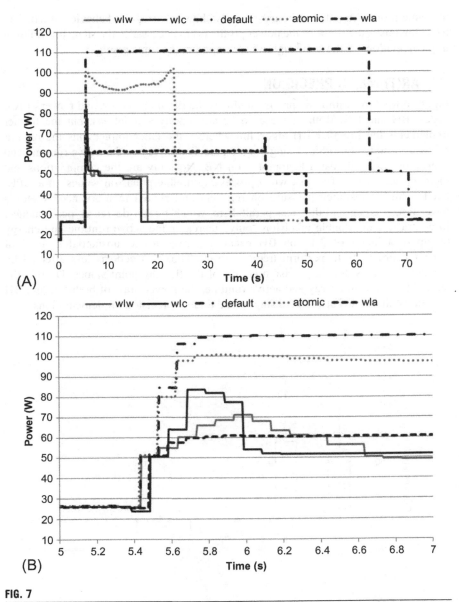

FIG. 7

(A) Power profiles of different implementations of BFS. (B) Power profiles of different implementations of BFS: zoomed in.

and hence work-efficient, that is, they do not perform unnecessary computations. This is why they are much faster. Both *wlw*'s and *wlc*'s profiles exhibit irregular wobbles, but the runtimes are too short to make the wobbles visible in Fig. 7A. Fig. 7B shows the same profiles zoomed in to more clearly show the irregular behavior of *wlw* and *wlc*. Obviously, the shape of the power profile is not necessarily the same for different implementations of the same algorithm computing the same results.

4.2 ARITHMETIC PRECISION

Fig. 8 shows how arithmetic precision affects the runtime, energy, and power of two codes: BH and NB. Both of these codes are *n*-body simulations, but the former implements the irregular BH algorithm whereas the latter implements the regular pairwise *n*-body algorithm. Using double precision increases the active runtime and energy by up to almost a factor of 4 on NB. Not only are the computations and memory accesses half as fast when processing double-precision values on a GPU, but the higher resource pressure on registers and shared memory necessitates a lower thread count and thus less parallelism, which further decreases performance. In contrast, using double precision "only" increases the active runtime and energy by up to a factor of 2.12 on BH because it executes a substantial number of integer instructions to perform tree traversals. Thus this code is less affected by the single- versus double-precision choice of the floating-point values. Despite the large differences in energy and active runtime, the power draw of both NB and BH are almost the same between the single- and double-precision implementations.

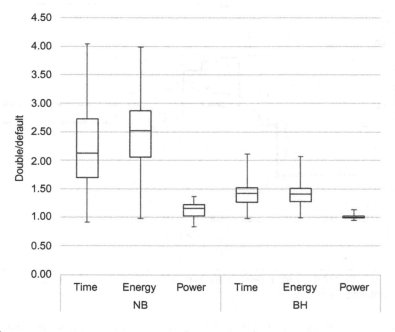

FIG. 8

Range of differences between single- and double-precision for floating point values.

4.3 CORE AND MEMORY CLOCK-FREQUENCY SCALING

The Tesla K20c GPU supports six clock frequency settings, of which we evaluate the following three. The "default" configuration uses a 705 MHz core frequency and a 2.6 GHz memory frequency. This is the fastest setting at which the GPU can run for a long time without throttling itself down to prevent overheating. The "614" configuration combines a 614 MHz core frequency with a 2.6 GHz memory frequency, which is the slowest available compute frequency at the default memory frequency. Finally, the "324" configuration uses a 324 MHz frequency for both the core and the memory. This is the slowest available setting.

4.3.1 Default to 614

Fig. 9 shows the relative change in active runtime, energy, and power when switching from the default frequency setting to the 614 setting. Values above 1.0 indicate an increase over the default. In the figure, the horizontal line where the two boxes touch represents the median, the boxes above and below extend to the first and third quartiles, and the whiskers indicate the maximum and minimum for the studied programs from each benchmark suite.

The 614 configuration has a core speed that is about 15% lower than the default, so one might expect to see roughly a 15% increase in active runtime. However, only a couple of the benchmark medians (CUDA SDK and LonestarGPU) and a few individual programs slow down anywhere near 15%. This is because going from

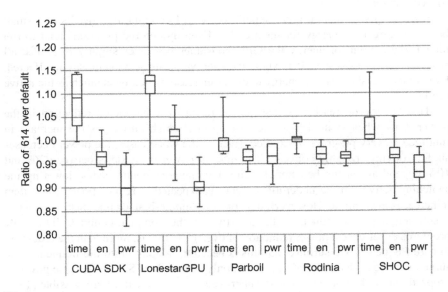

FIG. 9

Range of effects on runtime (time), energy (en), and power (pwr) when throttling the clock frequency from the default to the 614 setting.

default to 614 only lowers the core frequency but not the memory frequency. Hence memory-bound programs show little to no change, including many codes in the Parboil, Rodinia, and SHOC suites. In contrast, most of the tested SDK programs are compute-bound. A few programs show a slight speedup, but many of those measurements are within the margin of error (i.e., the average variability among repeated measurements).

Switching to the 614 configuration affects the LonestarGPU suite the most. In fact, this suite includes both the worst increase and the best decrease in active runtime as well as the highest median increase. At first glance, this may appear surprising as LonestarGPU contains only programs with irregular memory accesses, which tend to be memory-bound, particularly on GPUs where they often result in uncoalesced memory accesses [11]. Hence lowering the core frequency while keeping the memory frequency constant should not affect the runtime much. However, irregular programs, by definition, exhibit data-dependent runtime behavior, which frequently leads to timing-dependent behavior. This means that, if a computation is waiting for a value, the time at which the value becomes available can have unforeseen effects on the runtime behavior of the program. As a consequence, small changes in timing—for example, due to lowering the core frequency—can have a large effect on the runtime. This is why the active runtime of some LonestarGPU programs changes by more than the clock frequency. Note that this effect can be positive or negative, which explains why LonestarGPU exhibits the widest range in runtime change and includes both the program that is helped the most and the program that is hurt the most by going to the 614 configuration.

Interestingly, going from the default to the 614 configuration results in a small beneficial effect on energy for most codes. Even though the programs tend to run longer, the amount of energy the GPU consumes decreases slightly in almost all cases except for LonestarGPU, where the energy consumption is mostly unaffected. Even in the worst cases, the energy does not increase by nearly as much as the active runtime.

This general decrease in energy is the result of a significant reduction in the power draw when switching to the 614 setting, which outweighs the increase in runtime on every program we studied. Even in the worst cases, the power decreases slightly or stays roughly constant. The median power decrease is between 3% and 10% depending on the benchmark suite. For memory-bound codes, lowering the switching activity in the underutilized core is expected to reduce power more than it increases the runtime. However, some of the compute-bound codes also experience a substantial power reduction. In fact, two of the compute-bound CUDA SDK programs experience a power reduction of over 15%, that is, more than the reduction in core frequency. We surmise that this is because, in addition to the frequency, the supply voltage is also reduced as is commonly done in DVFS [12]. Because power is proportional to the voltage squared, superlinear power reductions are possible [13].

NB from the CUDA SDK sees the greatest savings in power (22%) for the reasons just stated. It also has one of the largest increases in active runtime (15%) as it is highly compute bound, resulting in a middling decrease in energy (7%). Interestingly, just behind NB for decrease in power is the irregular MST code

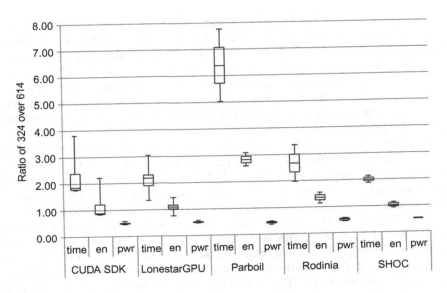

FIG. 10

Range of effects on runtime (time), energy (en), and power (pwr) when throttling the clock frequency from the 614 to the 324 setting.

from the LonestarGPU suite. It has the highest increase in active runtime of all the programs across all the benchmarks (25%) and the third highest increase in energy (8%) and saves 16% in power. SHOC's MF boasts the greatest savings in energy (14.3%) and one of the lowest increases in active runtime (1%). It saves 15% in power, making it the third best in terms of power reduction.

4.3.2 614 to 324

Fig. 10 is similar to Fig. 9 except it shows the relative change in active runtime, energy, and power when switching from the 614 to the 324 configuration. Note, however, that the two figures should not be compared directly as a number of programs did not yield sufficient power samples with the 324 configuration. Hence Fig. 10 is based on significantly fewer programs.

Switching from the 614 to the 324 configuration not only involves a 1.9-fold decrease in core frequency but, much more importantly, also an 8-fold decrease in memory frequency. The cumulative effect is an average increase in active runtime of over 110% across the studied programs. Except for some irregular programs, where the change in timing affects the load balance and the amount of parallelism (cf. the explanation in the previous section), all investigated programs are slowed down by at least a factor of 1.9 as expected.

Going from default to 614, two-thirds of the programs see a savings in energy, albeit small. In contrast, going from 614 to 324 increases the energy consumption of two-thirds of the programs, in one case by over 200%. Even in the best case, the energy savings do not exceed 30% and, on average, going from 614 to 324 results in an increase in energy. The reason for this change in behavior is the large slowdown in memory frequency when going to 324, which makes the programs more memory-bound, that is, the GPU cores end up idling more, thus wasting energy. The resulting increase in active runtime more than outweighs the decrease in power draw. In contrast, on the 614 configuration, the active runtime increases less than or roughly in proportion to the decrease in power draw, so the energy consumption decreases or stays roughly the same.

Looking at the individual codes, PTA from the LonestarGPU suite sees the smallest decrease in active runtime and the largest decrease in energy when going from 614 to 324, but because of the small drop in active runtime compared to the other programs, it also has one of the smallest savings in power. LBM from the Parboil suite sees the largest increase in active runtime (7.75×) and energy (2×).

According to Fig. 10, the Parboil suite experiences by far the largest increase in active runtime and energy. This is misleading, though, as only one of the Parboil programs (LBM) yielded usable results on the 324 configuration. In fact, the two LBM inputs used resulted in the two highest increases in runtime and energy out of all the programs we studied. This is a good example of how big an impact altering the memory frequency of the GPU can have on an already memory-bound code.

4.4 INPUT SENSITIVITY

Fig. 11 shows how using different inputs affects the power profile of the irregular PTA code. Clearly, each tested input yields a rather distinct profile. For example, pine results in an over 15 W higher average power draw than vim, and tshark yields a profile in which the power ramps up after an initial spike, whereas the other two inputs result in more spikes and exhibit a slightly decreasing trend in power draw over time. Because a change in input can have such a drastic effect on the power profile of irregular programs, it may not be possible to use information from one type of input to accurately characterize the behavior for a different input. In fact, even the early behavior of a running program may not be indicative of its later behavior during the same run, as tshark illustrates. These potential problems need to be taken into account when making profile-based design decisions or implementing feedback-driven and online code optimizations.

4.5 SOURCE-CODE OPTIMIZATIONS

In this section, we again look at the irregular memory-bound BH code from the LonestarGPU suite and compare it to the regular compute-bound NB code. We modified these two programs in a way that makes it possible to individually enable or disable specific source-code transformations. We study the effect of the these code optimizations on the runtime, energy, and power for different core and memory frequencies, with and without using error correcting codes (ECC) in main memory, and with single and double precision. As in the Core and Memory Frequency Scaling section, we use the default, 614, and 324 frequency settings

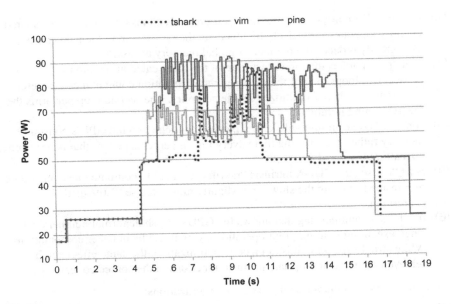

FIG. 11

Power profiles of PTA for different program inputs.

(see the aforementioned section for details). To these settings we add the "ECC" configuration, which combines ECC protection with the default clock frequency. On the K20c, enabling ECC has the effect of increasing the number of memory accesses a particular program makes without increasing the amount of computation done in software. All other tested configurations have ECC disabled. We also add the "double" configuration. By default, the evaluated programs use single-precision floating-point arithmetic, but we also wrote double-precision versions for comparison. Since CUDA-enabled GPUs require two registers to hold a double value and can store only half as many doubles as floats in shared memory, the "double" configuration has to run with fewer threads than the single-precision codes. Because of this, the single- and double-precision configurations used in this chapter are not directly comparable.

These experiments were conducted on three inputs varying both the number of bodies and the number of time steps. We found the differences in behavior between the inputs to be slight, so the results shown here are from just one set of inputs: 100,000 bodies with 100 time steps for NB, and 1 million bodies with 1 time step for BH.

For NB, we chose the following six code optimizations:

(1) unroll "u" uses a pragma to request unrolling of the innermost loop(s). Unrolling often allows the compiler to schedule instructions better and to eliminate redundancies, thus improving performance.

(2) shmem "s" employs blocking; that is, it preloads chunks of data into the shared memory, operates exclusively on this data, then moves on to the next chunk. This greatly reduces the number of global memory accesses.

(3) peel "p" separates the innermost loop of the force calculation into two consecutive loops, one of which has a known iteration count and can therefore presumably be better optimized by the compiler. The second loop performs the few remaining iterations.

(4) const "c" copies immutable kernel parameters once into the GPU's constant memory rather than passing them every time a kernel is called; that is, it lowers the calling overhead.

(5) rsqrt "r" uses the CUDA intrinsic "rsqrtf()" to quickly compute one over square root instead of using the slower but slightly more precise "1.0f/sqrtf()" expression.

(6) ftz "f" is a compiler flag that allows the GPU to flush denormal numbers to 0 when executing floating-point operations, which results in faster computations. While strictly speaking it is not a code optimization, the same effect can be achieved by using appropriate intrinsic functions in the source code.

For BH, we selected the following six code optimizations:

(1) vola "v" strategically copies some volatile variables into nonvolatile variables and uses those in code regions where it is known (due to lockstep execution of threads in a warp) that no other thread can have updated the value. This optimization serves to reduce memory accesses.

(2) ftz "f" is identical to the corresponding NB optimization.

(3) rsqrt "r" is also identical to its NB counterpart.

(4) sort "s" approximately sorts the bodies by spatial distance to minimize the tree prefix that needs to be traversed during the force calculation.

(5) warp "w" switches from a thread-based to a warp-based implementation that is much more efficient because it does not suffer from branch divergence and uses less memory because it records certain information on a per-warp instead of a per-thread basis.

(6) vote "V" employs thread voting instead of a shared memory-based code sequence to perform 32-element reductions.

Because we can individually enable or disable each optimization, there are 64 possible combinations of the 6 optimizations. Consequently, we evaluate 64 versions for both the NB and BH codes.

4.5.1 None vs all optimizations

Table 1 shows the measured active runtime and energy consumption as well as the average power draw of the five evaluated configurations for the second inputs when none and all of the optimizations are enabled.

Our first observation is that code optimizations can have a large impact not only on active runtime but also on energy and power. On NB, the energy consumption

Table 1 Active Runtime (s), Energy (J), and Power (W) With the Second Input When None and All of the Optimizations Are Enabled

		Default			614			324			ECC			Double		
		Runtime	Energy	Power	Runtime	Energy	Power	Runtime	Energy	Power	Runtime	Energy	Power	Runtime	Energy	Power
NB	None	63.88	7002	109.6	73.44	6902	94.0	135.85	6250	46.0	64.08	7078	110.5	154.64	17,857	115.5
	All	12.10	1828	151.1	13.88	1745	125.7	26.97	1580	58.6	12.16	1840	151.4	47.33	7137	150.8
BH	None	209.09	26,266	125.6	237.18	26,255	110.7	739.92	34,868	47.1	211.81	27,301	128.9	304.25	37,897	124.6
	All	16.15	1966	121.7	18.19	1952	107.3	40.72	2142	52.6	18.33	2277	124.2	26.18	3328	127.1

improves 2.5- to 4-fold due to the optimizations, and the performance improves 3.3- to 5.3-fold. At the same time, the power increases by up to 30% because the hardware is being used more effectively. On BH, the energy improves 11- to 16-fold and the performance 11.5- to 18-fold while the power increases by 10%. Clearly, code optimizations can drastically lower the active runtime and the energy, but tend to increase power.

The improvements are substantially lower on NB than on BH. We believe there are two main reasons for this difference. First, NB is a much simpler and shorter code, making it easier to implement efficiently without having to resort to sophisticated optimizations. Second, NB is a regular code with few data dependencies, enabling the compiler to generate quite efficient code even in the base case. As a consequence, the additional code optimizations we analyzed provide less benefit.

Focusing on the default configuration, we find that the optimizations help the active runtime of NB much more than the energy consumption, which is why the power increases greatly. On BH, the situation is different. Here, the optimizations reduce the energy consumption a little more than the active runtime, resulting in a slight decrease in power draw.

Comparing the default and the 614 configurations, we find that the 15% drop in core speed yields a 15% active runtime increase on NB, as previously discussed. The active runtime of BH increases only by 13%, because the memory accesses are not slowed down. Hence the drop in power draw is lower for BH than for NB. The 614 configuration consumes a little less energy than the default configuration. The reduction is within the margin of error for BH, but the 5% drop with all optimizations enabled on NB is significant. Overall, the 614 configuration primarily serves to lower the power draw. Because of a concomitant increase in active runtime, it does not affect the energy much. The benefit of all the various optimizations is fairly similar for the default and 614 configurations.

The 324 configuration behaves quite differently because it not only reduces the core frequency by a factor of 2 but also lowers the memory frequency by a factor of 8 relative to the 614 configuration. NB's increase in active runtime is in line with the twofold drop in core frequency because it is compute-bound, whereas BH's increase in active runtime is much larger due to its greater dependence on memory speed. As a consequence, there is a decrease in energy consumption on NB but a substantial increase on BH when comparing the 324 to the 614 configuration. Because the 324 configuration affects the active runtime much more than the energy, it results in a large decrease in power draw. Reducing power is the primary strength of the 324 configuration, which is otherwise not very useful and can greatly increase the energy consumption of memory-bound codes. Nevertheless, the code optimizations are just as effective on it as they are on the other configurations. In fact, on BH, they are more effective when using the 324 configuration because the optimizations eliminate some of the now extremely costly memory accesses.

Looking at the ECC configuration, we find that the energy, active runtime, and power numbers are almost identical to the default for NB. Since NB has excellent locality, which translates into many cache/shared-memory hits and good coalescing, even the version without our optimizations performs relatively few main memory accesses, which is why it is hardly affected by ECC. BH has less locality and accesses memory more frequently, which explains why it is affected more. Its active runtime and energy become 13% and 16% worse, respectively, when ECC is turned on and all optimizations are used. However, the active runtime and energy are only 1% and 4% worse with ECC when none of the optimizations are enabled. We believe the reason for this difference is that the optimizations improve the computation more than the memory accesses, thus making the optimized code, relatively speaking, more memory-bound.

Comparing the double configuration to the default, we observe that the active runtime and energy are 1.5–3.9 times worse, but the power is almost unchanged. Clearly, the double-precision code is substantially slower. While still highly effective (a factor of 2.5–11.6 improvement), the benefit of the code optimizations is lower for the double configuration. This is probably because the double-precision code is more memory-bound than the single-precision code, and as previously mentioned the optimizations improve the computation more than the memory accesses.

4.5.2 Effectiveness of optimizations

Fig. 12A and B shows the range of the effect of each optimization on the active runtime and the energy. The 64 versions of each program contain 32 instances that do not and 32 that do include any given optimization. The presented data show the maximum (top whisker), the minimum (bottom whisker), and the median (line between the two boxes) change when adding a specific optimization to the 32 versions that do not already include it. The boxes represent the first and third quartiles, respectively. Points below 1.0 indicate a slowdown or increase in energy consumption. It is clear from these figures that the effect of an optimization can depend greatly on what other optimizations are present.

The most effective optimization on NB is *rsqrt*. Using this special intrinsic improves the energy and particularly the active runtime because it targets the slowest and most complex operation in the innermost loop. Since *rsqrt* helps the active runtime more than the energy, it increases the power substantially. The other very effective optimization is *shmem*, that is, to use tiling in shared memory. It, too, improves the active runtime more than the energy, leading to an increase in power.

The impact of the remaining four optimizations is much smaller. *ftz* helps both energy and active runtime as it speeds up the processing of the many floating-point instructions. It is largely power-neutral because it improves energy and active runtime about equally. Except with the double configuration, *unroll* helps active runtime a little and energy a lot, thus lowering the power quite a bit. We are not sure why unrolling helps energy more. *const* hurts the energy consumption and the active runtime, but it is close to the margin of error. After all, this optimization only affects the infrequent kernel launches. *peel* hurts performance and energy, except in the double-precision code, but does not change the power much. Clearly, there are optimizations that help active runtime more (e.g., *rsqrt*) while others help energy

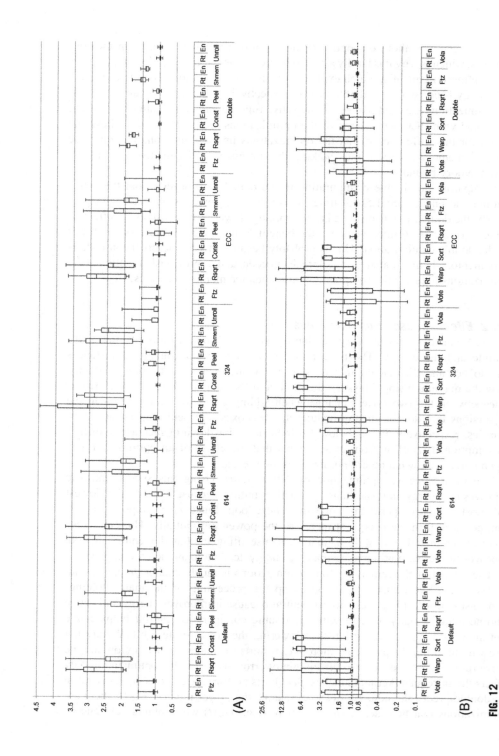

FIG. 12

(A) Improvement range of the active runtime (Rt) and energy (En) on NB. (B) Improvement range of the active runtime (Rt) and energy (En) on BH (log 2 scale).

more (e.g., *unroll*). Some optimizations help both active runtime and energy equally (e.g., *ftz*).

Most of the optimization benefits are quite similar across the different configurations. Notable 324 exceptions are *peel*, which hurts significantly more than in the other configurations, and *ftz* and *rsqrt*, which are more effective on 324. *shmem* and *unroll* are also more effective. Interestingly, the double configuration exhibits almost exactly the opposite behavior. *peel* is more effective on it than on the other configurations, whereas *ftz*, *rsqrt*, *shmem*, and *unroll* are substantially less effective.

The findings for BH are similar. There are also two optimizations that help a great deal. *warp*, the most effective optimization, improves energy a little less than active runtime, thus increasing the power draw. *sort*, the second most effective optimization, helps energy a little more than active runtime. *vola* and *rsqrt* also help both aspects but are much less effective and power-neutral. We are surprised by the effectiveness of *vola*. Apparently, it manages to reduce memory accesses significantly and therefore makes BH less memory-bound. *vote* helps energy substantially more than active runtime. Hence this optimization is particularly useful for reducing power. Interestingly, on some configurations, it hurts both energy and active runtime, on others only active runtime; yet on others, it helps both aspects. *ftz* is within the margin of error but seems to help a little. The reason why both *rsqrt* and *ftz* are much less effective on BH than on NB is because BH executes many integer instructions, which do not benefit from these optimizations.

Investigating the individual configurations, we again find that there is no significant difference in optimization effectiveness between default and 614 as well as between default and ECC on NB. For 324 on NB, *const* is unchanged, *peel* is less effective, and the other optimizations are more effective than with the default configuration. On BH, *warp* and *vola* are much more effective with the 324 configuration. This is because both optimizations reduce the number of memory accesses. For ECC on BH, *vote* is less effective, but the other optimizations are just as effective as they are with the default configuration.

Once again, the double configuration behaves quite differently. Most notably, *warp* is much less effective and *vola* somewhat less. However, *rsqrt* and especially *vote* are more effective. Note that in the double-precision code, the rsqrtf() intrinsic is followed by two Newton-Raphson steps to obtain double precision, which is apparently more efficient, both in terms of active runtime and energy, than performing a double-precision square root and division. Thread voting helps because it frees up shared memory that can then be used for other purposes. For NB, the double configuration results in *peel* being much more effective and all other optimizations except *const* being much less effective than using the default configuration. In particular, *rsqrt* and *shmem* are substantially less effective, the former because of the Newton-Raphson overhead, which is substantial in the tight inner loop of NB, and the latter because only half as many double values fit into the shared memory. Overall, the power is not much different for the double configuration with the exception of *unroll*, which does not lower the power draw in the double-precision code.

These results illustrate that the effect of a particular optimization is not always constant but can change depending on the regular or irregular nature of the code, the core and memory frequencies, the chosen floating-point precision, and the presence or absence of other source-code optimizations.

4.5.3 Lowest and highest settings

Fig. 13 displays the sets of optimizations that result in the highest and lowest active runtime and energy. In each case, a six-character string shows which optimizations are present (see the beginning of this section for which letter represents which optimization). The characters are always listed in the same order. An underscore indicates the absence of the corresponding optimization.

Interestingly, the worst performance and the highest energy are obtained when some optimizations are enabled, showing that it is possible for "optimizations" to hurt rather than help. In the worst case, which is NB 324, the energy consumption increases more than threefold when going from none of the optimizations to enabling *peel*. For all tested configurations, the best performance and the lowest energy consumption on BH are always obtained when all optimizations are enabled. This is also mostly the case for NB. Comparing the highest to the lowest values, we find that the worst and best configurations differ by over a factor of 12 (energy) and 14 (active runtime) on NB and by over a factor of 29 (energy) and 34 (active runtime) on BH. This highlights how large an effect code transformations can have on performance and energy consumption. The effect on the power is modest in comparison. It changes by up to 23% on BH and up to 60% on NB.

Looking at individual optimizations, we find that, except for the worst case with the double configuration, *peel* is always included in the best and the worst settings in NB. Clearly, *peel* is bad when used by itself or in combination with the *const* optimization. However, *peel* becomes beneficial when grouped with some other optimizations, demonstrating that the effect of an optimization cannot always be assessed in isolation but may depend on the context. To reach the lowest power on NB, *unroll*, *peel*, and *const* need to be enabled together.

In the case of BH, we find *sort* and *vote* to dominate the worst active runtime and energy settings. *sort* in the absence of *warp* does not help anything. *vote* generally hurts energy and often active runtime (cf. Section 3.3). Surprisingly, *ftz* is often included in the worst performance setting for BH. We expected *ftz* to never increase the active runtime. However, *ftz* also appears in all the best settings, showing that it does help in the presence of other optimizations.

Additionally, the best and worst settings are similar across the different configurations, illustrating that optimizations tend to behave consistently with respect to each other.

4.5.4 Energy efficiency vs performance

Table 2 shows the largest impact that adding a single optimization makes. We consider four scenarios, maximally hurting both active runtime and energy, hurting

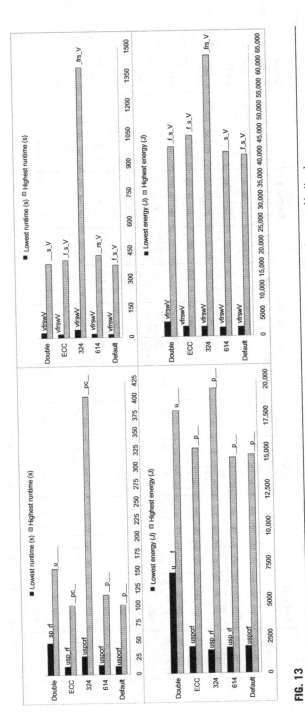

FIG. 13

Sets of NB (*left*) and BH (*right*) optimizations that yield the highest and lowest runtime (*top*) and energy (*bottom*).

Table 2 Base Setting and Added Optimization That Yields the Most Significant Positive/Negative Impact

		Default			614			324			ECC			Double		
		Setting & Opt	Impr. Factor		Setting & Opt	Impr. Factor		Setting & Opt	Impr. Factor		Setting & Opt	Impr. Factor		Setting & Opt	Impr. Factor	
			Time	Ener.		Time	Ener.		Time	Ener.		Time	Ener.		Time	Ener.
NB	rt+en+	___ & peel	0.63	0.47	___ & peel	0.63	0.47	___ & peel	0.34	0.32	___ & peel	0.63	0.46	__per & unrol	0.86	0.91
	rt+en−	__pc f & unrol	0.86	1.25	__pc f & unrol	0.86	1.24	__pc_f & unrol	0.97	1.26	__pc_f & unrol	0.86	1.28	__us_rf & const	1.00	1.00
	rt− en+	_sp_rf & const	1.01	1.00	_sp_rf & const	1.01	1.00	_sp_rf & const	1.00	0.99	_sp_rf & const	1.01	1.00	_us_cr & peel	1.00	0.97
	rt− en−	_P__ & rsqrt	2.97	3.65	_P__ & rsqrt	2.97	3.69	__pc__ & rsqrt	5.33	5.29	_P__ & rsqrt	2.98	3.74	_P__ & rsqrt	2.27	1.90
BH	rt+en+	_frs__ & vote	0.16	0.18	_frs__ & vote	0.16	0.18	_frs__ & vote	0.15	0.16	_frs__ & vote	0.15	0.17	_frs__ & vote	0.22	0.24
	rt+en−	__wV & vola	0.99	1.04	__wV & vola	1.00	1.05	v_rs__ & ftz	1.00	1.01	__wV & vola	0.99	1.04	___ & vote	0.96	1.07
	rt− en+	v_swV & ftz	n/a	n/a	v_swV & ftz	1.00	1.00	__w & ftz	1.00	1.00	__s__ & ftz	1.00	1.00	___V & ftz	1.00	1.00
	rt− en−	_frs_V & warp	19.06	17.04	_frs_V & warp	19.28	17.48	frs_V & warp	27.47	23.99	frs_V & warp	18.31	16.64	frs_V & warp	13.03	11.40

Notes: +, an increase; −, a decrease; en, energy; rt, active runtime.

active runtime but improving energy, improving active runtime but hurting energy, and improving both active runtime and energy.

With one exception, every configuration has examples of all four scenarios. The examples of decreasing the active runtime while increasing the energy consumption are within the margin of error and therefore probably not meaningful. However, the other three scenarios have significant examples. Excluding the double configuration for the moment, enabling just the *peel* optimization on NB increases the energy consumption by more than a factor of 2 and the active runtime by nearly as much (as noted in the previous section). Clearly, this "optimization" is a very bad choice by itself. However, adding *rsqrt* to the *peel* optimization improves the active runtime and energy by a factor of 3–5, making it the most effective addition of an optimization we have observed. Perhaps the most interesting case is adding *unroll* to *peel*, *const*, and *ftz*. It lowers the energy consumption by about 25% even though it increases the active runtime substantially. This example shows that performance and energy optimization are not always the same thing.

BH has similar examples. Adding *vote* to *ftz*, *rsqrt*, and *sort* greatly increases the active runtime and the energy consumption, making it the worst example of adding an optimization. In contrast, adding *warp* to *ftz*, *rsqrt*, and *sort* greatly reduces both active runtime and energy, making it the most effective addition of a single optimization we have observed. Again, decreasing the active runtime while increasing the energy is within the margin of error (or no such case exists). Finally, there are several examples of lowering the energy by a few percent while increasing the active runtime marginally. Although not as pronounced as with NB, these examples again show that there are cases that only help energy but not active runtime.

The base settings and the optimizations added that result in significant changes in energy and active runtime are consistent across the five configurations. Only the double configuration on NB differs substantially. However, even in this case, the effects of the optimizations are large. In fact, this configuration exhibits the most pronounced example of adding an optimization that lowers the active runtime (albeit within the margin of error) while increasing the energy consumption (by 3%).

4.5.5 Most biased optimizations
This section studies optimizations where the difference between how much they improve energy versus active runtime is maximal. Table 3 provides the results for the different configurations.

On NB, we find that adding *unroll* to *peel* and *const* improves energy by 18–56% more than active runtime except for double, where there is no strong example. In contrast, adding *rsqrt* to *unroll*, *shmem*, *peel*, and *const* improves active runtime by 31–46% more than energy, again with the exception of the double configuration, where the same optimization but on a different base setting yields 20% more benefit in active runtime than in energy.

On BH, there is no consistent setting or optimization that yields the highest benefit in energy over active runtime. Nevertheless, some code optimizations help energy between 5% and 18% more than active runtime. The best optimization for helping

Table 3 Base Setting and Added Optimization That Yields the Most Biased Impact on Energy Over Active Runtime and Vice Versa on the Second Input

		Default			614			324			ECC			Double		
		Setting & Opt	Impr. Factor		Setting & Opt	Impr. Factor		Setting & Opt	Impr. Factor		Setting & Opt	Impr. Factor		Setting & Opt	Impr. Factor	
			Time	Ener.		Time	Ener.		Time	Ener.		Time	Ener.		Time	Ener.
NB	max en over rt	_pc__ & unrol	1.19	1.82	_pc__ & unrol	1.19	1.80	_pc_f & unrol	0.97	1.26	_pc_ & unrol	1.19	1.86	_sp_r_ & ftz	1.01	1.02
	max rt ove ren	uspc__ & rsqrt	3.65	2.53	uspc__ & rsqrt	3.65	2.61	uspc__ & rsqrt	3.50	2.66	uspc__ & rsqrt	3.66	2.52	__p__ & rsqrt	2.27	1.90
BH	max en over rt	_wV & vola	0.99	1.04	_rs__ & warp	1.11	1.18	_wV & sort	3.01	3.16	_frs__ & warp	1.10	1.16	__ & vote	0.96	1.07
	max rt over en	__V & warp	4.36	3.81	v_rs__V & warp	18.13	16.13	_f__V & warp	7.56	6.25	__V & warp	4.99	4.29	vfrs_V & warp	11.59	10.13

active runtime more than energy is *warp*, but the base setting differs for the different configurations. It improves active runtime between 6% and 21% more than energy.

These results highlight that optimizations do not necessarily affect active runtime and energy in the same way. Rather, some source-code optimizations tend to improve one aspect substantially more than another.

5 SUMMARY

Understanding performance, energy, and power on GPUs is becoming more and more important as GPU-based accelerators are quickly spreading to every corner of computing, including handheld devices and supercomputers where reducing power and energy while maintaining performance is highly desirable and a key trade-off that has to be considered when designing new systems.

In this chapter, we show that the power profiles of regular codes are often similar to the expected "rectangular" power profile but that irregular codes often are not. Because of this, assumptions on the energy consumption of an irregular program based on that program's power profile from an earlier run may not be accurate.

We also made the following observations. Because of their more efficient use of the hardware, regular compute-bound codes tend to draw substantially more power than irregular memory-bound codes. Changing the implementation of programs can be a very effective tool to lower the power draw and active runtime, and thus the energy consumption. Lowering the GPU frequency is a good power-saving strategy but not useful as an energy-saving strategy, and doing so is bad for performance, as expected. Switching from single- to double-precision arithmetic has little effect on the power but drastically increases both the active runtime and the energy consumption of the GPU.

Using ECC with even slightly memory-bound programs not only results in a slowdown but also in a concomitant increase in energy consumption. ECC's cost is entirely dependent on how many main-memory accesses a program makes, so code transformations that reduce the number of (main) memory accesses are especially useful when ECC is active. Compute-bound codes are mostly unaffected by ECC in terms of performance, power draw, and energy consumption.

Source-code optimizations tend to increase the power draw and can have a large impact on energy. The effect of an optimization cannot always be assessed in isolation but may depend on the presence of other optimizations. Also, source-code optimizations do not necessarily affect active runtime and energy in the same way. Some optimizations hurt when used by themselves but can become beneficial when grouped with other optimizations, so optimizations should not be judged in isolation.

We identified several examples where code optimizations lower the energy while increasing the active runtime, showing that there are optimizations that help energy but not active runtime. In one case, the improvement in energy is 56% higher than the improvement in active runtime. In another case, the active runtime improvement is 46% higher than the energy improvement.

Our results demonstrate that programmers can optimize their source code for energy (or power), that such optimizations may be different from optimizations for performance, and that optimizations can make a large difference. Clearly, source-code optimizations have the potential to play an important role in making accelerators more energy-efficient.

Our results show that there are several software-based methods for controlling power draw and energy consumption, some of which certainly increase the active runtime, but others help active runtime. These methods include changing the GPU's clock frequency, altering the arithmetic precision, turning ECC on or off, utilizing a different algorithm, and employing source-code optimizations. Some of these methods are directly accessible to the end user, whereas others need to be implemented by the programmer.

We make the following recommendations for anyone interested in performing power and energy studies on GPUs:

(1) Use program inputs that result in long runtimes to obtain enough power samples to accurately analyze the energy and power behavior. However, avoid poor implementations that run slowly.
(2) Measure a broad spectrum of codes, including memory- and compute-bound programs as well as regular and irregular codes since they exhibit different behaviors.
(3) As none of the studied benchmark suites include all of these types of applications, use programs from different suites for conducting power and energy studies.
(4) Run irregular codes with multiple inputs that exercise different behaviors.
(5) Repeat experiments at various frequency and ECC settings if desired as the findings might change.

Portions of this chapter are based on published work that contains more detailed information [14–16].

APPENDIX

(1) *LonestarGPU*. The LonestarGPU suite is a collection of commonly used real-world applications that exhibit irregular behavior.
   (a) Barnes-Hut *n*-body simulation (BH): An algorithm that quickly approximates the forces between a set of bodies in lieu of performing precise force calculations.
   (b) Breadth-first search (L-BFS): Computes the level of each node from a source node in an unweighted graph using a topology-driven approach. In addition to the standard BFS implementation (topology-driven, one node per thread), we also study the atomic variation (topology-driven, one node per thread that uses atomics) and the wla variation (topology-driven, one flag per node, one node per thread). The wlw variation (data-driven, one

Table 4 Program Names, Number of Global Kernels (#K), and Inputs

Program	#K	Inputs	Program	#K	Inputs
EIP	2	None	SGEMM	1	"small" benchmark input
EP	2	None	STEN	1	"small" benchmark input
NB	1	100k, 250k, and lm bodies	TPACF	1	"small" benchmark input
SC	3	2^26 elements	BP	2	2^17 elements
BH	9	Bodies-timesteps; 10k-10k, 100k-10, lm-1	R-BFS	2	Random graphs; 100k and lm nodes
L-BFS	5	Roadmaps of Great Lakes Region (2.7m nodes, 7m edges), Western USA (6m nodes, 15m edges), and entire USA (24m nodes, 58m edges)	GE	2	2048 × 2048 matrix
DMR	4	250k, lm, and 5m node mesh files	MUM	3	100 and 25 bp
MST	7	Roadmaps of Great Lakes Region (2.7m nodes, 7m edges), Western USA (6m nodes, 15m edges), and entire USA (24m nodes, 58m edges)	NN	1	42k data points
PTA	40	vim (small), pine (medium), tshark (large)	NW	2	4096 and 16,384 items
SSSP	2	Roadmaps of Great Lakes Region (2.7m nodes, 7m edges), Western USA (6m nodes, 15m edges), and entire USA (24m nodes, 58m edges)	PF	1	Row length-column length-pyramid height; 100k-100-20, 200k-200-40
NSP	3	Clauses-literals-literals per clause; 16,800-4000-3, 42k-10k-3, 42k-10k-5	S-BFS	9	Default benchmark input
P-BFS	3	Roadmap of the San Francisco Bay Area (321k nodes, 800k edges)	FFT	2	Default benchmark input
CUTCP	1	watbox.sll00.pqr	MF	20	Default benchmark input
HISTO	4	Image file whose parameters "– are 20-4" according to documentation	MD	1	Default benchmark input
LBM	1	3000 and 100 timestep inputs	QTC	6	Default benchmark input
MRIQ	2	64 × 64 × 64 matrix	ST	5	Default benchmark input
SAD	3	Default input	S2D	1	Default benchmark input

node per thread) and the wlc variation (data-driven, one edge-per-thread version using Merrill's strategy [17]) were not used because they reduced the active runtime to the point that insufficient power samples could be recorded even with the largest available input.

(c) Delaunay mesh refinement (DMR): This implementation of the algorithm described by Kulkarni et al. [18] produces a guaranteed quality 2D Delaunay mesh, which is a Delaunay triangulation with the additional constraint that no angle in the mesh be less than 30 degrees.

(d) Minimum spanning tree (MST): This benchmark computes a minimum spanning tree in a weighted undirected graph using Boruvka's algorithm and is implemented by successive edge relaxations of the minimum weight edges.

(e) Points to analysis (PTA): Given a set of points-to-constraints, this code computes the points-to information for each pointer in a flow-insensitive, context-insensitive manner implemented in a topology-driven way.

(f) Single-source shortest paths (SSSP): Computes the shortest path from a source node to all nodes in a directed graph with nonnegative edge weights by using a modified Bellman-Ford algorithm. In addition to the standard SSSP implementation (topology-driven, one node per thread), we also used the wln variation (data-driven, one node per thread) and the wlc variation (data-driven, one edge per thread using Merrill's strategy adapted to SSSP).

(g) Survey propagation (NSP): A heuristic SAT-solver based on Bayesian inference. The algorithm represents the Boolean formula as a factor graph, which is a bipartite graph with variables on one side and clauses on the other.

(2) *Parboil.* Parboil is a set of applications used to study the performance of throughput-computing architectures and compilers.

(a) Breadth-first search (P-BFS): Computes the shortest-path cost from a single source to every other reachable node in a graph of uniform edge weights.

(b) Distance-cutoff Coulombic potential (CUTCP): Computes the short-range component of the Coulombic potential at each grid point over a 3D grid containing point charges representing an explicit-water biomolecular model.

(c) Saturating histogram (HISTO): Computes a 2D saturating histogram with a maximum bin count of 255.

(d) Lattice-Boltzmann method fluid dynamics (LBM): A fluid dynamics simulation of an enclosed, lid-driven cavity using the LBM.

(e) Magnetic resonance imaging—Q (MRIQ): Computes a matrix Q, representing the scanner configuration for calibration, used in 3D magnetic resonance image reconstruction algorithms in non-Cartesian space.

(f) Sum of absolute differences (SAD): SAD kernel, used in MPEG video encoders.

(g) General matrix multiply (SGEMM): A register-tiled matrix-matrix multiplication, with default column-major layout on matrix A and C, but with B transposed.

(h) 3D stencil operation (STEN): An iterative Jacobi stencil operation on a regular 3D grid.

(i) Two-point angular correlation function (TPACF): Statistical analysis of the distribution of astronomical bodies.

(3) *Rodinia.* Rodinia is designed for heterogeneous computing infrastructures with OpenMP, OpenCL, and CUDA implementations. Our study uses the following CUDA codes.

(a) Back propagation (BP): ML algorithm that trains the weights of connecting nodes on a layered neural network.

(b) Breadth-first search (R-BFS): Another GPU implementation of the BFS algorithm, which traverses all the connected components in a graph.

(c) Gaussian elimination (GE): Computes results row by row, solving for all of the variables in a linear system.

(d) MUMmerGPU (MUM): A local sequence alignment program that concurrently aligns multiple query sequences against a single reference sequence stored as a suffix tree.

(e) Nearest neighbor (NN): Finds the k-nearest neighbors in an unstructured data set.

(f) Needleman-Wunsch (NW): A nonlinear global optimization method for DNA sequence alignment.

(g) Pathfinder (PF): Uses dynamic programming to find a path on a 2D grid with the smallest accumulated weights, where each step of the path moves straight or diagonally.

(4) *SHOC.* The Scalable HeterOgeneous Computing benchmark suite is a collection of programs that are designed to test the performance of heterogeneous systems with multicore processors, graphics processors, reconfigurable processors, and so on.

(a) Breadth-first search (S-BFS): Measures the runtime of BFS on an undirected random k-way graph.

(b) Fast Fourier transform (FFT): Measures the speed of a single- and double-precision fast Fourier transform that computes the discrete Fourier transform and its inverse.

(c) MaxFlops (MF): Measures the maximum throughput for combinations of different floating-point operations.

(d) Molecular dynamics (MD): Measures the performance of an n-body computation (the Lennard-Jones potential from MD). The test problem is n atoms distributed at random over a 3D domain.

(e) Quality threshold clustering (QTC): Measures the performance of an algorithm designed to be an alternative method for data partitioning.

(f) Sort (ST): Measures the performance of a Radix Sort on unsigned integer key/value pairs.

> (g) Stencil2D (S2D): Measures the performance of a 2D, nine-point single-precision stencil computation.

(5) *CUDA-SDK.* The NVIDIA GPU Computing SDK includes dozens of sample codes. We use the following programs in our study.

> (a) MC_EstimatePiInlineP (EIP): Monte Carlo simulation for the estimation of pi using a Pseudo-Random Number Generator (PRNG). The inline implementation allows use inside GPU functions/kernels as well as in the host code.
>
> (b) MC_EstimatePiP (EP): Monte Carlo simulation for the estimation of pi using a PRNG. This implementation generates batches of random numbers.
>
> (c) *n*-body (NB): All-pairs *n*-body simulation.
>
> (d) Scan (SC): Demonstrates an efficient implementation of a parallel prefix sum, also known as "scan."

REFERENCES

[1] K. Bergman, S. Borkar, D. Campbell, W. Carlson, W. Dally, M. Denneau, P. Franzon, W. Harrod, J. Hiller, S. Karp, S. Keckler, D. Klein, R. Lucas, M. Richards, A. Scarpelli, S. Scott, A. Snavely, T. Sterling, R.S. Williams, K. Yelick, ExaScale computing study: technology challenges in achieving exascale systems, Editor & Study Lead Peter Kogge, 2008.

[2] V. Freeh, F. Pan, N. Kappiah, D. Lowenthal, R. Springer, Exploring the energy-time tradeoff in MPI programs on a power-scalable cluster, in: 19th IEEE International Parallel and Distributed Processing Symposium, March, 2005.

[3] S. Ghosh, S. Chandrasekaran, B. Chapman, Energy analysis of parallel scientific kernels on multiple GPUs, in: 2012 Symposium on Application Accelerators in High Performance Computing, July, 2012.

[4] V. Korthikanti, G. Agha, Towards optimizing energy costs of algorithms for shared memory architectures, in: 22nd Annual ACM Symposium on Parallelism in Algorithms and Architectures, June, 2010.

[5] LonestarGPU, 2016, http://iss.ices.utexas.edu/?p=projects/galois/lonestargpu.

[6] Parboil, 2016, http://impact.crhc.illinois.edu/Parboil/parboil.aspx.

[7] Rodinia, 2016, http://www.cs.virginia.edu/~skadron/wiki/rodinia/index.php/Main_Page.

[8] SHOC, 2016, https://github.com/vetter/shoc/wiki.

[9] CUDA SDK, 2016, https://developer.nvidia.com/cuda-toolkit.

[10] M. Burtscher, I. Zecena, Z. Zong, Measuring GPU power with the K20 built-in sensor, in: Seventh Workshop on General Purpose Processing on Graphics Processing Units, March, 2014.

[11] M. Burtscher, R. Nasre, K. Pingali, A quantitative study of irregular programs on GPUs, in: 2012 IEEE International Symposium on Workload Characterization, November, 2012, pp. 141–151.

[12] E. Le Sueur, G. Heiser, Dynamic voltage and frequency scaling: the laws of diminishing returns, in: Proceedings of the 2010 International Conference on Power Aware Computing and Systems (HotPower'10), USENIX Association, Berkeley, CA, USA, 2010, pp. 1–8.

[13] X. Zhong, Power management for networked embedded systems, PhD dissertation, Wayne State University, ProQuest/UMI (Publication No. AAT 3295990), Ann Arbor, 2007.

[14] J. Coplin, M. Burtscher, Power characteristics of irregular GPGPU programs, in: 2014 International Workshop on Green Programming, Computing, and Data Processing, November, 2014.

[15] J. Coplin, M. Burtscher, Effects of source-code optimizations on GPU performance and energy consumption, in: 8th Workshop on General Purpose Processing Using GPUs, February, 2015.

[16] J. Coplin, M. Burtscher, Energy, Power, and Performance Characterization of GPGPU Benchmark Programs. The 12th Workshop on High-Performance, Power-Aware Computing (HPPAC'16), May 2016.

[17] D. Merrill, M. Garland, A. Grimshaw, Scalable GPU graph traversal, in: Proceedings of the 17th ACM SIGPLAN Symposium on Principles and Practice of Parallel Programming (PPoPP'12), 2012, pp. 117–128.

[18] M. Kulkarni, K. Pingali, B. Walter, G. Ramanarayanan, K. Bala, L. Paul Chew, Optimistic parallelism requires abstractions, in: Proceedings of the ACM Conference on Programming Languages Design and Implementation (PLDI), June, 2007, pp. 211–222.

ABOUT THE AUTHORS

Jared Coplin is a Graduate Research Assistant in the Efficient Computing Laboratory at Texas State University, where he is currently pursuing his MS in Computer Science. He received his BS in Computer Science from Texas State University. His research interests include developing new algorithms for efficient parallel graph processing as well as performance, energy, and power assessment and optimization of GPU programs. He is a student member of the IEEE, its Computer Society, and the ACM. Coplin has coauthored four peer-reviewed scientific publications. He is the recipient of the 2016 Outstanding Undergraduate Researcher Award from the Computing Research Association, an Honorable Mention from the NSF's Graduate Research Fellowship Program, the 2015 Outstanding Undergraduate Award from the College of Science and Engineering at Texas State University, and multiple Research Excellence Awards and Scholorships from the Department of Computer Science at Texas State University.

Martin Burtscher is a Professor in the Department of Computer Science at Texas State University. He received the BS and MS degrees from ETH Zurich and the PhD degree from the University of Colorado at Boulder. Burtscher's research interests include efficient parallelization of programs for GPUs, high-speed data compression, and performance assessment and optimization. Burtscher has coauthored over 100 peer-reviewed scientific publications. He is a distinguished member of the ACM and a senior member of the IEEE and its Computer Society.

Architecting the last-level cache for GPUs using STT-MRAM nonvolatile memory

20

M.H. Samavatian[1], M. Arjomand[1], R. Bashizade[1], H. Sarbazi-Azad[1,2]

Sharif University of Technology, Tehran, Iran[1] Institute for Research in Fundamental Sciences (IPM), Tehran, Iran[2]

1 INTRODUCTION

During the past decade, graphics processor units (GPUs) became one of the mainstream technologies in many-core high-performance systems. GPU architecture is a type of single-instruction multiple-thread (SIMT) architecture, which tries to achieve massive thread-level parallelism (TLP) and improve the throughput. These characteristics led to the growing interest in general-purpose GPUs (GPGPUs). The main factor in this SIMT architecture is to keep the entire processor active and decrease the idle cycles by minimizing or covering stall cycles of threads. GPUs form logical groups of parallel threads belonging to the same instruction pack, named warps (or wavefront in AMD terminology) and schedule a number of them for interleaved execution on an SIMT core. This can lead to higher memory performance and reduce the problem of branch divergence. A large body of recent works [1–6] focused on this issue. Although these works diminish idle cycles by switching threads on stall times based on their proposed scheduling algorithms, high latency of main memory in GPUs causes significant idle times when all threads are stalled and no other threads exist for execution. On-chip memories play a substantial role in decreasing stall cycles of threads on memory accesses. Therefore, cache memories in GPU architectures become a critical issue due to the limited on-chip area available for them in GPUs.

In the same way, recent trends in GPU architecture show designers' interest in assigning most of the chip area to more compute cores rather than on-chip memories. Consequently, for supporting more thread executions in GPUs, besides compute cores, register file have priority to be placed on chip. While warp size is rather fixed through successive GPU generations (due to the overhead of branch divergence for

Advances in GPU Research and Practice. http://dx.doi.org/10.1016/B978-0-12-803738-6.00020-3

larger warps [1]), the number of warps assigned to one SIMT core have been steadily increasing in recent products (e.g., 64 warps per SIMT core in Kepler [7] compared to 24 in G80 [8]).

Scheduling more warps improves utilization and throughput of the GPU and can better cover access latency of the main memory. On the other hand, increasing the number of scheduled warps will increase the accesses to the L1 data cache. The emerging problem is that when a new warp is issued for execution, it may cause new accesses to the L1 data cache that cause prior scheduled warps data to be sent out, which is known as cache Thrashing. This phenomenon is made more tangible when studies on GPU cache hierarchy reveal that most L1 data cache hits result from intrawarp locality [2] rather than interwarp locality. The probability of cache Thrashing increases when the number of actively scheduled warps increases. Although increasing the number of active threads will improve throughput and core utilization, cache Thrashing is an aftereffect that degrades the performance of GPU. Hence, as Fig. 1 highlights, for a fixed L1 cache size of 32 KB, the gained performance is maximized when a specific number of warps are assigned to each SIMT core, that is, less or more warps than such a specific number will result in lower performance. Additionally, increasing the number of warps necessitates a larger L1 cache to sustain performance. Designers are also constrained from increasing L1 cache size for two reasons: first, the SIMT core is more dedicated to compute cores and register files than to memories (as previously mentioned); second, increasing intra-SIMT core memory size increases the access latency of the cache due to the larger data array and the cache controller. Higher access latency penalizes performance as a consequence.

With the constant L1 cache size and the growing number of warps scheduled per SIMT core, there are more access misses in the L1 cache, which results in more access traffic pressure being put on the L2 cache as the next level cache. If the L2 cache cannot handle the amount of accesses, the next memory in the memory hierarchy is accessed. In GPUs, the next memory hierarchy is the main memory with large gap in access latency toward L2 and L1 caches. Accesses to the lowest level

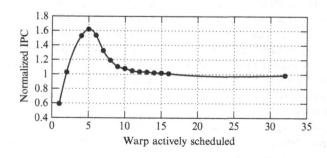

FIG. 1

Normalized IPC vs number of warps assigned to an SIMT core [2].

cause a long stall time. Thus the L2 cache size has to be increased in order to prevent long latency access to the main memory. Also, despite L1 caches, the L2 cache access latency is not so critical; however, the on-chip memory area remains a concern. The trend in recent GPU architectures also confirms the approach of increasing L2 cache size (e.g., L2 cache size increased from 786 KB in Fermi to 1536 KB in Kepler, both having a maximum of 48 KB L1 D-cache). In recent GPUs, the SRAM L2 cache size kept pace with this capacity demand. With current chips, maximum power budget being used, a further increase in the number of warps (requiring further growth of L2 cache size) will be very difficult. This is also true for increasing the number of cores in future GPUs.

Entering a deep nanometer technology era where leakage currently increases by 10 times per technology node, SRAM arrays confront serious scalability and power limitations [9]. Promising types of nonvolatile memories are now being introduced. Phase change memory (PCM), magnetic-RAM (MRAM), solid transfer-torque RAM (STT-RAM), racetrack memory, and resistive RAM (ReRAM) [10–14,67] are among the most popular nonvolatile memories. These memories have different specifications and characteristics, and based on that, each of these memories fit better than any of volatile memories. Density, low leakage power, and scalability are the most important advantages of nonvolatile memories over typical volatile memories such as SRAM and DRAM. Among the known technologies to replace SRAM is spin torque transfer RAM (STT-RAM) [15]. The STT-RAM cell has near-zero leakage power and is about $4\times$ denser than the SRAM cell. The promising characteristics of STT-RAM (especially its higher density and lower power consumption) make it a good candidate for building L2 caches of future GPUs. Nevertheless, writing to an STT-RAM cell requires the use of a large amount current for a long period of time. So, the realization of such a promising nonvolatile memory structure will face problems regarding latency and energy of memory accesses.

Several proposals, at both a circuit and an architectural levels [16–19], have been made to address the energy and latency challenges of STT-RAM writes. Another approach for mitigating the write problem of STT-RAM cells is device-level optimizations. Reducing the retention time of STT-RAM cells is one of the most effective optimizations; it was introduced in different works such as [20,21]. Reducing the retention time can further reduce write accesses latency and energy in STT-RAM drastically. On the other hand, reduction of STT-RAM cells requires accurate optimization based on observing applications on the targeted hardware platform.

Analyses for a wide range of GPGPU applications show a large variation in the intensity of writes to different blocks of the L2 cache. Some cache blocks get write access more than other cache blocks, and the distribution of write accesses are uneven between different blocks. For simplicity, we define write working set (WWS) as a data set that gets write access during an application's runtime. Based on observations in this chapter, WWS of the L2 cache has two specific features: the WWS of typical applications within a short period is small, and the rewrite interval (RI) time of the blocks in WWS is usually short (lower than 100 μs). Thus we refer to this portion of WWS as temporary WWS (TWWS). Consequently, a 10-year data retention in STT-RAM is not required for most of the blocks in WWS. These features give us the opportunity for device-level optimization for GPU cache as it has also been shown that physical and magnetization properties of an STT-RAM cell are a trade-off between device nonvolatility and latency/energy of write operations [20].

In this chapter, we propose an STT-RAM L2 cache architecture with two parts: a small-sized low-retention array (LR) optimized for write operations and a large-sized high-retention array (HR). LR cache is responsible for holding TWWS of the applications. HR cache, on the other hand, provides a high-capacity array, holding a large portion of L1 thrashed data that are mostly intended to be read-only or in frequently written. To increase the STT-RAM cache efficiency, the proposed architecture has three key differences from the traditional on-chip GPU caches: (1) A monitoring logic determines write-intensive data blocks forming TWWS of the running applications. The main features of this module are its low overhead and fast reaction to the changes in WWS. Furthermore, the monitoring logic adaptively monitors workload behavior in the runtime. Based on the monitored behavior, a decision is made in order to minimize the number of writes on HR, alongside minimizing the overhead of writes in proportion to the baseline; (2) the cache search mechanism is modified for better energy efficiency based on access types and data types that are more likely to be present in LR and HR; and (3) the cache eviction policy is changed slightly in order to keep more rewritten data blocks in LR and gain better energy efficiency. We use a simple buffer to take care of data expiration in LR based on the elapsed time of the data rewrites and postpone the refreshing of cache blocks until the last cycles of the retention period.

In the following section, we present a brief background on the baseline GPU architecture and its memory hierarchy. In addition to GPU architecture, STT-RAM concepts are briefly explained. Section 3 identifies previous related work on GPU memory hierarchy, STT-RAMs, and more details on employing STT-RAM in GPU architectures. The proposed architecture, from motivation to design, is presented in Sections 4 and 5. In Section 6, details of our implementation and its overhead are discussed. Section 7 presents evaluation results, and finally, Section 8 concludes the chapter.

2 BACKGROUND

2.1 GPU AND ITS MEMORY HIERARCHY

A GPU comprises multiple stream multiprocessors (SMs), called compute units in AMD architectures, each consisting of a rich memory hierarchy including register files, shared memory, cache arrays, and a number of simple cores called stream processor (SP). Generally, SMs are known as SIMT cores. GPUs use SMs as vector processors to achieve TLP by executing single instruction over multiple threads. A GPU application comprises one or more kernels. Each kernel launches a hierarchy of threads on GPU. Hundreds of threads create a grid composed of cooperative thread arrays (CTAs) or thread-blocks (TBs). The CTAs are allocated to SMs as single units of work. TBs decompose to groups of 32 threads for execution on an SM. These groups of threads are called warp in NVIDIA and wavefront in AMD terminologies, respectively. In other words, warps are the smallest fetched units within this hierarchy.

Each thread can access different data types that are annotated in GPGPU programming with separated address ranges in the main memory. These data types comprise *global*, *local*, *texture*, and *constant* data. A thread commonly accesses these data types through a rich memory hierarchy, as shown in Fig. 2B. The local data is usually placed in a dense register file array that is private to each SM. Global data refer to the data shared among all threads within a grid.

When a thread requests data from the off-chip main memory, the accesses pass through a two-level cache hierarchy. Each data type is placed in its specific cache memory in the first level of memory hierarchy. Local and global data are placed in D-caches while texture and constant data are placed in texture and constant caches, respectively. Instructions are placed in instruction caches. Additionally, unlike D-cache, which is a read-write cache memory, instruction, texture and constant caches are read-only caches. Each SM is also associated with a software-managed local memory for shared data accesses by threads within a TB. Note that shared data are not in this memory hierarchy and are directly placed in the shared memory. Shared memory is not the concern in this study; however, interested readers can refer to [22–25] for more details.

The existence of different data types and caches in GPU brings up different policies for read and write accesses. The L1 caches are private to SMs with no coherency among them because there is no data communication between SMs. Because L1 caches are not coherent, all write operations of global data are handled as write-evicts (on hit) or write-no-allocates (on miss). Local data are written into the associated L1 cache with a write-back mechanism (Fig. 2A). The L2 cache is a banked cache array shared by all SMs and backs all types of data. Each L2 bank

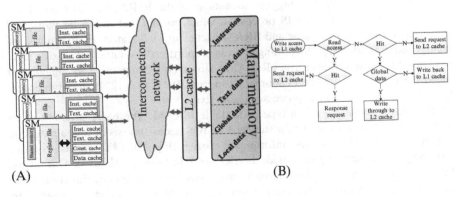

(A)   (B)

FIG. 2

(A) GPU memory hierarchy and (B) L1 data cache read/write policy diagram.

communicates with L1 caches of different cores through an interconnection network. L2 cache uses write-back policy with respect to the main memory. At the highest level of hierarchy, each L2 bank has a point-to-point connection with a dedicated off-chip memory controller. A more complete description of GPU memory system is available in Ref. [26].

The L1 data cache and shared memory in NVIDIA Fermi GPUs are uniform memory in each SM with the ability of reconfiguration and have a fixed total (L1 + shared memory) capacity of 64 KB per SM. L1 data cache and shared memory can be configured as (16 KB + 48 KB) and (48 KB + 16 KB). This gives flexibility to programmers to set cache and shared memory sizes based on the requirements of nonshared and shared data, respectively. In the new Kepler GK100 (32 KB + 32 KB), configuration is implemented, too. Moreover, texture and constant caches are unified as read-only data cache in the Kepler architecture. In the new NVIDIA Maxwell GM204 architecture, a fixed 64 KB dedicated shared memory is made possible by combining the functionality of the L1 and texture caches into a single unit [27].

2.2 NONVOLATILE MEMORIES

In this section, we briefly overview ReRAM, STT-RAM, and racetrack memory technologies because, among nonvolatile memories, they have features closer to SRAM. More detailed description can be found in Refs. [13,14,28]. Then we will focus on STT-RAM based on its capability of reducing retention in order to overcome one of its main challenges and and make its read latency comparable to SRAM's.

The ReRAM memory element consists of one inert electrode at the top (e.g., platinum), an electrochemically active electrode at the bottom (e.g., copper), and the oxide layer between inert and active electrodes. When a positive bias is applied to the active electrode, the metal ions are forced to migrate through the oxide and eventually reach the electrode on the other side (inert electrode). The ion path is highly conductive, and the cells, equivalent resistance value is low (1). The low-resistance state can be changed again to a high-resistance state by positively biasing the inert electrode (0). The biggest advantage of the ReRAM technology is the high compatibility with CMOS processes, which means that it can be fabricated at the same die that processor and SRAM caches are fabricated. Furthermore, the voltage required for ion path-forming process proportionally relates to the oxide layer thickness. These advantages gives ReRAM a strong cost-competitive advantage over SRAM. However, its low cell endurance (up to $\sim 10^{11}$ writes [29]) and high access latency limits its use at near-processor cache levels.

STT-RAM technology is a type of scalable MRAM. The basic structure of an STT-RAM cell is composed of a standard NMOS access transistor and a magnetic tunnel junction (MTJ) as the information carrier (Fig. 3). MTJ consists of two ferromagnetic layers and one oxide barrier layer in between (Fig. 3). One of the ferromagnetic layers (i.e., the reference layer) has a fixed magnetic direction while the magnetic direction of the other layer (i.e., the free layer) can be changed by directly passing a spin-polarized current. If these two layers are magnetized in

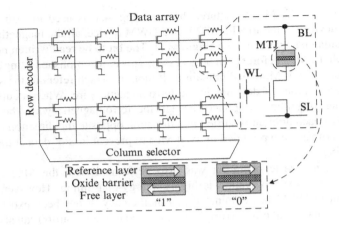

FIG. 3

1T1J memory element.

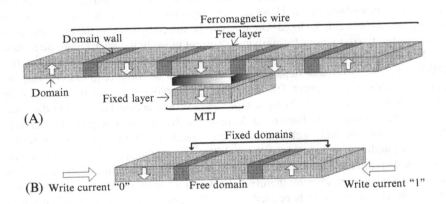

FIG. 4

(A) DWM device structure. (B) Shift-based write.

antiparallel (parallel) directions, the MTJ resistance is high (low), indicating bit "1" ("0"). STT-RAM has a limited write endurance per cell (up to $\sim 10^{12}$ writes [30]), and when the number of writes to a cell reach its maximum limit, the cell may lose its ability to change the magnetization status of the free layer, thus creating data errors.

Racetrack memory, also known as domain wall memory (DWM), is a spin-based memory technology, which represents information using the spin orientation of the magnetic domains in a ferromagnetic wire, as shown in Fig. 4A. Each of these domains can independently take any magnetic orientation (up-spin or down-spin). Therefore multiple bits of data can be packed into a single DWM device, resulting in very high density. Three basic operations can be performed on a DWM device: read, shift, and write. The MTJ structure, shown in Fig. 4A, is used to read data from the DWM device similar to STT-RAM. In a DWM device, all the magnetic domains in the ferromagnetic wire share a single MTJ. The bit to be read/written needs to be aligned with the MTJ before it can be accessed. This is accomplished using a property that is unique to DWM, called domain wall motion, which refers to the shifting of magnetic orientations of domains in the ferromagnetic wire. When a current pulse of a suitable magnitude is applied through the ferromagnetic wire, the magnetic orientation of each domain is shifted in a direction opposite the direction of current. Additional domains are provided in the device to prevent loss of data at the extrema while shifting.

Formerly, the write operation was also performed with the MTJ similar to STT-RAM. This write operation is highly energy-consuming. However, a recent development in DWM has eliminated this inefficiency. It has been experimentally shown that domain wall motion (originally intended to realize shifts) can also be used to perform fast, energy-efficient writes in DWMs. This operation, often referred to as shift-based writes, is demonstrated in Fig. 4B. The structure of the write operation consists of a ferromagnetic wire with three domains: two fixed domains and a free domain. The magnetization of the two fixed domains are hard-wired to up-spin and down-spin during fabrication. However, the magnetization of the free domain, which is sandwiched between the fixed domains, can be varied by shifting the magnetization of one of the fixed domains by applying a current pulse in the appropriate direction.

The main challenge of racetrack memory is the access latency to data stored in a DWM tape that is variable depending on the number of shifts required. Varying the number of bits stored in each DWM tape brings a unique trade-off between density (which increases with more bits-per-tape) and average access latency. On the other hand, there is another mechanism to decrease the write operation problems in MTJ cells. Reducing the MTJ cell retention time results in decreasing write operation energy, in addition to reducing cell reliability. In other words, there is a trade-off between data retention and write energy in MTJ cells. Reduction of the write time period results in more current; therefore, for faster write operations, a higher amount of current and more power is needed. Due to the constraint on maximum current in chips, the write pulse period must be increased in order for the write current to be decreased. By reducing the retention time, the level of write current decreases for different write pulses, so shorter write time becomes possible. Fig. 5 shows different write currents as a function of the width of write pulses for 10 years, 40 ms, and 100 µs retention times. More details on STT-RAM and the model used in this chapter can be found in Ref. [21].

3 RELATED WORK

In this section, we briefly review the recent research in GPU memory hierarchy and architectures exploiting STT-RAM, and we focus on the most important studies alleviating cache hierarchy shortcomings in GPU by using STT-RAM.

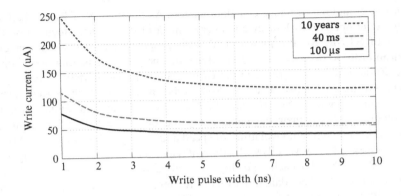

FIG. 5

Write current vs write pulse for different retention times.

GPU memory hierarchy

Many researchers have considered the memory hierarchy of GPUs to reduce access latency of the memory [31], improve memory access coalescing [23], and increase the parallelism among memory controllers [32]. DRAM scheduling [33] and prefetching [34] techniques have also been introduced for GPUs. In addition, a number of recent works concentrate on the GPU cache from various perspectives.

Jia et al. [35] specified the memory access patterns in GPUs. Based on such information, the suggested algorithm estimates how much of the bandwidth is required when cache memory is on/off and then decides which instruction data is placed in the cache. In Ref. [36], Tarjan et al. tried to quickly cross the interconnection network to access L2 by handling L1 misses using the copies kept at other L1 caches in other SMs. To do so, they used a sharing tracker to identify whether a missed data block in L1 cache is present in other L1 caches. Rogers et al. [2] presented a method called Cache-Conscious Wavefront that employs a hardware unit to examine intrawarp locality loss when a warp is selected for fetching. Hence, their mechanism prevents the issuing of new warps that might result in thrashing previously scheduled warps, data in the cache. Similarly, in Refs. [37–39], the same problem is tackled by modifying the cache indexing function, warp throttling, and detecting critical warps in order to maintain useful data in the cache. Gebhart et al. [40] designed a uniform memory that can be configured to be register file, cache, or shared memory regarding the requirements of the running application. Moreover some other works, such as [41,42], tried to reduce the power consumption of GPU by observing and considering GPU memory hierarchy from the main memory to the register file.

STT-RAM

Dong et al. [15] investigated the possibility of replacing SRAM with MRAM by introducing a model for power, area, and performance of MRAMs, which is used in our power and performance calculations, too. As the main STT-RAM challenges are the write operation's latency and energy, most of the research focused on these aspects of STT-RAM. Rasquinha et al. [19] proposed an energy-efficient cache design in order to decrease STT-RAM dynamic energy by managing operations on cache. Zhou et al. [18] introduced the early write termination (EWT) technique to prevent writing unchanged data bits. Some other researches such as Refs. [16,17] used a combination of MRAM and SRAM to overcome disadvantages of both technologies and use their advantages. On the other hand, Smullen et al. [20] considered, the relaxing nonvolatility of speed and energy-efficient STT-RAMs. Sun et al. [21] used STT-RAM cells with different retention times; they used a single low-retention STT-RAM L1 cache. For higher level caches, a two-retention STT-RAM structure was used, where data blocks with frequent writes are migrated to the cache blocks with low-retention time. In Refs. [43,44], different refreshing mechanisms are proposed to efficiently employ low-retention STT-RAM.

In Ref. [45], a two-part main memory consisting of a small DRAM part and a large PCM part is presented. In contrast to our proposal, DRAM and PCM parts are managed in a hierarchical manner, that is, DRAM works as a cache for the large PCM memory. Additionally, the differences between the features of the cache and main memory make this approach inapplicable for designing a cache. For instance, in Ref. [45], the writes are forwarded to the PCM part instead of DRAM, because it is assumed that the locality of the data evicted from the cache was already exploited. However, in the cache, due to the existence of data locality, there could be multiple writes on a block, so it is better to forward those to the write-friendly part.

GPU memory and STT-RAM

Recent work [46,47] used the nonvolatile DWM in both register files and the cache memory of GPUs. Also, Refs. [48–50] used STT-RAM in GPU register file with different approaches such as hybrid memory, write awareness, and multilevel cell design, respectively. Al-Maashri et al. [51] focused on using STT-RAM technology for 3D stacking of texture memory. They did not really address the use of GPUs for general-purpose high-performance computing but considered graphics applications. In research by Goswami et al. [52], a single and uniform low-retention time STT-RAM was used for the register file and constant and texture caches, and a hybrid memory (STT-RAM and SRAM) was employed for the shared memory of GPGPUs. To remedy the high-energy consumption of write operations, the EWT mechanism [18] with a higher granularity was used. Also, an SRAM write-back buffer was used to coalesce write operations of different threads to the STT-RAM register file.

Because L1 cache latency is critical to the overall application performance, in this chapter, we concentrate on studying trade-offs between STT-RAM retention time and write latency/energy and propose an architecture to surpass the cache shortcomings using this promising technology in GPU's last-level cache (LLC). The L2 cache is typically a unified large cache (e.g., 1.5 MB in Nvidia's GK110 and 2 MB in Nvidia's GM107), which is greater than the total L1 caches in terms of size. Additionally, L2 cache is responsible for improving the effective memory access bandwidth of the

SMs by reducing the number of off-chip memory accesses. Typically, the latency of L2 cache accesses is hidden by switching between multiple warps that are active in the SMs. Therefore implementing L2 cache using STT-RAM technology seems more reasonable and effective in GPUs.

4 TWO-PART L2 CACHE ARCHITECTURE

4.1 MOTIVATION

GPGPU applications perform different write patterns on cache blocks. In Ref. [53], the coefficient of variation (COV) parameter was used to indicate inter and intracache set write variations in chip multiprocessor (CMP) applications. Fig. 6 shows inter and intracache set writes COV for GPGPU workloads. Applications such as *bfs*, *bfs-p*, *lavaMD*, *leukocyte*, *RAY*, *STO*, *streamcluster*, and *stencil* have more writes on fewer cache blocks, whereas other applications have more balanced writes over L2 blocks. This justifies using an STT-RAM region having a reduced retention time that favors write operations. Ideally, we expect this region to hold data blocks with high rewrite frequency in order to minimize write energy and improve the cache performance.

Reducing the retention time of STT-RAM cells increases the error rate because of early data bit collapse (with respect to high-retention cells). Table 1 shows different magnetization stability heights ($\triangle$) and their corresponding retention times (RT), write operation energies (WE), and latencies (WL). The 10-year retention time STT-RAM cell has the most write energy and latency with no error rate because of its high data stability. Any reduction in the retention time of STT-RAM cells from this baseline reduces write operation energy and latency due to the reduction in the current needed for writing, but more refreshes are required to prevent data loss. This leads us to using a nonuniform STT-RAM cache structure with different retention times.

Utilizing low-retention STT-RAM is meaningful when it can hold WWS of an application to minimize the write energy. Also, refreshing overhead of cache blocks in low-retention part of the cache must be reasonable.

As mentioned before, the WWS of most GPGPU applications is small and within short periods of time. Fig. 7 schematically shows spatial and temporal distribution of write accesses to the LLC. At each TWWS (t_1 and t_2 in Fig. 7❶), a number of data blocks are accessed for write, and then there are no significant write accesses to the LLC for a while (t'_1 and t'_2 in Fig. 7❶). In a TWWS, each data block may be accessed one or more times. We define write-to-write time (W2W) as the time difference of two successive accesses to a block and use it indirectly to estimate the average TWWS duration for each workload. For this purpose, in the first phase, we count data blocks with W2W greater than a specific time range (time range 1 in Fig. 7❷). Then we increase the time range (time ranges 2, 3, ..., n in Fig. 7❷) and again count data blocks with W2W greater than each of the time ranges. This is repeated until a time range is found such that the number of data blocks with W2W greater than that remains almost unchanged (Time ranges 3, 4, ..., n in Fig. 7❷). This range marks the

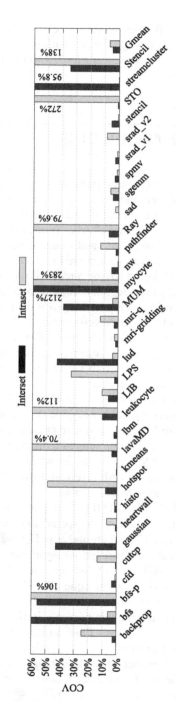

FIG. 6

Inter and intraset write variations.

Table 1 STT-RAM Parameters for Different Data Retention Times

Δ	RT	WL (ns)	WE (nJ)	Refreshing per Total Write
40.29	10 year	10	1.158	0
17.50	40 ms	5	0.91	8%
11.51	100 µs	0.8	0.070	68%

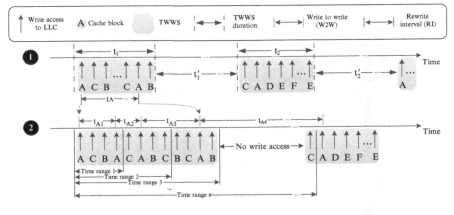

FIG. 7

Temporal and spatial distribution of write accesses to LLC.

end point for each workload and is an approximation for the time difference between the beginning of two consecutive TWWSs ($t_1 + t'_1$ in Fig. 7❶).

Afterward, to determine the length of TWWS, we observe the distribution of RI, the time difference between first and last accesses to a block in TWWS, for example, t_A in Fig. 7❶. We have chosen RI as a representative for TWWS duration, since a decline in accesses to most of the blocks constituting TWWS is observed in a short period of time. Therefore the time range that has the most RI distribution in it is probably the TWWS duration. For each workload, the TWWS duration is calculated based on this method. Table 2 shows the estimated TWWS durations in cycles.

Finally, Fig. 8 shows the distribution of data blocks whose RIs are in the estimated TWWS duration. More than 80% of rewrite accesses to the data blocks are under each workload's estimated TWWS duration, which proves our estimation accuracy. Moreover, this justifies the assumption that we have short-time periods in GPGPU applications with burst write accesses to a specific number of blocks in L2 cache. Additionally, Table 2 shows the maximum number of distinct cache blocks accessed

Table 2 TWWS Features for Different Workloads

Workloads	Est. TWWS Dur.[a] (Cycle)	WWS Size (No. of Blocks)	Avg. No. of Acc. per Block[b]	Workloads	Est. TWWS Dur. (Cycle)	WWS Size (No. of Blocks)	Avg. No. of Acc. per Block
backprop*	400	341	232	bfs-p*	1100	202	64
bfs	1000	284	356	cfd*	2500	206	117
cutcp	100	16	32	gaussian	400	267	70
heartwall*	4200	776	70	histo*	500	338	209
hotspot*	900	79	128	kmeaans	2200	46	26
lavaMD	200	297	313	lbm*	600	235	201
leukocyte*	1900	314	14	LIB	100	251	2
LPS	500	144	200	lud	400	237	79
mri-gridding*	1200	415	327	mri-q	2300	81	7
MUM*	100	222	2	myocyte	300	1	2
nw	600	201	142	pathfinder	500	52	74
RAY*	100	467	2	sad	4400	408	354
sgemm	2300	107	40	spmv	200	65	45
srad-v1	2800	295	59	srad-v2	700	451	416
stencil	300	297	215	STO	300	89	16
streamcluster	2600	26	9	Avg.	1177	232	100

[a]Estimated TWWS duration.
[b]Average number of accesses per block.
* Register file limitation is bottleneck for TLP.

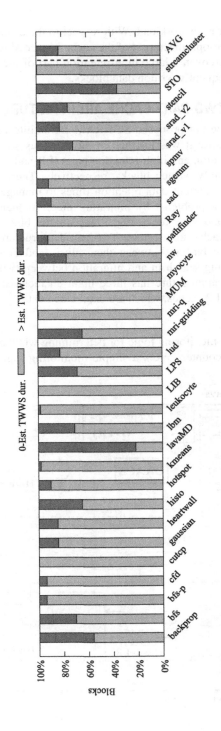

FIG. 8

Distribution of rewrite access interval.

in the TWWS duration for each workload. With respect to the average of maximum TWWS sizes, a small write-optimized part of the cache is needed for containing the TWWS of workloads. Moreover, a large high-retention part of the cache is used to hold read-only and less frequently written data blocks.

4.2 THE PROPOSED TWO-PART CACHE ARCHITECTURE

In this section, we describe our proposed STT-RAM L2 architecture for replacing SRAM L2 in GPUs. Because it was justified in the previous section, we need to have two parallel low-retention and high-retention parts (LR and HR) to keep more frequently and less frequently written blocks, respectively. Therefore, we propose a two-part L2 cache with different data retention times to manage write operation energy and data refreshing problems by migrating more frequently written data blocks from HR to LR, and vice versa. Fig. 9 depicts the block diagram of the proposed STT-RAM L2 cache architecture. Two parallel structures with different data retention times, swap buffers between themselves, and counters and some hardware logic for managing search in and migration between two cache parts are employed. Our L2 cache architecture has three main characteristics that make it distinct from typical GPU L2 caches, which are explained next.

Monitoring mechanism

The first characteristic is a monitoring logic for determining whether a data block is frequently written. Write counter (WC), a simple monitoring logic, is the counter

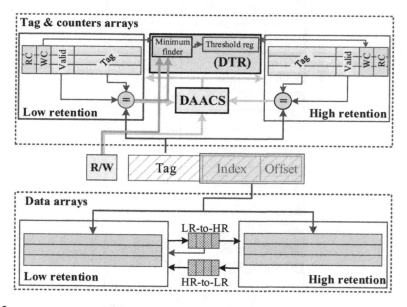

FIG. 9

Block diagram of the proposed L2 architecture.

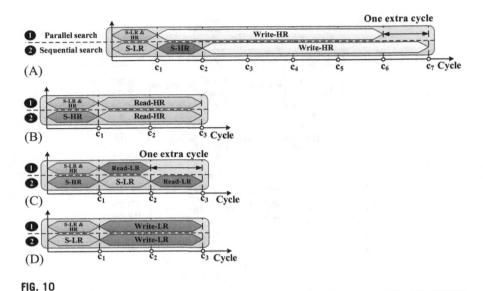

FIG. 10

Timing of sequential and parallel search mechanisms. (A) LR write miss-HR write hit. (B) LR read miss-HR write hit. (C) LR read hit-HR read miss. (D) LR write hit-HR write miss. *S-LR*, search LR tag array; *S-HR*, search HR tag array; *S-LR & HR*, search LR and HR tag array simultaneously; *Write-LR*, write on LR data array; *Read-LR*, read LR data array; *Write-HR*, write on HR data array; *Read-HR*, read HR data array.

responsible for this job. The WC of each cache line is incremented whenever a rewrite access is performed on that cache line. When the WC exceeds the threshold, its corresponding data block is detected as part of the TWWS, and then it will be migrated to LR. As HR is banked, a HR-to-LR buffer is necessary for data migration. Moreover, the write latency gap between HR and LR may cause problems when a block leaves LR part. So a small buffer is needed to support data block migration from LR to HR, too. Regulating write threshold (WT) value (i.e., a threshold based on which a decision is made regarding the migration of a block) is done by a dynamic mechanism during runtime by the dynamic threshold regulator (DTR), which is explained in the next section.

Search mechanism
The second difference is the search mechanism among two cache parts. Because we have two parallel cache arrays, different approaches can be considered in order to handle cache accesses. Two possible approaches include parallel and sequential searches in LR and HR. Searching in LR and HR in parallel results in better performance, but is more power-consuming. In contrast, sequential search may cause more latency, but saves power.

Fig. 10 shows the timing for both search mechanisms on different scenarios. Sequential search mechanism adds an extra cycle when the first cache selected

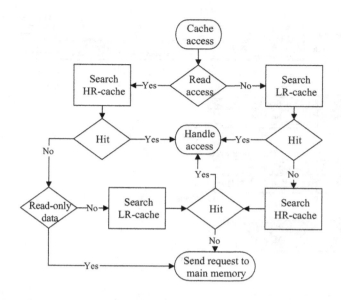

FIG. 11

Flow diagram of DAACS.

for searching does not hold the requested data block (Fig. 10A and C). However, the overhead of searching both LR and HR tag arrays can be avoided if the requested block is found in the first part (Fig. 10B and D). In order to address the shortcomings of each of the parallel and sequential search mechanisms, the data and access type aware cache search mechanism (DAACS), shown in Fig. 9, is employed.

The DAACS determines which part of the L2 cache must be searched first, regarding the access types (read or write) and data types (instruction, texture, constant, global or local data). If the requested data is not found in the first cache part, the second cache part will be searched. Obviously, as frequently written data are kept in LR, it is searched first for a write request. For read accesses, on the contrary, the HR part is searched first. Moreover, read-only data (i.e., texture and constant data and instructions) are never migrated to the LR part. Thus only the HR will be searched upon receiving access to these data types, regardless of whether the data exists in HR or not. Fig. 11 shows a flow diagram of the DAACS.

Eviction policy

The third difference is the eviction policy in our two-part cache. Inevitably, a short time after the migration of data blocks to LR, the small LR array will be fully utilized. Then, after each migration from HR to LR, a data block eviction is probable in both HR and LR. Clearly, a data block should be evicted from the LR cache when a new data block is migrated from HR to LR. If the evicted data block from LR returns to HR, it may cause an eviction from HR, too.

First, LR replacement policy is chosen to be write-LRU. Write-LRU is only sensitive to write accesses and read accesses does not change the LRU state. Because LR is the memory in which TWWS is placed, write-LRU helps to maintain data blocks on which more write operations are performed, rather than read operations. Second, when a data block is evicted from LR, two approaches are taken: the evicted data block is forced to be written back to the main memory (blocks in LR part are always dirty), or the evicted data block from LR is migrated to HR. The first approach causes traffic overhead in the main memory, but the second one, depending on the reserved place for the evicted LR data block in HR, may not impose a write-back to the main memory. The worst case occurs when the evicted data block from HR is also dirty, thus it additionally costs one read from HR and one write to the main memory. To minimize the overhead, we can take one of the two approaches dynamically based on LRU status of HR. This means that, if the LRU block in HR is dirty, then the LR's evicted block is written back to the main memory; otherwise, the evicted block is migrated to HR.

Refreshing mechanism

Because the retention time of the cache parts are reduced to favor write operations on STT-RAM cells, data refreshing is a new issue that needs to be addressed. Error prevention [54–56] or data recovery [57] are the common solutions, but they are not applicable here because of numerous bit collapses when a cache line with low-retention time expires. A simple mechanism based on Ref. [43] can be used to handle retention time expiration. In Ref. [43], a counter is used per cache line to keep track of the lifetime of the cache block. Similar to Ref. [43], in this work, we employ such a counter, retention counter (RC), with different policies. With respect to the value of RC, we can opt to refresh or invalidate the cache block, or perform a write-back to the data block. Our architecture uses all three approaches appropriately. If an RC saturates, this means that its corresponding cache block retention time has expired. Therefore the cache block will be invalidated. Note that before RC saturates (i.e., one cycle before counter saturation), the proper decision must be taken.

Fig. 12A shows that the RI distribution in LR. The 100 μs is a reasonable retention time due to its low write latency/energy and low overhead of refreshing. Most of the workloads have RIs lower than 100 μs. In order to refresh a cache block, it is read and pushed into a buffer and then rewritten in the cache to prevent data loss. The LR-to-HR buffer is used for refreshing cache blocks in LR. Because the LR-to-HR buffer is also used for data block migration between LR and HR, by using a tag in this buffer, the blocks migrating to HR and those needing to be refreshed are differentiated. When the LR-to-HR buffer is full, the cache block that needs refreshing is forced to be written back to the main memory before its retention time expires. Fig. 12B shows RIs for cache blocks in HR. We can draw two deductions from Fig. 12B. First, a 10-year retention time for HR is not needed, and 40-ms retention time covers the lifetime of more than 97% of cache blocks in HR. We can invalidate the few

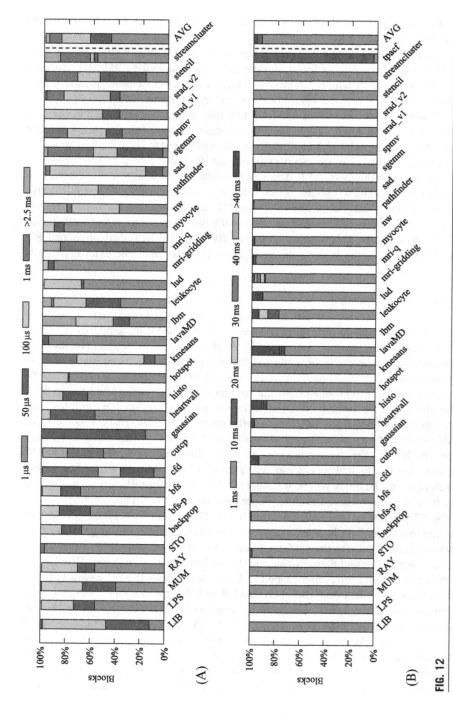

FIG. 12

Rewrite interval time distribution. (A) LR cache. (B) HR cache.

remaining cache blocks (i.e., less than 3%) with higher lifetimes and force them to be written back if they are dirty.

5 DYNAMIC WRITE THRESHOLD DETECTION MECHANISM

5.1 MOTIVATION

It is important to minimize the number of block transfers between HR and LR to reduce the overall write overhead with respect to the baseline architecture. Low WTs cause a high number of swaps between HR and LR and, consequently, increase the dynamic power. As dynamic power of STT-RAM memory is intrinsically more than that of SRAM, it is a critical factor for utilizing STT-RAM in our design. On the other hand, if WT is high, a lower number of blocks are migrated from HR to LR. As a result, more writes are performed on HR, and more dynamic power is consumed because of higher dynamic power of write operations in HR, whereas LR is left underutilized. This means that the effective size of cache decreases, which may cause performance degradation. Because of the different types of workloads on GPGPU regarding memory intensity and variation in the number of write operations, having a fixed threshold is not efficient. Fig. 13 shows the write cost in our two-part cache for different WTs. During various phases of runtime of an application, minimum write cost may be caused by different WTs. On the other hand, appropriate WTs may differ from one application to another. We design a dynamic architecture to regulate WT in the runtime based on the write costs of LR and HR, along with the number of block swaps between them.

5.2 THRESHOLD ANALYSIS

For designing an adaptive monitoring logic, we need to determine the parameters affecting cache write cost, and the affect of WT on these parameters. Eq. (1) indicates that the total cache write cost ($TWCost$) is composed of write costs of HR ($WCost_{HR}$) and LR ($WCost_{LR}$), each calculated by the multiplication of its write cost per block (WCB) and write rate (Eqs. 2, 3).

$$TWCost = WCost_{HR} + WCost_{LR} \qquad (1)$$
$$WCost_{HR} = W_{HR} * WCB_{HR} \qquad (2)$$
$$WCost_{LR} = W_{LR} * WCB_{LR} \qquad (3)$$

W_{HR} is the summation of write hits ($WHit_{HR}$), misses, and swaps (Eq. 4). The same parameters, excluding misses, form W_{LR} (Eq. 5). Misses are excluded from W_{LR}, because the missed data blocks are written in HR first.

$$W_{HR} = Miss + WHit_{HR} + Swap \qquad (4)$$
$$W_{LR} = WHit_{LR} + Swap \qquad (5)$$

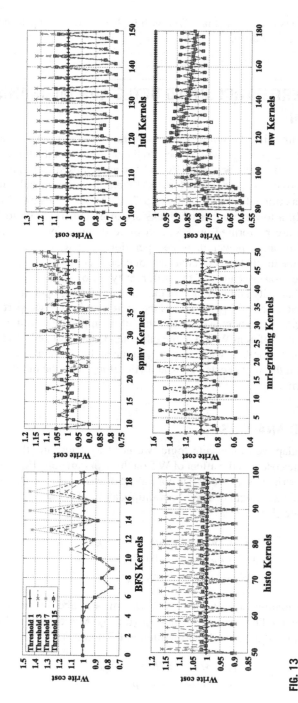

FIG. 13

Write cost for different workloads in runtime duration.

On the other hand, WCB_{HR} can be calculated as the product of WCB_{LR} and a constant factor (Eq. 6).

$$WCB_{HR} = n * WCB_{LR} \tag{6}$$

Therefore $TWCost$ can be calculated as:

$$TWCost = BWCost_{LR} * (n * WHit_{HR} + WHit_{LR} + n * Miss + (n + 1) * Swap) \tag{7}$$

Thus $Miss$, $Swap$, $WHit_{HR}$, and $WHit_{LR}$ are the factors that must be considered in regulating WT. Our observations show that the effect of WT changes on miss rate is less than 0.13%. Thus they can be ignored as an affecting parameter for the sake of simplicity. Table 3 explains the effects of the other three parameters on WT.

5.3 PROPOSED MECHANISM

Each of the parameters mentioned in Table 3 is a function of WT, which is dependent on the behavior of the applications themselves. The feedback from changes in these parameters during the runtime of an application can be used to regulate WT. However, such an approach is sensitive to the details of the implementation. In other words, the question, is how much should the variation in the aforementioned parameters change the WT? Additionally, the appropriate relation between these parameters and WT may differ in various applications. These complexities motivate us to employ a mechanism that has the least possible dependency to the behavior of running applications. To this end, we propose a new structure, DTR, in order to effectively take these parameters into account for regulating WT, without having to deal with the complexities mentioned before. Fig. 14 depicts DTR. It simply sets WT to the minimum value of WCs in LR.

Using the minimum value of WCs in LR mimics the desired behavior mentioned in Table 3. First, $WHit_{LR}$ is roughly related to the minimum value of WCs in LR. In other words, growth in $WHit_{LR}$ results in increase in the $min(WCs)$ most of the time, hence the WT goes up. Second, $min(WCs)$ creates meritorious data blocks into

Table 3 Effects of Write Cost Parameters on WT

Factor	Desirable Effect on WT	Description
$WHit_{HR}$	Decrease	WT must be decreased in order for highly written blocks to migrate to LR
$WHit_{LR}$	Increase	WT must be increased to prevent the migration of non-TWWS blocks to LR and LR thrashing
$Swap$	Increase	WT must be increased to avoid malignant swaps and entering of a large amount non-TWWS blocks to LR

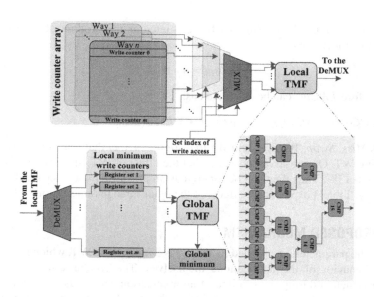

FIG. 14

Dynamic threshold regulator (DTR) architecture.

LR. This results in two desired consequences: first, unnecessary *Swap*s are avoided; second, *min(WCs)* will probably increase per swap.

WHit$_{HR}$ is another factor that must affect WT. However, *WHit$_{HR}$* cannot be considered directly by our proposal. To overcome this issue, we look at the number of writes per block in TWWS of different applications. By setting the maximum possible value of the WC to the average of writes per block in TWWS, the WCs will probably be reset at the end of the lifetime of the blocks in TWWS. This naturally prevents the WCs from keeping large values and hence averts directing the majority of write operations to HR.

We use two tree-structured minimum-finder (TMF) units, each comprising 15 comparators to find *min(WCs)*. One of the TMFs, the local TMF, is responsible for determining the minimum WC value per set. On each write access, the WCs' value of the corresponding set are directed to the local TMF by MUXes, and the minimum WCs of that set are updated via a DEMUX. The other TMF, the global TMF, updates the global minimum of the WCs in LR, using the local minima of sets.

The proposed mechanism can easily adapt itself to the behavior of applications, without having to deal with the complexities of determining the proper coefficients for *WHit$_{LR}$*, *WHit$_{HR}$*, and *Swap* values in making decisions about the value of WT. The only dependency of our design to the behavior of the application is the maximum possible value of WCs that we set to the average of writes per block in the TWWS of applications (see Table 2) in our experiments.

6 IMPLEMENTATION

In this section, we elaborate on the details of the implementation of our proposed architecture. The structure of LR, LR and HR retention times, bit-width of counters, and detailed parameters of cache latencies and power, in addition to the overhead of our design are discussed.

LR cache size and structure

Regarding the average size of TWWS in Table 2, we opt to set the size of LR to 256 blocks. Ideally, we want LR to keep the TWWS of the workload and HR to keep the read-only blocks. It is obvious that structures with higher associativities provide higher LR utilizations, but due to their higher complexity, they are not appropriate for large caches. On the other hand, direct-mapped structure has the least complexity, but the least utilization, too. Because the size of LR in our design is small, we adopt a high associativity. Fig. 15 shows different latency and energy values of LR with different associativities. By enhancing associativity, latency and dynamic power increase insignificantly, but LR utilization increases dramatically. Thus we set the associativity of LR to 16, because it yields proper utilization and reasonable energy/latency. In addition, with such an associativity level, our two comparator trees in DTR incur the least overhead of area and latency (i.e., two 15-comparator trees for our 16×16 LR structure).

LR and HR cache retention times

With respect to Fig. 12A and B, LR and HR retention times are selected to be 100 µs [52] and 40 ms [43], respectively. For each cache line, there are 4-bit counters working at 160 kHz in LR to track data retention, and 2-bit counters are used in HR working at 100 Hz. The use of larger RCs in LR is due to the lower retention

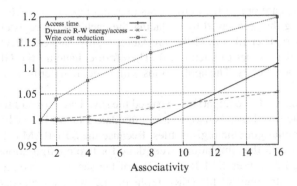

FIG. 15

Latencies, energies, and utilization of LR cache for different associativities.

time of blocks in this part of the cache, which requires a more accurate refreshing mechanism. Therefore a higher bit width enables tracking smaller slots of time, which leads to more accuracy [43].

As stated previously, the maximum possible value of WCs (i.e., 64) is selected based on the average write accesses per block in TWWS in Table 2.

The main overhead of the proposed architecture includes RCs, WCs, LR-to-HR and HR-to-LR buffers, and DAACS and DTR logics. The total capacity of RCs, WCs, and buffers is 6 KB, which is less than 1% of the cache capacity. Table 4 demonstrates the details of latencies and energies of LR, HR, and buffers extracted from CACTI 6.5 and its modified version [58,59]. DAACS and DTR logics, on the other hand, incur an area overhead of less than 3% in our design.

7 EVALUATION RESULT

To evaluate the proposed architecture, a GPGPU-Sim3.2.1 simulator [26] was used to simulate PTX commands at cycle level. The simulator mimics the behavior of SMs, L2 cache, interconnection network, and off-chip main memory, and three groups of benchmarks were considered: (1) benchmarks provided with the simulator [26], (2) Rodinia [60], and (3) Parboil [61]. We used the CUDA version of the benchmarks in our experiments.

According to the investigations carried out in Ref. [62], GPGPU applications are divided into two general categories based on their behavior: cache-insensitive and cache-sensitive, where the first is called a cache-unfriendly application and the latter is called a cache-friendly application. Note that increasing the cache size can increase the performance of some applications, while some other applications do not benefit from larger cache sizes. Of course, the area saved as a result of replacing the SRAM L2 by the STT-RAM L2 can be used to add new components that cause an application to run faster. We chose register files as a case study for two reasons: first, register files are one of the bottlenecks in assigning TBs to SMs in GPUs [63]; second, devoting the area saved by replacing the cache to the register files is a fair assumption, as register files in GPUs are large, highly banked SRAM arrays with a structure similar to that of cache [40]. Therefore enhancing the GPU with extra register files is beneficiary. The applications with larger register files are indicated by "*" in Table 2.

In order to have a fair comparison, we used the saved area for additional resources in two ways: the saved area is used to accommodate a larger L2 cache, or the saved area is used for enlarging the register files. Because the STT-RAM cell is 4× denser than the SRAM cell, the simulations were done for two configurations: extra cache (EC), replacing L2 with an STT-RAM cache of the same area (i.e., a 4× larger L2 cache); and an extra register file (ER), replacing L2 with a same-sized STT-RAM cache where the saved area is used for implementing 15% larger register files in SMs.

Table 4 Detailed Structural Parameters of L2 Cache

| Technology | Cache Size (KB) | Data Array | | | | Tag Array | | | | Leakage Power (mW) |
		RL (ns)	WL (ns)	RE (nJ)	WE (nJ)	RL (ns)	WL (ns)	RE (pJ)	WE (pJ)	
SRAM	384	0.596	0.538	0.048	0.021	0.242	0.157	1.03	0.520	48.79
STT-RAM (HR-LR)	1472–64	0.556–0.489	3.17–1.10	0.024–0.029	0.166–0.072	0.296–0.225	0.211–0.140	1.88–1.64	1.32–0.653	2.632
Buffer LR-to-HR	2	0.323	0.280	0.0105	0.0017	–	–	–	–	3.875
Buffer HR-to-LR	2	0.323	0.280	0.0105	0.0017	–	–	–	–	4.059

Notes: RE, read energy; RL, read latency; WE, write energy; WL, write latency.

Table 5 GPGPU-Sim Configurations

Baseline GPU	15 cluster, 1 SM/cluster, L1 D cache: 4-way 16 KB 128B line, Const. cache: 8 KB 128B line,
	Text. cache: 12 KB 64B line, Instr. cache: 2 KB 128 line, Shared memory: 48 KB, No. memory
	controller: 6, Interconnect topology: Butterfly, Technology node: 40 nm, 32,768 register
	32-bit width, 384 KB 8-way 256B line L2 cache
Baseline STT-RAM	32,768 register, 1536 KB 8-way L2 cache
EC	32,768 register, 1472 KB 8-way HR 64 KB 16-way LR L2 cache
ER	37,684 register, 320 KB 8-way HR 64 KB 16-way LR L2 cache

Note that because in our configuration, area of data array is at least $80\times$ that of tag array, we keep the tag array SRAM because it is fast and its area overhead remains insignificant. Table 5 shows these configurations based on the GTX480 structure. Simulation results are compared to the baseline GPU with SRAM L2 and EC and ER scenarios. We simulated baseline uniform caches with STT-RAM cells of 10-year and 40-ms retention times to show the effectiveness of our mechanism.

Fig. 16A and B shows the execution time and IPC values with respect to the SRAM baseline system. The applications are sorted in ascending order by the achieved IPC improvement in our proposal. As can be seen in Fig. 16A, the execution time of fixed and dynamic threshold mechanisms are, respectively, reduced by 16% and 17%.

About half of the applications (from *backprop* to *histo* in Fig. 16B) are not cache-sensitive; hence they do not benefit from the proposed architecture in terms of IPC. The other half (from *bfs-p* to *kmeans* in Fig. 16B), on the other hand, enjoy up to $2.7\times$ IPC gains. Overall, the proposed L2 architecture results in an average of 20.7% improvement in terms of IPC. It must be noted that these improvements are only 3% and 13.4% for baselines with STT-RAM cells of 10-year and 40-ms retention times, respectively. However, we could increase the IPC improvement to 18.8% and 20.7% by applying fixed and dynamic threshold techniques. A remarkable point is that applications like *MUM*, *lavaMD*, and *Gaussian* are cache-sensitive and suffer from high latency of the baseline STT-RAM L2 cache, and our proposal effectively overcomes this issue by employing the LR part for storing frequently written data blocks. For some of the applications marked with "*" in Table 2, no speedup is gained because the enhanced register file could not help the GPU assign more thread blocks to an SM.

Note that in most cases, IPC and execution time results have correlations, although in some cases, such as *streamcluster*, there is more improvement in the execution time.

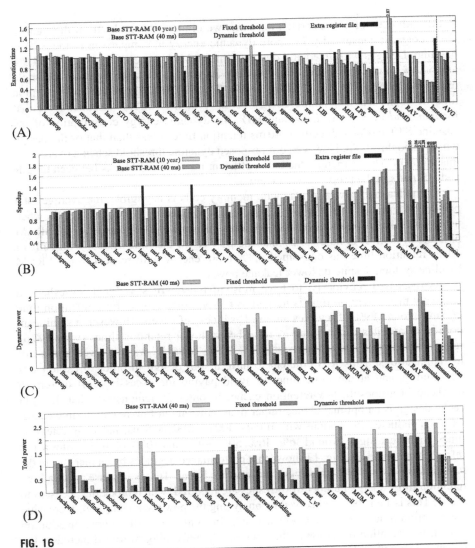

FIG. 16

(A) Execution time normalized to SRAM baseline. (B) IPC normalized to SRAM baseline.
(C) Dynamic energy consumption normalized to SRAM baseline. (D) Total power
normalized to SRAM baseline.

Fig. 16C shows the dynamic energy consumed by different architectures (normalized to that of the SRAM baseline system). Dynamic energy consumption in STT-RAM architectures is high due to the write energy of MTJ cells. The write energy in STT-RAM cells is more than SRAM cells even after reducing their retention time. Because of large values of the dynamic energy for baseline STT-

RAM with cells of 10-year retention time, we omitted its results from the figures. On average, it consumed 6.7× more dynamic energy in comparison to the SRAM baseline. Designs with fixed and dynamic thresholds impose an overhead of 74.9% and 52.6% to dynamic energy, respectively. As can be seen, the dynamic threshold technique reduces the overhead by 22.3%. The STT-RAM baseline with retention time of 40 ms has a dynamic energy of 2.5× of the SRAM baseline. Note that for *lbm, srad-v1, heartwall, nw,* and *RAY*, the dynamic energy consumption of the baseline STT-RAM with cells of 40 ms retention time is less than that of the design with a fixed threshold. However, our proposed dynamic threshold scheme overcomes this problem. This is mainly due to the efficient migration of blocks between the LR and HR parts in the proposed architecture.

As the leakage power of magnetic memory cells is negligible, the average total power consumption of the whole L2 cache has reduced by 20.3% and 28.9% when using fixed and dynamic threshold schemes, respectively, compared to the SRAM baseline system. It is noteworthy that the STT-RAM baseline system with cells of 40 ms retention time has consumed 9.9% more energy with respect to the SRAM baseline system, despite its lower leakage power.

As discussed previously, to have most of the rewrites as block refreshers, a relatively high-retention time is needed to be set. For example, for a retention time of 5 ms, around 89% of rewrites are used as block refreshers. However, a significant portion of rewrites can be used as refreshes in lower retention times (with 100 μs retention time, this fraction is around 36%). This behavior was observed in most of the applications. Thus it is efficient to have a split design in order to exploit this opportunity, and at the same time, to avoid paying the excessive cost of refresh overhead in a nonsplit low-retention cache. In order to demonstrate that the split cache design is an optimal choice rather than uniform but low-retention time cache, we also conducted simulations with 100 μs, 300 μs, 500 μs, 5 ms, and 40 ms retention times. In these designs, around 36%, 46%, 50%, 89%, and 100% of the rewrites act as refreshes, respectively. Fig. 17 shows that performance degrades by an increase in the retention time. However, this degradation is not linear. This is because, with a low-retention time, a large number of refreshes are required, which block the accesses to cache. This issue is better observed by analyzing the power consumption. Increasing the retention time to more than 500 μs results in significant write energy. In addition to that, for retention times lower than 500 μs, the refreshing overhead increases the power consumption. Our split cache design, however, outperforms all nonsplit cache designs in terms of performance and power consumption.

7.1 LIFETIME EVALUATION

Although endurance of the STT-RAM cache is not a concern in this work, we have investigated the effects of our proposed architecture on the lifetime of the cache. To do so, we used the equation presented in Ref. [53]. Fig. 18 demonstrates intra and interset variations for both HR and LR in the proposed architecture with respect to the baseline nonsplit STT-RAM cache. Using our dynamic threshold mechanism, intra

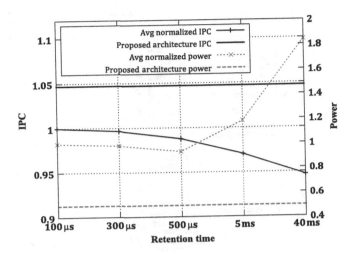

FIG. 17

Comparison of power and performance for uniform cache designs and our proposal.

and interset variations had improvements of 4.79% and 21.8%, respectively. This is due to the fact that we moved frequently written blocks to LR, and consequently the migration of data blocks from LR to HR results in a more even distribution of writes on cache blocks in HR, which is critical for lifetime. Intra and interset variation improvements for LR are 79% and 68%, respectively. The reason for these large improvements is that a significant portion of the writes are conducted in LR, with a relatively small size. This large number of writes in a small cache results in a more uniform write distribution. Because there are different retention times, write variation and count are not the only factors affecting the lifetime. It was shown that lifetime and write energy are directly related to each other [64–66]. This fact can be used to calculate the lifetime of the LR and HR part. Table 6 demonstrates the lifetime improvement (LI) values for LR and HR. The third column shows the LI for the whole cache structure, which is the minimum of the LI values of LR and HR parts. Our results show that the lifetime is improved by up to 336% (111%, on average) with respect to the baseline.

7.2 PARALLEL VS SEQUENTIAL SEARCH MECHANISM

Fig. 19 shows the dynamic power consumption reduction and performance overhead of the DAACS, in comparison to the parallel search mechanism. The figure shows an average reduction of 38.9% in the power consumption of the cache controller. Note that the performance overhead of using the power-efficient DAACS with respect to the parallel search mechanism is negligible (about 1%). This is mainly due to the efficient LR and HR block mapping and migration mechanisms we adopted.

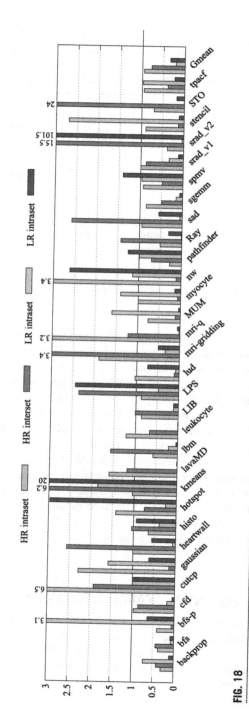

FIG. 18

Intra and interset variations for LR and HR with respect to the baseline.

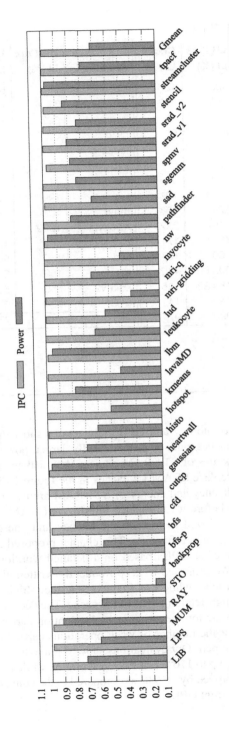

FIG. 19

IPC and power of DAACS normalized to parallel search.

Table 6 LI of HR and LR Parts

Workloads	HR Part LI (%)	LR Part LI (%)	Cache LI (%)	Workloads	HR Part LI (%)	LR Part LI (%)	Cache LI (%)
backprop	186	426	186	bfs-p	212	548	212
bfs	233	280	233	cfd	77	−4	−4
cutcp	30	32	30	gaussian	329	190	190
heartwall	83	409	83	histo	20	−30	−30
hotspot	76	1400	76	kmeans	17	−37	−37
lavaMD	53	239	53	lbm	158	37	37
leukocyte	51	198	51	LIB	91	1735	91
LPS	101	6861	101	lud	199	1993	199
mri-gridding	108	222	108	mri-q	102	7558	102
MUM	232	2194	232	myocyte	1039	336	336
nw	171	4531	171	pathfinder	56	13,142	56
RAY	127	560	127	sad	160	9652	160
sgemm	−27	90,768	−27	spmv	159	21,242	159
srad-v1	125	18,432	125	srad-v2	150	53,818	150
stencil	118	14	14	STO	184	510	184
tpacf	82	3260	9	Avg.	152	7760	111

8 CONCLUSION

Current trends in VLSI technology and GPU architectures show that future GPUs should have larger L2 caches with a proportionally larger power consumption. Due to the desirable properties of STT-RAM devices (low leakage power and high density), STT-RAM can replace SRAM L2 caches in the future GPU architectures. However, the high write latency and energy of STT-RAM are two main drawbacks that have to be dealt with before it can replace SRAM. STT-RAM cells with lower retention times can be employed to remedy the latency and energy problems of write operations, but they require refreshing. This chapter proposed a two-part STT-RAM L2 cache architecture for GPUs based on a detailed workload investigation of GPGPU applications. We proposed to keep frequently written blocks in a small low-retention part of the cache, while less frequently written, high frequently read blocks are mapped to the high-retention part of the cache. The decision regarding the mapping of data blocks to the low-retention or high-retention part was made based on a dynamic threshold for the number of write operations carried out on the data blocks in the high-retention part. Our evaluations showed that our architecture could effectively improve IPC by up to 170% (20.7%, on average), while average L2 cache energy consumption is improved by 28.9%, as compared to the conventional SRAM-based L2 architecture in current GPUs.

REFERENCES

[1] V. Narasiman, et al., Improving GPU performance via large warps and two-level warp scheduling, in: MICRO, ACM, 2011, pp. 308–317.

[2] T.G. Rogers, et al., Cache-conscious wavefront scheduling, in: MICRO, IEEE Computer Society, 2012, pp. 72–83.

[3] H.-K. Kuo, et al., Cache capacity aware thread scheduling for irregular memory access on many-core GPGPUs, in: ASP-DAC, IEEE, 2013, pp. 338–343.

[4] A. Jog, et al., OWL: cooperative thread array aware scheduling techniques for improving GPGPU performance, in: ACM SIGARCH Computer Architecture News, vol. 41, 2013, pp. 395–406.

[5] A. Jog, et al., Orchestrated scheduling and prefetching for GPGPUS, in: ISCA, ACM, 2013, pp. 332–343.

[6] T.G. Rogers, et al., Divergence-aware warp scheduling, in: MICRO, ACM, 2013, pp. 99–110.

[7] NVIDIA's next generation CUDA compute architecture: Kepler TM GK110, White Paper, 2013.

[8] E. Lindholm, et al., NVIDIA Tesla: a unified graphics and computing architecture, IEEE Micro 28 (2) (2008) 39–55.

[9] Emerging Research Devices, 2011, http://www.itrs.net/.

[10] M. Jalili, M. Arjomand, H.S. Azad, A reliable 3D MLC PCM architecture with resistance drift predictor, in: Proceedings of the 2014 44th Annual IEEE/IFIP International Conference on Dependable Systems and Networks, DSN '14, IEEE Computer Society, Washington, DC, USA, ISBN 978-1-4799-2233-8, 2014, pp. 204–215, http://dx.doi.org/10.1109/DSN.2014.31.

[11] M. Hoseinzadeh, M. Arjomand, H. Sarbazi-Azad, Reducing access latency of MLC PCMs through line striping, in: 2014 ACM/IEEE 41st International Symposium on Computer Architecture (ISCA), 2014, pp. 277–288, http://dx.doi.org/10.1109/ISCA.2014.6853228.

[12] M.H. Samavatian, M. Arjomand, R. Bashizade, H. Sarbazi-Azad, Architecting the last-level cache for GPUs using STT-RAM technology, ACM Trans. Des. Autom. Electron. Syst. 20 (4) (2015) 55:1–55:24, ISSN 1084-4309, http://dx.doi.org/10.1145/2764905.

[13] C. Zhang, G. Sun, X. Zhang, W. Zhang, W. Zhao, T. Wang, Y. Liang, Y. Liu, Y. Wang, J. Shu, Hi-Fi Playback: tolerating position errors in shift operations of racetrack memory, in: Proceedings of the 42nd Annual International Symposium on Computer Architecture, ISCA '15, ACM, New York, NY, USA, ISBN 978-1-4503-3402-0, 2015, pp. 694–706, http://dx.doi.org/10.1145/2749469.2750388.

[14] H. Akinaga, H. Shima, Resistive random access memory (ReRAM) based on metal oxides, Proc. IEEE 98 (12) (2010) 2237–2251, ISSN 0018-9219, http://dx.doi.org/10.1109/JPROC.2010.2070830.

[15] X. Dong, et al., Circuit and microarchitecture evaluation of 3D stacking magnetic RAM (MRAM) as a universal memory replacement, in: DAC, IEEE, 2008, pp. 554–559.

[16] X. Wu, et al., Power and performance of read-write aware hybrid caches with non-volatile memories, in: DATE, IEEE, 2009, pp. 737–742.

[17] J. Zhao, et al., Bandwidth-aware reconfigurable cache design with hybrid memory technologies, in: ICCAD, IEEE Press, 2010, pp. 48–55.

[18] P. Zhou, et al., Energy reduction for STT-RAM using early write termination, in: ICCAD, IEEE, 2009, pp. 264–268.

[19] M. Rasquinha, et al., An energy efficient cache design using spin torque transfer (STT) RAM, in: ISLPED, ACM, 2010, pp. 389–394.

[20] C.W. Smullen, et al., Relaxing non-volatility for fast and energy-efficient STT-RAM caches, in: HPCA, 2011, pp. 50–61.

[21] Z. Sun, et al., Multi retention level STT-RAM cache designs with a dynamic refresh scheme, in: MICRO, 2011, pp. 329–338.

[22] S. Ryoo, et al., Program optimization space pruning for a multithreaded GPU, in: CGO, ACM, 2008, pp. 195–204.

[23] Y. Yang, et al., A GPGPU compiler for memory optimization and parallelism management, in: ACM Sigplan Notices, vol. 45, ACM, 2010, pp. 86–97.

[24] M. Moazeni, A. Bui, M. Sarrafzadeh, A memory optimization technique for software-managed scratchpad memory in GPUs, in: SASP, IEEE, 2009, pp. 43–49.

[25] Y. Yang, et al., Shared memory multiplexing: a novel way to improve GPGPU throughput, in: Proceedings of the 21st International Conference on Parallel Architectures and Compilation Techniques, ACM, 2012, pp. 283–292.

[26] A. Bakhoda, et al., Analyzing CUDA workloads using a detailed GPU simulator, in: ISPASS, IEEE, 2009, pp. 163–174.

[27] NVIDIA GeForce GTX 980, White Paper 2014, http://international.download.nvidia.com/geforce-com/international/pdfs/GeForce_GTX_980_Whitepaper_FINAL.PDF.

[28] H. Li, X. Wang, Z.-L. Ong, W.-F. Wong, Y. Zhang, P. Wang, Y. Chen, Performance, power, and reliability tradeoffs of STT-RAM cell subject to architecture-level requirement, IEEE Trans. Magn. 47 (10) (2011) 2356–2359, ISSN 0018-9464, http://dx.doi.org/10.1109/TMAG.2011.2159262.

[29] Y.-B. Kim, S.R. Lee, D. Lee, C.B. Lee, M. Chang, J.H. Hur, M.-J. Lee, G.-S. Park, C.J. Kim, U.-I. Chung, I.-K. Yoo, K. Kim, Bi-layered RRAM with unlimited endurance and extremely uniform switching, in: 2011 Symposium on VLSI Technology (VLSIT), ISSN 0743-1562, 2011, pp. 52–53.

[30] Y. Huai, Spin-transfer torque MRAM (STT-MRAM): challenges and prospects, AAPPS Bull. 18 (6) (2008) 33–40.

[31] E.Z. Zhang, et al., Streamlining GPU applications on the fly: thread divergence elimination through runtime thread-data remapping, in: SC, ACM, 2010, pp. 115–126.

[32] I.-J. Sung, et al., Data layout transformation exploiting memory-level parallelism in structured grid many-core applications, in: PACT, ACM, 2010, pp. 513–522.

[33] N.B. Lakshminarayana, et al., DRAM scheduling policy for GPGPU architectures based on a potential function, IEEE Comput. Archit. Lett. 11 (2) (2012) 33–36.

[34] J. Lee, et al., Many-thread aware prefetching mechanisms for GPGPU applications, in: MICRO, IEEE, 2010, pp. 213–224.

[35] W. Jia, et al., Characterizing and improving the use of demand-fetched caches in GPUs, in: ICS, ACM, 2012, pp. 15–24.

[36] D. Tarjan, K. Skadron, The sharing tracker: using ideas from cache coherence hardware to reduce off-chip memory traffic with non-coherent caches, in: SC, IEEE Computer Society, 2010, pp. 1–10.

[37] M. Khairy, M. Zahran, A.G. Wassal, Efficient utilization of GPGPU cache hierarchy, in: Proceedings of the 8th Workshop on General Purpose Processing Using GPUs, GPGPU-8, ACM, New York, NY, USA, ISBN 978-1-4503-3407-5, 2015, pp. 36–47, http://dx.doi.org/10.1145/2716282.2716291.

[38] X. Chen, L.-W. Chang, C.I. Rodrigues, J. Lv, Z. Wang, W.-M. Hwu, Adaptive cache management for energy-efficient GPU computing, in: Proceedings of the 47th Annual IEEE/ACM International Symposium on Microarchitecture, MICRO-47, IEEE Computer Society, Washington, DC, USA, ISBN 978-1-4799-6998-2, 2014, pp. 343–355, http://dx.doi.org/10.1109/MICRO.2014.11.

[39] S.-Y. Lee, A. Arunkumar, C.-J. Wu, CAWA: coordinated warp scheduling and cache prioritization for critical warp acceleration of GPGPU Workloads, in: Proceedings of the 42nd Annual International Symposium on Computer Architecture, ISCA '15, ACM, New York, NY, USA, ISBN 978-1-4503-3402-0, 2015, pp. 515–527, http://dx.doi.org/10.1145/2749469.2750418.

[40] M. Gebhart, et al., Unifying primary cache, scratch, and register file memories in a throughput processor, in: MICRO, IEEE Computer Society, 2012, pp. 96–106.

[41] I. Paul, W. Huang, M. Arora, S. Yalamanchili, Harmonia: balancing compute and memory power in high-performance GPUs, in: Proceedings of the 42nd Annual International Symposium on Computer Architecture, ISCA '15, ACM, New York, NY, USA, ISBN 978-1-4503-3402-0, 2015, pp. 54–65, http://dx.doi.org/10.1145/2749469.2750404.

[42] S. Lee, K. Kim, G. Koo, H. Jeon, W.W. Ro, M. Annavaram, Warped-compression: enabling power efficient GPUs through register compression, in: Proceedings of the 42nd Annual International Symposium on Computer Architecture, ISCA '15, ACM, New York, NY, USA, ISBN 978-1-4503-3402-0, 2015, pp. 502–514, http://dx.doi.org/10.1145/2749469.2750417.

[43] A. Jog, et al., Cache revive: architecting volatile STT-RAM caches for enhanced performance in CMPs, in: DAC, 2012, pp. 243–252.

[44] J. Li, et al., Cache coherence enabled adaptive refresh for volatile STT-RAM, in: DATE, IEEE, 2013, pp. 1247–1250.

[45] T.J. Ham, et al., Disintegrated control for energy-efficient and heterogeneous memory systems, in: HPCA, IEEE, 2013, pp. 424–435.

[46] M. Mao, et al., Exploration of GPGPU register file architecture using domain-wall-shift-write based racetrack memory, in: DAC, ACM, 2014, pp. 1–6.

[47] R. Venkatesan, et al., STAG: spintronic-tape architecture for GPGPU cache hierarchies, in: ISCA, IEEE, 2014, pp. 253–264.

[48] J. Wang, Y. Xie, A write-aware STTRAM-based register file architecture for GPGPU, J. Emerg. Technol. Comput. Syst. 12 (1) (2015) 6:1–6:12, ISSN 1550-4832, http://dx.doi.org/10.1145/2700230.

[49] G. Li, X. Chen, G. Sun, H. Hoffmann, Y. Liu, Y. Wang, H. Yang, A STT-RAM-based low-power hybrid register file for GPGPUs, in: Proceedings of the 52nd Annual Design Automation Conference, DAC '15, ACM, New York, NY, USA, ISBN 978-1-4503-3520-1, 2015, pp. 103:1–103:6, http://dx.doi.org/10.1145/2744769.2744785.

[50] X. Liu, M. Mao, X. Bi, H. Li, Y. Chen, An efficient STT-RAM-based register file in GPU architectures, in: Design Automation Conference (ASP-DAC), 2015 20th Asia and South Pacific, 2015, pp. 490–495, http://dx.doi.org/10.1109/ASPDAC.2015.7059054.

[51] A. Maashri, et al., 3D GPU architecture using cache stacking: performance, cost, power and thermal analysis, in: ICCD, 2009, pp. 254–259.

[52] N. Goswami, et al., Power-performance co-optimization of throughput core architecture using resistive memory, in: HPCA, 2013, pp. 342–353.

[53] J. Wang, et al., i2WAP: improving non-volatile cache lifetime by reducing inter-and intra-set write variations, in: HPCA, 2013, pp. 234–245.

[54] D.H. Yoon, M. Erez, Flexible cache error protection using an ECC FIFO, in: SC, ACM, 2009, p. 49.

[55] D.H. Yoon, M. Erez, Memory mapped ECC: low-cost error protection for last level caches, in: ACM SIGARCH Computer Architecture News, vol. 37, ACM, 2009, pp. 116–127.

[56] D.H. Yoon, et al., FREE-p: protecting non-volatile memory against both hard and soft errors, in: HPCA, IEEE, 2011, pp. 466–477.

[57] C. Wilkerson, et al., Reducing cache power with low-cost, multi-bit error-correcting codes, in: ACM SIGARCH Computer Architecture News, vol. 38, 2010, pp. 83–93.

[58] N. Muralimanohar, et al., CACTI 6.0: A Tool to Model Large Caches, HP Laboratories, 2009.

[59] A. Jadidi, et al., High-endurance and performance-efficient design of hybrid cache architectures through adaptive line replacement, in: ISLPED, IEEE, 2011, pp. 79–84.

[60] S. Che, et al., Rodinia: a benchmark suite for heterogeneous computing, in: IEEE International Symposium on Workload Characterization, 2009, IISWC 2009, IEEE, 2009, pp. 44–54.

[61] J.A. Stratton, et al., Parboil: a revised benchmark suite for scientific and commercial throughput computing, in: Center for Reliable and High-Performance Computing, 2012.

[62] J. Lee, H. Kim, TAP: a TLP-aware cache management policy for a CPU-GPU heterogeneous architecture, in: HPCA, IEEE, 2012, pp. 1–12.

[63] E. Blem, et al., Challenge benchmarks that must be conquered to sustain the GPU revolution, CELL 1024 (8) (2011) 228.

[64] V. Young, et al., ACM, DEUCE: write-efficient encryption for non-volatile memories, in: ASPLOS, 2015, pp. 33–44.

[65] H.A. Khouzani, et al., Prolonging PCM lifetime through energy-efficient, segment-aware, and wear-resistant page allocation, in: ISLPED, ACM, 2014, pp. 327–330.

[66] M. Asadinia, et al., Variable resistance spectrum assignment in phase change memory systems, in: TVLSI, 2014.

[67] Samavatian, M. H., Abbasitabar, H., Arjomand, M., & Sarbazi-Azad, H. (2014, June). An efficient STT-RAM last level cache architecture for GPUs. In 2014 51st ACM/EDAC/IEEE Design Automation Conference (DAC) (pp. 1-6). IEEE. http://dl.acm.org/citation.cfm?id=2593086

Power management of mobile GPUs

21

T. Mitra, A. Prakash, A. Pathania*

National University of Singapore, Singapore, Singapore

1 INTRODUCTION

The system-on-chip (SoC) for mobile devices initially contained only a central processing unit (CPU), which would be considered very rudimentary by today's standard. As the CPUs became more capable over time, they also started rendering graphic applications (mostly games) by a process known as "software rendering." The CPU being designed for execution of sequential workloads was both performance-wise and power-wise inefficient when processing highly parallel graphic workloads. *Nvidia* introduced the first graphics processing unit (GPU) named *SC10* [1] for mobile devices in 2004. GPUs were later etched on the same die as the CPUs leading to the emergence of heterogeneous multiprocessor system-on-chips (HMPSoCs) [2]. Since then GPUs have continued to improve and in the process transformed the mobile landscape. For example, Fig. 1 shows how much mobile gaming has advanced over the years, from one of the first mobile games *Tetris* released in 1989 for *Nintendo Gameboy* devices to *Need for Speed No Limit* released in 2015 for *Android* devices.

This performance came at the price of high power consumption. At time of this writing, one of the most advanced HMPSoCs available is *Samsung's Exynos 7 Octa (7420)* fabricated on 14 nm technology. The *ARM Mali-760* GPU in this HMPSoC with eight cores can consume up to 6 W of power when operating at the highest frequency level, comparable to 7 W consumed by the octa-core *ARM big.Little* CPU on the same chip [3]. A mobile device is battery powered and high power consumption can quickly drain its limited-capacity battery [4]. High power consumption also leads to high die temperature, which can cause permanent damage to the mobile device given its restricted heat dissipation capacity [5]. Inevitably, many power management technologies, such as digital voltage and frequency scaling

---

*Author now works at Chair of Embedded System (CES), Karlsruhe Institute of Technology (KIT).

Advances in GPU Research and Practice. http://dx.doi.org/10.1016/B978-0-12-803738-6.00021-5

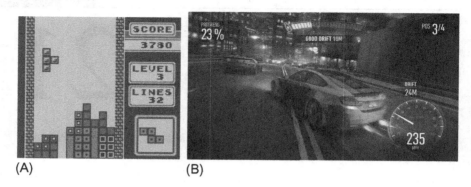

FIG. 1

Revolution in mobile gaming ushered by advancements in mobile GPUs. (A) *Tetris* (1989) *Source: GiantBomb*. (B) *NFS No Limits* (2015) *Source: GooglePlay*.

(DVFS) and dynamic power management (DPM), that are available for PC-class GPUs have now made their way to mobile GPUs [3].

DVFS scales the frequency (and voltage) of the GPU to reduce its power consumption. GPU consumes less power at lower frequencies but also provides less performance. DVFS thereby allows a power-performance trade-off. DPM allows idle cores of the GPU to be power-gated eliminating their idle power consumption. The operating system (OS) subroutines that use DVFS and/or DPM to reduce power consumption of devices are called "governors."

HMPSoCs, though similar in purpose to PC-class CPU-GPU systems, differ significantly in their architecture. Fig. 2 shows the abstracted block diagrams for both architectures. CPU and GPU are fabricated on separate dies in PC-class CPU-GPU systems, while in HMPSoCs they are on the same die. CPU and GPU have a different independent power supplies in PC-class CPU-GPU systems, while in HMPSoCs they share the power supply. Finally, CPU and GPU have their own private last-level memories (DRAM and graphics DRAM, respectively), while the last level memory is shared by them in HMPSoCs.

In addition to architecture, PC-class CPU-GPU systems also differ significantly in the management goals for their governors compared to the HMPSoCs. PC-class CPU-GPU systems are several times larger in size than HMPSoCs and are often accompanied by sophisticated cooling systems. They are also connected to a power supply and hence face no energy or thermal concerns. Governors designed for these systems mostly fixate on extracting maximum performance. On the other hand, HMPSoCs, being limited by their battery and cooling capacity, need their governors to provide acceptable performance in an energy/power-efficient fashion with no thermal violation. In HMPSoC, CPU and GPU share a common power budget called thermal dissipation power (TDP). Combined CPU and GPU power should not exceed beyond TDP. Without external cooling, TDP of most mobile platform is only

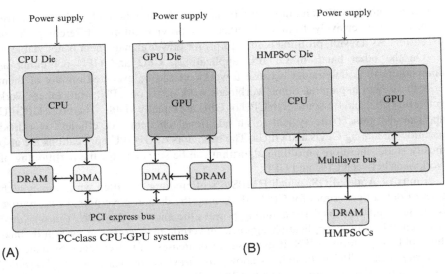

FIG. 2

Abstract architectural block diagrams of PC-class CPU-GPU systems and HMPSoCs.
(A) PC-class CPU-GPU systems. (B) HMPSoCs.

2–4 W, whereas the *Exynos* HMPSoC mentioned earlier (Samsungs Exynos 7 Octa 7420) can consume up to 13 W when both CPU and GPU are operating at their peak capacity.

The initial role for GPU in mobile devices was to unburden the CPU from the graphic processing for games. The ability to process highly parallel graphic workloads in a power-efficient manner turned out to be perfect for handling highly parallel general-purpose mobile workloads such as vision and image processing. Mobile GPUs also have now become sophisticated enough to run general-purpose computation on graphics processing unit (GPGPU) applications, similar to their PC-class counterparts. This capability allows them to help the CPU in tasks such as voice recognition and image processing, and even more interestingly opens up the possibility for large numbers of HMPSoCs to be put together to form low-power servers. Though GPU processing is similar for both games and GPGPU applications, the roles CPU plays in them are completely different.

While executing games, CPU and GPU need to work synergistically. Games use CPU for the general-purpose computation, for example, game physics and artificial intelligence (AI), while GPU is used for parallel 2D/3D graphics rendering. For games, CPU and GPU are in a producer-consumer relationship. To produce a game frame, the CPU first generates a frame, which it then passes on to the GPU for rendering. Games are also highly dynamic workloads that can change its requirements unpredictably depending on changes in the complexity of the scene being rendered. Thus games require a lightweight online governor that synchronously manages both the CPU and the GPU. In addition, being inherently user-interactive, games vary extensively from each other and provide infinite different paths of execution. As a result, profiling them a priori for power management is not viable.

On the other hand, in GPGPU applications, CPU and GPU act either as competitors or collaborators because a workload can be executed on any of them or both of them in parallel. Some workloads work better on CPU, while others work better on GPU, and for some both CPU or GPU are equally viable. Therefore GPGPU applications subject the system to an additional challenge of efficient workload partitioning among CPUs and GPUs. The behaviors of GPGPU applications are also mostly static; therefore an offline algorithm can be sufficient for the partitioning of workloads between CPU and GPU.

Linux or Android OS, which HMPSoCs often come installed with, comes with a set of default governors for CPU [6]. Among the default governors, *Conservative* is the governor designed for attaining power-efficiency on the CPU. *Conservative* is a general-purpose application agnostic governor that works on system-defined thresholds to perform DVFS. It increases or decreases CPU frequency by a step of *freq_step* when CPU utilization is above *up_threshold* or below *down_threshold*, respectively. The interval at which CPU utilization is measured is defined by *sampling_down_factor*. On the other hand, GPU DVFS is performed by a closed-source GPU driver, and it is not known what governor (or algorithm) the driver employs.

The separate CPU and GPU governor approach that Linux employs lacks synergy and does not reflect the complex interrelationships they have when executing games or GPGPU workloads. The problem, however, has been addressed in recent research in the form of specialized gaming or GPGPU governors. In this chapter, we characterize gaming and GPGPU workloads and present some of the current state-of-the-art governors designed for them. Finally, we discuss some of the open research problems that provide opportunities for further reduction in power consumption of a mobile GPU.

2 GPU POWER MANAGEMENT FOR MOBILE GAMES

We first measure the power consumption while executing gaming workloads on an *Odroid XU+E* board with *Exynos 5 Octa (5410)* HMPSoC as shown in Fig. 3. *Exynos 5 Octa (5410)* HMPSoC combines a powerful quad-core *Cortex-A15* CPU with a sophisticated tri-core *PowerVR SGX544* GPU. Both CPU and GPU support DVFS but neither CPU nor GPU can perform DPM. In the *Samsung Exynos* series HMPSoCs, DPM arrived in CPU and GPU with the introduction of *Exynos 5 Octa (5422)* and *Exynos 7 Octa (7420)*, respectively [3].

As expected, the games turn out to be extremely power hungry. Fig. 4 shows the average power consumption of some of the latest mobile games, while running at peak performance with the highest CPU-GPU frequency setting. Fig. 4 shows that the games use both CPU and GPU for execution. Still some games consume more

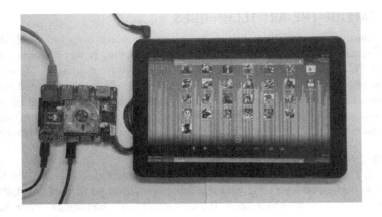

FIG. 3

Odroid-XU+E with Exynos 5 Octa (5410) HMPSoC.

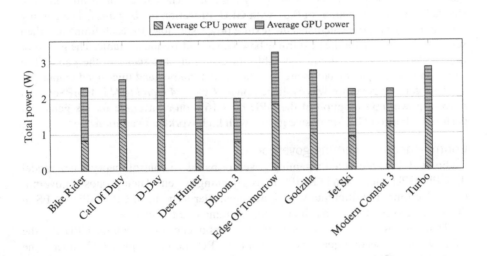

FIG. 4

Average CPU and GPU power consumption for latest mobile games.

CPU power, while others consume more GPU power. This is indicative of substantial variation in the workloads that different games produce and the challenges involved in their power management.

We begin by describing some of the state-of-the-art gaming governors proposed in research. We then present our in-depth characterization of mobile gaming workloads, followed by details of our approach to reducing the power consumption of mobile games running on HMPSoCs.

2.1 STATE-OF-THE-ART TECHNIQUES

Power consumption during mobile gaming was a concern even before HMPSoCs were introduced [7]. Early works [8,9] focused on reducing power consumption of a mobile CPU running open-source games through software rendering. These works are now obsolete as the introduction of mobile GPUs radically changed the way the games are executed on current mobile devices. Furthermore, most of the games played today are closed-source games. Therefore, in this section, we present details of only those works that can be applied to closed-source games running on HMPSoCs.

Texture-directed gaming governor

Sun et al. [10] show that there is a strong positive correlation between the texture operations performed on a CPU with rendering operations performed on a GPU in a HMPSoC. Based on this observation, the authors present a gaming governor that sets the frequency of the GPU reactively based on the texture processing load that a game places on the CPU.

Texture processing load is calculated from the number of times a call is made to the OpenGL function *glBindTexture ()* by the game. The call count of this function showed a strong correlation of 0.87 with GPU utilization in six games. The gaming governor they propose calculates the texture processing load for each frame and then sets GPU frequency for the next frame based on a load-frequency table. The governor is provided with a load-frequency table for each playable scene in the game. The values in load-frequency tables are empirically determined and fine-tuned manually.

This gaming governor was evaluated on an *Exynos 4 Quad (4412)* HMPSoC and reduces power consumption of the GPU by 7.16% on an average for six games. It performed best on GPU-intensive games with high workload variations.

Control-theoretic gaming governor

Kadjo et al. [11] presented a gaming governor based on control theory. They model the CPU-GPU interaction in HMPSoC as a queuing system. Their proposed governor uses a multiinput multioutput state space controller to perform CPU-GPU DVFS in the queuing system so as to achieve a target frame rate for a game.

There are two queues in the system. The first queue is between the CPU and the GPU, while the second queue is between the GPU and the display. CPU injects the work in CPU-GPU queue, which is ejected by the GPU. The injection rate in CPU-GPU queue is determined by CPU frequency, while the ejection rate is determined by GPU frequency. Similarly, the GPU acts as an injector in the GPU-display queue, and the display acts as an ejector. Injection rate in GPU-display queue is determined by GPU frequency, while ejection rate is determined by the display's refresh rate. The controller takes a game's frame rate as an input parameter and ensures that there is sufficient work in both queues at all times by adjusting injection and ejection rates using CPU-GPU DVFS to prevent any stall.

This control-theoretic gaming governor was implemented on *Intel Baytrail* HMPSoC. The governor operated at a granularity of 50 ms and achieves an average power savings of 20% and 17% on the CPU and GPU, respectively.

Regression-based gaming governor

We presented a regression-based gaming governor in Ref. [12]. In our work [13], we extensively characterized the producer-consumer relationships between CPU and GPU when games are executed on an HMPSoC. Based on this characterization, we developed a power-performance model using linear regression and employed this model to drive CPU-GPU DVFS to run a game at target performance with minimal power consumption. We cover this governor in detail in this chapter.

2.2 CPU-GPU RELATIONSHIP

The performance of a game is measured in frames per second (FPS). To produce a frame, the game requires both CPU and GPU to perform substantial calculations. CPU performs the game's physics and AI-associated calculations based on which location of objects in a playable 3D scene is generated. This information is then sent to GPU for processing that creates a 2D image (frame) from the 3D scene, visually reflecting the current state of the scene. The frame produced by the GPU is then displayed on the screen.

Fig. 5 shows a simplified abstraction of how a game's code is written. In the code, there is a one major loop that performs most of the processing. CPU's part of the code is performed first, followed by GPU's part of the code in the loop. Each iteration of the loop produces a single frame for the game. Fig. 5 clearly shows the producer-consumer relationship between CPU and GPU. Until CPU finishes processing a frame, GPU cannot start frame processing. Similarly, until GPU finishes processing the last frame, CPU cannot start processing the next frame.

CPU's part of a game's code works on real-system clock time, and an object in the game will always behave similarly on the screen in a given time interval irrespective of how fast the game loop executes (provided no user interaction happens in between and game code is deterministic). But, if the loop executes faster, then more frames are produced to reflect the behavior of the object. For example, Fig. 5 shows movement

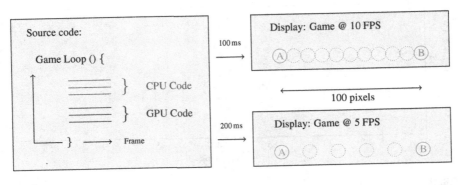

FIG. 5

Production of frames by a game loop in source code.

of a ball from points A to B separated by a distance of 100 pixels on the display. Assume that the ball is moving at 100 pixels/s. If the loop runs at 100 ms, then the movement of the ball will be shown to the user using 10 frames in a second. If the same loop runs at 200 ms, then the ball's movement will be displayed using 5 frames in a second. Understandably, quality of service (QoS) experienced by the user will be superior in 10 FPS than 5 FPS as the user will visually perceive a smoother animation.

2.3 POWER-PERFORMANCE TRADE-OFF

Exynos 5 Octa (5410) can perform CPU DVFS from 800 to 1600 MHz in nine discrete steps and GPU DVFS from 177 to 640 MHz in six discrete steps. In total, a game can be run on 54 static CPU-GPU DVFS settings. We run the *Asphalt 7* racing game deterministically on each setting for 5 min and report the observed average FPS and power consumption in Fig. 6. The *Asphalt 7* game loop runs at different speeds in different settings, resulting in a different average FPS for the game at each setting. Fig. 6 shows that a game can achieve the same level of FPS with different settings, whose power consumption can differ substantially. Fig. 6 also shows that reducing the FPS of a game can significantly reduce its power consumption. The challenge for a gaming governor is to choose the most power-efficient CPU-GPU DVFS setting for a given FPS among all settings. The most power-efficient setting will change over time as a game scene changes in complexity during the gameplay, but not substantially.

We chose FPS per unit CPU power and FPS per unit GPU power as a measure for CPU and GPU power-efficiency, respectively. Fig. 7A (or Fig. 7B) shows the power-efficiency of a CPU (or GPU) for the *Asphalt 7* game when CPU (or GPU) frequency is increased, while keeping GPU (or CPU) at the highest frequency. Fig. 7

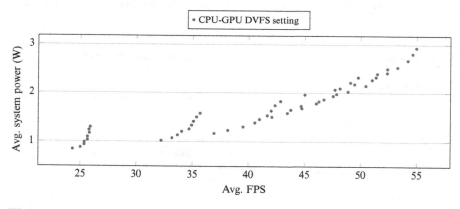

FIG. 6

Power-performance trade-off possible in *Asphalt 7* game.

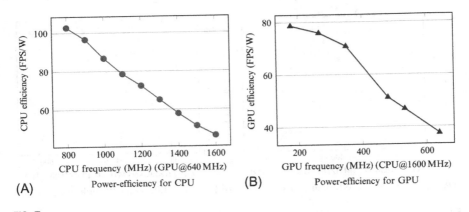

FIG. 7

CPU and GPU power-efficiency measured in FPS/watt at different frequencies.
(A) Power-efficiency for CPU. (B) Power-efficiency for GPU.

shows that the power-efficiency of both CPU and GPU decreases as their frequency is increased. We made a similar observation for almost all games. This observation greatly simplifies the power management algorithm for the gaming governor, since we know that if the desired FPS can be met by multiple different CPU (or GPU) frequencies, then the lowest among them will prove to be the most power-efficient.

2.4 GAMING BOTTLENECKS

Producer-consumer relationships between CPU and GPU in games as shown in Fig. 5 are subject to bottlenecks like any other producer-consumer relationship. If either CPU or GPU becomes a bottleneck, game performance cannot be increased irrespective of how fast the other component operates. The nonbottleneck component just ends up wasting power. In addition to resource bottlenecks, OS on HMPSoCs also limits the performance of the game to the refresh rate of the display (generally 60 Hz). If the game produces more than 60 FPS, then either CPU or GPU or both are operating faster than necessary, thereby wasting power. A game's FPS can be directly measured from the OS kernel. For detecting resource bottlenecks, we found CPU and GPU utilizations as sufficient measures that are available on all platforms. We now show how these bottlenecks manifest themselves in real games.

Fig. 8 shows the effect of increasing GPU frequency for the CPU-bound game *Edge of Tomorrow*, when CPU is fixed at its highest frequency. Fig. 8A shows that FPS first increases with increase in GPU frequency, but then stops responding to GPU DVFS after 480 MHz and beyond. Fig. 8B shows that CPU utilization for the game reaches 100% at 480 MHz making CPU a bottleneck, and further performance gain from GPU DVFS beyond 480 MHz impossible. Fig. 9 similarly shows that saturation of GPU (100% utilization) is responsible for a GPU-bound game *Bike Rider*'s FPS to

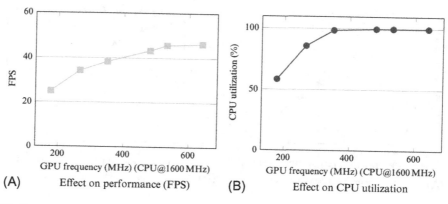

FIG. 8

Effect of increasing GPU frequency on CPU-bound game *Edge of Tomorrow*. (A) Effect on performance (FPS). (B) Effect on CPU utilization.

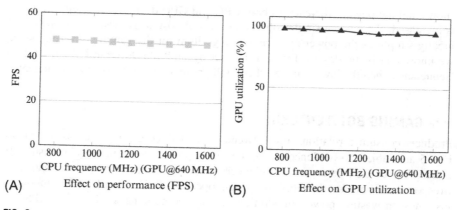

FIG. 9

Effect of increasing CPU frequency on GPU-bound game *Bike Rider*. (A) Effect on performance (FPS). (B) Effect on GPU utilization.

never respond to CPU DVFS. Finally, Fig. 10 shows the relatively simple FPS-bound game *Deer Hunter* whose FPS hits 60 FPS at the lowest CPU-GPU DVFS settings, leaving no further scope of increase in FPS with either CPU or GPU DVFS.

2.5 PERFORMANCE MODELING

Based on Section 2.4, a game's FPS will increase with increase in a component's frequency (CPU or GPU) as long as it does not reach the upper limit of 60 FPS or the

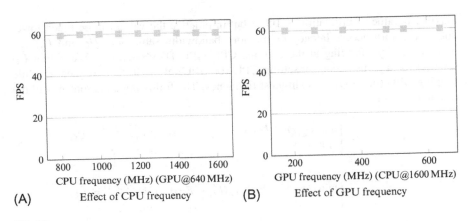

FIG. 10

Effect of increasing CPU and GPU frequency on FPS-bound game *Deer Hunter*. (A) Effect of CPU frequency. (B) Effect of GPU frequency.

other component (GPU or CPU) becomes a bottleneck. We capture this behavior in the form of a linear mathematical model. All the constants in the model are determined using linear regression on data obtained from ten games.

Let F_C and F_G represent the current CPU and GPU frequency, respectively. $Q^{(F_C,F_G)}$, $U_C^{(F_C,F_G)}$, and $U_G^{(F_C,F_G)}$ represent the FPS, CPU utilization, and GPU utilization at the CPU-GPU DVFS setting (F_C, F_G), respectively. We now attempt to estimate FPS at a higher frequency setting (F_C', F_G') from the current frequency setting (F_C, F_G). We assume a linear relationship between FPS and different CPU/GPU frequencies in the absence of a bottleneck. The relationship is captured using

$$Q^{(F_C',F_G)} = Q^{(F_C,F_G)} + \gamma_1(F_C' - F_C) \tag{1}$$

$$Q^{(F_C,F_G')} = Q^{(F_C,F_G)} + \gamma_2(F_G' - F_G) \tag{2}$$

where γ_1 and γ_2 are constants obtained through linear regression.

Now we add the FPS bottleneck to the model. Let $\hat{Q}$ represent the maximum FPS a game can attain on the HMPSoC. Theoretically, it is the same as the display refresh rate (60 FPS) but some games also employ internal FPS control, which can limit a game's FPS to a much lower value. $\hat{Q}$ for a game scene can be easily obtained by setting CPU and GPU together at their highest frequency, while the game scene is executing. The following equations model the FPS bottleneck.

$$Q^{(F_C',F_G)} = \min\left(\hat{Q}, Q^{(F_C,F_G)} + \gamma_1(F_C' - F_C)\right) \tag{3}$$

$$Q^{(F_C,F_G')} = \min\left(\hat{Q}, Q^{(F_C,F_G)} + \gamma_2(F_G' - F_G)\right) \tag{4}$$

Now we add the resource bottlenecks to the model. Let $\hat{U}_C$ and $\hat{U}_G$ represent the maximum CPU and GPU utilization for a game, respectively. Theoretically, maximum value of utilization is 100% but in practice the value can be much lower due to memory access latency or memory bandwidth saturation. $\hat{U}_C$ and $\hat{U}_G$ can be obtained by sampling at the extreme CPU-GPU DVFS settings. We obtain $\hat{U}_C$ (or $\hat{U}_G$) for a game scene by setting CPU (or GPU) at the lowest frequency, while keeping GPU (or CPU) at the highest frequency. The following equations model the resource bottlenecks.

$$Q^{(F'_C, F_G)} = \begin{cases} \min\ (\hat{Q}, Q^{(F_C, F_G)} + \gamma_1 (F'_C - F_C)) & \text{if } U_G^{(F_C, F_G)} \neq \hat{U}_G \\ Q^{(F_C, F_G)} & \text{otherwise} \end{cases} \quad (5)$$

$$Q^{(F_C, F'_G)} = \begin{cases} \min\ (\hat{Q}, Q^{(F_C, F_G)} + \gamma_2 (F'_G - F_G)) & \text{if } U_C^{(F_C, F_G)} \neq \hat{U}_C \\ Q^{(F_C, F_G)} & \text{otherwise} \end{cases} \quad (6)$$

2.6 UTILIZATION MODELS

We also need a utilization model to predict bottlenecks before they happen. When a component's frequency is increased and the FPS remains unchanged, then the component's utilization must decrease. This will be true only if the component is not itself a bottleneck and holding the FPS back. Utilization of a component will remain unchanged if it is the bottleneck because the component will be able to process more frames (and hence more utilization) with an increase in its clock frequency. This is captured mathematically by

$$U_C^{(F'_C, F_G)} = \begin{cases} U_C^{(F_C, F_G)} + \alpha_1 (F'_C - F_C) & \text{if } U_C^{(F_C, F_G)} \neq \hat{U}_C \\ U_C^{(F_C, F_G)} & \text{otherwise} \end{cases} \quad (7)$$

$$U_G^{(F_C, F'_G)} = \begin{cases} U_G^{(F_C, F_G)} + \beta_1 (F'_G - F_G) & \text{if } U_G^{(F_C, F_G)} \neq \hat{U}_G \\ U_G^{(F_C, F_G)} & \text{otherwise} \end{cases} \quad (8)$$

where α_1 and β_1 are constants.

Utilization of a component (CPU or GPU) is also affected by a change in frequency of the other component (GPU or CPU) even if the frequency of the component of interest (CPU or GPU) is kept constant. This is because if the other component (GPU or CPU) frequency is increased, then the fixed frequency component (CPU or GPU) will have more work to do in the form of more frames to process at the same frequency. This behavior is captured by

$$U_C^{(F_C, F'_G)} = U_C^{(F_C, F_G)} + \alpha_2 (Q^{(F_C, F'_G)} - Q^{(F_C, F_G)}) \quad (9)$$

$$U_G^{(F'_C, F_G)} = U_G^{(F_C, F_G)} + \beta_2 (Q^{(F'_C, F_G)} - Q^{(F_C, F_G)}) \quad (10)$$

where α_2 and β_2 are constants.

2.7 GAMING GOVERNOR

Based on our models presented in previous sections, we design a governor for mobile games. The goal of the gaming governor we design is to execute a game at a target FPS provided by the user with minimal power consumption. It was already shown in Section 2.3 that a game consumes less power at a lower FPS, but an acceptable level of FPS will differ from one user to another. For a professional gamer with eyes very attuned to a high refresh rate, anything less than 60 FPS will be unacceptable. On the other hand, for a casual gamer, 30 FPS will be sufficient. Therefore it is best for the user to provide the desired level of performance manually.

Further, it was also shown in Section 2.3 that the lowest power-consuming CPU-GPU DVFS setting for a given FPS is the setting in which CPU and GPU frequencies are the lowest possible under the FPS constraint. Thus the goal of our gaming governor is to find the lowest CPU-GPU DVFS setting where the user-defined FPS can be met. Our gaming governor operates at a granularity of 1 Hz.

When a game scene starts, we take three samples (each of duration 1 s) to obtain game-specific upper-bound constants $\hat{U}_C$, $\hat{U}_G$, and $\hat{Q}$. Game scenes generally last a long time, and the benefits of taking these samples in the beginning far outweighs the momentary drop in user experience. These samples greatly enhance the accuracy of our models and also avoid any requirement of prior offline profiling.

Initially in the models, we use coefficients that are obtained from our regression analysis. This provides a good estimate to set initial CPU-GPU frequencies for achieving the target FPS. As the game progresses, a sample is taken from the game every second. These samples from additional data to further refine our regression models online and tailor the models to the scene currently being rendered. This runtime regression has a very low overhead of approximately 0.08% on the CPU. The governor's total overhead on the CPU is 2%, attributed mostly to the complex process of extracting FPS information from kernel log dumps.

Our governor can target any FPS, but to simplify the explanation, we assume the highest FPS $\hat{Q}$ as our target. At the present CPU-GPU DVFS setting (F_C, F_G), we can either be below the maximum FPS $(Q^{(F_C, F_G)} < \hat{Q})$ or at it $(Q^{(F_C, F_G)} = \hat{Q})$.

Meeting FPS

If $Q^{(F_C, F_G)} < \hat{Q}$, then either CPU is the bottleneck $(U_C^{(F_C, F_G)} = \hat{U}_C)$ or GPU is the bottleneck $(U_G^{(F_C, F_G)} = \hat{U}_G)$. We need to identify the bottleneck component and increase its frequency to increase FPS. Let us assume the required DVFS setting is (F'_C, F'_G), where $F'_C \geq F_C$ and $F'_G \geq F_G$.

If CPU is the bottleneck, then we need to increase CPU frequency using the following equation derived from Eq. (3).

$$F'_C = \frac{\hat{Q} - Q^{(F_C, F_G)}}{\gamma_1} + F_C \qquad (11)$$

This increased CPU frequency should increase the FPS, but it may happen that we may still not see $\hat{Q}$ because bottlenecks switch, and GPU now becomes a bottleneck at its current frequency F_G. GPU utilization at F_C' is given by the following equation derived from Eq. (10).

$$U_G^{(F_C',F_G)} = U_G^{(F_C,F_G)} + \beta_2(\hat{Q} - Q^{(F_C,F_G)}) \tag{12}$$

If $U_G^{(F_C',F_G)} > \hat{U}_G$, then GPU will become a bottleneck that has to be widened to realize FPS $\hat{Q}$ by increasing GPU frequency to F_G'. F_G' is given by the following equation derived from Eq. (8).

$$F_G' = \frac{U_G^{(F_C',F_G)} - \hat{U}_G}{\beta_1} + F_G \tag{13}$$

Similarly, if GPU were the bottleneck instead of CPU to begin with, then we would have evaluated F_G' first using Eq. (4). We would have checked for a possible CPU bottleneck using Eq. (9) and if required set it to a higher frequency F_C', based on Eq. (7).

Saving power

Now we focus on the other possibility where we are meeting the maximum FPS requirement on our current DVFS setting itself $Q^{(F_C,F_G)} = \hat{Q}$. This setting, though meeting our demand, may still be wasting power if CPU and/or GPU are not at their maximum utilization. If $U_C^{(F_C,F_G)} \neq \hat{U}_C$, then we can save power by reducing CPU frequency to F_C'' using the following equation derived from Eq. (7).

$$F_C'' = \frac{\hat{U}_C - U_C^{(F_C,F_G)}}{\alpha_1} + F_C \tag{14}$$

Similarly, if $U_G^{(F_C,F_G)} \neq \hat{U}_G$, then we can save power by reducing the GPU frequency to F_G'' using following equation derived from Eq. (8).

$$F_G'' = \frac{\hat{U}_G - U_G^{(F_C,F_G)}}{\beta_1} + F_G \tag{15}$$

2.8 RESULTS

We use 20 games in our work. We divide them into two equal sets of 10 games each. We use the first set as the learning set to train our regression model. The second set is used as the testing set to evaluate the model in making predictions on unseen games. Tables 1 and 2 show the average error of our model in predicting performance at all DVFS setting for games in the learning and the test set, respectively. Average error in predicting FPS is only 3.87%.

Table 1 FPS Prediction Errors for Games in the Learning Set

Edge of Tomorrow	Deer Hunter	Call of Duty	Jet Ski	Dhoom 3	Bike Rider	D-Day	Turbo	MC3	Godzilla
2.39%	0.08%	2.11%	3.63%	3.48%	11.41%	3.32%	13.91%	11.41%	1.30%

Table 2 FPS Prediction Errors for Games in the Testing Set

Farmville	Contract Killer	RoboCop	Dark Meadow	Revolt	AVP	Asphalt	I, Gladiator	Call of Dead	B&G
0.26%	0.21%	5.23%	5.48%	4.58%	0.02%	0.09%	7.64%	4.90%	1.02%

We then test our approach against the default Linux *Conservative* governor [6] on a set of 10 games, chosen equally from the learning and the test set. The results are presented in Fig. 11. Linux always aims for the highest performance, so we also set maximum FPS as the target for our gaming governor. Both governors result in the same performance ($\approx$ 60 FPS) for the games but consume different amounts of power. Therefore HMPSoC's power-efficiency under the two approaches when measured as FPS per unit power is directly comparable. Evaluations show our proposed gaming governor can provide on average 29% additional power-efficiency.

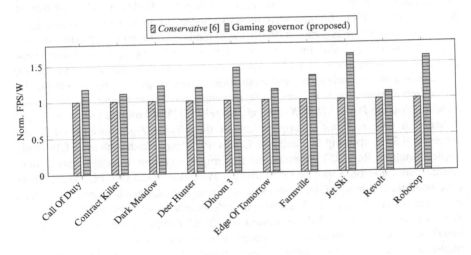

FIG. 11

Power-efficiency of our gaming governor against default *Conservative* governor [6].

3 GPU POWER MANAGEMENT FOR GPGPU APPLICATIONS

In the previous section, we discussed the state-of-the-art power management techniques to reduce power consumption of mobile games running on HMPSoCs. Recent advancements in the mobile GPUs have empowered the user to run not only games but also GPGPU applications. This section discusses the state-of-the-art techniques proposed for executing such applications on mobile GPUs.

3.1 STATE-OF-THE-ART TECHNIQUES

There has been tremendous interest in optimization techniques for performance and power-efficiency in heterogeneous platforms containing GPUs [14–17]. Conventionally, the multicore CPUs in these heterogeneous systems are used for general-purpose tasks, while the data-parallel tasks in the applications exploit the integrated or discrete GPU for accelerated execution [15]. However, most of the research in the past focused on PC-class CPU-GPU systems [14–18]. Unlike PC-class CPU-GPU systems, GPGPU applications executing on HMPSoCs also need to deal with the effects of resource sharing between CPU and GPU [19–21]. This necessitates appropriate consideration to coordinate both the CPU and the GPU so as to maximize performance. Wang et al. [19] took the total chip power budget of the *AMD Trinity* single-chip heterogeneous platform into consideration to propose a runtime algorithm that partitions the workload as well as the power budget between the CPU and the GPU to improve throughput. Wang et al. [21] also showed that in coordinated CPU-GPU runs on a similar *AMD* platform, there is a higher possibility of the CPU and the GPU accessing the same bank because of the similarity of memory access patterns, resulting in memory contention. Paul et al. [20] proposed techniques to address the issue of shared resources in integrated GPUs in *AMD* platforms. Additionally, DVFS techniques were used to achieve energy-efficient executions.

In the context of targeting GPGPU workloads toward mobile platforms, several early works [22–26] only explored image processing and computer vision applications on mobile GPUs [27]. Work presented in Refs. [22,23] explored the implementation, optimization, and evaluation of image processing and computer vision applications, such as cartoon-style nonphotorealistic rendering, and stereo matching, on the *PowerVR SGX530* and *PowerVR SGX540* mobile GPUs. Ref. [24] executed a face recognition application on the *Nvidia Tegra* mobile GPU and achieved $4.25\times$ speedup by using a CPU-GPU design rather than a CPU-only implementation. Ref. [25] presented the first implementation of local binary pattern feature extraction on a mobile GPU using a *PowerVR SGX535* GPU. The authors concluded that, although GPU alone was not enough to achieve high performance, a combination of CPU and GPU improved performance as well as energy-efficiency. Work presented in Ref. [26] showcased an efficient implementation of the scale-invariant feature transform (SIFT) feature detection algorithm on several mobile platforms such as the *Snapdragon S4* development kit, *Nvidia Tegra 3*-based *Nexus 7* among others. The authors partitioned the SIFT application so as to execute different parts of the application in CPU and GPU in a producer-consumer fashion. They achieved considerable speedup for CPU-only optimized design, while also improving energy-efficiency.

While all of these early works focused only on image processing and related algorithms as GPGPU applications, the current mobile GPUs have advanced to the point of implementing a wide range of parallel applications [27]. Moreover, the growing popularity and support for OpenCL in mobile GPUs has also simplified GPU computing, thereby enabling several other types of GPGPU applications [27,28].

Maghazeh et al. [28] explored GPGPU applications on a low power *Vivante GC2000*-embedded GPU on the *i.MX6 Sabre Lite* development board and compared it to a PC-class *Nvidia Tesla* GPU. Their platform supports OpenCL Embedded Profile 1.1, which implements a subset of the OpenCL Full Profile 1.1 APIs. The authors demonstrated that different applications behave differently on CPU and GPU and argued for the benefit of using CPU and GPU simultaneously for performance and energy-efficiency.

Grasso et al. [27] focused on examining the performance of the *Mali* GPU for high-performance computing workloads. They identified several OpenCL optimization techniques for both the host and the device kernel code so as to use the GPU more efficiently. In order to exploit the unified memory system in the HMPSoC, they optimized the memory allocations and mappings in the host code. They also proposed to manually tune the work-group size of the OpenCL kernels in order to maximize the resource utilization of the GPU, thereby achieving higher performance. Several other optimization techniques for the kernel code, such as vectorization based on the GPU architecture and thread divergence issue for GPUs, were also proposed in their work to improve performance of the GPU. This work mainly targeted the GPU, without considering the CPU to further improve performance.

Chandramohan et al. [29] presented a workload partitioning algorithm for HMPSoCs, while considering shared resources and synchronization. Their HMPSoC contained dual-core *Cortex-A9* processor, dual-core *Cortex M3* processor, and *C64X+* digital signal processor (DSP). They tested several workload partitioning policies on these compute devices based on the individual throughput, frequency, and so on, and ultimately proposed an iterative partitioning technique based on load balancing to achieve high performance. However, they missed the opportunity to use the mobile GPU for executing any part of the workload. Furthermore, their iterative technique is shown to perform worse than the best possible results achievable on their platform, as found from exhaustive design space exploration.

Jo et al. [30] designed their OpenCL framework to support specifically *ARM* CPUs. A similar open-source framework, *FreeOCL* [31], was also developed for *ARM* CPUs to enable the CPU to act as the host processor as well as an OpenCL compute device. In an effort to improve cache utilization and load balancing, Seo et al. [32] proposed a technique to automatically select the optimum work-group size for OpenCL kernels on multicore CPUs. The ideas proposed in their work can also be used to improve performance in mobile GPUs.

Existing literature on exploiting mobile GPUs for general-purpose computing is quite sparse. They also do not consider the DVFS capabilities of the latest

HMPSoCs in order to save power and energy. Moreover, with the increasing number of cores in the accompanying CPUs, it is equally important to exploit CPU and GPU *concurrently* for a single kernel in order to achieve increased performance as well as energy-efficiency. However, it is a nontrivial task to obtain optimal load partitioning of a single kernel on the CPU and GPU, especially while considering the effect of resource contention in a HMPSoC.

We now proceed to discuss techniques proposed in our recent work [33] to exploit the GPU along with the accompanying CPU in HMPSoCs to achieve high performance for diverse GPGPU kernels. Furthermore, we demonstrate a way to obtain the best DVFS settings for GPU and CPU in order to improve energy-efficiency.

3.2 BACKGROUND

3.2.1 Hardware environment

While the gaming workloads were evaluated on the *Odroid XU+E* development platform, we explore the GPGPU applications on the *Odroid XU3* [34] mobile application development platform as shown in Fig. 12. This platform features the *Exynos 5 Octa (5422)* HMPSoC comprising a quad-core *Cortex*-A15 CPU cluster, a quad-core *Cortex*-A7 CPU cluster, and a hexa-core (arranged in two clusters of 4-core and 2-core) *Mali-T628* GPU. Unlike the *Exynos 5 Octa (5410)* HMPSoC in the *Odroid XU+E* platform, the *Exynos 5 Octa (5422)* HMPSoC allows all the eight CPU cores to function simultaneously. This feature is extremely important for GPGPU applications in order to employ all eight cores of the two CPU clusters for OpenCL execution, unlike only one CPU cluster being available at any given time in

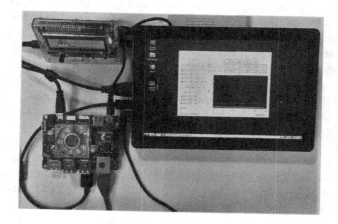

FIG. 12

Experimental platform using *Odroid-XU3*: a state-of-the-art mobile development platform featuring *Samsung Exynos 5 Octa (5422)* HMPSoC.

the *Exynos 5 Octa (5410)* HMPSoC. Furthermore, all eight cores of the CPU and four cores (only the four-core cluster of this GPU supports OpenCL) of the GPU support *concurrent* execution of OpenCL kernels.

Each of the CPU clusters, namely the *A15* and *A7*, allows extensive DVFS settings for power and thermal management. The frequency of the *A15* cluster, for example, can be set between 200 and 2000 MHz, while the *A7* cluster can be clocked between 200 and 1400 MHz, both at an interval of 100 MHz. The accompanying *Mali-T628 MP6* GPU on this platform is based on the *ARM*'s *Midgard* architecture and implements six shader cores that can execute both graphics and general-purpose computing workloads. However, the OpenCL runtime uses only four shader cores during OpenCL execution. The GPU L2 cache (128 KB) is shared between the shader cores. However, the GPU L2 cache is not kept coherent with the CPU L2 cache, even though the GPU is allowed to read from the CPU cache. The main component of the shader core is a programmable massively multithreaded tri-pipe processing engine. Each tri-pipe consists of a load-store pipeline, two arithmetic pipelines and one texture pipeline. The texture pipelines are not used during OpenCL execution. The arithmetic pipeline is a very long instruction word (VLIW) design with single-instruction multiple-data (SIMD) vector characteristics that operate on registers of 128-bit width. This means that the arithmetic pipeline contains a mixture of scalar and vector (SIMD) arithmetic logic units that can execute a single long instruction word. The load-store pipeline of each shader core has 16 KB L1 data cache. The tri-pipe is capable of concurrently executing hundreds of hardware threads. The memory latency of threads that are waiting on memory can be effectively hidden by executing other threads in the arithmetic pipeline. The *ARM Midgard* architecture used in this GPU differs significantly from other GPU architectures in the sense that the arithmetic pipelines are independent and can execute threads that are different, for example, in case of divergent branches and memory stalls. The available voltage-frequency settings for this GPU are shown in Table 3.

3.2.2 Software environment
In our work we heavily rely on OpenCL, a parallel programming language, to exploit the heterogeneity in our platform to achieve energy-efficiency. In this section, we briefly explain the OpenCL programming model followed by our technique of partitioning the application across the CPU and GPU cores.

OpenCL background
OpenCL is an open-source programming language for cross-platform parallel programming in modern heterogeneous platforms. It can be used develop applications that are portable across devices with varied architectures such as CPU, GPU,

Table 3 The Available Voltage-Frequency Settings for GPU

Frequency (MHz)	600	543	480	420	350	266	177
Voltage (mV)	975	962.5	912.5	875	850	975	762.5

field-programmable gate array (FPGA), etc. Device vendors are responsible for providing OpenCL runtime as well as compilation tools to support OpenCL on their devices. Moreover, multiple OpenCL runtime software can coexist on a single platform, thereby allowing applications to concurrently exploit various devices in the platform.

The OpenCL programming model allows a *host* code segment that runs on the CPU to schedule the computations using the OpenCL *kernels* on one or more *compute devices*. A CPU, GPU, DSP, or even FPGA can act as a compute device. The initialization and setup of these compute devices is performed by the host code, which then uses OpenCL API functions to schedule kernels for execution. The host code is also responsible for transferring the data to and from the compute devices before and after the kernel execution, respectively. The kernel or device code is built on the host CPU with the help of OpenCL APIs during runtime before getting scheduled on the compute device for execution.

Each of the compute devices (e.g., GPU) consist of several *compute units* (e.g., shader cores in *Mali*), whereas the compute units consist of *processing elements* (e.g., arithmetic pipelines). A *work-item* refers to a kernel instance that operates on a single data point and is executed on a processing element. A *work-group* contains a group of work-items that are simultaneously executed on the processing elements of a single compute unit. The term *NDRange* refers to the index space of the input data for data-parallel applications. All work-items of an OpenCL program operate along this *NDRange* and execute identical codes. However, they may follow different control paths based on the input data instance on which they operate. The OpenCL execution model can be related to the popular Compute Unified Device Architecture (CUDA) model by visualizing the OpenCL work-item as a CUDA thread, work-group as a thread-block, and NDRange as the grid. The OpenCL work-items have a private memory, whereas every work-group has a local memory that is shared by all the work-items within the work-group. The work-groups also have access to a global memory that can also be accessed by the host. The memory model defined in OpenCL mandates memory consistency across work-items within a work-group; however, this is not required among various work-groups. This feature allows different work-groups to be scheduled on different compute devices (e.g., CPU and GPU) without a need to ensure memory consistency among the devices.

OpenCL runtime

ARM supplies the OpenCL runtime software for the *Mali* GPU to promote the usage of the GPU for GPGPU applications. On the other hand, current HMPSoCs typically do not ship with OpenCL support for their *ARM* CPUs [30]. Hence, in order to explore the concurrent execution of OpenCL applications on CPU alongside the GPU, we compile and install an open-source OpenCL runtime called *FreeOCL* [31] on our HMPSoC. This enables usage of all the eight CPU cores (four big and four small cores) as OpenCL compute units. From the perspective of the OpenCL programmer, there is no difference between the different core types. Moreover, unlike other open-source OpenCL runtimes such as [35], *FreeOCL* also enables us to launch an OpenCL kernel concurrently on all CPU cores and GPU.

OpenCL code partitioning across CPU-GPU

The pseudocode shown in Algorithm 1 describes the strategy used in partitioning an OpenCL application workload across the CPU and GPU cores. Given an application, the fraction of work-items to be executed on each device is obtained statically. During OpenCL execution, the workload (global_work_size) on both CPU and GPU needs to be a multiple of the work-group size (Line 1). Hence *splittingPoint*, which is used as the reference point for splitting, is obtained as the number of work-groups nearest to the desired fraction of the CPU workload (split_fraction). Subsequently, the global work-size and offset values for the CPU and GPU are obtained based on this splittingPoint as shown in the pseudocode (Lines 2–7). The partitioned workload is then executed by enqueuing kernels on both devices with the new global work-size and offset values (Lines 9–10).

ALGORITHM 1 PSEUDOCODE FOR PARTITIONING WORKLOAD ON CPU AND GPU

1: $splittingPoint = (global\_work\_size * split\_fraction)/work\_group\_size$;
2: // Parameters for workload on CPU
3: $globalWorkSizeCPU = splittingPoint * work\_group\_size$;
4: $offsetCPU = 0$;
5: // Parameters for workload on GPU
6: $globalWorkSizeGPU = \left(\frac{global\_work\_size}{work\_group\_size} - splittingPoint \right) * work\_group\_size$;
7: $offsetGPU = splittingPoint * work\_group\_size$;
8: // Enqueue OpenCL kernels
9: $clEnqueueNDRangeKernel(clCPUCommandQue, clCPUKernel, dim, offsetCPU,$
    $globalWorkSizeCPU, work\_group\_size, 0, NULL, NULL)$;
10: $clEnqueueNDRangeKernel(clGPUCommandQue, clGPUKernel, dim, offsetGPU,$
    $globalWorkSizeGPU, work\_group\_size, 0, NULL, NULL)$;

3.3 GPGPU APPLICATIONS ON MOBILE GPUs

The *y*-axis in Fig. 13 shows that the runtime execution for the OpenCL kernels from the *PolyBench* benchmark suite [36] on all CPU cores (4 *A7* + 4 *A15*), GPU cores, and when optimally partitioned for performance across the CPU and GPU cores. Each cluster is set to run at its maximum frequency for this experiment. We reinforce additional environmental cooling to maintain the chip below its thermal design power in order to avoid thermal throttling. It can be seen from the figure that, while many applications run significantly faster on the GPU, others exhibit shorter runtimes on the CPU. However, most of the applications run significantly faster while running on both the CPU and the GPU. The percentage of runtime improvement for CPU + GPU execution over the best of the CPU-only and GPU-only executions is shown on

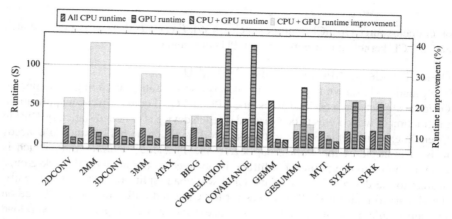

FIG. 13

Runtime improvement with CPU and GPU partitioning.

the secondary y-axis. The improvement in runtime can be up to 40% and on average 19% across all the benchmarks. This experiment clearly establishes that even those GPGPU applications that run much faster when running only on the GPU than on the CPU, can also benefit significantly from concurrent CPU + GPU execution.

3.4 DVFS FOR IMPROVING POWER/ENERGY-EFFICIENCY

While the concurrent execution helps in terms of performance as shown in the previous section, we also need to explore the various DVFS settings in order to achieve high power/energy-efficiency. Fig. 14 illustrates the energy-performance trade-off for *2DCONV* and *SYR2K* applications from the *PolyBench* suite, while executing on CPU alone, GPU alone, and when optimally partitioned between CPU and GPU, with various DVFS settings of the CPU and GPU. The y-axis shows the energy consumption in Joules, while the x-axis plots the execution time in seconds in log scale. Table 4 shows the DVFS settings used for these experiments.

It can be observed from Fig. 14 that different applications behave very differently based on their individual characteristics. The *2DCONV* application benefits significantly from the GPU (GPU-bound), and therefore the GPU-only execution points are close to the Pareto-front with very low-energy consumption, whereas

Table 4 DVFS Settings for Design Space Exploration

Test Configuration	A7 Frequency (MHz)	A15 Frequency (MHz)	GPU Frequency (MHz)
CPU-only (A7 +A15)	1400	1000–2000	Not applicable
GPU-only	Not applicable	Not applicable	177–600
CPU + GPU (A7 +A15 + GPU)	1400	1000–2000	177–600

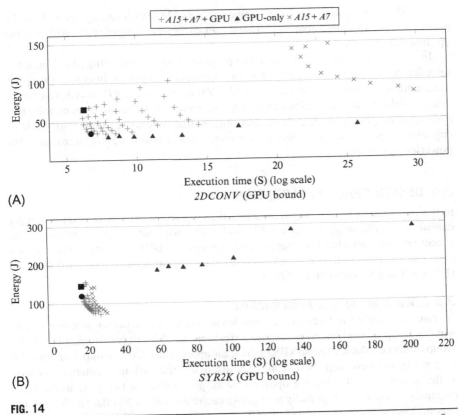

FIG. 14

Design space for *2DCONV* and *SYR2K* applications. *Black circles* represent optimal ED^2. (A) *2DCONV* (GPU bound). (B) *SYR2K* (GPU bound).

the CPU-only design points are much farther away. On the other hand, the *SYR2K* application is heavily reliant on the CPU (CPU-bound), and therefore the CPU-only (*A7 +A15*) execution points are closer to the Pareto-front with higher performance (low execution time) than the GPU-only designs.

In addition, it can also be seen that energy-efficiency can be improved by running at lower DVFS settings (black circles), when compared to the highest frequency settings (black boxes), without significant degradation in the performance of the execution time. The design space for the *2DCONV* and *SYR2K* applications as shown in Fig. 14, include the optimal ED^2 point, highlighted as a black circle on the Pareto-front. The CPU-GPU (*A7, A15*—GPU) frequency (in MHz) combination, and the CPU workload fraction (in %) for the optimal ED^2 point for *2DCONV* and *SYR2K* applications are (1400, 1000–600, 21%) and (1400, 1600–600, 71%), respectively. Power consumption is also reduced significantly at these points (black circles) since the energy reduces significantly, while the execution time increases by only a small margin. However, due to the large number of possible DVFS settings as well as the application partitioning between CPU and GPU, it is a challenging task to choose the optimal design point.

In the next section, we introduce the proposed static partitioning plus frequency selection technique to generate the Pareto-optimal design points. In order to simplify the quantitative evaluation of the proposed solution, we use the ED^2 metric (energy × delay × delay) that encapsulates the energy-performance trade-off. This metric gives additional weightage to the *delay* term to ensure that we choose points with the least degradation in the execution time performance, while achieving the largest possible power/energy savings.

3.5 DESIGN SPACE EXPLORATION

In the previous section, it was shown that the concurrent execution of an optimally partitioned application between CPU and GPU not only helps in reducing the execution time but also the energy with appropriate DVFS settings. This section discusses the proposed techniques to obtain the appropriate workload partitions and DVFS settings for the optimal ED^2 value.

3.5.1 Work-group size manipulation

As discussed earlier in Section 3.2, each kernel instance in OpenCL is a work-item, while a group of work-items constitute a work-group. Prior to partitioning the work-groups between the CPU and GPU cores, an appropriate work-group size must be selected in the first step. Seo et al. [32] discussed the various challenges as well as the benefits of selecting the optimum work-group size for OpenCL applications executing on the CPU, especially to improve cache utilization. Similar challenges and benefits also apply to executing OpenCL applications on the GPU, and even more so in case of mobile GPUs because of the limited amount of cache available in these devices. We observe that the work-group size does not impact the CPU performance on our platform because of sufficient cache capacity, but it significantly affects the GPU performance. Therefore we find the optimal work-group size for the GPU and use the same value of the work-group size for both CPU and GPU.

The maximum work-group size that can be selected for *Mali GPU* is 256 [37]. However, this maximum size cannot be guaranteed for all applications. OpenCL provides API to obtain the maximum possible work-group size for a given kernel, but this may not necessarily be the optimal work-group size. The OpenCL runtime can also be employed to automatically select a work-group size for the kernel if there is no data sharing among work-items [37]. This does not always produce the best results [27].

In order to obtain the best work-group size for an application, we employ a simple technique. It is noteworthy that the value of the work-group size is preferred to be in powers of two [37]. Hence we exhaustively explore all work-group size in powers of two up to the maximum possible work-group size for the given application and select the one that provides the best performance. Fig. 15 shows the improvement

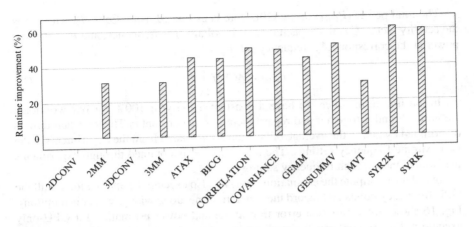

FIG. 15

Runtime improvement with best work-group size.

in execution time with selected work-group size compared to the default work-group size as originally specified in the *PolyBench* suite. Some applications such as *2DCONV* and *3DCONV* show minimum or no improvement in performance as the default work-group size is itself the optimal value. Overall, using the best work-group size can lead to an average of 40% performance improvement. We perform the subsequent partitioning and frequency selection for applications with this best work-group size.

3.5.2 Execution time and power estimation

In order to select the appropriate DVFS point for the GPU and CPU clusters, we first model the impact of frequency scaling on the power-performance behavior of an OpenCL kernel. After estimating the behavior of GPU and CPU independently, we subsequently include the impact of memory contention between the two.

GPU estimation

In order to estimate the power-performance of a given application on the GPU, we first sample its runtime and power at the minimum (177 MHz) and maximum (600 MHz) GPU frequencies. We then predict the performance and power for the remaining frequency points. During the execution of OpenCL kernels on the GPU, the utilization always stays at 100%. Hence the runtime can be safely modeled using a linear relationship, as shown in Eq. (16).

$$T = \alpha/f + \beta \tag{16}$$

Here T is the execution time, f is the frequency, and α, β are constants obtained through interpolation from the runtime at two extreme points.

The total power (P_{total}) of the GPU core is estimated using Eq. (17), where A is the activity factor, C is the capacitance, V is voltage, f is frequency, and P_i is the idle power at the corresponding frequency setting.

$$P_{total} = ACV^2f + P_i \tag{17}$$

In the first term, since we have a constant activity of 100% for our workload, we group C and A together and regard them as one constant c. This constant term is determined by taking the average of the values calculated from the experiments at the two extreme frequency settings. The idle power P_i is obtained through experiments performed once at each frequency setting.

In order to compute the estimation error, we also execute the applications at all the GPU frequency points and record the actual runtime along with power consumptions. Fig. 16 shows the estimation error in runtime and power estimation for GPU-only execution. Fig. 16 confirms the applicability of the linear model, which results in a low average estimation error of ≈ 0.5% in runtime and ≈ 1% in power consumption.

CPU estimation

Similar to the estimation for the execution time and power consumption during GPU-only execution, we also obtain the model for CPU-only execution. In order to estimate the effect of DVFS, we sample the execution time and power consumption of the OpenCL kernel at the minimum (200 MHz for $A15$, 200 MHz for $A7$) and maximum (2000 MHz for $A15$, 1400 MHz for $A7$) frequencies for each cluster. We then predict the performance and power for the remaining frequency points. During the OpenCL kernel execution, all the CPU cores are utilized to the maximum 100%

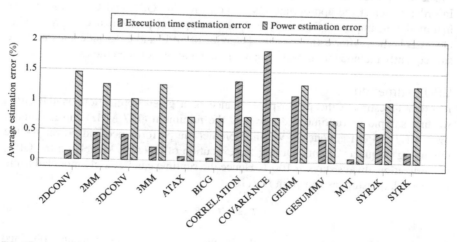

FIG. 16

Estimation error for GPU-only execution averaged across frequencies.

as the *FreeOCL* runtime schedules multiple work-groups to a single CPU core similar to Ref. [30]. Therefore similar to the GPU-only execution, we use the linear model in Eq. (16) to estimate the execution time and Eq. (17) for power consumption at the other CPU frequency settings between the two extremes.

In order to evaluate the accuracy of the proposed technique, we also run the kernel at all possible frequency values to obtain the actual runtime and power consumption for each application. Fig. 17A and B shows this average error in execution time and power estimation for *A15* and *A7* clusters, respectively. The linear model serves well

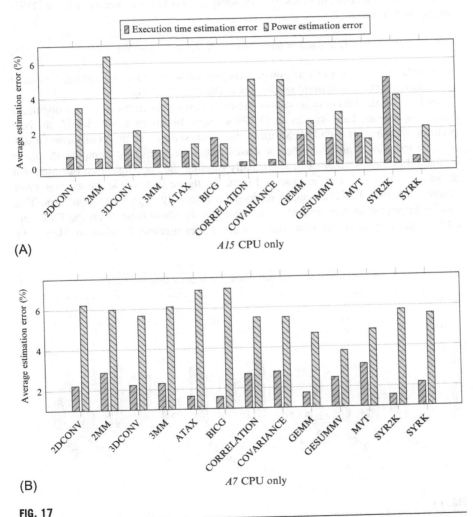

(A) *A15* CPU only

(B) *A7* CPU only

FIG. 17

Estimation error for *A15* CPU-only and *A7* CPU-only executions averaged across frequencies. (A) *A15* CPU only. (B) *A7* CPU only.

in this case and leads to an average estimation error of less than 2% in execution time and less than 6% in power consumption.

Concurrent execution and effect of memory contention

While running the application kernels concurrently on CPU and GPU cores, let us assume that we select a fraction N of the work-items to run on the CPU cores, while the rest run on the GPU at a particular DVFS setting. Now, we need to estimate the execution time and power for concurrent execution. Eq. (18) estimates the runtime for the entire application after partitioning between CPU and GPU, where T_{CPU} and T_{GPU} are the estimated runtimes for CPU-only and GPU-only execution at the DVFS setting, respectively.

$$T_{concurrent} = \max\left(T_{CPU} \times N, T_{GPU} \times (1 - N)\right) \tag{18}$$

In order to estimate the total power consumption in this case, we add the estimated power consumption of individual devices at the DVFS setting.

In Fig. 18, the first columns show the estimation error in runtime for concurrent execution, averaged across various DVFS settings. In this case, we identify the best partitioning point for each DVFS setting (the method to derive this is discussed next), observe the power and runtime for concurrent executions and compute the error compared to values obtained from actually running the application on our platform at similar settings. It can be observed from the figure that, while the average error remains less than 10%, few applications incur relatively large estimation error. This can be attributed to the contention for memory bandwidth between the CPU and GPU, especially in applications that demand larger memory bandwidth. Hence the

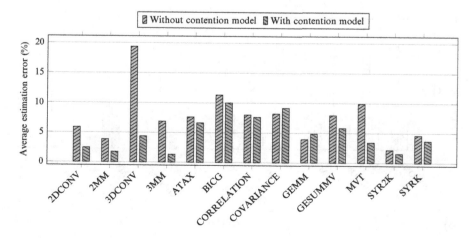

FIG. 18

Runtime estimation error for concurrent execution averaged across different frequency settings.

effect of memory contention must be accounted for while estimating the execution time for concurrent execution.

We model the impact of this contention by obtaining the reduction in the instructions per cycle (IPC) value of a compute device when executing concurrently with another compute device. We first set the GPU at the lowest (177 MHz) and highest (600 MHz) frequencies, while keeping the CPU idle and running the GPU-only portion of the partitioned workload. Next, we again set the GPU at the two extreme frequencies, but this time the CPU runs in parallel with its portion of the partitioned workload. Fig. 19 shows the reduction in the IPC of the GPU because of the sharing of memory bandwidth with the CPU during concurrent execution when compared to the GPU-only execution at the highest GPU frequency. Similar results are also observed at the lowest GPU frequency setting. We used this reduction in IPC at the two extreme GPU frequencies in a linear model to account for the memory contention at other GPU frequencies. This contention effect (reduction in IPC) is then considered while estimating concurrent execution time in order to reduce the estimation error. The second column in Fig. 18 shows the estimation error in execution time averaged across various DVFS settings after incorporating this factor. It can be clearly seen that not only does the average estimation error drop from 7.6% to 4.8%, but also there is a significant reduction in the maximum error. Fig. 20 plots the power estimation error averaged across all DVFS points. It can be seen that the power estimation results are also quite accurate with an average estimation error of 5.1%.

CPU-GPU partitioning ratio

Now we focus on judiciously partitioning the kernels of an OpenCL application between the CPU and GPU based on their individual capabilities. We use a load balancing strategy for each application based on its runtime for CPU-only and

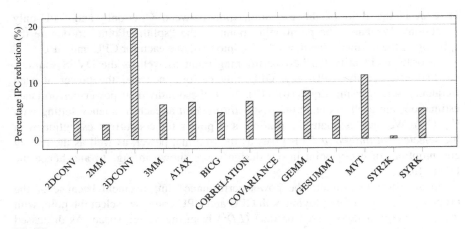

FIG. 19

IPC difference for GPU because of concurrent execution with CPU.

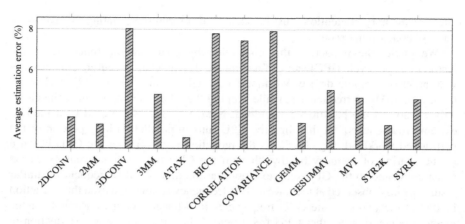

FIG. 20

Power estimation error for concurrent execution averaged across different frequency settings.

GPU-only executions. In essence, this strategy splits the workload between CPU and GPU such that both compute devices take the same amount of time to finish executing their assigned workload portion. We partition the input data (*global_work_size*) of the OpenCL kernels for CPU and GPU before launching them concurrently on the two compute devices. Eq. (19) can be used to obtain the fraction (*split_fraction*) of the *global_work_size* of the application that should be executed on the CPU for the optimal load balancing.

$$N = \frac{1}{(1+m)} \tag{19}$$

Here *m* is the ratio of the execution time between CPU-only and GPU-only executions. We name the partitioning point as the "splittingPoint" to denote the splitting of the original *global_work_size* into two, one each for CPU and GPU.

In order to identify the best partitioning point as well as the DVFS settings, we first estimate the CPU-only, GPU-only performance and the power at each frequency setting using Eqs. (16), (17). Next, these individual power-performance estimations are used to obtain the best *splittingPoint* at each frequency setting with Eq. (19). We then estimate the runtime and power for concurrent execution with the selected *splittingPoint*. This gives us the runtime, power, as well as the energy consumption for every point in our design space shown in Fig. 14 and hence the Pareto-front.

In an effort to evaluate the power-performance improvement because of the proposed approach of employing both GPU and CPU cores, we select the point with the best energy-delay-squared product (ED^2) from the design space. As discussed earlier in Section 3.4, the ED^2 metric gives more weight to the execution time, which ensures minimal execution time degradation while still providing significant power and energy savings. Table 5 shows the DVFS settings (*A15* CPU and GPU) and CPU workload fraction for the best ED^2 design points. The frequency of the *A7* CPU is set at 1400 MHz; however, this is not shown in the table to maintain clarity. Lastly, Fig. 21 shows the respective performance degradation and power savings at optimal ED^2 point (similar to black circles in Fig. 14 for *2DCONV* and *SYR2K* applications) compared to maximum frequency settings (similar to black boxes in Fig. 14 for *2DCONV* and *SYR2K* applications). Most applications exhibit significant power savings with negligible degradation in execution time (less than 10%).

Table 5 Frequency Setting and CPU Workload Fraction for Optimal ED^2

App. Name	Frequency (MHz)		CPU Workload Fraction	App. Name	Frequency (MHz)		CPU Workload Fraction
	CPU	GPU			CPU	GPU	
2DCONV	1000	600	0.21	COVAR	1800	600	0.52
2MM	1600	600	0.37	GEMM	1000	600	0.12
3DCONV	1400	600	0.29	GESUM	1600	600	0.77
3MM	1400	600	0.28	MVT	1000	600	0.30
ATAX	1200	600	0.20	SYR2K	1600	600	0.71
BICG	1000	600	0.22	SYRK	1600	600	0.70
CORR	1800	600	0.52				

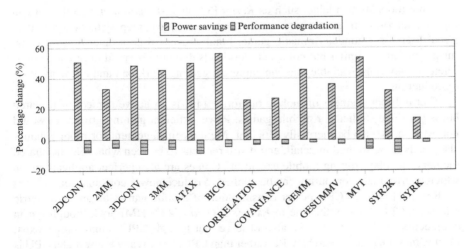

FIG. 21

Power savings and corresponding performance degradation.

4 FUTURE OUTLOOK

We now discuss some problems we believe are still open in power management for mobile GPUs when running gaming or GPGPU applications.

4.1 OPEN PROBLEMS FOR GAMING APPLICATIONS

In this chapter, we presented a gaming governor that operates efficiently by virtue of being sensitive to the complex relationship that mobile CPUs and GPUs exhibit when running mobile games. Still, many questions remain unanswered.

Ideal granularity at which a gaming governor should operate is yet to be found. The gaming governor we presented operated at a granularity of 1 s. In another approach, the gaming governor operates at a granularity of 50 ms [11]. The finer granularity a gaming governor operates at, the more variation in gaming workload it can exploit; but at the same time there is a power cost involved in doing DVFS. It is not clear which approach is better because a direct comparison between the two approaches with same games and same platform is yet to be made.

Research in gaming is held up by the unavailability of sufficient tools. There is no open-source GPU simulator that supports OpenGL; as a result, the impact of change in GPU architecture on power and performance of mobile games cannot be studied. There is also no standardized set of games that forms a comprehensive benchmark suite, where superiority of a gaming governor over other governors can be clearly established. Furthermore, there is no open-source OpenGL game that can match the sophistication of popular closed source games that are now ubiquitous on mobile platforms. This severely limits the ability of researchers to study the impact of source code and openGL compiler optimizations on a mobile game's power-efficiency.

Some tools are available, such as *Reran* [38] and *MonkeyGamer* [39], that can replay a deterministic game, but no tool allows automatic gameplay that can simulate a real user for a nondeterministic game. Finally, every time a deterministic game runs, it produces similar but not exact workloads that are observed in previous runs. There are no tools available that can capture a gaming workload and allow its exact reproduction.

Thermal management of mobile platforms [40] is an active subject of research but is yet to be studied for mobile games. Power-efficient gaming governors would not necessarily also be thermally efficient. Memory management for mobile games also needs to be studied in detail, and it still remains to be seen what role the shared memory bus plays during mobile execution. Games are also perfect applications on which approximate computing can be applied to reduce power consumption.

Ref. [41] reduces CPU power consumption of mobile games on an asymmetric multicore CPU such as the one in *Exynos 5 Octa (5422)* HMPSoC, though not in conjunction with the GPU. We also observe that though CPU-bound games exist, most games are constrained by GPU rather than CPU. We already know that a CPU is capable of performing GPU workloads, so a GPU workload division can be explored similar to the workload partitioning performed in GPGPU applications.

4.2 OPEN PROBLEMS FOR GPGPU APPLICATIONS

In this chapter, we discussed the identification of energy-efficient design points for GPGPU applications targeting mobile GPUs. However, we also observed that at higher frequencies (close to the maximum frequency), the HMPSoC quickly exhausts its thermal headroom and begins to throttle the CPU and GPU. This leads to a less than expected performance and also raises reliability concerns. In our current setup, we reinforced our HMPSoC with additional cooling measures to avoid such a scenario. In the future, the thermal budget can be taken into account while selecting the DVFS settings in order to proactively avoid hitting the thermal wall [42].

In addition, more complex applications, such as image processing and speech recognition, with multiple kernels can also be targeted toward mobile GPUs. However, as discussed in the Section 3, the accompanying CPU cores in the HMPSoC will also play an important role in these applications in order to achieve both performance and energy-efficiency. The workload partitioning between the GPU and CPU cores is a nontrivial task in the face of different power-performance trade-offs, multiple DVFS settings, and dynamic core scaling possibilities in such platforms.

The shared memory bandwidth between the CPU and GPU in a HMPSoC also poses additional challenges, as discussed earlier. The static solution proposed in this work might not provide optimal results in mobile phones when multiple applications are launched randomly to run on the CPU or GPU. Hence a runtime technique is necessary in such cases to monitor the memory traffic and perform appropriate DVFS of CPU and/or GPU to mitigate this effect.

The latest HMPSoCs discussed in this chapter contain performance heterogeneous *ARM big.Little* CPUs. The OpenCL runtime, however, treats them as similar processing elements and schedules the threads evenly across all CPU cores. In the future, the OpenCL runtime can be improved to take into account the performance heterogeneity of the processors, while also considering the CPU-GPU functional heterogeneity.

5 CONCLUSIONS

In this chapter, we first described the current state-of-the-art techniques for power management in mobile devices for both games and GPGPU applications. After identifying the limitations of the existing work, we discussed our latest power management techniques for these applications.

For games, a gaming-specific governor was presented that detects bottlenecks in CPU and GPU, and then accordingly increases the frequency of the bottlenecked component just enough to meet the game's FPS target. The proposed governor reduced a HMPSoC's power on average by 29% in comparison to the on-board stock Linux governor.

Next, we presented a static approach to save power and energy for GPGPU applications running on HMPSoCs. We considered the effect of contention because of the shared memory resources in a HMPSoC. Along with the appropriate partitioning of the OpenCL kernels to run on both CPU and GPU concurrently, suitable CPU-GPU DVFS settings were identified to save power and energy without a significant loss in performance. The approach saved more than 39% of power with minimal loss in performance when compared to the execution of GPGPU applications at the highest CPU-GPU DVFS setting.

Finally, we also identified possible future directions for research on reducing the power consumption of mobile GPUs while executing games or GPGPU applications. The rapid growth in the capabilities of the mobile GPUs as well as the other processing elements on HMPSoCs will continue to demand more sophisticated power management techniques.

ACKNOWLEDGMENTS

This work was partially supported by Singapore Ministry of Education Academic Research Fund Tier 2 MOE2012-T2-1-115 and CSR research funding.

REFERENCES

[1] E. Hutchins, SC10: a video processor and pixel-shading GPU for handheld devices, in: Hot Chips Conference, 2004.

[2] T. Mitra, Heterogeneous Multi-core architectures, IPSJ Transactions on System LSI Design Methodology, 8 (2015) 51–62.

[3] AnandTech, http://www.anandtech.com/.

[4] M. Shafique, S. Garg, T. Mitra, S. Parameswaran, J. Henkel, Dark silicon as a challenge for hardware/software co-design, in: Conference on Hardware/Software Codesign and System Synthesis (CODES + ISSS), 2014.

[5] J. Henkel, H. Khdr, S. Pagani, M. Shafique, New trends in dark silicon, in: Design Automation Conference (DAC), 2015.

[6] V. Pallipadi, A. Starikovskiy, The ondemand governor, in: Linux Symposium, 2006.

[7] Y. Gu, S. Chakraborty, W.T. Ooi, Games are up for DVFS, in: Design Automation Conference (DAC), 2006.

[8] S.-R. Kuang, K.-Y. Wu, B.-C. Ke, J.-H. Yeh, H.-Y. Jheng, Efficient architecture and hardware implementation of hybrid Fuzzy-Kalman filter for workload prediction, Integr. VLSI J. 47 (2014) 408–416.

[9] B. Anand, A.L. Ananda, M.C. Chan, L.T. Le, R.K. Balan, Game action based power management for multiplayer online game, in: Workshop on Networking, Systems, and Applications for Mobile Handhelds (MOBIHeld), 2009.

[10] B. Sun, X. Li, J. Song, Z. Cheng, Y. Xu, X. Zhou, Texture-directed mobile GPU power management for closed-source games, in: International Conf on High Performance Computing and Communications (HPCC), 2014.

[11] D. Kadjo, R. Ayoub, M. Kishinevsky, P.V. Gratz, A control-theoretic approach for energy efficient CPU-GPU subsystem in mobile platforms, in: Design Automation Conference (DAC), ACM, 2015.

[12] A. Pathania, A.E. Irimiea, A. Prakash, T. Mitra, Power-performance modelling of mobile gaming workloads on heterogeneous MPSoCs, in: Design Automation Conference (DAC), 2015.

[13] A. Pathania, Q. Jiao, A. Prakash, T. Mitra, Integrated CPU-GPU power management for 3D mobile games, in: Design Automation Conference (DAC), 2014.

[14] D. Grewe, Z. Wang, M.F.P. OBoyle, OpenCL task partitioning in the presence of GPU contention, in: International Workshop on Languages and Compilers for Parallel Computing (LCPC), 2014 .

[15] C.-K. Luk, S. Hong, H. Kim, Qilin: exploiting parallelism on heterogeneous multi-processors with adaptive mapping, in: International Symposium on Microarchitecture (MICRO), 2009.

[16] P. Pandit, R. Govindarajan, Fluidic kernels: cooperative execution of OpenCL programs on multiple heterogeneous devices, in: International Symposium on Code Generation and Optimization (CGO), 2014.

[17] Y. Wen, Z. Wang, M. OBoyle, Smart multi-task scheduling for OpenCL programs on CPU/GPU heterogeneous platforms, in: International Conference on High Performance Computing (HiPC), 2014.

[18] D. Grewe, M.F.P. OBoyle, A static task partitioning approach for heterogeneous systems using OpenCL, in: Compiler Construction (CC), 2011 .

[19] H. Wang, V. Sathish, R. Singh, M.J. Schulte, N.S. Kim, Workload and power budget partitioning for single-chip heterogeneous processors, in: International Conference on Parallel Architectures and Compilation Techniques (PACT), 2012.

[20] I. Paul, V. Ravi, S. Manne, M. Arora, S. Yalamanchili, Coordinated energy management in heterogeneous processors, in: Scientific Programming (SP), 2013.

[21] H. Wang, R. Singh, M.J. Schulte, N.S. Kim, Memory scheduling towards high-throughput cooperative heterogeneous computing, in: International Conference on Parallel Architectures and Compilation Techniques (PACT), 2014.

[22] N. Singhal, I.K. Park, S. Cho, Implementation and optimization of image process-ing algorithms on handheld GPU, in: International Conference on Image Processing (ICIP), 2010.

[23] N. Singhal, J.W. Yoo, H.Y. Choi, I.K. Park, Implementation and optimization of image processing algorithms on embedded GPU, IEICE Trans. Inf. Syst. E95.D (2012) 1475–1484.

[24] K.-T. Cheng, Y.-C. Wang, Using mobile GPU for general-purpose computing—a case study of face recognition on smartphones, in: International Symposium on VLSI Design, Automation and Test (VLSI-DAT), 2011.

[25] M.B. Lopez, H. Nykanen, J. Hannuksela, O. Silvén, M. Vehviläinen, Accelerating image recognition on mobile devices using GPGPU, SPIE Electron. Imaging 7872 (2011) 78720R.

[26] B. Rister, G. Wang, M. Wu, J. R Cavallaro, A fast and efficient SIFT detector using the mobile GPU, in: International Conference on Acoustics, Speech and Signal Processing (ICASSP), 2013.

[27] I. Grasso, P. Radojkovic, N. Rajovic, I. Gelado, A. Ramirez, Energy efficient HPC on embedded SoCs: optimization techniques for mali GPU, in: Parallel and Distributed Processing Symposium (PDPS), 2014.

[28] A. Maghazeh, U.D. Bordoloi, P. Eles, Z. Peng, General purpose computing on low-power embedded GPUs: has it come of age?, in: International Conference on Embedded Computer Systems: Architectures, Modeling, and Simulation (SAMOS), 2013.

[29] K. Chandramohan, M.F.P. O'Boyle, Partitioning data-parallel programs for heterogeneous MPSoCs: time and energy design space exploration, in: Conference on Languages, Compilers and Tools for Embedded System (LCTES), 2014.

[30] G. Jo, W.J. Jeon, W. Jung, G. Taft, J. Lee, OpenCL framework for ARM processors with NEON support, in: Workshop on Programming models for SIMD/Vector processing (WPMVP), 2014.

[31] FreeOCL: multi-platform implementation of OpenCL 1.2 targeting CPUs, https://goo.gl/qWL1Eg.

[32] S. Seo, J. Lee, G. Jo, J. Lee, Automatic OpenCL work-group size selection for multicore CPUs, in: International Conference on Parallel Architectures and Compilation Techniques (PACT), 2013.

[33] A. Prakash, S. Wang, A.E. Irimiea, T. Mitra, Energy-efficient execution of data-parallel applications on heterogeneous mobile platforms, in: International Conference on Computer Design (ICCD), 2015.

[34] Odroid-XU3, http://goo.gl/Nn6z3O.

[35] POCL: portable computing language, http://portablecl.org/.

[36] S. Grauer-Gray, L. Xu, R. Searles, S. Ayalasomayajula, J. Cavazos, Auto-tuning a high-level language targeted to GPU codes, in: Innovative Parallel Computing (InPar), 2012.

[37] ARM Mali-T600 series GPU OpenCL, version 2.0, developer guide, http://goo.gl/R0FKs8.

[38] L. Gomez, I. Neamtiu, T. Azim, T. Millstein, Reran: timing-and touch-sensitive record and replay for Android, in: International Conference on Software Engineering (ICSE), 2013.

[39] J.M. Santos, S. Nadjm-Tehrani, A.P. Bianzino, Monkey Gamer: automatic profiling of Android games, in: International Conference on Mobile Computing, Applications and Services (MobiCASE), 2014.

[40] O. Sahin, P.T. Varghese, A.K. Coskun, Just enough is more: achieving sustainable performance in mobile devices under thermal limitations, in: International Conference on Computer-Aided Design (ICCAD), 2015.

[41] A. Pathania, S. Pagani, M. Shafique, J. Henkel, Power management for mobile games on asymmetric multi-cores, in: International Symposium on Low Power Electronics and Design (ISLPED), 2015.

[42] S. Pagani, H. Khdr, W. Munawar, J.-J. Chen, M. Shafique, M. Li, J. Henkel, TSP: thermal safe power: efficient power budgeting for many-core systems in dark silicon, in: Conference on Hardware/Software Codesign and System Synthesis (CODES + ISSS), 2014.

Advances in GPU reliability research 22

J. Wadden, K. Skadron

University of Virginia, Charlottesville, VA, United States

1 INTRODUCTION

When writing any type of software, programmers must rely on a set contract that describes the instructions and the exact instruction semantics for a particular architecture. This contract can be as low-level as the instruction set architecture (ISA) for a particular processor, or as high-level as a programming language such as C or Compute Unified Device Architecture (CUDA). Whatever the contract, it must be consulted to ensure correct implementation of an algorithm on the underlying machine model.

While hardware/software contracts may vary between different architectures and programming languages, we generally assume one underlying premise: *executed instructions will behave according to the contract*. In other words, the contract is *never* broken by the hardware. This is a simple and perhaps obvious assumption that is often overlooked by programmers. However, in practice, this assumption is impossible to guarantee. For example, an ISA might include an addition instruction that says $1 + 1$ will return 2 when executed, but manufacturing defects, voltage noise, malicious attacks, or acts of nature might cause the processor to return 3! Note that some errors may occur from limitations of precision (e.g., in floating point) or from undefined behavior (e.g., $\times 86$ integer overflow), but these errors are known properties of the system and thus considered a part of the contract. In computing environments where breaches of the hardware/software contract are becoming increasingly hard to prevent, we must acknowledge in both hardware and software architecture some nontrivial chance of unexpected, incorrect behavior.

In this chapter, we will motivate GPU reliability as an important, if often overlooked problem, and discuss the current state-of-the-art in GPU reliability research. Unsurprisingly, GPUs are designed and sold primarily to satisfy graphics applications, which traditionally require a low level of reliability. However, computing's recent adoption of GPUs as high-throughput, data-parallel coprocessors has elevated their reliability requirements almost to that of server processors. Unfortunately, for

Advances in GPU Research and Practice. http://dx.doi.org/10.1016/B978-0-12-803738-6.00022-7

617

both economic and practical reasons, architectural enhancements for improving GPU reliability have lagged significantly behind this new use case, motivating intense research focus in this area.

Section 1.1 will first present common reliability terminology, how GPUs fail in real systems, and the difficulty in preventing radiation-induced soft errors. Section 1.2 will present a brief history of GPUs as coprocessors, their economics, and will frame the current issues with GPU reliability. Section 1.3 will present results from studies on real distributed systems and supercomputers showing alarming rates of soft errors, and motivating reliability as a first-class design constraint for future GPUs. The rest of the sections in this chapter will discuss different proposed methods of evaluating and improving GPU reliability. Section 2 will introduce studies of architectural vulnerability factor (AVF) and program vulnerability factor (PVF) modeling (Section 2.1), fault-injection (Section 2.2), and accelerated beam testing (Section 2.3) as methods for evaluating and predicting reliability of real systems. Section 3 will survey state-of-the-art approaches to improving reliability via hardware enhancements to a GPU's micro-architecture. Section 4 will then survey state-of-the-art approaches to improving reliability via software enhancements to kernel code running on the GPU.

1.1 RADIATION-INDUCED SOFT ERRORS

While we often assume that combinational logic and storage elements on CPUs and GPUs always work correct any processors constructed using a traditional complementary metal oxide semiconductor manufacturing process are vulnerable to both permanent (hard) and transient (soft) failures or faults. Permanent faults are failures that manifest as stuck-at bits in the architecture, that is, lines that always carry the logical signal "0" or "1" as the result of a short or open circuit. These faults can be caused by many different physical processes from normal operation, for example, thermal stress, electromigration, hot carrier injection, gate oxide wear-out, and negative bias temperature instability (see Shubu Mukherjee's book on architecture design for soft errors [1] for a more detailed discussion of these failure modes). While permanent faults may cause undesirable behavior, they are relatively easy to identify and eliminate because their incorrect output is consistent and they are isolated to a particular piece of hardware. To reduce the likelihood of permanent faults, techniques such as "burn-in" can be used to stress test hardware and identify failures before a processor enters its useful lifetime [1]. Periodic stress and check tests can also be run on the system in question to determine if permanent faults have developed over time [2]. Not only are permanent faults fairly easy to identify, they are also fairly easy to eliminate, because faulty hardware can simply be fixed or replaced. Because of this, researchers generally focus their efforts on protecting CPUs and GPUs against the more insidious *transient fault*. We therefore focus this chapter on state-of-the-art research into mitigating the effects of transient faults.

As the name suggests, transient faults are not permanent and may cause only a transistor or gate to malfunction for a short period of time. Transient faults can be caused by crosstalk between wires, voltage noise, and other types of electromagnetic interference. However, we typically associate transient faults with random high-energy particle strikes [3]. Particles that strike a chip have the potential to inject charge into the silicon, and if enough charge is injected, the transistor or gate may drive the wrong value temporarily. We call these temporary faults single-event upsets (SEUs) or, if more than one gate is affected, single-event multibit upsets (SEMUs) [1]. SEUs may be harmless if they are not permanently recorded; however, if an SEU occurs directly within a storage cell, such as a flip-flop on-chip, an incorrect value may be captured; if an SEU occurs in combinational logic, it may propagate incorrect values to storage cells. SEUs that are captured and committed to program output are referred to as silent data corruptions (SDC).

While the words *fault* and *error* are often used interchangeably, we use the same definitions in Shubu Mukherjee's book on architecture design for soft errors [1] to distinguish between the two. A *fault* is any failure, for example, the device, for example, an SEU or SEMU; an *error* is a user-identified fault within a particular protection domain. A fault that goes undetected but ultimately changes user-visible program output is an SDC. A fault that does not ultimately affect program output is said to be *masked*. Errors that are known, but cannot be recovered from are referred to as detected unrecoverable errors (DUEs). At first glance, an SDC and DUE may seem equally terrible, in both situations our data have been corrupted! However, it is hard to overstate how much more insidious SDCs are than DUEs. Not knowing if an output is correct or incorrect means that your results may be wrong. For important calculations with high correctness requirements, this is simply unacceptable. SDCs represent a breach in the software/hardware contract that software developers may not be able to tolerate. If we could at least guarantee that all SDCs be converted to DUEs, a system could guide a user to conclude that some portion of their results are useless, and should be discarded, or to engage an appropriate recovery mechanisms such as reverting to the last checkpoint, or restarting the computation. Our goal is therefore to practically eliminate the occurrence of SDCs, and preserve the integrity of the software/hardware contract, while keeping DUEs (that might require time-consuming recovery computation) to a minimum.

Fortunately, transient faults and soft errors are rare occurrences, and may happen on the order of one in tens-of-thousands of operating hours per device. We refer to this as the *soft-error rate* (SER) of a device, and it is a closely guarded secret of any silicon device vendor. Because typically, suspected SERs are longer than the useful lifetime of many GPUs, and the fact that GPUs are generally used for low-stakes gaming or graphics applications, GPU reliability has traditionally been ignored [4]. In the next section, we will look at evidence to support why GPU reliability has been considered a low priority, the economics hindering GPU vendors from adopting more aggressive soft error protection, and the pitfalls of using unreliable hardware in large-node high-performance computing (HPC) systems.

1.2 GPUs AS HPC COPROCESSORS

Even in high-stakes computation, a single SDC every 5 years might be a low enough SER to ignore. However, in high-node-count data centers or HPC supercomputers, with tens of thousands of nodes, an application using the whole system might experience an SDC on the order of hours or even minutes! This means that any product that is used in HPC (including GPUs) must be extremely robust. Because of this, GPUs were not even considered for high-node-count clusters until after they first gained error correcting code (ECC) support. NVIDIA's Fermi microarchitecture was the first GPU to include ECC on all off-chip GDDR RAM and on-chip static RAM (SRAM) structures in 2009 [5]. Fermi was immediately adopted for HPC use and powered three out of the top five supercomputers in the world in 2010 [6]. Titan, Oak Ridge National Labs' supercomputer, the second largest supercomputer in the world as of the writing of this chapter, originally had 18,688 NVIDIA Fermi GPUs, but was upgraded to house newer Kepler GPUs in 2013. Adding features to GPU architectures (such as more resilient cell design or ECC to even more SRAM regions) to gain parity with server CPU reliability standards is a logical next step over ECC support; however, this is prohibitively expensive for the vendor because HPC does not support a large enough proportion of total revenue to justify the cost.

GPGPU-specific products like NVIDIA's Tesla line are a growing part of overall GPU vendor revenue, but graphics processing units (GPUs) are and will continue to be sold primarily for gaming and graphics applications in the near future. NVIDIA does not publish the proportion of GPU cards sold for GPGPU applications versus gaming, but the company has mentioned yearly revenue from GPGPU products being on the order of "several hundred million dollars" [7]. Given that NVIDIA's yearly revenue is almost 5 billion dollars, the GPGPU market probably accounts for between 5–8% of total revenue. While this is a significant portion, and is a quickly growing segment of NVIDIA's total revenue, it is not enough to justify architectural changes to improve reliability if those changes do not also positively impact the graphics business. In the future we may see scientific computing and HPC become healthy enough businesses to justify their own derivative product, but for now GPUs will remain focused on increasing gaming and graphics performance.

1.3 EVIDENCE OF SOFT ERRORS IN HPC SYSTEMS

Because device SER rates are so closely guarded by CPU, GPU, and DRAM vendors, identifying even rough SER estimates for large node supercomputers is challenging, if not impossible. However, many CPUs and GPUs contain special registers that log parity, and ECC events, and other pipeline exceptions. By querying these counters in the field, researchers can get a reasonable approximation for the SER for individual components. In this section we present the state-of-the-art field studies analyzing GPU failures and SER in real systems. Following sections will present other methods for evaluating GPU SER rates, but we present field studies on real HPC systems here to motivate GPU reliability as an important problem and to motivate research into practical GPU reliability solutions.

Field studies examining failures in DRAM because of hard and soft errors were first conducted on large distributed systems by Li et al. [8] and Schroeder et al. [9]. This work showed that hard faults could be distinguished from soft faults by looking at temporal locality of errors. The main insight being that it is extremely unlikely that frequent errors in the same memory location are caused by random and infrequent particle strikes, thus recurring errors in the same location are most likely hard errors. Results showed failures were mainly dominated by hard errors in DRAM modules, but the study ultimately could not reliably distinguish between hard and soft errors without root access to machines. Sridharan et al. conducted a larger and more precise study of DRAM failures on Los Alamos National Lab's Jaguar supercomputer [10]. Jaguar was an ideal choice for examining hard and SERs for two reasons: (1) it had an extremely high node count (18,688 CPUs) with every node containing identical hardware, and (2) it resides at a high altitude (7500 ft) where cosmic radiation is measurably more intense than at sea level. Results showed that approximately 30% of all DRAM failures could be attributed to soft faults, and that the entire system experienced about 900 faults per month, or a little more than 1 fault per hour! Newer studies suggest that soft faults are a smaller proportion of overall faults, and may be as low as 1.5% when accounting for faults in the entire memory path (including memory controllers, busses, channels), rather than just memory modules [11].

While DRAM is an important piece of a system, the preceding studies did not look at on-die SRAM or logic failure rates in CPUs and GPUs. Modern studies have taken care to distinguish between DRAM and SRAM failures and have found that SRAM faults are dominated by transient faults. Sridharan et al. conducted an experiment on the Cielo and Jaguar supercomputers that showed 98% of faults in L2 and L3 SRAM structures were transient faults [12]. Interestingly, the same study also showed a correlation between error rates and position of the processor in a server rack. The higher the processor, the more likely it was to experience a soft fault, indicating that CPUs in lower racks may be shielded from cosmic rays by the upper racks.

The first large-scale field study of GPU failure rates was conducted on the Blue Waters supercomputer at the University of Illinois [13]. The study showed that GPU DDR5 had 10× more soft errors than the DDR3 main memory and that GPU cards were by far the least reliable component in the system, but the authors did not study on-chip SRAM failures. Haque et al. [2] conducted a study on the Folding@Home network of distributed computers looking at DRAM memory errors in consumer-grade GPU cards. Controlled experiments found no errors, but examination of consumer-grade GPUs from the large scale, 20,000 GPU-distributed system revealed patterned hard errors in two-thirds of the cards. These errors were highly correlated with GPU architecture, indicating that the memory systems of more modern GPU architectures and server-grade compute GPUs such as the NVIDIA's Tesla line were indeed more reliable than gaming products—although the reason for this difference was not identified. More recently, a study looked at GPU DRAM and on-chip SRAM error rates in nodes on the Titan supercomputer at Oak Ridge National Labs and the Moonlight cluster at Los Alamos National Labs. Experiments on the Titan showed that over 18 months, 899 of the 18,688 GPUs experienced at least 1 error, an average of 1.66 per day across the entire system [14].

Ultimately, because SDCs must be identified by comparing program output to a gold standard, the SERs identified in these studies underestimate the total number of data corruptions. While the SDC and SER rates are hard to experimentally verify, the next chapter discusses how to evaluate how vulnerable GPUs are to soft errors using accelerated particle beam testing, and simulated fault-injection vulnerability analysis.

2 EVALUATING GPU RELIABILITY

Field studies give us a very broad, blunt tool to examine both hard and soft faults on systems, but the practical difficulty of conducting such experiments and the imprecise nature of their results and conclusions lead researchers to examine artificially injected faults in architectural simulations as an alternative tool to asses processor and program reliability. Such simulations allow architects to glean information about reliability of structures in an architecture and the relative susceptibility of programs to soft errors, without the need for large and expensive experiments on real hardware. In the extreme case, researchers will use particle accelerators to greatly increase the SER rate in a single chip in a real system. "Beam tests" can quickly isolate the effects of hard errors from soft errors and isolate failures in a single piece of silicon from failures in the rest of the system, without the need for an arduous field study. The following sections present current efforts in GPU software simulation and architectural vulnerability analysis in simulation, fault-injection tools for simulating faults in real hardware, and current, state-of-the-art beam testing practice.

2.1 ARCHITECTURAL AND PROGRAM VULNERABILITY ANALYSIS

When adding any features to a processor, simulation is often used to perform a cost-benefit analysis. Does the feature increase instructions per cycle (IPC) in benchmark suites enough to justify the transistor real estate and engineering effort necessary to include it in the next iteration? This analysis is relatively straightforward in simulation because one can easily measure improvements in IPC, memory system performance, and utilization, but how would we quantify increased reliability? Architectural vulnerability analysis attempts this feat by tracking every bit in an architecture during the run of a program and calculating how likely it is to affect the program output.

Consider a bit stored in any sequential logic or memory cell in a processor; if we change the value of that bit, will it cause incorrect program output? Naively we might assume "of course!" but there are many structures in CPUs and GPUs where state is either stored solely for performance enhancement, or never read at all. Take, for instance, a branch target buffer where predicted addresses are stored in an SRAM structure on-chip. If we flip a bit in a target address, how will this affect the *correctness* of the program if that target address is read as a prediction? If the address is a correct prediction before the SEU and the bit-flip creates an incorrect prediction, then we have simply wasted a performance opportunity and forced a mispredict. In the off chance it was an incorrect prediction, and the bit-flip created a correct prediction, then the fault accidentally increased performance. In either case, the performance of the program may have been affected, but the correctness was never compromised. In this sense, the bits in a branch target buffer are *invulnerable*, in that they are not required for architecturally correct execution (ACE). We refer to these invulnerable bits as *un-ACE*, and any bits required for correct execution as ACE. All idle or invalid state, misspeculated state, and predictor structures are un-ACE. State that is never read is un-ACE, and instructions that produce state that is never read are un-ACE! We refer to these instructions that never affect program output as *dynamically dead*. We refer to instructions whose results are used only by dynamically dead instructions as *transitively dynamically dead*, as they are also not required for correct execution.

An example of a structure where bits are ACE most of the time is the CPU's program counter. If we flip a bit in the program counter, will it affect correct execution? Probably! Jumping to random locations in a program would almost certainly cause incorrect output or a program exception. However, some bits, even those in the program counter, are not ACE all the time. Consider the program counter just before a new instruction address is written to the register. The program counter could literally have *any* value before being written to, and therefore the bits are un-ACE until immediately after the write. An entire instruction becomes dynamically dead if its results are never read or never used for ACE computation, for example, if the program halts.

Because the ACEness of a bit or instruction may depend on dynamic behavior, we use the proportion of cycles a bit is ACE over the total number of program cycles as a measure of vulnerability to soft errors. This ratio is called the *architectural vulnerability factor* or AVF and is a measure of the likelihood a change in any individual bit will result in incorrect program output. Because practically calculating the AVF of every individual bit in an architecture requires fast and accurate register transfer language (RTL) models of processors, researchers often use Little's Law [1] to calculate the average AVF of bits in a structure. Little's Law states that the AVF of a bit in a structure is the bandwidth of ACE bits entering the structure per cycle, times the average number of cycles a bit resides in the structure, divided by the total number of bits in the structure. This method of AVF calculation allows for relatively easy integration into existing performance simulators. Once estimated, AVFs can be used to navigate the cost/benefit of enhancing the reliability of structures in a CPU or GPU. For instance, why add expensive ECC to the entries of the branch target buffer if it has an AVF near zero and is rarely required for correct execution?

Because AVF is derived from runs of many different programs, and ignores program specific reliability, Sridharan et al. introduced the concept of PVF [15]. PVF is a micro-architecturally independent measurement of architectural program reliability. Sridharan adapted ACE analysis such that the reliability of software resources can be measured, just as traditional ACE analysis can identify the AVF of hardware resources of a micro-architecture. PVF works by calculating the ACEness of instruction-level resources, such as a register, during the lifetime of that instruction, until it is committed. In this way, PVF calculation of architectural program resources (such as registers) can approximate the vulnerability of the program across any micro-architecture.

CPU AVF analysis has been well researched since it was introduced by Shubu Mukherjee in 2003 [16]. Results from their simulations of an Itanium2 processor found that only 46% of instructions were ACE for combined integer and floating-point benchmarks [1]. Today, AVF continues to be an important part of reliability, availability, and serviceability (RAS) architecture strategy.

GPU AVF analysis was only recently motivated after GPU inclusion into HPC systems. Previously, single node reliability was never important enough to justify fine-grained analysis. When first included in HPC systems, GPU architects simply added single error correct, double error detect (SEC-DED) ECC on all of their large SRAM structures such as the instruction and data L1 caches, L2 cache, and register files. This is a reasonable but conservative and expensive strategy for reliability, and does not address the reliability of every part of a GPU's pipeline. Ideally AVF analysis could identify which high-priority structures require the most protection, and conversely which presumed high-priority structures are overprotected.

Tan et al. [17] and Farazmand et al. [18] were the first to study AVFs of GPU structures. Their studies showed that GPU AVFs varied highly depending on the studied software and the software's relative utilization of different hardware structures on the GPU, where higher utilization of a structure corresponded with a higher AVF of that structure. Farazmand et al. were the first to study GPU AVF in comparison to CPUs and found that the AVFs of relatively larger GPU structures, like the GPU's massive vector register files, were usually much lower than corresponding structures in CPUs. These low AVFs can be attributed to low thread occupancy, or low utilization of the register file, or the GPU's scratchpad memory. Intuitively, this makes sense; if a GPU streaming multiprocessor (SM) contains a massive 256 KB register file, but threads are only allocated 25 KB of registers, the AVF for that structure should be approximately $10\times$ lower than a fully utilized structure. In contrast, a CPU's register file state is generally much smaller, on the order of 1 KB, but usually has a much higher utilization than a GPU's register file.

Jeon et al. [19] performed the first integrated CPU-GPU AVF analysis (called accelerated processing units or APUs in Advanced Micro Devices (AMD) terminology) and showed how AVFs of structures in the CPU and integrated GPU varied over time. The motivation for this study lies in the uniqueness of a truly heterogeneous integrated system with a shared memory hierarchy, where both CPU and GPU AVF must be accounted for wholistically. This work presented two interesting conclusions that highlight the complexity of GPU AVF in contrast to CPU AVF analysis.

(1) *AVF of massive GPU structures is generally low, but corresponding SERs can be extremely high.* Similar to prior studies, GPU register file AVF was found to be very low (around 0–1.5% depending on the application) because of low utilization in the structure, that is, any individual bit-flip has a low likelihood of affecting program output. However, even though the per-bit AVF of the register file may be low, because a GPU's register file is so large, the overall failure rate of the structure is *extremely* high. To calculate the SER of a structure, per-bit AVF must be multiplied by the size of the structure and the transistor process dependent raw failure rate. Jeon et al. found that after adjusting for these factors, the GPU's, register file SER was up to three orders of magnitude larger than the CPU's, due primarily to the fact that a CPU's register file is hundreds of times smaller than the register file of even a single GPU SM or compute unit (CU). This finding motivates *higher* levels of protection on the GPU's register file, rather than lower levels the simple AVF would suggest. As an architect, this is frustrating. We would like our ECC to have a large bang for its buck, but in the case of the massive register files in GPUs, ECC is necessary on every bit but rarely taken advantage of because of GPU register file underutilization.

(2) *AVF is highly time dependent in an integrated CPU-GPU architecture.* If the CPU is doing computation, and not offloading computation to the GPU, the AVF of a GPU's structures is implicitly zero. On the other hand, when the GPU is doing computation, the AVF or SER of structures can be extremely high. Just as the size of GPU structures decreases the "bang for the buck" of ECC, this "bursty" nature of GPU vulnerability also reduces the "bang for the buck" of ECC protection. While average AVF may be low over the runtime of an application across GPUs and CPUs, some GPU structures intermittently require very high reliability and protection. Thus ECC is a required addition to the architecture, but is rarely used on average.

2.2 FAULT-INJECTION

AVF analysis is extremely useful for doing fast design-space exploration and for setting early upper bounds on the vulnerability of processor structures. However, it is fundamentally a conservative analysis, as it assumes that a bit is ACE until it is proven to be otherwise. Both a lack of micro-architectural detail in performance simulators and a difficulty in adding such detail (either because of a lack of proprietary knowledge or prohibitive engineering effort) contribute to underestimating the practical reliability of the architecture [20]. Furthermore, even if one has access to a representative cycle-accurate simulator, or RTL description, AVF analysis fails to account for fault-induced changes in program behavior that may not actually affect program output. AVF analysis usually does not consider a program's final result and instead analytically arrives at a probability of incorrect execution, whether or not that incorrect execution causes a user-visible error.

A much more straightforward, but more reactive, approach to examining reliability of architectures is *fault-injection*. Fault-injection randomly induces a bit-flip into a running program, either architecturally in the ISA, micro-architecturally into a structure such as a register file, or into a storage bit in an architecture at the RTL model level. Once a fault is injected, the fault-injection tool looks for changes in user-visible output by comparing to a precomputed golden run; if a change is exhibited, the fault is manifested as an SDC, and is recorded. By looking at injected faults and how they affect program output, architects can get a broad sense for how reliable structures are, at least in relation to each other.

Fault-injection can be done on either presilicon (such as on an RTL-level processor simulator) or on real hardware to evaluate the reliability of production GPUs. In simulation, fault-injection is useful for evaluating the reliability gained from proposed reliability enhancing structures such as ECC, redundant execution units, or redundantly executed code, things which AVF and ACE analysis do not consider. In our upcoming discussion, we will present tools capable of performing fault-injection on real GPUs. Simulated fault-injection studies and methodologies will be discussed as a part of the proposed hardware-based reliability research.

Performing fault-injection is a fairly simple task: stop the simulation or processor, pick a structure in the GPU to inject a fault in a systematic and controlled manner, modify that structure to reflect a hypothetical transient fault, let the program run, and record whether or not the output recorded an SDC. While simple, fault-injection can be extremely time consuming. There are an extremely large number of configurations that the GPU could be in at any one time. On every cycle, any one of literally thousands to hundreds of thousands of GPU thread contexts could be affected. Therefore, fault-injection experiments on both CPUs and GPUs suffer from a dilemma. We can either perform a fast experiment with a low number of injected faults, but at the risk of not properly characterizing the reliability of the GPU, or we can spend a large amount of computational power, over tens of thousands of trials, over many benchmarks, properly characterizing the reliability of a GPU. For the purposes of properly executed science, researchers, begrudgingly, are forced to choose the latter option.

To address this issue, researchers have decided to inject faults at a higher level of abstraction than at the RTL model layer. Yim et al. developed SWIFI [21], a fault-injection framework that uses a source-to-source translator to modify programs before they are run. SWIFI was able to perform 10,000 fault-injection experiments per tested application. Unfortunately, SWIFI's source-level software abstraction is too coarse-grained to accurately reflect the impact of faults at the micro-architectural level or the assembly instruction layer.

GPU-Qin [22], developed by Bo et al, attempts to solve this problem by injecting faults at the GPU architectural layer, using the debugging tool *cuda-gdb* [23]. Cuda-gdb can be used as an external hook into a running CUDA program to selectively trace and modify values in the CUDA programs code or data. At runtime, GPU-Qin first profiles the CUDA application and classifies threads into groups with identical program traces. For each fault-injection run, GPU-Qin then selects a thread from each group and identifies an instruction to halt the program and inject a fault. Faults are injected in proportion to the size of the groups to reflect to overall proportion of threads executing on the GPU. Instructions are chosen uniformly over time to represent the uniformly random nature of radiation-induced transient faults. To simulate a fault in an arithmetic instruction, faults are injected into the destination operand of the instruction. To simulate a fault in a memory instruction, GPU-Qin injects faults into the destination operand or the address operand for load/store instructions, respectively. For control flow instructions, cuda-gdb does not allow for the modification of predicate registers, which control the behavior of individual threads within a CUDA single-instruction multiple-data (SIMD) instruction or "warp"; therefore GPU-Qin injects a fault into the control flow instructions of an entire warp. Once a fault is injected, the outcome of the execution (crash, program hang, SDC, or normal) is recorded.

SASSI [24] is a compiler-based GPU assembly instrumentation framework, which also leverages cuda-gdb. SASSIFI [25] is a fault-injection framework built around SASSI, which has similar functionality to GPU-Qin. SASSIFI randomly injects single bit-flips into the destination values of all executing instructions. Unlike GPU-Qin, SASSIFI is *unbiased*, meaning that each instruction is given equal weight, rather than weighting injections based on the number of times an instruction is dynamically executed like GPU-Qin.

All of these tools are extremely helpful for characterizing the reliability of existing architectures and identifying particular properties of programs that make them more unreliable. However, current GPU fault-injection tools are in their infancy and still need extensive validation and correlation with physical fault models. In the next section, we will take fault-injection to its extreme and look at studies that physically induce transient faults into real hardware using accelerated neutron or alpha particle beams.

2.3 ACCELERATED PARTICLE BEAM TESTING

While AVF analysis is useful for bounding reliability of structures early in the design process and fault-injection in hardware is useful for analyzing how faults affect program output, both of these techniques ignore the physical rate and manifestation of *actual* soft errors. Ideally, just as in field studies of large node supercomputers, we want to design experiments to identify both the rate and effects of transient faults on processors, rather than just the vulnerability of a particular architecture. Field studies of soft errors in real systems (previously presented) can roughly identify how vulnerable individual nodes are, but these field studies are extremely difficult to do, requiring thousands of nodes and years of observation to acquire data that often does not correspond to processor reliability. Also, because field studies are done on real systems, this limits the experiments that can be performed, as they may interfere with higher priority user-level programs and experiments. To overcome these issues, researchers turned to radioactive particle sources and particle accelerators to approximate the effects of soft errors from natural sources in real systems.

By placing silicon in the path of a beam of alpha particles or neutrons, researchers can get a sense for the effects of soft errors in nature in a fraction of the time. Dubbed "beam tests," these experiments can isolate effects of radiation-induced faults on a single silicon die [26]. Accelerated alpha particle beam tests can be accomplished by exposing silicon to radioactive sources that emit alpha particles (such as thorium 232) and must be placed in close proximity to the actual silicon as alpha particles easily interact with packaging. Accelerated neutron beam tests are accomplished by placing silicon directly in the path of a neutron high-energy neutron source. To approximate the effects of atmospheric radiation on silicon, the energy profile of the neutrons in the neutron beam should at least approximately match those experienced on the Earth's surface. Such beams are called "white neutron sources" and exist at several US national laboratories. The neutron beam at the Los Alamos Neutron Science Center (LANSCE) is often sourced for such tests.

Beam tests are extremely useful as they allow a real-world evaluation of current silicon reliability, trends in silicon reliability over generations of products, and evaluation of the efficacy of software and hardware reliability mechanisms, but they also have major drawbacks. Firstly, they are extremely expensive and inconvenient. While not nearly as expensive and time consuming as collecting field data from performance counters on large supercomputers, access to neutron beam time is still expensive and competitive. Secondly, unlike in fault-injection, where the source and rate of faults that manifest as errors is exactly known, beam tests still require root cause analysis. We can probably assume that a user-visible error during a beam test was most likely caused by a transient fault induced by the neutron source, but exactly in what structure and on which cycle the transient fault occurred might be unknowable. Error causes and locations can be approximated by checking special GPU exception registers. SDC rate can be approximated by comparing program output to a gold standard. In the remainder of this section, we will look at the only published study of accelerated beam testing on GPUs, and examine implications of this study on GPU architecture.

The first, and only, published study on accelerated neutron beam testing on GPUs was done by Tiwari et al. using the white (i.e., approximating the energy distribution of cosmic rays) neutron beam at LANSCE [14]. Because errors in systems might be caused by many different sources, such as application or driver bugs, Tiwari et al. focused on gathering data reported by internal exception registers in NVIDIA GPUs. Two systems were set up with two different NVIDIA GPUs, one Fermi-based C2050 and one Kepler-based K20. Each GPU was suspended in the line-of-fire of the beam and connected to a motherboard using a PCIe extender cable. To measure the raw sensitivity of the SRAM structures on-chip to transient faults, ECC support on internal SRAMs was disabled, patterns of 0s and 1s were stored to these structures, and the chip was exposed to the neutron beam. The researchers then calculated the *cross-section* of the structures, which is the number of errors in the structure divided by the neutron *fluence* (flux per unit area). Per-bit cross-sections were calculated using patterns of all 0s and all 1s and reported for each GPU's L2 cache and register file. Three interesting results were highlighted from this experiment.

(1) *Per-bit failure rates for the older 40 nm C2050 Fermi architecture was 2× to 3× higher than the newer 28 nm Kepler-based K20.* These failure rates contradict many assumptions that reliability automatically decreases as transistor feature sizes decrease, and were instead attributed to better bit-cell design, although the exact details of the improvement are proprietary. When normalized for the larger sizes of the L2 and register file in Kepler, the K20 still was found to be more resilient to errors.

(2) *Bits in the L2 that are set to 0 are 40% more likely to be corrupted than bits set to 1.* This trend was not seen for the register file, and thus indicates that asymmetric design of the cells in the cache (vs the symmetric bit-cell design in the register file) is what caused the discrepancy.

Both of these results highlight the need for attention to bit-cell design to increase base GPU resiliency. Unfortunately, such changes are only one-time adjustments, and the ability to continue to increase cell-level reliability cheaply is improbable. These results also suggest that fault-injection tools should account for this discrepancy in future studies.

(3) *NVIDIA's K20 GPU is six times more likely than the C2050 to experience a double-bit error (DBE) from a particle strike.* This is hypothesized to be due to the fact that the K20 uses a 28 nm process, while the C2050 uses a 40 nm process. Because transistors in the K20 are smaller and have a lower critical charge, it is easier for a neutron to interact with multiple bit cells. Overall, DBE rate was relatively low in both GPUs, 1% for the C2050 and 6% for the K20, and no triple-bit errors were identified. Thus SEC-DED ECC for SRAM protection is effective for current process node GPUs. However, as GPUs are implemented in 16 nm and smaller process nodes, the DBE rate and the occurrence of triple-bit errors will most likely rise, keeping cell design constant. Even though SEC-DED ECC is sufficient protection for SRAMs on current GPUs, it will most likely not be sufficient protection in the future.

The preceding experiment was only designed to test the sensitivity of writable SRAM structures. To evaluate the susceptibility of the entire architecture to transient faults, Tiwari et al. ran a set of benchmarks while exposing the GPU to the neutron beam. Two failure modes were observed: crashes, where the GPU program either failed or timed out, and incorrect output (SDC), where the result of the computation failed to match that of a precomputed golden output. Results showed a wide range of failure rates that ultimately depend on the resource utilization and AVF of a particular application, and the accelerated data supports the crash rates seen in the field data mentioned previously. Two interesting observations were made by the authors about this data:

(1) *ECC reduces the SDC rate by up to 10×, but increases crashes because of ECC exceptions from benign DBE that cannot be corrected.* Because faults may not occur in ACE bits, ECC is fundamentally a conservative mechanism. It does not distinguish between benign DBEs faults (false positives) and faults that will propagate to user-visible output. Therefore, even with higher protection from SDCs, (the priority) crash rates can increase. This is not a bad thing. An order of magnitude decrease in SDC rate is a welcome (and perhaps a required) improvement for usability, even at the cost of an increased crash rate.

(2) *Pipeline logic, queues, flip-flops, and schedulers are all unprotected.* ECC is implemented only on caches and the register files in modern GPUs, leaving the rest of the architecture vulnerable to the same kinds of upsets. Tiwari et al. showed that single-bit SRAM faults account for up to ~90% of all SDCs, meaning that more than 10% of SDCs, a nonnegligible amount, were due to faults in other structures.

(3) *Compute-bound kernels such as dgemm have higher crash rates.* Of the two matrix multiplication kernels (dgemm and MxM) *dgemm*, which is compute-bound, had a 2× higher crash rate than the memory-bound *MxM*. The authors hypothesize that this is because compute-bound applications have higher utilization (and therefore AVF) of unprotected structures such as the instruction scheduler and instruction queues, leading to a higher rate of control-flow errors and crashes.

While the preceding experiments show ECC is most likely good enough for protecting SRAM structures in current generation GPUs, it does not come without its drawbacks. Firstly, ECC is inherently *eager* in its assumption that an error will be user-visible, and therefore will lead to false positives. Secondly, ECC is not able to cover pipeline logic or other combinational circuits. Thirdly, ECC is not always required; architects pay an expensive area and power cost for a structure that sometimes may be rarely used or required. Researchers have attempted to find solutions to these drawbacks, identifying cheaper solutions that provide higher reliability for GPUs. In the following sections, we will examine research in both enhancements to the hardware and purely software techniques to improve reliability over current SEC-DED ECC methods.

3 HARDWARE RELIABILITY ENHANCEMENTS

The previous sections surveyed the current state of the art in evaluation of GPU reliability and showed that while GPUs themselves are not that much different from CPUs physically, their organization (e.g., the size of the register file, SIMD execution) makes addressing their reliability needs a little more complex. In the next few sections, we will discuss currently known techniques for enhancing GPU reliability using modifications to the hardware and new research on low-cost architectural and circuit techniques for improved protection.

3.1 PROTECTING SRAM STRUCTURES

We mentioned ECC in previous sections as a solution for protecting memory cells, such as a GPU's cache and register file, from soft errors. Instead of rehashing how ECC works [1], we instead briefly give an overview on ECC functionality, types of ECC and its overhead and protection, and research on how to make error coding schemes cheaper and more effective. ECC is normally implemented as SEC-DED code meaning that values with single bit-flips can be recovered (i.e., an SDC can be converted to the original value and execution can continue), while double bit-flips can be at least detected (i.e., an SDC can be converted to a DUE), and cause an exception, usually leading to a program crash. SEC-DED ECC accomplishes this by using a unique code word based on the data and a parity check matrix shared among all code words. When multiplied together, the parity check matrix and a code word can identify the location of a single flipped bit in the data. Once identified, correction is simple, flip the bit again! SEC-DED ECC can detect whether a DBE occurred, but it cannot identify the locations of the two bits, and therefore cannot correct the error. The size of the code word determines how much change can be detected and corrected. Double-error correct, triple-error detect (DEC-TED) ECC and any other granularity of ECC is implementable, but with a harsh penalty in the state required for each code word. For a 64-bit word, we need at least 7 bits to implement SEC-DED ECC (a 7% overhead) and 13 bits to implement DED-TED ECC (a 22% overhead) [1]. Many other error correction coding techniques exist that are able to correct more bits, with varying performance and state trade-offs, but we omit discussion of these codes and refer the reader to Shubu Mukherjee's book on architecture design for soft errors [1] for further study.

NVIDIA's Fermi architecture was the first NVIDIA GPU microarchitecture to support SEC-DED ECC protection on its SRAMs. Although exact details of the implementation are unavailable, assuming conservatively that all ECC protection is at double-word granularity (64 bits) for all caches, scratchpads, and register files, this translates to an 11% overhead in area! NVIDIA's Kepler architecture most likely did not drastically change the ECC organization for the register file, scratchpad, L1, or L2, but did include a clever optimization to reduce the need for ECC on its read-only data cache. Because inclusive caches are essentially redundant, lower-level inclusive caches do not need ECC, and only need parity to detect whether an error has occurred. If an error is detected, the line in the inclusive cache can simply be invalidated. Unfortunately, because of the relaxed memory consistency model of GPUs, both L1 cache designs, as well as the scratchpads, of current generations of AMD and NVIDIA GPUs are exclusive. However, the read-only data cache in Kepler *is* inclusive, and therefore requires parity protection for only single bit correction [27].

Tan et al. [28] observed via AVF analysis that the register files and instruction buffers of GPUs carry the most architectural state and are essentially reliability "hotspots" in the GPU. To avoid the high cost associated with adding ECC protection to a GPU's large register files, Tan proposed using the GPU's often underutilized scratchpad memory to store ECCs for the register file. Dubbed SHARP (SHAred memory to Register Protection), the technique adds hardware structures for ECC generation and recording and a checker structure to identify possible errors in the register file. SHARP reduces normalized AVF of the register file by an average of 41%, supplying similar protection as ECC, with an estimated 18% reduction in power. To avoid the cost of adding ECC protection to the GPU's instruction buffers, Tan observed that many instructions in a GPU's streaming architecture share the same PC and can therefore share ECCs. Tan proposed a technique called SAWP (Similarity-AWare Protection) to take advantage of this phenomenon. SAWP adds a small ECC table to the hardware as well as an ECC generator, a checker, and hardware to support identifying different SIMD instructions that share the same PC. SAWP reduced the AVF of the instruction buffer by 68% on average, and has an estimated 17% reduction in power over a full SEC-DED ECC implementation.

3.2 PROTECTING PIPELINE STRUCTURES

ECC has proved to be an extremely powerful, successful protection mechanism and has become a necessary requirement for any architecture expecting to satisfy consumers demanding reliable computation. However, ECC suffers from two main drawbacks; it is limited in the number of errors it can detect and correct, and it only protects SRAM structures on-chip and does not protect pipeline logic or other processor structures. In this section we will discuss new research on proposed hardware mechanisms that enhance reliability of nonstorage logic in GPUs.

Sheaffer et al. [29] proposed some purely architectural-level techniques to address the inherent unreliability of shader arithmetic logic units (ALUs) and raster operations units in early GPGPU pipelines. By replicating ALUs and placing a comparator on the critical path, they built in redundant shader computation with more than $2\times$ area overhead on the many shaders in a GPU. To protect the raster hardware, fragments are issued to the raster pipeline twice, essentially hardware-assisted redundant instructions. To support reissue of incorrect computation, Sheaffer et al. add a domain buffer to the data path to store inputs. If an error is detected in the raster operations unit, the fragments are reissued into the pipeline. Redundant hardware is expensive, though, and must be paid for by casual users such as gamers who do not demand the strictest reliability. Schaeffer et al. reported a ~50% performance degradation because of reissued operations, but noted that this was much less than the 100% overhead expected from naive redundant execution. This was due to increased memory locality and thus more ideal cache behavior for the second of the two redundant instructions.

3.3 TAKING ADVANTAGE OF UNDERUTILIZATION

Because most modern GPUs use an SIMD model for computation, GPUs suffer from the same classic disadvantages of SIMD processors. One particular inefficiency that arises with lock-stepped execution of threads in SIMD architectures is that they are hard to utilize to their full potential, and are often underutilized if the program has irregular parallelism. Software may have dynamically changing needs for parallelism, but the GPU's SIMD units, load/store units, and special functional units (SFUs) are obviously fixed resources.

Underutilization of GPU SM resources in NVIDIA GPUs happens for two main reasons: (1) underutilization within SIMD units because of mismatches between thread-block size and SIMD width, thread divergence, memory stalls, and so on, and (2) underutilization of entire SIMD, load/store units, or SFUs because of a lack of ready instructions from the instruction scheduler. Jeon et al. [30] attempt to take advantage of both of these sources of underutilization to improve GPU reliability by opportunistically executing redundant computation in idle GPU SMs, or SIMD units. Dubbed *Warped-DMR* (DMR stands for *dual-modular redundancy*), the technique offers two main operating modes: *intrawarp* and *interwarp* DMR. Intrawarp DMR takes advantage of underutilization within SIMD instructions or "warps." If any of the threads in a warp are inactive (i.e., masked from execution because of SIMD divergence), intrawarp DMR uses the inactive threads (empty SIMD lanes) to verify the execution of the active threads. If all of the threads in a warp are active, and intrawarp DMR cannot execute, interwarp DMR reexecutes the SIMD instruction in an idle execution unit. Warped-DMR cannot be done efficiently in pure software; therefore, Jeon introduces architectural support to facilitate efficient redundant execution. For intrawarp DMR, registers from active threads must be forwarded to the inactive threads doing redundant computation, thus a *register forwarding unit* is added to the architecture, which funnels correct data to redundant lanes. Furthermore, comparators are included to compare the results of redundant execution. Interwarp DMR requires the addition of a *replay queue* to buffer executed instructions for reexecution in idle execution units. In their work, Jeon et al. [30] set the size of the replay queue to be 5KB for each SM; while this is not extremely large, it is not an insignificant addition in area and power to the GPU SM architecture. A *replay checker* also needs to be added to the SM to coordinate redundant execution and validation of correct execution. Error coverage is reported as the percentage of instructions that execute redundantly. Warped-DMR has 96% instruction coverage, with only 16% performance overhead (mainly from interwarp DMR) on average. The lower the utilization of the SIMD units, the lower the overhead of Warped-DMR.

Tan et al. [31] propose a similar approach to Jeon et al. called *RISE* (Recycling the streaming processors Idle time for Soft-Error detection). Full-RISE uses the same intuition that warps themselves often stall to wait on long-latency operations such as memory accesses. Request pending aware full-RISE (RP-FRISE) takes advantage of this latency by predicting long latency operations. Once predicted, RP-FRISE inserts extra redundant computation after the long latency operation. Full-RISE requires three additions to the GPU architecture to support redundant execution. The first is a storage array and an ALU for keeping track of and calculating the latency of different memory requests. Once this latency is calculated, it is sent to the SM along with the requested data, and an appropriate number of redundant instructions are executed. Tan et al. take this methodology one step further and proposes idle SM aware Full-Rise (IS-FRISE). IS-FRISE looks at imbalances in how SMs on a GPU are processing thread-blocks. If an SM is known to be underutilized (because an SM can handle more thread-blocks than were scheduled to it), the work of a thread-block in that SM is duplicated. The hardware overhead required to support RP-FRISE and IS-FRISE is small, calculated to be only 3% additional area in each memory controller, and 1% extra area in each SM.

Tan et al. also propose Partial-RISE, which takes advantage of empty SIMD lanes due to thread divergence to execute redundant computation with little or no extra cost. In contrast to intrawarp DMR, which replicated computation within warps, Partial-RISE works by looking for SIMD instructions that diverge and then picking a ready SIMD instruction with the same PC to execute. Threads from the ready instruction are replicated into the empty lanes of the divergent warp, replicating their computation. Once the first warp is executed, results from the redundant threads are stored in a buffer and compared to the results of the second warp once it finishes its execution. To support Partial-RISE, comparators for comparing the active masks of two warps with the same PC and buffers to hold temporary results that must be added to the SM pipeline. This extra hardware leads to a 1% area overhead per SM. Both performance degradation and AVF were calculated for Full-Rise and Partial-Rise techniques. When combined, Full-RISE and Partial-RISE techniques cause a miniscule 4% performance degradation because of extra computation, and reduce the AVF of a particular SIMD processor by 43%.

Argus-G [32] is an extension of Argus [33], the hardware error-detection scheme developed for CPUs, retargeted specifically for GPUs. Argus makes the observation that von-Neumann architectures do four basic computations: (1) control flow, (2) computation, (3) data flow, and (4) memory. If these four operations can be checked, Argus can detect all errors in the core. Argus-G does this by extending an SM architecture with control flow, dataflow, and computation checkers. Data flow checking is accomplished by comparing the dynamic data flow graph of each thread to a precomputed static data flow graph. If the graphs differ, an error occurred in the monitored thread's execution. This analysis implicitly checks control flow within basic blocks, but does not account for control flow between basic blocks. Control flow between basic blocks is checked by calculating both a data flow and a control flow signature. A check for the signature for each legal predecessor block is then included in the code of each basic block just before the branch or exit instruction. If the signature does not match, a control flow error was encountered. Computation is checked using the identical method used in Argus, by simply replicating functional units in hardware. More efficient checkers can be implemented, and this is an open and active area of research. Argus-G uses the identical computation checking method as Argus, although each checker is implemented many more times to account for the wider SIMD functional units in GPU hardware. Both Argus and Argus-G claim to have 100% coverage over the architecture and can provably catch all transient and permanent errors in a core; however, in later experiments, the same authors reported that 7% of injected faults ended up as SDCs and that Argus-G was able to detect only 66% of injected faults that would have ended up as SDCs if not for Argus-G Performance of GPU applications utilizing Argus-G was mainly impacted by the insertion of signature checking code at the end of basic blocks. For some applications, this overhead was not insignificant (close to 20%), but for most, overhead was negligible. On average runtime increased by only 4% over all tested benchmarks. Applications with smaller basic blocks have higher performance penalties because of an increased ratio of signature code to useful code.

All of these techniques provide fairly impressive improvements in reliability, with relatively low overheads. It is reasonable to think that some customers would sacrifice 10% performance on average for large improvements in reliability, especially as data-center GPU and HPC GPU use increases. However, in practical terms, most if not all of these research efforts are unlikely to be implemented in mainstream GPUs. The economics of GPU organization and design are driven mainly by consumers who do not require reliable computation: gamers. In the heated competition between AMD and NVIDIA for the gaming and professional graphics market, there is little to no room to spend engineering dollars on ultra-reliable hardware. Having said that GPUs are being used in supercomputers! This motivates the need for configurable software reliability solutions that can be turned on and paid for by those who desire it, but does not increase the cost of GPU design and manufacture. The next section deals exclusively with software reliability solutions and the attempt by researchers to identify cheap and practical alternatives for hardware reliability solutions.

4 SOFTWARE RELIABILITY ENHANCEMENTS

Perhaps the most obvious method for providing cheap, hardware-agnostic GPU reliability is to run a GPU application twice. If the outputs of the two runs differ, then an error must have occurred somewhere in the computation of one of the program runs, and users know that they must run their application again. If the outputs of the two program runs agree, an error most likely did not occur, and a single copy can be committed as program output. As previously mentioned, this technique is referred to as *dual-modular redundancy* or DMR. DMR can detect nearly 100% of errors, but note that DMR cannot *correct* errors. If an error is detected via DMR, the application in question must be reexecuted from a recoverable checkpoint, as we have no evidence of which thread encountered the error! For DMR techniques, any structures that are used in redundant execution are said to be within the *Sphere of Replication* or SoR, and are generally assumed to have 100% coverage. This is not entirely true as a permanent fault may cause the same error to manifest in both redundant threads (called the *hidden error problem*), but as discussed previously, we are focused on the detection and mitigation of soft faults and assume the hidden error problem for transient faults is statistically impossible. Later on we will see how the hidden error problem can emerge when considering soft faults in SIMD architectures. Values that enter the SoR must be replicated, called "input replication," and redundant value pairs that leave the SoR must be shared and compared before a single value is allowed to exit, called "output comparison."

While DMR provides nearly 100% coverage of all faults on every structure in the SoR, it is expensive. Full redundant execution naively either requires twice as much time for computation or twice as much hardware. Furthermore, the sharing and comparison of program output between redundant threads can be expensive, adding to this assumed 2× overhead. Even with this high cost, program reexecution is used as a practical, common sense approach for verification of program runs with high-reliability needs. A 2× or even 3× slowdown is expensive, but may be a quick and dirty option for scientists or engineers who must guarantee correctness, but do not have access to other hardware or software options. This high overhead can generally be improved upon by executing redundant computation at the same time, amortizing the cost of data and instruction fetch over two computations. In the next section, we will look at some research techniques for software reliability enhancements on CPUs and how these concepts have been adapted for GPU kernels and architectures. In the following section we will also look at an attempt to sacrifice the high coverage provided by software replication in exchange for performance improvements by using opportunistic and probabilistic protection.

4.1 REDUNDANT MULTITHREADING

Redundant multithreading (RMT) is a DMR concept that replicates computation at the granularity of a software context. Two thread contexts are launched and execute redundantly until a result must be committed outside of the SoR, for example, on a store to main memory, or an I/O event. When a result needs to be committed, the threads share this value, compare the two copies, and commit the result outside the SoR if they both agree on the value, called "output comparison." Hardware extensions to support efficient RMT have been evaluated on CPUs for simultaneous multithreaded (SMT) cores [34,35], identifying fairly reasonable average overheads of 32% [34] and 10–30% [35], with nearly 100% fault detection coverage. However, both techniques add special hardware structures to allow the architecture to efficiently coordinate redundant execution and output comparison.

Wang et al. [36] were the first to automate pure software redundant multithreading in a compiler and conduct experiments on real hardware. They show an impressive 19% overhead for redundant execution in simulation, but included the benefits of simulated low-latency intercore communication queues that do not exist in real hardware. When implemented on real SMT architectures, using software-only communication queues, their redundant multithreading technique saw a ~500% increase in runtimes on average. Wang found that frequent communication of values between threads for output comparison was the main bottleneck. Even if threads were executing on the same SMT core, they had to use the cache hierarchy to communicate values, often passing values via the L4 cache. Using SMT threads as redundant thread pairs, values could be passed via the L1 cache, but performance of both threads would suffer because of contention for shared intracore resources such as execution units, L1 cache, and memory bandwidth. This is an interesting result and lesson: redundant threads that execute in separate cores are generally bottlenecked by communication latency, whereas redundant threads that execute in the same core are generally bottlenecked by computation resources designed for a single thread. Unlike CPUs, GPUs have a much different design and execution philosophy—and as we have seen in previous sections, their SIMD units are often underutilized—and thus may allow for much more efficient software RMT.

Dimitrov et al. [37] were the first to evaluate the performance impact of software redundancy on GPUs. Dimitrov investigated three ways of implementing software redundancy: (1) *R-Naive*, where a GPU kernel, including data copies to and from the host CPU is simply executed twice, (2) *R-Scatter*, where unused instruction-level parallelism in under-packed VLIW instructions is used for redundant instructions, and (3) *R-Thread*, where CUDA thread blocks are duplicated in a single kernel call. R-Naive works by first allocating twice as much memory in the GPU's main memory and duplicating the memory copies from the host CPU's main memory to the GPU. This means that the GPU's main memory is included in the SoR at the cost of twice as much space. This is fine, as long as the GPU's main memory is underutilized by half, but may be an untenable requirement for kernels that have high memory utilization. Dimitrov reported that R-Naive increased runtimes by an average (with low variance) of 99%, essentially the same cost as running the kernels in serial. This indicates that coarse-grained software replication may be unable to take advantage of fine-grained architectural underutilization, motivating finer-grained replication.

R-Scatter is more complex, and relies on underutilization in the VLIW-based architectures of older Array Technologies Inc. (ATI) or AMD graphics cards. Dimitrov et al. analyzed this technique on an R670, 5-way VLIW GPU. R-Scatter works by duplicating variable declarations, definitions, and all computations in the original code, essentially replicating every line of code in the original program with an identical, redundant version. In this way, there are always twice as many instructions without dependencies that can be scheduled into any VLIW instruction. Just like R-Naive, memory allocations and data transfers are duplicated (input replication), and redundant threads are guided to read to and write from these redundant structures. Dimitrov reported that R-Scatter increased runtimes by an average of 93%, indicating that there was perhaps not much underutilization in the VLIW schedule to begin with.

R-Thread works by launching a single GPU kernel call, but with twice as many blocks. Just as in R-Scatter and R-Naive, memory allocations and copies are duplicated, and the redundant threads in the redundant thread blocks are guided to do computation using these separate values. R-Thread was reported to increase overhead by a disappointing 97%, again indicating that thread-blocks were too coarse-grained to take advantage of unused thread-level parallelism, if it existed at all in the benchmarks on that architecture.

Based on this study alone, it seems that GPUs respond poorly to pure software redundancy, but there still may be room for replication at a finer granularity. R-Thread replicated computation at the thread-block level, and thus was unable to take advantage of SIMD-level underutilization. This study indicated that GPU SMs are usually highly utilized, and so thread-block-level redundancy may not be as cheap as researchers had hoped. However, the hardware reliability enhancements presented in the previous section indicate that SIMD underutilization is ripe for the taking, and thus GPU RMT might still have a place in practical reliability solutions if it is properly tuned.

Another issue with Dimitrov's kernel-level replication is the duplication of memory allocations and copies. Modern day applications most likely will not be able to tolerate a $2\times$ memory overhead (both $2\times$ memory capacity and $2\times$ memory bandwidth), especially over the PCIe bus. ECC is also already fairly standard on server class GPU DRAM and on-chip caches, and so increasing the strength of this ECC may be a better approach than duplicating allocations and data transfers. Further complicating matters is the danger in allowing any errors to exist in memory, even if they are backed up by redundant state. Extreme care must be taken to ensure that a fault cannot propagate to other accelerators, or storage via paging or DMAs, before being checked. In many cases, this is impossible to guarantee, motivating a protection domain, and output comparison that exists on-chip. Wang et al. attempted this method, requiring comparisons before commit for every shared memory operation, but found that intercore communication for output comparison was a large bottleneck.

Wadden et al. [38] reexamined GPU RMT on modern SIMD GPU architectures. Dimitrov attempted to exploit fine-grained parallelism in VLIW architectures; however, most modern GPU designs (at least AMD and NVIDIA architectures) have settled on a combined SIMD/vector model, instead of VLIW, thus Wadden focused exclusively on this type of execution model. Wadden took a similar approach to Wang et al. by implementing GPU RMT directly into AMD's OpenCL compiler stack, thus maintaining transparency to the software developer, while also excluding the memory hierarchy from the SoR. Wadden explored two granularities of GPU thread replication: (1) intergroup RMT, similar to Dimitrov's R-Thread, where kernels are launched with twice as many thread-blocks (work-groups), and (2) intragroup RMT, where each OpenCL work-group is inflated, and twice as many single instruction multiple threads (SIMT) execute per work-group. While these two techniques may seem very similar, they have extremely different overheads and different fault detection coverage. Both techniques and their differences in protection are described in the remainder of the section.

Intragroup RMT works by first modifying the host program to double the size of each work-group being launched in the kernel. Once this is accomplished, the kernel code intermediate representation (IR) is transformed during compilation to guide adjacent threads in adjacent SIMD lanes to do the same computation by forcing adjacent threads to query the same thread IDs. Because the only thing that distinguishes computation between threads is their thread IDs, two threads that read the same IDs will have identical behavior, albeit while using different registers! When a redundant thread pair encounters a store operation—and a single correct value must be committed outside the SoR to the memory hierarchy—one thread passes a value to the other thread via a communication buffer allocated in the GPU's scratchpad memory. The receiving thread then compares its private value to the passed value and then executes the store instruction if the values agree. In this way, all replicated structures that are used to execute these two threads are within the SoR; however, structures that are shared between threads in an SIMD instruction, such as the L1 cache, instruction fetch and decode logic, and scalar instruction unit, are not protected at all by this technique. This is an interesting result.

(1) *Intragroup RMT does not protect against faults in structures shared by threads in one SIMD instruction.* This is an example of the *hidden error* problem. Hidden errors are usually defined as faults encountered by both redundant CPU threads, such as redundant threads using the same faulty ALU. In this context, hidden errors arise because of the SIMD programming model. A single fault in an SIMD instruction in an SM's instruction queue will cause all threads in that instruction to misbehave in the same way! Therefore the adjacent redundant threads in one SIMD instruction will not be able to detect the fault. As previously mentioned, instruction and data caches, the GPU's scalar support unit, branch unit, instruction fetch, decode, and scheduling logic are all left unprotected. However, the large register files and SIMD ALUs are protected.

Because modern GPU SMs include managed scratchpad memories that are not included in the global memory hierarchy, this structure can be either included (covered) or excluded (uncovered) from the SoR. If the scratchpad memory is included, its allocations and memory traffic must be duplicated. If the application cannot tolerate an increase in the scratchpad size, the scratchpad memory can be excluded from the SoR. In this case, the scratchpad must be treated just like main memory; every time a redundant thread pair wants to store a value to the scratchpad, their values must be shared and compared via an interthread communication buffer in the scratchpad first, resulting in an increase in scratchpad traffic. Results show a few interesting conclusions.

(2) *Overheads of DMR are either high (~100%) or low (0–10%) depending on how memory-bound the application is.* Because memory instructions are not replicated, redundant computation and communication of redundant thread pairs can be hidden behind these long latency instructions, especially if the kernel is bottlenecked by memory operations. This is a very interesting result, as anecdotally, many real-world HPC benchmarks are memory-bound, and so this type of fine-grained RMT may be a viable solution for fault coverage in real systems. Applications that were already compute-bound had predictable ~2× increases in runtime when run with twice as many threads.

(3) *Interthread communication via the scratchpad is very expensive.* While the latency of communication traffic via the scratchpad can be hidden behind the latency of long latency main memory stores, that same latency cannot be hidden behind stores to the scratchpad with identical latency. Thus excluding the scratchpad from the SoR and forcing communication via a communication buffer in the same structure has a large impact on performance if scratchpad traffic was high in the original kernel.

(4) *Doubling the size of the work-groups is expensive when capacity (registers, scratchpad) is a scarce resource.* This is a specific example of a broader lesson: if you have to double usage of a resource that bottlenecks your application, expect a near ~100% (or greater because of overheads!) increase in runtime.

Because intragroup RMT guarantees that redundant thread pairs execute in lockstep in adjacent SIMD lanes, Wadden et al. also experimented with using register *swizzle* operations to accomplish interthread communication without the need for explicit scratchpad buffers. This optimization had a large impact on performance when intrathread communication was expensive, decreasing communication overhead to nearly zero and decreasing kernel runtime overheads by as much as 90%.

Intergroup RMT works similarly to Dimitrov's R-Thread thread-block-level replication of computation. Instead of increasing the size of a kernel's work-groups, intergroup RMT increases the number of work-groups by two. Therefore redundant computation is accomplished by a redundant work-group pair, and redundant thread pairs are in separate work-groups, possibly executing on entirely separate SMs. Unlike intragroup RMT threads, which were forced to execute in lockstep in adjacent lanes of an SIMD instruction, intergroup threads execute in different SIMD instructions, and therefore require explicit synchronization. Furthermore, because threads in different work-groups cannot be guaranteed to execute on the same SM, they cannot communicate through an SM's scratchpad memory, and must communicate via a buffer in main memory. Intergroup RMT has higher coverage than intragroup RMT because threads executing in different work-groups are using completely redundant instruction streams. Therefore the instruction fetch, decode, scheduling logic, as well as the branch and scalar units of the AMD GPUs are protected with this technique. Unsurprisingly, intergroup RMT greatly increases kernel runtimes. The chapter presented these interesting conclusions.

1 *Memory-bound applications are bottlenecked by the extra memory traffic needed to synchronize and communicate redundant values.* Some applications experience devastating slowdowns of $3.4\times$ to $9.5\times$, similar in scale to those experienced by Wang et al. for CPU threads. As concluded by Wang et al., this motivates high-speed communication buffers between SMs, but perhaps indicates finer-grained RMT is a better target for practical software-based RMT on GPUs.

2 *SM underutilization can allow for low-cost execution of redundant work-groups, but underutilization at this granularity is most likely not a realistic scenario.* GPUs gain advantage on extremely large, embarrassingly parallel problems, thus it is usually not the case that a GPU is ever starved for work-groups waiting to execute. Some applications with dynamic parallelism, like a reduction, may experience SM underutilization in later stages of computation, but this is not the dominant use of GPUs.

3 *Compute-bound applications have predicted $\sim 2\times$ slowdowns.* If the memory system is underutilized, it can handle extra traffic introduced by synchronization and communication code, and kernels run with twice as many work-groups and experience expected $\sim 2\times$ slowdowns.

4.2 SYMPTOM-BASED FAULT DETECTION AND DYNAMIC-RELIABILITY MANAGEMENT

As we saw in the previous sections, hardware protection provides high error detection coverage, but requires (most likely) economically infeasible additions to the hardware. Software-redundant multithreading can be accomplished cheaply, but can be accompanied by extremely high performance overhead, depending on the level of protection required and the dynamic behavior of the application. To address these issues, researchers have looked toward *probabilistic protection*, sacrificing identification of some percentage of SDCs within a protection domain for a decrease in overhead. In this section we look at a few techniques that attempt to implement this trade-off.

Yim et al. propose Hauberk [21], an error detection framework that selectively protects sections of code with software checkers. Instead of using DMR and duplicating every instruction within a vulnerable region, Hauberk selectively places different types of software checkers that look for symptoms that a transient fault has affected program output. This is a subtle but important difference in reliability philosophy and DMR. Redundancy checks for *faults* via direct comparison of values within an SoR while symptom-based techniques such as Hauberk check for *symptoms of faults* in a possibly nonredundant domain using checkers. Full redundancy might have higher reliability guarantees, as it can detect 100% of faults within the SoR, but unfortunately it raises alarms for all false-positive faults that might never manifest as SDCs or DUEs in program output. Symptom-based detection ignores most false positives by looking for evidence of errors, but may allow for some SDCs that would have been caught by full replication. Hauberk attempts to optimize this trade-off by using relatively expensive checksum-based live range value checkers to protect important code that is executed infrequently, and low-overhead, accumulator-based software checkers to selectively protect values in frequently executed loop bodies in GPU kernel code.

Yim et al. first do an in-depth analysis of failures due to faults in GPU HPC codes. Using the SWIFI fault-injection tool discussed previously, Yim et al. describe two important observations that affect the design of their reliability scheme:

1 *Because integer and pointer data are more likely to be used for important data values and program control, they are also more likely to cause user-visible errors or program crashes.* However, floating point data are just as likely to cause SDCs (as opposed to crashes) as integer data. Therefore control data in loop bodies is most likely less important to protect because it is more likely to cause a user-visible crash rather than the more insidious SDC.

2 *87% of kernel execution time was spent in loop code (five out of seven applications spent > 98% of their time in looping code!).* Therefore a small added overhead to a loop may have a large impact on overall performance, and software checkers in loops should be as lightweight as possible.

Using these observations, Hauberk first profiles a GPU kernel to determine which lines of code have the highest impact on performance, placing strong error detection (dynamic reliability management, DRM) around nonlooping code, and lightweight checking code inside loop bodies. Strong detection for nonlooping code involves duplicating the definitions (assignments) to all virtual variables. Once this computation is duplicated (and checked to make sure that the duplicated variables match in value), the value is XORd with a checksum variable shared among all duplicated variables. After the last use of this variable (at the end of the variable's live range), the variable is again XORd with the checksum. Therefore, if all defined values XOR with the checksum twice, at the end of the kernel, the checksum must be zero. If the checksum is not zero, then the kernel has seen a fault, and an error can be reported. For lightweight loop-based detectors, Hauberk uses accumulators inserted into loop bodies that accumulate the value of a variable. After the execution of the loop, Hauberk compares the accumulator values against values gathered from profiling runs. Dubbed "value-accumulation-based range checking," Hauberk simply checks whether an accumulator value is within a reasonable range of the stored profile value based on how many iterations were executed. If the value is suspiciously far away from the profiled results, it is flagged as a potential error.

Potential errors are then distinguished from false positives using a diagnosis and tolerance algorithm. Experiments conducted on real hardware revealed that Hauberk was able to capture 86.8% of injected faults on average, leaving 13.2% of injected faults to lead to SDCs. It should be noted that this type of coverage metric does not provide any type of reliability guarantee on any part of the system, and so should again be distinguished from DMR. Probabilistic protection provides an average probability of fault-detection over the entire architecture, where DMR provides 100% fault-detection within an SoR that may only cover portions of the architecture. Performance overheads were 15% on average, ranging from very low (1.9%) to very high ($\sim$52%) depending on the time spent by a GPU kernel in loop versus nonloop code.

Li et al. also examined overheads of probabilistic symptom-based protection on real GPU hardware [39]. Li used the Lynx dynamic instrumentation tool for NVIDIA GPU kernels [40] to instrument PTX IR of real GPU kernels with error checking code. Li implements three different software checkers: (1) alignment checkers for errors in memory address operands, (2) array bounds checkers for detecting errors in array addresses, and (3) control flow checkers for errors in branch addresses. Alignment checkers look at whether the target address of each memory instruction has the same multiple of bytes as the target data size based on the base address. If not, error-logging code is inserted after the check to write error data out to a memory log such that the CPU can take appropriate action (e.g., rerun the GPU kernel). Array bounds checkers look to see if address operands of memory instructions are within known global allocations. A table of these global allocations is computed at compile time and queried by the checker on every single memory access. Li's control flow checkers use the same control flow checking technique implemented for CPUs by Oh et al. [41] and are inserted into each GPU basic block. Control flow checkers place a unique signature at the beginning of each basic block corresponding to any legal basic block predecessors. If the calculated signature from the entry block does not match the unique signature determined by legal predecessors, the entry into the block was not a legal one, and an error is presumed. Probabilistic error coverage was not calculated for these techniques via ACE analysis or fault-injection. Total overheads for all evaluated benchmarks ranged from 1% to 737%, with the most expensive overheads contributed by the alignment and array bounds checkers.

In separate but related research with AMD Research, Li et al. proposed combining parts of Hauberk and the software checkers from their previous work into a single introspective reliability runtime framework [42]. Dubbed dynamic reliability management or DRM, the framework monitors a GPU kernel at runtime and selectively applies different software reliability enhancements (SRE) via just-in-time compilation (JIT) depending on the vulnerability of the running kernel. To characterize the vulnerability of the kernel, Li calculates the kernel's PVF previously discussed. PVF can be calculated by doing a static data-flow analysis, and thus can be done offline on a kernel's IR, and does not affect runtime performance. Once PVF is calculated, the overhead of each SRE is calculated using an SRE-specific performance model. Once the PVF and overhead are calculated, the model within DRM decides whether or not to apply the SRE. Once executed, profile information about the kernel can be gathered and used to update the SRE-specific performance model. The different SREs that can be applied to the kernel are (1) Hauberk's checksum-based, value live-range checks, (2) instruction duplication, and (3) control flow checkers as previously described. Li et al. conducted an experiment to measure the overhead of individual SREs applied to matrix multiplication, and showed that runtimes for instruction duplication ranged from $1.10\times$, $1.34\times$, and $1.37\times$ depending on whether the computation was integer, floating point, or a memory load, respectively. Control flow checking only added 1% to the runtime of the matrix multiplication kernel. Register live-range, however, increased the kernel runtime by $2.51\times$.

5 SUMMARY

This chapter surveyed the current state-of-the-art research into GPU reliability. We first described some mechanisms for failures in GPUs, the most insidious of which is the radiation-induced transient fault. Transient or "soft" faults are caused by cosmic radiation that can inject charge into silicon, flipping a bit to an incorrect value. These types of faults are more difficult to detect than permanent hardware failures because they are rare and nondeterministic. If a fault silently propagates to program output, we call this a silent data corruption or SDC. SDCs are the worst possible outcome of a fault because at least when an unrecoverable fault is detected, the known error can motivate some sort of recovery mechanism.

We then framed GPU reliability as an important problem. Many high-node-count data centers and supercomputers experience transient faults much more often than single GPUs, and field data gathered from real supercomputing systems supports this claim. Therefore, although GPUs are gaming products, they must have similar reliability guarantees as server class CPUs. This problem is made more difficult by the fact that the economics driving changes to GPU architecture and design are still dominated by the gaming and graphics markets, rather than scientific or HPC use cases.

We then looked at the state-of-the-art research in hardware reliability enhancements for GPUs, showcasing various hardware structures that were much less expensive than full hardware redundancy, while greatly increasing protection against SDCs. One technique looked at using underutilized GPU scratchpad memory to implement ECC, without the large overhead in area and power associated with ECC. While reducing the cost of ECC is a net benefit, ECC and SRAM protection techniques do not protect pipeline logic. To address this shortcoming, one technique used special redundant ALUs and buffers to address this reliability hole. Other techniques addressed this shortcoming by attempting to take advantage of underutilization in SIMD hardware to execute extra redundant instructions at a low cost.

Finally, we surveyed current attempts to provide reliability for GPU hardware with purely software reliability enhancements. Hardware reliability enhancements generally protect against a large percentage of possible SDCs, but cannot be applied to legacy hardware and are extremely expensive (in dollars, engineering hours, GPU performance, power, etc.) to include in future hardware. Therefore software reliability enhancements are proposed as a cheap, practical alternative as long as added reliability and additional performance and power overheads are acceptable. An application can simply be run twice, gaining ~100% protection against SDCs, but this generally incurs a ~100% performance overhead. More fine-grained replication can be accomplished, taking advantage of the same SIMD underutilization previously mentioned, but this often comes at the cost of reduced coverage: redundant threads in the same SIMD instruction do not protect against faults in shared structures such as a GPU's SIMD instruction buffer. While redundant threads protect a subset of a GPU from ~100% of SDCs, probabilistic software reliability techniques provide an average probability of catching an SDC over the runtime of the program. This compromise generally leads to lower overhead, but is harder to consider as there are no reliability guarantees provided anywhere by the hardware or software. Probabilistic coverage is implemented as special checker instructions, selective reexecution, and duplication of instructions and data. Such selective techniques can be employed in an introspective manner so that profiling or runtime information can guide the system to employ the best reliability scheme with the lowest performance penalty.

Whereas CPU reliability research spans decades, GPU reliability research is a relatively young field. And while GPUs face similar challenges as CPUs, because of a GPU's unique architecture, potential solutions to these problems may carry very different protection, and performance and power overheads. Thus practical solutions to GPU reliability may look different than those used to help protect server class CPUs, and may also be much more costly. One possible path forward is to codify unreliable behavior into an architecture's ISA. This line of thinking asserts that if we cannot uphold the hardware/software contract provided by the ISA, then we should notify programmers and force them to account for the consequences. Though it is unclear whether speedy "approximate computing" will ever be accepted by programmers, future research should consider these techniques, and practical implementations.

REFERENCES

[1] S. Mukherjee, Architecture Design for Soft Errors, Morgan Kaufmann Publishers Inc., Burlington MA, 2008.
[2] I.S. Haque, V.S. Pande, Hard data on soft errors: a large-scale assessment of real-world error rates in GPGPU, in: 2010 10th IEEE/ACM International Conference on Cluster, Cloud and Grid Computing (CCGrid), May 17–20, 2010.
[3] C. Constantinescu, Trends and challenges in VLSI circuit reliability, IEEE Micro 23 (4) (2003) 14–19.

[4] J.W. Sheaffer, D.P. Luebke, K. Skadron, The visual vulnerability spectrum: characterizing architectural vulnerability for graphics hardware, in: Proceedings of the 21st ACM SIGGRAPH/EUROGRAPHICS Symposium on Graphics Hardware, ACM, Vienna, Austria, 2006, pp. 9–16.

[5] NVIDIA, NVIDIA's Next Generation CUDA Compute Architecture: Fermi, 2009.

[6] E. Strohmaier, J. Dongarra, H. Simon, M. Meuer, TOP500 Lists, November, 2010, http://www.top500.org/lists/2010/11/.

[7] T.P. Morgan, Tesla Compute Drives NVIDIA Upwards, 2015.

[8] X. Li, K. Shen, M.C. Huang, L. Chu, A memory soft error measurement on production systems, in: 2007 USENIX Annual Technical Conference on Proceedings of the USENIX Annual Technical Conference, USENIX Association, Santa Clara, CA, 2007, pp. 1–6.

[9] B. Schroeder, E. Pinheiro, W.D. Weber, DRAM errors in the wild: a large-scale field study, in: Proceedings of the Eleventh International Joint Conference on Measurement and Modeling of Computer Systems, ACM, Seattle, WA, USA, 2009, pp. 193–204.

[10] V. Sridharan, D. Liberty, A study of DRAM failures in the field, in: Proceedings of the International Conference on High Performance Computing, Networking, Storage and Analysis, IEEE Computer Society Press, Salt Lake City, UT, 2012, pp. 1–11.

[11] T. Siddiqua, A.E. Papathanasiou, A. Biswas, S. Gurumurthi, Analysis and modeling of memory errors from large-scale field data collection, in: Workshop on Silicon Errors in Logic-System Effects (SELSE), 2013.

[12] V. Sridharan, J. Stearley, N. DeBardeleben, S. Blanchard, S. Gurumurthi, Feng Shui of supercomputer memory: positional effects in DRAM and SRAM faults, in: Proceedings of the International Conference on High Performance Computing, Networking, Storage and Analysis, ACM, Denver, CO, 2013, pp. 1–11.

[13] C. Di Martino, Z. Kalbarczyk, R.K. Iyer, F. Baccanico, J. Fullop, W. Kramer, Lessons learned from the analysis of system failures at petascale: the case of blue waters, in: 2014 44th Annual IEEE/IFIP International Conference on Dependable Systems and Networks (DSN), June 23–26, 2014.

[14] D. Tiwari, S. Gupta, J. Rogers, D. Maxwell, P. Rech, S. Vazhkudai, D. Oliveira, D. Londo, N. DeBardeleben, P. Navaux, L. Carro, A. Bland, Understanding GPU errors on large-scale HPC systems and the implications for system design and operation, in: 2015 IEEE 21st International Symposium on High Performance Computer Architecture (HPCA), February 7–11, 2015.

[15] V. Sridharan, D.R. Kaeli, Quantifying software vulnerability, in: Proceedings of the 2008 Workshop on Radiation effects and Fault Tolerance in Nanometer Technologies, ACM, Ischia, Italy, 2008, pp. 323–328.

[16] S.S. Mukherjee, C. Weaver, J. Emer, S.K. Reinhardt, T. Austin, A systematic methodology to compute the architectural vulnerability factors for a high-performance microprocessor, in: Proceedings of the 36th Annual IEEE/ACM International Symposium on Microarchitecture, 2003 (MICRO-36), December 3–5, 2003.

[17] T. Jingweijia, N. Goswami, L. Tao, F. Xin, Analyzing soft-error vulnerability on GPGPU microarchitecture, in: 2011 IEEE International Symposium on Workload Characterization (IISWC), November 6–8, 2011.

[18] N. Farazmand, R. Ubal, D. Kaeli, Statistical fault injection-based AVF analysis of a GPU architecture, in: Workshop on Silicon Errors in Logic-System Effects (SELSE), 2012.

[19] H. Jeon, M. Wilkening, V. Sridharan, S. Gurumurthi, G. Loh, Architectural vulnerability modeling and analysis of integrated graphics processors, in: Workshop on Silicon Errors in Logic-System Effects (SELSE), 2013.

[20] N.J. Wang, A. Mahesri, S.J. Patel, Examining ACE analysis reliability estimates using fault-injection, in: Proceedings of the 34th Annual International Symposium on Computer Architecture, ACM, San Diego, CA, USA, 2007, pp. 460–469.

[21] Y.K. Soo, P. Cuong, M. Saleheen, Z. Kalbarczyk, R. Iyer, Hauberk: lightweight silent data corruption error detector for GPGPU, in: 2011 IEEE International Parallel & Distributed Processing Symposium (IPDPS), May 16–20, 2011.

[22] F. Bo, K. Pattabiraman, M. Ripeanu, S. Gurumurthi, GPU-Qin: a methodology for evaluating the error resilience of GPGPU applications, in: 2014 IEEE International Symposium on Performance Analysis of Systems and Software (ISPASS), March 23–25, 2014.

[23] NVIDIA, CUDA-GDB, 2015, http://docs.nvidia.com/cuda/cuda-gdb/.

[24] M. Stephenson, S.K.S. Hari, Y. Lee, E. Ebrahimi, D.R. Johnson, D. Nellans, M. O'Connor, S.W. Keckler, Flexible software profiling of GPU architectures, in: Proceedings of the 42nd Annual International Symposium on Computer Architecture, ACM, Portland, OR, 2015, pp. 185–197.

[25] S.K.S. Hari, T. Tsai, M. Stephenson, S. Keckler, J. Emer, SASSIFI: evaluating resilience of GPU applications, in: 11th Workshop on Silicon Errors in Logic-System Effects (SELSE), Austin, TX, 2015.

[26] P. Rech, L. Carro, N. Wang, T. Tsai, S.K.S. Hari, S.W. Keckler, Measuring the radiation reliability of SRAM structures in GPUS designed for HPC, in: Workshop on Silicon Errors in Logic-System Effects (SELSE), 2014.

[27] NVIDIA, NVIDIA's Next Generation CUDA Compute Architecture: Kepler GK110, 2012, https://www.nvidia.com/content/PDF/kepler/NVIDIA-Kepler-GK110-Architecture-Whitepaper.pdf.

[28] J. Tan, Z. Li, X. Fu, Cost-effective soft-error protection for SRAM-based structures in GPGPUs, in: Proceedings of the ACM International Conference on Computing Frontiers, ACM, Ischia, Italy, 2013, pp. 1–10.

[29] J.W. Sheaffer, D.P. Luebke, K. Skadron, A hardware redundancy and recovery mechanism for reliable scientific computation on graphics processors, in: Proceedings of the 22nd ACM SIGGRAPH/EUROGRAPHICS symposium on Graphics hardware, Eurographics Association, San Diego, CA, 2007, pp. 55–64.

[30] H. Jeon, M. Annavaram, Warped-DMR: light-weight error detection for GPGPU, in: Proceedings of the 2012 45th Annual IEEE/ACM International Symposium on Microarchitecture, IEEE Computer Society, 2012, pp. 37–47.

[31] J. Tan, X. Fu, RISE: improving the streaming processors reliability against soft errors in GPGPUs, in: Proceedings of the 21st International Conference on Parallel Architectures and Compilation Techniques, ACM, Minneapolis, MN, USA, 2012, pp. 191–200.

[32] R. Nathan, D.J. Sorin, Argus-G: comprehensive, low-cost error detection for GPGPU cores, Comput. Archit. Lett. 14 (1) (2015) 13–16.

[33] A. Meixner, M.E. Bauer, D.J. Sorin, Argus: low-cost, comprehensive error detection in simple cores, in: 40th Annual IEEE/ACM International Symposium on Microarchitecture, 2007 (MICRO 2007), December 1–5, 2007.

[34] S.S. Mukherjee, M. Kontz, S.K. Reinhardt, Detailed design and evaluation of redundant multi-threading alternatives, in: Proceedings of the 29th Annual International Symposium on Computer Architecture, 2002.

[35] E. Rotenberg, AR-SMT: a microarchitectural approach to fault tolerance in microprocessors, in: Twenty-Ninth Annual International Symposium on Fault-Tolerant Computing, 1999, Digest of Papers, June 15–18, 1999.

[36] C. Wang, H.S. Kim, Y. Wu, V. Ying, Compiler-managed software-based redundant multi-threading for transient fault detection, in: Proceedings of the International Symposium on Code Generation and Optimization, IEEE Computer Society, 2007, pp. 244–258.

[37] M. Dimitrov, M. Mantor, H. Zhou, Understanding software approaches for GPGPU reliability, in: Proceedings of 2nd Workshop on General Purpose Processing on Graphics Processing Units, Washington, DC, USA, ACM, 2009, pp. 94–104.

[38] J. Wadden, A. Lyashevsky, S. Gurumurthi, V. Sridharan, K. Skadron, Real-world design and evaluation of compiler-managed GPU redundant multithreading, in: Proceeding of the 41st Annual International Symposium on Computer Architecuture, Minneapolis, MN, USA, IEEE Press, 2014, pp. 73–84.

[39] S. Li, N. Farooqui, S. Yalamanchili, Software reliability enhancements for GPU applications, in: IEEE Workshop on Silicon Errors in Logic-System Effects (SELSE), 2013.

[40] N. Farooqui, A. Kerr, G. Eisenhauer, K. Schwan, S. Yalamanchili, Lynx: a dynamic instrumentation system for data-parallel applications on GPGPU architectures, in: 2012 IEEE International Symposium on Performance Analysis of Systems and Software (ISPASS), April 1–3, 2012.

[41] N. Oh, P.P. Shirvani, E.J. McCluskey, Control-flow checking by software signatures, IEEE Trans. Reliab. 51 (1) (2002) 111–122.

[42] S. Li, V. Sridharan, S. Gurumurthi, S. Yalamanchili, Software-based dynamic reliability management for GPU applications, in: IEEE Workshop on Silicon Errors in Logic-System Effects (SELSE), April, 2015.

Addressing hardware reliability challenges in general-purpose GPUs

23

J. Tan, X. Fu

University of Houston, Houston, TX, United States

1 INTRODUCTION

Modern graphics processing units (GPUs) support thousands of concurrent threads and provide remarkably higher computational throughput than CPUs on parallel computing, which is key for the large-scale high-performance computing (HPC) in science and engineering. In addition, the programming models (e.g., NVIDIA CUDA [1], AMD Stream [2], OpenCL [3]) significantly reduce the development effort to parallelize general-purpose applications on GPUs. With these increasing computing power and improved programmability, general-purpose computing on GPUs (GPGPUs) emerge as a highly attractive platform for a wide range of HPC applications exhibiting strong data-level or thread-level parallelism. For example, as the second most powerful supercomputer in the world, Oak Ridge National Laboratory's Titan uses GPUs in addition to the traditional CPUs [4].

This extensive usage of GPGPU makes reliability a critical concern. Traditionally, the dominant workloads on GPUs are graphic processing applications that can effectively mask errors and have relaxed request on computation correctness. For example, Sheaffer et al. [5] observed that errors in video applications are usually masked since they impact only a few pixels, or the corrupted image is quickly recomputed in the next frame. Therefore the error detection and fault tolerance on GPUs receive little attention. However, the newly adopted HPC applications, such as the scientific computing, financial application, and medical data processing, have rigorous requirements on execution correctness. For example, in the HPC application computing correlation function [6], 1% of value errors in any of the program output elements is treated as a silent data corruption (SDC) error and cannot be tolerated. This makes reliability a growing concern in GPGPU architecture design. Even worse, the shrinking of feature sizes allows the manufacture of billions of transistors on a single GPGPU processor chip that concurrently runs thousands of threads. This further emphasizes the need for characterizing and addressing reliability in GPGPU architecture design.

There are two paramount hardware reliability challenges in GPGPUs, particle strikes induced soft errors and manufacturing process variations (PVs).

(i) Soft errors, also called transient faults, are failures caused by high-energy neutron or alpha particle strikes in integrated circuits. These faults are said to be "soft" in contrast to hard-faults, which are permanent in the device. They may silently corrupt the data and lead to erroneous computation results. Soft-error rate (SER) has been predicted to increase exponentially because of the shrinking of feature sizes and growing integration density [7,8]. GPGPUs with hundreds of cores integrated in a single chip are prone to suffer severe soft-error attacks [9–15]. For example, 8 soft errors were observed in a 72-h testing program on 60 NVIDIA GeForce 8800GTS 512 [10]; and transient faults were found in two-thirds of evaluated commodity GPUs [9]. It was also found that the SDC ratio in commodity GPUs is 16–33% [16], while the ratio is smaller than 2.3% in CPUs that have comparatively developed fault tolerance techniques. The increasing SER becomes the major obstacle to current and future GPGPUs by either preventing them from scaling down to smaller feature sizes or resulting in imprecise operations from these systems.

(ii) PV is the divergence of device parameters from their nominal values, which is caused by the challenging manufacture process at very small feature technologies. PV induces substantial variability in circuit path delay and causes timing errors [17–19]. This impact is further exacerbated in GPGPUs that contain tremendous amounts of parallel critical paths [20,21]. The frequency ratio of the fastest to the slowest computing core in GPGPUs increases up to 1.4 under the impact of PV [20].

In this chapter, we mainly target at the preceding two types of reliability issues. We explore a set of mechanisms to leverage the unique GPGPU architectural features to effectively optimize the GPGPUs' reliability.

This chapter is organized as follows: Section 2 provides the background on the state-of-the-art GPGPUs; Section 3 models and characterizes GPGPU reliability in the presence of soft errors; Section 4 improves the soft-error robustness of GPGPUs; and Section 5 discusses mitigating the susceptibility of GPUs to PVs.

2 GPGPUs ARCHITECTURE

Fig. 1A shows an overview of the state-of-the-art GPUs [1]. They consist of a scalable number of in-order streaming multiprocessors (SM) that can access multiple memory controllers via an on-chip interconnection network. The GPU device has its own off-chip external memory (e.g., global memory) connected to the on-chip memory controllers. Fig. 1B illustrates a zoom-in view of the SM [22]. It contains

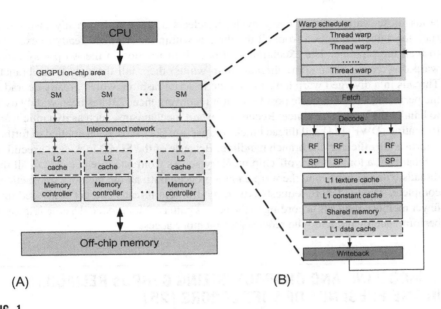

FIG. 1

General-purpose computing on graphic processing units (GPGPU) architecture. (A) An overview. (B) SM microarchitecture.

the warp scheduler, register files (RF), streaming processors (SP), constant cache, texture cache, shared memory, and so on.

To facilitate GPGPUs' application development, several programming models have been developed (e.g., NVIDIA CUDA [1], AMD Stream [2], OpenCL [3]). In this chapter, we take the NVIDIA CUDA programming model as an example; the basic concepts will hold for most programming models. In CUDA, the GPU is treated as a coprocessor that executes highly parallel kernel functions launched by the CPU. The kernel is composed of a grid of lightweight threads; a grid is divided into a set of blocks (referred to as cooperative thread arrays [CTA] in CUDA); each block is composed of hundreds of threads. Threads are distributed to the SMs at the granularity of blocks, and threads within a single block communicate via shared memory and synchronize at a barrier if needed. Per-block resources, such as registers files, shared memory, and thread slots in an SM, are not released until all the threads in the block finish execution. More than one block can be assigned to a single SM concurrently if there are sufficient per-block resources.

Threads in the SM execute in the SIMD fashion. A number of individual threads (e.g., 32 threads) from the same block are grouped together, which is called a warp. In the pipeline, threads within a warp execute the same instruction but with different data values. Fig. 1B also presents the details of SM microarchitecture. Each SM interleaves multiple warps (e.g., 32) on a cycle-by-cycle basis; the warp scheduler holds those warps, and at every cycle, it selects a warp with a ready instruction (i.e., the same instruction from all the threads within the warp are ready to execute) to feed the pipeline. The execution of a branch instruction in the warp may cause warp divergence when some threads jump while others fall through at the branch. Threads in a diverged warp have to execute in serial fashion, which greatly degrades the performance. Immediate postdominator reconvergence [23] has been widely used to handle the warp divergence. Recently, several mechanisms, such as dynamic warp formation (DWF) [24] and thread block compaction [22], have been applied to further improve the efficiency of branch handling. Because of the SIMD lock-step execution mechanism, a long-latency off-chip memory access from one thread can stall all the threads within a warp, and the warp cannot proceed until all the memory transactions complete. The load/store requests issued by different threads can get coalesced into fewer memory requests according to the access pattern. Memory coalescing improves performance by reducing the requests for memory access.

3 MODELING AND CHARACTERIZING GPGPUs RELIABILITY IN THE PRESENCE OF SOFT ERRORS [25]

3.1 MICROARCHITECTURE-LEVEL SOFT-ERROR VULNERABILITY ANALYSIS

A key observation of soft-error behavior at a microarchitecture level is that a transient fault may not affect processor states required for correct program execution. At a microarchitecture level, the overall hardware structure's SER is decided by two factors [26]: the FIT rate (failures in time, which is the raw SER at circuit level) per bit, mainly determined by circuit design and processing technology; and the architecture vulnerability factor (AVF) [27]. A hardware structure's AVF refers to the probability that a transient fault in that hardware structure will result in incorrect program results. Therefore the AVF, which can be used as a metric to estimate how vulnerable the hardware is to soft errors during program execution, is determined by the processor's state bits required for architecturally correct execution (ACE). At the instruction-level, an instruction is defined as ACE (un-ACE) instruction if its computation result affects (or does not affect) the program final output, and AVF is primarily determined by the quantity of ACE instructions per cycle and their residency time within the structure [27]. In this chapter, we use AVF as the major metric to estimate structure soft-error vulnerability.

3.2 SOFT-ERROR VULNERABILITY MODELING IN GPGPU MICROARCHITECTURE

In order to characterize and optimize the soft-error vulnerability of emerging GPGPU architecture, a tool to estimate the impact of soft errors on GPGPUs is highly desired. Recently, a Sim-SODA [28] was developed to compute AVF of CPU microarchitecture structures. Compared to the general-purpose CPU cores, GPGPU SM's implement in-order SIMD pipeline and have significantly different architecture and data/control flow from traditional CPUs. Sim-SODA is not applicable to the GPGPU architecture. For instance, in order to calculate AVF of structures buffering in-flight instructions (e.g., issue queue and reorder buffer in the CPU core, the warp scheduler in SM), the framework needs to identify ACE instructions by tracing the data dependence chains on the instruction output(s). Sim-SODA is built upon Alpha ISA, and only supports the analysis on instructions with two inputs and one output. However, instructions in GPGPUs are likely to consume/produce vector input/output, which requires a more complicated analysis considering all the data dependencies among the vector inputs and outputs. Moreover, Sim-SODA mainly targets single-thread uniprocessors in which the AVF computation is relatively simple. On the contrary, GPGPU contains tens of SMs with thousands of parallel threads running simultaneously, and threads within a block share data via the per-core shared memory. Hence error propagation from one thread to another thread is possible. In other words, the instruction output from one thread could affect the correct execution of a different thread. When estimating the GPGPU's microarchitecture vulnerability, a comprehensive methodology is required to consider the vector input/output and thread-level error propagation in ACE instruction identification, which is obviously far beyond the capability of Sim-SODA.

We build GPGPU-SODA (GPGPU SOftware Dependability Analysis) on a cycle-accurate, open-source, and publicly available simulator GPGPU-Sim [29]; it supports CUDA parallel thread execution (PTX) ISA. GPGPU-SODA is capable of estimating the vulnerability of the major microarchitecture structures in each SM, including the warp scheduler, streaming processors, registers, shared memory, and L1 texture and constant caches. The structures in SMs are classified as two types: address-based structures keeping computation data values (e.g., registers, shared memory, and L1 caches) and structures buffering instructions (e.g., warp scheduler). To compute AVF for address-based structure, GPGPU-SODA summarizes the ACE components [30] of each bit's lifetime in the structure. In order to calculate AVF for structures buffering instructions, GPGPU-SODA implements an instruction analysis window [27] for each thread. It explores data dependence chains for instructions with multiple inputs and outputs to perform the comprehensive ACE instruction identification. Note that even threads within a warp share the same PC; an analysis window on one thread for the entire warp is not sufficient. Because it ignores the data dependencies across threads caused by the interthread data sharing, an ACE instruction may be incorrectly identified as un-ACE. In CPU processors, an analysis window with a size of 40,000 instructions is required to determine un-ACE instructions. Since GPGPUs workloads are composed of lightweight threads, the window size is largely reduced to 1000 instructions in GPGPU-SODA. We classify the instruction as vulnerability-unknown if its vulnerability cannot be determined by our 1000-instruction analysis window. The percentage of unknown instructions is mostly lower than 5%. We use synthetic microbenchmarks that have small amounts of instructions to validate the analysis windows. Their reports on un-ACE instructions match our expectations.

3.3 SOFT-ERROR VULNERABILITY ANALYSIS ON GPGPUs

3.3.1 Experimental methodologies

We use the developed GPGPU-SODA to obtain the GPGPU reliability and performance statistics. Our baseline GPGPU configuration models the Nvidia Fermi-style architecture: the GPU contains 28 SMs; the warp size is 32; each SM supports 1024 threads and 8 blocks at most; each SM contains 64 KB registers, and 16 KB shared memory; the scheduler applies the round-robin among the ready warps scheduling policy.

We collected a large set of available GPGPU workloads from Nvidia CUDA SDK [31], Rodinia Benchmark [32], and Parboil Benchmark [6]. We list them as follows: *64H* (64 bin histogram), *BFS* (breadth-first search), *BP* (back propagation), *BS* (Black-Scholes option pricing), *CP* (Columbic potential), *FWT* (fast walsh transform), *HS* (hot spot), *KM* (K-means), *LIB* (LIBOR), *LPS* (3D Laplace solver), *LV* (Levenshtein edit-distance calculation), *MRIF* (magnetic resonance imaging FHD), *MT* (matrix transpose), *NE* (nearest neighbor), *NN* (neural network), *NW* (Needleman Wunsch), *SLA* (scan of large arrays), *SP* (scalar product), *SRAD* (speckle reducing anisotropic diffusion), *ST3D* (stencil 3D), and *STO* (store GPU). The workloads show significant diversities according to their kernel characteristics, divergence characteristics, memory access patterns, and so on. They are compiled into PTX assembly, and GPGPU-SODA takes the produced PTX assembly instructions associated with the information on thread-level registers, shared memory, and memory usages to perform the simulation. We simulate most benchmarks to completion, except a few that causing an extremely long simulation time. AVF is used as the basic metric to estimate how susceptible a GPGPU microarchitecture structure is to soft-error attacks.

3.3.2 Soft-error vulnerability of the GPGPU microarchitecture structures

Fig. 2 profiles the instruction vulnerability characteristics in various benchmarks. It shows the percentage of ACE, un-ACE, and vulnerability-unknown instructions for each workload. The un-ACE instructions are further classified as first dynamically dead (FDD) instructions whose results are not consumed by any other instructions [27], and transitively dynamically dead (TDD) instructions whose results are only read by FDD or TDD instructions [27]. On average, there are 88% ACE, 8% un-ACE, and 4% vulnerability-unknown instructions across the benchmarks. As shown in Fig. 2, most benchmarks have a large number of ACE instructions, with benchmark *SLA* the exception as it contains only 41% ACE instructions. Generally, threads running in GPGPUs are mainly composed of loops, and un-ACE instructions that appear in the loop will be repeatedly executed and will contribute to a large number of un-ACE instructions in the workload. This is the case in *SLA* whose un-ACE instructions mainly exist in the loops. Our GPGPU-SODA framework reports 1% FDD and 8% TDD instructions, which dominate the un-ACE instructions. This is different from the general-purpose workloads in CPU processors that have 10–30%

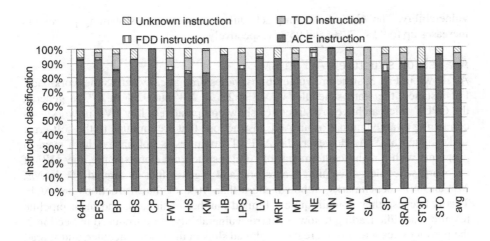

FIG. 2

The percentage of ACE, FDD, TDD, and unknown instructions.

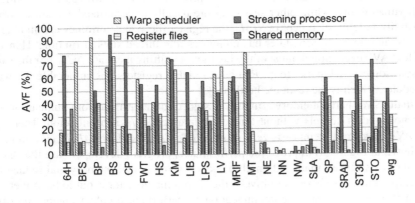

FIG. 3

The AVF of GPGPU SM microarchitecture structures.

NOP (No Operation) instructions, which are usually inserted for pipeline flushing or instruction alignment in VLIW processors [27,28,33].

Fig. 3 shows the soft-error vulnerability of several key structures in GPGPU SMs with the baseline GPGPU configuration. We present the averaged result across the SMs. The AVF of L1, constant, and texture caches are not shown in Fig. 3. This is because the workloads we studied either do not or rarely use those structures, and their AVF is even lower than 4%. As shown in Fig. 3, the primary microarchitecture structures (e.g., warp scheduler, registers) that are heavily utilized exhibit high vulnerability. The AVF of the warp scheduler, registers, and streaming processors increases up to 92%, 77%, and 95%, respectively.

Analysis on structure's AVF in SM

As shown in Fig. 3, structure vulnerability varies dramatically across the workloads. For instance, the warp scheduler's AVF is 2% in *NW* but 92% in *BP*. In general, the GPUs' microarchitecture structures show comparatively low AVF in workloads containing a large number of un-ACE instructions that are immune to the soft-error strikes, such as *SLA*. However, the AVF of structures is not always high even in programs with a significant amount of ACE instructions. For example, the AVF of the warp scheduler, streaming processors, and register files is around 5% in *NE*, *NN*, and *NW* benchmarks, although more than 90% of the instructions are ACE. This is because they contain quite a limited number of threads, and most pipeline resources are idle leading to low soft-error vulnerability. As introduced in Section 2, the per-block resources (e.g., registers, thread slots in the warp scheduler, and shared memory) will not be released until the block completes execution, which limits the maximum number of blocks that can be simultaneously assigned to an SM. Different per-block resources become the bottleneck for kernels that have different resource requirements. The bottleneck structure is prone to be fully utilized and manifests high vulnerability, while other structures are usually underutilized and show strong capability in fault tolerance. In *ST3D*, the register file size determines the number of blocks, and the warp scheduler has numerous idle thread slots at runtime. Hence it has low AVF even though most of the instructions sitting there are ACE. For the same reason, some benchmarks (e.g., *BP*) have reliable registers but vulnerable the warp scheduler, which is the resource bottleneck.

In the SM, shared memory is mainly designed for interthread communication, and it is not used in kernels without thread communication/synchronization. Therefore the AVF of shared memory is zero in *BFS*, *BS*, *CP*, *KM*, *LIB*, *MRIF*, *NE*, and *NN*, as shown in Fig. 3. To improve the performance, program developers use the shared memory as software managed on-chip cache for the global memory and reduce the off-chip memory accesses. Intuitively, the shared memory turns out to be vulnerable when it is used for thread communication or performance enhancement purposes, and becomes the resource bottleneck during the block allocation. However, its AVF still stays as low as 12% on average across the benchmarks that use the shared memory. Shared memory is highly banked. The bank selected to hold a data value is determined by the data address, which leads to the unbalanced bank usage in a block. The number of blocks that each bank can support is different, and the minimum number finally limits the number of blocks the shared memory can support. Even though shared memory becomes the resource bottleneck, most banks in it may be underutilized, and the vulnerability of the entire structure is low. Fig. 4 presents the percentage of used entries in the shared memory for each benchmark. On average, it is only 24%. In workloads whose block resource allocation is limited by the share memory (e.g., *64H*, *LPS*, *NW*, *SP*, *SRAD*, and *STO*), more than 40% of entries are never used during the entire execution time. The used entries are written/read in a

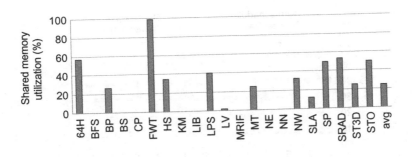

FIG. 4

Shared memory utilization in percentage.

very short period and become free the majority of the time. Therefore the shared memory has very low vulnerability.

As shown in Fig. 3, the streaming processors' AVF has strong correlation to the number of ACE instructions in most benchmarks. Since the instruction execution time in streaming processors is constant, the ACE instruction quantity per cycle becomes the major factor to determine the AVF. However, streaming processors' AVF is only 10% in *BFS* even 92% instructions in it are ACE. BFS has heavy branch divergences and long-latency off-chip memory accesses. The diverged threads within the warp have to execute sequentially, which causes tremendous performance penalty. In our baseline machine configuration, the immediate postdominator-based reconvergence is applied to reconverge threads at the immediate postdominator (detailed explanation can be found in Ref. [23]) to handle the branch divergences. However, it has limited capability to efficiently recover the performance loss. Furthermore, the long-latency memory accesses increase the streaming processors' idle time. Accordingly, the parallelized streaming processors are highly underutilized in *BFS*, and the AVF is low.

Vulnerability variations at streaming multiprocessor level

A GPGPU processor contains tens of SMs. Generally, they are equally utilized and exhibit similar vulnerability behavior. Fig. 5A shows the AVF of the major microarchitecture structures in each SM when executing *HS*. The figure shows a small AVF divergence among the SMs. However, this is not the case for some benchmarks.

Fig. 5B demonstrates an example of *BP* with its streaming processors' AVF varying significantly across SMs. For example, the streaming processors' AVF is 80% in SM 9, but drops to 29% in SM 27. This happens because the threads running in each SM have a different memory access pattern, which determines the quantity of memory requests that can get coalesced (more coalesced requests implies fewer off-chip memory transactions), and the severity of memory contentions among requests affects the memory access latency. SM 27 experiences more off-chip memory accesses compared to SM 9; the streaming processors in SM 27 are idle in

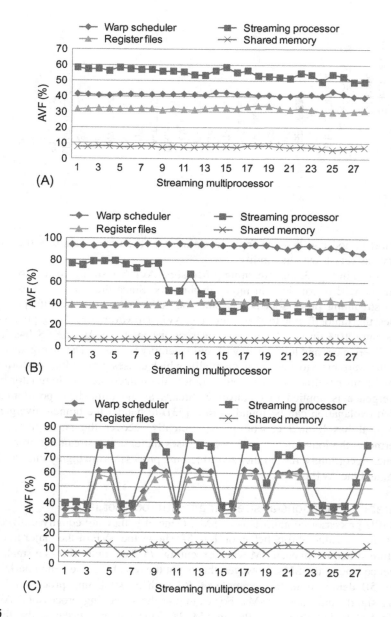

FIG. 5

The AVF of microarchitecture structures in each SM while running (A) FWT, (B) LPS, and (C) SP.

majority of the time, and correspondingly, they are more robust against the soft-error strikes. Interestingly, the AVF of warp scheduler, register files, and shared memory does not show much difference among SMs. During the kernel launch process, all its blocks may not be able to distribute to the SMs and start the execution simultaneously since the maximum number of blocks an SM can support is limited. The block that cannot be allocated to the SM at the kernel launch time has to wait until one block finishes and its resources in the SM are released. By doing this, the execution time of each SM tends to be balanced. Furthermore, SMs with a long block execution time caused by the frequent memory accesses execute fewer blocks and have a smaller quantity of ACE instructions in the storage-based pipeline structures (e.g., warp scheduler) through the entire execution time. However, instructions have to remain in those structures during the off-chip memory accesses, and their residency time increases. As a result, the AVF of the warp scheduler, register files, and shared memory are nearly the same across SMs.

Fig. 5C shows another example of *SP*; the structure of the AVF differs substantially across SMs, and structures in the same SM show similar vulnerability behaviors. Take SM 7 and 9 for example; the vulnerability of the major structures including the warp scheduler, streaming processors, and registers is low in SM 7 but is much higher in SM 9. This is caused by the uneven distribution of blocks among SMs. SM 7 is assigned 3 blocks for execution, while the number of blocks allocated to SM 9 is doubled, leading to a much larger number of ACE instructions. Moreover, different from *BP*, the execution time of SMs in *SP* varies significantly; SM 7 finishes its workloads much earlier than SM 9, which implies that the residency time of ACE instructions in both SMs are similar. Therefore structures in SM 9 are more vulnerable to soft errors because of their numerous ACE instructions.

When a thread encounters a barrier instruction, it has to wait until the synchronization in the block finishes. In other words, warps will stall upon the synchronization requests. Similar to the long-latency off-chip memory accesses, the barrier instructions may increase execution time, thus affecting the structure of soft-error robustness. Since warps are issued to the pipeline in a round-robin order, in our baseline GPGPU's machine, threads within the block usually proceed at a similar rate; the warp waiting time at the barrier is short compared to that for the off-chip memory access. Furthermore, barrier instructions account for only 2.5% of the total instructions in most benchmarks. Their impact on structure vulnerability is trivial.

In summary, we observe that the GPGPU's microarchitecture vulnerability is highly related to workload characteristics such as the percentage of un-ACE instructions, the per-block resource requirements, the branch divergences, the memory access pattern (e.g., memory coalescing, memory resource contentions, and memory access latency), the block allocation that determines the execution time, and the amount of workload executed in each SM.

3.3.3 Impact of architecture optimizations on GPGPU microarchitecture-level soft-error vulnerability

In this section, we evaluate the impact of several popular architectural design optimizations on the soft-error vulnerability of GPGPUs microarchitecture.

Dynamic warp formation

Branch divergence is a major cause for performance degradation in GPGPUs. As we discussed earlier, the immediate postdominator (PDOM) lacks the capability to reconverge threads at the beginning for branch divergence to further improve the performance. DWF is proposed in Ref. [24] to efficiently handle the threads' divergence. It groups threads from multiple warps but branching to the same target into a new and complete warp, and issues it into the SIMD pipeline. Therefore the parallel streaming processors in the SM are fully utilized, and their performance is enhanced.

In our baseline GPGPUs, a warp splits into multiple warps at the occurrence of the branch divergence; those spawned warps have to consume the issued bandwidth to leave the warp scheduler. They delay the issue time of other warps and increase the warp residency time. DWF regroups the divergent threads into new warps. It reduces the number of warps competing for the issue bandwidth and shrinks the warp waiting time. Meanwhile, DWF aims to improve the performance and reduce the kernel execution time. Note that reducing the warp waiting time and correspondingly the ACE instruction residency time can help to decrease AVF, but shrinking the execution time will increase the AVF as it increases the ACE instruction quantity per cycle [27]. Therefore the impact of DWF on the warp scheduler's vulnerability can be negative or positive, depending on the warp residency time and the kernel execution time. When the reduction of warp residency time dominates that of the kernel execution time, the warp scheduler AVF decreases, and vice versa. Since the warps enter the SIMD pipeline earlier, registers are written/read faster, which helps to reduce their lifetime. Similar to the warp scheduler, the DWF could increase/decrease the registers' AVF.

Fig. 6 presents the structures' AVF under the impact of DWF; they are normalized to the baseline case with PDOM applied for comparison. Benchmarks *KM*, *LIB*, *MRIF*, *NN*, and *ST3D* cannot execute when DWF is enabled, so we eliminated those benchmarks from this figure. The results of the L1 caches and shared memory are not shown in Fig. 6 and the following figures since they are always robust to the soft-error strikes under different architectural optimizations. On average, DWF optimizes the warp scheduler and the registers' reliability by 5% and 5%, respectively. Obviously, most benchmarks studied here fall into the category in which DWF has positive effect on those two structures reliability. Note that the capability of DWF to optimize a structure's reliability is significantly affected by the percentage of branch divergence operations in the benchmark. When there are few branch divergences, DWF has limited opportunities to explore the warp formation, whose effect on reliability is trivial. For example, the warp scheduler AVF decreases only 1% in *CP* with 2% branch divergence operations. On the other hand, DWF

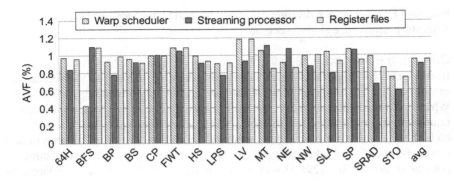

FIG. 6

The normalized AVF of GPGPU streaming multiprocessor microarchitecture structures under the impact of DWF.

helps to improve the warps scheduler's reliability by 60% in *BFS* with 40% branch divergence operations.

The streaming processors' AVF is highly related to the kernel execution time. Since the instruction computation time is mainly determined by the instruction type, a shorter kernel execution time implies an increased quantity of ACE instructions per cycle in the streaming processors. And the streaming processors are more susceptible to soft errors when the execution time shrinks. Intuitively, DWF would hurt the streaming processors' soft-error vulnerability because it targets on optimizing performance and reduces the kernel execution time. Interestingly, DWF decreases streaming processors' AVF by 10% on average as shown in Fig. 6. This is because DWF decreases the IPC in a number of benchmarks (as shown in Fig. 7). When randomly regrouping threads into new warps, DWF may lose opportunities to combine memory accesses originally from the same warp, and introduce extra off-chip memory transactions, which negatively affect the performance. When the

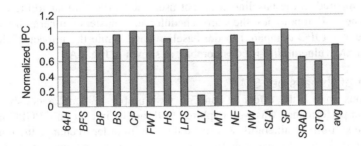

FIG. 7

The normalized IPC under DWF.

benefit of DWF in branch divergences is outweighed by the increased memory access requests, performance starts to degrade.

Off-chip memory access

In the GPGPUs' applications, all threads in a kernel execute the same code and exhibit similar execution progress in the fine-grained multithreading environment. When one thread encounters an off-chip memory access, other threads are likely to issue requests at approximately the same time, leading to severe resource contentions on both the on-chip network and the memory controllers. The effect of interconnect topologies and request scheduling policies in the memory controller on GPU throughput was studied in Ref. [29]. However, their impact on GPU microarchitecture soft-error vulnerability is largely ignored.

Fig. 8A shows the vulnerability of SM structures when applying the FIFO scheduling policy in the memory controller and two interconnect network topologies (i.e., Torus and Fly), respectively. Results are normalized to our baseline configuration with mesh topology and first-ready first-come first-serve (FR-FCFS) scheduling policy. As it shows, even though the performance is hurt considerably while using the Torus network topology (Fig. 8B also presents the normalized IPC for the vulnerability analysis), in general the interconnect network topology has little impact on the vulnerability of the warp scheduler and register files. For instance, the two structures' AVF is similar to the baseline case, while the IPC decreases 23% in NE under the Torus topology. The reduced IPC implies fewer ACE instructions per cycle in the warp scheduler; however, the instructions spend longer time in the structure, and its vulnerability remains almost the same as the baseline case. A similar case occurs in the register files. On the other hand, the streaming processors' AVF varies noticeably in NE under the Torus topology, because it exhibits strong correlation with the GPU performance.

The FIFO scheduling policy simply serves the memory requests in the order of their arrival time in the memory controller. It causes a frequent switch among DRAM rows, which increases the request service time and the memory access latency. FR-FCFS gives the memory requests that hit the open DRAM row higher priority to access the DRAM. Therefore the IPC decreases 22% under the FIFO scheduling policy compared to the baseline case that uses FR-FCFS. Similar to the case with different network topologies, the warp scheduler and registers' vulnerability changes slightly under FIFO compared to the baseline case, while the impact of the FIFO policy on SM vulnerability is considerable, as shown in Fig. 8A.

Number of threads per SM

In previous works, the effect of altering the number of simultaneously running threads on performance was well explored [29], but its impact on GPGPU microarchitecture soft-error vulnerability is still unknown. In order to change the number of parallel threads per SM, we scale the per-block resources (the amount of maximum blocks, shared memory, and registers) between 50% and 200% to the baseline case, which supports 1024 threads.

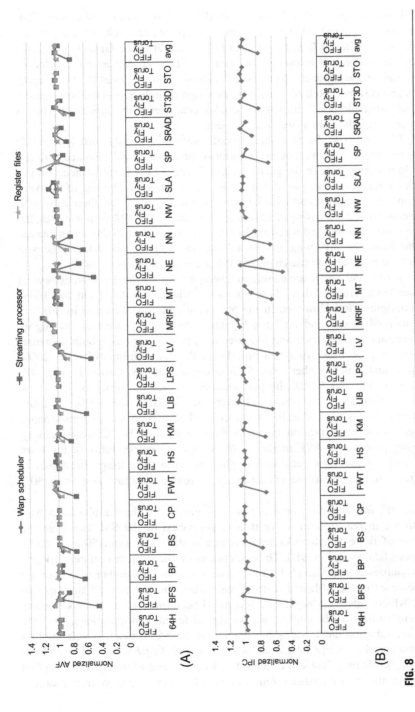

(A)

(B)

FIG. 8

The normalized (A) AVF and (B) IPC of GPGPU microarchitecture structures when applying the FIFO scheduling policy in the memory controller, the Fly, and the Torus network topology, respectively. Both memory controller scheduling and network topology have considerable impact on streaming processors' AVF and have little impact on the vulnerability of the warp scheduler and register files.

Fig. 9 shows the AVF and IPC results with different amounts of threads per SM. The results are normalized to the baseline case. When the per-block resources shrink to 50%, the kernels in *FWT*, *KM*, and *STO* fail to launch in the GPGPU processor because of the insufficient resources for even one block. Therefore the results for *FWT*, *KM*, and *STO* are missing from the 50% reduced thread count (512) in Fig. 9. As Fig. 9A and B shows, both AVF and IPC vary significantly across the benchmarks with the increasing number of threads per SM. We characterize the benchmarks based on their reliability behaviors as we describe next.

In *CP*, *LIB*, and *NW*, the 50% thread configuration is already sufficient for all the blocks to execute simultaneously; additional thread slots and resources are not used and do not contribute to the performance. Therefore the performance of these benchmarks remains the same as shown in Fig. 9B. In that case, the size of the warp scheduler and registers scales up with the increasing thread count, but their utilization reduces because of the increasing idle entries. Therefore, as Fig. 9A demonstrates, the AVF of the warp scheduler and registers decreases as the number of threads increases. On the other hand, the streaming processors' size and utilization do not change with thread count; hence there is little change in the streaming processors' AVF.

Similarly, *LPS* and *SRAD* are unable to leverage the additional resources beyond the baseline configuration; they show the same behavior as *CP* from the 100% to 200% configurations. However, in the 50% configuration, there are insufficient resources to hold blocks and feed the pipeline. Streaming processors are highly underutilized, and performance and the streaming processors' AVF both decrease. The performance of these two benchmarks is the same from 100% to 200% configuration and much higher than 50% configuration, as shown in Fig. 9B. For *FWT*, *SLA*, *SP*, and *ST3D*, the performance reaches the peak for the 150% configuration; they show the same behaviors as *CP* from the 150% to 200% configurations. *NN* is able to utilize the increased resources, so the performance is improved as the configuration increases from 50% to 200%. Correspondingly, the streaming processors' AVF increases. Moreover, the vulnerability of the warp scheduler and register files decreases slightly, because their usage decreases to some degree with regard to the continuously increased structure size from 50% to 200%.

In *BFS*, *BP*, *BS*, and *NE*, there are enough blocks for the simultaneous execution with the increasing number of threads supported by the SM. However, the performance of these benchmarks remains nearly the same from 50% to 200% configurations (shown in Fig. 9B). The contentions on the interconnect network and memory resources among threads become more severe as the number of concurrent threads increases in the SM, and instructions spend a longer time in the pipeline structures, which induces a negative effect GPU performance. As a consequence, the structure utilization is similar across the different configurations, and the configuration variation has a negligible impact on the SM structure's vulnerability in those benchmarks, except *BFS* as shown in Fig. 9A. In *BFS* the majority of the SMs are idle, while only few still execute blocks at the end of the kernel execution time. As the configuration changes from 50% to 200%, there are more free resources

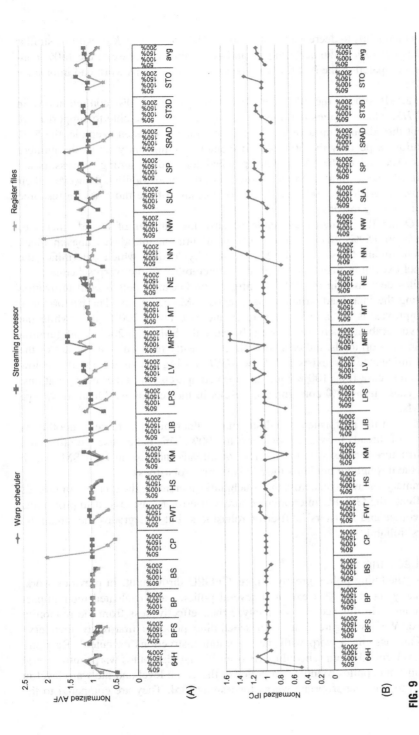

FIG. 9

The normalized (A) AVF and (B) IPC of GPGPU microarchitecture structures when the number of threads per SM is 50% (512 threads), 150% (1536 threads), and 200% (2048 threads) compare to the baseline case. Increasing the quantity of threads improves the warp scheduler and registers' soft-error robustness, but degrades the streaming processors' reliability.

in SMs, which helps to decrease the structures' AVF. Moreover, *KM* exhibits similar behavior as *BP*, except the performance and vulnerability decease in the 150% configuration compared to the baseline case because of the serious workload imbalance among SMs.

As Fig. 9B shows, the IPC increases from 50% to 150% configurations in 64*H* and *HS*, which implies that the increasing resources are able to support more concurrent threads and improve the throughput. Take *64H* as an example, the 50% configuration (especially the 50% shared memory) significantly limits the number of blocks executed in the SM and warp scheduler, and streaming processors are underutilized and exhibit extremely low soft-error vulnerability. However, their performance degrades at 200% configuration because of the more severe resource contentions among threads.

In *STO* the IPC remains the same because the number of threads increases from 100% to 150%. Because the 150% configuration introduces uneven block distribution among SMs, several SMs are heavily loaded, which determines the total kernel execution time. Moreover, the vulnerability of the warp scheduler and register files decreases in the 150% configuration because their overall utilization (considering the increased structure size) across SMs decreases. The performance further improves as the number of threads increase up to 200%, meanwhile the structure vulnerability increases as well. Because the SMs with 200% configuration have balanced workloads, the execution time is greatly reduced. The impact of the workload imbalance also exists in *LV* and *MRIF*. As Fig. 9B shows, the IPC is low in the baseline case (i.e., 100% configuration) compared with other configurations. This is because the 100% configuration results in the serious workload imbalance among SMs.

In *MT*, both the performance and structure vulnerability increases smoothly as the number of threads increases from 50% to 200%. This is because the utilization of each structure increases as the number of threads increase in each SM, which improves the throughput but hurts the SM soft-error robustness.

In summary, on average, across the benchmarks increasing the quantity of threads greatly affects the GPGPU microarchitecture soft-error robustness. It improves the warp scheduler and registers' soft-error robustness, but it degrades the streaming processors' reliability.

Warp scheduling

The warp scheduling policy greatly affects GPGPU throughput. In previous work, Lakshminarayana et al. [34] explored several policies and evaluated their impact on performance. In this section, we analyze their effectiveness from the reliability perspective. We investigate four warp scheduling policies: first-ready first-serve (FRFS), Fair (issuing a warp with the minimum instructions executed), Random, and two-level, round-robin scheduling (two-level) that distributes warps into several fetch groups and applies round-robin policy at the group level and the warp level in each group to select appropriate warps for issuing [35]. They are compared to the baseline case of round-robin scheduling. Fig. 10 presents the normalized AVF and IPC under the impact of various policies.

As Fig. 10 shows, on average, across the benchmarks, the structure AVF varies less than 8% under different scheduling policies when compared to the baseline case, and the IPC variation is even less than 5%. The structure vulnerability under the FRFS and Random scheduling policies is similar to the baseline case, but the vulnerability variation is more noticeable in several benchmarks (e.g., *LPS, LV, MRIF, ST3D*, and so on) when Fair and two-level polices are enabled. The Fair policy keeps the uniform progress among warps. It may increase the opportunities for interwarp memory coalescing when threads across warps have similar memory access patterns, and it reduces the warp waiting time. However, when it fails to merge the interwarp memory accesses, a large number of memory requests are generated in a very short time span, which results in heavy memory resource contention and extends the warp stall time. Hence the warp scheduler's AVF increases when the total execution time has a minor increase, such as *MT* shown in Fig. 10A. When a significant number of off-chip memory transactions fail to get coalesced, and the workload execution time severely extends, the significantly reduced number of ACE instructions per cycle dominate the increased instruction residency time in the pipeline structure, and as a result, the structure AVF decreases considerably (e.g., *SLA, SP,* and *ST3D*). The two-level scheduling policy aims to hide the long-latency memory accesses and improve performance; therefore, the number of ACE instructions per cycle increases and structures become more susceptible to soft errors (e.g., *LV* and *MRIF*).

To conclude, in this section, we first develop GPGPU-SODA to evaluate the GPGPU microarchitecture soft-error vulnerability. As our GPGPU-SODA suggests, the majority of the structures in GPGPUs (e.g., warp scheduler, streaming processors, and register files) are highly vulnerable, so a comprehensive technique is needed to protect them against the soft-error attacks. We observe that the structure's vulnerability is largely affected by the workload characteristics. For example, both branch divergences and long-latency memory accesses decrease the streaming processors' vulnerability. Moreover, SMs in a single GPGPU processor may manifest significantly different reliability characteristics. We further analyze the impact of several architecture optimizations on GPGPUs' microarchitecture vulnerability. For example, increasing the thread quantity per SM improves the warp scheduler and register files' reliability, but degrades the streaming processors' soft-error robustness. We also found that the structure vulnerability is insensitive to the warp scheduling polices. The observations of the microarchitecture structure's vulnerability characteristics made in this section provide useful guidance in building future resilient GPGPUs. Based on these observations, we suggest the GPGPU reliability-optimization technique should consider all the GPGPUs' microarchitecture structures and workload characteristics and that a technique focusing on one particular structure will not be an efficient, resilient solution for GPGPUs.

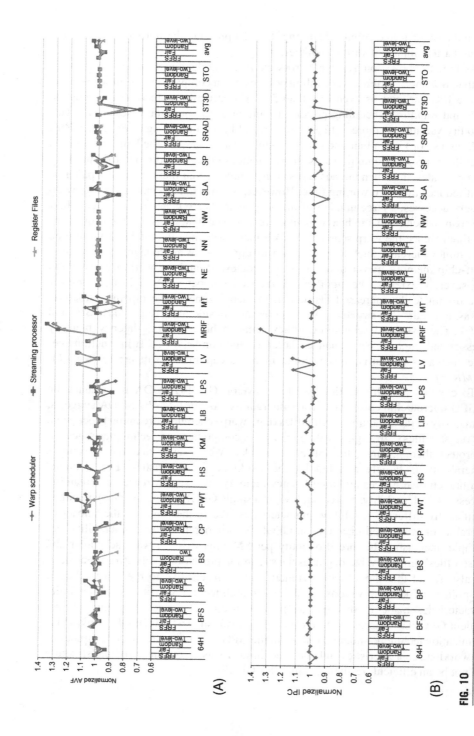

FIG. 10

The normalized (A) AVF and (B) IPC of GPGPU microarchitecture structures under the impact of FRFS, Fair, Random, and two-level warp scheduling policies, respectively. The structure vulnerability is insensitive to the warp scheduling polices.

4 RISE: IMPROVING THE STREAMING PROCESSORS' RELIABILITY AGAINST SOFT ERRORS IN GPGPUS [36]

In each GPGPU streaming multiprocessor, there are several parallel streaming processors (SPs). They perform the fundamental computing operations and play an important role in exploiting the parallel computing. In the GPGPUs with thousands of parallel threads, SPs execute numerous instructions and expose them to neutron and alpha particle strikes, leading to the high SER. We evaluate the SPs soft-error vulnerability by computing its AVF, which estimates the possibility that a transient fault in the structure will produce incorrect computation output, and find that the AVF is 53% on average (detailed description on AVF can be found in Section 3.1). In addition, as the key and representative combinational logic-based structure in the GPGPUs, SPs occupy a large portion of the chip area, and the SER of SPs becomes the major contributor to the overall SER of a GPGPU processor. Effectively protecting SPs becomes the essential first step to building a the resilient GPGPU architecture.

To overcome the reliability challenge, duplication [37] is the well-known classical technique: all instructions can be redundantly executed in the SPs, and two copies are compared for soft-error detection. However, the simple duplication will lead to a high-performance penalty. For example, software duplication causes more than 100% a performance penalties [38]. In our experiments, we also evaluate a simple hardware mechanism that duplicates all warp instructions (we refer it as full redundancy). Based on the experiments on various benchmarks, we found that on average, the full redundancy results in 58% performance degradation. The high computing throughput is the critical feature provided by GPGPUs. In general, substantially sacrificing the performance to achieve the perfect error coverage is not an efficient solution to the reliability issue in GPGPUs. A good trade-off between performance and reliability is more acceptable and desirable in future commodity GPGPU design.

As introduced in Section 2, GPGPU exploits TLP by grouping a number of threads into a warp that simultaneously executes the same instruction from each thread, and warps are interleaved on a cycle-by-cycle basis to hide the latency caused by the data dependence between consecutive instructions from a single warp. However, SPs are unused when all warps stall in the pipeline because of the long-latency operations (e.g., off-chip memory access). In addition, threads in the same warp may take different paths at a branch. They execute sequentially in the diverged warp, and partial SPs in the GPU core become idle [35]. We investigate a large set of GPGPU benchmarks and find that on average all SPs in a GPU core are idle during 35% of the total execution time, and the case that the SPs are partially idle appears 11% of the execution time. The large portion of the SPs' idle time provides great opportunities to trigger the partial redundancy and to trade a little performance degradation for maximal reliability improvement. In this section, we propose *RISE (Recycling the streaming processors Idle time for Soft-Error detection)*, which intelligently leverages the underutilized SPs to perform the redundancy and to substantially improve the SPs, reliability with negligible performance loss.

The details of this work are as follows:

- We propose Full-RISE, which effectively reuses the fully idled SPs in the GPU core caused by the long-latency memory accesses and the load imbalance among cores for soft-error detection. Full-RISE comprises the request pending aware Full-RISE (RP-FRISE) and the idle SMs aware Full-RISE (IS-FRISE). RP-FRISE predicts the warp stall time for its next off-chip memory access and appropriately delays the warp progress via the redundant execution, thereby successfully recycling the stall time for redundancy without degrading the performance. IS-FRISE estimates the load imbalances among cores and smartly triggers the redundancy in cores that are predicted to execute fewer threads.
- We propose Partial-RISE that redundantly executes a number of threads from a warp by combining their execution with the diverged warp, thereby utilizing the partially idled SPs during the branch divergence for reliability optimization.
- Our experiments show that both Full-RISE and Partial-RISE are capable of optimizing the SPs soft-error robustness substantially with negligible performance penalty. As the integration of the two techniques, RISE is able to reduce the SPs' vulnerability by 43% with only 4% performance loss. Based on our sensitivity analysis, RISE is also applicable to GPU architecture designs with various performance optimization schemes.

The rest of this section is organized as follows: Sections 4.1 and 4.2 present our Full-RISE and Partial-RISE techniques, respectively. Section 4.3 introduces the integrate RISE technique. Section 4.4 describes our experimental methodologies and evaluates the proposed techniques.

4.1 FULL-RISE

When implementing the redundant multithreading (RMT) technique in CPUs, the main and redundant threads share the pipeline resources, and no extra hardware resources are required to support the redundant thread. However, every parallel thread in GPGPU has statically allocated resources, including the register files and on-chip shared memory. Those per-thread resources have to be double-sized to successfully launch the main and redundant threads simultaneously in the GPU core, which leads to high use of resources and high power consumption. For example, Wadden et al. evaluate the software RMT in GPUs and observe that the intragroup RMT causes more than 100% slowdown in several applications [38]. In order to avoid this high overhead, the redundant thread in our study will use the same per-thread resources with the main thread. In other words, the redundant thread follows the main thread immediately; they interleave on an instruction-by-instruction basis and execute at the same speed.

In previous work, the opportunistic transient-fault detection in CPUs was proposed by Gomma et al. [39]. It keeps the progress difference between the main and redundant threads and triggers the redundant thread when the main thread stalls for the long-latency operations. Therefore the redundant thread can efficiently leverage the underutilized pipeline resources to perform the redundancy without degrading the performance. However, the technique is not applicable to the SPs' soft-error detection in the GPGPUs in our study. As previously described, both main and redundant threads in our study share the same resources thus they keep the same execution progress and stall at the same time. A novel technique is desired to intelligently trigger the redundant thread ahead of the pipeline stalls in the SM. In this section, we propose Full-RISE, which is composed of two methodologies: request pending aware Full-RISE and idle SMs aware Full-RISE.

In this study, we focus on the single-bit error model, which has the first-order impact on the failure rate in processors [40]. Note that SPs will operate the computations from main and redundant threads in two consecutive cycles; our technique is sufficient to detect the single-bit errors in SPs. Moreover, it is also able to catch the multiple-bit errors occurring simultaneously in the SPs resulting from either a single upset event or multiple, independent upsets. The particle-strikes, which could last for more than a cycle in a single bit, are not considered in this section.

4.1.1 Request pending aware Full-RISE

The observation on resource contentions among memory requests

In the CUDA programming model, all threads in a kernel execute the same code. Moreover, warps in the GPU SMs interleave on a cycle-by-cycle basis and exhibit similar execution progress. When one warp sends out a request for off-chip memory access, other warps are likely to issue requests at approximately the same time. The sudden burst of memory requests will cause congestion in the interconnect network and the memory controller, leading to severe resource contentions. In particular, the input buffer in the memory controller will quickly fill up by because of the requests. Generally, the out-of-order (OoO) FR-FCFS scheduling policy is applied in the memory controller. It grants higher priority to the requests that hit an open row in the DRAM and saves the time spent on precharge and activation to open a new row. However, its impact on alleviating request congestion is ambiguous because a limited number of requests (e.g., only one) can be serviced at a time, and most requests are experiencing a long waiting time.

Fig. 11 shows a case observed in a CUDA benchmark, *BP*. A large number of memory requests from the SM are routed to the memory controller in a short period. Because of the serious resource contentions, the off-chip memory access takes up to thousands of cycles. At the same time, the SM suffers extremely long pipeline stall, and SPs remain idle (as shown in Fig. 11A). Instead of sending the memory requests at a similar time and then stalling for a long time, warps can run at a slower pace, which prolongs their request issues (e.g., req2 ~ reqn in Fig. 11B) and avoids possible resource contentions and thereby having their requests serviced without any delay in the input buffer. Because of the dramatically reduced memory operation latency, the total warp execution time remains the same or even decreases. This provides a great opportunity for temporal redundancy, whose negative effect on performance can be positively used to postpone the warp execution progress and

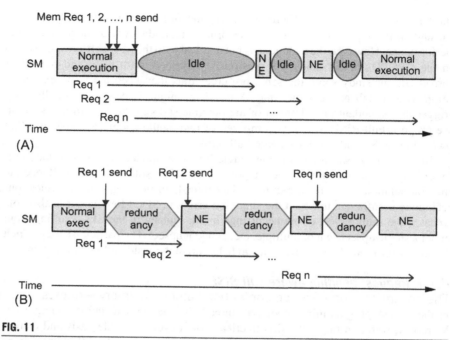

FIG. 11

SPs' idle time (A) caused by resource contentions among memory requests, and (B) recycled for partial redundancy. *NE*, normal execution.

their requests' issue time. The SPs' idle time caused by the request pending in the memory controller (highlighted in oval in Fig. 11A) is successfully recycled for the redundancy (highlighted with Hexagon in Fig. 11B). Note that the redundant and normal executions are interleaved at cycle level. We mark the redundancy separately from the normal execution in Fig. 11B for easy understanding of the impact of redundancy. By running a large number of benchmarks, we observe that the request pending contributes 65% of the time that all SPs in the SM are free. This implies that the SPs soft-error reliability can be substantially improved with no performance penalty.

The concept of request pending aware Full-RISE

As just discussed, the partial redundancy (relative to the full redundancy) can be treated as the knob to control the warp progress. In order to use the SPs' idle time without hurting performance, the partial redundancy has to be carefully tuned: overadjustment will result in excessive redundancy and unnecessary delay, consequentially degrading the performance significantly. On the other hand, the insufficient adjustment cannot effectively leverage the SPs' idle time for reliability enhancement. Moreover, different warps should spend different amounts of time on redundancy in order to separate their memory requests. That is, the warp progress should adapt well to its memory access pattern to achieve the SPs' optimal soft-error robustness. Obviously, statically determining the period for performing the partial redundancy fails to meet the goal since workloads have various memory access patterns. In this study, we propose RP-FRISE (for request pending aware Full-RISE) which dynamically tunes the knob (i.e., partial redundancy) per warp and recycles the SPs' idle time to maximize the error coverage in SPs.

Since the major resource contentions occur in the memory controller, the request waiting time in the input buffer is a good indicator for the necessity of slowing down the warp. A long waiting time implies a serious resource contention and that the warp that issues the request should have been delayed. While a short waiting time means that the request is issued appropriately, postponing the warp progress may degrade the performance. In the ideal case, a memory request gets serviced once it arrives at the memory controller: the period that allows a warp to perform the redundant execution should be equal to its request waiting time. In RP-FRISE we use the previous request pending time to predict the delay in the following memory transaction and tune the partial redundancy in the warp.

Note that the warp progress was already postponed after finishing the previous memory access, further slowing it down by the same amount of the previous request waiting time may serious prolong the warp computation. The example in Fig. 12 illustrates the challenge: warp0 and warp1 exhibit a different execution progress after the first memory access, and their following memory requests have less interference. Using the previous request waiting time leads to excessive redundancy and degrades the performance. On the other hand, although warps run at different rates after a long-latency memory access, the interference is still severe. Fig. 13 demonstrates the case. When the second memory request is issued from warp0, it interferes with the unfinished memory access from warp1, and the waiting time increases. The extended memory access in warp0 further affects the warp1, and setting the redundancy time as the preceding request waiting time for warp1 is appropriate. Note that warp1 may not delay the scheduled redundancy time as long, even when performing the full redundancy for the computation between its two memory accesses (highlighted by the light gray rectangular in Fig. 13). In that case, it will be stalled after finishing the redundancy because of the interference with warp0. Therefore the required redundancy time still accurately predicts the necessary delay in warp1. As can be seen in Figs. 12 and 13, generally the excessive redundancy occurs when the kernel is more computation-intensive, and the time spent on the normal computation alleviates the memory contentions among threads. While the brief normal computation in the memory-intensive kernel cannot effectively separate the memory requests, a longer redundant execution is desired.

In our study, we sample the memory access latency periodically when running a kernel and use it to adjust the number of cycles that the warp executes the redundant threads. Eq. (1) describes the analytical model to dynamically determine the redundancy cycles (represented by RC) in the warp based on its previous request pending time (represented by T_P) and the latest sampled memory access latency (represented by T_{acc_lat}).

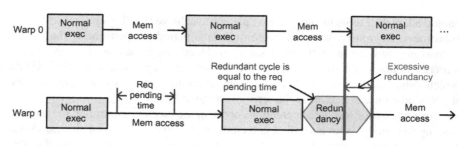

FIG. 12

An example of excessive redundancy.

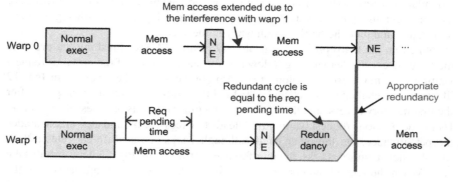

FIG. 13

An example of appropriate redundancy.

$$RC = \begin{cases} 0, & \text{if } T_P \leq T_{thr\_pend} \\ \left\lceil \frac{T_{acc\_lat}}{T_{ref\_lat}} \times T_P \right\rceil, & \text{if } T_{acc\_lat} < T_{ref\_lat}, T_P > T_{thr\_pend} \\ T_P, & \text{if } T_{acc\_lat} \geq T_{ref\_lat}, T_P > T_{thr\_pend} \end{cases} \tag{1}$$

Here T_{thr_pend} is the threshold of the request pending time. It is possible that the previous memory access is delayed by the redundancy and that the improper delay (implied in the prior request pending time) cannot further propagate to the following execution. T_{thr_pend} plays an important role in filtering the excessive redundancy out. Only when T_P is longer than T_{thr_pend} is warp redundancy enabled; otherwise, it is disabled to maintain performance. T_{ref_lat} is the referred memory access latency describing the memory access time with moderate resource contentions. When T_{acc_lat} is higher than T_{ref_lat}, it implies that the kernel currently exhibits memory-intensive characteristics and aggressive redundancy (i.e., directly setting the redundancy cycles as the request pending time) should be applied to it. To the contrary, a lower T_{acc_lat}

means that the kernel involves heavier computation and that the redundancy period should be scaled down according to the ratio of T_{acc_lat} to T_{ref_lat}.

Recall that threads in a warp execute the same instruction, and triggering the redundancy at the warp level becomes the first choice in RP-FRISE. However, all threads in the block have to synchronize at barriers if there exist, and large progress differences among warps belonging to the same block will extend the faster warps' waiting time at the barrier and hurt performance. Additionally, GPGPU programmers are encouraged to make consecutive threads access consecutive memory locations, and warps in a block tend to show the strong spatial locality [1,41]. The memory requests issued by those warps are likely to be directed to the same row in the DRAM, which is called row locality [35]. When they are sent out simultaneously, the pending time in the input buffer of the memory controller tends to be similar under the OoO memory scheduling policy. On the other hand, it will take even longer time to complete the memory transactions if issued separately, because the row locality among warps is broken, and the row switches more frequently. In order to maintain performance, RP-FRISE performs block-level redundancy. Since the redundant time is computed on the basis of memory requests, a single warp may have more than one option for setting the redundancy cycles, and there are numerous choices when extending to a block. With RP-FRISE the redundancy time will be incorporated into the response packet from the memory to the SM. For a block, the first packet arriving after it finishes the previously assigned redundant execution sets the new redundancy cycles, which should be applied to all its warps.

4.1.2 Idle SMs aware Full-RISE

While a kernel is launched into the GPUs, its blocks may not be evenly distributed across the SMs. A number of SMs are free when approaching the end of the kernel execution, and they have to wait for other busy SMs to finish their tasks. In other words, an SP becomes idle when no more blocks can be assigned to the SM. We found that this case contributes to 35% of the time that all SPs are free in the SM. Those free SPs can be leveraged for redundant execution. One straightforward method is to redundantly execute the blocks that are currently running in other SMs. This will cause the challenges for memory synchronization between the original and redundant blocks and introduce more memory transactions from the redundant blocks.

Instead of implementing the redundancy when the SM is free, we propose to do so at the beginning of the kernel execution so that the SMs' execution time is aligned and the SPs' idle time is effectively recycled for redundancy. This technique is called IS-FRISE, as the abbreviation for idle SMs aware Full-RISE. Based on the information obtained during the kernel launch process (e.g., the total number of blocks, the maximum concurrent blocks a single SM supports when running the specific kernel), a simple calculation is done to roughly estimate the total number of blocks assigned to each SM through the entire kernel execution ignoring the possible memory access delay. We conservatively assume that there is only one block difference among SMs, and divide the block quantity by the number of SMs. If there is a remainder, we expect that some SMs may be free at the end of the kernel execution, and the remainder determines the quantity of SMs (which are randomly selected among all the SMs) running an additional block. Once the kernel is launched, the full redundancy is applied to one of the currently executed blocks in SMs that are predicted to run fewer blocks; thus the total loads including the redundancy are balanced across SMs and performance remains the same. Note that the load imbalance among SMs can be larger than one block since faster SMs will take more blocks, but predicting a large load difference is likely to cause an overestimate of the SMs' idle time, which leads to aggressive redundancy and will hurt performance.

When integrating the two Full-RISE techniques simultaneously, some blocks may perform the redundancy, twice which is a waste of resources. Considering that IS-FRISE has an effect on only a small set of blocks, the redundant execution scheduled by RP-FRISE on those blocks will be ignored. Although there is an overlapped effect between the two techniques, their positive interaction minimizes the potential of excessive redundancy in RP-FRISE. Recall that RP-FRISE depends on the previous requests pending time to determine the redundancy cycles for the following execution, and it loses the opportunities to perform redundant execution before the blocks issue their first memory requests. The memory contentions among the first memory transactions tend to be severe. Using the first request's pending time for redundancy cycles calculation would over delay the block progress, and this negative effect is likely to propagate toward the end of the kernel execution. IS-FRISE triggers the full redundancy on certain blocks at the very beginning of the kernel execution, and it differentiates the block progress across SMs and mitigates the resource contentions even before the first memory requests, effectively reducing the possibility of unnecessary redundancy.

4.1.3 The implementation of Full-RISE

Fig. 14 shows the implementation of the request pending aware Full-RISE in the GPGPU architecture. In the memory controller, a timer is attached to each input buffer entry, and an arithmetic logic unit (ALU) is added to calculate the redundancy cycles (in our study, we assume that only one request is serviced at a time and that one ALU is sufficient to perform the calculation). When a memory request is written into the input buffer, the timer is set to zero and automatically increments every cycle. It records the request pending cycles that will be sent to the ALU when the request is issued out for DRAM access. The sampled memory access latency threshold pending time and referred access latency are used as the input to the ALU as well. Its output is combined with the response packet and sent back to the SM. Considering that ALU operation has to be done per memory request and the major computation in it is the division (as shown in Eq. 1) that lasts for tens of cycles, we set the referred access latency at 2 to the power of n and translate the division into logical shift. This shift operation will operate based on the product of the average access latency and the pending time. We performed the detailed sensitivity analysis on the referred access latency and found that RP-FRISE achieves optimal trade-off between reliability and performance when it is set at $2^7 = 128$ cycles. Note that the

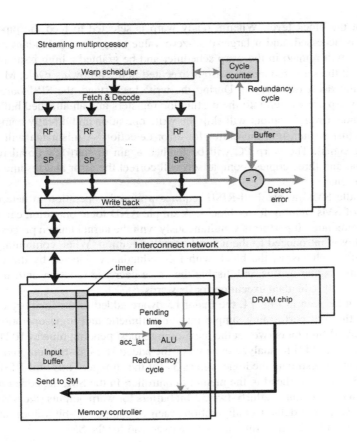

FIG. 14

Implementation of request pending aware Full-RISE.

redundancy time computation occurs in parallel with the data access in DRAM, and it does not introduce any extra delay to the critical path in the memory controller.

As Fig. 14 shows, each block in the SM is allocated a cycle counter that keeps the redundancy cycles. The amount of counters per SM is determined by the maximum number of concurrent blocks an SM supports (e.g., eight in our default configuration). When a response packet arrives at the SM, we can determine its corresponding cycle counter based on the warp it returns to. If the counter is larger than zero, it implies that the block is already under the redundancy mode, and the new redundancy time (in cycles) will be ignored. Otherwise, it is multiplied by the number of warps in the block, and the result will be written into the counter, which implies the desired total amount of redundancy cycles applied to all warps in the block. In this study, instead of controlling each warp in a block to spend the same amount of time in redundancy mode, we apply a relaxed mechanism to manage the total redundancy cycles at the block level. When a ready warp is selected to feed the pipeline, the counter is accessed, and a larger-than-zero value suggests a redundant execution. The warp will remain in the warp scheduler and be granted a high issue priority to ensure that the same redundant warp is executed in the following cycle. Meanwhile, the counter decreases by one. During the write-back stage, the SPs' output of the original warp are written into the destination registers and an attached buffer, while the redundant warp's output will skip the write operation and directly compare it to the data just written into the buffer for error detection. A mismatch will raise the recovery signal. The warp PC will be fetched again to start additional redundant execution, and three copies' comparison will correct the error and resume the warp computation.

The idle SMs' aware Full-RISE requires a modulo operation to determine the number of SMs running fewer blocks. A simple AND logic operation can compute out the remainder. It performs simultaneously with the kernel launch process, and no extra delay is introduced to the normal kernel execution. When combining the two Full-RISE mechanisms, the block with full redundancy selected by the IS-FRISE will set its counter as one and disable the value decrease function until it finishes, ensuring a full redundant execution for its warps.

As can be seen in Fig. 14, the major hardware added to the memory controller includes the unit performing simple integer arithmetic and logic operations and a number of 10-bit timers (we set the maximum request pending time as 1024 cycles). We use CACTI [42] to analyze the area of the added storage structure under 32 nm technology. We estimate the logic area as $3\times$ of the storage. Thus Full-RISE creates about a 3% area overhead in the memory controller. In the SM, the added hardware contains 8 cycle counters, thirty-two 32-bit buffers for warp outputs (the SM pipeline width is 32 in the default configuration, each SP output 32-bit value), and some combinational logics, resulting in 1% area overhead for the SM.

4.2 PARTIAL-RISE

4.2.1 The concept of Partial-RISE

When the warp diverges at the branch instruction, several SPs in the SM are idle. In the workload encountering frequent branch divergences, SPs are partially free the majority of the time. For instance, the case occurs during 52% of the total kernel execution time in a CUDA benchmark, *HS*. Unfortunately, Full-RISE fails to leverage such a large portion of SPs' idle time for reliability optimization because of its nature of performing the redundancy via using all SPs. In this section, we propose Partial-RISE, which intelligently combines redundant threads in a diverged warp to utilize the partially idled SPs, thus improving the SPs' error coverage and maintaining performance.

As described in Section 4.1, GPGPUs have a unique microarchitecture characteristic (e.g., warps interleave at cycle level, and all threads execute the same code), and typically there are numerous warps in the SM warp scheduler. When a ready warp is issued into the pipeline, it is highly possible that another ready warp sharing the same PC is sitting in the scheduler. Similarly, the diverged ready warp can usually find another ready warp (not necessarily diverges), and both are going to perform the same operation in SPs. A number of threads from a warp with the same PC can join the execution of the diverged warp. Therefore the warp is partially protected as the idle SPs in the diverged warp are effectively utilized to execute redundant threads. Moreover, the warp will be issued in the following cycle so that the output for both the main and the redundant threads can be compared immediately for the error detection. We name this technique Partial-RISE. Fig. 15 shows an example. In Fig. 15A, at cycle m, the warps i and j have the same PC, and the active mask shows that warp i diverges. When it is issued into the pipeline, threads from warp j will take the free slots in warp i based on its active mask. When the outputs of warp j are available, they will be sent to the buffer instead of being written to the registers. During the cycle $m + 1$ (shown in Fig. 15B), warp j is issued, and it outputs are compared to the data saved in the buffer in the previous cycle.

Finding the warp with the same PC is critical to Partial-RISE. We investigate various benchmarks, and Fig. 16 plots the percentage of warp divergence cycles that at least one ready warp has the identical PC with the current issued diverged warp (shown as the left bars). The round-robin policy is applied to the warp scheduling. The benchmarks with quite a few branch divergences are not shown in the Fig. 16 because the Partial-RISE is rarely triggered in that case. As the figure shows, more

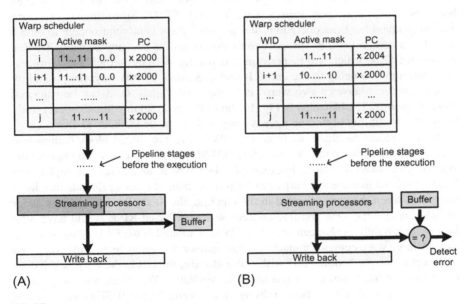

(A)   (B)

FIG. 15

An example of Partial-RISE. (A) warp j is issued together with warp i. (B) warp j is issued in the next cycle.

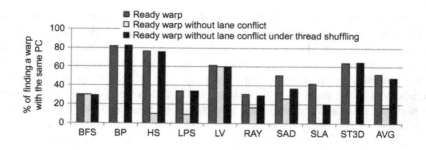

FIG. 16

Possibility of a diverged warp finding a warp with identical PC.

than half of the time, the diverged warp has the opportunity to combine with another warp by searching across the warp scheduler. However, the two warps are likely to use the SP and registers belonging to the same lane and encounter lane conflict. This becomes a major obstacle for Partial-RISE. As shown in Fig. 15A, although warp $i + 1$ has the identical PC with warp i, Partial-RISE cannot be used because both of them have the same active mask. Fig. 16 also shows the possibility that a diverged warp can be combined with another warp without lane conflict (shown in the middle bars). As can be seen, the possibility decreases significantly down to 16%, and even becomes zero in some benchmarks (e.g., *BP, SLA, ST3D*). Since threads in a warp are independent but their operations are the same, there is no requirement to bind a thread to a certain lane. We propose to randomly shuffle the threads while sending them to the SMs, which will be performed in parallel with the kernel launch process and with no extra delay to the entire kernel execution. In this way, the possibility of lane conflicts between two warps decreases and Partial-RISE can be triggered more frequently. The black bar in Fig. 16 shows that rearranging threads successfully brings the possibility of finding a ready warp with the same PC back to 48%.

Several recent mechanisms (e.g., the DWF [24], the thread block compaction [22], and the large warp microarchitecture (LWM) [35]) are proposed to improve the efficiency of branch handling. For example, the LWM as an example, it implements larger warps so that the subwarps can be formed from the active threads in a large warp, and when they are executed in the pipeline, the SPs' idle time reduces under branch divergences. One possible concern was that Partial-RISE would have little benefit for reliability enhancement when LWM is applied in the GPU. This is not the case. A large warp contains a much smaller number of threads (e.g., 256) compared to the entire warp scheduler. It is unable to find active threads in the warp, and it does not provide a mechanism to avoid the lane conflicts. LWM does not always fully utilize the idled SPs during branch divergences. While Partial-RISE searches warps across the entire scheduler and is equipped with the thread shuffling technique, it can efficiently use those idled SPs in LWM for redundant execution. We observe that Partial-RISE has an effect 20% of the time when LWM fails to fully utilize the SPs.

In some benchmarks (e.g., *NN*, *NW*), the block contains few threads (e.g., 16) so that it has only one warp and all threads in that warp cannot fill up the SIMT pipeline width. Since several lanes keep idle through the entire kernel execution, Partial-RISE will perform the intrawarp duplication that leverages those idle lanes to provide the spatial redundancy for some threads contained in the warp.

4.2.2 The implementation of Partial-RISE

In the SM pipeline, when the warp enters to the final pipeline stage (i.e., write-back stage), its PC and active mask are updated, and its status becomes ready for issue in the following cycle. To implement the Partial-RISE technique, a comparator is attached to each warp entry in the warp scheduler. While updating the warp status, its PC (active mask) will be compared with other ready warp PCs (active masks) in the scheduler to seek a warp for joined execution. The comparison is executed along with the write-back stage, with no impact on the critical path delay. If successful, the scheduler will be notified to issue the diverged warp, and threads from its matched warp simultaneously in the next cycle, followed by the normal issue of the matched warp. Partial-RISE will reuse the hardware (e.g., buffer, comparator) in Full-RISE to perform the error detection. In total, Partial-RISE adds an additional 1% area overhead to the SM equipped with Full-RISE.

4.3 RISE: PUTTING IT ALL TOGETHER

Because Full-RISE and Partial-RISE aim to recycle the SPs' idle time caused by two different cases for reliability improvement, they can be integrated into RISE. While implementing RISE, the warp under the redundancy mode due to the Full-RISE will not be considered in Partial-RISE. Although Full-RISE differentiates the block execution progress, it does not degrade the efficiency of Partial-RISE in finding appropriate warps for redundancy. We find that the Partial-RISE trigger time even increases by 2% when combined with Full-RISE. This happens because the row locality leads to similar redundancy cycles and consequently to similar progress among blocks in the same SM under Full-RISE. Thus the block progress difference generally happens at the SM level.

4.4 EVALUATIONS

4.4.1 Experimental setup

We use AVF [27] to evaluate the error coverage of our proposed RISE. A hardware structure's AVF refers to the probability that a transient fault in that hardware structure will result in incorrect program results. Therefore the AVF, which can be used as a metric to estimate how vulnerable the hardware is to soft errors during program execution, is determined by the processor state bits required for ACE. The structure's AVF in a given cycle is the percentage of ACE bits that the structure holds, and its overall AVF during program execution is the average AVF at any point in time. We apply the methodology proposed by Mukherjee et al. [27] to identify the

ACE bits and their residency time in the structure and to compute the AVF of GPGPU microarchitecture structures. We build our vulnerability estimation framework based on the cycle-accurate, open-source, and publicly available simulator GPGPU-Sim [29] and to obtain the GPGPU reliability and performance statistics. Our baseline GPGPU configuration is set as follows: there are 28 SMs in the GPU; SM pipeline width is 32; warp size is 32; each SM supports 1024 threads and 8 blocks at most; each SM contains 16384 32-bit registers, 16 KB shared memory, 8 KB constant cache, and 64 KB texture cache; the warp scheduler applies the round-robin scheduling policy; the immediate postdominator reconvergence [23] is used to handle the branch divergences; the GPU includes 8 DRAM controllers, each controller has a 32-entry input buffer and applies OoO FR-FCFS scheduling policy; the interconnect topologies are Mesh, and the dimension order routing algorithm is used in the interconnect. We collect a large set of available GPGPU workloads from Nvidia CUDA SDK [31], Rodinia Benchmark [32], Parboil Benchmark [6], and some third-party applications. The workloads show significant diversity according to their kernel characteristics, divergence characteristics, memory access patterns, and so on.

4.4.2 Effectiveness of RISE

To better analyze the technique's effectiveness, we classify the benchmarks in four categories based on their workload characteristics. The first category includes memory-intensive benchmarks such as *64H*, *BFS*, *BP*, *HY*, *LIB*, *LV*, *MT*, *NE*, *NN*, *NW*, *PR*, and *SLA*. The second category contains benchmarks that cause load imbalance across SMs in our baseline GPGPU configuration. They are *BN*, *CP*, *FWT*, *HY*, *KM*, *LV*, *MRIF*, *NW*, *PR*, *SLA*, *SP*, *SRAD*, and *ST3D*. The third category includes benchmarks usually utilizing partial SPs (caused by the frequent branch divergences or the partially full warps), such as *BFS*, *BP*, *HS*, *LPS*, *LV*, *NN*, *NE*, *NW*, *SAD*, *SLA*, and *ST3D*. The last category includes computation-intensive benchmarks such as *BS*, *CS*, *MM*, and *RAY*. Note that the preceding categories are not exclusive (i.e., one benchmark can be classified into different categories).

Fig. 17 shows (A) the execution time and (B) the AVF of streaming processors when running various benchmarks under the impact of IS-FRISE, RP-FRISE, Full-RISE, Partial-RISE, and RISE, respectively. The execution time of full redundancy is demonstrated in Fig. 17A as well for comparison. As can be seen, on average, full redundancy results in 58% performance degradation. Because the full redundancy achieves 100% error coverage (i.e., AVF is zero), its results are not shown in Fig. 17B. We present the averaged results across SMs, and the results are normalized to the baseline case without optimization. As Fig. 17 shows, RP-FRISE exhibits strong capability in improving the SPs' soft-error vulnerability with little performance loss when executing the memory-intensive benchmarks (classified as the first category). Take the *MT* as an example. The SPs' AVF decreases by 90% with only 4% performance penalty, which implies that the redundancy cycles are properly set by RP-FRISE and the SPs' idle time in the baseline cases is effectively recycled for redundant execution. One may notice that the AVF reduction under RP-FRISE is

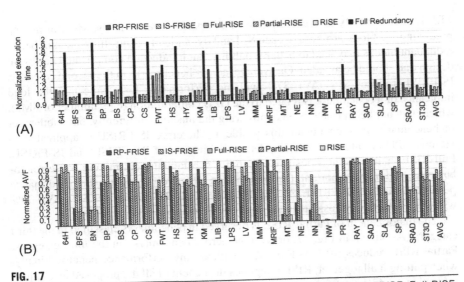

FIG. 17

The normalized (A) execution time and (B) SPs' AVF under IS-FRISE, RP-FRISE, Full-RISE, Partial-RISE, RISE, and full redundancy techniques.

less obvious in *PR*, although the warps spend 17% of the execution time waiting for the memory transactions. This is because their memory requests were already well separated during the execution phase. Also, the memory access latency is generally short, and the pipeline only stalls for a couple of cycles for the memory transaction. Postponing the warp progress would easily cause substantial damage to the performance; therefore RP-FRISE is seldom triggered. While improving the SPs' AVF, RP-FRISE degrades performance in some benchmarks such as *FWT*, *LIB*, and *SLA*. Because RP-FRISE uses the last request pending time to predict the next request waiting time and to determine the corresponding redundancy cycles, its prediction accuracy is affected when the next memory access pattern differs greatly from the last one. As a result, excessive redundancy is applied, which hurts the performance. On average, across the benchmarks in the first category, RP-FRISE enhances the SPs soft-error robustness by 57% with 8% performance loss.

The impact of IS-FRISE on improving the SPs' error coverage is impressive in benchmarks belonging to the second category. For example, the SPs free time caused by the imbalanced block distribution is completely recycled for redundancy in *BN*, and the AVF decreases 75% with 0.1% performance loss. Recall that IS-FRISE conservatively assumes one block difference among SMs to maintain the kernel execution time, while the difference is larger in some benchmarks (e.g., *LV*). In the GPU, a block is assigned once there is an empty slot in a certain SM. It is possible that an SM commits multiple blocks at similar times and that the remaining unexecuted blocks are all allocated to it. Although other SMs finish the block execution in the very near future, they have to remain idle until the kernel completes. In that case, IS-

FRISE does not fully leverage the idle SPs to perform redundancy. Monitoring and predicting the block progress in each SM and dynamically controlling the number of redundant blocks may lead to better reliability, but it induces a complicated hardware design that should be avoided. On average, across benchmarks in the second category, IS-FRISE reduces SPs' AVF 37% with no performance loss. Note that the load imbalance of a benchmark is related to the GPU configuration (e.g., number of SMs), which may not be an issue when configuring the machine differently, but another set of benchmarks may encounter this problem. Therefore IS-FRISE is applicable to various GPU architecture designs. As a combination of RP-FRISE and IS-FRISE, Full-RISE maintains their positive effects for substantially optimizing soft-error robustness, and more important, their interaction effectively mitigates the performance penalty caused by RP-FRISE. As Fig. 17 shows, Full-RISE improves SPs' AVF 39% with 4% performance loss on average across all investigated benchmarks.

The major benefit of Partial-RISE is observed in benchmarks classified in the third category. As shown in Fig. 17, on average across benchmarks in the third category, Partial-RISE reduces SPs' AVF by 32% without any performance penalty. Finally, when putting it all together, RISE integrates the benefit of all the proposed techniques by achieving 43% of SPs' soft-error reliability enhancement and minimizes (only 4%) the performance loss. In the computation-intensive benchmarks, the effect of RISE is less impressive because of the SPs' limited idle time. Note that RISE optimizes the SPs' vulnerability via redundancy; the SPs' AVF does not migrate to any other microarchitecture structures.

4.4.3 Sensitivity analysis

Various techniques have been proposed on warp scheduling and warp formation to improve the GPGPU throughput, such as Fair, which issues the instruction for the warp with a minimum number of instructions executed [34], FRFS, LWM, and two-level round-robin warp scheduling that effectively hides long memory access latency and improves the SPs utilization [35]. Fig. 18 shows (A) the execution time and (B) SPs' AVF under RISE when those optimization schemes are enabled. Results are normalized to the baseline case with the corresponding optimizations, respectively. The results obtained when using the default scheduling policy (i.e., round robin) is also shown in Fig. 18 for comparison. As the figure shows, the effectiveness of RISE is not affected when running with different schemes; on average, the SPs' AVF reduction stays around 42% with 6% performance loss. Take the scheme of LWM+two_ level as an example. It reduces the SPs' idle time to some degree to shrink the kernel execution time, so one would expect that it largely diminishes the opportunities to trigger RISE. However, this only occurs in a limited number of benchmarks (i.e., *BFS, HS, MT*), which shrinks the reliability optimization to around 12%. As we described in Section 4.2.1, LWM finds only active threads in the warp scope and cannot avoid the lane conflicts; it leaves sufficient room for Partial-RISE in RISE to further use the partially idled SPs for redundant execution. Moreover, the two-level round-robin scheduling cannot totally avoid the memory contentions and

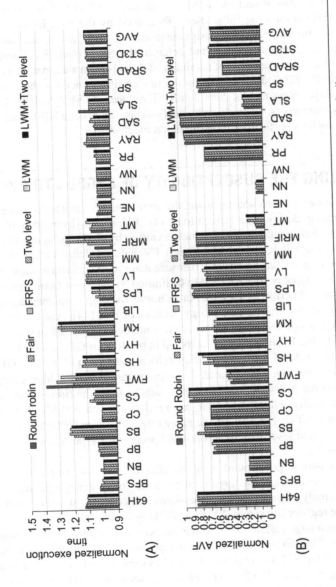

FIG. 18

The normalized (A) execution time and (B) SPs' AVF under various scheduling policies and performance optimizations.

the load imbalance across SMs; therefore, the Full-RISE in RISE can be frequently triggered to recycle the SPs' free time for reliability enhancement.

To conclude, in this section, we propose RISE to effectively recycle the SPs' idle time for soft-error detection. RISE is composed of Full-RISE and Partial-RISE. Full-RISE exploits the fully idled SPs caused by the long-latency memory transactions and imbalanced load assignment among GPU cores, and uses them to perform the redundant execution and enhance the SPs' reliability. Partial-RISE combines the redundant execution of a number of threads from a warp with a diverged warp to recycle the SPs' idle time during the branch divergence for their reliability optimization. Experiment results show that RISE reduces the SPs' AVF by 43% with only 4% performance loss. Our sensitivity analysis also shows that RISE is applicable to GPUs with various performance optimization mechanisms.

5 MITIGATING THE SUSCEPTIBILITY OF GPGPUs TO PVs [43]

As process technology keeps scaling down, the increasing PV have become a growing threat to processor design and fabrication [44]. PV is the divergence of device parameters from their nominal values, which is caused by challenging manufacturing processes at very small feature technologies. PV induces delay variations among critical paths and causes timing errors. To ensure that processors run as expected, the maximum clock frequency (FMAX) has to be limited by the worst critical path delay, leading to substantial performance loss. For example, the chip frequency degrades as much as 22% in 45 nm process technology because of PVs [44]. And the frequency degradation becomes more significant with the continuous shrinking in feature size.

Unfortunately, the PV impact is exacerbated in modern GPGPUs. This is because FMAX is strongly related to the number of critical paths in a chip [45]. GPGPUs contain a tremendous amount of parallel critical paths to deliver high computing throughput. Thus the possibility that one path fails to meet the timing speculations increases substantially, which forces a severe decrease on FMAX in GPGPUs compared to that in CPUs [21,46]. The negative effect of PV on GPGPUs' frequency has recently motivated several architecture-level proposals for performance boosting under PV [21,46–52].

GPGPUs support a great number of parallel threads and implement a zero overhead context switch among threads to hide the long-latency operations. This requires an extremely large RF to keep the states and contents of all active threads. For instance, the register file size is 2 MB in NVIDIA Fermi [53] and 6 MB in AMD Cayman [54]. Such large register files include numerous parallel critical paths and are quite sensitive to PVs. Even worse, to afford a greater number of threads executing simultaneously in the SM, the register file size has continuously increased in recent GPUs' product generations [53,55]. Therefore register files have become one of the major units that affect frequency and performance [56], and it is crucial to mitigate the PV impact in them.

The unique, that is, highly banked, register architecture design in GPGPUs provides a promising direction to efficiently tolerate the PV effect. However, generic

PV mitigation techniques, such as adaptive body biasing (ABB) [57] and gate sizing [58], fail to exploit this unique feature and could cause considerable power and area overhead when directly applied to GPGPUs' register file. In this section, we propose to characterize and further leverage this highly banked architecture feature to effectively mitigate the susceptibility of GPGPUs' register file to PVs. Note that we assume other PV-sensitive structures, such as streaming processors, are handled by conventional PV tolerance mechanisms (e.g., ABB).

There have been several PV tolerant techniques explored to optimize the multiported register file in CPUs [59,60]. For instance, Liang et al. [59] proposed $n\%$ variable-latency RF ($n\%$ VL-RF) to put all registers' read ports in fast and slow categories. The slowest $(100 - n)\%$ ports are marked as slow and are accessed in two cycles. They are not considered in determining the frequency so that the chip frequency increases in the presence of PV. When a slow port is assigned to read a register, a port switching technique is triggered to switch to a fast port attached to the same register and to avoid the extra cycle delay. However, port switching is not applicable to modern GPGPUs' register file. This is because implementing multiple ports to a sizeable register file in GPGPUs is not practical, and the highly banked register architecture has become a widely accepted design to provide high register access bandwidth [29,61–63]. Although the VL technique can be simply extended to GPGPUs' registers by exploring the fast and slow registers based on their access delay to attain the optimal frequency improvement, such a fine-grain register classification causes extremely high IPC degradation. This is because multiple (e.g., 32) same-named registers are accessed simultaneously in GPGPUs, and the access latency increases when one slow register gets involved.

In this section, we first develop a novel fast and slow register classification mechanism to maximize the frequency improvement in the highly banked register architecture. We then exploit the unique features in GPGPU applications to intelligently tolerate the extra access delay to the slow registers.

The contributions of this work are as follows:

- We observe that PV exhibits much stronger systematic effects in the vertical direction than in the horizontal direction within each RF bank in the state-of-the-art GPGPU register file floor plan [61,62]. We then propose a coarse-grain register classification mechanism by vertically dividing each RF bank into subbanks, and applying the variable-latency technique at the subbank level (VL-SB). VL-SB is able to attain the same frequency improvement as the fine-grain classification at the register level.
- We further propose RF bank reorganization (RF-BRO) to virtually combine subbanks with the same speed type (i.e., fast and slow). Therefore the same-named registers in an RF bank entry share the uniform access delay, and the newly formed RF banks can be classified in fast and slow categories. We also show that the proposed VL-SB and RF-BRO techniques are applicable to other register file architecture designs [64,65].
- In order to mitigate the IPC loss caused by the slow RF banks' access under VL-SB + RF-BRO, we propose to grant warps that heavily use fast RF banks a

higher issue priority (in GPGPUs, threads are executed in warps). This forces fast RF banks to serve more threads and minimizes the use of slow RF banks, and also appropriately enlarges the progress difference among warps to effectively hide stalls caused by long-latency operations.

By combining all the explored techniques, we achieve 15% frequency improvement compared to the baseline case without optimization under PV, and 24% IPC improvement compared to the fine-grain register classification mechanism (i.e., VL-RF technique).

The rest of this section is organized as follows: Section 5.1 provides background on the highly banked register file in GPGPUs. Section 5.2 presents the register classification mechanism to achieve the most desirable frequency optimization. Section 5.3 proposes a set of techniques to hide the access delay overhead on slow registers. Section 5.4 evaluates the proposed mechanisms.

5.1 BACKGROUND: HIGHLY BANKED REGISTER FILE IN GPGPUs

In Nvidia PTX standard, an instruction can read up to four registers and write to one register. Therefore the register file in the SM is heavily banked (e.g., 16 or 32 banks) instead of multiported to provide high bandwidth, and multiple register operands required by one instruction can be read from different banks concurrently [1,29,61–65]. Each RF bank is equipped with dual ports to support one read and one write per cycle. Each entry in the bank is 128 bytes wide to hold 32 same-named registers [61,62]. During the register access, the RF bank ID is obtained based on the warp ID and register ID, and the port attached to that RF bank is activated to serve the access request.

Ideally, the register access for an instruction warp finishes in one cycle [61]. This is not the case when multiple register access requests map to the same bank and cause a bank conflict. In that case, requests have to be served sequentially, which extends the register access time to multiple cycles and hurts the performance. In order to reduce the possibility of bank conflicts, registers in a warp are distributed across the RF banks. Since multiple source operands for an instruction warp may not be read at the same cycle due to the bank conflicts, operand collectors are applied to buffer the operands. One instruction warp will be allocated one operand collector once issued by the scheduler. When all required operands are ready in their assigned operand collector, the instruction warp proceeds to the execution stage and releases its operand collector resources.

5.2 FREQUENCY OPTIMIZATION FOR GPGPUs' REGISTER FILE UNDER PVs

5.2.1 Modeling PV impact on GPGPUs' register file

PVs are a combination of random effects (e.g., due to random dopant fluctuations) and systematic effects (e.g., due to lithographic lens aberrations) that occur during transistor manufacturing. Random variations refer to random fluctuations in parameters from die to die and device to device. Systematic variations refer to layout-dependent variations that cause nearby devices to share similar parameters. Die-to-die (D2D) variations mainly exhibit as random variations, and within-die (WID) variations consist of both random and systematic variations. We focus on WID variations since D2D effect can be modeled as an offset value to all the devices in the chip. Among the design parameters, effective channel length (L_{eff}) and threshold voltage (V_{th}) are two key parameters subject to large variations [66]. The high V_{th} and L_{eff} variations cause high variations in transistor switching speed.

An architectural model of PVs, VARIUS [66], has been developed to quantitatively characterize the frequency variation in CPUs. In this study, we leverage the SRAM timing error model in VARIUS and modify it to model the PV effects on GPGPUs' register file. We focus on the 32 nm process technology that is generally used in the state-of-the-art GPUs [30]. We set the WID correlation distance coefficient ϕ as 0.5, and assume V_{th}'s $\sigma/\mu = 12\%$, L_{eff}'s $\sigma/\mu = 6\%$ [19,66], and the random and systematic components have equal variances for both V_{th} and L_{eff} [19,66,67]. Fig. 19 shows an example of V_{th} variation map for GPGPUs' register file. We generate 100 chips for statistical analysis and present the averaged result.

Note that each SM in GPGPUs exhibits different FMAX under PV. We model SM-to-SM variations as the ratio of frequencies of the fastest and the slowest SM in a GPGPUs' chip, and model the within-SM variations as the ratio of frequencies of the fastest and slowest critical path. Based on our experimental results, within-SM variations are 1.7, which is larger than SM-to-SM variations that are around 1.3. This is because each SM has numerous parallel critical paths, while there are only tens of SMs. SM-to-SM variations have been smoothed out as the FMAX of each SM is determined by the slowest critical path in it. Moreover, there are techniques letting each SM in GPGPUs run at their own FMAX for PV mitigation [46]. We thus perform the variability analysis within the SM. As previously mentioned, the register file is one of the major structures that limit the SM frequency, and we assume other PV-sensitive structures are handled by conventional PV tolerance mechanisms. Thus the SM frequency is determined by the register file frequency, which is the reciprocal of the slowest register access time. Fig. 20A demonstrates the register file frequency distribution over 100 chips. There are 15 SMs in the Fermi architecture, and we use the averaged register file frequency across SMs to represent the frequency for one chip. Therefore Fig. 20A mainly shows the impact of within-SM variations on frequency. As the figure shows, the mean frequency degradation is 40% compared to

FIG. 19

V_{th} variation map of GPGPUs' register file.

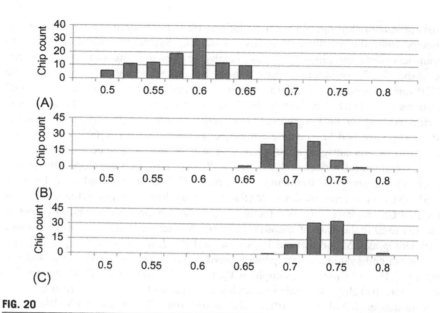

FIG. 20

Register file frequency distribution. (A) Frequency distribution (baseline without optimization). (B) Frequency distribution (70% VL register vectors). (C) Frequency distribution (70% VL sub-banks).

GPUs without PV. This is because numerous critical paths in GPGPUs' register file lead to the large within-SM variation, which significantly decreases the frequency.

5.2.2 Variable-latency subbanks (VL-SB) in GPGPUs register file
Extending VL-RF to GPGPUs RF

In our baseline RF design, each SM is equipped with a 128 KB register file that is composed of 32 KB 32-bit registers. In order to reduce the impact of the extremely slow register and boost the frequency under PV, one can apply the $n\%$ variable-latency RF technique [29] to divide those 32 KB registers contained in the SM into fast and slow categories depending on their access delay. Based on our sensitivity analysis, setting $n\%$ as 70% delivers the optimal trade-off between frequency and the amount of slow registers. We implement the 70% variable-latency register file (70% VL-RF); the slowest 30% registers are classified in the slow category and will take two cycles to finish the read/write operation; frequency is determined by the slowest register of the remaining 70% registers in the fast category.

However, the variable-latency RF causes serious IPC loss. Recall that one operand access in an instruction warp involves the parallel accesses to 32 same-named registers from all threads within the warp. As long as there is 1 slow register among those 32 registers, the operand access latency is 2 cycles. In our baseline RF design [61,62], although the 32 same-named registers are implemented close to each other and included in a single entry of the RF bank, the PV exhibits weak systematic effects for such a 1024-bit wide entry. As a result, most 32 same-named registers contain at least 1 slow register, and the operand access latency is generally extended. We observe 23% IPC degradation under 70% VL-RF compared to the baseline case without optimization under PV. Moreover, the variable-latency technique requires an extra bit per register to record the speed information as fast or slow, leading to high power and area overhead.

An alternative design to avoid the large IPC degradation is to consider each 32 same-named registers as a group, called register vector, and apply the 70% variable-latency technique at the register vector level, namely, 70% VL-RV. Similar to VL-RF, VL-RV requires an extra bit per register vector and causes considerable power and area overhead. More importantly, there is large delay variability among registers within a register vector, but the slowest one determines its access delay. In other words, the variations at register level are significantly smoothed out at the register vector level. Thus dividing register vectors into fast and slow categories has a limited effect on frequency optimization.

Variable-latency subbanks (VL-SB) in RF

In our baseline RF design [61,62], each RF bank holds sixty-four 1024-bit wide entries. Therefore PV exhibits much stronger systematic effects in the vertical direction than that in the horizontal direction within each RF bank. In this study, we focus on this wide-entry RF architecture containing 16 banks, and the explored techniques perfectly fit to other RF architecture, which is discussed in Section 5.2.4.

We propose $n\%$ variable-latency subbanks in GPGPUs' register file (named VL-SB) that vertically divides each RF bank into several subbanks, and registers within each subbank share the same access speed that is constrained by the slowest one. Subbanks exhibit distinct access delay, and the slowest $(100 - n)\%$ ones are marked as slow. There is small delay variability among registers contained in a subbank because of the systematic effects; therefore the large variations at register level are well maintained at the subbank level in VL-SB, which maximizes the frequency improvement under the VL technique.

Note that both read and write delay are considered in VL-SB. We observe that subbanks with long (short) read delay are highly likely to exhibit long (short) write delay under the impact of systematic variations. This makes the subbanks' classification quite straightforward, and leads to only two categories that are fast read + fast write (i.e., fast subbank) and slow read + slow write (i.e., slow subbank). We choose to divide each RF bank into two subbanks because further aggressively performing the fine-grain partition (i.e., four subbanks or more) does not lead to an obvious frequency increase based on our sensitivity analysis. As can be seen, only 32 bits are required to keep the speed information for the 32 subbanks in VL-SB, which causes negligible area overhead.

Since PV also causes delay variability among SMs in the same GPGPUs chip, one can change the value of $n\%$ during the subbanks' partition in different SMs to ensure the uniform frequency across SMs. In that case, each SM has a distinct number of fast subbanks that may affect the IPC. It is a good idea to employ the per-SM clocking as discussed in Ref. [46]; we thus keep the uniform partition criterion (i.e., 70%)

for each SM, and our techniques are orthogonal to the previously explored inter-SM level PV mitigation mechanisms [46].

Fig. 20B and C justifies the effectiveness of 70% VL register vectors and 70% VL subbanks by showing the RF frequency distribution when the two techniques are enabled, respectively. Every 32 nearby register vectors in VL-RV are grouped into an array to keep the same area overhead as VL-SB for a fair comparison. This makes 32 arrays in total, and the slowest one in the fastest 70% arrays decides the frequency. As Fig. 20B demonstrates, the mean frequency in 70% VL-RV increases 10% compared to the baseline case presented in Fig. 20A, while 70% VL-SB in Fig. 20C is able to boost the mean frequency by 15%.

Note that the structural redundancy technique [21], which adds redundant structures to the processor as spares, is not applicable to eliminate the slowest $x\%$ critical paths in GPGPUs' RF for frequency boosting. If just applying redundancy to replace the slowest $x\%$ register vectors, which may distribute across all the RF banks, the register mapping becomes extremely complicated and impractical. Applying redundancy to replace the slowest $x\%$ RF banks will cause considerable area overhead. Moreover, selective word-line voltage boosting [68], which was applied to reduce the cache line access latency under the PV effect, is not applicable to GPGPUs' RF. Since RF is accessed more frequently than caches, selective word-line voltage boosting will cause considerable energy overhead to GPGPUs' RF.

5.2.3 Register file bank reorganization

The VL-SB technique faces the same challenge as VL-RF, because it distributes registers belonging to the same register entry (i.e., register vector) to two subbanks, which may be classified in different categories. We further propose RF-BRO on top of VL-SB that virtually combines two subbanks from the same category to form a new RF bank. RF-BRO ensures the uniform access latency during the parallel accesses to 32 same-named registers. An operand access from an instruction warp is able to finish in one cycle as long as it is mapped to the newly formed RF bank that is composed of two fast subbanks.

Fig. 21 shows an example of applying 70% VL-SB with RF-BRO on GPGPUs RF. When VL-SB is applied (step I in Fig. 21), the 16 RF banks are vertically divided into 32 subbanks, and 22 of them are fast based on the 70% partition criterion (only 5 RF banks are shown in Fig. 21 for the illustration purpose). However, 10 RF banks still need two cycles to finish the read/write operation because they all contain slow subbanks. With the help of RF-BRO (step II in Fig. 21), subbanks with the same type are virtually grouped to rebuild the RF banks. For example, the new RF bank 0 is composed of subbank 0 and 5, and its access delay decreases to one cycle as it gets rid of the slow subbank 1. As a result, there are only five RF banks exhibiting a two-cycle access delay. In other words, the percentage of slow RF banks reduces from 62.5% to 31.25% under RF-BRO.

5.2.4 Implementation

We divide the word-line in each RF bank into two segments to obtain the subbanks. This is a widely used method in SRAM-based structures to reduce the delay because

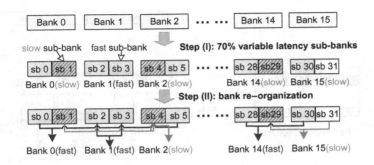

FIG. 21

An example of applying 70% VL-SB (step I) and RF-BRO (step II). *sb*, subbank.

of word-line [42] or to save dynamic power when a single word needs to be accessed in a large cache [69]. Each word-line segment in the subbank is equipped with a local decoder in our VL-SB.

The implementation of VL-SB is similar to that of the VL-RF technique [59]: the speed information for each RF subbank will be collected by using BSIT [70] at chip test time. This information is used to mark each subbank as fast or slow, and also to set an appropriate SM frequency. Note that the bank reorganization does not physically move any subbank during the chip fabrication. It virtually rebuilds the RF banks by introducing a 16-entry bank organization table; each entry in the table records the IDs of 2 subbanks that are assigned to the newly formed RF bank. In order to implement the bank reorganization technique, the IDs and the type (fast or slow) of every two same-type subbanks are configured into a ROM at the chip test time. They will be loaded from the ROM and written into the SRAM-based bank organization table once GPUs are powered on. Based on our gate-level modeling, the access latency of the bank organization table is negligible because of its small size, thus it does not increase the cycle time of the pipeline stage.

Fig. 22 depicts the implementation of the two proposed techniques. During an operand access to the 32 same-named registers, the RF bank ID obtained from the warp and register IDs is used to index the bank organization table and retrieve IDs and the speed type of corresponding subbanks. The same entry in those two subbanks will be activated simultaneously for operand access. For example, when RF bank 2 is accessed, subbanks 1 and 4 are enabled as shown in Fig. 22. Meanwhile, the speed type obtained from the table will be ANDed with a busy signal, and a slow type leads to a distribution of the signal to all subbanks. Only subbanks that are activated to fulfill this operand access will receive the busy signal and save it into the attached latch. This is used to prevent the precharge at the next cycle to ensure that the register read lasts for two cycles and finishes correctly. In GPGPUs RF, an arbitrator is applied to select a group of nonconflicting accesses and send it to the RF banks at every cycle [29,61,62]. Therefore the busy signal is also sent to the RF arbitrator to stall the following register read/write to the same RF bank.

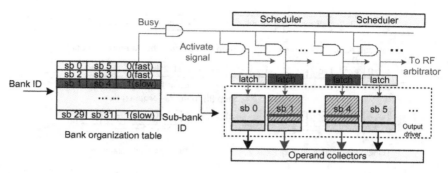

FIG. 22

Hardware implementation of variable-latency subbanks (VL-SB) and register file bank reorganization (RF-BRO).

5.2.5 Feasibility in alternative register file architecture

Alternative register file architectures are used in contemporary GPGPUs. One example is to group four SIMD lanes in an SM into a cluster, and eight clusters form a complete 32-wide SM [64,65]. In this case, each cluster contains four register banks, and each entry in a bank is only 16 bytes wide and contains the register values for four threads in a warp (i.e., four same-named registers). Thus 32 same-named registers are distributed into eight banks (one bank per cluster), and the same entries from eight RF banks are accessed simultaneously for one operand access. As can be seen, the systematic effects for those 32 same-named registers are weak since they are evenly distributed to different clusters. Neither the VL-RF technique nor the VL-RV technique could deliver good frequency improvement. We can consider this narrow-width style RF architecture as vertically dividing the 1024-bit wide register vectors (i.e., 32 same-named registers) into eight subbanks. Thus the proposed RF-BRO technique can be directly applied for the performance optimization under PV; we will not subdivide each register bank, instead we adopt the VL technique to those 16-byte wide banks, and virtually reorganize eight banks with the same speed to form the 32 same-named registers. In summary, our VL-SB RF design and the RF-BRO mechanism built upon it are applicable to other GPGPUs RF design.

5.3 MITIGATING THE IPC DEGRADATION UNDER VL-SB AND RF-BRO

Although the VL-SB + RF-BRO technique explored in Section 5.3 largely optimizes the GPGPUs RF frequency under PV impacts, there are still about 30% slow banks among the virtually reorganized RF banks, leading to around 9% IPC degradation based on our experimental results shown in Section 5.4. We further propose a set of techniques that harness the unique characteristics in GPGPUs' applications to minimize the IPC loss. Note that the slow (fast) RF banks mentioned in this section are RF banks that are virtually composed of two slow (fast) subbanks under RF-BRO.

5.3.1 Register mapping under VL-SB and RF-BRO

The SM in Fermi-style architecture is armed with two warp schedulers. Warps with odd and even IDs are dispatched into those two schedulers, respectively. At every cycle, two instruction warps are issued based on the round-robin scheduling policy, and they are likely to have identical PC since all threads in a kernel execute the same code. Mapping the same-ID registers from different warps into the same bank seriously exacerbates the bank conflicts, because different entries within a bank may be requested by the two simultaneously issued instruction warps. Therefore the register-to-bank mapping mechanism follows Eq. (2)

$$\text{bank\_ID} = (\text{warp\_ID} + \text{register\_ID})\% \quad \text{(the number of banks)} \qquad (2)$$

to ensure that different banks hold the same-ID registers across the warps. As Eq. (2) shows, consecutive warps tend to map their same-ID registers into nearby RF banks. For instance, R1 from warp0 and warp1 are mapped to bank 1 and bank 2, respectively. Generally, consecutive warps exhibit strong data locality [35], so their same-ID registers should be allocated to RF banks with the same speed type to ensure that they execute at a similar progress. We propose to save IDs of same-type subbanks into consecutive entries in the ROM at the chip test time; therefore bank0–bank10 are fast and bank11–bank15 are slow in the bank organization table under VL-SB and RF-BRO techniques. By using Eq. (2), there are a number of registers per warp mapping to the slow RF banks. And the slow bank keeps registers with different IDs at the warp level. Fig. 23 demonstrates an example of register mapping: R11–R15 from warp0 while R0–R4 from warp11 are assigned to the slow RF bank11–bank15.

5.3.2 Fast-bank aware register mapping

It has been observed that around 50% of registers are not even allocated by the compiler for the application execution [63]. This unique feature can be leveraged to minimize the use of slow RF banks by mapping registers to fast banks to the maximum degree during the kernel launch time. For the benchmarks that have high RF utilization, slow banks are used to ensure high level TLP. We find that a small set of registers have much higher access frequency than other registers allocated to the same warp, and they are usually the registers with small IDs. For instance, each warp in benchmark BN (detailed experiment methodologies are in Section 5.4) is assigned 14 register vectors, and R0–R2 are used 250% more frequently than R3–R13. This is because the compiler tends to reuse the small-ID registers. We explore a novel fast-bank aware register mapping mechanism (named FBA-RM) that consists of two steps: (1) obtaining the register resource requirements at the kernel launch time, and mapping registers only to fast banks if they are large enough to hold all registers needed by the parallel threads (i.e., reducing the number of RF banks to 11 in Eq. (1) during the mapping); (2) allocating the large-ID registers to slow RF banks when they have to be used, which means that the slow banks are rarely accessed. In

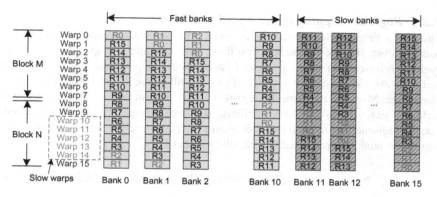

FIG. 23

The idea of FWAS. R0–R2 are frequently accessed small-ID registers. Warp 10–14 in block N are slow warps.

that case, Eq. (1) is used for small-ID registers to fast banks mapping and large-ID registers to slow banks mapping, respectively.

The major disadvantage of the FBA-RM technique is the increased bank conflicts because most RF accesses are limited to fast banks, and the technique fails to effectively mitigate the IPC degradation. In Section 5.4, we perform the detailed evaluation about FBA-RM by comparing it to other proposed techniques in the following sections.

5.3.3 Fast-warp aware scheduling (FWAS) policy
Considering that modifying the register mapping mechanism to minimize the use of slow banks has little impact on performance optimization, we thus adopt the default mapping mechanism in Fermi and propose a set of methods to hide the extra access delay on slow banks.

As Fig. 23 shows, the frequently accessed small-ID registers in a number of warps (e.g., warp 11) are mapped to slow RF banks, which seriously delays their execution progress. And we define this kind of warp as slow warp. We further define warps whose frequent register accesses in fast banks as fast warps (e.g., warp 0). The execution progress for fast warps is delayed somehow when the default warp scheduling policy (i.e., round-robin) is applied. This is because the round-robin policy gives each warp the same issue priority, and when the slow warps occupy the pipeline resources (e.g., the issue and write slot), the ready fast warps cannot leverage those resources for execution. As a result, there is a small progress difference between fast and slow warps within the same SM.

We propose the fast-warp aware scheduling policy (named FWAS) that assigns fast warps higher issue priority than slow warps to maximize the progress difference between them. This explores the unique opportunities to mitigate the IPC loss as follows:

(1) The fast warps have a shorter execution time, thus the RF resources allocated to these warps are able to serve more warps during execution. This is effective for kernels including a large number of blocks that cannot be fully distributed to SMs at one time.

Fig. 23 explains this opportunity in detail. Generally, there are multiple blocks executing concurrently in an SM. Fig. 23 shows an example SM with two blocks: block M and block N, each block contains eight warps. The frequently accessed registers (i.e., R0–R2) of all warps in block M (i.e., warp 0–7) are mapped to fast banks, so all warps belonging to block M are fast warps. On the contrary, in block N, most of their frequently accessed registers in warp 10–14 are mapped to slow banks, thus these warps are considered as slow warps. During program execution, FWAS prioritizes fast warps and allows them to finish earlier. As a result, warp 10–14 will left behind and become the bottleneck for block N. When all warps in block M finish execution, the incoming block within the same kernel will be assigned to take the resources (e.g., warp slots, registers) just released by block M. It also contains more fast warps (i.e., use those fast banks) because its warps will be assigned the same warp IDs as those warps in block M. On the other hand, block N will not release its resource until all its slow warps finish execution. As a result, the number of blocks that contain a larger amount of fast warps increases (in other words, fast banks are able to serve more warps) during the entire kernel execution, leading to the IPC improvement.

(2) The fast warps are able to start their off-chip memory accesses earlier, which alleviates the memory contention under the round-robin policy and reduces the pipeline stall time. This is quite effective in memory-intensive benchmarks.

In order to implement the FWAS policy, the fast warps have to be identified at the issue stage. However, there is no clear boundary between fast and slow warps, because the frequently accessed registers in a few warps are allocated to both fast and slow banks under the default mapping mechanism, for example, the heavily used R0–R2 in warp9–warp10 in Fig. 23. Although slow warps also access fast banks, it is highly possible that an instruction with fast bank access belongs to a fast warp. Instead of performing the accurate fast and slow warp identification, we choose to simply give the instruction warp that requires fast bank accesses higher issue priority. At the decode stage an instruction warp is marked as fast if it has fast RF read/write. Note that only when all its operands reads are mapped to fast RF banks is an instruction warp considered as possessing fast RF read. The one-bit fast/slow information combined with the ready bit is sent to the selection logic during the issue stage to perform the FWAS policy.

5.4 EVALUATIONS

We use a cycle-accurate, open-source, and publicly available simulator GPGPU-Sim (v3.1.0) [29] to evaluate the IPC optimization under our proposed methodologies. Note that our 70% variable-latency technique causes the frequency variations among

SMs, and we model that SM level frequency difference into the simulator as well. Our baseline GPGPU configuration models the Nvidia Fermi-style architecture: the GPU contains 15 SMs; the warp size is 32; each SM supports 1536 threads and 8 blocks at most; each SM contains 128 KB registers, 16 KB L1 data cache, and 48 KB shared memory; L2 cache size is 768 KB; the scheduler applies the round-robin among ready warps scheduling policy. The experimental methodology to model the PV impact and evaluate the frequency optimization under various variable-latency techniques is described in Section 5.2.1.

We collect a large set of GPGPU workloads from Nvidia CUDA SDK [31], Rodinia Benchmark [32], and Parboil Benchmark [6]. The benchmarks show significant diversity according to their kernel characteristics, divergence characteristics, memory access patterns, and so on.

5.4.1 IPC improvement
Evaluation of VL-SB with RF-BRO

To evaluate the effectiveness of VL-SBs with RF-BRO, we compare it to the VL-RF technique explored by Liang et al. [59]. Fig. 24 shows the IPC of the investigated benchmarks when those two PV mitigation techniques are enabled. The results are normalized to the baseline case without optimization (i.e., frequency is determined by the slowest critical path). As discussed in Section 5.3.1, bank0–bank10 are always fast while bank11–bank15 are always slow in all chips under RF-BRO. The IPC results are identical for all chips and only one chip's IPC results for RF-BRO-based techniques are shown in Figs. 24 and 25. The averaged IPC results across all 100 chips are shown for 70% of the VL-RF technique. In the baseline case, all registers have one-cycle access latency, and it has the same IPC as the ideal case without PV. Note that the 70% variable-latency register vector (VL-RV) technique discussed in Section 5.2.2 can also partition the banks into fast and slow subbanks, thus achieving the same IPC results as VL-SB + RF-BRO. However, the frequency improvement of VL-RV is lower than VL-SB + RF-BRO. Therefore VL-RV is not included in Fig. 24. As the figure shows, when compared with the VL-RF mechanism, VL-SB + RF-BRO successfully reduces the IPC loss from 23% to 9% on average across all the benchmarks because it reorganizes subbanks to deliver a considerable number of fast RF banks. VL-RF focuses at a quite fine-grain register-level classification, making it

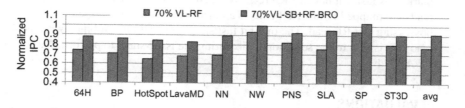

FIG. 24

Normalized IPC results under 70% VL-RF and 70% VL-SB + RF-BRO.

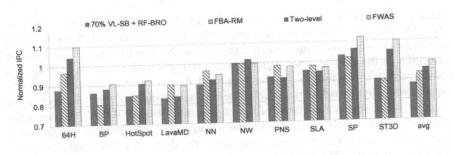

FIG. 25

Normalized IPC results under FBA-RM, two-level, and FWAS.

impossible to apply the RF-BRO for fast RF bank reorganization, and almost all the register vectors accesses take two cycles.

Interestingly, the IPCs of benchmark NW under both VL-RF and VL-SB + RF-BRO are already approaching 1. This is because NW includes very few threads, and there are insufficient warps running concurrently in the SM to hide the stalls for true data dependencies between consecutive instructions from a single warp (in absence of the long memory operations). As a result, the extra register access time is well absorbed by those stall cycles and has little impact on the IPC. On the other hand, the IPC decreases considerably in several computation-intensive benchmarks under VL-SB + RF-BRO, because few stall cycles are helping to hide long RF access delays. For instance, the IPC reduction is 18% in benchmark LavaMD that makes SM active 80% of the total execution time.

Evaluation of FWAS

Fig. 25 presents the normalized IPC results when the fast-warp aware scheduling policy (FWAS) is enabled. We compare FWAS with the fast-bank aware register mapping (named FBA-RM) discussed in Section 5.3.2. A two-level scheduling policy was proposed to boost performance [35]. This policy splits warps into groups and triggers the round-robin warp scheduling policy at intragroup and intergroup levels, respectively. By doing this, each group's warps reach a long-latency instruction at different points in time, which can also alleviate the memory contentions and tolerate the latency. We thus introduce the two-level policy into VL-SB + RF-BRO and compare it with our proposed FWAS policy. As shown in Fig. 25, all three techniques are able to mitigate the IPC reduction compared to the VL-SB+RF-BRO technique; the IPC losses under FBA-RM, two-level, and FWAS are 7%, 5%, and 1%, respectively.

The effectiveness of FBA-RM is highly related to the register utilization. For instance, NN uses less than 10% of the register file through the entire execution. The fast RF banks are by far enough to support the requirement. Moreover, since very few registers are utilized per warp in NN, pushing them to the fast banks negligibly increases the bank conflicts. As a result, the IPC loss of NN decreases from 11% under VL-SB + RF-BRO to only 4% under FBA-RM. Note that VL-SB + RF-BRO applies the default register mapping mechanism, so the slow RF banks have the same utilization as the fast ones no matter how many registers are needed, leading to a considerable IPC loss for NN. On the other hand, the performance penalty is severely exacerbated when benchmarks need more register resources. Take HotSpot as an example, it requires around 80% of the register file. When FBA-RM allocates the frequently used register to fast banks, the negative impact caused by the increased bank conflicts outweighs the positive effect of the decreased slow banks accesses, and results in a 16% IPC degradation.

As Fig. 25 shows, the two-level technique integrated with VL-SB + RF-BRO can effectively improve IPC on multiple memory-intensive benchmarks, such as *64H* and *ST3D*, because it decreases stall cycles caused by long-latency memory operations. For example, the IPC of *ST3D* is even 1% higher than that in the baseline case. As an exception, its effect on PNS is quite limited. The group size is fixed (i.e., eight warps) in the two-level policy, and there are only eight warps—that is, one group— in most SMs when executing PNS. The intergroup level round-robin in the two-level is inactive.

Similar to the two-level technique, FWAS shows the strong capability to mitigate the IPC loss for memory-intensive benchmarks. Moreover, FWAS does not have any constraint on warp grouping, and it successfully mitigates the IPC loss of PNS to only 2%, which is far better than that under the two-level technique. On average, across the memory-intensive benchmarks (i.e., *64H*, *NW*, *PNS*, and *ST3D*), FWAS boosts the IPC to 105% when normalized to the baseline case, which implies a 12% performance improvement compared to VL-SB + RF-BRO. Additionally, FWAS can effectively optimize the IPC for computation-intensive benchmarks, especially those including numerous blocks, because it makes the fast RF banks support warps at the utmost degree. For instance, it induces 8% IPC gains for both HotSpot and LavaMD compared to VL-SB + RF-BRO.

5.4.2 Overall performance improvement

Fig. 26 compares the overall performance (IPC × frequency) under the baseline case without optimization, 70% VL-RF, and our FWAS mechanism by presenting the performance distribution over the 100 investigated chips, respectively. The performance is normalized to the ideal case without PV impacts. As the figure shows, FWAS significantly improves the mean performance by 15% over the baseline case; 70% VL-RF achieves slightly higher frequency (i.e., 2%) than our FWAS technique because it performs at a fine-grain register-level; however, our technique outperforms the 70% VL-RF by 17% because of the substantial (i.e., 24%) IPC improvement.

To conclude, this section aims to mitigate the susceptibility of GPGPUs' register file to PV. We first propose to vertically divide RF banks into subbanks and explore the variable-latency technique at a subbank level to perform the coarse-grain register classification, which maximizes the frequency optimization under PV. We then propose to reorganize the RF banks by virtually combining the same-type subbanks,

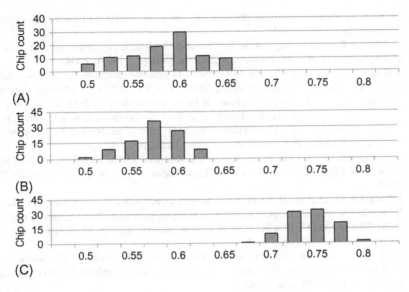

FIG. 26

Overall performance (IPC × frequency) distribution. (A) Overall performance distribution (baseline). (B) Overall performance distribution (70% VL-RF). (C) Overall performance distribution (all-together).

leading to the fast and slow RF bank categories. The IPC degrades when using the slow RF banks during the kernel execution. We further explore the FWAS technique that leverages the unique features in GPGPU applications to minimize the use of slow RF banks and thus mitigate the IPC loss. Our PV mitigation techniques achieves 15% overall performance improvement compared to the baseline case without optimization.

REFERENCES

[1] NVIDIA CUDA Programming Guide Version 3.0, 2010.
[2] Advanced Micro Devices Inc., AMD Brook+, 2016, http://ati.amd.com/technology/streamcomputing/AMD-Brookplus.pdf.
[3] Khronos, OpenCL—the open standard for parallel programming of heterogeneous systems, http://www.khronos.org/opencl/.
[4] http://www.top500.org/lists/2015/11/.
[5] J. Sheaffer, D. Luebke, K. Skadron, A hardware redundancy and recovery mechanism for reliable scientific computation on graphics processors, in: Proceedings of Graphics Hardware, 2007.
[6] Parboil Benchmark suite, 2016, http://impact.crhc.illinois.edu/ parboil.php.

[7] N. Wang, S. Patel, ReStore: symptom based soft error detection in microprocessors, in: Proceedings of DSN, 2005.

[8] C. Weaver, J. Emer, S. Mukherjee, S. Reinhardt, Techniques to reduce the soft error rate of a high-performance microprocessor, in: Proceedings of ISCA, 2004.

[9] I. Haque, V. Pande, Hard data on soft errors: a large-scale assessment of real-world error rates in GPGPU, in: Proceedings of the 2010 10th IEEE/ACM International Conference on Cluster, Cloud and Grid Computing, IEEE Computer Society, 2010, pp. 691–696.

[10] N. Maruyama, A. Nukada, S. Matsuoka, A high-performance fault tolerant software framework for memory on commodity GPUS, in: 2010 IEEE International Symposium on Parallel & Distributed Processing (IPDPS), IEEE, pp. 1–12.

[11] N. Maruyama, A. Nukada, S. Matsuoka, Software-based ECC for GPUs, in: 2009 Symposium on Application Accelerators in High Performance Computing (SAAHPC'09), 2009.

[12] J. Sheaffer, D. Luebke, K. Skadron, A hardware redundancy and recovery mechanism for reliable scientific computation on graphics processors, in: Proceedings of the 22nd ACM SIGGRAPH/EUROGRAPHICS Symposium on Graphics Hardware, Eurographics Association, 2007, pp. 55–64.

[13] G. Shi, J. Enos, M. Showerman, V. Kindratenko, On testing GPU memory for hard and soft errors, in: Proceedings of Symposium on Application Accelerators in High-Performance Computing, 2009.

[14] K. Yim, R. Iyer, Hauberk: lightweight silent data corruption error detectors for GPGPU, in: Proceedings of the 17th Humantech Thesis Prize (also in IPDPS 2011), 2011.

[15] C. Ding, C. Karlsson, H. Liu, T. Davies, Z. Chen, Matrix multiplication on GPUs with on-line fault tolerance, in: Proceedings of the 9th IEEE International Symposium on Parallel and Distributed Processing with Applications (ISPA 2011), IEEE Computer Society Press, 2011.

[16] K. Yim, R. Iyer, Hauberk: lightweight silent data corruption error detectors for GPGPU, in: Proceedings of the 17th Humantech Thesis Prize (also in IPDPS 2011), 2011.

[17] S. Dighe, S. Vangal, P. Aseron, S. Kumar, T. Jacob, K. Bowman, J. Howard, J. Tschanz, V. Erraguntla, N. Borkar, V. De, S. Borkar, Within-die variation-aware dynamic-voltage-frequency-scaling with optimal core allocation and thread hopping for the 80-core TeraFLOPS processor, J. Solid-State Circuits 46 (1) (2011) 184–193.

[18] R. Teodorescu, J. Torrellas, Variation-aware application scheduling and power management for chip multiprocessors, in: 35th International Symposium on Computer Architecture, 2008 (ISCA'08), June 21–25, 2008, pp. 363–374.

[19] U.R. Karpuzcu, K.B. Kolluru, N.S. Kim, J. Torrellas, VARIUS-NTV: a microarchitectural model to capture the increased sensitivity of many-cores to process variations at near-threshold voltages, in: Proceedings of the 2012 42nd Annual IEEE/IFIP International Conference on Dependable Systems and Networks (DSN) (DSN'12), 2012, pp. 1–11.

[20] J. Lee, P. Ajgaonkar, N.S. Kim, Analyzing performance impact of process variations on GPGPU throughput, in: Proceedings of ISPASS, 2011.

[21] S. Seo, R.G. Dreslinski, M. Woh, Y. Park, C. Charkrabari, S. Mahlke, D. Blaauw, T. Mudge, Process variation in near-threshold wide SIMD architectures, in: Proceedings of DAC, 2012.

[22] W.W.L. Fung, T. Aamodt, Thread block compaction for efficient SIMT control flow, in: Proceedings of HPCA, 2011.

[23] S.S. Muchnick, Advanced Compiler Design and Implementation, Morgan Kaufmann, San Francisco, CA, USA, 1997.

[24] W.W.L. Fung, I. Sham, G. Yuan, T.M. Aamodt, Dynamic warp formation and scheduling for efficient GPU control flow, in: Proceedings of MICRO, 2007.

[25] J. Tan, Y. Yi, F. Shen, X. Fu, Modeling and characterizing GPGPU reliability in the presence of soft errors, J. Parallel Comput. 39 (9) (2013) 520–532.

[26] N. Soundararajan, A. Parashar, A. Sivasubramaniam, Mechanisms for bounding vulnerabilities of processor structures, in: Proceedings of ISCA, 2007.

[27] S.S. Mukherjee, C. Weaver, J. Emer, S.K. Reinhardt, T. Austin, A systematic methodology to compute the architectural vulnerability factors for a high-performance microprocessor, in: Proceedings of MICRO, 2003.

[28] X. Fu, T. Li, J. Fortes, Sim-SODA: a unified framework for architectural level software reliability analysis, in: Workshop on Modeling, Benchmarking and Simulation, 2006.

[29] A. Bakhoda, G.L. Yuan, W.W.L. Fung, H. Wong, T.M. Aamodt, Analyzing CUDA workloads using a detailed GPU simulator, in: Proceedings of ISPASS, 2009.

[30] A. Biswas, R. Cheveresan, J. Emer, S.S. Mukherjee, P.B. Racunas, R. Rangan, Computing architectural vulnerability factors for address-based structures, in: Proceedings of ISCA, 2005.

[31] http://www.nvidia.com/object/cuda_sdks.html.

[32] S. Che, M. Boyer, J. Meng, D. Tarjan, J. Sheaffer, S. Lee, K. Skadron, Rodinia: a benchmark suite for heterogeneous computing, in: Proceedings of IISWC, 2009.

[33] B. Fahs, S. Bose, M. Crum, B. Slechta, F. Spadini, T. Tung, S.J. Patel, S.S. Lumetta, Performance characterization of a hardware mechanism for dynamic optimization, in: Proceedings of MICRO, 2001.

[34] N.B. Lakshminarayana, H. Kim, Effect of instruction fetch and memory scheduling on GPU performance, in: Workshop on Language, Compiler, and Architecture Support for GPGPU, 2010.

[35] V. Narasiman, M. Shebanow, C.J. Lee, R. Miftakhutdinov, O. Mutlu, Y.N. Patt, Improving GPU performance via large warps and two-level warp scheduling, in: Proceedings of MICRO, 2011.

[36] J. Tan, X. Fu, RISE: improving streaming processors reliability against soft errors in GPGPUs, in: International Conference on Parallel Architectures and Compilation Techniques (PACT), September, 2012.

[37] S.K. Reinhardt, S.S. Mukherjee, Transient fault detection via simultaneous multithreading, in: Proceedings of ISCA, 2000.

[38] J. Wadden, L. Alexander, G. Sudhanva, S. Vilas, S. Kevin, Real-world design and evaluation of compiler-managed GPU redundant multithreading, in: Proceeding of the 41st Annual International Symposium on Computer Architecture (ISCA), 2014.

[39] M.A. Gomaa, T.N. Vijaykumar, Opportunistic transient-fault detection, in: Proceedings of ISCA, 2005.

[40] S.S. Mukherjee, J. Emer, S.K. Reinhardt, The soft error problem: an architectural perspective, in: Proceedings of HPCA, 2005.

[41] D. Kirk, W.W. Hwu, Programming Massively Parallel Processors: A Hands-on Approach, in: (1st ed.) Morgan Kaufmann Publishers Inc., San Francisco, CA, USA, 2010.

[42] N. Muralimanohar, R. Balasubramonian, N.P. Jouppi, Cacti 6.0: a tool to understand large caches, Technical report, University of Utah and Hewlett Packard Laboratories, 2007.

[43] J. Tan, X. Fu, Mitigating the susceptibility of GPGPUs register file to process variations, in: International Parallel & Distributed Processing Symposium (IPDPS), May, 2015.

[44] S. Sarangi, B. Greskamp, A. Tiwari, J. Torrellas, EVAL: utilizing processors with variation-induced timing errors, in: 2008 41st IEEE/ACM International Symposium on Microarchitecture, November 8–12, 2008, pp. 423–434.

[45] N.S. Kim, T. Kgil, K. Bowman, V. De, T. Mudge, Total power optimal pipelining and parallel processing under process variations in nanometer technology, in: IEEE/ACM International Conference on Computer-Aided Design, 2005 (ICCAD-2005), November 6–10, 2005, pp. 535–540.

[46] J. Lee, P. Ajgaonkar, N.S. Kim, Analyzing throughput of GPGPUs exploiting within-die core-to-core frequency variation, in: Proceedings of ISPASS, 2011.

[47] E. Krimer, P. Chiang, M. Erez, Lane decoupling for improving the timing-error resiliency of wide-SIMD architectures, in: Proceedings of the 39th Annual International Symposium on Computer Architecture (ISCA'12), 2012, pp. 237–248.

[48] E. Krimer, R. Pawlowski, M. Erez, P. Chiang, Synctium: a near-threshold stream processor for energy-constrained parallel applications, in: IEEE Computer Architecture Letters, 9 (1), 2010, pp. 21–24.

[49] R. Pawlowski, E. Krimer, J. Crop, J. Postman, N. Moezzi-Madani, M. Erez, P. Chiang, A 530 mV 10-lane SIMD processor with variation resiliency in 45 nm SOI, in: 2012 IEEE International Solid-State Circuits Conference, February 19–23, 2012, pp. 492–494.

[50] A. Rahimi, L. Benini, R.K. Gupta, Spatial memoization: concurrent instruction reuse to correct timing errors in SIMD architectures, IEEE Trans. Circuits Syst. Express Briefs 60 (12) (2013) 847–851.

[51] A. Rahimi, L. Benini, R.K. Gupta, Hierarchically focused guardbanding: an adaptive approach to mitigate PVT variations and aging, in: Proceedings of the Conference on Design, Automation and Test in Europe (DATE'13), 2013, pp. 1695–1700.

[52] P. Aguilera, J. Lee, A. Farmahini-Farahani, K. Morrow, M. Schulte, N.S. Kim, Process variation-aware workload partitioning algorithms for GPUs supporting spatial-multitasking, in: Proceedings of the conference on Design, Automation & Test in Europe (DATE'14), 2014.

[53] NVIDIA's Next Generation CUDA Compute Architecture: Fermi, 2016, http://www.nvidia.com/content/PDF/fermi_white_papers/NVIDIA_Fermi_Compute_Architecture_Whitepaper.pdf.

[54] D. Kanter, AMD's Cayman GPU architecture, 2010, http://realworldtech.com/page.cfm?ArticleID=RWT121410213827.

[55] NVIDIA's Next Generation CUDA Compute Architecture: KeplerGK110, 2016, http://www.nvidia.com/content/PDF/kepler/NVIDIA-Kepler-GK110-Architecture-Whitepaper.pdf.

[56] N. Goswami, B. Cao, T. Li, Power-performance co-optimization of throughput core architecture using resistive memory, in: 2013 IEEE 19th International Symposium on High Performance Computer Architecture (HPCA2013), February 23–27, 2013, pp. 342–353.

[57] J. Tschanz, J. Kao, S. Narendra, Adaptive body bias for reducing impacts of die-to-die and within-die parameter variations on microprocessor frequency and leakage, J. Solid-State Circuits 37 (11) (2002) 1396–1402.

[58] A. Agarwal, B.C. Paul, H. Mahmoodi, A. Datta, K. Roy, A process-tolerant cache architecture for improved yield in nanoscale technologies, IEEE Trans. Very Large Scale Integr. Syst. 13 (1) (2005) 27–38.

[59] X. Liang, D. Brooks, Mitigating the impact of process variations on processor register files and execution units, in: 2006 39th Annual IEEE/ACM International Symposium on Microarchitecture (MICRO'06), 2006, pp. 504–514.

[60] R. Teodorescu, J. Nakano, A. Tiwari, J. Torrellas, Mitigating parameter variation with dynamic fine-gain body biasing, in: 40th Annual IEEE/ACM International Symposium on Microarchitecture (MICRO 2007), December 1–5, 2007, pp. 27–42.

[61] Y. Lu, S. Ganapathy, Z. Mao, M.I. Guo, R. Canal, N. Jing, Y. Shen, X. Liang, An energy-efficient and scalable eDRAM-based register file architecture for GPGPU, in: Proceedings of the 40th Annual International Symposium on Computer Architecture (ISCA'13), 2013, pp. 344–355.

[62] J. Leng, T. Hetherington, A. ElTantawy, S. Gilani, N.S. Kim, T.M. Aamodt, V.J. Reddi, GPUWattch: enabling energy optimizations in GPGPUs, in: Proceedings of the 40th Annual International Symposium on Computer Architecture (ISCA'13), 2013, pp. 487–498.

[63] M. Abdel-Majeed, M. Annavaram, Warped register file: a power efficient register file for GPGPUs, in: Proceedings of the 2013 IEEE 19th International Symposium on High Performance Computer Architecture (HPCA) (HPCA'13), 2013, pp. 412–423.

[64] M. Gebhart, D.R. Johnson, D. Tarjan, S.W. Keckler, W.J. Dally, E. Lindholm, K. Skadron, Energy-efficient mechanisms for managing thread context in throughput processors, in: Proceedings of the 38th Annual International Symposium on Computer Architecture (ISCA'11), 2011, pp. 235–246.

[65] M. Gebhart, S.W. Keckler, W.J. Dally, A compile-time managed multi-level register file hierarchy, in: Proceedings of the 44th Annual IEEE/ACM International Symposium on Microarchitecture (MICRO-44), 2011, pp. 465–476.

[66] S. Sarangi, B. Greskamp, R. Teodorescu, J. Nakano, A. Tiwari, J. Torrellas, VARIUS: a model of process variation and resulting timing errors for microarchitects, Trans. Semicond. Manuf. 21 (1) (2008) 3–13.

[67] A. Agrawal, A. Ansari, J. Torrellas, Mosaic: exploiting the spatial locality of process variation to reduce refresh energy in on chip eDRAM modules, in: International Symposium on High Performance Computer Architecture (20th HPCA), Minneapolis, 2014, pp. 84–95.

[68] Y. Pan, J. Kong, S. Ozdemir, G. Memik, S.W. Chung, Selective wordline voltage boosting for caches to manage yield under process variations, in: Proceedings of the 46th Annual Design Automation Conference (DAC'09), 2009, pp. 57–62.

[69] M. Yoshimoto, K. Anami, H. Shinohara, T. Yoshihara, H. Takagi, S. Nagao, S. Kayano, T. Nakano, A divided word-line structure in the static RAM and its application to a 64K full CMOS RAM, IEEE J. Solid-State Circuits 18 (5) (1983) 479–485.

[70] M. Tehranipour, Z. Navabi, S. Falkhrai, An efficient BIST method for testing of embedded SRAMs, in: The 2001 IEEE International Symposium on Circuits and Systems, 2001 (ISCAS 2001), vol. 5, 2001, pp. 73–76.

Author Index

Subject Index

Note: Page numbers followed by *b* indicate boxes, *f* indicate figures and *t* indicate tables.

727

Printed in the United States
By Bookmasters